TRAVELER'S GUIDE TO

EUROPEAN CAMPING

Explore Europe With RV Or Tent

Mike and Terri Church

Rolling Homes Press

ROLLING HOMES PRESS

Published by
Rolling Homes Press
P.O. Box 2099
Kirkland, WA 98083-2099

www.rollinghomes.com

Printed in the United States of America
First Edition 1996
Second Edition 1999

Publisher's Cataloging in Publication

Church, Mike, 1951-
Traveler's Guide To European Camping : explore Europe with RV or tent / Mike and Terri Church
p.cm
Includes index
Preassigned LCCN: 99-70202
ISBN 0-9652968-3-0

1. Europe--Guidebooks. 2. Camping--Europe--Guidebooks. I. Church, Terri. II. Title.

D909.C48 1999 914.04/559--dc21

This book is dedicated
to our parents

With Love and Appreciation

WARNING, DISCLOSURE, AND COMMUNICATION WITH THE AUTHORS AND PUBLISHERS

Half the fun of travel is the unexpected, and self-guided camping travel can produce much in the way of unexpected pleasures, and alternately, complications and problems. This book is designed to increase the pleasures of European camping and reduce the number of unexpected problems you may encounter. You can help ensure a smooth trip by doing additional advance research, planning ahead, and exercising caution as appropriate. There can be no guarantee that your trip will be trouble free.

Although the authors and publisher have done their best to ensure that the information presented in this book was correct at the time of publication they do not assume and hereby disclaim any liability to any party for any loss or damage caused by errors, omissions, or any other cause.

In a book like this it is inevitable that there will be omissions or mistakes, especially as things do change over time. If you find inaccuracies we would like to hear about them so that they can be corrected in future editions. We would also like to hear about your enjoyable experiences. If you come upon an outstanding campground or destination please let us know, those kinds of things may also find their way to future versions of the guide. You can reach us by mail at:

Rolling Homes Press
P.O. Box 2099
Kirkland, WA 98083-2099

www.rollinghomes.com

Other Books by Mike and Terri Church
and
Rolling Homes Press

Traveler's Guide To Mexican Camping
Traveler's Guide To Alaskan Camping

A brief summary of the above books is provided on pages 446 and 447

TABLE OF CONTENTS

Chapter 12

Chapter 13

INTRODUCTION

This second edition of our camping guide to Europe was even more fun to produce than the first edition. During the writing of the first edition we traveled in a Volkswagen camping van, our year-and-a-half-long odyssey was the experience of a lifetime and a trip we will never forget. For many people, however, it is difficult to find the time for such a long trip.

For the travel needed for this update we tried a different approach. Instead of buying a camping van we rented automobiles and tent camped during our stays. We had traveled this way in Europe before, but never for such long periods. We used a big roomy tent and found the experience very enjoyable. It was inexpensive and comfortable. It was also very convenient. We could make reservations for a vehicle in the U.S., pack our camping gear into two large duffel bags, and hit the road running when we arrived in Europe by picking up the car at the airport and spending the first night in a campground. We found that the method works well for a one-week visit or a two-month trip.

Whether you tent camp out of a rented car, rent or buy a European van, or bring your own rig from home, we are convinced that there is no better place to camp than Europe. If you have been touring North America in your RV and you would like to try something different but at the same time familiar, try Europe. Camping there is no more difficult than in North America, not much more expensive, and certainly just as much fun. If you want to tour Europe in the most economical and flexible way possible, camping is the best way to go.

This book is part how-to book, part travel guide, and part campground guide. Many of our readers probably know more about camping or European culture than we will ever know. They've just never been introduced to the European version of camping or the camping version of traveling. The only information widely available has been directed at younger travelers trying to see Europe inexpensively and just incidentally doing it by camping. The camping side of the story usually gets a very short treatment, and leaves a lot of questions unanswered. For example – it is sufficient to tell a

Eurailpass train traveler that you get to a campground by taking the Number 6 bus from the train station. This doesn't help an RVer arriving on the autobahn.

You will find that many cities and regions are covered within these pages. However, there are many thousands of European campgrounds that are not included. There are just too many of them. We think that a person could spent ten years of summers wandering around Europe and not visit everything he or she would like to see, not to mention the places to be visited for a second, third or fourth time.

We've tried to write the book in a manner that allows you to pick it up and start reading almost anywhere. Chapter 1 describing the concept of European camping and Chapter 2 about equipping yourself with a rig are probably best read in one sitting each. Chapter 3 about the myriad details can be referenced as needed, the remaining chapters about destinations can be browsed before the trip to familiarize yourself, plan, and dream; or used during the trip to assist you in finding a pleasant place to stay or locate that hard-to-find campground.

Our purpose in writing this book is to help you decide to go, to help you select your camping vehicle and get it properly equipped, and to make your European camping experience as enjoyable as possible. By camping vehicle we mean to include trains, bikes, and rental cars in addition to camping vans, motorhomes and caravans. This is the book we searched for but couldn't find when we were planning to go to Europe. It should save you some time and money. It will give you a head start so that you can do more, see more, miss less, and spend less than you otherwise would have. We're sure you will have as much fun camping in Europe as we do and perhaps even as much fun as we have had writing about it.

EUROPE

Top Row Left: Amalfi, Italy
Top Row Right: Neuschwanstein Castle in Germany
Bottom Row Left: Tent camping on the Island of Mýkonos in Greece
Bottom Row Right: The Island of Burano near Venice

CHAPTER 1

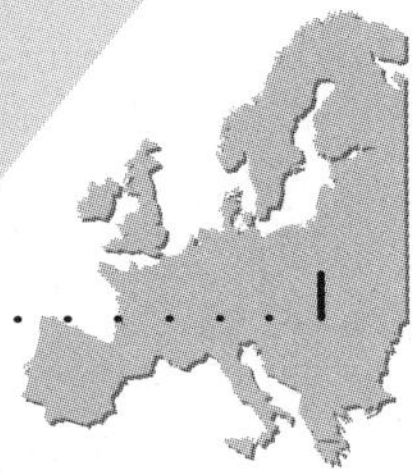

WHY CAMP EUROPE?

For most of us a trip to Europe is the ultimate dream vacation. Sure, the swaying palm trees and golden sands of tropical islands have a certain attraction, but we've grown up hearing about Europe and Europeans, and we want to see them for ourselves. Hundreds of thousands of Americans head off to Europe each year, some on business trips but mostly for pleasure. Few of these people go as campers, but that is certain to change as the word gets out.

The Attractions of European Camping

Camping is every bit as popular in Europe as it is in North America. The autobahns and motorways of Europe are full of camping vehicles, as are the country roads. France is said to have 10,000 campgrounds and other European countries aren't far behind. There is a good campground near virtually any European destination you are likely to want to visit, just take a look at Chapters 5 through 13 of this book.

Europeans camp in tents and they camp in well-designed camping rigs of every description. Chapter 2 of this book will tell you more about this. The European campground is similar to the ones we are accustomed to, but there are differences. Many European campers have small rigs so the facilities in campgrounds are more important than they are in North America and they tend to be more extensive. Most campgrounds have showers, clothes-washing machines, dish-washing sinks, and often even covered cooking areas. Many campgrounds also have bars, restaurants, food markets, and lounge areas.

The actual camping sites within the campgrounds are also different than the ones we are accustomed to. It is not unusual to find that individual sites are not delineated. Campers park where they like, often in a grassy field or in an old fruit-tree grove or vineyard. Electricity is usually limited to an amperage suitable only for lights and refrigerators. There are usually no picnic tables, campers bring along their own folding versions. People spend a lot of time outdoors and you will find that you will meet more people than in a campground in North America. There are no fire rings, campfires are almost never a part of European camping.

Most Europeans camp during July and August. Veteran visitors to Europe know that the whole continent goes on vacation during these months, many European vacationers head for the campgrounds. Fortunately most European campers go to the seashores and the mountains, campgrounds near the cities are not really crowded. Outside these months, from May to early July and also in September and October, campgrounds are half-full at best, you'll have no trouble finding a place to stay and you will not have to deal with crowds.

Europe has its snowbirds, just like North America. In North America they winter in Texas, Arizona, and Mexico. In Europe they fill campgrounds in southern Spain and Portugal, and also in Greece and Turkey. If you want to visit Europe in the winter you can join these snowbirds.

You will find a convenient campground near almost any destination you would want to visit in Europe. In big cities the campground is generally located away from the city center in a quiet suburb. There is almost always convenient public transportation to whisk you in to town. Using the maps provided in this guide you will have no trouble driving right to these outlying campgrounds, there is no reason to take your vehicle into the crowded city centers.

The use of a vehicle is by far the best way to see Europe. Imagine trying to see the U.S. from the window of a train or airplane. Think of what you would miss. Yet this is the way most visitors see Europe. They miss the countryside, arguably the best part of Europe. A vehicle also gives you unmatched flexibility. You can go where you want, change your mind at any time, and travel without reservations. Best of all, you don't have to carry suitcases or backpacks.

The camping lifestyle is a great way to meet Europeans. Most visitors from North America only meet people who make their livings dealing with tourists, people working as taxi drivers, desk clerks, or waiters. As a camper you'll meet Europeans who almost never see tourists, they certainly don't meet American campers. You'll be more popular than you think!

You'll also save a lot of money. Camping in Europe costs about the same thing as camping in the United States or Canada. Chapter 3 has more information about costs. If you are a group of two or more you will probably find that it is cheaper to rent a car and camp than it would be to travel on a Eurailpass and spend the nights in hostels.

As a camper you can eat in restaurants or you can cook your own food. This can save you lots of money, it can also be one of the best parts of the travel experience. The small restaurants at the campgrounds tend to be inexpensive, they won't break your budget. If you choose to buy groceries and cook you will be living off the local economy, not paying extortionate tourist prices. Almost all European countries have great supermarkets, small shops, and street markets full of interesting things to eat. You can try something new or cook the familiar dishes from home that other travelers miss while they are on the road. On the other hand, there is no reason that you can't join the others and visit some of the best restaurants in the world.

Camping is an excellent way to travel with children, they love it. Foreign campgrounds are interesting and the great outdoors offers lots of opportunities to use up youthful exuberance. Many campgrounds have playgrounds, bike trails, swimming pools, water slides or beaches. A family pays little more for a camping vacation than a couple does so you'll save lots of money over a hotel tour. Finally, you can cook the things that your family will eat, you won't have to deal with unfamiliar restaurant food.

A Camping Grand Tour

Probably the best way to show what camping in Europe is like is to outline an itinerary for a camping trip to Europe. This is one of a million possible itineraries, there really is no limit to the possible camping tours of Europe. This is a two-month tour, you could easily plan a one-week tour or a six-month tour. Remember, flexibility is one of the big advantages to camping travel. If you decide that you want to spend more time anywhere along the route you can do so and make up the time or skip a destination later in your trip.

The tour outlined here will give you just a taste of France, Italy, Austria, Germany, Benelux and the British Isles. Another good way to travel would be to concentrate on just one chapter of this book at a time, plan on at least a month to thoroughly explore the area covered in each chapter. Using this rule of thumb you can see that it would take a little over a year in Europe to begin to exhaust the possibilities outlined in this

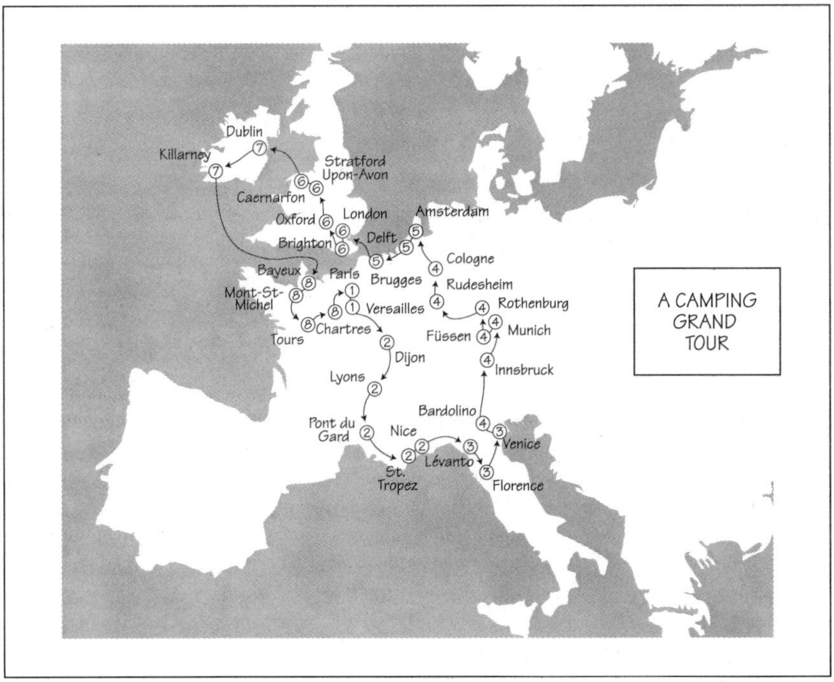

guide, or you could make many shorter visits over a number of years.

This tour starts in Paris, but it could just as easily start in London, Amsterdam, or Frankfort. Each of these cities is a popular gateway to Europe with vehicles readily available.

As you will see in the following chapter, there are many ways to camp. For this trip you could rent a car and tent camp or rent an RV and travel in true comfort, the choice is yours.

Week 1 - Arrive in **Paris** and pick up your vehicle, perhaps right at the airport. Paris has lots to see so you should plan to spend a few days here. A good place to stay is Camping du Bois de Boulogne. From the campground it is easy to travel in to the center of the city on the Metro.

One of the most interesting sights near Paris is **Versailles**. There's a campground nearby, Camping Municipal de Porchefontaine, so before leaving the Ile de France spend a night there and visit the palace.

Week 2 - Time to drive south and sample the pleasures of the Riviera. An interesting route would be to stop in campgrounds at **Dijon**, **Lyons**, the **Pont du Gard** near **Avignon**, then a couple of nights each at **St. Tropez** and Villeneuve-Loubet-Plage near **Nice**. Avoid the autoroutes if you really want to enjoy the French countryside.

Week 3 - This is the week for Italy. Use the Italian autostradas, they'll let you cover a lot of ground quickly. Spend your first and second nights in Italy at **Lévanto** near the **Cinque Terre** coast, you can spend the day hiking one of the most popular routes in Europe. Use the railroad running through a tunnel inside the cliffs to get to the beginning of the hike and come home when you are tired. From there head directly to **Florence**, well worth a two-day stop. Camping Michelangelo is within walking distance of the city center, you'll probably have a great view overlooking the city from your site. **Venice** is next, again demanding at least two days, three would give you more time to wander the streets and canals of this magical place. Camp across the lagoon from the city and travel in by water taxi.

Week 4 - From Venice it is time to head north. We suggest a stop at **Bardolino** on the shore of **Lake Garda**. You've probably heard of this village's wine. The next day drive over the **Brenner Pass** to **Innsbruck** and then to **Munich**. This Bavarian city demands two days, then drive westward to see **Neuschwanstein Castle** and camp on the shores of the Forggensee at Ferienplatz Brunnen am Forggensee near Füssen. The next day follow the **Romantic Road** north to mediaeval **Rothenburg**, tour the town with the watchman in the evening. Drive west the next day to the **Rhine** at **Rüdesheim** where you can spend the night next to the river and walk in to town in the evening to have dinner and a glass of Riesling in a restaurant along the Drosselgasse. From Rüdesheim follow the river north to **Cologne** and another riverside campground. Don't miss the cathedral.

Week 5 - **Amsterdam** is an easy day's drive from Cologne. Camp at Gaasper Camping so you can zip into town on the subway. After Amsterdam spend the remainder of the week working your way westward through picturesque Holland and Belgium to Calais. We recommend stops at **Delft** and **Brugge**.

TOUR BOAT ON THE MOSELLE

Week 6 - Take a ferry or the Chunnel (Le Shuttle) across or under the **English Channel** to **London**. There are a number of excellent campgrounds there. If you wish you can explore the surrounding countryside using your vehicle, distances are manageable. **Brighton** and **Oxford** make interesting destinations near London, toward the end of the week start east toward the ferry port at **Holyhead** in northwestern Wales. **Stratford-upon-Avon** and **Caernarfon** are good places to stay along this route.

Week 7 - Time for **Ireland**. The ferry arrives in **Dublin**, and you'll want to spend a couple of days there. The rest of the week should be spent in the countryside, we suggest a base at **Killarney** and perhaps a drive around the **Ring of Kerry**.

Week 8 - A ferry from Ireland directly to Cherbourg, France will save a lot of time, but during some months of the year you may have to travel via England. Once in France head for **Bayeux** which makes an excellent base for your first night back in France, the **Normandy D-Day invasion beaches** are nearby. From there travel southwest and make a stop at **Mont-St-Michel** before heading south again to Tours. Explore the **château along the Cher and the Loire Valley**, you won't want to leave. When it's time to make the drive to Paris make sure to stop in Chartres for one last cathedral before leaving for home.

CHAPTER 2

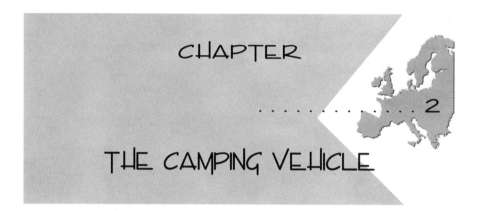

THE CAMPING VEHICLE

INTRODUCTION

We suspect that most of the users of this book will be camping out of a vehicle of some kind. Even backpackers and Eurailpass travelers will benefit from the convenience of occasionally renting a bike or automobile. You just won't want to miss some of the places that can only be conveniently explored using your own set of wheels.

Choosing your vehicle is important. It will affect almost everything else about your trip. There are many questions to consider. How long will your trip last? How much are you willing to pay? What weather are you likely to run into? Will you travel alone, with a friend, or bring a family? How important is comfort to you?

Europe's remote location (for North Americans anyway) means that you must make a decision about bringing your vehicle and camping equipment from home or renting, leasing, or purchasing the equipment and vehicle in Europe. The length of your visit will help determine the answer to this question. High European taxes and falling freight rates mean that the answer might not be what you expect.

An Important Note

In this chapter we list many firms that you may choose to use when you visit Europe. Please be aware that we do not specifically recommend any of them. Although they are the companies that are most active in their respective businesses we have not personally used many of them so we can make no guarantees. We do not receive commissions or remuneration from any of them. We would love to hear from you about your experiences if you choose to use them.

FIVE STRATEGIES

We'll sum up your options for traveling and camping in Europe as five basic strategies. You can probably think of many others.

Travel using airplanes, trains, busses, and perhaps even occasionally hitchhike. Carry everything you need in a backpack, including a tent for camping. You sacrifice comfort and lose some flexibility but this is an affordable method, particularly if you do not have the option of sharing the cost of a vehicle with a partner.

Travel by bicycle and supplement this mode of travel with train and bus transportation. Spend the nights in campgrounds. This can be a rewarding and inexpensive form of travel, but you'd better be in shape and you give up flexibility and comfort.

Travel by motorcycle and carry camping equipment. When the weather is good this is a great way to travel but you can't carry much and it can be even more expensive than a car if the number of people in your party means that you must have several bikes.

Travel by automobile spending your evenings at campgrounds sleeping in a tent. A great compromise: economy, flexibility, and with a large tent a surprising amount of comfort. If you do it properly you can rent a vehicle in Europe for a reasonable price.

Travel using a recreational vehicle (RV) or van. The RV could be a van, pickup camper, tent trailer, camping trailer (caravan), or full-size motorhome (motor caravan). Rent it in Europe, buy it there, or bring it from North America. This is the ultimate solution for both short comfortable vacations and extended visits. While it is the most expensive option you will find that the cost is very comparable with doing the same thing in North America.

Backpacking And Rail Travel

Backpacking and rail travel through Europe are without a doubt the most popular modes of travel for budget travelers. Low-priced rail passes (often called Eurailpasses, but there are other European rail pass deals) allowing virtually unlimited railroad travel can be supplemented by buses, boats, ferries, rental bicycles, rental automobiles, and even hitchhiking. Your overnight accommodation may often be a bench on the train, but options also include rail compartments, hostels, bed-and-breakfasts, budget hotels, and camping–both free and in campgrounds.

The disadvantage of camping for backpackers is that camping equipment adds lots of bulk and weight to the load on your back. A tent, stove, and sleeping bag can easily double the weight of your pack or force you to leave things at home that you would like to have along (like extra clothes or travel guides). On the other hand, modern backpacking tents and other equipment are much lighter than they used to be. A good tent, stove, mattress, cooking utensils, and sleeping bag can add no more than 10 pounds to the weight of your pack. Two people traveling together can share the weight of the tent and cooking equipment.

Buy your camping gear in the North America before coming to Europe. Costs are much lower and the selection of backpacking gear much better. Limitations on the weight of baggage that can be checked as luggage on your flight shouldn't be a problem since you should limit your pack to no more than 40 pounds for men or 30 for women. Any more is just too much to carry around on a daily basis. Less is always better.

Before you decide that railroad passes and backpacking are your best option for visiting Europe make sure you check out the cost of the rail pass you will need. The standard one-month Eurailpass (which does not include the British Isles) now costs almost nine hundred dollars. Also take a look at some of the rail and drive combinations. These give you some days on trains and some with a rental car. Our web site at www.rollinghome.com has links to organizations that sell rail passes. A good one is Rick Steve's Europe Through The Back Door, Inc. at (425) 771-8303.

Living out of a backpack works just fine on a short trip but gets very old after a while. In a month or so you'll yearn for four walls to call your own.

Bicycles

Bicycles make a great way to explore the European countryside. Most countries have areas with quiet roads and lots of scenery and ambiance. Especially good are Denmark, the Netherlands, Belgium, France, and the Danube Valley because they're flat and they have lots of quiet roads or bike paths. Your bicycle itinerary will probably be limited, don't expect to cover too much ground. Abilities differ but bicycle travelers can easily cover from 50 to 100 kilometers per day. If you plan to ride too far you'll find yourself without the time or energy to investigate interesting places along your route. Remember too that bicycle riders are subject to the vagrancies of wind, rain, and sun so be sure to pick the season of your visit with this in mind.

To cover more ground you may want to supplement your bicycle riding with rail and bus travel. Trains are good for traveling those last few miles into big towns (to avoid city traffic) or to move from one region to another. In most European countries it is relatively easy to bring your bike right along with you when riding the rails.

You will probably want to bring your bike from North America. European selection can be quite good, but prices are not. Bringing equipment from home means that you can try it out before you leave to make sure that both you and the bike are up to the challenges.

Take the time to do some research about the bicycle you will use. You want it to be efficient, sturdy, able to carry a load, and comfortable. Obviously this means that there are going to be compromises. You are going to have to spend a lot of time on that bike and you will want to enjoy it. In view of the other costs involved in your trip you should definitely consider buying a new bicycle if the one you own is not right. Make sure the gearing is appropriate for touring, you'll be carrying a lot of weight and you'll have to deal with the wind and hills. Don't forget accessories like bike bags, helmets, locks, a bell, tools and spares, a bicycle computer, and appropriate clothes (including rain gear).

Traveling by bicycle has some of the same disadvantages as backpacking. Living out of a small tent with limited equipment can get old in a short time, especially if the weather does not cooperate.

Motorcycles

Motorcycles are very popular in Europe, if you are an enthusiast this can be the best choice for your European visit. High European fuel costs help make a motorcycle a sensible alternative to an automobile. Camping meshes well with motorcycles. You can easily carry light camping gear and mobility is no problem.

The use of motorcycles may not be more economical than an automobile, especially if there will be two or more in your party. With the required crating it costs almost the same thing to ship a motorcycle to Europe as to ship a car, but you will probably be able to do it by air so you'll be without your bike for a shorter time than if it were to go by ship as an automobile must. You will also have to pay for Green Card liability insurance for all of the bikes.

The decision to buy a new motorcycle in Europe is much like the one to buy a new car or RV. You should take a look at the discussion about buying an RV below because the same factors apply. Taxes on new vehicles in Europe are high. If you buy a used motorcycle you will be taking the risk that you will have unexpected mechanical problems. If you want to leave the bike in Europe when you are finished with it you will have to take the time to sell it. If you want to bring it home the regulations are likely to be a little less onerous than for a car, but check to make sure. If you want to check prices you can contact **Shipside Tax Free World on Wheels B.V., Shipside Building, P.O. Box 430, 2130 AK Hoofddorp, The Netherlands (31 20 6533333, Fax 31 20 6533241).** They can handle inquiries in English.

Automobiles

An automobile is probably the best compromise for a medium-term visit, say up to three months. This assumes that you will be traveling at a time of year when the weather is decent. Automobiles are available on lease plans which make them affordable and you can carry enough camping gear in the trunk to be comfortable at night. Especially important is a large tent, one that has a high ceiling allowing you to stand. A small collection of folding furniture (chairs, table, and folding cots), a stove with two burners (or two one-burner stoves), maybe an ice chest, and perhaps an electric heater will give you a comfortable home-away-from-home.

Camping in a tent does have some disadvantages. Probably the worst is that you must pitch the tent and set up camp when you arrive and reverse the process when you depart. The burden can be lessened by using the campground as a base for day trips rather than moving your camp each night. We often travel this way and find that we soon become really proficient at setting up and tearing down our camp. It takes about 15 minutes to set up and 20 minutes to hit the road. That isn't much longer than it takes with a van and is just as fast as a caravan.

The considerations involved in renting, purchasing, or bringing an automobile from home are much the same as those discussed below in the RV section. There are some important wrinkles, however.

In past years many people have traveled to Europe to buy an automobile. They would drive it during their tour and then ship it back home. These cars were special models manufactured to U.S. or Canadian specifications so that they could be imported with no problems. European specification vehicles are almost impossible to bring into North America. While it sounds appealing, very few people buy their car in Europe today because there are usually no savings. Also, many European manufacturers now build their cars for the North American market in North America. At the date of publication of this book only Volvo, BMW, and Mercedes have European delivery programs for North American specification cars. On the other hand, the rising dollar may once again make this a popular option. There are no programs for North American specification campers, not even Volkswagens. If you want to inquire about the possibility of purchasing with European delivery you can check with a dealer in the U.S. You can also check with **Shipside Tax Free World on Wheels B.V., P.O. Box 430, 2130 AK Hoofddorp, The Netherlands (31 20 6533333, Fax 31 20 6533241).** This is a Dutch outfit (they speak English too) that can sell you a European car from any of the manufacturers having European delivery programs for convenient pickup in Europe. They also arrange shipment of the car back to the U.S. Be sure to check to see about North American taxes before doing this. Taxes that may apply include import duties, sales or use taxes, the gas-guzzler tax, and even the luxury car tax.

If you decide to rent and if you are going to need a car for more than 17 days you will find that the best deal is a Renault purchase-repurchase lease. You are actually buying a brand-new Renault and then reselling it when you are done. The beauty of the deal is that you don't have to really come up with the purchase price. You pay a fee up front which basically includes the difference between purchase and resale price, interest on the deal, and insurance. A very small car will run about $1,300 for two months. The longer you have the car the better the deal. Arrange your lease-repurchase while you're still in North America with one of these companies:

Europe by Car (800 223-1516)
Renault Eurodrive (800 221-1052)
Rob Liddiard Travel (800 272-3299)

You can pick up or turn in these cars at most major European cities by paying a small delivery charge. Check to see if the car you are interested in comes in a diesel model, you'll save a lot of money on fuel.

If your European trip is for a short time you will probably decide on a normal weekly rental. Most of the companies you are familiar with in the U.S. and Canada also have European operations. However, you should be aware that car rental rates vary considerably from country to country. The least expensive countries are Great Britain, Belgium, and Germany. In France, Ireland, and Italy you can easily pay twice as much for the same car. In the Scandinavian countries the price starts to approach three times as much. It definitely pays to shop around. Alamo, Avis, Budget, Dollar, Hertz, National Car Rental, Payless and Thrifty all have rental operations in Europe. You can also try:

Auto Europe (800 223-5555)
Rob Liddiard Travel (800 272-3299)

DER Travel Services (800 782-2424)
Europe By Car (800 223-1516)

You'll probably get a better rental rate if you book in North America before leaving for Europe.

Recreational Vehicles

For an extended camping visit to Europe a recreational vehicle (RV) of some kind is essential. We find that two months is about our limit for a tent-camping trip. For early spring, late fall, and winter camping an RV is the only way to go.

The most popular types of European RVs are what North American RVers know as van conversions (Class B's), Class C's, Class A's, and camping trailers. This is no surprise since these are also the popular rigs in North America. If you plan to use a European camping vehicle it will probably be one of these. You will find that there are almost no pickup-type slide off campers in Europe, in fact, there are very few pick-ups. If you plan to bring your own rig, however, this type of camper should work quite well because it is so compact.

Vehicle size is an important consideration in Europe. Their camping rigs are smaller than we are accustomed to for several reasons. Fuel is expensive and small means better mileage. Camp sites are often smaller, anything longer than 6.5 meters (22 feet) may be difficult to fit into some campgrounds. Ferry travel and toll roads are cheaper for smaller rigs. While roads are generally fine for larger rigs there are some inviting destinations where a larger RVs just won't fit. Street parking is often difficult for smaller rigs but impossible for larger ones. Finally, when you do decide to free camp it is usually better to be smaller and less conspicuous.

Fuel will probably be your largest expense during your visit so don't ignore fuel consumption when deciding on an RV. This means that you must consider more than just the size of the rig. Fuel type is important too. Your choices will probably be between gasoline and diesel. If you happen to be buying a rig in The Netherlands you may also find vehicles set up to burn both propane and gasoline, selectable at the turn of a switch. You can expect a European RV to get at least 18 miles per gallon, some get as high as 30. Take a look at the discussion of fuel prices in Chapter 3 of this book to see how important this is.

Van Conversions (Class B's)

Van conversions have traditionally been the popular choice for North Americans, Australians, and New Zealanders visiting Europe. The Volkswagen camper van was ubiquitous at one time. These rear-engine vans remain the least expensive choice. They are inexpensive, simple, and more comfortable than sleeping on the ground. Unfortunately good ones are becoming difficult to find. Volkswagen stopped manufacturing them years ago when it replaced them with the modern T4 front-wheel drive model. Many are disappearing into Eastern Europe. Their age is making them maintenance risks, you don't want to have to worry about the health of your wheels during your entire visit.

A COMFORTABLE CAMPSITE (NOTE SATELLITE ANTENNA ON VAN)

Modern vans are taking their place. These vans, manufactured by Volkswagen, Ford, Fiat, Renault, Mercedes, Citroën and Peugeot are efficient and handle well. Most have front mounted engines and front-wheel drive and offer mileage in the range of 20 to 30 miles per gallon.

Conversion companies in Great Britain and Germany produce comfortable and attractive camping vans based upon these vehicles. They are particularly popular in England because they can be used as primary transportation when not on a camping trip. Some top brands are Auto-Sleepers, Reimo, and Autohomes. You'll also find quite a few vans that have been modified by owners, parts for converting vans are readily available in Europe. A fully equipped van will sleep two to four, have a gas/electric refrigerator, a gas two-burner stove (with grill on English rigs), a gas/electric space heater, a portable or cassette toilet, and perhaps (on extended-length versions) even a gas-heated hot water system with shower. Some have raised roofs to give standing room and others offer pop-tops that can be extended while parked to give the same kind of interior stand-up convenience. You'll give up some mileage and gain storage room and weather tightness with the permanently-raised tops. Something else to consider is that some parking spots in garages and lots that are protected by barrier bars are off-limits to extended top rigs.

Van conversions have the advantage of fuel economy, maneuverability, unobtrusiveness (for free camping) and ease of handling. They have the disadvantage of being quite cramped, traveling with more than two people in a van conversion is difficult. Good weather helps, you can set up a table and chairs and move the living and dining rooms outside.

Prices for van conversions in England start at about $3,000 for old units in poor mechanical condition. Expect to pay at least $6,000 for an older VW in reasonable condition. If you want to buy a new unit you can find beautiful rigs starting at $40,000.

Class C's

The next step up the affordability ladder are the Class C's. These RVs have a camping body added to the back of a specially manufactured truck chassis. This arrangement has the advantage of offering more living room in the rear while retaining the factory-built driving cockpit engineered by the vehicle manufacturer. You can expect to find all of the features of a van conversion in a Class C, plus more sleeping room, a usable shower arrangement, and larger tank capacities.

Class C's seem to be even more popular than van conversions on the continent. The French, Germans, Italians, and English all manufacture good units. Names to remember are Herald (British), Auto-Sleeper (British), Auto-Trail (British), Gruppo Ci (Italian), Hymer (German), Roller (German), and Pilote (French).

Advantages of Class C camping rigs are that they have more internal room than vans, they usually can sleep 4 comfortably, and often they have higher capacity tanks for fresh water and gray-water waste (from showers and dishwashing sinks). Disadvantages relate to increased size: reduced maneuverability, reduced road performance, reduced fuel economy and increased parking difficulty.

In England used Class C's start at about $10,000. $40,000 will buy you a brand-new example of one of the smaller Italian-built rigs now being sold in England.

Class A's

A Class A motorhome is one where the entire body is built in an RV factory. The cockpit area is not built by the chassis manufacturer, it is part of the camper structure. Class A's are increasingly popular in Europe, especially in Germany and France.

Most European Class A's are much smaller than those we are accustomed to in North America. The reason is that most European countries require a special driving license for large RVs. This won't affect you if you bring your own large rig from home because you will drive using your North American driving license, but it does mean that few European RVs are really big.

The plusses and minuses of Class A's are very much like Class C's. They tend to be the largest RVs. Some people like them because the cockpit area is much more a part of the living area than in other kinds of rigs, this makes the living area seem larger. Others do not like them because they think the cockpit area is not as well designed or functional as the cockpit in Class C's that are designed and built by motor vehicle manufacturers. You may appreciate their high seating position and the view it gives you when driving. American Class A motorhomes are enjoying a surge of popularity in England because they are as big as anything built in Europe and much less expensive. The dealers who import them, however, spend many thousands of dollars rewiring and replumbing them to European specifications.

Camping Trailers or Caravans

Far and away the most popular camping RV in Europe is the camping trailer. These are usually called caravans. Most caravans range in size from 3.5 meters (12 feet) to 5 meters (17 feet) for the actual living area excluding the hitch. You'll find much longer ones in Germany. Features vary considerably. You can expect to be able to sleep from 2 to 6 in a caravan and have all of the amenities of a motorhome (except an engine). Price for decent used caravans in England start at about $4,500.

For some reason caravans are not used much by visitors from North America. They are definitely an option that you should consider, particularly if you plan to visit Europe several times over a multi-year period. Used caravans are readily available and are much less expensive than motorhomes. They also tend to depreciate much less, particularly if you buy a used one. Finally, storing a caravan is less worrisome than storing a motorhome since you do not have to worry about deterioration of expensive engines and running gear.

Of course you will need an automobile to pull your caravan. European caravans are designed to be pulled by much smaller cars than you might expect. You'll find units that can be pulled by cars as small as a Peugeot 306, Renault 19, Honda Civic, or Volkswagen Polo.

One of the reasons that caravans are not as popular with tourists is that they must be hitched and unhitched each time you stop. This is not much of a problem if you are going to be in a campground for several days. In fact, the ability to leave your caravan safe in a campground while touring in the tow car is a real advantage. With practice you will find that the process of hitching or unhitching doesn't really require more than a few minutes. European caravans are so small and light that most are easily manhandled if the camp site has difficult access.

Another theoretical problem with caravans in that they are difficult to tow. Handling a caravan does require some skills that not all drivers have, but they are easily acquired skills. Pulling a caravan is quite comparable in difficulty to driving a larger motorhome. Automobile/caravan combinations are prohibited from some mountain roads in Switzerland but there are generally alternative routes. These same roads are not advised for large motorhomes either.

Before considering a caravan you should make sure that the tow vehicle you plan to use is acceptable. Leased automobiles may have contract provisions prohibiting use as tow vehicles and insurance may be a problem.

TYPICAL CAMPER LAYOUTS

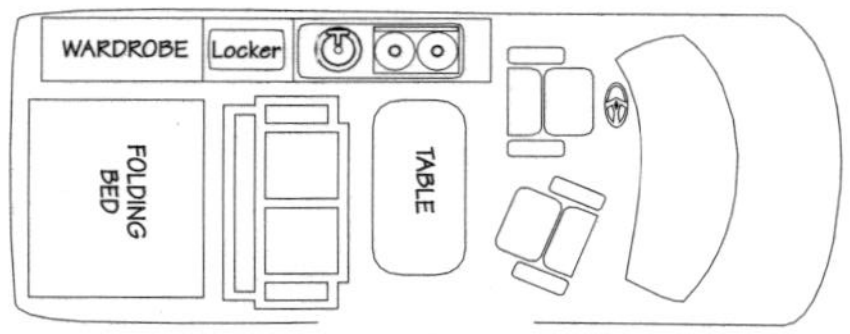

15 Ft. Van Conversion

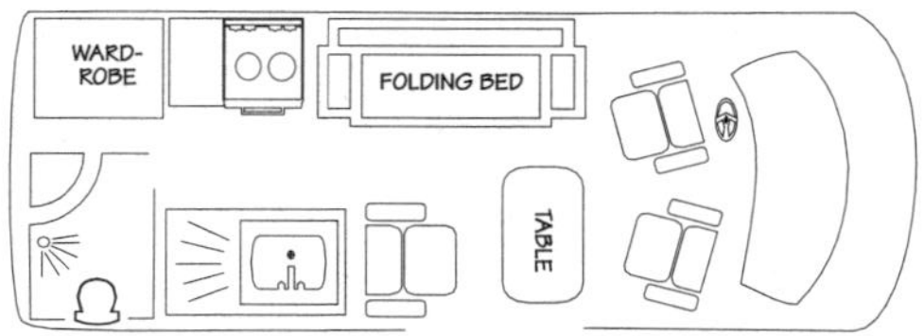

17 Ft. Van Conversion

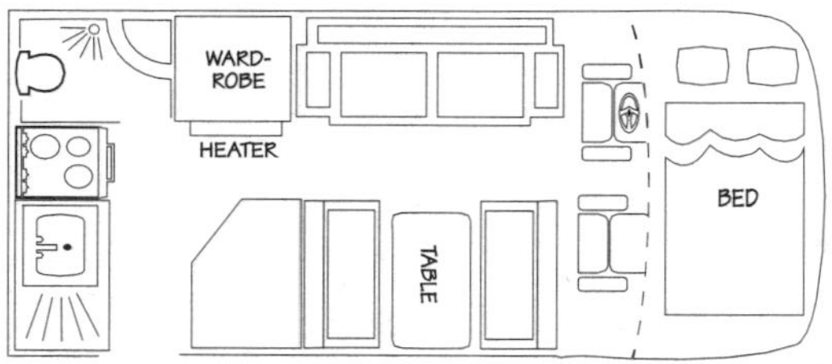

21 Ft. Class C

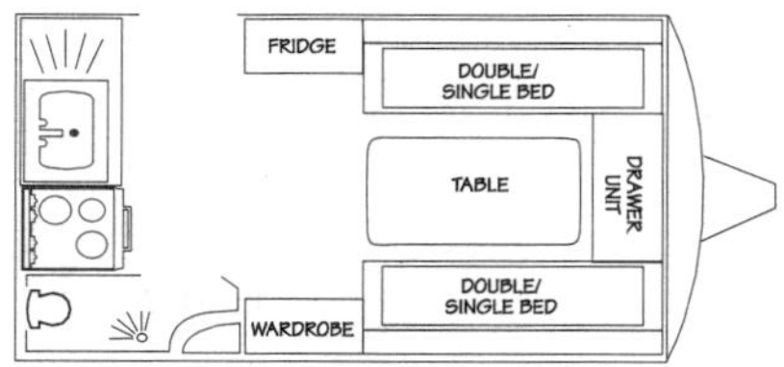

Small Caravan (British)

RENT, BUY, OR BRING IT WITH YOU

Renting an RV

If you are planning to visit Europe for a short time, say less than a month, you will probably want to rent an RV. Renting an RV for a short vacation is quite practical, you can start your trip in any of the larger cities thereby limiting the amount of driving you must do. There are dozens of rental operations in Europe. Many locals rent for their own vacations. Prices will vary considerably depending upon time of year, size of rig, and country. There are basically three seasons although the months do vary from dealer to dealer: high (usually June, July, August), middle or shoulder season (usually May, September), and low (usually October through April). Typical prices are about $65 per day in Amsterdam or England during the low season for an almost-new van conversion that sleeps two. This would go to $75 per day during the shoulder season and $85 during the high season. A larger rig that would sleep six would be about $120 during the summer from the same outfit. During the low season it is sometimes possible to rent for longer periods for lower rates. If these prices seem high you should check on the price of renting an RV in North America. Remember, you won't have an expensive hotel room, you have your own transportation, and you will probably save a bundle on food.

Make your reservations early because RV rental companies tend to get fully booked during the summer months.

Many travel agencies in North America can make motorhome reservations for your trip to Europe. Ask your normal travel agent or try contacting:

Hertz (800 654-3001)
Auto Europe (800 223-5555)
European Car Reservations (800 535-3303)
Owasco Car and Camper Rentals, 1425 Dundas Street, Whitby, Ontario, Canada L1N 2K6 (905 686-6410)
Rob Liddiard Travel, 4809 Laurelgrove Ave., #203, Valley Village, CA 91607 (800 272-3299 or 818 980-9133)

It is also possible but a little more difficult to deal directly with the European RV rental firms. You will probably find better prices by doing this. To call overseas from the U.S. dial 011, then the country code listed below, then the number given for the company. Many of these outfits have web sites and you will find links from ours at www.rollinghomes.com.

United Kingdom (country code 44) **:**

Bowers Motorcaravans, Greenlawns Kinsbourne Green, Harpenden AL5 3FN, U.K. (1582 713094)
Motorhome Rentals Ltd., 37-39 Upper Halliford Road, Shepperton, Middlesex, TW17 8RX, U.K. (193 770765).
Sunseeker Rentals Ltd., 27D Stable Way, London W10 6QX, U.K. (181 960 5747).

Turners Motorcaravan Hire, 11a Barry Road, East Dulwich, London SE22 OHX, U.K. (181 693 1132)

The Netherlands (country code 31, all firms can deal with you in English):

A-Point B.V. Volkswagen, Kollenbergweg 11, NL-1101 AR Amsterdam Zuidoost, Netherlands (20 4301600)

Braitman & Woudenberg, Droogbak 4A, NL-1013 6E Amsterdam, Neterlands (20 6221168)

Campanje Campervans and Campers, P.O. Box 9332, NL-3506 GH Utrecht, Netherlands (30-2447070)

Germany (country code 49):

Reise-Profi Service GmbH, Offenbachstr.6, D-Westoverledingen, Germany (4955-920905)

TRV Trading Corp, Am Hohenstein 3-5, D-65779 Kelkheim, Germany (6195-960507)

Switzerland (country code 41)

Moby Campers, Postfach 20, Möslistrasse 12, Postfach 20, CH-4532 Feldbrunnen, Schweiz-Switzerland (32 6229610).

Here are a few extras that you should ask about. Does the rate include unlimited mileage, is there a weekly limit or a per kilometer charge? Rental RVs usually come equipped with cooking equipment, linens, and bedding, see if there is an extra charge for this. Rental rates should include insurance, note that the collision damage waiver on your credit card may not apply to the rental of a van or RV. There are often some setup and possibly cleaning charges in addition to the daily rate. Many companies arrange transportation from the airport, see if the cost is included in your rental rate.

Buying an RV

Traditionally there have been three places where most people go to buy a European rig: England, Amsterdam, or Germany (Frankfort or Munich). Each place has advantages and disadvantages. The important considerations are licensing laws, language, availability, and cost.

Licensing laws and taxation of vehicles have become more difficult in recent years. Most countries require that the owner of a vehicle licensed in that country have a local mailing address. This is primarily to assist in the collection of taxes.

England seems to allow the most flexibility here, often nonresident buyers use a dealer's or an individual seller's address. This may or may not be absolutely legal, but it is done. The Netherlands and Germany have recently initiated very restrictive policies requiring that the registration address be the owner's actual residence. Dealers there seem to be having some success in dealing with this by using quasi-leases or keeping the vehicle in the dealers name instead of the purchase/repurchase agreements that were formerly used. Exercise caution if you decide to do something like this since you are placing a great deal of trust in the seller by giving him your money and also letting him keep the vehicle in his own name.

Even with the registration problems outlined here the fact remains that each year hundreds of nonresidents buy RVs to travel around Europe. If you plan to do the same make sure your I's are dotted and T's crossed. ***Europe By Van and Motorhome*** by David Shore and Patty Campbell, and mentioned in the Reference Books section of Chapter 3 covers purchase of an RV in the U.K., The Netherlands, and Germany.

In London vehicle registration can be taken care of at the Department of Transport, Vehicle Registration Office, 1 Zoar Street, London SE1 OSY. They have a booklet (V100) that covers the registration process. The Automobile Association of Great Britain (AA) can sell you insurance and also give you registration help. Dealers are excellent sources of registration information, that is one reason many people buy from them. Insurance brokers are another good information source, insurance is either required before registration or before driving the vehicle (depending upon the county) so they tend to be knowledgeable.

All three countries; the U.K., the Netherlands, and Germany; have mechanical inspection programs in place that require inspections every year or two years. Evidence of inspection is a dated sticker on the windshield or rear license. You should make sure the inspection sticker on the vehicle you are considering is current. It may be very expensive to have it renewed. Germany is notorious for requiring extensive repairs, even for any rust on a vehicle. You should consider requiring a new MOT (U.K.), AKP (The Netherlands), or TUV (Germany) inspection before buying the vehicle.

If you only speak English you'll want to buy your rig in a place where you can talk to the sellers. England is the best place for this, of course. In the Netherlands and Germany (less so) many people do speak English and you will probably have little trouble if you do business with a dealer. Calling on classified newspaper advertisements may be more problematic, especially in Germany.

England now has the best prices and offers an excellent choice of vehicles. The British pound is a softer currency than the German mark or Dutch guilder. You'll get a better exchange rate when you buy them with your U.S. dollars.

One problem with English vehicles is that most have right-hand drive. This is fine for traveling in England but not ideal for the continent. Driving from the right gives poor visibility in passing situations but is otherwise not difficult to deal with. Some dealers do have a few left hand drive units but they are not really common. English units (motorhomes and caravans) are also unusual in having the entrance door to the living area on the left side but this is rarely a problem in the campground.

Here are a selection of European dealers in the United Kingdom and The Netherlands. To call from the U.S. dial 011, then the country code given below, then the telephone number. Many of these firms have internet sites, you'll find links on our web site at www.rollinghomes.com.

There are a large number of dealers in the **United Kingdom**, these are in or near London (country code is 44):

Bilbo's Trading Co., Eastbourne Road, South Godstone, Surrey, RH9 8JQ, UK (1342 892499)

Bromley Motor Caravans, 55-65 Abbey Road, Belvedere, Kent DA17 5DG, UK (181 3113500)

Sunseeker Rentals Ltd., 27D Stable Way, London W10 6QX, UK (181 9605747)(a rental operator also offering used RVs)

Turners of London, 11a Barry Road, East Dulwich, London SE22 OHX, UK (181 6931132)

In **The Netherlands** (country code 31) you can purchase RV's and caravans from:

A-Point B.V., Kollenbergweg 11, 1101 AR Amsterdam Zuidoost, Postbus 12888, 1101 AR Amsterdam Zuidoost, Netherlands (20 4301600)

Braitman & Woudenberg, Droogbak 4A, 1013 GE Amsterdam, Nether lands (20 6221168)

Campanje Campervans and Campers, P.O. Box 9332, NL-3506 GH Utrecht, Netherlands (30 2447070)

You can write to these dealers to get a listing of their stock and an idea of the selection you will have when you arrive. Ask about licensing, registration, warranties, and buyback schemes. You should probably wait until your arrival, however, to make a final decision. A few days shopping around will let you familiarize yourself with the market and be well worth the time and effort.

Many dealers offer purchase/repurchase agreements for overseas visitors. Commonly they guarantee to repurchase the RV for a fixed percentage of the purchase price after a set period of time. They also often include a warranty of some kind. Exercise caution in depending upon such an agreement. Enforcement would be very difficult if there were problems, you are really relying on the honesty of the dealer. Repurchase agreements do take a load off your mind because you don't have to worry about the uncertainty of trying to sell your rig before heading back home. A relatively standard buyback agreement would pay you 70% of the purchase price after three months, 65% after six months, and 60% after a year.

It is not difficult to purchase a rig from an individual in England. Every newsstand has a large selection of camping magazines with classified sections. A daily newspaper, *Loot,* is also available on newsstands and has a large used RV and caravan classified section. You'll probably also find a number of small dealers listed in *Loot* that specialize in camper vans for Australians and New Zealanders.

London has a famous RV street market. Sellers park their rigs along the road each day and buyers have a large selection, especially in the early spring and late fall. Many of the inexpensive rigs that are handed from one tourist to the next change hands here. Be careful buying one of these rigs, many are real beaters.

The market tends to move. Most recently we found it on Market Road, about 2 kilometers north of the King's Cross underground station and near the Caledonian Road station on the purple Piccadilly line. The best way to find the current location is to ask at one of the local campgrounds.

Money From Home

If you decide to buy a rig in Europe you will have to find a way to transfer quite a large sum of money. There are several ways to do this.

The most flexible method is traveler's checks. Consider purchasing the checks in the currency of the country where you plan to buy your vehicle, this can save some hassles when it comes time to cash them. You must try to minimize fees, a 3% fee on $10,000 is $300, a significant amount of money to most of us. With traveler's checks there are usually fees charged at each end, one or two percent when you buy them and sometimes even more when you cash them. You can get around the purchase fee if you are a member of the American Automobile Association, they issue free traveler's checks to members. Some banks do the same thing for customers with special checking accounts. Check around to see if you can find any deals, it can be worth your time. In Europe you will have to find a good place to cash the checks. If the seller or dealer won't accept them (he might if they are denominated in his currency) you will have to cash them. Don't try to do this at a money changing kiosk. Check with several banks and let them know that you wish to change a substantial amount. Don't be surprised if some banks or dealers don't want to cash large amounts, counterfeit traveler's checks are a big problem in Europe. Eventually, however, you'll probably find a bank willing to cash your checks for a small fee, perhaps well under one percent.

It is sometimes possible to pay for a purchased vehicle with your credit card. This will only work with a dealer, of course. Many people now have cards with large credit limits or debit cards that draw directly on their bank accounts. An advantage here is that you avoid fees and get a good exchange rate. We've even had a dealer transfer money back to us by crediting our account when he repurchased our RV.

A bank wire transfer is an excellent way to transfer money overseas if you know where you want the money to go. You'll need to know the bank identification number and account number of the seller and you'll have to arrange to make the transfer while you're still in North America since your signature is required. Your bank can probably make a transfer based on a call from you if you arrange it before you leave. The advantage of a bank transfer is that it only costs about $25 and you get a good exchange rate. Be advised that it can take up to a week to make a wire transfer.

Shipping a Vehicle from North America

Low shipping costs now make bringing a vehicle from home a practical alternative. Motorcycles, automobiles, and RVs can all be economically shipped. Rates are expected to decline even more in the near future. If you already own a suitable rig this is our recommended method of getting an RV in Europe, especially if you will be making an extended visit.

A word of warning. You will probably hear that you can sell your North American RV in Europe for a good profit, thereby making your trip much less expensive. While Europeans are indeed intrigued by American motorhomes, there are significant barriers to licensing one in Europe. Once buyers start looking into the nuts and bolts of such a transaction their ardor usually cools. Do the necessary research before counting on selling your American rig overseas.

To get information about shipping a vehicle check the yellow pages in port cities for freight forwarders specializing in vehicles. If you don't live in a port city you can find a phone book at a library. They can give you a quote, arrange for shipment, or refer you to someone else if they don't deal with shipping vehicles to Europe. Costs vary considerably but we were recently quoted the following approximate rates for shipment from New Jersey to Germany: Motorcycle - $500, Automobile - $800, 19-foot RV (7.5 ft. high) - $1,200. These rates do not include insurance which can run about 1.5% to 2.5% of the value of the vehicle. Also check to see if there are additional paperwork charges. You should definitely shop around because rates vary considerably. The rates are based upon the cubic volume of your rig so big RVs cost a lot more than small ones. Ask about transit time, expect it to be between two and four weeks. Rates from the east coast are cheaper than those from the west coast.

Seabridge International specializes in shipping automobiles and RV's to and from Europe from both coasts of the U.S.. Contact them at Point Breeze Maritime Center, 2310 Broening Highway, Suite 130, Baltimore, MD 21224 (410 633-0550). Also check our web site at www.rollinghomes.com for links to freight forwarders specializing in vehicles.

Theft of contents is a major problem if you ship your RV. Minimize your exposure by not shipping anything of value in the unit. Obtain insurance on contents if you can but this is difficult. Even things of little resale value are often stolen: linens, kitchen utensils, tools. Since you probably will end up leaving some things in the rig you can minimize the risk of theft if you don't leave the unit sitting on the dock any longer than necessary. There is little risk when the unit is actually aboard the ship. Deliver it as late as possible and pick it up at the other end at the earliest possible moment.

Is the rig you own in North America suitable for Europe? Size is probably the most important consideration. Any rig over 22 feet long will give you problems. Camp sites and roads are smaller in Europe and gas is much more expensive. You will be way ahead if your rig burns diesel.

You won't want to plug your 110 volt rig into the 220 volt current used throughout Europe. The wiring is not suitable and your appliances would be ruined. This includes things like battery chargers, microwaves, and refrigerators. When U.S. rigs are imported by British dealers (as they increasingly are) they are entirely rewired. You won't want to do this as it is very expensive and involves replacing a lot of equipment. A better solution is the purchase of a voltage converter to step the voltage down to 110 before it even enters your rig. Portable converters to do this are available from British RV dealers. In Germany they can be found around American military bases, you may find it easiest to make a military friend to buy you one on base. Even the use of a converter will not allow you to use all of your appliances everywhere. Most continental campgrounds don't provide enough amperage for microwaves, air conditioners, or powerful electric heaters. You must also make sure that the slower 50 cycle current won't damage appliances.

Another problem area is black-water (toilet) waste tanks. Many European campgrounds do not have any dump facility at all. Others only have provisions for dumping gray water (sink and shower water) tanks. European rigs almost all use portable or cassette (removable tank) toilets and sometimes portable gray-water tanks that are carried or wheeled to a disposal room or toilet. To empty the tanks on your rig you will need a portable tank and hand trolley to empty the waste. You can buy this in Europe at RV supply stores but it would probably be easier to find one in the U.S.

If you bring a vehicle from home don't forget to bring along some spares. Replacement light bulbs, belts, hoses, filters and even tires in North American sizes may be difficult to locate in Europe. Have the vehicle thoroughly gone over before leaving home because maintenance is much cheaper and easier in North America. Consider replacement of tires, belts, and hoses even if they have a few thousand more miles left in them. Also have a complete tune-up and oil change. The tune-up will mean better mileage and save gas money.

INSURANCE

You must have European liability insurance to operate a car, RV, or motorcycle in Europe. If your vehicle is licensed in the U.S. one place you can obtain this insurance is from AIU North America, Inc. at 800 343-5761. If you buy from a dealer in Europe he will be able to assist you in buying insurance. Rates can vary considerably. You should try to bring proof of a good driving record with you from home, perhaps a letter from your current insurance company and a copy of your driving record if you can get it. It might help you get a lower rate. We were able to obtain insurance for a much lower price the second time we purchased it because we had established a good record with the same company on a previous visit. You may have better luck getting insurance at a reasonable rate if you have done a quasi-lease transaction with the vehicle remaining in the dealer's name.

Make sure that the insurance that you buy covers you in all of the countries that you plan to visit, and also make sure that it includes Spanish bail bond coverage. Liability-only policies will cost you from $2 to $6 per day, more per day for short visits and less for long ones, and assuming you have a decent driving record. Like everything else it pays to shop around for your insurance.

MAGAZINES AND INFORMATION SOURCES

There are many camping magazines published in the U.K. They are a good way to educate yourself about European camping and also have many classified advertisements. If you know someone traveling through London have them pick up a pile of them from a newsstand. Failing that try giving some of these magazines a call to purchase recent issues or a subscription: **Motorcaravan Motorhome Monthly**, **Which Motorcaravan**, and **Caravan Life** are all available at 44 1778 391153, **Motor Caravan World** at 44 181 3026069, **Caravan Magazine** at 44 181 6466672. Caravan Life and Caravan Magazine deal with caravans (camping trailers) only.

The Caravan Club offers a wealth of information including a magazine, European and U.K. camping guides, and more. Consider joining before your visit, you'll save enough on campgrounds while in the U.K. to pay for the fees. Their address is East Grinstead House, East Grinstead, West Sussex RH19 1UA (44 342 326944). There's a link to their web site on ours, www.rollinghomes.com.

CHAPTER

3

DETAILS, DETAILS, DETAILS

Alternate Accommodations

There is no reason that you have to camp every night during your visit to Europe. A hotel room can be a pleasant change after several days in a tent or RV. There are many types of alternative accommodation, many of them almost as economical as the campgrounds.

After camping, hostels are probably the least expensive form of accommodation. They are not just for students, there is not an upper age limit for guests except in Bavaria, where it is 26. You must generally be a member of the International Youth Hostel Federation (IYHF), but nonmembers can pay extra for a temporary pass. Accommodation is generally a bed in a dormitory room and there are either kitchen facilities that you can use or a cafeteria/restaurant. If you're young or young at heart you will probably enjoy the occasional hostel visit.

The next level of accommodation is what we would call a bed-and-breakfast in North America. Sometimes they are just a room in a private home, sometimes something more elaborate. These are found throughout Europe, although they may have another name. In Britain they are called bed-and-breakfast, in Germany they may be called a Gasthäuser or Zimmer, and in other countries pensions or guest houses. Prices vary considerably, the local tourist office can often book you or point you in the right direction. Many of these places have signs out front, don't hesitate to inquire.

When you travel the highways you're likely to see a type of hotel that rail travelers don't even know about. Some European countries, especially France, have "subbudget" hotels along the freeways. Names to look for are Formule 1, Fasthotel, Liberté, Bonsai, Nuit d'Hotel, and Première Class. You get about 100 square feet with a double bed and share a restroom down the hall. All of this for $30 or so. If you're looking for a little better motel similar to the budget hotels in North America try Campanile, Balladins, Relais Bleu or Climat de France. Expect to pay between $60 and $75 a night. In Italy you might also try the AGIP chain which has many motels along the autostradas.

Finally, there are all of the other hotels. These come in all price ranges, of course. Probably the best place to find inexpensive hotels is near train stations. Often the bathroom will be down the hall. Tourist offices are a good place to get help in finding a hotel room or room in a private home, it is one of their main functions.

Automobile Clubs

You will find that automobile clubs are much more popular in Europe than in North America. In many countries auto clubs are in charge of a national breakdown service, even nonmembers can get help for a fee. The American Automobile Association (AAA), Canadian Automobile Association (CAA) and other clubs around the world are members of two international associations of automobile clubs, the AIT and FIA, and have reciprocal agreements. These agreements give members limited access to automobile club services in other countries. Services provided vary from country to country and often involve fees. We've included phone numbers for some of the most popular European auto clubs in each of the country chapters. More information can be found in a free booklet available from the AAA, ***Offices to Serve You Abroad***.

Bathroom/Shower Facilities in Campgrounds

It is time for a little honesty about the bathroom/shower facilities in Europe. You are going to find yourself at a few campgrounds where the toilets and showers are not up to North American standards, or European standards either for that matter.

First, there are the toilets. Pit toilets like you sometimes find in the U.S., Mexico, and Canada are unusual. Most campgrounds do have plumbing. Many of them just don't make the best use of it.

In much of southern Europe you will find that normal seat-type toilets are scarce. Instead you will find what are often indelicately called "squatters" by most North American visitors. These consist of a ceramic fixture looking a lot like the floor of a shower stall. There is a hole in the floor with two platforms in front that are obviously places to put your feet. After you've done your business you had better stand back before you pull the flush cord, because the deluge that follows may wet your shoes. To be fair these things are common in other places around the world, some people swear by them. It must take a lifetime of use to attain proficiency.

Even if you do find a sit-down toilet your problems may not be over. The toilets in many campgrounds do not have seats. I suppose the theory here is that they are easier to clean. Your guess is as good as mine.

European toilet paper as been a joke for a long time. The quality has been poor, sometimes the proverbial Sears catalog seems like it would be an improvement. Now you can buy good toilet paper in the stores. You had better do so because most campgrounds do not provide it for you.

The other problem area in campground bathrooms is the showers. Energy is expensive in Europe and campground designers do not want you to waste it. They have developed many ways to limit your use of hot water. Some campgrounds require that you buy a token to insert into a slot to get hot water. Others require that you push on a button on the wall the entire time you are in the shower. Many do not let you adjust the temperature of the water, you must be happy with what you get. This would be fine if the water were hot enough, but we have been in many where it was much too cool, and none where it was too hot.

An additional shower problem is that there often is nowhere to undress or leave your clothes. You must do this in the shower, and then you must invent some way to keep everything dry while you are taking the shower.

European campers get around the shower problem just as you will. They carry their toilet articles in a plastic bag that can be hung on the shower door. They wear plastic slippers that can get wet. They don't wear a lot when they go in to take their showers. In fact, this can be a problem too. It isn't unusual to see men heading for the shower in just their underwear. We advise you to take a robe or a sweat suit if you don't want to do the same.

Don't be surprised to see references to the showers when we write about campgrounds we visit later in this book. If a campground has particularly good or bad showers we may feel compelled to mention it. After a few weeks camping in Europe you will come to appreciate the information.

Bicycles

A bicycle is much more useful in Europe than in the North America. Since few people tow a car behind rigs in Europe (it is often illegal) you might try some bicycles instead. In many countries bicycles are commonly used for transportation. This means that there are often bicycle paths going where you want to go. You can leave your RV in the campground where it is safe and use the bicycle for shopping and sightseeing, not to mention staying in shape. We've found that large supermarkets, particularly in Great Britain and France, are good places to pick up new bikes at decent prices. Don't pay too much, you don't want to spend much time worrying about your bike being stolen. Racks for carrying your bike on the back of your rig are available in bike shops and at RV dealers.

Budget

In the table below we've tried to give you some idea of the cost of a camping visit to Europe using one of the several options open to you. You can see that the daily cost varies from $33 to about $71 per person per day. The length of your stay has a major effect upon the daily cost. We've made many estimates and assumptions in producing the table and it certainly does not include all costs that you will incur. Costs not considered include but are not limited to transportation to Europe, the cost of purchasing camping equipment if you don't already own it, public transportation, tolls and ferries, restaurant meals and alcohol, entrance fees and entertainment, medical costs, additional insurance, and vehicle maintenance. All of these things are highly variable and will depend upon your destination and style of living.

	Eurailpass	Car Rental	Car Lease	RV Rental	Van Purchase & Resale	RV From Home
Number of People	1	2	2	2	2	2
Length of Visit (Days)	30	14	60	14	120	180
Transportation Costs:						
Eurailpass	890	0	0	0	0	0
Rent or Net Cost of Owning	0	400	1200	1150	2000	0
Shipping	0	0	0	0	0	3000
Insurance (Liability Only)	0	0	0	0	500	550
Total	890	400	1200	1150	2500	3550
Total Per Day	30	29	20	82	21	20
Daily Living Expenses:						
Meals	10	20	20	20	20	20
Fuel	0	15	15	25	25	35
Campgrounds	8	10	10	15	15	15
Totaly Daily	18	45	45	60	60	70
Total Transportation and Daily	48	74	65	142	81	90
Total Per Person	48	37	33	71	40	45

There are some ways to save money:

1. We have assumed that you will spend every night in a campground. Many people free camp at least half the time, sometimes much more. Take a look at the Free Camping section below.

2. A $10 a day food budget is more than adequate if there are more than a singleperson in your party. It is a little tight for one person. Most meals would be picnic style or prepared at the campground. Quantity purchase economies will allow you to save money or eat better. To save money consider giving up meat for some meals or even the occasional bottle of beer or wine.

3. In our cost calculation for the purchase of a van we have assumed that the vehicle will depreciate or require repairs totaling $2,000 over a three month period. This is really the net cost of a purchase and resale, if you are skillful or lucky or have the time to do a thorough job you can reduce this cost substantially. Even if you enter into a purchase/repurchase agreement with a dealer you usually have the option of selling the vehicle yourself. For the most inexpensive long term visit the purchase and sale of a European rig is probably the way to go.

4. Fuel is a huge variable cost. Our table assumes that you average 250 kilometers per day and pay $3.50 a gallon for gas. You can save a considerable amount of money if you drive fewer kilometers, use diesel fuel, or visit countries with cheaper gasoline. Take a look at the Fuel Price and Distances sections below and the individual mileage charts in the campground chapters.

Bookstores and Magazines

Since books are heavy you'll probably not want to pack much of a library to bring from home. If you're starting in England this doesn't present much of a problem, you'll be able to pick up a good selection of books before heading for the Continent. Once there, however, English language books are harder to find.

Most of the capital cities have an English language bookstore or two. We've found them in Amsterdam, Brussels, Vienna, Paris, Lyons, Berlin, Munich, Rome, Florence, and Milan. Even if you don't find a store specializing in English you will probably be able to find bookstores with small English language sections. Many people catch up on their classics while in Europe, these seem to be the easiest books to find and the least expensive. Countries where a language other than English, German, French, Spanish, or Italian is spoken often have good selections of English language books in their stores because only a limited number of books are printed in the local language.

English language newspapers are easy to find in major towns. Often you'll find them at newsstands on major streets or at train stations. The most common are the International Herald Tribune and USA Today, sometimes you can find the Wall Street Journal. Time and Newsweek are also often available. A good selection of papers from England is available in tourist areas.

Children

There can be no better way to travel in Europe with children than by camping. Children generally love camping and the opportunities it provides to be outdoors, meet other youngsters, and live in a way that is different and exciting.

Most campgrounds provide facilities for kids. They range from playground equipment and playing fields to swimming pools, beaches, and water slides, to bike trails to video games.

For most of us camping is the only way we can afford to bring the children to Europe for an extended tour. It costs little more to bring four or six to a campground than to bring two, and cooking for your family is much less expensive than taking them to a restaurant.

It is entirely possible to travel with children during the school year. Home schooling is now quite popular and most school districts will allow it, especially if it is only for a year or so and the object is to travel in an educational place like Europe. Policies vary, you may find that the school district will provide a lesson plan, give you assistance with your own, or require the use of a correspondence school. Check with your school or state department of education about the legalities and procedures. Don't forget about the advantages of a laptop computer with CD ROM drive. There is more and more reference and educational material available in a compact format on disk. Home schooling requires discipline but can be very rewarding.

Clothes

The key to a good camping wardrobe is to keep it simple. Europe is not at all formal these days. Jeans and T-shirts will do for some people, you may be accustomed to dressing a little more formally than that even in North America. You can plan on wearing about the same thing you would at home. One set of more formal clothes for visits to nice restaurants, shows, or casinos is about all you'll want, hanging space is scarce in an RV.

You'll probably want something to wear to the shower. A robe or sweat suit works well, you'll see Europeans with even less. A pair of plastic shower sandals will also come in handy. You will appreciate some kind of hanging bag to hold your toilet articles, shelf space in bathrooms is usually nonexistent.

Outdoor clothing will be necessary since you'll be spending a lot of time outdoors. Bring some light rain gear including rain pants, they're very useful in a heavy rainstorm. Make sure your rain gear is as light and compact as possible so you don't leave it at home when you plan an all-day expedition. Synthetic fleece sweaters and coats are a good choice for staying warm, they'll continue to do their job when wet and they dry almost immediately when you wash them. You will also really appreciate a collapsible umbrella.

Compass

We know, when you think of a compass you think of those cheap dash mounted things. In Europe, however, they are really handy. Not the dash variety, although even one of those has its place. You'll find a small hand-held compass very useful when wandering around European cities. Your sense of direction can abandon you when you emerge from a subway on a cloudy day. A compass will set you straight and save you a lot of uncomfortable moments.

Credit Cards

Credit cards really are widely used in Europe. Most countries in Western Europe are moving more and more towards their use. Some, like Spain, already use them more than we do. Gasoline, however, in some countries is difficult to buy with a credit card.

The cards you will find most useful are Visa, Master Card, American Express, and Diners Club. American Express and Diners Club are used much more than in the U.S., and American Express offers some services at their offices in Europe that can be quite handy, so if you don't have all of these cards you might try to get them before you go.

A problem with credit cards is that you must pay them on a monthly basis, which can be inconvenient if you are overseas. One solution to this is to prepay your cards, in effect turning them into debit cards. Unfortunately the credit card companies hate to leave a positive balance on your card. Even with a letter of explanation from us we've only had so-so luck prepaying. Once our prepayment was refunded while we were gone and we ended up over our credit limit on the card. This is as good a reason as any to carry several cards. Debit cards, which draw directly out of your bank account also work quite well. Another solution to the payment problem is American Express, you can pay your statement balance with a check at American Express offices in Europe.

Probably the best thing about using a credit or debit card is that you don't have to worry about getting the best exchange rate, the exchange rate you get with a card will probably be better than any you can get with traveler's checks at a European bank or money exchange counter.

Distances

Gas is expensive in Europe so it's a good thing that the distances are short. We usually try to drive no more than 250 kilometers per day. On the freeway this takes less than three hours. In the States we think nothing of driving three hundred miles and taking almost six hours to do it. We just don't have to travel as far in Europe. The following distances are from Amsterdam, a common starting point for a European tour.

Amsterdam, The Netherlands to:

	KM	Miles
Barcelona, Spain	1,551	961
Berlin, Germany	660	409
Lisbon, Portugal	2,317	1,436
London, England	530	328
Madrid, Spain	1,775	1,100
Marseilles, France	1,265	784
Paris, France	506	314
Rome, Italy	1,712	1,061

If you're really in a hurry and use the freeways it is quite easy to do 600 to 700 kilometers per day for days on end.

Documents

You will have to have a passport to even get into Europe. After your arrival you are likely to never have to show it at a border again. For U.S. or Canadian citizens visas are not required unless an extended stay in one country is planned. Three months is the usual cutoff. Border checks in western Europe are mostly a thing of the past. On the other hand, you will probably have to produce you passport quite often at campgrounds and hotels. They may use it to register you with the police. Some countries require that you register within three days of entering the country and campgrounds and hotels take care of this for you. Often they will want to keep it overnight and you have no choice but to let them. This can be inconvenient because the other place you'll probably need it is when you are getting cash (unless you use cash machines).

Campgrounds will often accept a Camping Card International (also called a Camping Carnet or International Camping Card) instead of a passport, this is just one of the reasons you need one. Camping Cards are also required at some campgrounds, if you don't have one you can't stay there. In other campgrounds you'll get a substantial discount. In North America you can get a Camping Card International by joining the Family Campers and RVers, Inc., 4804 Transit Road, Building 2, Depew, NY 14043 (716 668-6242). AAA (American Automobile Association) members can get one through the International Documents Department at the affiliated CAA (Canadian Automobile Association), 1145 Hunt Club Road, Suite 200, Ottawa, Ontario K1V 0Y3 (613 247-0117).You can survive in Europe without a Camping Card but there is no reason to do so.

An International Driving Licenses is just a standard form that translates the information on your national driving license into several languages. It also has a picture. They are easy to get at American Automobile Association offices, even if you are not a member. Even though these are really not specifically required in any Western European country you will find that some countries, like Italy and Spain, do require that you carry a translation of your driver's license. The International Driving License is the easiest way to comply with this requirement.

ONE REASON YOU DON'T WANT TO TAKE YOUR VAN INTO TOWN

Driving in Europe

Driving in Europe is really no more difficult than driving in North America. Each year the traffic rules seem to get more like ours (or ours like theirs). There are a few differences but they should give you no real problems.

Traffic signs are fairly uniform throughout Europe. The many languages spoken on the continent have forced the use of international pictorial signs. You'll find representations of them in many guide books, they are largely self-explanatory and you'll soon become accustomed to them.

Safety regulations similar to those in place in North America are now also effective in most European countries. Seat belts are required and there is no tolerance for drinking and driving. Children 12 and under must not ride in the front seat unless there in no other seat available. Child safety seats are required for infants. On freeways you must never pass on the right.

There are also some differences from what we are accustomed to. In most countries the police can issue tickets and collect fines on the spot. There is usually no provision for making a right turn at a red light after a stop. You must have a green light. You'll often come to intersections that have no stop or yield signs. Just as in North America the person on the right has the right-of-way, and in Europe he is much more likely to assume that you know he has it. You must be alert.

European roads are generally very good. Almost all countries now have extensive freeway systems, some free and others toll systems. In the introduction to each of our country chapters we have described the driving situation in the individual countries including idiosyncrasies like driving on the left in the British Isles. Large trucks use these roads just as they do at home, most roads have plenty of room for even the largest RV.

Electrical Appliances

Almost all European countries use 220 to 250 volt current rather than the 110 volt we are accustomed to in the US, Canada, and Mexico. They also use different plug shapes than we do, and these vary from country to country.

As a camper the plug shape dilemma is not too much of a problem. Inside your RV you will have outlets like those of the country that manufactured your RV. Once you adapt your RV service cord to the area you are visiting you will be able to use the same appliances in all countries. See the Electrical Service In The Campgrounds section below about that concern.

The use of 220 volt current is the major problem. There are converters available to convert 220 volt to 110 volt, Radio Shack carries some good ones. However, you probably won't be happy with this solution. Some appliances, particularly hair dryers, do not work too well using adapters because the current throughout Europe cycles at 50 cycles per second rather than the 60 cycles our North American appliances are designed for. Any motors in your appliances will run too slowly. We find that purchasing inexpensive European appliances is well worth the money, they will work better than the ones you bring from home.

Most campground electrical service is limited to 500 to 600 watts. This means that most heating appliances will not work. If you buy a heater or hair dryer make sure that it draws no more than 500 watts.

We have had very good luck with portable computers in Europe. Most of these have power packs that adapt automatically to the 220 volt current, take a look at the information plate on yours to see if it does before plugging it in. We have never used surge protectors on our portables, even in campgrounds, where power surges must be quite common. You may not feel comfortable doing this, we certainly don't know enough about the technical details to guarantee that you won't have any problems.

Electrical Service in Campgrounds

European campgrounds do not provide as much electricity to campers as is usually available at North American campgrounds. You will find that the individual campground descriptions in this book often give the amperage of electrical service offered. You'll almost never find more than 16 amps and occasionally as little as 2 amps.

You can calculate the amps required by your appliances if you know their wattage. Amps are equal to watts divided by volts. Since most countries in Europe use 220 volt current you can see that a 1,000 watt appliance draws about 4.5 amps. Here are average numbers for some frequently used appliances:

Refrigerator	0.5 amps
Microwave	5.0 amps
Battery Charger	0.1 amps
Fluorescent Lights	0.5 amps
500 Watt Heater	2.3 amps
1,000 Watt Heater	4.5 amps
2,000 Watt Heater	9.0 amps

You'll find that you become quite knowledgeable about the amount of current you need because not all campgrounds have easily accessible breaker switches. If you trip the switch you have to find someone to reset it.

There are several types of plugs used in Europe. The newest and most common is the CEE17 plug. It is commonly used in Great Britain and at new campgrounds throughout the continent. Usually blue in color, it has three prongs and a protective plastic collar, a hefty design. Both the Germans and French have their own plug style, it has two round prongs and a ground. The only difference is that the German type uses grounding strips on the outside of the plug and the French type uses a grounding prong mounted on the electrical outlet. The two plugs are not interchangeable but you can buy a plug which can be used for both systems, it incorporates both grounding systems. Finally, the Swiss use an entirely different plug (also used in Liechtenstein and at some Spanish sites). You'll want to have your main service cord fitted with a CEE17 plug and also carry an adapter that works for both the German and French styles. In Switzerland the campgrounds generally supply you with the adapter or you can easily find one to buy. Finally, in some small older campgrounds you'll find only old or indoor style outlets. The management will probably have a selection of adapters to get you plugged in.

You will probably notice that we often mention that a long cord is required for a campground in the campground section of this book. That is because we tried to make do with a 10 meter cord (to save storage space). If you plan to use electricity much this is not enough. Go to a hardware store and buy a 25 meter (80 foot) cord on a convenient reel. If it is not already equipped with them add a CEE17 plug to the end. The experts say this is the longest length that is safe, it should be adequate.

Free Camping

Not everyone who camps spends every night in a campground. One way to dramatically cut the costs of visiting Europe is to free camp. Many people visit a campground only every second or third night for a chance to take a hot shower. We have met some people who almost never visit a campground.

While laws vary from country to country, even from city to city or district to district, you can safely assume that you're probably breaking some kind of law when you free camp in a spot that is not private property. Most jurisdictions have laws that they can use to control unwanted vagrants. That doesn't mean that free camping won't be allowed. Often free campers are tolerated if they are unobtrusive. Never camp where there are signs prohibiting it, you are likely to be socked with a fine on the spot, or worse. We give some suggestions about the local free camping situation in each country chapter.

You can often find a place to camp on private property, especially in the country. Always ask permission if you can find anyone around. You might consider offering a reasonable fee. Having permission will give you a lot of peace of mind during the night.

Freeway rest areas are often used by free campers. As in North America this may be frowned upon but you can usually get away with an overnight stay if you are inconspicuous and don't set up a camp. Officials don't want people driving if they're likely to fall asleep.

Safety is an important consideration if you decide to free camp. For this reason we do not recommend it unless you are in an area with other campers or help nearby.

Fuel

As you've probably heard fuel is quite expensive in Europe, it is heavily taxed. Here are some representative prices from the fall of 1998. Prices are in U.S. dollars per U.S. gallon.

Unleaded has different names in different countries. Here are some of them:

Austria	Bleifrei
Belgium	Normale sans plomb or ongelood
Czech Republic	Natural
Denmark	Blyfri benzin
Finland	Lyijyton polttoaine
France	Essence sans plomb
Germany	Bleifrei normal

Greece	Amoliwdi wensina
Italy	Benzina sensa plombo
The Netherlands	Loodvrije benzine
Norway	Blyfritt kraftstoff
Portugal	Gasolina sin plomo
Spain	Gasolina sin plombo
Sweden	Blyfri
Switzerland	Same as Germany, France or Italy
Turkey	Kursunsuz benzin

We've not listed leaded gas but where it is available (not all countries) it is usually a little more expensive than the cheapest unleaded. You can generally identify unleaded gas because it is in the green pump.

	Unleaded	Diesel	Propane
Austria	3.73	2.96	2.75
Denmark	3.86	3.45	2.90
Finland	4.11	2.78	N/A
France	3.83	2.71	1.80
Germany	3.49	2.52	N/A
Gibraltar	2.42	1.90	N/A
Greece	2.78	2.21	N/A
United Kingdom	3.78	3.84	N/A
Italy	3.79	2.98	1.80
Luxembourg	2.59	2.10	2.17
Netherlands	4.09	2.72	1.25
Norway	4.79	3.87	1.95
Portugal	3.48	2.38	2.20
Republic of Ireland	3.62	3.62	2.23
Spain	2.88	2.44	N/A
Sweden	3.75	2.90	2.17
Switzerland	2.98	3.11	N/A
Turkey	2.25	1.37	1.42

You will note that diesel is often a much better deal than gasoline. The fact that diesel yields about 25% better mileage than gas makes it an even better buy. The diesel pump is not normally hard to identify, it will probably be marked Diesel or Gasoil. When in doubt ask, attendants will recognize either the word Diesel or the word Gasoil in any country.

If you examine the chart closely you'll see that it often makes sense to plan your gas purchases. Prices are becoming more uniform throughout the E.C. but Luxembourg still stands out as a good place to stop for a fill-up in northern Europe.

Some vehicles, especially in The Netherlands, Belgium, France, and Italy run on propane. Often you can run them on either gasoline or propane with the flip of a switch. Propane yields about 80% of the mileage that gasoline does, but it is a great deal in some countries. We've listed the propane price only in countries where it is available at service stations. Although listed in Denmark, Norway and Sweden propane is difficult to find in these countries. A guidebook to stations with propane really helps, we've found them at stations in The Netherlands.

Health Matters

Europe is a modern, healthy place with no significant health risks that you wouldn't run into in North America. No special immunizations are required for the countries covered in this book. Health services in all of these countries are quite good.

You should review your health insurance coverage before any extended foreign trip. Check to see if your health expenditures will be reimbursed by your carrier and what procedures should be followed. If there is no coverage you may wish to consider supplemental travel insurance.

Internet

As the internet matures it is becoming a wonderful tool for research and communication. Rather than fill the text of our books with web site addresses we have set up our own web site. At **www.rollinghomes.com** you will find links to pages about the following:

European Camping Clubs
European Used RV Dealers
RV Rental Companies in Europe
Shipping Companies Specializing in Vehicles
European Ferry Companies
Tourist Information
Campground Listings
European Cell Phone Providers
Internet Cafes in Europe

It is possible to use the internet for communication while you are in Europe, but e-mail is not yet the most economical or convenient way to keep in touch with home. Internet cafes are not difficult to find, but the fees and time involved make using the phone the preferable communication alternative.

Laundry

Fortunately, camping allows you to wear simple clothing that is relatively easy to care for. The reason that this is fortunate is that the laundry facilities in Europe leave a lot to be desired.

In most European countries self-service laundries are hard to find. When you do find them they are very expensive. Campgrounds often have their own facilities, but these are usually quite limited, consisting of one or two machines to service the whole campground. The cost of doing a load of clothes in one of these machines can be extraordinarily high compared with what we are accustomed to in North America, often well over $5.00 to wash and dry a load, sometimes over $10.00.

The solution that most campers use is to hand wash their small, easy to wash articles.

Things like underwear and socks are easily washed on a daily basis and will dry pretty quickly, even if you have to hang them on a line in the van while you drive on to the next destination. Lines of drying clothes are commonplace in European campgrounds. We like to save difficult-to-wash clothes for the rare campground where we can gain access to a decent washer. This means that when we pack our clothes to take to Europe we bring along a large selection of jeans and shirts so that we don't have to visit the laundry room very often. Summer travel is easier since shorts and T-shirts are pretty easy to wash by hand.

Maps

You will need good maps to navigate. The standard is probably the Michelin series which covers almost all of Europe, but there are many other companies offering similar products.

European maps, except those in Great Britain, use the metric system. This works quite well when measuring distances on the map. On a 1:200,000 scale map, our favorite scale for detailed navigation, 1 centimeter is equal to 2 kilometers. On a 1:400,000 scale 1 centimeter would equal 4 kilometers.

You should consider buying the beautiful small-scale motoring atlases that Michelin and others offer. These are easy to handle in a vehicle where sheet maps are difficult to manipulate. They seem expensive at first but the individual sheet maps you'll accumulate can add up to even more. Michelin prints atlases covering France (1:200,000, their best), Germany, Spain and Portugal, Great Britain and Ireland, Italy, and one for all of Europe.

When you are evaluating a map take a look to see if it shows campgrounds. None of them show all campgrounds but some show quite a few. This can be very useful.

Keep your eyes peeled for discount prices on last year's atlases. Roads don't change much in a year and prices are often much lower for these out-of-date-maps.

In Britain you can find inexpensive small scale road atlases in the big supermarkets. These work great and are a real deal when you compare their price with a Michelin atlas.

Mail

If you are going to be in Europe for any length of time you are going to have to find a way to receive mail. There are several ways to do this.

American Express offers Client Letter Service at many of their offices. This is a letter service only, no parcels or registered mail. This is a free service for American Express card holders and people who are using their traveler's checks. Otherwise there is a fee. You can obtain a small booklet containing a complete list of all of their offices which also tells which ones accept mail. Call American Express and ask for a copy of *American Express Worldwide Traveler's Companion*. The booklet is compact and has other useful information like international access codes for AT&T, Sprint, and MCI and embassy addresses.

The other good option is to have your mail sent to any city in Europe C/O Poste Restante. This is the European name for General Delivery. In large towns Poste Restante mail usually goes to the main office.

You can have your mail sent in care of a campground. We hesitate to recommend this unless you have been there before, are sure of the address, and are sure that the mail will be handled properly. For important mail this is really only a practical option if you make prior arrangements with the management.

For really frequent visits or long stays in Europe you may want to set up a permanent mail drop. British Monomarks Limited in London can provide you with a permanent mailing address and will forward mail to you as you direct. Contact them at Monomark House, 27 Old Gloucester Street, London WC1N 3XX (0171-4054442)

Money Exchange

You've no doubt heard of the euro, a new common currency that will make travel in Europe very easy because everyone will use the same type of money. Unfortunately that day isn't here yet. The euro will not go into circulation until January 1, 2002. It will trade in the countries that are being called Euroland: Austria, Belgium, Finland, France, Germany, Ireland, Italy, Luxembourg, The Netherlands, Portugal and Spain. Between now and then it is possible that a few other countries will join the group, the others will continue to have their own currencies.

For now very country in Europe has its own currency, a traveler never really gets away from the frustrations of changing money. Just when you start to feel like you're on top of the situation you cross a border and suddenly you're penniless.

Most travel guides recommend that you carry traveler's checks. This is old technology. In a year of traveling in Europe we only had to cash traveler's checks twice, once to get money to pay for the purchase of a van and once when the magnetic strip on our only debit card went south. It took a week to get a new one from home.

With a credit or debit card and pin number you may never have to visit a currency exchange booth at all. Cash machines are everywhere, we used them without any problems in every country covered in this book except Turkey. The exchange rate you get will be better than what you could get at any exchange booth and the machine is a lot easier to deal with than most exchange booth or bank tellers.

Not all cards will work with all machines. We have cards that will work with both the Plus network and the Cirrus network. We use the Cirrus card most of the time and found that if a machine wouldn't take it (very unusual) we could use the Plus card. If we were willing to look around a little we could usually find a Cirrus machine. Our U.S. pin number worked without a hitch, you might check with your bank to make sure that you don't need an international number with yours. You will need a pin number if you want to use your card in automated tellers so check to see if you can get one with your Visa or Master Card. Generally it must be a four digit number to work in Europe.

You should be aware that most cards have a daily limit on cash withdrawals of about $400 dollars. This isn't enough for the occasional emergency. See if you can get that daily limit raised before leaving home.

If your magnetic strip stops working or if your bank decides to cut you off for no good reason you should have a back-up plan. A few hundred dollars of traveler's checks is good insurance. Another possibility is American Express, if you have one of their cards they will cash your personal check (if you happen to have brought along your check book).

Pets

You should not even consider bringing a pet to Europe. Several countries, including the U.K. and Sweden, require very long quarantines (four months and longer) before a pet will be allowed to join you in your rig. The reason for this appears to be a fear of disease, especially rabies, and the rules are not likely to become much looser in the foreseeable future.

Propane

Most campers and RVs use either propane or butane for cooking, heating hot water, and space heating. Both propane and butane are available in all western European countries, some places make it easier to obtain than others.

You will find that most U.K. rigs have removable propane or butane bottles. It is easy to get either one of these refilled in the British Isles, not so easy elsewhere. Most French rigs seem to be designed for removable butane while German and Dutch RVs often have a permanently-mounted propane bottle and these sometimes present problems in the British Isles. However, campers from all three countries regularly travel everywhere and they all manage to find fuel. Many campgrounds will have replacement bottles or facilities for refilling bottles. As a last resort you can always ask a neighbor for advice. There's bound to be someone with a system like yours.

You'll need a propane filling adapter for your North American rig. These are generally available at RV supply stores, especially in the British Isles were they import a lot of American motorhomes. If you can't find a set of adapters you can always have one made, or alternatively, have a European valve installed on your RV.

In some European countries it is very easy to find propane because they use it to fuel cars. Propane pumps (labeled GPL, LPG, or Autogas) are ubiquitous in The Netherlands, Belgium, Ireland, and Italy. They are slightly harder to find but still plentiful in France. The Scandinavian countries also have a few stations. All of these countries use their own special filler designs, but the stations usually have adapters that they will loan you. They probably won't have one to adapt to an American rig, however. It is possible that in some countries the propane in gas stations is only supposed to be used for fueling cars, the rules tend to be obscure and intricate in these matters, but we've never had anyone refuse to let us fill our RV's tank.

Public Transportation

Most North Americans are not accustomed to efficient and convenient public transportation. An amazing number of European cities have subway systems, all have excellent bus systems often augmented by trams or even an aerial lift of one kind or another. Don't be afraid to use any of them, you're as safe on the subways as on the streets.

Almost all of the city campgrounds in this book are serviced by public transportation. Don't even think of taking your rig into town, in most European cities a car is a liability. Why risk the traffic, narrow streets, and impossible parking to park it unprotected on the street. You can leave it safe in your campground and be whisked into town by a local specialist, the bus driver.

Radio

Long periods in foreign countries will really make you feel isolated unless you can get some news and hear an English speaker occasionally. The radio is a good way to do this.

Radios in European vehicles have three settings: MW (AM), UKW (FM), and KW or SW (shortwave) With one of these you can pick up English programs from several sources. In places where there are American military bases you can often hear Armed Forces Radio. It has U.S. news, music, and sometimes even sports from home. Frequencies vary. You can also often hear the Voice of America (VOA) and British Broadcasting Service (BBC) on car radios. For the BBC in northern France, northern Germany, and the Benelux countries listen at 648kHz (MW), or 198 (UKW). For a better selection of stations you should consider purchasing one of the small digital shortwave radios, in the evening you can pick up English language broadcasts from all over the world. Our internet site at www.rollinghomes.com has links to the BBC, Voice America, and the Armed Services Network for frequency and schedule information that you can print out to take with you to Europe.

Reference Books

A small set of reference books can make your trip more enjoyable. If you travel in your own vehicle they're much easier to bring along.

Europe By Van And Motorhome by David Shore and Patty Campbell (Travel Keys Books, 1994, ISBN 0938297082) will help you raise your enthusiasm level about camping in Europe. It also has very good information about purchasing a van and evaluation of a used vehicle. When we decided to go camping in Europe this was the only directly applicable book we could find in the U.S.

Budget travel guides like those published by **Lonely Planet**, the **Rough Guides**, and the **Let's Go** series are very useful for information about inexpensive restaurants and brief guides to what to see. They also list quite a few campgrounds, especially ones near cities useful to backpackers. You can find these in most bookstores.

The **Michelin Green Guides** go into a great deal of detail about the sights you will see. If you use them for that purpose and not your primary guide you will love them. They do tend to be a little dry. These are also widely available. In Europe you can find them almost everywhere.

Guidebooks produced by **Fodor's**, **Fielding**, **Access**, and others seem to be written for folks willing to spend a lot of money for food and lodging so their sections about hotels and restaurants may not be very useful. On the other hand they often have very informative sections about things worth seeing. The best ones have beautiful modern graphics and good maps and are a pleasure to use.

A very complete campground guide available in the U.S. is ***Europa Camping and Caravanning Guide International*** (Drei Brunnen Verlag GmbH & Co, Stuttgart, Germany, annually). It seems to be directed largely at German campers but is relatively complete and is written in German, French, and English. We have found some of the English portions to be less complete than the German and this sometimes makes finding the campgrounds listed a little difficult. In fact, it is usually best to use the guide to get in the general neighborhood and then follow signs. This guide can be difficult to find in the U.S., try REI Co-op in Seattle, Washington (but with stores in many other places around the country). You may have to order it by phone. Amazon.com on the internet also lists the book.

The best camping guides to Europe in English are published by The Caravan Club in the U.K. Their address and phone number are published in the Camping section of the British Isles chapter. We highly recommend both the organization and their two-volume ***Continental Sites Guide & Handbook***. You should consider giving them a call to join and get a copy of this guide, especially if you aren't planning to visit the U.K. at the start of your visit to Europe.

If you are a hiking buff you might find ***100 Hikes in the Alps*** by Vicky Spring and Harvey Edwards (Mountaineers Books, 1992, ISBN 0898863333) well worth bringing along. English language outdoor guides are not always easy to find in Europe. This guide covers the Alps in France, Switzerland, Germany, Austria and Italy and also lists several hikes in the Pyrenees between France and Spain.

If you find that you are short in background knowledge about European history and art you might enjoy two books by budget travel writer and tour operator Rick Steves. These are ***Europe 101*** by Rick Steves and Gene Openshaw (John Muir Publications, 1996, ISBN 1562612468) about European history and art in general and ***Mona Winks: Self-Guided Tours of Europe's Top Museums*** by Rick Steves and Gene Openshaw (John Muir Publications, 1998, ISBN 1562614215) which has easy to follow guides to the some of the most important museums all over Europe.

We like to have a dictionary covering the language of each country we visit. Language can be one of the most enjoyable parts of your trip if you are approaching it with a learning attitude.

Camping means that you will cook a great deal of your own food. Since you will be traveling in foreign countries you will probably enjoy knowing about their food and wine. There's nothing like a visit to a supermarket to pique your curiosity. We enjoy cook books and wine guides, but I have not found any that I would really recommend as both compact and outstanding. We're still looking, and carrying more of them than we probably should.

A technical manual for your rig is sometimes worth its weight in gold. The one supplied with our VW was in Dutch, however. Foreign languages may be fun but our patience is limited when working on a car. Fortunately we brought a guide that covered some aspects of the vehicle from the U.S. We used it.

Reservations

We have found campground reservations to be a lot more trouble than they are worth. In a year of camping in Europe, moving almost every day, we were turned away from a campground only one time and we never made any reservations.

One reason for this is that some European campgrounds never fill up, they just get more and more crowded. Many of them have large grassy fields designed for campers who do not require hook-ups. If you can get along without hook-ups too you'll be able to find a place.

Another reason that reservations really are not necessary is that European campgrounds are really only crowded during the July and August school vacations. The rest of the year you'll be surprised to find one even half full. You should always be able to find a place even in July and August if you travel early in the day and arrive at the campground by three or four in the afternoon.

In most countries reservations are not easy to make. It is customary to make them by mail, usually with a substantial deposit required. Make reservations only if you want to reserve a great spot for a substantial period of time. You can make your reservation by calling the campground and checking on availability and the preferred procedure, you may get lucky and be able to make the reservation using a credit card.

Chains of campgrounds like the camping clubs in the British Isles, the Scandinavian countries, Germany and Switzerland or the commercial chains in France and Portugal often have reservation systems that are easier to work with. You might consider using them to make a few reservations if you happen to be traveling during the high season and find that it is necessary.

Safety Equipment

Certain items of safety equipment are required to be carried in your vehicle in most European countries. Other things will just make things easier if you should encounter problems.

A safety triangle is a must in Europe and required by law. Most are collapsible and stow away in a bag or case. They also work pretty well to mark your campsite if you leave temporarily to go shopping or sightseeing.

An extra bulb kit for your rig is required in many European countries. Seems like it would be handy to have anyway, I don't know why we don't have this requirement in the U.S. Maybe because bulbs are pretty easy to get at home. Extra bulb kits are readily available in Europe at auto supply stores and service stations.

Several countries require that you carry a first aid kit and will ticket you if you are asked for one and can't produce it. They also are available in European auto parts stores.

Spare tire, lug wrench, and jack. Need I say more? Also convenient is an aerosol can of sealant for times when you must get a flat squared away quickly. Good tires are important in Europe too, and bad ones can get you in just as much trouble as they can in the U.S.

If you are a member of the American Automobile Association you have reciprocal rights with many European auto clubs. Before leaving the US you can get a copy of their foreign driving guide entitled ***Offices To Serve You Abroad*** which gives numbers to call in all European countries for assistance and a tow. Your Europe trip may be a good reason to join, they have a package for RV owners and they offer free American Express travelers checks. We've also given emergency phone numbers in our country chapters under the Roads and Driving heading.

When you buy insurance for your driving in Europe you will probably be given an accident record form. Make sure you understand both it and the procedure to follow in case of an accident. Keep it somewhere handy where you can find it in a stressful situation.

While it is not a safety item there is one final purchase you should make to complete outfitting your rig. European regulations used to require that you have a sticker on the rear of your vehicle indicating the country of registration. Many people don't have one and no one seems to care any longer, but it is fun to check out where other campers are from. Some people put two on their rig, one for the country of registration and one for their own nationality. This can head off embarrassing interchanges in the campground when your neighbor might expect you to speak Dutch or German.

Security

Europeans think that the U.S. is a very dangerous place. Statistics show that there is a lot more violent crime at home than there is in Europe. Don't let that make you overconfident during your trip. It is true that you are less likely to be murdered with a handgun in Europe but living in an RV leaves you relatively exposed to criminals.

Personal safety shouldn't be a problem if you make sure that you spend the nights in secure areas and avoid high crime areas in large cities. Europe really is safer than the U.S. in this way.

The security of your belongings, however, is another matter. It takes a thief almost no time to enter a locked vehicle. You yourself have probably seen the tool that tow truck drivers use to enter locked cars. Those tools are easy to get. Police always advise not leaving anything in a car that would attract a thief, but it is difficult to take this advice with an RV, you can't carry all your possessions with you everywhere you go. You might, however, consider strictly limiting the valuable items you bring to Europe to what you can comfortably carry along with you when you leave your rig.

You might consider equipping your rig with a burglar alarm. It will give you a great deal of peace of mind on the occasions when you must leave your vehicle unprotected on the street or in a parking lot. An alarm is not infallible, but it may give a thief second thoughts about breaking in to your RV when he sees that blinking light and those decals on the window, or it might chase him away.

Don't leave valuable things in sight in your RV if you can help it. Why tempt someone.

Finally, park in safe places. Campgrounds are great places to leave your rig. Public transportation is almost everywhere in Europe. Most campgrounds in this book have service. Use it to get in to the center of town while your RV sits safely in the campground. If you must park on the street do it where there are a lot of people or where there is security of some kind, like a parking attendant. And don't forget to turn on that alarm.

Another aspect of security is the security of the things that you carry with you. Pickpockets and purse snatchers are common in the places that tourists visit. We recommend that before you leave for Europe you make a Xerox copy of all of your documents including passports and both sides of the credit cards you will take with you. Keep the copies hidden somewhere safe in your RV so that if you do have your things stolen you will be able to accurately report the loss. Most cards have a phone number to report losses on the back, you will have a copy of this.

Buy and use a money belt or purse that you carry inside your clothing. You can carry most of your cards, money and documents in it so that if your purse or wallet are stolen you won't lose everything.

Telephones

In the last few years Europe has been taken by storm by prepaid phone cards. They can be purchased at post offices and shops and are the cheapest way to make calls, including international ones back home. The cards are inserted into slots in public phones and have a programmable chip preloaded with varying values of money. The cost of the call you make is deducted from the total in the chip, you can insert a new card in the middle of your call if your card runs out. Instructions in your choice of languages (including English) show on a screen on the phone, as does a running balance of the funds or time remaining on your card. Almost all European countries now have these phones.

An alternative is a phone card from home (AT&T, MCI, or Sprint). These companies now have special numbers that you can call in all western European countries to reach an English-speaking operator (or you can direct dial if you're at a touch-tone phone), the call will be charged to your card. You can also use them to call anywhere else in Europe. There are different access phone numbers for each country so you need a list, these are distributed by the companies wherever there are tourists in any numbers. Sometimes they are even on the front page of *USA Today*. You may have to prime the public phone with some small change but only until you get through to the operator. It is more expensive to use this system than it is to use prepaid phone cards.

More and more people carry cell phones, especially in Europe. This is an excellent but expensive way to stay in touch. Europe uses a completely different system (called GSM) for cell phones than the U.S. and Canada. Your cell phone from North America won't work in Europe. You can purchase a Europe-capable cell phone from AT&T in the U.S. and establish service. Do this before leaving for Europe because you probably won't be able to set up service when you arrive because you won't have a European address. There is a link to the AT&T internet site on our internet site at www.rollinghomes.com.

The phone systems in Europe vary quite a bit. In general, the phone numbers in all countries have a two or three digit country code; a two, three, or four digit area code; and then individual subscriber numbers that vary from four to eight digits in length. Sometimes the same country will have varying length subscriber numbers, even in the same city. The area code always starts with a zero or a 9. If you are calling from outside the country you dial the country code but not this initial digit of the area code, if you are calling from inside the country you don't dial the country code but you do dial the leading 0 or 9 of the area code. You'll find some information about phone systems in individual countries under the Shopping, Currency, Credit Cards and Fuel heading in our country chapters.

Country codes for Europe are as follows: Austria 43, Belgium 32, Czech Republic 42, Denmark 45, Finland 358, France 33, Germany 49, Greece 30, Gibraltar 350, Ireland 353, Italy 39, Liechtenstein 41, Luxembourg 352, The Netherlands 31, Norway 47, Portugal 351, Spain 34, Sweden 46, Switzerland 41, Turkey 90, the U.K. 44.

Tourist Offices

Almost every city, town, or village in Europe with any tourist potential at all has a tourist office. You will find them very useful. They are often the best place get assistance in finding a room if you wish to spend the night indoors. They also usually have information about local campgrounds, sometimes with great maps, and also information about interesting local attractions.

Units of Measurement

One of the things that makes Europe really seem foreign is the fact that they use different units of measurement for almost everything; gas, distance, speed, money, temperature, food weight and volume, and even clothing sizes. If you are a Canadian you have already learned how to deal with most of this, you're lucky. For the rest of us it takes just a short time of working with all of these things, and there is no way to avoid it, to start to feel at home. Conversion tables and factors are available in most guide books but you will probably remember a few critical conversion numbers as we have.

For distance runners like ourselves, kilometers were easy. A kilometer is .62 miles. We can remember this because a 10 kilometer race is 6.2 miles long. For converting miles to kilometers, divide the number of miles by .62. For converting kilometers to miles, multiply the kilometers by .62. Since kilometers are shorter than miles the number of kilometers after the conversion will always be more than the number of miles, if they aren't you divided when you should have multiplied.

For liquid measurement it is usually enough to know that a liter is about the same as a quart. When you need more accuracy, like when you are trying to make some sense out of your miles per gallon calculations, there are 3.79 liters in a U.S. gallon.

Weight measurement is important when you're trying to decide how much cheese or hamburger you need to make a meal. Since a kilogram is about 2.2 pounds we just round to two pounds. This makes a half pound equal to about 250 grams and a pound equal to 500 grams. It's not exact, but it certainly works in the grocery store, and we get a little more than we expected for dinner.

Temperature is our biggest conversion problem. The easiest method is to just carry around a conversion chart of some kind. If you don't have it with you just remember a few key temperatures and interpolate. Freezing, of course is 32 F and 0 C. Water boils at 212 F and 100 C. A nice 70 F day is 21 C. A cooler 50 F day is 10 C. An extremely hot 90 F day is 32 C. Since 50 - 90 F is our comfort zone we know that we're OK as long as the temperature in Europe is between 10 C and 32 C.

Here are a few useful conversion factors:

1 kilometer = .62 mile
1 mile = 1.61 kilometers
1 meter = 3.28 feet
1 foot = .30 meters
1 liter = .26 U.S. gallon
1 U.S. gallon = 3.79 liters
1 kilogram = 2.21 pounds
1 pound = .45 kilograms
convert from °F to °C by subtracting 32 and multiplying by 5/9
convert from °C to °F by multiplying by 1.8 and adding 32

Useful Gadgets

There are many useful gadgets available that will make the camping life more comfortable for you. Some are difficult to find in Europe and should be purchased before you leave, others are only available in Europe.

If you are going to try to access a message machine of some kind from European telephones you will need a small hand held device that makes touch tone beeps when you hold it up to a telephone mouthpiece. These are not hard to find in the U.S., try Radio Shack. Many telephones in Europe are still rotary, not touch tone, especially the pay phones. Some phones, particularly in rural areas, have such poor sound quality that these gadgets won't work. If you run into this problem just try another phone.

Keep your eyes open for a 220 volt, 400 watt electrical space heater. It won't put out a lot of heat but will add a lot of comfort in countries that limit amperage in campgrounds. Three amps will run it and it will keep you comfortable if temperatures don't drop very low. We found a good one at a British RV show, it was invaluable.

A laptop computer with a CD drive and a library of disks can be very useful. Laptops will generally accept a wide range of voltages, usually you can use the machine you buy in North America in Europe with no changes. Take a look at the plate on the AC to DC converter.

Walking

This is a word of warning. We run marathons for fun and exercise. The up side of this is that during our daily training runs we see a great deal of the neighborhood around campgrounds and sometimes discover interesting things to pass along to you. The down side is that we love to walk and are sometimes willing to walk a distance that you will find unacceptable. When talking about walking in to town from a campsite we usually try to give the actual distance, we find that it usually takes about twelve and a half minutes to walk a kilometer. That is a three-mile-an-hour pace and doesn't allow for lollygaging. Fifteen minutes per kilometer might be more reasonable. Even if the distance seems a little long for a walk it is probably great for a bike ride.

Water

The water throughout Europe is usually fine to drink. You might suspect that this is not the case because Europeans drink an astonishing volume of bottled water. Unless a water source is labeled as non-potable you can feel safe in drinking it, if in doubt ask. We've only run into non-potable water in southern Italy, Greece, and Turkey. If in doubt go ahead and buy bottled water at the grocery store, those exclusive European brands are cheaper in Europe.

When To Go, or The Weather

As a camper the weather is an important factor in your decision about the time of your visit. Of course, you may not have the luxury of timing your visit perfectly, other commitments tend to shape travel plans. If they do you can take comfort in the fact that off-season camping in an appropriate rig (one with a reliable heater) is entirely possible.

Northern Europe has some nasty winter weather: Lots of rain (or snow in the far north) and temperatures near or below freezing. Even southern Italy and southern Spain, the warmest regions, are coolish during November to March.

The camping season with a heated rig runs from April to October in most of Europe. Tent campers won't be comfortable in northern continental Europe until May and should be out of the high country and the north by the end of September. Northern Scotland and Scandinavia are comfortable only during June, July, and August. Southern Italy, southern Iberia, southern Greece and coastal Turkey are comfortable throughout the winter.

Crowded campgrounds during July and August make the months of May, June, September, and October the prime European camping months. We call this the shoulder season, it is our favorite time to be in Europe. Don't let July and August bother you however. You can spend them in the north where campgrounds are less crowded. You can visit the cities which are not as popular as the seaside with European campers on vacation. Or you can go where the Europeans go: the mountains and seashore, and cope by traveling less or early in the day and arriving early enough to get a camp site.

CHAPTER 4

HOW TO USE THE DESTINATION CHAPTERS

Chapters 5 through 13 contain information about some of the many destinations you will undoubtedly visit during your visit to Europe. The chapters are arranged by country, in some cases where countries fall into logical groups due to culture or geography there may be more than one country included in the chapter.

Introductory Material

Each chapter starts with an introduction giving important information about the country or countries covered in the chapter. Most of this information is important to a camping traveler and much of it is not necessarily included in normal tourist guides. On the other hand, much information that is readily available in normal tourist guides will not be found in this book. Other books do a good job of covering things like currency information, hotels, restaurants, language, and tour details. This book is designed to be a supplement to normal tourist guides, not to replace them. It provides a framework, other guides must be used to fill it the details.

Chapter Overview Maps

At the beginning of each chapter is a map of the country or countries covered in that chapter. The cities shown on these maps are all included in the chapter and have individual sections with information about the city and about at least one campground nearby.

Some of the maps also show the outline of an interesting district or region. These regions have their own individual sections at the end of each chapter. Each region section has information about interesting attractions and several campgrounds.

You can use the country maps as a supplemental table of contents to the cities and districts covered in the chapter.

Distance Tables

Each chapter introduction also includes a distance table. These tables show the distance between the cities in the chapter. Each also shows the distance to a few cities located outside the country covered in the chapter but covered in other chapters. We have done this to allow you to easily calculate distances when you move from one country to another. A few chapters cover areas that are separated by water where you have a choice of ferry routes (Scandinavia, Greece and Turkey, and the British Isles). On the distance tables for these chapters we have omitted some distances where there might be confusion about which ferry route you might use. You can calculate distances in this case by adding together distances to the ferry ports you intend to use. All distances on the distance chart are given in kilometers because this is the scale used most often on European maps and roads and the scale you yourself will undoubtedly soon become most comfortable using.

City Descriptions

Following the introductory material in each chapter is the Selected Cities and Campgrounds section. Cities are listed alphabetically in this segment. Each city has a few paragraphs describing the local attractions, then information about at least one campground. In some cases there is also information about interesting side trips that you may wish to take while continuing to use this particular town and campground as a base. Some of the destinations are famous and well known, others less familiar but still well worth a visit. We've made a big effort to select those places most interesting to visitors from outside Europe.

Our descriptions of the destinations in this book are intended to give you an idea of what the city or region has to offer. They are by no means complete, you will undoubtedly need additional guides during your visit. Exploring travel guides is almost as much fun as exploring the destinations themselves, you will no doubt acquire a small library before you finish your travels.

Campground Maps

Most of the campground descriptions include a small map to assist you in finding the campground. They show enough freeways and other identifying features to allow you to tie them into the country and city maps you will be using for primary navigation. You can use these maps to assist you in your search for campgrounds, they are meant to be used in conjunction with the written directions that we have included in the campground descriptions. A picture often **IS** worth a thousand words, even if it only serves to give you a general idea of the campground location. We hope these maps will do more than that, we've spent many hours searching for campgrounds with only a brief description from other campground guides to guide us. May you never have to do the same.

While the maps are for the most part self explanatory here is a key.

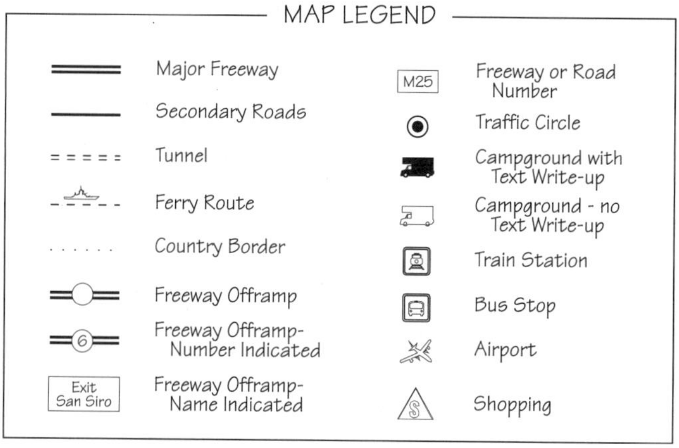

Campground Descriptions

Each campground section begins with address and telephone number. While it is not generally necessary to obtain reservations in Europe it is sometimes desirable to check ahead. This is particularly true during the busy July and August school holidays. You'll quickly become attuned to whether reservations are desirable in your locality at your time of year.

One thing you will not find in our campground descriptions is a rating with some kind of system of stars, checks, or tree icons. Hopefully we've included enough information in our campground description to let you make your own analysis. We have found that the rating systems used by different organizations don't tell us much about what to expect in a campground. The things important to you may be different than the things important to us so we'll let you rely on the written information. While there are thousands of campgrounds in Europe, there are not really so many near the places you will want to see that you can afford to choose them by their amenities. Location is the most important factor in selecting a campground.

Campground prices vary considerably and are based upon different things in different countries. The price you pay depends upon the type of rig you drive, the number in your party, your use of electricity and the time of year.

Generally you can expect that tents are least expensive, followed by either caravans or four-wheeled RV's (including vans). The different prices paid by caravans and motorhomes is a contentious issue, particularly in England. Motorhomes are sometimes charged more because they must have a flatter parking pad, European rigs seldom have hydraulic levelers. Caravans, on the other hand, need space for both the trailer and a car.

You'll almost always pay two or three dollars for electricity. Sometimes electricity is metered, sometimes there is a flat fee. Showers, too, are often extra. We've noted information about showers and electricity in the write-ups.

A final price consideration is the value of the U.S. or Canadian dollar. Our prices were determined during late 1998.

We've grouped campground fees into the following categories:

Inexpensive	Less than $15 U.S.
Moderate	$15 to $25 U.S.
Expensive	More than $25 U.S.

All of these prices are summer high season prices for a van conversion with two people using electricity and taking a shower. While methods of determining charges and prices vary you can come reasonably close by deducting $3-5 for visits out of high season, adding $3 per person over two people, deducting $2 if you don't use electricity, and deducting $3 if you are using a tent.

Campground icons can be useful for a quick overview of campground facilities or if you are quickly looking for a particular feature.

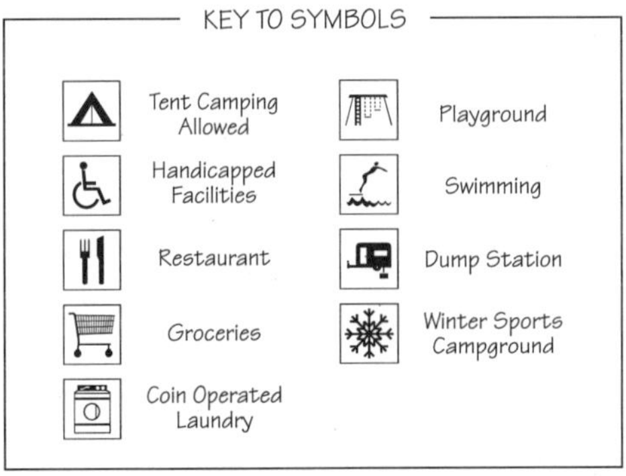

Europe is becoming more friendly to those with handicaps. It has quite a distance to go to catch up with the U.S. and Canada but more and more campgrounds have handicapped facilities. Unfortunately they are often limited.

All of the campgrounds in this book accept RV's but not all accept tent campers. We've included the tent symbol for all campgrounds that do accept tents.

An on-site or nearby restaurant can provide a welcome change and a good way to meet people. In Europe most restaurants also include some kind of a bar provision. Campgrounds sporting this symbol have food service, they range from temporary kiosks with take-away items to full-service, white-tablecloth restaurants.

If we've given the campground a shopping cart icon then it has some groceries. This could be a few items in the reception area or a large store with grocery carts. Check the write-up for more information. The write-up will often mention a larger store located conveniently near the campground.

The dump station icon means that the campground has a dump station designed for motorhomes. Many of these stations are meant for only gray water because while many European RV's have gray-water systems for showers and sinks, few have black-water toilet systems. Check with the campground manager before using them for black water.

Campground with the winter sports snowflake icon are near a winter sports area (generally skiing) and are open during the winter. These places are popular during the winter, reservations are recommended.

Campgrounds with the playground icon have a playground facility of some kind, most have playground equipment and play fields.

A swimming icon means that the campground has swimming either on-site or nearby. This may be a pool or the beach at an ocean or lake.

You'll find that this book has a much larger campground description than most guidebooks. We've tried to include detailed information about the campground itself so you know what to expect when you arrive as well as information about the availability and use of public transportation for traveling into town. While most campgrounds have a map we've also included a paragraph giving even more instructions about finding the campground.

Side Trips

The Side Trip section included for some towns describes interesting places you may want to visit. Tenters and caravanners can leave their camp set up at the base and avoiding pulling a caravan or setting up camp each night. Even if you are in a van or motorhome and do take your camp along with you the base city always provides a place to return to if you can find no acceptable alternate campground during your side trip.

Region Descriptions

Many regions of Europe are particularly appealing. They may include major cities or they may be largely rural. Toward the end of several of our chapters we've included regional descriptions of some of these areas. They include information about the features of the regions including major towns or attractions. As in the town write-ups we've also included regional maps and many campgrounds. Many of the regions have attractions that are not located near the campgrounds we have chosen to report so they are included in side trip sections, often with brief mention of additional campgrounds.

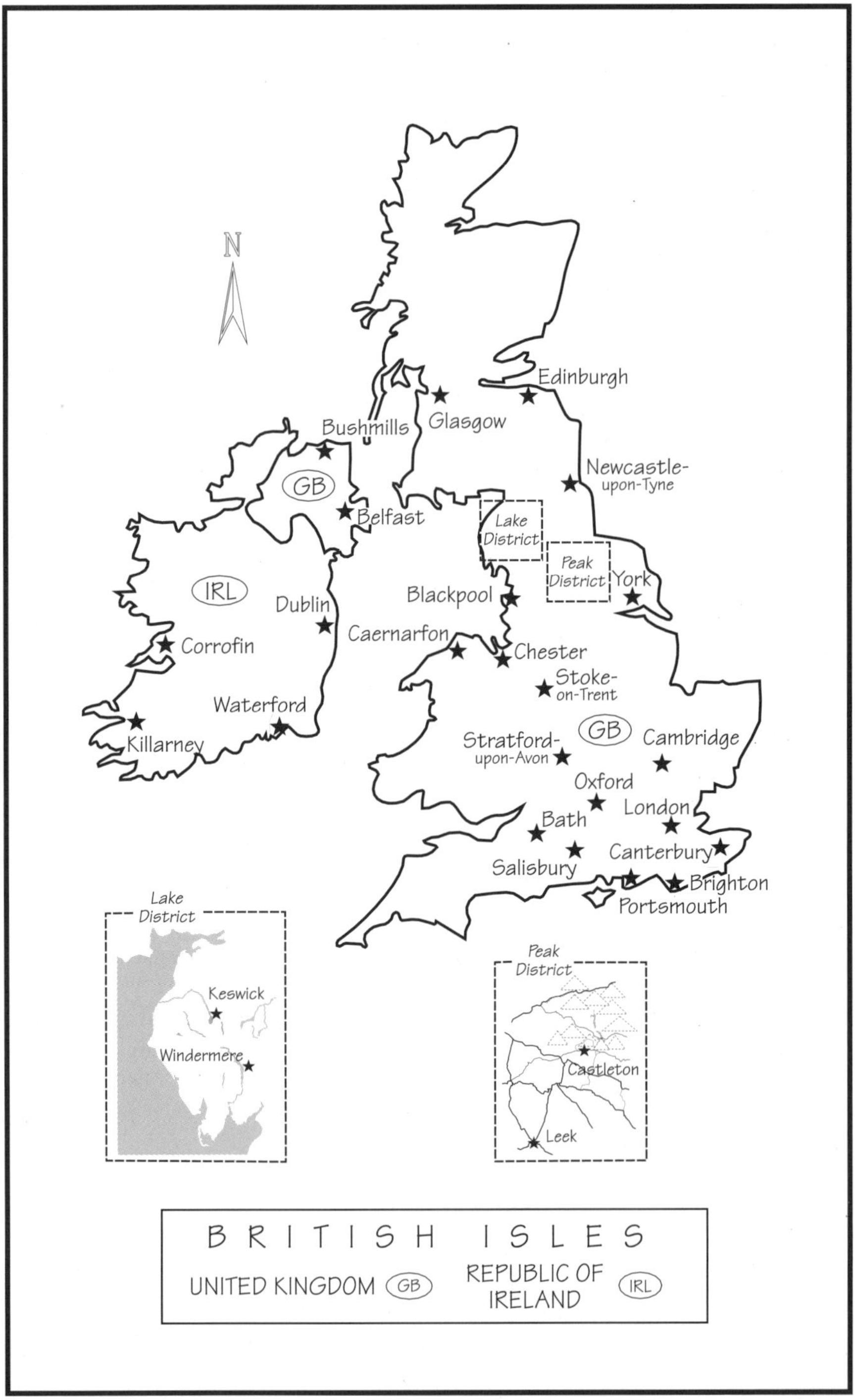
N
Edinburgh
Glasgow
Bushmills
Newcastle-
upon-Tyne
GB
Belfast
Lake
District
Peak
District
York
IRL
Dublin
Blackpool
Caernarfon
Corrofin
Chester
Stoke-
on-Trent
Waterford
Killarney
GB
Stratford-
upon-Avon
Cambridge
Oxford
London
Bath
Canterbury
Salisbury
Brighton
Portsmouth
Lake
District
Keswick
Windermere
Peak
District
Castleton
Leek
BRITISH ISLES
UNITED KINGDOM
GB
REPUBLIC OF
IRELAND
IRL

CHAPTER

5

BRITISH ISLES: GREAT BRITAIN AND IRELAND

INTRODUCTION

We consider the British Isles to be one of the top camping regions in Europe. The attractions of the countries themselves are manifold. England, Scotland, Wales, and Ireland are full of destinations you've heard about and probably want to see. Many of us from North America have roots somewhere in the British Isles.

The campgrounds are another attraction. We think British campgrounds are the best in Europe. Standards of cleanliness, quality of the facilities, and the friendly management are all outstanding.

Finally, as you might expect, virtually everyone (except perhaps in parts of Ireland or Wales) speaks English. This will go a long way toward making you feel more comfortable and is a good reason to start your European camping visit in the British Isles.

The British Isles are really composed of two countries: the United Kingdom and the Republic of Ireland. Most of us are accustomed to thinking of the United Kingdom in terms of its components: England, Wales, Scotland, and Northern Ireland. Great Britain is the largest island of the British Isles and contains England, Scotland and Wales.

Roads and Driving

The biggest concern most people have about driving in the British Isles is learning to drive on the left side of the road. You'll find that you adapt quickly, if you are driving a vehicle with the steering wheel on the left just remember to keep your side of the car next to the curb. The most persistent problem for many people is left or right turns onto intersecting streets, be alert when you make turns and you'll be fine. First thing in the morning as we pull out of the campground we often find ourselves on the wrong side of the road, old habits are hard to break.

The United Kingdom is the only place in Western Europe that has not adopted the metric system for its road signs. Maybe the familiar measurement system will offset some of the anxiety that folks from the U.S. will feel when driving on the left side of the road.

Since England is an island you'll inevitably find yourself using ferries. To get to England from France you now have a choice, the Chunnel under the English Channel has been opened to motorhomes. Reservations are not required but you can purchase tickets in advance from travel agents. You'll pull up, be loaded aboard a railway car (you ride in your vehicle), and be unloaded some 30 minutes later. In England the Chunnel entrance is Exit 11A on the M20 motorway near Folkestone. In France the entrance is from the A16 Autoroute west of Calais.

The procedure for riding a ferry from Dover to Calais is much the same. You can buy your ticket at the dock, there are lots of boats, and the crossing takes only an hour and fifteen minutes. The price you pay for crossing the channel can vary considerably so it does pay to shop, there are several companies providing ferry service. During busy times the ships are sometimes fully booked so reservations during the middle of the summer are a good idea.

The Chunnel and ferries are competing fiercely which is keeping fares down. Recently it has been much cheaper to buy a short-term excursion fare (over and back) than a one way ticket. This is true even if you have a vehicle. You just throw away the return portion and end up paying about a quarter of the one way fare. The best way to comparison shop is through a travel agent, many handle ferry and tunnel tickets. The cheaper excursion fares are limited so you might want to shop several days before you plan to cross. Cheap fares are usually unavailable during peak crossing times.

While the Dover to Calais ferries and Folkestone to Calais tunnel routes are the shortest there are many other ferry routes from Great Britain. Across the channel you can choose to travel Harwich to Hoek van Holland, The Netherlands; Felixstowe to Zeebrugge, Belgium; Ramsgate to Öostende, Belgium; Ramsgate to Dunkerque, France; Folkestone to Boulogne, France; Newhaven to Dieppe, France; Portsmouth to Le Havre, France; Portsmouth to Caen, France; Portsmouth to Cherbourg, France; Poole to Cherbourg, France; Poole to St-Malo, France; Plymouth to Roscoff, France; Cork, Republic of Ireland to Brest France; Cork to Roscoff, France; or Rosslare, Republic of Ireland to Cherbourg, France. The longer routes are more expensive but you may be able to save time and gas money to offset the higher fares.

Even longer runs are also possible. The ferries on these runs are a lot like cruise ships with lots of facilities and even staterooms. Ferries run from Newcastle-upon-Tyne to Bergen, Norway; Stavanger, Norway; Gothenburg, Sweden; Esbjerg, Denmark, and Bremen, Germany. Ferries from Harwich also run to most of these cities. They also run from Plymouth to Santander, Spain and from Portsmouth to Bilbao, Spain.

A visit to Ireland also requires riding on a ferry and these can be surprisingly expensive considering the length of the run. There is no competition from a tunnel to keep them down. Major routes are Stranraer, Scotland to Larne, North Ireland; Holyhead,

Wales to Dublin, Ireland; and Fishguard, Swansea and Pembroke, Wales to Rosslare, Ireland.

English freeways, called motorways, are plentiful and free. The island is small by our standards and it is easy to cover ground quickly on the motorways. Avoid motorways near large cities during the morning and evening commute just as you would in North America. Outside England, in the Republic of Ireland, Northern Ireland, Wales and even Scotland there are few four-lane roads and traffic is often held up by slow-moving farm tractors and trucks.

Motorways are designated on maps with the letter "M". Secondary roads are designated with an "A" and a number, fewer digits indicate a more heavily used and direct route. There are also "B" roads, these are small local roads.

The British are heavy users of their automobile club breakdown services. The AAA has a reciprocal agreement with the Automobile Association (AA) which can be reached at 0800 88 77 66 in the UK and 1800 66 77 88 in the Republic of Ireland. The all-in-one police/ambulance/road help number in the British Isles is 999.

Camping

The campground scene in England is dominated by two camping clubs: **The Caravan Club** and **The Camping and Caravanning Club**. Both have excellent campgrounds in useful locations. While you can use some of their campgrounds without joining (with a Camping Card International, see Documents in Chapter 3), you will find that there are advantages to being a member. Both clubs offer discounts to members so that if you camp in their sites for ten days or so during your visit you will save at least the cost of the membership. Both clubs also have reservation systems and excellent guidebooks with maps and directions for finding each campground. The Caravan Club also has hundreds of inexpensive Certified Locations. These are orchards or farms with limited facilities scattered throughout the country. One other benefit of the Caravan Club is its *Continental Sites Guide and Handbook*. This two-volume guide to campgrounds on the continent is the best European campground guide we've found, it is prepared from reports by members, covers more campgrounds than anything else available in English, and has good driving directions for finding each listing. It is amazingly accurate, perhaps because the information comes from amateur inspectors (the members) who have learned the hard way that accurate information is important. You can join these clubs at any of their campgrounds or contact them before you head for Europe. Contact the Caravan Club at East Grinstead House, East Grinstead, West Sussex RH19 1UA (phone 1342 326944) Contact The Camping and Caravanning Club at Greenfields House, Westwood Way, Coventry CV4 8JH (phone 1203 694995). Check our web site at www.rollinghomes.com for links to these camping clubs. A Camping Card International is required for many campgrounds in the British Isles including the club sites.

The club campgrounds generally have extremely friendly and helpful managers (called wardens). Most also have first class shower/toilet buildings with lots of hot water. They do not have a lot of additional amenities like swimming pools, grocery shops, or restaurants. Those things are generally available nearby but off site.

Great Britain also has a lot of campgrounds that are not run by the camping clubs. These campgrounds vary considerably, many have a lot more amenities than club sites.

You can usually make reservations in England over the telephone directly with the campground office using your credit card. Being able to speak the language is a big help.

Electricity in British campgrounds is generally better than that available on the continent. Sixteen amperes are usually available and modern CEE17 plugs are the standard. Current is 220 volt, 50 cycles.

Free camping in Britain is possible but sometimes difficult. In the past many visitors free camped in motorway rest areas. This is sometimes allowed but a fee may now be charged. Some rest areas have special overnight parking areas. Open flames are not allowed in motorway rest areas so you are not allowed to use your propane or butane stove or refrigerator. Off the motorways barrier bars (to block high vehicles) are often placed at the entrances to large parking lots to discourage overnight camping. As an alternative consider The Caravan Club's small Certified Locations.

British local tourist offices can be a good place to get information about camping. Many can provide small guidebooks to camping sites, but usually not for free.

Shopping, Currency, Credit Cards and Fuel

Despite what you may have heard about British cooking the British Isles offer the best selection of familiar foods in Europe. Modern hypermarket-type supermarkets like Sainsbury's, Tesco, and Safeway are easy to find and offer good prices.

British pubs provide more than a place to drink a pint of beer. They're one of the best places to find an economical meal. They also provide an opportunity to meet some of the local people and, especially in Ireland, often provide entertainment.

Credit cards are easy to use in the British Isles and cash machines are generally located at banks. You'll find them throughout both the United Kingdom and the Republic of Ireland.

The best place to buy gasoline is the hypermarkets, many have gas stations in their parking lots and offer gasoline as a loss leader to attract shoppers. You can use credit cards to buy gas at most stations.

Itinerary Suggestions

In The British Isles, just as in the rest of Europe, you have to deal with the July and August vacation crush. Our favorite time for a visit is May and June, the crowds haven't arrived and the weather can be good. If you must visit during the summer you can deal with the crowds at campgrounds by making telephone credit card reservations and traveling early in the day.

British weather tends to be wet. The best weather months are July and August. The spring weather can be quite good at times and this is also a good time for flowers and a green countryside if you are willing to risk traveling then. September can also be a good weather month, many people think this is a good time for visiting Scotland because the countryside is at its most colorful.

London is one of Europe's top tourist destinations, and for good reason. Plan on at least a week in one of the city's comfortable campgrounds.

All of England, Wales, and Scotland are easy to reach using the excellent motorway system. We have included many cities in this chapter that are attractive to travelers but they are just the start. The British Isles are full of places you'll enjoy.

Don't neglect Ireland. The green countryside is ideal for a camping visit and there are convenient campgrounds for visits to Dublin and other smaller cities.

For one of the least developed and most open countrysides in Europe you might want to venture into highland Scotland, the region north of Glasgow and Edinburgh. There are plenty of campgrounds.

You can request campground and general tourist information from the **British Tourist Authority, 551 Fifth Avenue, Suite 701, New York, NY 10176-0799 (800-462-2748)**. In Canada the address is **111 Avenue Road, Suite 450, Toronto, ON M5R 3J8 (888-VISIT UK)**. Ask for a copy of their booklet *Camping and Caravan Parks: England, Northern Ireland, Scotland, Wales.* Visit www.rollinghomes.com for links to information sources on the internet.

CAERNARFON CASTLE AND HARBOR IN WALES

BRITISH ISLES DISTANCE TABLE

In Kilometers

Kms X .62 = Miles

	Bath England	Belfast N. Ireland	Blackpool England	Brighton England	Bushmills N. Ireland	Caernarfon Wales	Cambridge England	Canterbury England	Castleton England	Chester England	Corrofin Republic Of Ireland	Dublin Republic Of Ireland	Edinburgh Scotland	Glasgow Scotland	Keswick England	Killarney Republic Of Ireland	Leek England	London England	Newcastle-upon-Tyne England	Oxford England	Portsmouth England	Salisbury England	Stoke-on-Trent England	Stratford-upon-Avon England	Waterford Republic Of Ireland	Windermere England
Belfast N. Ireland	--																									
Blackpool England	347	--																								
Brighton England	204	--	518																							
Bushmills N. Ireland	--	130	--	--																						
Caernarfon Wales	367	--	237	521	--																					
Cambridge England	275	--	330	193	--	370																				
Canterbury England	293	--	541	143	--	539	169																			
Castleton England	346	--	196	416	--	266	233	402																		
Chester England	282	--	118	402	--	119	275	477	258																	
Corrofin Republic Of Ireland	--	328	--	--	393	--	--	--	--	--																
Dublin Republic Of Ireland	--	171	--	--	301	--	--	--	--	--	229															
Edinburgh Scotland	623	--	322	729	--	517	520	689	423	398	--	--														
Glasgow Scotland	613	--	317	747	--	512	596	764	459	393	--	--	76													
Keswick England	441	--	140	570	--	335	405	574	258	216	--	--	214	209												
Killarney Republic Of Ireland	--	474	--	--	551	--	--	--	--	--	159	303	--	--	--											
Leek England	229	--	156	363	--	196	237	423	88	77	--	--	426	422	245	--										
London England	188	--	411	85	--	422	97	95	333	316	--	--	617	636	473	--	277									
Newcastle-upon-Tyne England	497	--	250	555	--	414	362	531	259	295	--	--	158	233	156	--	323	459								
Oxford England	106	--	316	165	--	356	163	226	290	251	--	--	564	582	405	--	198	97	406							
Portsmouth England	133	--	447	71	--	487	219	195	421	832	--	--	695	713	536	--	329	119	537	131						
Salisbury England	66	--	412	138	--	433	245	246	425	348	--	--	699	678	501	--	294	158	541	135	67					
Stoke-on-Trent England	210	--	137	344	--	177	217	404	107	58	--	--	407	403	226	--	19	258	304	179	310	275				
Stratford-upon-Avon England	138	--	261	225	--	301	145	286	231	213	--	--	522	527	337	--	130	157	364	60	191	195	111			
Waterford Republic Of Ireland	--	329	--	--	459	--	--	--	--	--	177	158	--	--	--	206	--	--	--	--	--	--	--	--		
Windermere England	407	--	107	536	--	301	371	540	224	182	--	--	248	243	34	--	211	436	190	371	502	467	192	303	--	
York England	370	--	159	440	--	290	247	416	148	171	--	--	285	328	192	--	196	336	127	282	410	417	177	237	--	158

SELECTED CITIES AND CAMPGROUNDS

BATH, ENGLAND

Population 88,000

Bath was England's 18th-century destination resort. Instead of golf courses or ski hills there were baths and gardens. Much of the Georgian architecture remains, and Bath still draws many visitors. There are lots of expensive shops where you can spend your money. Even if you don't shop you'll admire Bath's handsome streets and gardens. Recommended reading before your visit are Jane Austen's novels *Persuasion* and *Northanger Abbey.*

Probably the best examples of Georgian architecture in town are **The Circus** and the nearby **Royal Crescent**, both situated northwest of the central area near **Royal Victoria Park**. East of the Circus on Alfred Street are the **Assembly Rooms** where the balls Austen wrote about were held, downstairs is a museum with examples of costumes including some from the days of Beau Nash, the fashion plate of Bath's golden era. **Bath Abbey** marks the center of the city, nearby is the **Pump Room** and the well-preserved **Roman Baths**. You'll also want to see **Pulteney Bridge**, built in 1771, it is similar to the Ponte Vecchio in Florence with shops on either side of the roadway.

Bath Campground

✦ BATH MARINA AND CARAVAN PARK

Address: Brassmill Lane, Bath BA1 3JT
Telephone: 01225 428778
Price: Moderate

Open all year

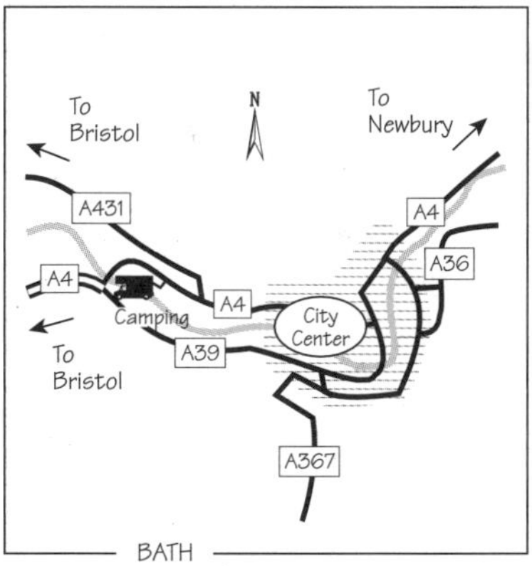

The campground is next to the River Avon and is only about five kilometers from central Bath.

This is a medium-sized campground with nice facilities. All of the sites are paved and level and all have electricity. There is good separation between the sites and they have electrical outlets (16 amps). The shower/toilet buildings are modern and clean, they have hot water for showers (premixed), bathroom basins, and dishwashing. There is also a laundry room with coin-operated machines. Unfortunately, the campground does not accommodate tents. There is a nice restaurant nearby overlooking the river.

Access to Bath from the campground is quite easy. There is a park-and-ride nearby with frequent bus service to the city center. On Sundays the park and ride is not in service but city busses pass near the campground. If you don't mind walking the city center is about 5 kilometers away by a path along the river, this makes a good bike route once you have covered the somewhat overgrown first kilometer or so.

The campground is located west of Bath on the route from central Bath to the A4 and Bristol. If you are entering town on the A4 from the west watch for a Murco service station on the right just after you cross the River Avon. The campground is behind the Murco station, follow Brassmill Lane about 100 meters to reach the entrance. If you are arriving on the A4 from the east you can follow signs through town and will see the Murco station on your left about 3 kilometers out of town.

Side Trips from Bath

The city of **Bristol** is only 20 kilometers northwest of Bath on the A4 motorway. This is a large city but the riverfront area is attractive and entertaining with yacht harbors and restaurants. You can see the **SS. Great Britain**, the first oceangoing iron-hulled screw-driven ship. It was in service from 1843 to 1886 and was brought back to Bristol from the Falkland Islands in 1970.

Wells is England's smallest cathedral town with the country's oldest gothic cathedral, the **Cathedral of St. Andrew**. The medieval town is well worth the 37-kilometer drive down Highway A39 from Bath.

BELFAST, NORTHERN IRELAND

Population 420,000

Belfast is a modern industrial city with a bad reputation stemming from the "Troubles", the long-running struggle between the Protestant and Catholic citizens of the area. If you are there during a quiet period you may want to visit some of the more notorious trouble spots like the Protestant **Shankill Road** and the Catholic **Falls Road**. Both of these are west of the city center.

In the central city area **Donegall Square** marks the center with the **City Hall**, gardens, and the city bus station. **Donegall Place** is a pedestrian shopping street that runs north from the square. Most bars, restaurants, and night life are along the **Golden Mile** on Great Victoria Street which is southwest of Donegall Square. Here you'll find the **Crown Liquor Saloon**, a Victorian pub owned by the National Trust.

If you enter Northern Ireland by ferry via the shortest route, from Stranraer in Scotland, you'll land at Larne which is about 25 kilometers north of Belfast. If you want to visit Belfast you should base yourself right in Larne. Campgrounds around Belfast are not too good, but Larne has a nice municipal campground and good transportation to Belfast.

Belfast Campground

✦ CURRAN PARK CARAVAN AND CAMPING SITE

Address: 131 Curran Road, Larne BT40 1RU
Telephone: 0154 273797
Price: Inexpensive

Open Easter to September 30

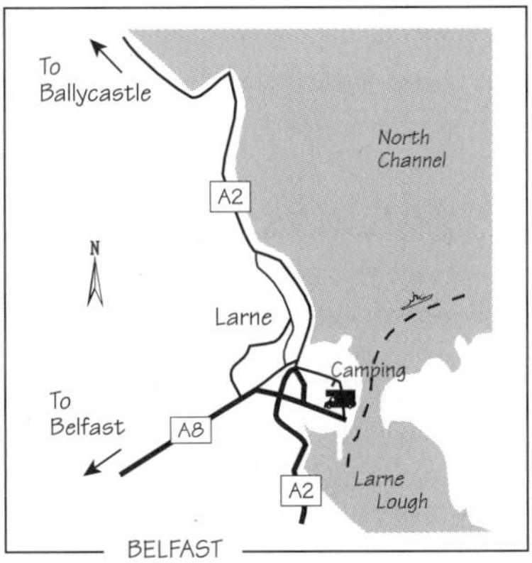

This campground is a jewel of a municipal campground. Ideally located near ferry docks, train station, and the center of town, the price is right and the facilities are more than adequate.

This medium-sized campground is a grassy site sitting in a residential area near the ferry dock. There are about 30 hard-surfaced parking spots for caravans or motorhomes and a large grassy area for tents or even vans if the campground is crowded. Electricity is scarce, only a few sites have it. The shower/toilet building has free hot water in sinks, showers and laundry room, also a coin-operated washer and dryer. There is a playground next door for the kids and three supermarkets are less than 10 minutes away on foot in the center of town.

Larne is a ferry port and as such has outstanding train connections to Belfast. Trains leave at least every hour, the trip takes about an hour, and a round trip costs roughly six dollars. This is so convenient and reasonably priced that we wouldn't even think of staying somewhere nearer to Belfast.

If you arrive by ferry turn right immediately after leaving the port gate, the campground is about 1 kilometer directly toward town, it will be on your left. If you arrive from any other direction follow signs toward the center of town and then proceed east on the main street which will soon become Curran Road. In a short distance you'll see the campground on your right.

Side Trips from Belfast

The **Ulster Folk Museum** and **Ulster Transport Museum** are located 11 kilometers northeast of Belfast toward Bangor on the A2 motorway. The folk museum is a European-style open-air museum with typical buildings from around Northern Ireland.

Northwest of Larne the sometimes narrow and steep road runs along the very scenic Antrim coast past the famous **Antrim Glens**, small wooded river valleys running down from the hills. At Glenariff you can drive up to **Glenariff Forest Park** which has hikes, a waterfall, and even a decent campground. If you're not driving a big rig turn toward the sea when you reach Cushendun and follow the impressively scenic but less easily navigated coastal loop to Ballycastle.

BLACKPOOL, ENGLAND

Population 150,000

Blackpool is Britain's top seaside resort. Expect fun, not sophistication. While Blackpool was a popular 19th-century resort some would argue that this town's golden era is right now.

Along the **oceanfront promenade** you'll find every variety of cheap and gaudy entertainment. There are also **three entertainment piers** and the **Blackpool Tower**, an Eiffel-inspired tower built in 1894. **Pleasure Beach** is a huge amusement park just south of the center of town, nearby is the **Sandcastle** leisure complex with indoor swimming pools and man-made waves. If you visit only one seaside resort in Great Britain make it this one. The **Blackpool Illuminations** during September and October extend the desirable season for a visit to this resort.

Blackpool Campground

✦ BLACKPOOL SOUTH CARAVAN CLUB SITE

Address: Cropper Rd, Marton, Blackpool, Lancs. FY4 5LB
Telephone: 01253 762051
Price: Moderate

Open March 19 to January 4, varies slightly

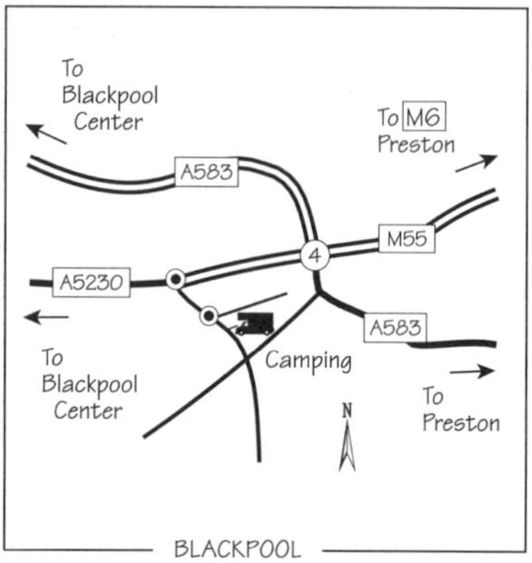

Blackpool South is a typically well run and outfitted Caravan Club site and probably the most convenient campground to Blackpool. You can take a bus or ride your bike downtown.

The medium-sized campground is a flat parcel with gravel sites, hedges provide separation for some sites and all are quite large. The shower/toilet building is clean and has everything necessary: hot water for showers, bathroom basins, dishwashing sinks and laundry tubs. Laundry facilities include a coin-operated washer and dryer. There is a dump station. Unfortunately, the campground does not accept tenters. It is also a members-only campground, have you joined the Caravan Club yet?

The easiest way to find the campground is from M55 which approaches Blackpool from the east. If you come into Blackpool from some other direction you can head out the M55 and then turn around at Junction 4 to head back in. Heading west, just after Junction 4 the M55 enters a traffic circle, take the first exit to the left. After a short distance you'll come to another traffic circle, this time take the second exit on the left. The campground is on your left about 200 meters down this road.

Side Trips from Blackpool

Lytham St. Anne's, just south of Blackpool, has several excellent golf courses that are open to visitors.

Liverpool, about 100 kilometers south of Blackpool by motorway, is fun to visit. Along the waterfront you'll find **Albert Dock**, an area of renovated docks and warehouses now housing offices, restaurants, and shops. It also houses **The Beatles Story** (a Beatles museum), a branch of London's **Tate Gallery** displaying contemporary art, and the **Merseyside Maritime Museum**. The excellent **Walker Art Gallery** is also located in Liverpool.

The 14th-century **Lancaster Castle** is in the historic port of Lancaster, 40 kilometers northeast of Blackpool.

You might also consider visiting the industrial metropolis of **Manchester**, 75 kilometers southeast of Blackpool. The **Museum of Science and Industry** has exhibits showcasing Manchester's industrial heritage. Two good art museums are the **City Art Galleries** and the **Whitworth Art Gallery**.

BRIGHTON, ENGLAND

Population 235,000 (Including the neighboring town of Hove)

Of all the British seaside resorts Brighton must be the most well known. The town became very popular in the second half of the 18th century when doctors began to prescribe seawater bathing. Brighton has everything you expect: a long multitiered seaside promenade, the **Palace Pier**, shopping and restaurants in the old town area known as **The Lanes**, the **Sea Life Centre** aquarium, and even a fantasy Indian palace built for King George IV in 1815 during the Regency period and known as the **Royal Pavilion**.

All of this is easily reached from a conveniently-located Caravan Club campground just 4 kilometers east of the city center.

Brighton Campground

✦ SHEEPCOTE VALLEY CARAVAN CLUB SITE

Address: East Brighton Park, Brighton, East Sussex BN2 5TS
Telephone: 01273 626546
Price: Moderate

Open all year

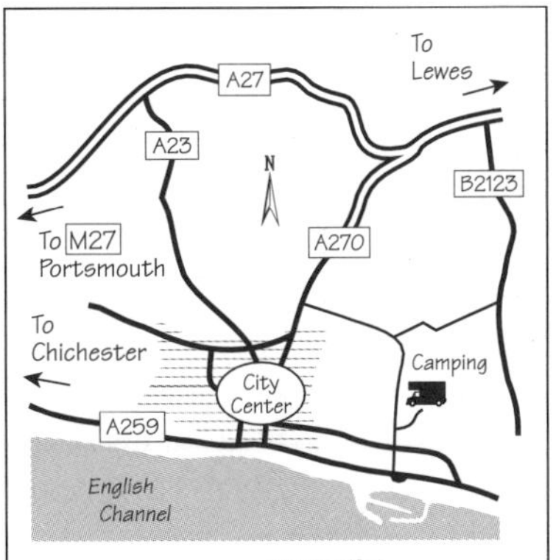

BRIGHTON

This is a relatively new Caravan Club site and as such is quite nice. It is large for a Caravan Club campground and has lots of room even for tents. The campground sits in an amphitheater-shaped valley in the South Downs about a kilometer inland from the ocean and next to a golf course. Individual sites are both grass and gravel, they have convenient electrical service boxes (CEE17 plugs, 16 amps), and the other facilities are first rate. The shower/toilet buildings are heated, have hot water for showers (adjustable), bathroom basins, dishwashing sinks, and laundry with coin-operated machines. There is a conveniently-located supermarket about a kilometer away, it's in a large shopping complex complete with marina and cinemas that is located on the waterfront directly to the south of the caravan park. You do not need to be a member of the Caravan Club to camp here and tents are allowed.

There is bus service to town from above the marina shopping complex. It is a nice 4 kilometer stroll or bike ride into town along the waterfront promenade.

The easiest way to find the campground is to drive east from the Brighton pier along the waterfront. In about 3 kilometers follow the campground signs as they lead you to an off ramp (also signed for Brighton Marina Village), lead you through a U-turn, and then right into Wilson Avenue. Drive 100 meters away from the water and then turn right into East Brighton Park and follow the driveway about a kilometer to the campground.

Side Trips from Brighton

Royal Tunbridge Wells is about 50 kilometers northwest of Brighton on A27 and then A26. In a fairly extended area surrounding this town (which is much like Bath) are many impressive castles and manors. These include **Penshurst Place**, **Hever Castle**, **Chartwell** (Winston Churchill's home), **Knole House**, **Ightham Mote**, **Leeds Castle**, **Lamberhurst**, **Bateman's** (Rudyard Kipling's home), **Rochester Castle**, **Finchcocks**, **Bodiam Castle**, and **Sissinghurst Castle Gardens**. You'll need a good guidebook to find all of these places but they are within easy driving distance of the town and fun to visit. A convenient place to stay is CROWBOROUGH CAMPING AND CARAVANNING CLUB SITE just north of Crowborough which is about 11 kilometers south of Tunbridge Wells on A26. The campground's season is March 27 to October 30.

If you enjoy hiking you'll want to walk at least part of either the **South Downs Way** (Eastbourne to Winchester, 171 kilometers) or the **North Downs Way** (Dover to Farnham, 227 kilometers).

BUSHMILLS, NORTHERN IRELAND

Population 1,500

Bushmills is a small town that is well located for exploring one of the most inderesting areas of Northern Ireland, the western Antrim Coast. Nearby you'll find the **Giant's Causeway**, long sandy beaches, and of course the **Bushmills Irish Whiskey Distillery** which offers frequent tours.

Bushmills Campground

✦ PORT BALLINTRAE CARAVAN PARK

Address: Ballaghmore Avenue, Port Ballintrae, Bushmills, Co. Antrim BT57 8RX
Telephone: 01265 731478
Price: Inexpensive

Open Easter to October 7

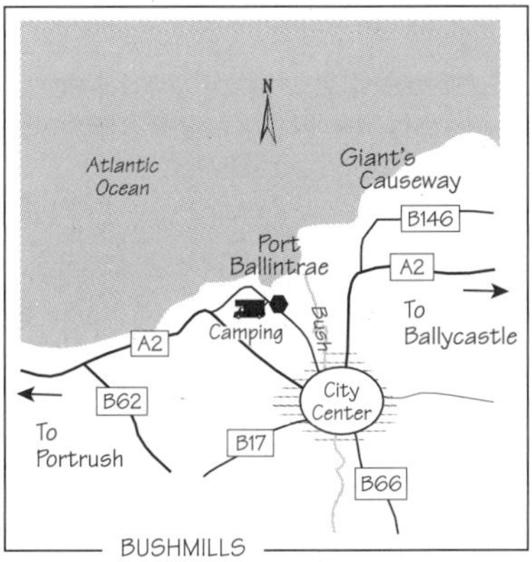

This is a large caravan park, but it is almost entirely filled with mobile home units used as summer cottages by people from nearby Londonderry. The warden told us that these units were quite popular during the "Troubles". There is a medium-sized area set aside for tourist rigs, however, and a lot of folks use the campground because the location is very handy.

The tourist area has room for about 50 campers, both hard sites with electricity and tent sites. The hard sites are well separated and laid out, the tent sites are delineated with lines in the grass. The shower/toilet building has one shower each for men and women but hot water is available for showers, bathroom basins, dishes, and laundry. There is a coin-operated washer and dryer. A back entrance to the park opens onto a road running along the ocean. You'll find a small pocket of sandy beach there, or if you walk about a kilometer east you'll find a long sandy beach backed with dunes where the Bush River reaches the ocean.

The campground is actually located about 3 kilometers from Bushmills in the small town of Port Ballintrae. Starting in Bushmills drive about one kilometer west on Highway A2 toward Portrush. You'll see the campground sign pointing to the right and Port Ballintrae. Follow the Port Ballintrae road for about 1.5 kilometers until you see another campground sign pointing left. The campground entrance is straight ahead down this side road.

Side Trips from Bushmills

The **Giant's Causeway**, a favorite Northern Ireland tourist attraction, is just 6 kilometers away by car. The causeway is an unusual rock formation of octagonal-shaped basalt columns that almost appear to be the remains of a causeway leading into the sea toward Scotland. If you wish you can ride a bike from the campground to the causeway using a bike trail on an abandoned tram right-of-way, the distance this way is about 5 kilometers as the route is more direct than the road. Once you reach the Causeway Visitor's Center you have access to another 16 kilometers of trail running eastward along the coast as far as White Park Bay.

Farther east along the coast is **Carrick-a-Rede rope bridge**. This is a precarious rope bridge that crosses to a small island used for commercial salmon fishing during the summer. The seabird rookery is fascinating, especially if you like puffins, and the rope bridge you have to use to get there is challenging, especially if heights make you nervous. There's a nice paved 1 kilometer path along the rocky shoreline from the parking lot to the bridge.

Bushmills Distillery gives a popular half-hour tour culminating in a tasting. This is probably the best known Irish Whiskey label to Americans and the distillery tour is fun, lots of good smells.

CAERNARFON, WALES

Population 10,000

Caernarfon is a fun little Welsh town with all the conveniences a "caravanner" needs and a famous castle too. Another nearby attraction is Snowdonia, a National Park lying just a few miles to the east.

The Caernarfon castle was built in 1283 (and earlier) on the coast so that it could be supplied by sea, and was one of many castles constructed under King Edward I of England to subdue Wales. His son, Edward II, was the first of a long line of Princes of Wales who were eventually to become kings of England. The Prince of Wales traditionally continues to have his investiture at the castle.

There is a picturesque small harbor just under the walls. Caernarfon also has Roman roots, the **Roman Fortress of Segontium** is near the town. You can visit the excavations and an excellent museum.

Caernarfon Campground

✦ COED HELEN CARAVAN CLUB SITE

Address: Coed Helen, Caernarfon, LL54 5RS
Telephone: 01286 676770
Price: Inexpensive

Open March 26 to November 1, varies slightly

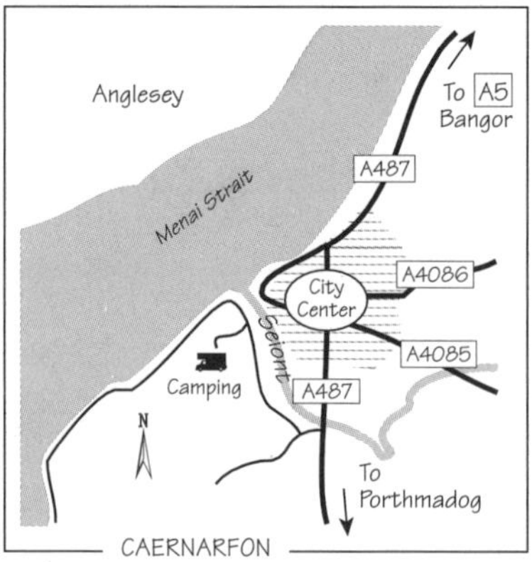

This is a medium-sized campground run by the Caravanning Club on the grounds of a park that has many static mobile home type units. The static trailers are in a separate area, they have a store, bar and swimming pool that are available to the campers from the caravan site.

The campground is a grassy, mostly level field with trees along the borders. Electrical boxes are relatively abundant but not all sites have one nearby. There is no physical separation between sites. The shower/toilet building is small, there are only four toilets and four showers in total, not many for a European campground where most people use them. The water in showers, bathroom basins, dishwashing sinks, and laundry area is hot, however, and the shower area is heated. There is a coin-operated washer and dryer. You do not need to be a member of the Caravan Club to camp here and tents are allowed.

Our favorite feature of the campground is its location. You can walk past the boat harbor and across a pedestrian bridge to the walled town and castle in five minutes. In town are pubs and restaurants. Just a little farther (10 minutes) is a modern Safeway supermarket, so if you don't feel like driving you can always walk for any groceries you might not be able to find at the campground's small store. In the other direction you can walk or ride a bike for 5 kilometers along a small road paralleling the rocky beach to a bird sanctuary.

The campground is harder to find in your car than on foot. Pass south through Caernarfon on A487. Just south of town you'll cross a bridge over the Seiont River. Turn right as soon as possible. You'll immediately see a camping sign pointed left, turn right instead and follow the small lane (Coed Helen Rd.). In about one kilometer you'll pass the site on your left, turn left at the T to drive along the site's border and then enter.

Side Trips from Caernarfon

If you drive about 8 kilometers east of Caernarfon on A4086 you will enter **Snowdonia National Park**. This region of mountains is a popular holiday destination, it's full of tourist sites as well as lots of good walking trails. You can either take a tram to the top of **Mount Snowdon** or hike one of five trails to the top at 1,085 meters. Further on you'll drive across the **Pass of Llanberis** on a tiny road closely bordered by rock fences and then descend into the lush **Gwydyr Forest Park** area around **Betws-y-coed**.

Caernarfon Castle is one of many built by the English king Edward I in the 13th century as an "iron ring" to protect his conquest of northern Wales. Others in the area that make good day trips are **Beaumaris Castle** on Anglesey Island and **Conwy Castle** to the east in Conwy near the coastal resort town of **Llandudno**.

The most impressive castle in the district, **Penrhyn Castle**, was only built in the 1820's. It is located about 5 kilometers east of Bangor near the point where A5 and A55 meet. The castle is owned by the National Trust and is considered a masterpiece of Norman revival architecture. It also has great gardens.

CAMBRIDGE, ENGLAND

Population 105,000

The first or second university town in England, depending upon your information source, Cambridge is not quite as old as Oxford. The university originated in the 12th century with Benedictine monk teachers from the nearby cathedral town of Ely. Residential colleges eventually opened and gradually became today's university town. Your visit to the British Isles won't be complete if you don't visit **King's College Chapel,** a Perpendicular Gothic style church inspired by St-Chapelle in Paris. You can also rent a punt and tour the **"The Backs"**, the lawns and waterways behind the colleges. Actually Cambridge is fun and easily visited from the campground. Don't miss the **Fitzwilliam Museum** with a fine collection including French Impressionists and English paintings by Hogarth, Gainsborough, Constable and Turner.

Cambridge Campground

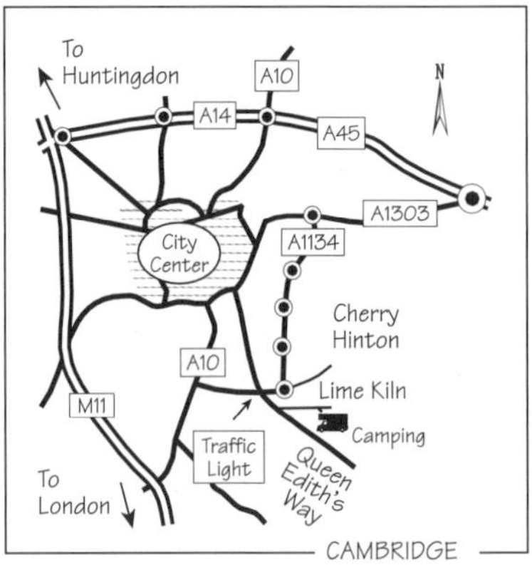

✦ CHERRY HINTON CARAVAN CLUB SITE

Address: Lime Kiln Road, Cherry Hinton, Cambridge CB1 8NQ
Telephone: 01223 244088
Price: Moderate

Open March 26 to January 4, dates vary slightly

This medium-sized Caravan Club site is unusual because it is located in an old limestone quarry. Now covered with grass and plants the sites are arranged in groups beneath the quarry walls. Parking is on grass in marked sites off paved access roads. Electricity is available at all sites except in the area set aside for tents. The shower/toilet building is a typical heated Caravan Club type with plentiful hot water for showers, bathroom basins, dishwashing and laundry. A coin-operated washer and dryer are available. The campground is relatively new and has a dump station for motor caravans. There is also a small self service information building with lots of pamphlets and maps of the area. You do not need to be a member of the Caravan Club to camp here and tents are allowed.

PUNTING IN CAMBRIDGE

Transportation to Cambridge is quite good. A bus stop is located about 500 meters from the site with the trip to town taking about 10 minutes. Bus 44 or bus 45 will work although others using slightly different routes will get you to and from town. The stop is known as "Robin Hood" after the pub across the road. If you elect to walk you can do so in about 45 minutes, the distance is about 3.5 kilometers.

This campground is not easy to find without good instructions as there are few signs. The best route is from the A45 running east/west north of town. Take the exit for A1303 and at the roundabout located at the exit follow the signs for Cambridge and A1303. In two kilometers turn left following the sign for Cherry Hinton. In 1.5 kilometers you will come to a roundabout, turn left into Gazelle Way following signs to Fulbourn. Pass through two roundabouts continuing straight and at the third (after 1.5 kilometers) turn right. At the traffic light in 1 kilometer turn left into Queen Edith's Way and then in a short distance turn left into Lime Kiln Road. The campground is up this road about 200 meters on the right.

Side Trips from Cambridge

North of Cambridge lie the **Fenlands**, a large swampy area, much of which has been drained for farming. The most important city of the Fenlands is **Ely**. Building of the **Ely Cathedral** or "Ship of the Fens" began in 1083. Ely is where Oliver Cromwell headquartered during the civil wars against King Charles I, his house is now the tourist office. To reach Ely drive 25 kilometers north from Cambridge on A10.

Eighteen kilometers south of Cambridge is **Duxford Airfield**, now the location of the aviation exhibits of the Imperial War Museum. This was a World War II air base and many of the exhibits reflect this, although there is also a Concorde, a Harrier, and a U-2. This may be the best aviation museum in Europe, aviation buffs shouldn't miss it!

The wool trade made East Anglia a very rich area during the 15th and 16th centuries. Towns built showpiece churches and the merchants and weavers had impressive homes. Two of the best towns to visit are **Lavenham** and **Long Melford**. They are located about 80 kilometers east of Cambridge.

Canterbury, England

Population 40,000

Canterbury is probably best known for **Canterbury Cathedral.** The original dated from about 600 AD. and was founded by St. Augustine. In 1170 Thomas à Becket, the archbishop at the time, was murdered here and was soon canonized as a martyr. Four years later the church burned and was soon replaced by the present cathedral. Pilgrims began flocking to Canterbury, Chaucer's 14th-century classic *Canterbury Tales* is about a group of such pilgrims.

Canterbury is very convenient to the ferries to the continent at Dover and Folkestone, both are about 30 kilometers away. This is a good first stop when you arrive or last stop before you leave Britain.

Canterbury Campground

✦ CANTERBURY CAMPING AND CARAVANNING CLUB SITE

Address: Bekesbourne Lane,
Canterbury CT3 4AB
Telephone: 01227 463217
Price: Inexpensive

Open all year

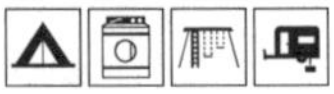

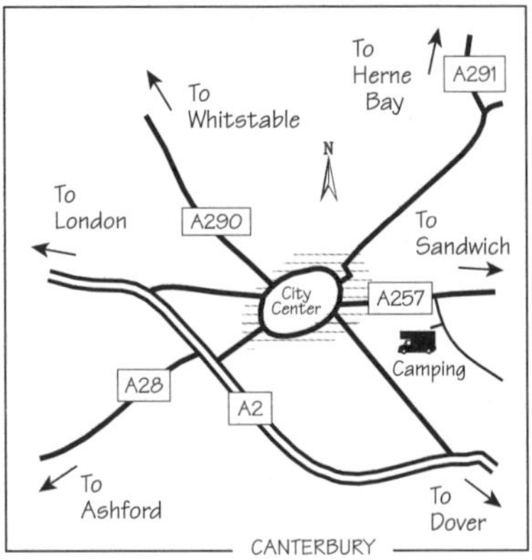

This is a large site with over 200 spaces. It is a grassy field with unnumbered sites, however, vehicles and tents are carefully placed by the warden. You don't need to worry about someone parking too close or taking your place if you drive down to the nearby Safeway store. The shower/toilet buildings are clean and well maintained, showers have preset hot water with spring loaded buttons. Bathroom basins and dishwashing sinks also have free hot water and coin-operated washers and dryers are available.

It takes about 25 minutes to walk from the campground to the cathedral so bus service, while available and convenient, is almost unnecessary. There is a Safeway store near where Highway 257 enters town.

To reach the campground take Highway 257 east from Canterbury toward Sandwich. The campground is on the right 1.5 kilometers from the town's ring road, it is well signed.

Side Trips From Canterbury

Canterbury makes a good base for exploring the Cinque Port towns of the southern coast. The **Cinque Ports** were Sandwich, Dover, Hythe, Romney and Hastings. During the Middle Ages they were responsible for patrolling the English Channel against invasion. Additional sights along the coast are **Deal** and **Walmer Castles** built by Henry VIII, and **Dover Castle** perched high atop the **White Cliffs** with the **Hellfire Caves** beneath.

CHESTER, ENGLAND

Population 125,000

Chester is a very old town, it was once an important Roman camp. Today it is probably best known for two features. The first is the **city walls**. They are over three kilometers long and completely circle the older part of town, you can walk the top of the walls for the complete circle. The second feature is the **Rows**. These are two-story shopping arcades (covered walkways) along the front of the old city buildings that date from the Middle Ages. Chester also has many "magpie" black and white half-timbered buildings.

Chester Campground

✦ CHESTER SOUTHERLY CARAVAN PARK

Address: Balderton Lane, Roughill,
Marlston-cum-Lache, Chester CH4 9LB
Telephone: 0976 743888
Price: Inexpensive

Open March 1 to November 30

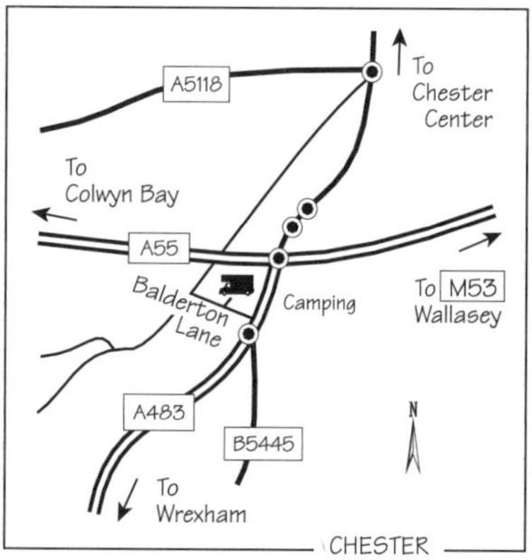

The campground is located 5 kilometers south of Chester next to the A55 freeway. It is a simple site in a country setting. Road noise from the freeway is present but really just serves as "white noise". Surrounding dairy farms are noticeable if the winds are wrong. Convenient bus service in to town and the fact that the campground is easy to find make this the best choice for a base to explore Chester.

This is a flat grassy campground with most sites on grass. Each site is marked with a number so distance between rigs is maintained. There is one shower/toilet building for the campground, it has hot water showers with hot water available to all bathroom, dishwashing and laundry sinks. There is a clothes-washing machine and dryer and the campground has a small grocery store and a playground. Access to town is by a bus that stops about a half kilometer away or by bicycle.

To drive to the campground take the A483 exit from A55 as it passes south of Chester. You'll have seen the campground just south of A55 if you've come from the west. Just south of the exit traffic circle from A55 on A483 you'll see the campground sign pointing west on Balderton Lane. The campground is a short distance down the lane on the right.

Side Trips from Chester

Sixty-five kilometers south of Chester is a famous market town, **Shrewsbury**. The **Severn River Gorge** with its **Museum of Iron** and **Museum of the River** is just to the southeast of Shrewsbury. Many consider this area the birthplace of the industrial revolution, it is the place where the process of using coke to produce iron was developed.

CORROFIN, REPUBLIC OF IRELAND

Corrofin is located in County Clare just south of the Burren (see the Side Trip section below). In addition to being a wonderful place to stay while exploring the park Corrofin has its own attractions. It is the home of the **Clare Heritage Center** which displays the historical way of life in this region. Another destination is the **Dysert O'Dea Castle Archaeology Center**. This castle is surrounded by Burren antiquities, all described and explained in an exhibition. Corrofin also is a pleasant place to spend the evening, we counted nine pubs on the two-block-long main street, several of them with live music. This small village is well prepared for tourists, in addition to the campground and its accompanying hostel there are many bed-and-breakfast establishments in the surrounding countryside. This is also a popular trout fishing area.

Corrofin Campground

✦ CORROFIN VILLAGE CARAVAN AND CAMPING PARK

Address: Corrofin, Co. Clare
Telephone: 065 37683
Price: Inexpensive

Open all year

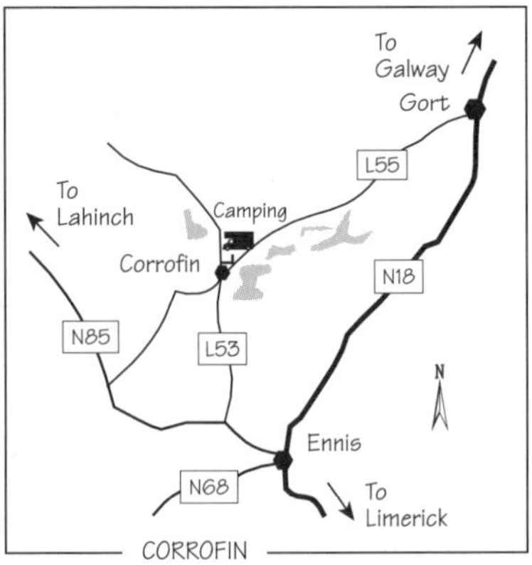

This small campground is located behind a hostel just off the main street of Corrofin village. It is a grass field with eight electrical hookups and room for a total of approximately 20 rigs. The campground is almost new so the facilities are quite nice. The shower/toilet building has hot water for showers, bathroom basins, and the combination laundry room and dishwashing area. There is a coin-operated washer and dryer. You need only walk about 50 meters to reach the nearest pub for dinner and music, yet the campground is surprisingly quiet.

The campground is located right in the center of Corrofin, if you find the village you've found the campground. Corrofin is located 13 kilometers northwest of Ennis on Highways N85 and L53 (R476).

Side Trips from Corrofin

North of Corrofin the **Burren** district is well worth a visit. The treeless limestone plateau bordering the Atlantic is filled with sights including the impressive **Cliffs of Moher** with walking trails, the **Ailwee Caves**, and the **Burren Display Center** in Kilfenora. **Lisdoonvarna** is a spa town which hosts a matchmaking festival in September and October and **Doolin** is a tiny village that is known for its pubs and traditional Irish music.

DUBLIN, REPUBLIC OF IRELAND

Population 950,000

This is the only really large urban center in the Republic of Ireland, Dublin's one million or so people comprise about a third of the Republic's inhabitants. Although a large city Dublin is easy for a camper to visit with a convenient campground and good public transportation to get you in to town.

Dublin is bisected by the west to east-flowing River Liffey. O'Connel Street, running north from the river, is the central thoroughfare and a good point of reference. The north half of Dublin was the posh area during the 18th century, but it is a little run down today. It contains much that you'll want to see, **O'Connel Street** is probably the best known boulevard in Dublin. Near the street's north end you'll find **Parnell Square**, home to the **Hugh Lane Municipal Art Gallery**, the **Gate Theater** and the **Dublin Writer's Museum**. About half way up O'Connel a major shopping street, **Henry Street**, runs westward.

South of the Liffey the streets are smaller and more crowded and the sights more concentrated. This is the home of **Trinity College** and its **Book of Kells**. You'll also find **Dublin Castle** and **St. Stephen's Green** here. **Merrion Square** is east of Stephen's Green and home of the excellent **National Gallery of Ireland**. Good shopping streets are **Nassau Street** which runs south of Trinity College and **Grafton Street**, a pedestrian street running from College Green in front of the Trinity College to St. Stephen's Green.

There are some attractions upstream of the town center to the west. Best known is probably the **Guinness Brewery** with its museum and recreated 19th-century pub. The giant **Phoenix Park** has flowers, a castle, and the **Dublin Zoo**.

Dublin is known for its pubs. The drink of choice is Guinness, of course. There's an organized Literary Pub Crawl tour or you can select your own pubs. Look for some of the best along Grafton Street or in the **Temple Bar Area** which is just south of the Liffey near the Ha'penny Bridge crossing.

Dublin Campground

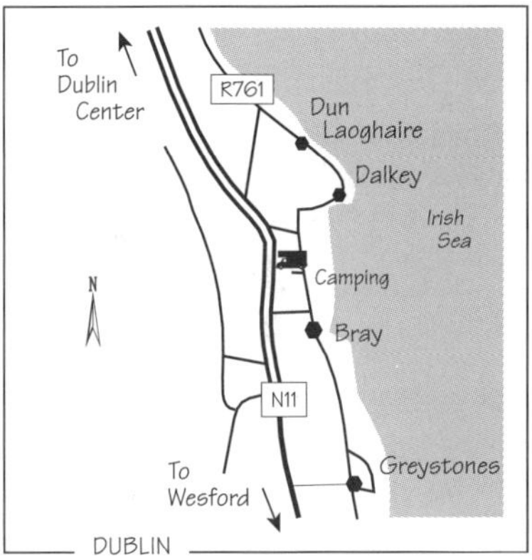

✦ Shankill Caravan and Camping Park

Address: Sherrington Park, Shankill, Dublin
Telephone: 01 2820011
Price: Inexpensive

Open all year

This medium to large campground is really two small grassy fields with paved roads threading through them. Early arriving campers park somewhat haphazardly in spots that seem convenient or pleasant and later arrivals fill in around them. Electrical outlets are a little scarce and scattered. The one shower/toilet building is old but adequate, hot showers require a token but bathroom basins, dishwashing sinks, and laundry sinks have free hot water. There is also a coin-operated washer and dryer. About one kilometer north of the campground in the town of Shankill you'll find small grocery shops and pubs. About 3 kilometers south is the town of Bray which has larger stores, a long ocean-side promenade and also a good cliff-side trail that leads above the ocean for 10 kilometers south to Greystones.

Busses to Dublin are double deckers, numbers 45 and 84 both will get you there. The stop is just outside the campground entrance and the trip takes about 45 minutes. You can also make the trip by train from the Shankill station.

To find the campground head south on N11 from Dublin toward Wexford. About 16 kilometers south of Dublin you may see a campground sign pointing east. At any rate, follow signs for Shankill or Bray to get established on the small highway that runs north and south between N11 and the ocean (R761). About 3 kilometers north of Bray you'll find the campground on the west side of this highway.

Side Trips from Dublin

The area around Dublin, known as "the Pale" during the years of English occupation has many rewarding side trip destinations. One of the most prosperous English communities was at **Dun Laoghaire**, located on the coast between the campground and Dublin. If you ride the Dart train in to town from the campground you pass through Dun Laoghaire. Today the town is a pleasant ferry port for the run to Holyhead in north Wales but it also is home to the **James Joyce Martello Tower Museum.**

Just a few kilometers south of the campground and inland from Bray near Enniskerry are the **Powerscourt Gardens**. Powerscourt House was damaged by fire in 1974 but the gardens remain, some consider them the best in the Europe. Five kilometers south of the gardens is the tallest waterfall in the British Isles, the 400 foot **Powerscourt Waterfall**.

From Enniskerry continue another 25 kilometers south on R755 into the **Wicklow Mountains**, through the village of Roundwood, to the **Glendalough Valley**. There are two mountain lakes, the ruins of a monastery founded by St. Kevin, and a visitor center to explain the valley's history to you. Return north via the Military Road (R115) for more great scenery.

Fifteen kilometers north of Dublin is Malahide village and **Malahide Castle**. You can tour the castle which houses part of the **Portrait Collection of the National Gallery** and the **Fry Model Railroad Museum** and wander the surrounding gardens.

EDINBURGH, SCOTLAND

Population 450,000

Edinburgh is a great town to visit. This is no secret, you will probably see more foreign tourists here than any other city you visit in the British Isles, excepting maybe London. Don't let that put you off, however. The campground here is very convenient to the city and there's lots to see.

As a visitor you'll find that Edinburgh's attractions are in two areas: the **Royal Mile** which stretches from the Edinburgh Castle to Holyrood Palace, and the **New Town** to the north. These are separated by a deep chasm, now the **Prince Street Gardens**, which is spanned by several bridges and paths. Busses from the campground will drop you in either place, but the whole central city area is quite compact. Both **Edinburgh Castle** and **Holyrood Palace** can be toured and the **Royal Mile** between them is full of worthwhile stops like the **Scotch Whiskey Heritage Center** where you can plan your tour of highland distilleries (see Side Trips below). Between the old and new town you'll find the **National Gallery of Scotland**, filled with a wide selection of European paintings from the 15th to the 19th century.

Edinburgh Campground

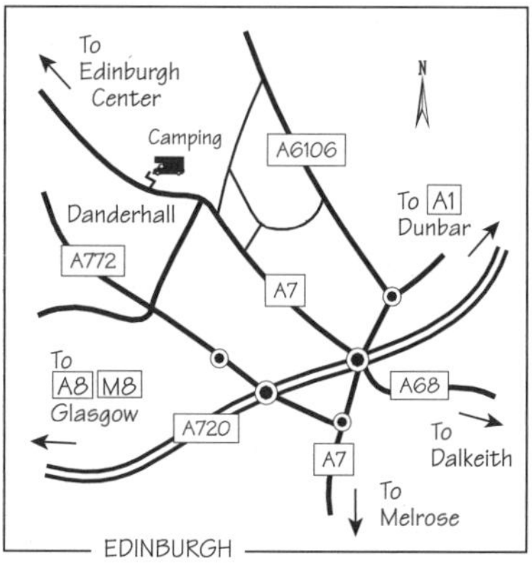

✦ LITTLE FRANCE CARAVAN PARK

Address: 219 Dalkeith Road,
Edinburgh EH16 4SU
Telephone: 01316 66 23 26
Price: Inexpensive

Open April to October

Little France Caravan Park sits about five kilometers south of the city in a green belt area of woods and farms. It is easy to reach from the ring road around the city and has convenient bus service to town.

The campground is a large open grassy field with a few paved access roads. Individual camping sites aren't marked in areas where there is no electricity. The sites with electricity are more regimented because campers park in front of the individual outlets. Toilet/shower buildings (2) are clean and heated, hot water is provided for showers and sinks. Laundry facilities include coin-operated washers and dryers. There is no store at the campground but a nearby gas station has limited supplies. Two kilometers toward town there is a large supermarket complex, coming back from Edinburgh on the bus you can get off here and then either catch another bus or walk home.

Bus service to town is a double decker, the number 33 works best for coming out from town, going in almost anything that stops will work. Busses run every 10 minutes or so during most of the day and the stop is just outside the campground entrance road.

Best access to the campground is from A720 south of the city. Drive north on A7, you'll see the campground on the right.

Side Trips from Edinburgh

Golfers will want to take a drive up to **St. Andrews** for a day on the links in the town where the game was born. Drive 15 kilometers west and cross the Firth of Forth on the Forth Road Bridge. From there it is 70 kilometers north to the town and St. Andrews Links which have six courses: Old Course, New Course, Strathyrum, Jubilee, Eden, and Balgrove (only 9 holes). You can camp near St. Andrews at CRAIGTON MEADOWS HOLIDAY PARK located west of town and open from March through October.

Whiskey lovers have their own important tour route from Edinburgh or Glasgow. The Spey River which runs northeast into the Moray Firth is home to many **Scotch Whiskey distilleries**. To get there you must drive north about 250 kilometers or 3 hours from either Edinburgh or Glasgow. This is quite a drive but you'll see a great deal of the highlands and can easily overnight at a campground in the Spey valley. You could even take a short side trip to the famous **Loch Ness** and **Inverness**. The Caravan Club has a campground about 9 kilometers east of Inverness on B9006 called CULLODEN MOOR that is open from the end of March to the first part of October.

The area around Edinburgh is **Sir Walter Scott country**. The famous novelist immortalized many sights in the region including **Glamis Castle** (also associated with Shakespeare's *Macbeth*), **Inveraray Castle**, and **Melrose Abbey**. Scott's home, **Abbotsford**, is situated south of Edinburgh.

GLASGOW, SCOTLAND

Population 700,000

Glasgow is a bustling, modern city which has kept its Victorian-era buildings. The train station has one of the warmest atmospheres and may be the most attractive that we have seen. There is a pedestrian street, **Sauchiehall St.**, on the northern edge of the downtown area. Although Glasgow has a subway you'll probably find the downtown area compact enough to explore on foot. Find time to take a look at the **Glasgow Cathedral** which was built over the grave of Glasgow's patron Saint Mungo and visit the excellent **Glasgow Art Gallery and Museum**. About 5 kilometers south of central Glasgow in an area of parkland are two more worthwhile art museums, **Pollok House** and **The Burrell Collection**.

Glasgow Campground

✦ STRATHCLYDE CARAVANNING AND CAMPING PARK

Address: 366 Hamilton Road, Motherwell ML1 4ED
Telephone: 01698 266155
Price: Inexpensive

Open Easter to October 31

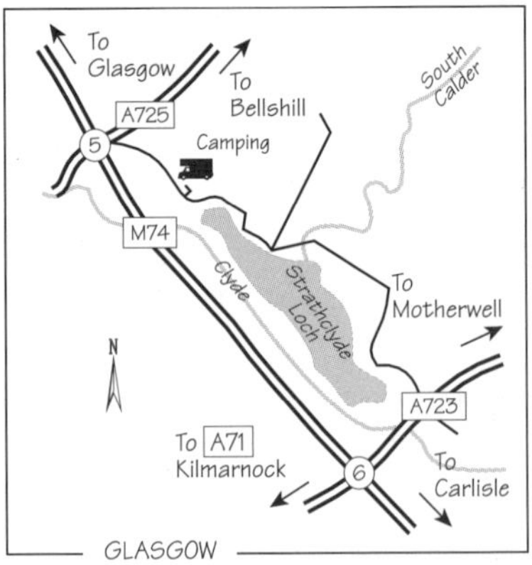

This very large county campground is located within a large park with a lake, tennis, golf, and even the ruins of a Roman bathhouse. It is conveniently placed for access by car but public transportation service to downtown Glasgow is a just a shade too far from the campground to really be called convenient. This might not be a problem if you are willing to drive downtown, parking isn't hard to find in Glasgow if you look outside the city center area.

The campground is composed of several grassy parking areas separated by hedges and trees with paved access roads. Sites are grass. There is also a large field for tent camping. Electricity is readily available if required. There are many shower/toilet buildings, each with hot water showers, dishwashing, and laundry areas. All are quite clean and well maintained. Coin-operated washers and dryers are available. Limited supplies are available at the reception desk but you'll find that you have to drive or walk to get to a supermarket.

The nearest shopping and rail station are at Bellshill. This is a twenty-five minute walk from the campground towards Glasgow. There are many shops and stores including a large Safeway. There is also a train station where you can catch a train for Glasgow, only fifteen minutes and $2.00 per round trip away.

To get to the campground take Highway M74 southeast from Glasgow. Take Exit 5 and then follow signs no more than 1 kilometer to the campground.

Side Trips from Glasgow

About 50 kilometers north of Glasgow on the east side of Lock Lomond are the **Trossachs**, a very scenic region of mountains and lakes. The **West Highland Way** footpath threads its way along the east shore of the lake.

Stirling Castle played an important part in Scottish history and remains an impressive and interesting destination. It is located about 50 kilometers northeast of Glasgow on the M80 motorway. Many important battles were fought nearby, including the long-remembered defeat of the English by Robert the Bruce at the Battle of Bannockburn in 1314. The **Bannockburn Heritage Centre** stands on the field of battle some 3 kilometers south of Stirling Castle.

Killarney, Republic of Ireland

Population 9,000

Killarney has a deserved reputation as a tourist town and it is an excellent base for exploring this part of Ireland. On days when a longer trip doesn't sound attractive you'll want to visit closer attractions in the **Killarney National Park** which is discussed under Side Trips below. A good way to explore nearby attractions is by bike, if you didn't bring one along you can always rent one at the campground.

Killarney Campground

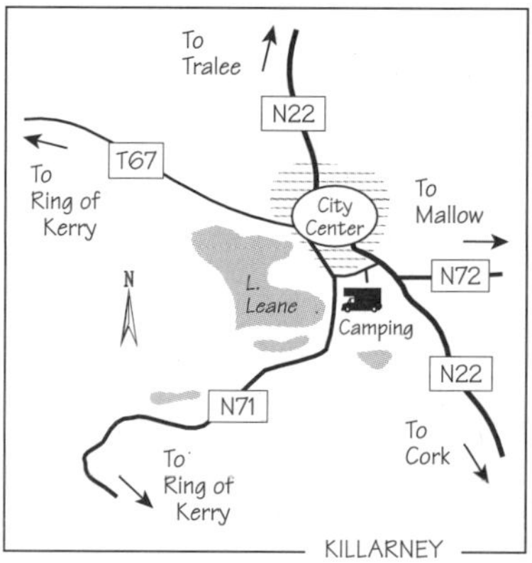

✦ Flemings White Bridge Caravan and Camping Park

Address: Ballycasheen, Killarney, Co. Kerry
Telephone: 064 31590
Price: Inexpensive

Open March 15 to October 31

White Bridge is a large well kept campground about 2 kilometers from the center of Killarney next to the River Flesk. It covers two large grassy fields. A few pitches near the entrance have hard all-weather surfaces, the remainder of the campground sites are on the grass and not delineated in any way. Adequate electrical outlets (10 amps) are provided. There are three shower/toilet buildings with hot water for showers, dishes and laundry. Showers require a token. There is a small grocery store on site and bicycles for rent. You do not need to be a member of the Caravan Club to camp here and tents are allowed.

You'll find the campground on the southeast edge of town, just off Highway N22. A sign on the highway will show you where to turn. If you approach town from the southwest on N71 a sign just outside the central area of town will direct you to the right along a convenient route south of town.

Side Trips from Killarney

Killarney is perfectly situated for a circular day trip around the **Ring of Kerry.** The circuit is about 175 kilometers when done from Killarney but many of the roads are slow and narrow. There are also many places to stop and explore. You will find several campgrounds along the south coast of the peninsula so you might want to make a two-day (or week-long) expedition of the circuit. WAVECREST CARAVAN AND CAMPING PARK is located just outside the town of Caherdaniel and is open from the first of April to the end of September.

The **Dingle Peninsula**, just north of the Iveragh Peninsula and the Ring of Kerry, is just as scenic and much less crowded. The drive out the peninsula and back is about 160 kilometers.

The three **Lakes of Killarney** (Lough Leane, Muckross Lake, and Upper Lake) are famed for their scenery. They are within the **Killarney National Park** and located just southwest of Killarney. There are many attractions including **Muckross Abbey**, **Muckross House**, **Ross Castle and Torc Waterfall**. You can take a boat out to Innisfallen Island or hike or bike the **Gap of Dunloe.**

Cork and the nearby **Blarney Castle** are only 90 kilometers southeast of Killarney. You can easily visit the castle, kiss the **Blarney stone**, and tour Cork on a day trip. You could also choose to spend the night at BLARNEY CARAVAN AND CAMPING PARK, only 2.5 kilometers from Blarney Castle.

LONDON, ENGLAND

Population 7,700,000

Like Paris and Rome, London is circled by a freeway ring road, the M25 London Orbital Motorway. This one, however, is huge, you will cover 200 kilometers if you drive around it. For this reason we've included four campgrounds to use when visiting the city, when you arrive you can pick the closest because they're all good.

Transportation in London means subways (the tube), busses (many double deckers), and suburban railways. Don't bring your vehicle in to town, the combined difficulties of overcrowded streets and driving on the left are no fun. Avoid arriving in London during rush hours.

London is arguably the most entertaining city in the world. The possibilities are endless, they include a **theater district** second to none. Museums are plentiful and include the **British Museum**, **National Gallery**, **National Portrait Gallery** and the **Tate Gallery**. There are monuments and sights to keep you busy for weeks: **Big Ben's clock tower**, the **Parliament Buildings**, **Buckingham Palace**, **The Tower of London**, **The Monument, St. Paul's Cathedral, The Tower Bridge, Kew Gardens** and much more.

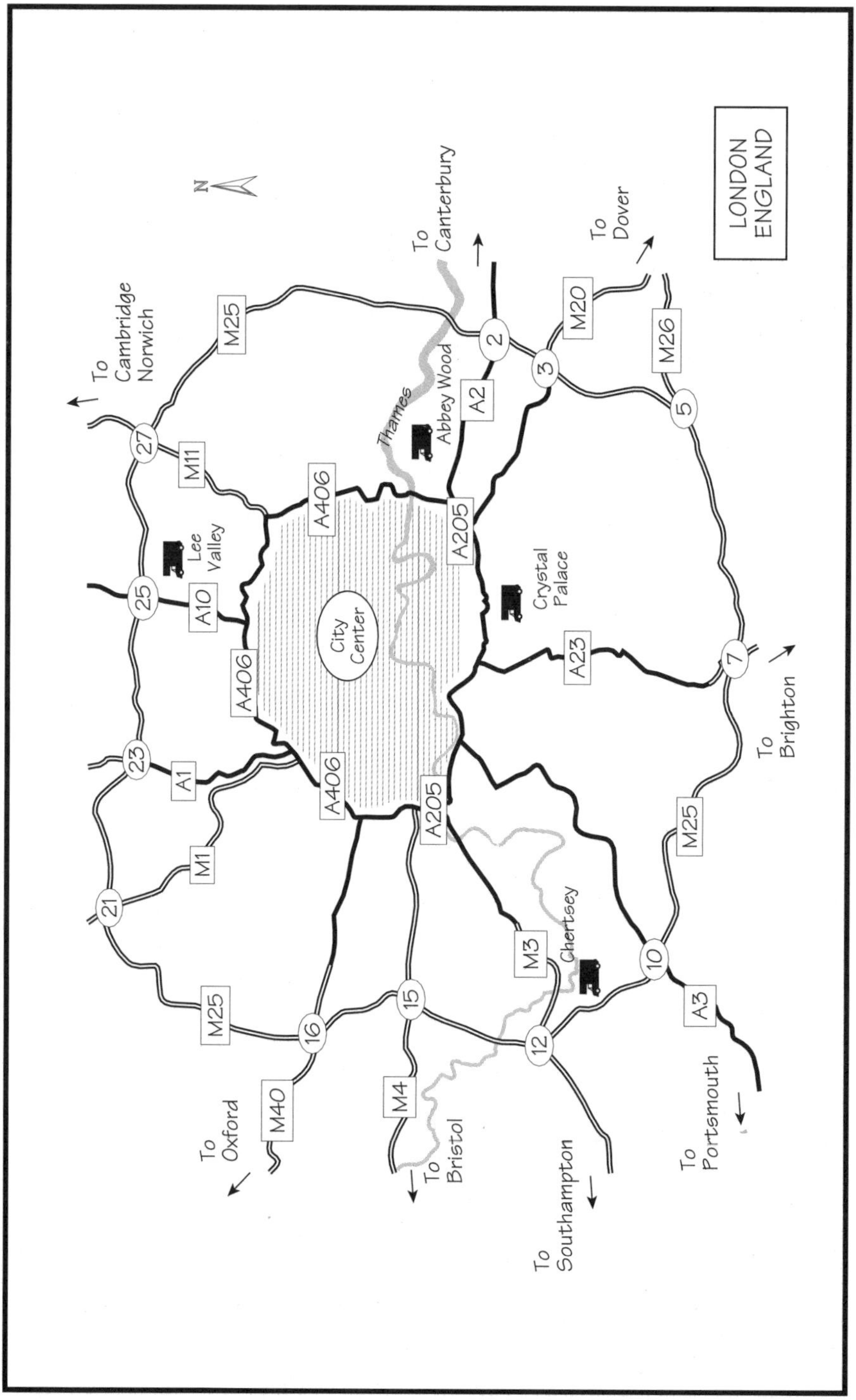
LONDON
ENGLAND
N
To Cambridge Norwich
To Canterbury
To Dover
To Brighton
To Portsmouth
To Southampton
To Bristol
To Oxford
City Center
Thames
Lee Valley
Abbey Wood
Crystal Palace
Chertsey
M25
M11
M20
M26
M1
M40
M4
M3
A406
A205
A2
A23
A10
A1
A3
2
3
5
7
10
12
15
16
21
23
25
27

There's no point in covering London in much detail here. There are information sources everywhere, start by checking with the campground reception office. You'll use public transportation quite a bit so buy daily pass tickets allowing unlimited use of subways and busses. The various sightseeing tours on double-decker busses are a good introduction to the city but you'll probably soon start thinking of locations in terms of tube stations. Best of all, almost everyone speaks English.

London Campgrounds

✦ CRYSTAL PALACE CARAVAN CLUB SITE

Address: Crystal Palace Parade,
London SE19 1UF
Telephone: 0181 7787155
Price: Moderate

Open all year

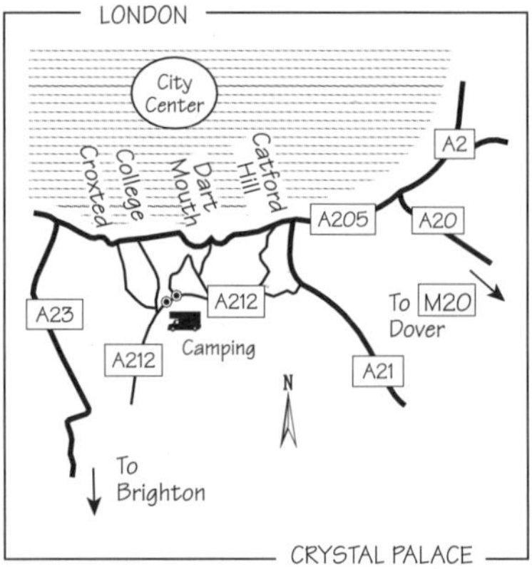

One of two Caravan Club campgrounds in suburban southwest London this campground may be the most convenient place to stay while visiting the city. A forty-five minute ride on a double-decker bus will take you to Oxford Circus or Trafalgar Square. Crystal Palace is a nearby park with pleasant walking avenues. After the 1851 Great London Exhibition the giant Crystal Palace greenhouse was reerected here but it burned to the ground in 1936. You may find the high BBC television tower next to the campground helpful in locating it. You do not need to be a member of the Caravan Club to camp here and tents are allowed. In the summer this campground is very busy, arrive early or make reservations. Try the Abbey Wood campground if you don't get lucky here.

The medium-sized campground is spread across a hillside but has flat, mostly gravel sites with convenient electrical outlets (CEE17 plugs, 16 amps). It is nicely landscaped with some shade. The one shower/toilet building is immaculate and has lots of hot water for showers (adjustable), bathroom basins, and washing dishes. While there is no store at the campground you will find a very modern Safeway about 2 kilometers away. Ask at the reception desk for directions. Many other shops and restaurants are much closer.

You can get downtown by taking the bus, it stops about 100 meters from the campground entrance. The campground reception desk sells daily tickets good for all London public transportation.

Directions for this campground will seem complicated but it is well signed once you are on the A205. Start on the London ring road east of the city. Exit the M25 ring road at Exit 2 and join A2. After 14 kilometers take the exit for and turn left onto A205. You'll be going west toward Catford. Continue for 5.6 kilometers, then take the left onto A212. The campground is on the left in 4.4 kilometers.

✦ ABBEY WOOD CARAVAN CLUB SITE

Address: Federation Road, Abbey Wood, London SE2 OLS
Telephone: 0181 3117708
Price: Moderate

Open all year

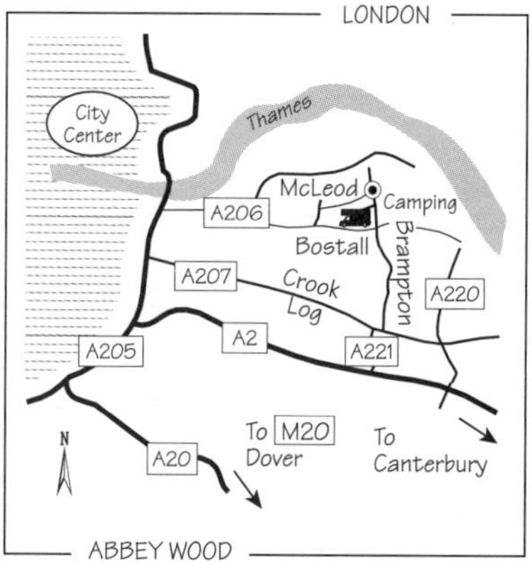

Another Caravan Club campground that is close to London, this one has a lot of room and excellent access to the city.

Abbey Wood is not a typical Caravan Club campground. It is a large campground spread across a hillside with some open grass, some gravel, and a large tent area. Electricity is available to many sites but you may find it difficult to level your rig if you have a four-wheeled rig like a van or motorhome. The shower/toilet buildings are old and not up to Caravan Club standards, but they have plenty of hot water for showers, bathroom basins, and dishes. There is a small shop on site and you'll find several grocery stores within a kilometer of the campground. You do not need to be a member of the Caravan Club to camp here and tents are allowed.

Access to London is by suburban railroad. The Abbey Wood station is about one kilometer down the hill. The normal London Travel Card will work from this station, trains are frequent and it takes a half-hour to reach the Charing Cross station in the center of the theater district. At Abbey Woods you're very near Greenwich, the train stops at the Greenwich station on the way in to London.

To reach the campground start on the M25 ring road east of London and then take Exit 2 onto A2 toward London. Take the A221 exit for Bexleyheath and proceed north on Danson Road. When you reach Crook Log Road you have to jog right and then left onto Brampton Road. Follow Brampton for 2.4 kilometers and turn left onto Bostall Hill Road at a stop light. You're now very near the campground but have to take a circular route to make the easiest entrance. Drive 1.2 kilometers down the hill and turn right at the light onto Basildon Road. In .3 kilometer turn right again on McLeod road. Proceed .8 kilometer to a roundabout, turn right onto Knee Hill Road, then after .1 kilometer turn right into Federation Road. The campground is on the left after about 100 meters. This entire route is well signposted, fortunately.

✦ LEE VALLEY CAMPSITE

Address: Sewardstone Road, Chingford,
London E4 7RA
Telephone: 0181 5295689
Price: Moderate

Open April 1 to October 30

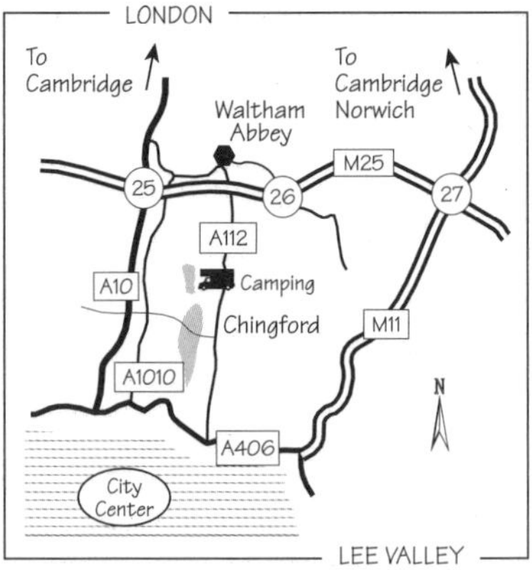

This large campground is on the north side of London near the ring road. It is one of four sites in the area run by Lee Valley Park. Access to London takes about an hour and fifteen minutes via double decker and then subway. You're really outside London and in the countryside at this campground.

The campground is a large flat field with trees separating it into several areas. Individual sites are not separated from each other. Electricity is available to about half the sites. The shower/toilet buildings are modern and clean, hot showers are available. The campground also has coin-operated washing machines, a grocery shop, and a playground.

To get to London you walk about 1 kilometer south and catch the number 215 double decker to Walthamstow Underground Station. This is on the Victoria line and is a long way north, it's a long tube ride to central London. During the middle of the summer some of the number 215 busses actually stop at the campground so you don't have to walk that first kilometer.

From the M25 ring road take the exit at Junction 26, follow the signs to Waltham Abbey on A121 along the north side of the freeway. Turn left at the traffic lights following A112 south toward Chingford, you'll cross to the south side of the freeway and see the campground on the right in about 3 kilometers.

✦ CHERTSEY CAMPING AND CARAVANNING CLUB SITE

Address: Bridge Road, Chertsey,
Surrey KT16 8JX
Telephone: 01932 562405
Price: Moderate

Open all year

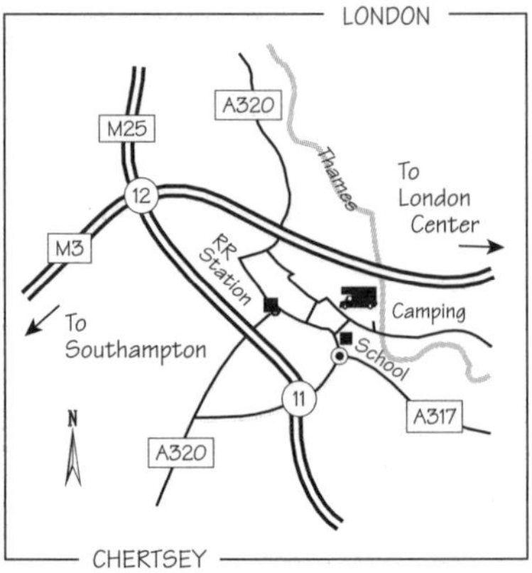

A good choice for camping on the west side of London, Chertsey is a Camping and Caravanning Club Site, which means it's nice. Situated on the bank of the Thames, Chertsey is closer to Windsor Castle than it is to London, so it makes a good base for visiting the castle as well as being a convenient London campground.

The campground is a large grassy field running back from the banks of the river with the shower/toilet building in the center. Camp sites are carefully assigned by the warden in person, fire regulations require good separation. Electricity is available to may sites. The shower/toilet building is very good, it is heated and has hot water for showers, bathroom basins, dishwashing and laundry. There are coin-operated laundry machines. There's a large supermarket in Chertsey about a kilometer from the campground, unfortunately it has barrier bars to prevent campers from entering its parking lot so you'll have to walk, ride your bike, or find a parking space somewhere else if you have a high-topped rig.

To reach central London from Chertsey you use the suburban rail lines. The Chertsey station has pretty good service but if you have the time walk up the left bank of the Thames to the Staines station at least once. The walk along the river is extremely pleasant and Staines has more frequent train service. Make sure to check schedules back to Chertsey if you plan to come back late in the evening, service to Chertsey at night stops about midnight, we almost had to walk from Staines one night.

To find the campground take the Junction 11 exit from A25 London ring road. From the roundabout just east of the junction head northwest toward Chertsey on A317. Pass through Chertsey making sure to continue straight just past the school building and at the T (B375) turn right. You'll see the campground entrance on the left in a short distance before the road crosses the Thames.

Side Trips from London

Windsor Castle is one of the queen's residences, in fact her family is named for it. Windsor is located west of London just outside the London Ring Road. You can most easily visit by using the suburban rail lines. From the Chertsey campground it doesn't take long at all to get there, from central London about forty minutes. At the castle you can tour the **State Apartments** if the family isn't in residence and also take a look at the Perpendicular Gothic **St. George's Chapel**.

NEWCASTLE UPON TYNE, ENGLAND

Population 205,000

This large city in the northeast corner of England will probably be on your visiting card because it is a port for ferries to Scandinavia and is also on the east-coast routes to and from Scotland. The campground we like is outside town on a pretty stretch of coast, bus service to town is convenient.

The most interesting area of Newcastle is near the river. The old **Norman castle** keep there is the "new castle" that the city is named for, it dates from the 11th century, an indication of the long history of the city. Newcastle also has a very large modern shopping center, the **Metro Center**, largest in Europe.

Newcastle-upon-Tyne Campground

✦ OLD HARTLEY CARAVAN CLUB SITE
Address: Whitley Bay, NE26 4RL
Telephone: 0191 2370256
Price: Inexpensive

Open March 26 to November 1, dates vary slightly

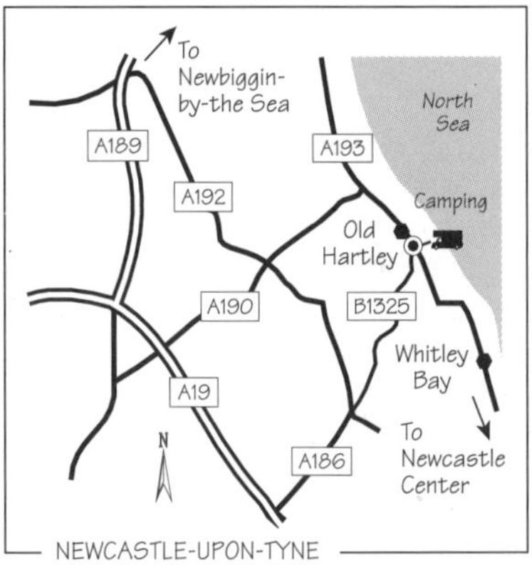

This is another Caravan Club campground with the order, cleanliness, and superior facilities that you expect from them. It is a popular members-only site so if you haven't popped for the Caravan Club membership you might try a holiday park with tourist sites just south along the coast toward Whitley Bay. It is called WHITLEY BAY H0LIDAY PARK and is open from March to December.

Old Hartley is a medium-sized site on a sloping meadow above cliffs that overlook the ocean and St. Mary's Island. The island has a lighthouse and road access that disappears under the sea at every high tide. Like all normal Caravan Club campgrounds this one has friendly wardens, electricity (CEE17 plugs, 16 amps) at every site, hard pads for parking, and good heated sanitary facilities with hot water for showers, bathroom basins, and dish and clothes washing sinks. The laundry room has a coin-operated washer and dryer. This campground does not accept tent campers. There is a coastal footpath that runs right past the campground.

To find the campground just head for the coast in the neighborhood of Whitley Bay north of the mouth of the Tyne River. As you drive north from Whitley Bay on A193 it jogs inland and then turns north again. There is a small traffic circle just before Seaton Sluice where the B1325 meets A193, you can identify the circle by the Delaval Arms Hotel sitting next to it. The caravan park is on the ocean side of this circle, it is difficult to see from the road but access is good.

Side Trips from Newcastle

About 30 kilometers south of Newcastle is **Durham**, northern England's university town, third oldest in the country after Oxford and Cambridge. The town is known for it's **Norman cathedral** and **Durham Castle**.

Driving north along the coast from Newcastle you'll find several castles. The first is **Ainwick Castle**, it is inland and about 50 kilometers north of Newcastle, then on the coast are **Dunstanburgh Castle** which was featured in the movie *Hamlet* starring Mel Gibson and also **Bamburgh Castle**.

The Romans built **Hadrian's Wall** to protect their northern border. One end started near Newcastle and portions are still standing. Start your tour of the wall at the **Roman Army Museum** near Greenhead which is 50 kilometers west of Newcastle. From there drive east on B6318 which follows the wall's route almost the entire distance back to Newcastle, signs will direct you to points of interest. Incidentally,

Greenhead is also on the **Pennine Way**, a 400-kilometer hiking trail running from Edale in the Peaks District to just north of the Scottish border.

OXFORD, ENGLAND

Population 115,000

As you travel up the Thames from London you'll pass through **Windsor** with its castle and **Eaton College**, bypass the industrial town of Reading if at all possible, and finally reach the university town of Oxford. Oxford has been a university town longer than most, since at least the 11th century. Today almost a tenth of the city's population are students. On the other hand, Oxford is also home of the Rover automobile factory.

The central part of town is a virtual architectural museum. It is quite compact and easy to get around on foot. You'll want to tour several of the colleges, check with the Tourist Information Center in the middle of town, they actually conduct a walking tour although it is possible to visit on your own during scheduled visiting hours. Many colleges are arranged around quadrangles, famous names you'll probably recognize are **All Souls College**, **Christ Church College**, **Magdalen College**, **Merton College** and **Trinity College**. Book fans will want to join a tour of the three-million-volume **Bodleian Library** and visit **Blackwells's**, one of the world's largest bookstores.

Oxford Campground

✦ OXFORD CAMPING INTERNATIONAL

Address: 426 Abandon Rd. Oxford OX1 4XN
Telephone: 01865 246551
Price: Inexpensive

Open all year

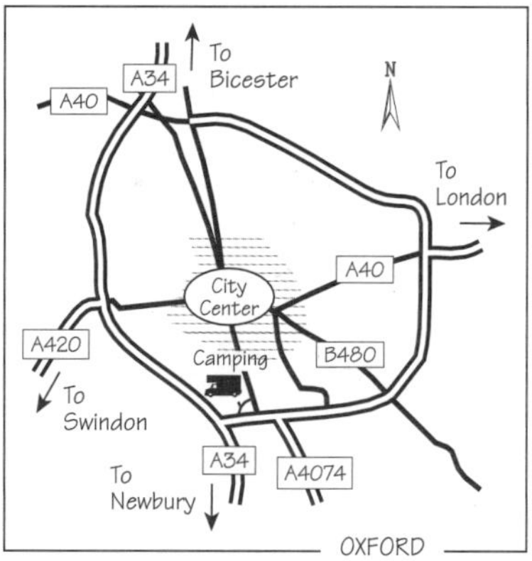

Oxford Camping International is a medium-sized campground on the southern outskirts of town. It is a grassy field with camp sites marked by small signs, many have electricity conveniently located nearby. If the campground is full you may find yourself quite close to your neighbor. The shower/toilet building has coin-operated hot showers but free hot water for bathroom basins and washing dishes. There is a small grocery store at the campground. You'll also find a large Sainsbury's supermarket about one kilometer east on the ring road, there's a good bike path right to it.

To get into town you can take a bus that stops near the campground or follow a well-marked bike route that runs through a quiet residential neighborhood and several small parks. The distance is about 2 kilometers.

To find the campground follow the signs from the ring road on the south side of town. There are quite a few signs for campgrounds along this stretch of road, you want the ones that point north since the campground is just inside the ring road. Once heading toward town watch closely for another sign pointing at the campground entrance. If you're not careful you'll be past before you see it since you can't see the campground from the road.

Side Trips from Oxford

Blenheim Palace is located in the village of Woodstock, about 13 kilometers north of Oxford. Blenheim was the birthplace of Winston Churchill but not his home. It is the home of the Dukes of Marlborough and was given to the original Duke of Marlborough by Queen Anne in 1705 as a reward for winning the battle of Blenheim. Winston Churchill's father was a later duke's younger brother. Blenheim is one of Britain's largest palaces, the grounds cover over 200 acres, tours are quite entertaining. Winston himself is buried three kilometers south in Bladon.

Thirty kilometers south of Oxford near the village of **Uffington** the giant outline of a **white horse** is cut into a hillside. It was apparently created about 3000 BC. The chalk hills in England made this art form popular with the early inhabitants of the island, but this figure has been unusually well maintained over the years.

PORTSMOUTH, ENGLAND
Population 185,000

Although Portsmouth is not generally a popular tourist overnight stop it has good camping facilities and plenty to do. The big draw is the **Royal Navy Heritage Area**. You can tour two very famous ships here: Admiral Nelson's flagship the **H.M.S. Victory** (in service for 150 years) and the **H.M.S. Warrior**, a Victorian-era square-rigged ironclad that was unbeatable when built. You can also see the salvaged remains of the **Mary Rose**, Henry VIII's ill-fated favorite. This ship capsized and sank in the harbor in 1545 and was raised in 1982.

Portsmouth Campground

✦ SOUTHSEA CARAVAN PARK

Address: Melville Road, Southsea, Hampshire PO4 9PT
Telephone: 01705 735070
Price: Moderate

Open all year

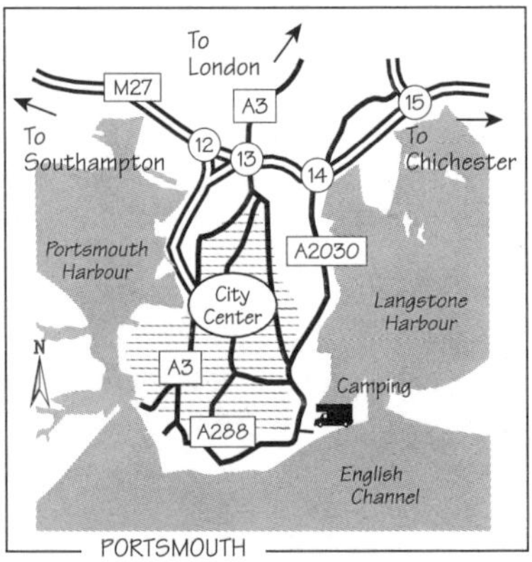

Southsea is located next to the ocean about 5 kilometers east of downtown Portsmouth. There is a berm between the campground and the ocean but access to the beach is easy.

This is a large campground with many permanently-located rental caravans as well as large areas for tourist campers. The sites are covered with dry grass and sand, they are numbered but not separated by shrubbery. Electricity is convenient to most sites. The shower/toilet buildings have hot water for showers (premixed push button), bathroom basins, and dishwashing sinks. There is a laundry area with coin-operated machines, a swimming pool, a small grocery shop, a restaurant and two bars.

Bus service to downtown Portsmouth is convenient to the campground. You can also walk or ride a bike in to town, the wide paved ocean-side promenade stretches almost the entire distance.

To find the campground take the A2030 exit from the A27 motorway and drive south. You'll soon start seeing camp signs and even possibly see another campground as you pass it. Continue to follow signs, turning onto A288 after about 5 kilometers until you reach the campground at the ocean. From Portsmouth just follow the seaside promenade east as far as you can go, the campground is located at the end of the promenade.

Side Trips from Portsmouth

You can catch a ferry to the **Isle of Wight** from Portsmouth. There are several campgrounds on this mostly-rural island, also sandy beaches and chalk cliffs. King Charles I was imprisoned in the island's **Carisbrooke Castle** which is open to visitors. There's a 65 kilometer hiking trail, the **Isle of Wight Coastal Path**, all the way around the island. If you wish to camp on the island try ADGESTONE CAMPING PARK located just north of Sandown which is open from April to September.

SALISBURY, ENGLAND

Population 37,000

Salisbury has two big attractions. **Stonehenge** is nearby and **Salisbury Cathedral** is one of England's most famous. The cathedral was built in an unusually short period between 1220 and 1258 and houses one of the four original copies of the Magna Carta, here since the 13th century. The cathedral has the highest spire in England and sits in an open park-like setting. Salisbury is also a real market town with market days being Tuesday and Saturday. Don't miss the walkways along the Avon River with lots of shops and even a pub or two.

Salisbury Campground

✦ SALISBURY CAMPING AND CARAVANNING CLUB SITE

Address: Hudson's Field, Castle Road, Salisbury, Wiltshire SP1 3RR
Telephone: 01722 32 07 13
Price: Moderate

Open March 22 to November 1, dates vary slightly

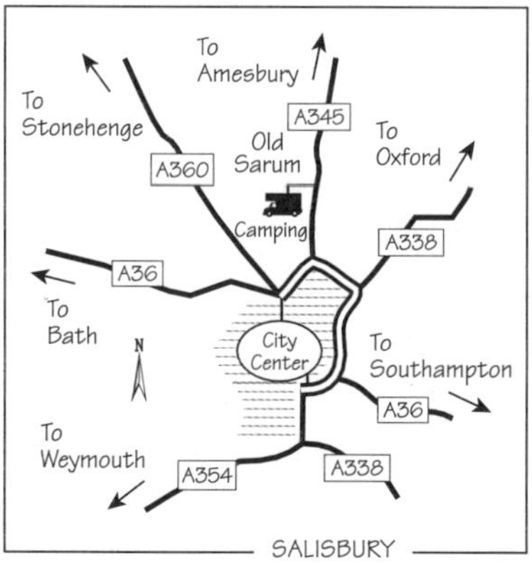

This medium-sized site is really just a fenced-off section of a big grassy field known as Hudson's Field. A line of electrical posts and a few water faucets have been installed and a portable shower/toilet building hauled in. The managers are friendly and the view is great since the campground sits at the top of a small hill with vistas to the north and west towards the Salisbury plain. The shower/toilet building has hot water for showers and bathroom basins, there is also a separate area for dishes and hand washing of clothes, also with hot water.

The campground is quite convenient to downtown Salisbury. There is a bus stop nearby or you can walk downtown, it takes 30 minutes to walk from the campground through the old town to the cathedral.

The easiest way to find the campground is to head out of town to the north from the ring road on A345. The entry road will be on your left at about 1 kilometer, you turn and drive down across the field on a hard-surfaced driveway and then left up to the campground.

Side Trips from Salisbury

A bike ride to **Stonehenge** on quiet back roads is easy from Salisbury. You'll pass through the tiny villages of Lower, Middle and Upper Woodford, Wilsford, and West Amesbury. The distance is about 15 kilometers each way.

If Stonehenge piques your interest in prehistoric monuments consider driving 55 kilometers north from Salisbury on A345 to the less crowded and more extensive monuments in the Marlborough Downs around Avebury. You'll find the **Silbury Hill** burial mound, the **Kennett Stone Avenue** processional way, and the giant **Avebury Monument**, similar to Stonehenge. There's also the much more recent **Cherhill Down hillside horse outline** dating from the late eighteenth century.

Winchester is only 40 kilometers east of Salisbury. The town is very old and known for its **cathedral**. Both Jane Austin and Izaak Walton are buried there.

The **New Forest**, centered around the town of Lyndhurst about 45 kilometers south of Salisbury, is a popular British camping destination. Originally set aside as a royal hunting preserve by William the Conqueror in 1079 today the New Forest is a 145-square-mile area of unfenced woodlands with free-ranging New Forest ponies and deer.

If you're a Thomas Hardy fan you probably know that his fictional **Wessex region** is modeled after the area around Dorchester. This city is 60 kilometers southwest of Salisbury on A354.

STOKE-ON-TRENT, ENGLAND

Population 250,000

The area around Stoke-on-Trent is known as the **Potteries**. Wedgwood, Royal Dalton, Spode, and others have factories here. Many visitor centers, museums and factory tours are available in the area, if you're a bone china fan you'll love it, if not you will probably enjoy a tour and become quite knowledgeable anyway. The towns of the Potteries region, jointly administered as the city of Stoke-on-Trent, are Stoke, Burslem,

Hanley, Tunstall, Fenton, and Longton. A vehicle is necessary for conveniently getting around but much of the area is rural so a camping vehicle is an ideal way to visit.

Stoke-on-Trent Campground

✦ Trentham Gardens Caravan and Camping Park

Address: Trentham, N. Staffs. ST4 8AX
Telephone: 01782 65 73 41
Price: Inexpensive

Open all year

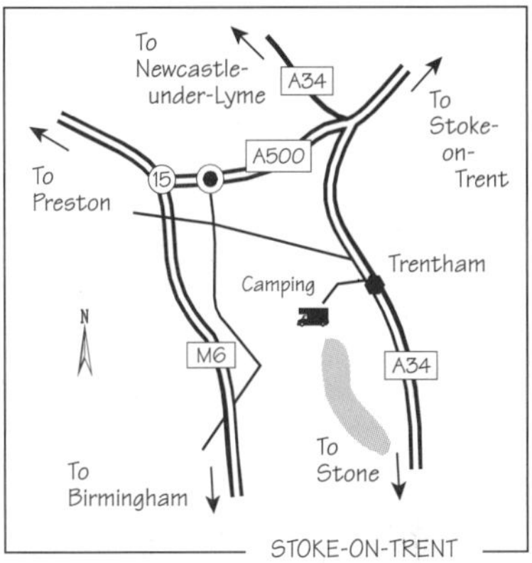

The camping area is really just a small part of a large entertainment complex known as Trentham Gardens. The gardens were once an estate of the Dukes of Sutherland, the main house is gone but extensive gardens, a large lake, and a church remain. More recent additions include a children's zoo, several restaurants, an indoor go-kart track, a pitch-and-putt golf course, and of course the camping area. The location near the M6 motorway to the north makes this a good place to stop for the night even if you aren't interested in the local sights.

The very large camping area sits on a sloping grass-covered field above the lake. There are a few scattered trees, you can find shade if you want it. You can set up your camp pretty much where you want to, there is an area of graveled hard sites, good for wet weather, large grassy areas with many electrical outlets scattered throughout, and large grassy tent areas. Sanitary facilities are plentiful if not particularly attractive, they are located in ugly factory built mobile modules, but provide lots of facilities including plenty of hot water for showers. There is a small grocery store on site and also a restaurant down by the lake, not to mention the other restaurants that are part of the complex located an easy five minute walk across the Italian Garden.

The campground is located off the M6 just south of Stoke near the small town of Trentham. There is good signage. Take the exit at Junction 15 on M6, you can follow signs from there to Trentham and the campground.

Stratford-upon-Avon

Population 21,000

Stratford is totally dedicated to the memory of William Shakespeare, any fan will find lots of places to visit. The Shakespeare Birthplace Trust operates and issues a joint ticket for **the Shakespeare Centre and Birthplace**, **Nash's House and New Place**, **Hall's Croft**, **Anne Hathaway's Cottage**, and **Mary Arden's House**. The Royal Shakespeare Company plays in the **Royal Shakespeare Theatre** from March to late January so you can spend several pleasant evenings attending shows if you can manage to get tickets.

Stratford is also home to an event that might be of interest to you as an RVer in Europe, the **Stratford Motor Caravan Fair**, which is held some time during the first half of June each year. You can find out the exact date by checking with an RV dealer or picking up one of the many motor caravan magazines from a newsstand. This show will let you examine first hand the van conversions, motorhomes, and caravans (camp trailers) that the English excel in producing.

The Motor Caravan Fair is held at the Stratford Race Course (horses). This race course also has a camp area with electrical outlets and sanitary facilities so if you are interested in the horse racing scene or are a Dick Francis mystery novel fan you might consider overnighting at the course instead of at the campground described below.

Stratford-upon-Avon Campground

✦ AVON CARAVAN PARK

Address: Warwick Road, Stratford-upon-Avon CV37 ONS
Telephone: 01789 293438
Price: Moderate

Open March 1 to October 31.

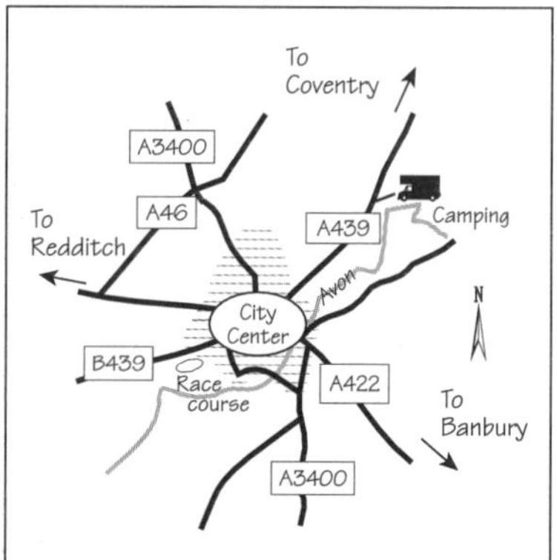

STRATFORD-UPON-AVON

This campground is located just outside Stratford on the bank of the Avon River. It makes a convenient place to stay while you visit the town or make day trips south into the Cotswold Hills.

The medium-sized campground is a grass-covered meadow next to the river. There is no shade and the sites are not separated by shrubbery. The sites next to the river carry a small surcharge, take a look first to decide if you really think they are any better than the rest of the sites. Electrical outlets are conveniently located near the sites. There are a large number of mobile home-type holiday homes set behind the tourist-camper area. The shower/toilet building is back behind the permanent units near the reception area. Hot water showers require payment. There's also a laundry room with a machine and dish and clothes washing sinks with hot water. Tents are not allowed at this campground.

Bus transportation into Stratford is handy although the walk in to town only takes fifteen to twenty minutes. There is also a boat that makes hourly trips on certain days.

To find the campground leave Stratford on A439 toward Warwick. After about 1.5 kilometers you will see campground warning signs. The campground is on the right.

Side Trips from Stratford

The **Cotswold Hills**, a well-loved area of small villages and rolling countryside filled with herds of sheep lies just south of Stratford. You have an excellent opportunity that is denied to most tourists since you have transportation at your disposal and can wander through the region at your own pace. The area actually runs southeast as far as Bath.

Just northwest of Stratford about 12 kilometers is Warwick and **Warwick Castle**. This is one of the most interesting castles in England to visit, it is very tourist oriented but the ramparts are impressive, as are the exhibits.

WATERFORD, REPUBLIC OF IRELAND

Population 40,000

The big draw here may be obvious, the **Waterford Crystal Factory**. Waterford was originally a Viking town, some of the city walls built by them still remain. The Waterford area also has sandy beaches along the coast and is a major port.

Waterford Campground

✦ CASEY'S CARAVAN AND CAMPING PARK

Address: Clonea, Dungarvan, Co. Waterford
Telephone: 058 41919
Price: Moderate

Open May 14 to September 8.

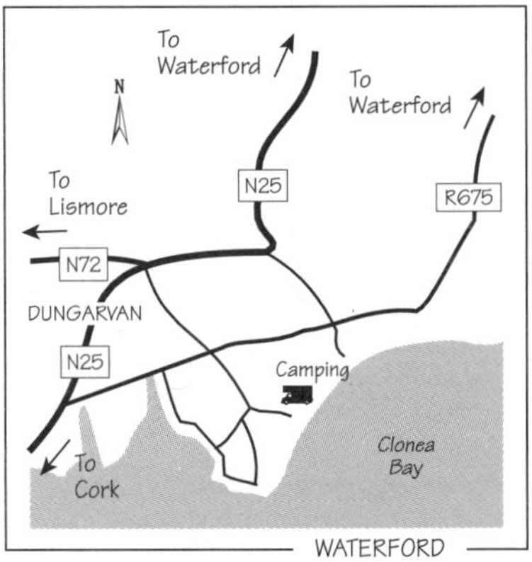

Since there are no campgrounds that are conveniently close to Waterford it makes sense to stay in a pleasant area nearby. Casey's overlooks the beach on Clonea Strand near Dungarvan, about 45 kilometers southwest of Waterford.

This campground is very large, it has many permanently-located mobile homes plus room for many tourist rigs. The sites are on grass with paved access roads. Some electricity is available but most sites are without service. The shower/toilet facilities are limited for such a large campground, on weekends you had better plan your shower time carefully or you'll have to wait in line. There is hot water for showers, dishes, and laundry although you'll have to buy a shower token. There's also a coin-operated washer and dryer. The campground has a large game room with pool tables and Ping-Pong, a TV room and miniature golf. Nearby are two small stores, a hotel and restaurant, and a good beach.

The easiest way to get to Waterford is to drive your own car. The Waterford Crystal factory is on the left before you actually reach the town. There's lots of parking and a good tour and store.

To get to the campground drive to Dungarvan which is on the coast about 44 kilometers southwest of Waterford. From Dungarvan take the coast road, R675, east. You'll soon see signs for Clonea Strand and Casey's pointing toward the ocean on the right.

Side Trips from Waterford

From the campground near Dungarvan it is an easy matter to drive some 75 kilometers inland to the **Rock of Cashel**, the historic religious and civil center of power in

Ireland. En route you can also visit the **Mitchelstown Caves** near Ballyporeen and **Cahir Castle**. There is hiking in the **Comeragh Mountains** near Clonmel. If the area appeals consider staying at POWER'S THE POT, a small campground 9 kilometers southeast of Clonmel off R678 and open from May 1 to October 15.

YORK, ENGLAND

Population 100,000

While Newcastle is the major city of northeast England the city of York must certainly be the tourist capital. A smaller town, bisected by the tranquil River Ouse, and partially surrounded by medieval walls, York's streets teem with tourists shopping at dozens of large and small shops and restaurants. When you've had your fill of shopping and crowd watching you might want to visit **York Minster**, the largest Gothic cathedral in northern Europe or take a stroll along the top of the **old city walls**.

York was also a Roman and Viking city as you'll see if you visit some of the city's many museums including the **Undercroft Museum and Treasury** in the Minster and the **Jorvik Viking Centre** with its "time cars" and recreated Viking town streets. York also has the **National Railway Museum**, the world's largest train museum.

Fortunately York is one of the easiest towns in Europe for the camper to visit. The Rowntree Park Caravan Club Site is almost inside the city walls, it sits next to the river and is no more than five minutes walk from the action.

York Campground

✦ ROWNTREE PARK CARAVAN CLUB SITE

Address: Terry Avenue, York YO2 IJQ
Telephone: 01904 658997
Price: Moderate

Open all year

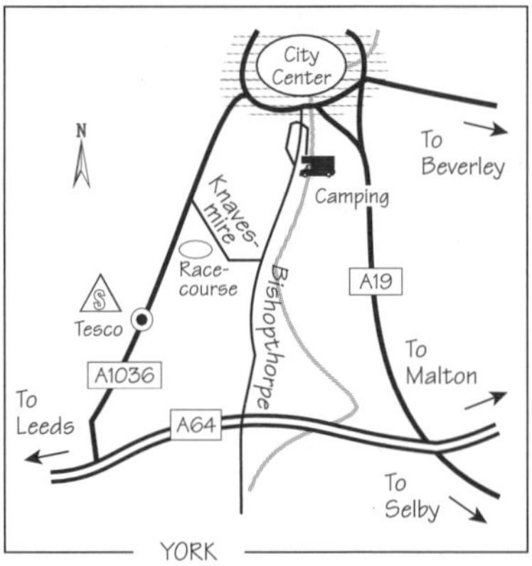

This medium to large campground is a classic Caravan Club Site. It has hard-surfaced gravel sites in small groups surrounded by well-clipped grass and separated by tall hedges. Each site has a convenient electrical outlet. The shower/toilet building is heated and has lots of hot water for showers, bathroom basins, and dish and clothes washing. A coin-operated washer and dryer are available. Unlike some Caravan Club sites this one accepts tent campers. Since this is a very popular campground you'll want to make reservations or arrive early. You do not need to be a member of the Caravan Club to camp here.

The campground's location is extremely handy. You can walk in to town by heading out the gate, turning left to walk along the river for a short distance, and then crossing a bridge into the central area. You pass a large Tesco supermarket while driving to the site if you follow the directions below.

Driving around inner York is difficult because traffic is heavy and roads are cramped. The easiest access to the campground is from the south. From the A64 passing south of York take the York West exit. The campground is pretty well marked with signs from this point. In about 2 kilometers you will reach a traffic circle that has a large Tesco supermarket next to it. Follow signs toward the city center (Highway 1036). After 1.2 kilometers you will see a horse racing track on your right. Turn right after passing this racetrack (1.9 kilometers from the Tesco traffic circle) onto Knavesmire. Follow Knavesmire as it passes the racetrack and curves left until it comes to a T junction in 1.3 kilometers. Turn left here on Bishopthorpe Rd. and proceed 1 kilometer until you are forced to turn left into Nunnery Lane. Your object now is to pass clockwise around the block on this one-way circle so turn sharply right in a short distance into Prices Lane and then get into the right lane so that at the next intersection you can cross Bishopthorpe Rd. and enter the small road next to the Swan Hotel. Proceed down this small lane to the river, turn right and follow Terry Avenue a short distance to the campground on the right. Don't arrive before noon because Terry Avenue is narrow and the campground has a policy of turning early arrivals away to discourage traffic problems. Before noon Terry is full of campers on their way out.

Side Trips from York

Studley Royal and the ruins of **Fountains Abbey** are run by the National Trust and have impressive gardens. The complex is located 40 kilometers northwest of York near Ripon.

Castle Howard, setting for the TV series "Brideshead Revisited", is about 25 kilometers northeast of York via A64 near Malton. The house and gardens are the most impressive in the region.

The **North York Moors National Park** is easily visited. It is 70 kilometers north of York and east of Whitby.

TWO OUTSTANDING REGIONS AND THEIR CAMPGROUNDS

LAKE DISTRICT

The English Lake District is a region of long lakes and small but often rugged mountains. The whole area covers about 1,200 square miles (35 miles to a side), the longest lake is 11 miles long, and the highest peak in the Lakes District is also the highest in England at 3,210 feet. It is a region with many literary associations, the best known are William Wordsworth and the Romantic Poets and the children's writer Beatrix Potter, creator of stories about Peter Rabbit, Benjamin Bunny, and Jemima Puddle-Duck. The region can be easily explored from two bases, Windermere and Keswick.

WINDERMERE

Population 10,000

Located on the east side of Lake Windermere, the region's largest lake, Windermere can be considered the center of the district's tourist trade. This is actually a double town, Bowness-on-Windermere was originally a lakeside town separate from

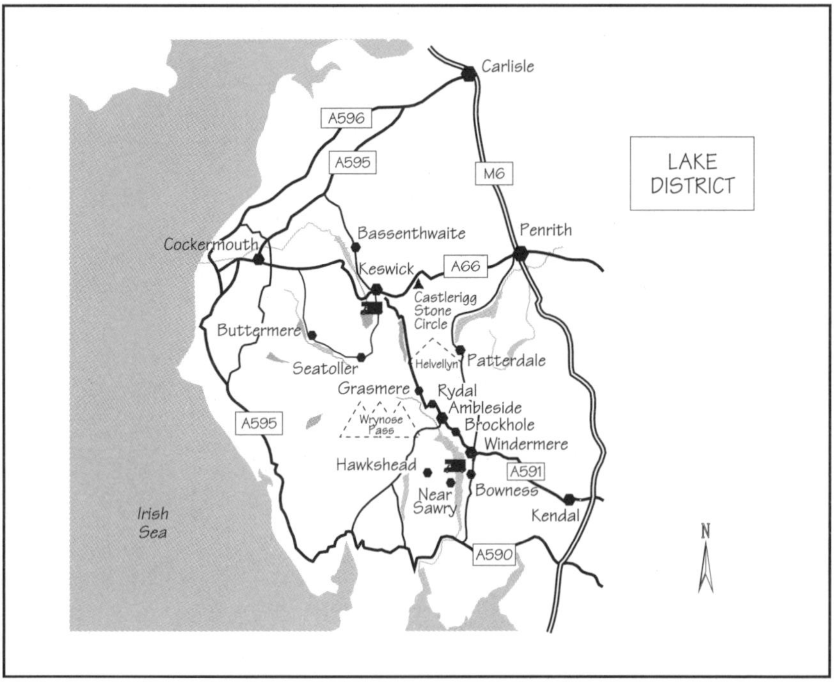

Windermere but the two have grown together.

The lake shore and docks are quite attractive, you can ride one of the lake cruise boats or catch a cable-propelled car and pedestrian ferry to the far side of the lake where things are much quieter and the walking is good on the small quiet lanes around Near Sawrey. The **Windermere Steamboat Museum** has a collection of lake boats and, as you would expect, the town is full of restaurants and shops oriented toward the tourist trade.

The Braithwaite Fold campground is popular and often full. If it is, try driving north along the lake about a kilometer where you'll find another campground that will probably have more room and is just as convenient.

Windermere Campground

✦ **Braithwaite Fold Caravan Club Site**

Address: Glebe Road, Bowness-on-Windermere, Windermere LA23 3GZ
Telephone: 015394 442177
Price: Moderate

Open March 26 to November 1, dates vary slightly

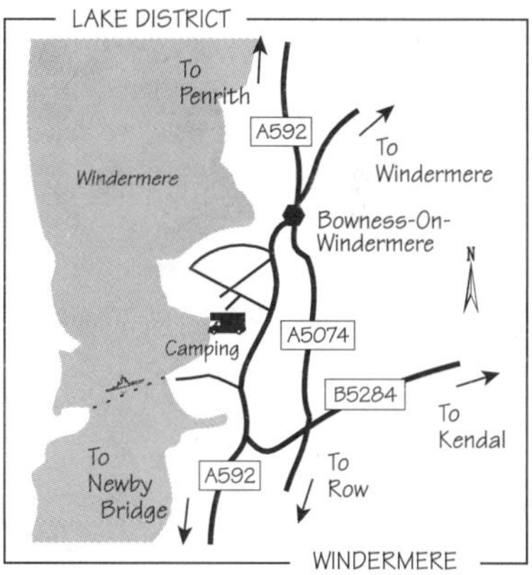

This Caravan Club site is located just about as close to the action on Windermere as you can get. The site is just south of Windermere's lakeside companion town, Bowness. The medium-sized campground is an open, grassy field, separated into three smaller sections by hedge, with cement strips to park your rig on. The campground is so popular that the warden says it is full every evening from June through August. You would be well-advised to make reservations if you wish to spend some time here. The shower/toilet building is not standard Caravan Club issue (unfortunately) but does offer hot water for showers, bathroom basins, and laundry tub. There are no dishwashing stations but there is a coin-operated washer and dryer. Tenters are not accepted here but membership in the Caravan Club is not required.

The campground is located at the south end of Bowness. It is well signed from the pier and tourist information office area.

Side Trips from Windermere

For your Wordsworth tour drive north along the east side of Lake Windermere for about 5 kilometers to Brockhole, and the **Lake District National Park Visitor Center**. You'll find information about the region and also about its literary legacy. Continue north through Ambleside to two lakes that are in the heart of Wordsworth country: Rydal Water and Grasmere. Two of Wordsworth's former residences are in the area, Rydal Mount and Dove Cottage. Dove Cottage is the headquarters of the Centre for British Romanticism and is full of information for those with an interest.

For your Beatrix Potter tour either drive around the south end of Lake Windermere or take the ferry across the lake. Near Sawry and Hawkshead on Esthwaite Water, you'll find the **Hill House**, her home and the **Beatrix Potter Gallery**. You may also wish to visit the World of **Beatrix Potter Exhibition** in Bowness.

If you want to get out and see the high country try hiking to the top of 3,118 foot **Helvellyn**. The trail starts at Patterdale which is north of Windermere on A592. A much shorter walk will take you in to the waterfalls at **Aira Force**, 5 miles north. To see the high country from the comfort of your vehicle try crossing **Wrynose Pass**, located just west of Ambleside. You'll climb to 1,280 feet on a very tiny paved road with very steep grades. Don't try this in wet weather or with a motorhome or trailer, it is sometimes possible in a lightly loaded VW van (a short section of slope exceeds one in three).

KESWICK

Population 6,000

Keswick is a small town on the north shore of Derwentwater, one of the region's most scenic lakes. Think of the town as a base for hiking, there are few attractions within the village. An exception is the **Cumberland Pencil Museum**, this is the first place in the world where they were manufactured.

Check at the Tourist Information Center for information about hiking routes in the area. A nice local stroll is the **Friar's Crag path** to a viewpoint over the lake. Several trails start in Keswick that head west into the Skiddaw and Latrigg Mountains.

Keswick Campground

✦ DERWENTWATER CAMPING AND CARAVANNING CLUB SITE

Address: Crowe Park Road, Keswick, Cumbria CA12 5EP
Telephone: 01768 772392
Price: Moderate

Open February 1 to November 9, dates vary slightly

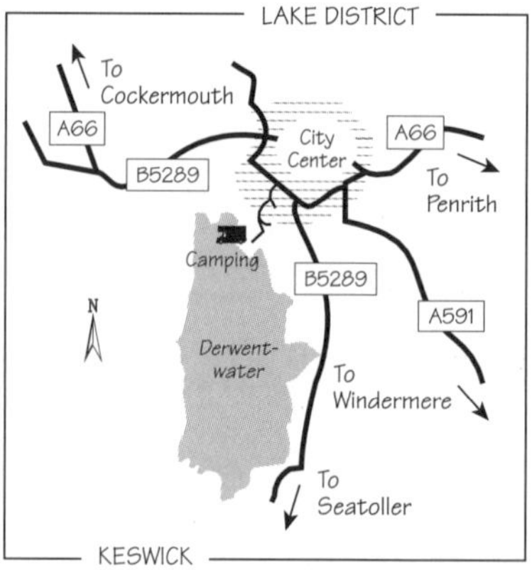

This Camping and Caravanning Club Site is handily located on the shore of Derwentwater in the town of Keswick. It has its own beach so it is convenient for kayakers and sailboarders and the walk into town for shopping, a meal, or a movie takes only five minutes.

The Derwentwater campground is a large one, it is two large grassy meadows on the shore of the lake. Electrical hook-ups are available and conveniently located. There are two shower/toilet buildings with hot water for showers, bathroom basins, washing dishes and laundry tubs. The campground also has its own grocery shop although there is a nice supermarket just outside the campground entrance. There is also a boat launch facility.

The campground is one of two that are next to each other on the north shore of Derwentwater which is just southwest of Keswick. Keep these relative locations in mind and you'll have no problems finding the campground. It is well signed from the roads coming into Keswick and from the town center.

Side Trips from Keswick

Just east of Keswick is the **Castlerigg Stone Circle**. Follow signposts to this circle of stones dating from before Stonehenge.

For a nice driving tour head south from Keswick along the east side of Derwentwater on Highway B5289. Take a look at the **Ladore Waterfall** near the south end of the lake and then drive on to **Seatoller**. There's another information center here, Seatoller is the starting point for several hiking routes. From here you can drive on through **Honister Pass** to **Buttermere** and then return to Keswick over **Newlands Pass**.

THE PEAK DISTRICT

The Peak District National Park will give you a chance to see some country that passes for "wild" country in England. It is a region of mostly treeless rolling hills and protected valleys. The most popular recreational pursuits here are hiking and caving.

The Peaks District is in central England, it is surrounded by the Potteries on the south-

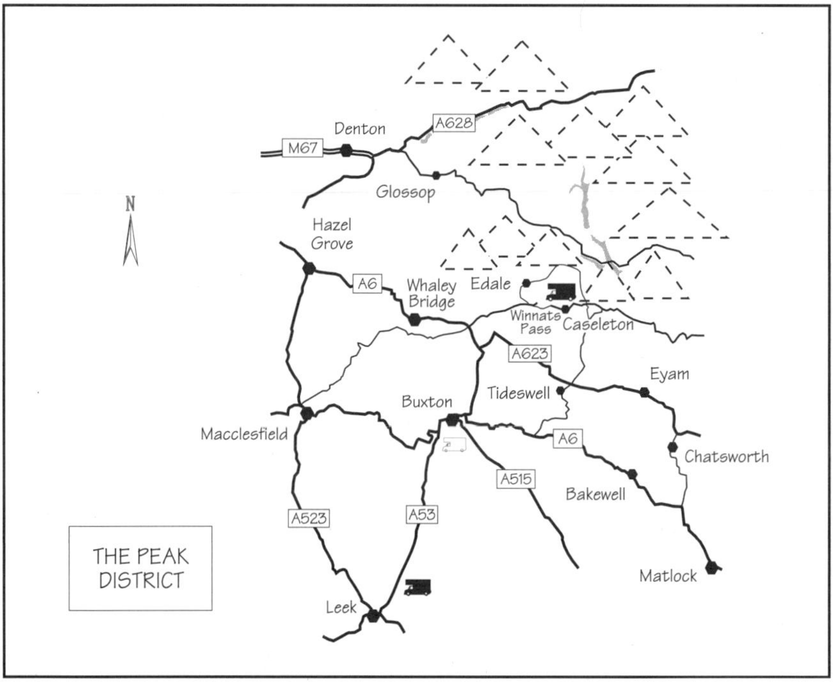

west, Manchester on the west, and Sheffield on the east. The region is quite small. It measures about 30 kilometers east to west and about 60 kilometers north to south.

If you enter the Park from the direction of the Potteries and Leek you'll pass by our first featured campground, Blackshaw Moor.

Blackshaw Moor Campground

✦ BLACKSHAW MOOR CARAVAN CLUB SITE

Address: Leek, Staffs ST13 8TW
Telephone: 01538 300203
Price: Moderate

Open March 26 to November 8, dates vary slightly

This almost-new campground, operated by the Caravan Club, is located at a gateway to the Peaks region. There's a excellent view of Hen Cloud, a rugged-looking limestone peak, to the northwest.

The medium-sized campground sits on a sloping hillside well above the highway and its noise. Paved access roads are lined with gravel pads which are separated by plots of grass. No shade is provided, but you probably won't want it here anyway. Electricity (CEE17 plugs, high amps) is available at each site. There's a convenient water supply and dump station. The shower/toilet buildings are heated and have free hot showers (adjustable), and hot water in bathroom basins and dishwashing sinks. The laundry room has a coin-operated washer and dryer. There's a restaurant across the road and 100 meters or so to the south. You can order milk and bread at the reception desk for delivery the next morning. You do not need to be a member of the Caravan Club to camp here and tents are allowed.

Blackshaw Moor is located on Highway A53 which runs north from Leek to Buxton. It is about 3 kilometers north of Leek on the right side of the road as you head north.

Side Trips from Blackshaw Moor

The largest town in the Peaks district is **Buxton**, a small spa town with some of the features of Bath including its own **Crescent** and an impressive **Opera House**. **Poole's Cavern** is a large limestone cave located just southwest of town with a visitors center and nature trail. You can camp near Buxton at GRIN LOW CARAVAN CLUB SITE located about 3 kilometers south off A53 and open from early April to early November.

In the center of the Peaks District is Castleton. The town is surrounded by caves and hiking routes and has a good campground.

CASTLETON

Population 1,000

This small town offers shopping, restaurants, and pubs. It is best described as a tourist town. The only real sights in Castleton itself are the ruins of **Peveril Castle** sitting on a small peak just south of town and the **Peak Cavern** under the castle.

There are many other caves and mines in the surrounding hills. Just three kilometers west of Castleton is the **Speedwell Cavern**. Here you ride a boat through floodlit galleries. Even farther west and on the upper side of Winnats Pass is the **Blue John Cavern** where a blue fluospar called Blue John is mined. Also nearby is the **Treak Cliff Cavern**.

Castleton Campground

✦ LOSEHILL CARAVAN CLUB SITE

Address: Castleton, Hope Valley, Derbyshire S33 8WB
Telephone: 01433 620636
Price: Moderate

Open May 26 to January 4

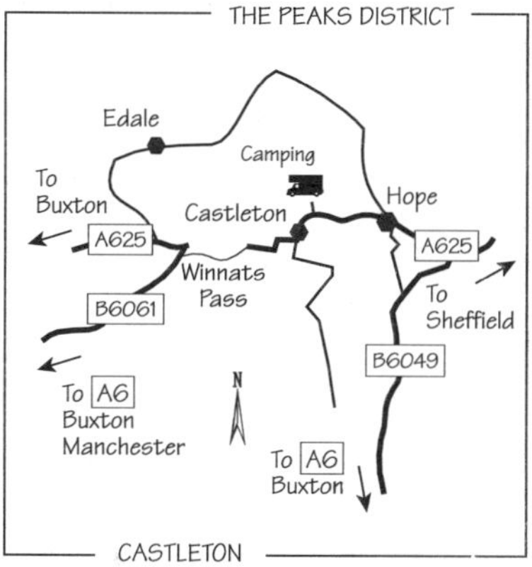

This is a medium-sized level campground with well-trimmed grass surrounding hard, well-drained gravel-surfaced sites. The campground is newly improved and refurbished and offers very nice facilities. Electrical (CEE17 plugs, high amps) outlets are near each site, there is a water fill area and dump station. The shower/toilet building is heated with hot showers and hot water in bathroom basins. Dishwashing sinks have hot water and the laundry tubs are indoors. There is a coin-operated washer and dryer and even a heated area for drying clothes on lines. You do not need to be a member of the Caravan Club to camp here and tents are allowed.

To find the campground follow your map to Castleton in the heart of the Peaks region. The campground is about one kilometer to the east. Incidentally, maps sometimes show access to Castleton on a small road from the west that runs down Winnats Pass, this road is very small and steep and not suitable for large motorhomes or trailers.

Side Trips from Castleton

If you drive east down the valley to Hope and then turn north you'll soon arrive in **Edale**. The 400-kilometer **Pennine Way** hiking route starts here. You don't have to hike all the way to Scotland however, the trails here also give access to Edale Moor, Kinder Scout, The Peak and The Edge.

Twenty-six kilometers southeast of Castleton is **Chatsworth House**, the "Palace of the Peak". First built in 1555 the house has been virtually rebuilt several times. The surrounding gardens and grounds are almost as impressive as the house.

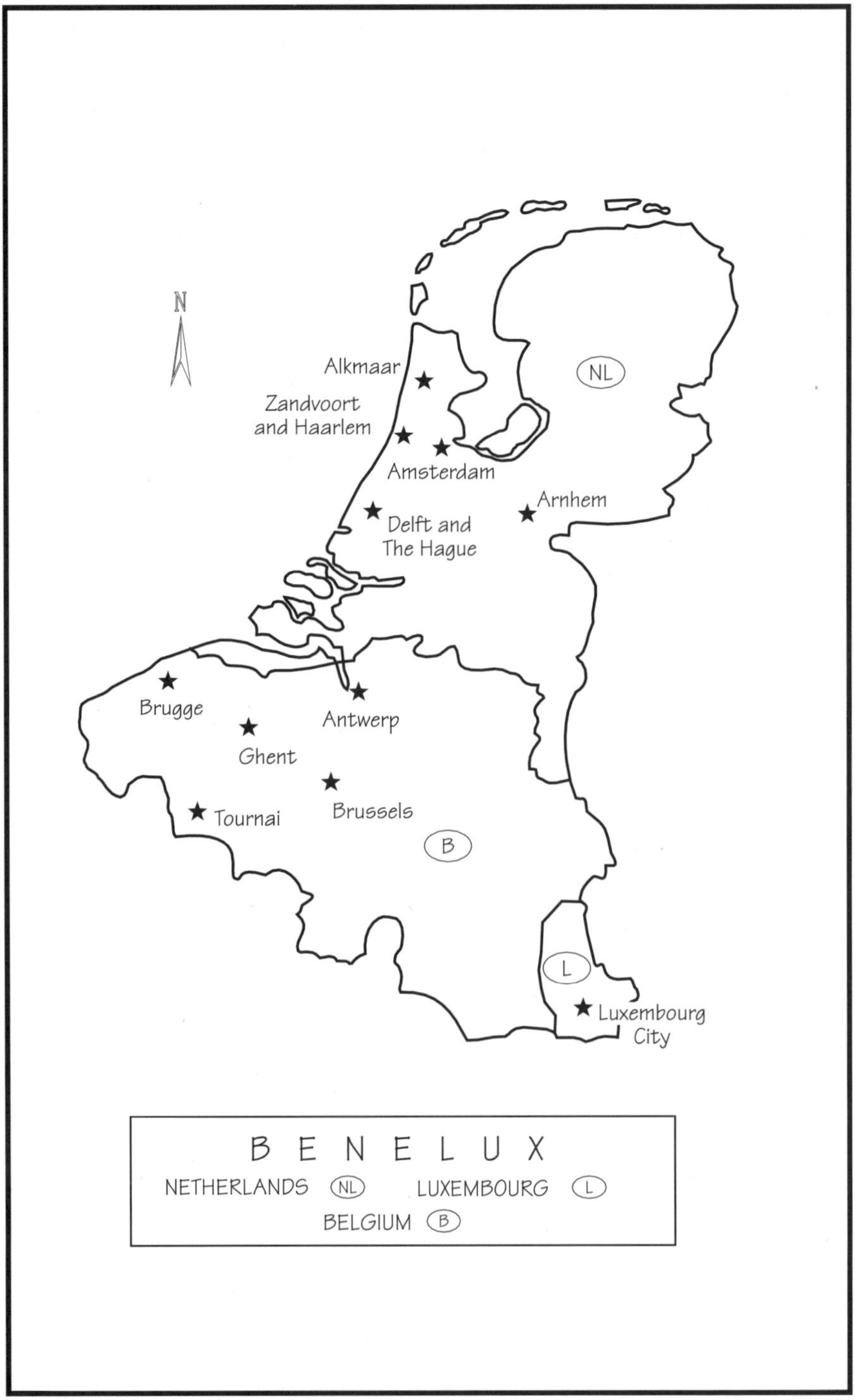
N
Alkmaar
Zandvoort
and Haarlem
Amsterdam
Delft and
The Hague
Arnhem
NL
Brugge
Antwerp
Ghent
Brussels
Tournai
B
L
Luxembourg
City
BENELUX
NETHERLANDS NL
LUXEMBOURG L
BELGIUM B

CHAPTER 6

BENELUX COUNTRIES

INTRODUCTION

The Benelux countries: Belgium, The Netherlands, and Luxembourg; combine to form a relatively small area of about 28,800 square miles, about the same size as the states of West Virginia or North Carolina. They have a large population for their size, 26 million people or about one tenth the population of the U.S. Despite the large number of people in such a small area there is lots of countryside although it is definitely not being wasted. Every spare square meter seems to be well tended and under cultivation.

The Netherlands and Belgium are also called the Low Countries, they're so low that parts are below sea level. The Netherlands (often called Holland) is very flat, some of it on land reclaimed from the sea. Dutch is spoken, of course, but English is also very widely understood, especially by the younger people. You'll probably have fun with the Dutch Language. It is considered closer to English than any other European language but is different enough to seem very bizarre. Much of The Netherlands's coast is parkland composed of sand dunes and there are several good campgrounds along the North Sea.

Belgium is split ethnically with Walloon and Flemish areas speaking respectively French and a form of Dutch. The landscape is low and flat like Holland in the north, more hilly in the south, especially in the Ardennes region. In this chapter you'll often find three versions of town names, the first is English, the second Flemish (Dutch) and the third Walloon (French).

Luxembourg is by far the smallest of the Benelux countries with an area of less than 1,000 square miles. It is rural and mountainous in the north and more developed and populous in the south. Both French and German are spoken but the country has its own language – Letzeburgesch.

Roads and Driving

Holland and Belgium have very good freeway systems, they are free but often crowded. While distances are short in these countries you will find yourself on the freeways if you want to make any kind of decent progress. International highways use the "E" prefix, national freeways use "A", and major secondary roads are designated as "N" roads.

Belgium and especially Holland are great for bicycle trips. There are often separated bike paths along the roads with their own traffic signs. Be alert since riders sometimes seem oblivious to automobiles, often because they have the right-of-way.

Both Belgium and The Netherlands have important ferry ports with service to the British Isles and Scandinavia. Available routes include Ostend, Belgium to Ramsgate, England; Zeebrugge, Belgium to Dover, England; Hoek van Holland, The Netherlands to Harwich, England; and Amsterdam, The Netherlands to either Gothenburg, Sweden or Stavanger, Norway.

All three Benelux countries have different phone numbers for emergency help. In The Netherlands emergency police number is 112. Road help is available at 0800-0888. The AAA affiliated auto club is the Koninklijke Nederlandse Toeristenbond ANWB (ANWB) at 70-314 77 14. In Belgium the emergency phone number for the police is 101 and the AAA affiliated auto club is the Touring Club Royal de Belgique (TCB) at 2-233-22-11. For breakdown service call 070 344 777, there is a charge. Finally, in Luxembourg the police are at 113 and the auto club is the Automobile Club du Grand-Duché de Luxembourg (ACL) at 352 45 00 45. The breakdown number is 45 00 45-1.

Camping

All of these countries have a good selection of campgrounds. Many are holiday parks with lots of amenities. Many also have large contingents of permanently-located caravans used primarily as weekend country retreats by city dwellers. You'll be impressed by the gardens in the yards of some of these. Usually the permanent units are in separate areas and do not really affect the overall atmosphere of the campground for tourists.

The Camping Card International is generally not required in the Benelux countries, but it is appreciated and often will get you a discount. Without one you may have to leave your passport at the office overnight.

Energy seems to be at a premium in these countries, particularly The Netherlands. Electricity is often metered or quite expensive, showers are likewise often metered and often not quite as hot as one would like.

Free camping is not allowed in Holland, fines are often levied and it is difficult to be inconspicuous. Belgium also restricts free camping.

Shopping, Currency, Credit Cards and Fuel

Belgium, The Netherlands, and Luxembourg are thoroughly modern countries with good supermarkets and wide use of credit cards and cash machines. Prices are toward the high side of the European Economic Union scale, not as high as Scandinavia nor as low as Greece or Portugal.

You'll find a few hypermarkets and many smaller supermarkets in these countries. They are sometimes hard to find, especially in Holland, because many are tucked into residential areas away from the highways and often don't have much in the way of signs. The best way to find one is to ask at the campground or on the street.

Service stations in these countries are modern and easy to find. Most of them accept credit cards. You may be interested in the Dutch propane dispensing system. The pumps are self-service and cleaner and faster than gasoline pumps.

Itinerary Suggestions

The Benelux countries are small and nothing is really far away. Trains are often a good way to make side trips since the system is quick, clean, and easy to use. Ticket people usually speak enough English to explain all you need to know. Bicycles are frequently available for rent at train stations and are easy to bring along on train expeditions.

In The Netherlands the old capital city of Amsterdam is by far the most popular destination. You could easily stay in Amsterdam during your entire visit to the county and use the train system to visit places of interest. It is more fun, however, to stay in the campgrounds in places like Delft, Alkmaar, and Haarlem where you can go in to town in the evening and be part of the community. Holland's seacoast, particularly around Zandvoort and The Hague, is nice for a shot of nature after too much time in urban areas. Another good natural area is the Hoge Veluwe National Park near Arnhem.

Belgium has an excellent selection of historical towns that make good destinations: Brugge, Antwerp, Gent, and Tournai. Brussels is also well worth a visit even though it is not particularly camper friendly. South toward Luxembourg the Ardennes region is scenic and quiet.

Northern Luxembourg shares the characteristics of Belgium's Ardennes Mountains while the south around Luxembourg city is historically industrial. Still, Luxembourg City is a popular destination while immediately east is the very attractive Moselle River valley, covered in detail in our Germany chapter.

For information about The Netherlands contact **Netherlands Board of Tourism, 225 N. Michigan Ave., Chicago, IL 60601 (312 819-1500 or 888-GO HOLLAND)**. In Canada contact **Netherlands Board of Tourism, 25 Adelaide Street East, Suite 710, Toronto, ON M5C 1Y2 (416 363-1470)**. For information about Belgium contact the **Belgium Tourist Office, 780 Third Avenue, Suite 1501, New York, NY 10017 (212 758-8130)**. For information about Luxembourg contact **Luxembourg National Tourist Office, 17 Beekman Place, New York, NY 10022 (222 935-8888)**. Links to internet sites with information about the Benelux countries can be found at www.rollinghomes.com.

BENELUX DISTANCE TABLE

In Kilometers

Kms X .62 = Miles

	Alkmaar Netherlands	Amsterdam Netherlands	Antwerp Belgium	Arnhem Netherlands	Bremen Germany	Brugge Belgium	Brussels Belgium	Calais France	Cologne Germany	Delft Netherlands	Ghent Belgium	Luxembourg City Luxembourg	Rheims France	Tournai Belgium
Amsterdam Netherlands	33													
Antwerp Belgium	185	143												
Arnhem Netherlands	137	100	154											
Bremen Germany	400	363	417	263										
Brugge Belgium	285	243	100	254	517									
Brussels Belgium	232	190	47	201	464	96								
Calais France	412	370	227	381	644	134	226							
Cologne Germany	307	274	212	172	325	289	193	419						
Delft Netherlands	87	61	110	114	377	210	157	337	295					
Ghent Belgium	240	198	55	209	472	45	50	169	243	165				
Luxembourg City Luxembourg	440	395	255	344	572	303	208	430	200	365	258			
Rheims France	441	399	256	410	673	304	209	274	376	366	259	254		
Tournai Belgium	305	263	120	274	537	71	76	146	269	230	65	284	236	
Zandvoort Netherlands	46	28	180	128	391	280	227	407	302	71	235	435	427	291

SELECTED CITIES AND CAMPGROUNDS

Alkmaar, The Netherlands

Population 92,000

Alkmaar is probably best known for its **Cheese Market** on the **Waagplein,** held on Friday mornings at 10 AM from the middle of April to the middle of September. This is a staged cheese auction for tourists, during the high season you'll be lucky to get close enough to even take pictures because of the crowds. Don't be put off, however. The armies of tourists drawn to the cheese market draw an interesting group of street vendors. Get there early for a good location to take pictures of the market activities then listen to a mechanical music cart, watch wooden shoes being carved, or sample Dutch culinary treats. Alkmaar has a pleasant central pedestrian area that you'll enjoy exploring. There's also a centrally-located **Cheese Museum (Kaasmuseum)** and a **Beer Museum (Biermuseum)**. A bonus is that Alkmaar and the campground are near a recreation area of dunes running along the North Sea coast.

Alkmaar Campground

✦ Molengroet Recreatieverblijven

Address: Molengroet 1/Postbus 200, NL-1722 ZL Noord-Scharwoude
Telephone: 0226 393444 Fax: 0226 391426
Price: Moderate

Open all year

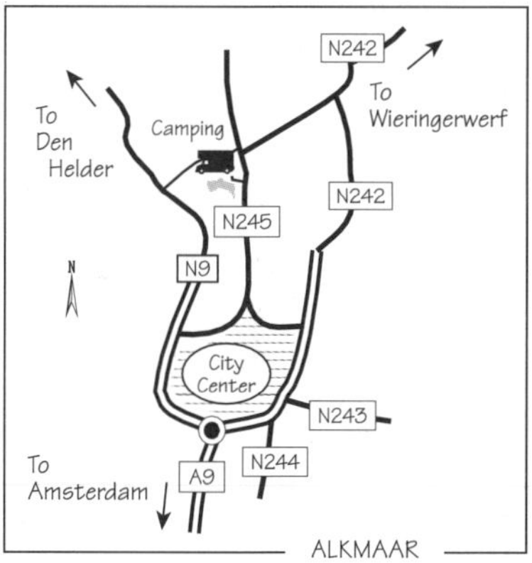

Molengroet is a large and very complete camping resort about six kilometers north of Alkmaar. The resort is located in a park area that has a large lake complete with bathing beaches, restaurants, and bike trails. The campground's own bus provides transportation to Alkmaar, and also to the nearby beach.

The campground has grass camping sites in groups separated by hedges. They are numbered and assigned to you at the reception desk when you check in. A warden will direct you to your site. Electrical outlets (10 amps) are conveniently located. Shower/toilet buildings are very modern and clean. Showers require that you buy a token but are adjustable, they have an annoying pressure-activated valve. There is also hot water in bathroom sinks and for washing dishes. The campground has a large restaurant/bar, a snack bar, a large grocery shop, a children's farm, a recreation room, a disco and laundry facilities. The campground's bus provides shuttle service to Alkmaar although the distance is about right for a good bike ride, bicycle rentals are available.

To reach the campground drive north on Highway 245 from the Alkmaar ring road. You can most easily do this by turning left onto the ring road when you arrive in town on the A9 freeway from the south, then turn right on 245 after circling around to the northwest of town. The campground is on the left 7.2 kilometers from the turn onto 245.

AMSTERDAM, THE NETHERLANDS

Population 680,000

Amsterdam is the first city visited by many travelers to Europe from North America and it is a great introduction to the continent's charms. Schiphol Airport is an important entry point, fortunately there's easy-to-use train service to Amsterdam from the airport because taxis are extremely expensive. The central city is the perfect size, not so large that it is intimidating but large enough to keep you busy for many days. The quiet streets along canals and the residential central city area with walking streets and bicycles are unlike anything you're likely to have seen at home but are a great preview to the best European cities.

Amsterdam's central area is arranged in a half-circle fronting on the Central Railroad Station. Half-rings of canals define the city's shape. This layout was initiated in 1585 and is an excellent example of early city planning. While most of the sights are within walking distance of each other there are so many things to see that the good tram, bus, and subway system is a lifesaver. Making the whole thing even better is the fact that most Dutch people seem to speak fluent English (and other languages too).

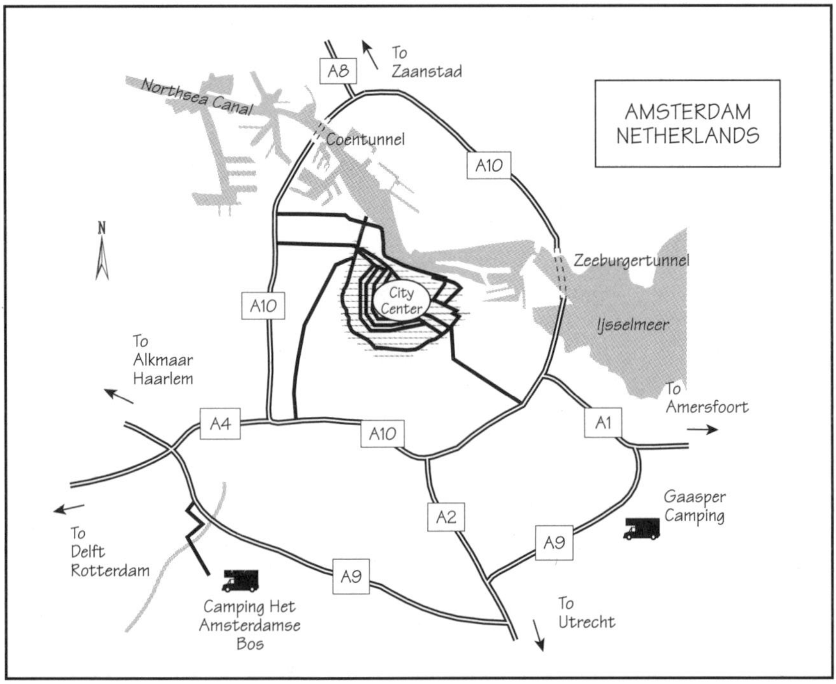

While in Amsterdam there are several must-see museums. First on the list is the **National Museum (Rijksmuseum)** with its unsurpassed collection of Dutch masters. Next stop is the **Van Gogh Museum (Rijksmuseum Vincent Van Gogh),** which has the best collection anywhere of paintings by this popular artist. Other interesting museums include **Ann Frank's House (Anne Frankhuis),** the **Jewish Historical Museum (Joods Historisch Museum), Rembrandt's House (Rembrandthuis),** the **Stedelijk Modern Art Museum (Stedelijk Museum),** and even the **Netherlands Maritime Museum (Nederlands Scheepvaart Museum).**

If you're sick of museums you can take the popular **Heineken Brewery (Heineken Brouwerij) Tour**, visit a **diamond-cutting workshop**, or stroll through the strange **red light district** just east of the Central Station.

Shopping is lots of fun in Amsterdam. There are several large department stores like De Bijenkorf on Dam Square but you can walk the Kalverstraat and Nieuwendijk pedestrian shopping streets and have as much fun watching the people as buying things. From there take a short side trip to the flower market barges on the Singel Canal. There is also an excellent English-language book store in Amsterdam, W.H. Smith at Kalverstraat 152.

Amsterdam Campgrounds

✦ GAASPER CAMPING AMSTERDAM

Address: Loosdrechtdreef 7,
NL-1108 AZ Amsterdam
Telephone: 020 6967326   Fax: 020 6969369
Price: Moderate

Open March 15 to December 31

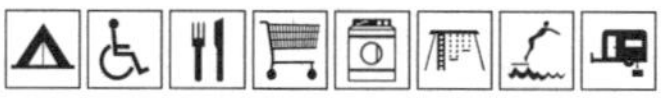

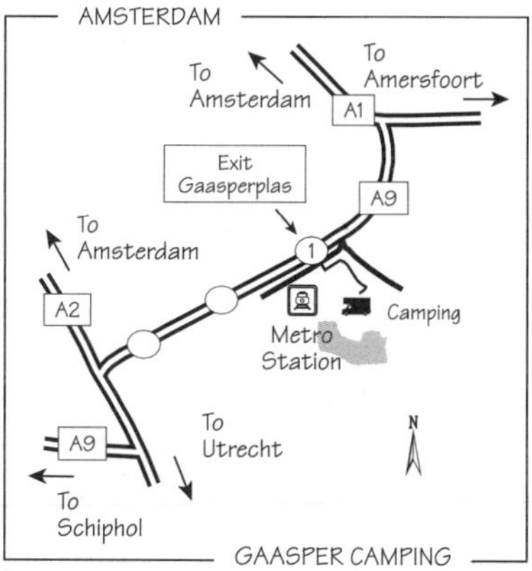

Gaasper Camping is a large, modern campground located south of Amsterdam at the end of the subway line. Quick, easy access to central Amsterdam and good (although sometimes almost overzealous) management make this our favorite Amsterdam campground.

The campground is a very large grass field somewhat broken up by hedges. Some parts have paved access roads and numbered sites, others are large grassy fields intended for tent camping. All sites are grass. Sites are assigned at the reception desk and the warden will lead you to your assigned space. There are a large number of permanent resident rigs here with landscaped yards, they are isolated from the remainder of the campground and do not dominate it. Electrical plugs are provided for individual sites (CEE17 plugs, some 4 amps, some 10 amps). Some sites also have gray-water drains and there is a dump station. The shower/toilet buildings are modern but Spartan, showers are warm, not hot, and require purchased tokens (push button, preset), bathroom sinks are cold water only and hot water for dishwashing requires a purchased token. There is a restaurant and a grocery shop. The campground is adjacent to a large park area with bike trails, a swimming lake, and playgrounds.

BARGES ON THE AMSTEL RIVER IN AMSTERDAM

Gaasper Camping is at the far south end of the easternmost fork of the Amsterdam subway line. The subway station is about 500 meters from the campground and the ride to the Amsterdam Central Station takes no more than 20 minutes.

The campground is just south of the A9 freeway south of Amsterdam. It is on the section of A9 between the A2 freeway and the A1 freeway. Take the Gaasperplas exit and follow the campground signs a very short distance to the gate. Park outside and walk in to register.

✦ KAMPEERTERREIN HET AMSTERDAMSE BOS

Address: Kleine Noorddijk 1,
NL-1432 CC Aalsmeer
Telephone: 020 6416868 Fax: 020 6402378
Price: Moderate

Open April 1 to October 31

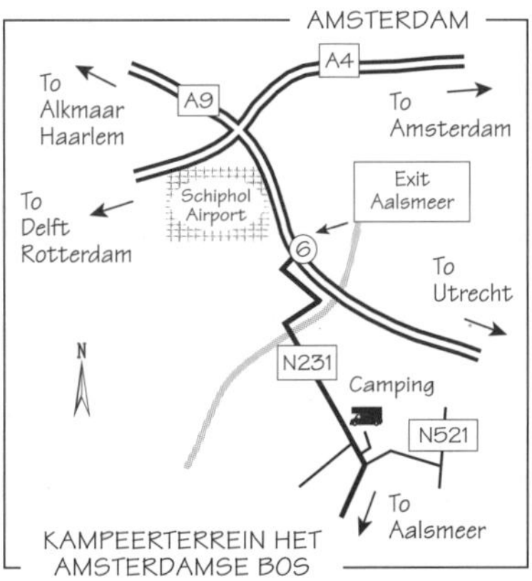

This is a very large campground in the town of Aalsmeer near Schiphol international airport. There is convenient bus service into Amsterdam and a large wooded area next to the campground for walking and biking.

Het Amsterdamse Bos has over 400 campsites,

they are located on several fields of various sizes and separated by hedges so the feeling is of a smaller campground. This is a popular stop for the camping-bus tours visiting Amsterdam. There are quite a few resident rigs here but they are concentrated in an area away from the tourist campers and don't affect the atmosphere of the campground. The camp sites are on grass with a few paved spots for the winter use of vehicle campers. They are unmarked and unassigned, the reception person will usually assign you a general area but not a space. Electricity (CEE17 plugs, 5 or 10 amps) is available to about a third of the sites. Shower/toilet buildings are scattered around the campground and have free hot showers, hot water is available in the sinks but requires payment. The campground has a grocery store and small restaurant. There are no dogs allowed at this campground so you'll see a lot of rabbits at dusk. There is a good supermarket about 2 kilometers from the campground, ask at the reception desk for directions.

Access to Amsterdam is by bus from this campground. The number 171 bus leaves from a stop about 300 meters from the campground and the ride to the Central Station takes some 45 minutes. During the busiest summer months there is even a Camping Bus that leaves right from the campground.

Take the Aalsmeer exit (No. 6) from Highway A9 near Schiphol. This exit is just southeast of where A9 meets A4. Head south on N231 along the canal and then turn left and cross the canal following the Aalsmeer direction signs. After a 1.5 kilometers you'll see the campground sign pointing to your left near a set of traffic lights. Het Amsterdamse Bos is about 100 meters back along the access road.

Side Trips from Amsterdam

A short drive northeast along the shore of the Markermeer through the Waterland is quite rewarding. Follow the causeway out to **Marken** and visit **Volendam** to see traditional costumes. A little farther on you'll come to the attractive towns of **Edam** (famous for its cheese), **Hoorn**, and **Enkhuizen**.

ANTWERP (ANTWERPEN OR ANVERS), BELGIUM

Population 491,000

Although Antwerp is Belgium's second largest city you can make it actually seem intimate by staying at Camping De Molen. The campground is located in a quiet suburb yet you can be right in the middle of the interesting and friendly old center of town with only a short walk. This is an easy way to take advantage of the lively night life that the city offers.

Antwerp became an economic power in late fifteenth and early sixteenth century under Charles V of Spain. At that time the Zwyn estuary at Brugge was silting up and traders transferred their business to Antwerp. For a time the city was the economic capital of Europe. Antwerp quickly declined under Philip II, Charles' son, as a result of the struggles of the inquisition. Today the city acts as the unofficial capital of Flemish Belgium and is an important port even though it is located some 90 kilometers from the North Sea.

To tourists the town of Antwerp is synonymous with the prolific painter **Peter Paul Rubens**. You can visit his home and workshop, called the **Rubens' House (Rubens Huis),** and see his paintings in the **Royal Art Gallery** or Belgium's largest cathedral, the **Onze Lieve Vrouwe Kathedraal**. Antwerp is also a diamond trading town, you can watch the action on **Pelikaanstraat** in the Jewish Quarter near the Central Station or visit the **Diamond Museum**. Antwerp also has a good centrally-located **zoo**.

Antwerp Campground

✦ CAMPING DE MOLEN

Address: Antwerpen-Strand, Thonetlaan,
St. Annastrand, B-2020 Antwerp
Telephone: 3 2196090
Price: April 1 to September 30

Open April 1 to November 30

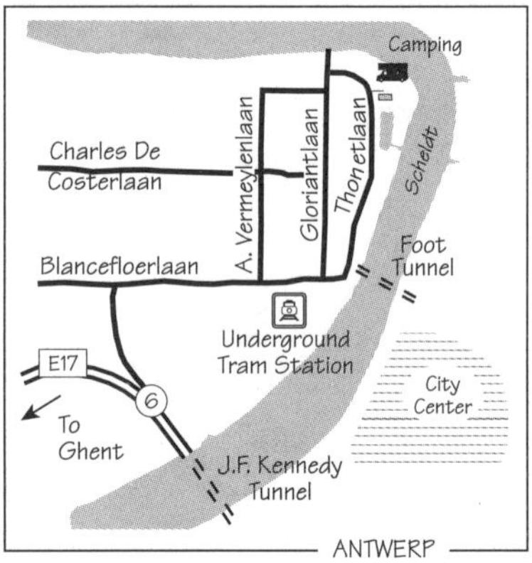

Camping De Molen will surprise you with how close it really is to downtown Antwerp. Located on the left bank of the Scheldt River it is seemingly far from the bustle and noise of the city. Yet if you stroll along the water for 10 minutes, then cross the river through an underwater pedestrian tunnel, you'll find yourself near the center of town.

This is a medium-sized campground on a grassy plot in the St. Annastrand district of Antwerp on the west side of the river. There are quite a few resident caravans here, but also room for quite a few tourists. Camping is on numbered grass sites that are assigned at the reception office. Electricity is convenient to most sites. The shower/toilet building is modern and showers are hot and free. There is also hot water available in bathroom sinks and for washing dishes. You'll find a small supermarket near the metro station less than a kilometer away.

To reach downtown you can take a bus from near the campground entrance or walk about 10 minutes south to reach either a metro station or a pedestrian walkway that will take you under the river to central Antwerp. Bikes seem to be acceptable in the underground tunnel and there are escalators at each end.

To find the campground take the first exit west of the Kennedy tunnel on the R1 ring road freeway, Exit 6. Turn right at the traffic lights and proceed east on Blancefloerlaan. When you reach the river turn left on Thonetlaan and drive about 1 kilometer. You'll see the campground sign on your right.

ARNHEM, THE NETHERLANDS

Population 130,000

Arnhem is a large modern Dutch city mostly rebuilt after heavy damage in World War II. The town is interesting because of it's World War II history and because it in near the Hoge Veluwe, the largest Dutch national park.

Arnhem was the scene of the disastrous World War II Operation Market Garden depicted in Cornelius Ryan's book *A Bridge Too Far*. The World War II sites to see are the **Airborne Museum** in Oosterbeek and the **Airborne Cemetery** nearby.

The **Hoge Veluwe** is a double attraction. The **Kröller-Müller Museum** in the park is one of Europe's most important museums with many Van Gogh paintings and a great outdoor sculpture garden. The park itself is a very large natural area with miles of bike paths and free bikes for the use of visitors. You may even see a red deer or two.

The Arnhem area is home to two other well known attractions. The **Burgers Zoo** is the largest in Holland and has very well designed natural enclosures. **Nederlands Openlucht Museum** is one of the ubiquitous European open-air museums with preserved traditional buildings, costumes, and demonstrations.

Arnhem Campground

✦ CAMPING WARNSBORN

Address: Bakenberseweg 257, NL-6816 TB Arnhem
Telephone: 026 4423469
Price: Moderate

Open April 1 to October 31

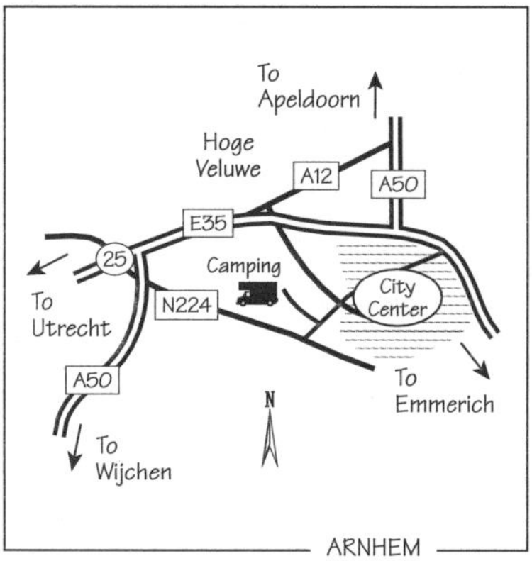

This is a medium-sized quiet campground located in a wooded area about 4 kilometers northwest of central Arnhem. Like most Dutch campgrounds there are permanently situated caravans here but also room for quite a few tourists. Sites are numbered and assigned, the warden will guide you to your spot. Most surfaces are grass and electricity is convenient to most sites (CEE17 plugs, 4 amps). The shower/toilet buildings are older but clean and in good shape, hot showers require that you buy a token. There is a small grocery shop.

Campers with bikes will be very happy here. Hoge Veluwe is about 3 kilometers away on good trails and in the opposite direction the Airborne Museum and central Arnhem are also convenient and about the same distance. Bus transportation is available near the campground.

To find the Camping Warnsborn take Exit 25 from the E35 freeway running east/west northwest of Arnhem. Head southeast on N224 towards Arnhem. Turn left at the third set of traffic lights and again left at next traffic light you come to. You should see a camping sign at this second light and will find the campground straight ahead.

BRUGGE (BRUGGE OR BRUGES), BELGIUM

Population 120,000

Although small, Brugge is probably Belgium's most popular tourist town. The popularity stems from the town's medieval buildings and streets dating from an extremely prosperous period in the fourteenth and fifteenth centuries. The old town was preserved because the Zwijn estuary silted up in the early sixteenth century cutting the town off from the sea and stalling the economy. Today the river is filled with pleasure boats and the town with visitors. A ring of water circles the center of town, you can wander at will on foot, boat, bike, or horse-drawn cab with little chance of becoming seriously lost.

The **Burg** and **Markt**, two squares, are at the center of town. The **Belfry** next to the Markt is a good place to climb for the view while the buildings around the Burg are genuinely medieval. The cluster of museums a few blocks south of the squares includes the **Memling Museum** and the **Groeninge Museum** , both with Flemish masterpieces.

Brugge Campground

✦ CAMPING ST. MICHIEL

Address: Tillegemstraat 55, B-8200 St. Michiel, Brugge
Telephone: 050 380819 Fax: 059 806824
Price: Moderate

Open all year

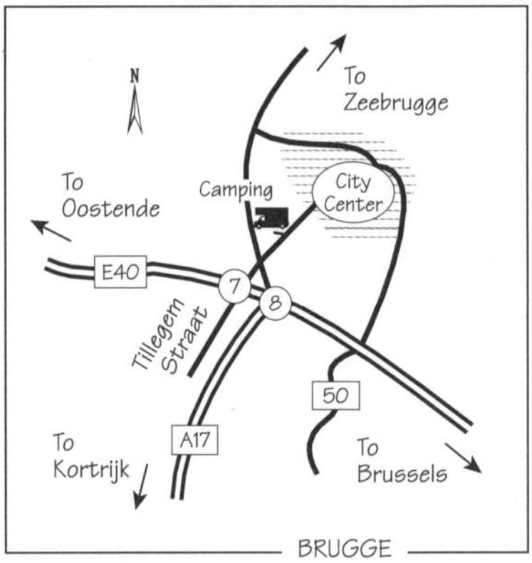

This large campground has a convenient location. It is less than four kilometers from the center of Brugge and convenient to the freeway. Brugge itself is convenient because it is on the direct route between the cross-channel ferry ports and continental destinations to the east. This is the first night's stop for many British campers headed south on holiday.

The campground is a large grassy plot with most individual sites separated by hedges. While there are quite a few permanently-located caravans there are also a lot of sites reserved for tourist campers. Parking is on grass and electrical outlets (CEE17 plugs, 5 amps) are conveniently located. The toilet/shower building is large (perhaps even a little cavernous, damp, and dark) but the water in the showers (preset) and sinks is hot. Coin-operated washers and dryers are available. The campground also has a grocery shop and a good restaurant.

You can easily reach town by walking or riding a bike, the distance is about 4 kilometers and takes about 40 minutes to walk. Bus service is also available (Number 7).

To find the campground take Exit 8 from E40. Follow the signs towards Brugge. Turn right at the intersection that follows the first set of traffic lights. You will soon see the campground entrance on the left.

BRUSSELS (BRUSSEL OR BRUXELLES), BELGIUM

Population 950,000

Brussels is both a modern and a medieval city, home to the European Community, NATO, and an attractive 15th-century old town. Visits to the old city center around the **Grand' Place**, a large square lined with medieval **Guild Halls**. Just a few blocks away you'll find the **Manneken Pis**, the statue of a small peeing boy that must be the top tourist attraction in town. Also interesting are the narrow streets filled with cafes and shops, some in glass-covered galleries to protect shoppers from the often inclement weather.

Just southeast of the old city you'll find the **Parc de Bruxelles** with the **Palais Royal** on one end and the **Palais de la Nation** on the other. From this higher area you have views over the old town and are near several good museums including the **Musée d'Art Moderne** and the **Musée Royale d'Art Ancien**.

Brussels Campground

✦ WEZEMBEEK CAMPING

Address: Warandberg 52, B-1970 Wezembeek
Telephone: 02 7821009
Price: Inexpensive

Open April 1 to September 30

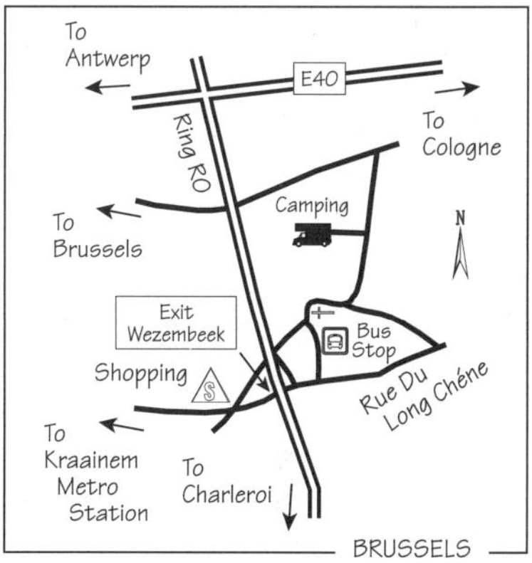

This is a well-tended medium-sized site operated by the Belgian Camping Club in the Brussels suburb of Wezembeek. Trees and shrubs provide shade and some separation between rigs. Access to downtown Brussels is not difficult and you don't have to brave the city traffic to reach the campground.

There are many static caravans here but about 30 sites are set aside for tourist rigs. These sites are numbered and assigned when you check in, the surface is grass, some have gravel wheel pads, all are relatively flat. Electricity (CEE17 plugs, 6 amps) is available, you may need a longer cord for some sites. The campground has hot showers (push valve, not adjustable) and two clean toilet buildings, hot water is available in the shaving sinks but not for dishwashing. An area for hand washing laundry and hanging clothes to dry inside is also provided. A clubhouse building provides inside seating and some snacks.

The Kraainem metro station is about 3 kilometers from the campground. You can reach it by taking the local bus, number 30, from a stop that is about one-half kilometer from the campground. Using the combination of bus and metro you can reach downtown in about 45 minutes, we found that even by walking to the metro station we could be there in under an hour. There is a shopping center with two large supermarkets about 2 kilometers from the campground in the direction of the metro station.

To find the campground take Exit 2 from the Brussels ring road near the point where Highway E40 intersects. Turn towards Wezembeek and then almost immediately take one of the first possible left turns, it is marked with an inconspicuous camping sign. From here follow more inconspicuous signs about 1 kilometer to the campground.

Side Trips from Brussels

Napoleon was finally defeated by combined English and Prussian forces in June 1815 at the village of Waterloo which is just south of Brussels. Follow the RO ring road south along the east side of Brussels to Exit 23 for Waterloo. There are several sites and museums relating to the battle in the area. You can climb the **Lion's Mound (Butte du Lion)** for a view of the battle area.

Beersel castle, dating from the thirteenth century, is an impressively restored castle located just southwest of the city. Take Exit 14 from the A7 freeway running around the west side of Brussels.

About 12 kilometers east of Brussels in the town of Tervuren is the **Royal Museum of Central Africa (Musée Royal de l'Afrique Centrale).** This museum is the legacy of Belgium's days as an imperial power controlling what was then called the Belgian Congo. It has an excellent collection of African art.

DUTCH WINDMILLS

Delft and The Hague (Den Haag), The Netherlands

Population of Delft 90,000, Population of The Hague 695,000

Delft is most famous for **Delftware porcelain** which is white with blue patterns. The town is a popular day trip from other cities in Holland, you can beat the crowds by staying just outside of town and spending the mornings and evenings wandering the very attractive streets with their canals and old houses. Delft has many of the most attractive features of Amsterdam.

Delftware is actually copied from examples of Chinese Ming porcelain captured by Dutch pirates from a Portuguese ship in 1604. Porcelain manufacturers in Delft quickly began producing Delftware to meet the huge demand created when the limited cargo was auctioned in Amsterdam. Delft was also the home of the famous Dutch painter of quiet interiors, Jan Vermeer.

Visits to several porcelain works are possible, the reception desk at the campground can steer you in the right direction or even arrange tours. The shops and sights around the central **Markt** or square are interesting and Delft offers an exceptionally large number of restaurants.

Delft Campground

✦ Camping Delftse Hout

Address: Korftlaan 5, NL-2616 LJ, Delft
Telephone: 015 2130040 Fax: 015 2131293
Price: Moderate

Open all year

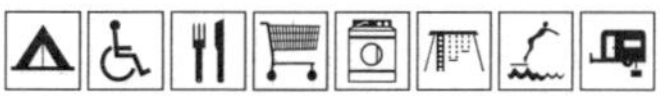

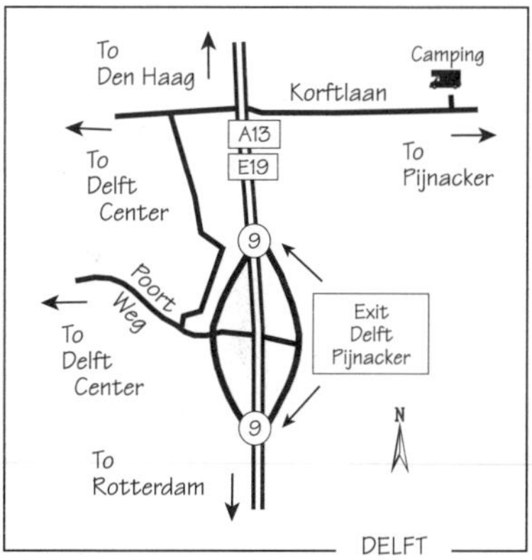

This is a very nice, and therefore often crowded, campground at the edge of the village of Delft. It makes a good place to stay for visiting Rotterdam and The Hague, not to mention Delft.

Camping Delftse Hout is a large campground with lots of amenities and good modern facilities. There are many permanently-located rigs here, over 200 tourist sites are located in an area separated from them. Campsites are mostly on grass, some have brick driveways. High hedges break the campground into small friendly groupings. Electrical outlets (CEE17 plugs, 4 or 10 amps) are conveniently located near each site. The shower/toilet facilities are in the main building near the campground entrance and are modern and clean. Free hot water is provided for showers, bathroom sinks, dishes and laundry. There is also a restaurant, a grocery shop, a recreation room that sometimes shows English language movies (Dutch subtitles), and a small swimming pool. The campground is located next to a large park with a lake and many walking and biking paths. Rental bicycles are available.

The campground is close enough to central Delft to allow you to stroll to the central square in 20 minutes. There is also bus service. Bus and train service to The Hague and Rotterdam from central Delft is quite convenient.

Heading north on Highway A13 take the second Delft exit and follow signs toward Pijnacker. You'll soon see the campground signs and by following them will pass under the freeway to the campground just east of Delft.

Side Trips from Delft

Delft is centrally located for visits to several interesting cities. **Den Haag** and **Rotterdam**, close by but in opposite directions, are easy to reach by train or bus from Delft.

Rotterdam is a giant modern city, often thought of as Holland's Manhattan, but this is a newer town than Manhattan since most of it has been rebuilt since World War II. Consider taking a **harbor tour**, Rotterdam has the world's largest commercial harbor. You could take the nine-hour version but there is also one that takes about an hour and a quarter. The boat pier is near the Leuvenhaven Station of the Metro's blue line.

Den Haag is the center of government in The Netherlands although Amsterdam is nominally the capital. Parliament meets in the **Binnenhof**, the building dates from 1248. The area around the Binnenhoff is the old section of town. Don't miss the **Royal Picture Gallery** in the **Mauritshuis** with its excellent collection of Dutch Master paintings. **Madurodam**, north of The Hague, is a 1/25 scale model of a Dutch city complete with moving airplanes and cars. Along the ocean near The Hague is the resort town of **Scheveningen.** Take the bus to Den Haag and then a tram to the beach.

There is a very popular campground located about 7 kilometers north of Den Haag in the town of Wassenaar. This is CAMPING DUINRELL, it is located on the grounds of a large water park. It is a great place to stay if you have kids along and is open all year.

The well known cheese town of **Gouda** is about 25 kilometers east of Delft. Drive north on A13, jog northwest on A4 for a couple of kilometers, then take A12 east to Gouda. There's a cheese market every Thursday morning in July and August. There are also some traditional Dutch windmills at the edge of town. For more windmills you can make your way about 20 kilometers southwest from Gouda to **Krimpen**. Just south of Krimpen at **Kinderdijk** is the largest collection of windmills in Holland. They are actually put into operation each Saturday afternoon in July and August.

GHENT (GENT, GAND), BELGIUM

Population 238,000

You might not guess it today, but at one time during the Middle Ages Ghent was Europe's second largest city, bowing only to Paris. The source of this prosperity was the production of cloth from wool imported from England.

Today the core of the town centers around a chain of squares and historic buildings: **St. Baaf's Cathedral**, the **Belfry**, and **St. Nicholas' Church**. A few blocks away is the massive 12th century **Gravensteen Castle** which has dungeons and torture machines on display. Inside St. Baaf's Cathedral is the huge painting by Jan van Eyck called **Adoration of the Lamb.** One of the earliest oil paintings, it is probably the most famous painting in Belgium. The **Museum voor Schone Kunsten** (Museum of Fine Arts) contains Flemish masters paintings from the 16th and 17th centuries. Well preserved **medieval guildhouses** line the Graslei Quay.

Access to all of this is easy. The campground is located only three kilometers from the city center, you can take the city bus or easily walk in to town along the banks of the Leie River.

Ghent Campground

✦ KAMPEERTERREIN BLAARMEERSEN

Address: Zuiderlaan 12, Watersportlaan,
B-9000 Gent
Telephone: 09 2215399
Price: Moderate

Open March 1 to October 15

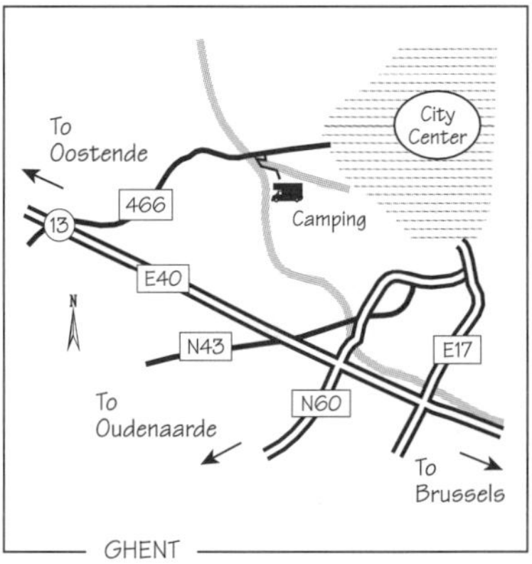

Blaarmeersen is a very large, well-equipped, well-run municipal site that is part of a large sports area just outside downtown Ghent. Besides the campground you'll find a lake with a swimming beach, many tennis courts, a plastic-surfaced summer ski hill, walking and jogging trails, and much more. This is a popular stop for campers from Great Britain who cross the channel and are looking for a spot to spend the night before moving on so you'll probably run in to some folks who speak your language.

The campground has over 200 sites, none of them occupied by permanent residents. Sites are grass with hard driveways enclosed by hedges and are quite large, there's lots of privacy. They are numbered and assigned when you check in. Electricity is 10 amps with CEE17 (some with German) plugs and the outlet spacing may require a cord just a little longer than 10 meters. The shower/toilet facilities are first rate, modern buildings house lots of showers with adjustable hot water, hot water in the shaving sinks, and hot water for dish and clothes washing. Coin-operated washers and a dryer are available. There's a restaurant, a frit (as in French fry) or snack shop, and a grocery store. There's also a dump station.

Bus access to downtown Gent is from a stop located about 500 meters from the campground. The bus number is 38 and it runs right to the center of town, and to the train station. You can easily walk in to town in about a half-hour, the distance is 3 kilometers and a map is available at the reception office.

The best way to reach the campground is to take exit number 13 from Highway E40 which runs east west on the south side of town. Exit 13 is west of Gent and is marked Gent-West. Follow signs toward Gent-West. After about 5 kilometers you'll see a sign for the campground pointing to the right. Follow signs from here around a large canal-like lake to the campground which is located near another lake that you can't see from the road.

LUXEMBOURG CITY, LUXEMBOURG

Population 79,000

Luxembourg City, the capital of the country, is 1,000 years old, but it also has a very modern face. This city is heavily involved in modern Europolitics. It is home to the Court of Justice of the European Union, the Court of Auditors of the E.U., the General Secretariat of the European Parliament, the Consultative Committee, the European Investment Bank, and the European Monetary Fund. The city is compact and easy to tour on foot.

Luxembourg City was one of the Middle Ages most impressive fortresses, it sits on an easily defended rock plateau. The fortress was torn down in the late 1800's and for the most part the ramparts are now parks. You can tour some of the 23 kilometers of underground passages that once were part of the fortifications at two places: the **Petrusse Casemates** and the **Bock**. Also take a stroll along the **Chemin de la Corniche** and visit the **National Museum** for a better idea of Luxembourg City's history.

Luxembourg City Campground

✦ CAMPING KOCKELSCHEUER

Address: 22 Route de Bettembourg,
L-1899 Kockelscheuer
Telephone: 47 18 15 Fax: 40 12 43
Price: Moderate

Open April 4 to October 31

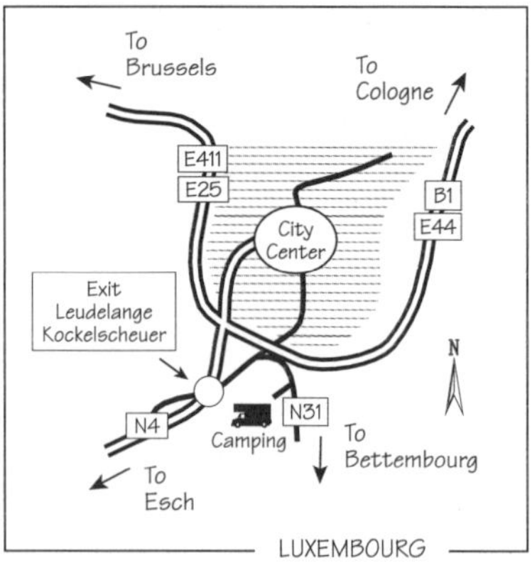

Kockelscheuer is the most convenient campground for a visit to Luxembourg City. It is only 4 kilometers south of the city with a convenient bus connection.

The campground is quite large, sites are arranged in rows that spill down a gentle terraced hillside onto a flat field. All sites are assigned at the reception desk when you arrive and a warden on a motor scooter will guide you to your campsite. There are no permanent residents. Sites are grass covered with no separating vegetation. Electrical service is from pedestals at each site (CEE17 plugs, 16 amps) The sanitary facilities are in modern buildings with hot showers (push-button valves), shaving sinks have hot water while the dishwashing sinks do not. Coin-operated clothes washers and dryers are available. There is a grocery shop in the campground and a restaurant next door in a sports facility with swimming, tennis, bowling, artificial ice rink, and sauna. Otherwise the campground is quite isolated with no other facilities nearby. There is a dump station.

Access to central Luxembourg City is good. You can walk the 4 kilometers (about 45 minutes) or take the bus which stops about 500 meters from the campground, bus number 2. This bus stops at the train station in town.

To find the campground begin on the freeway which rings the city to the south. Take the Esch exit which will take you south on Highway N4. Take the first exit, Leudelange/ Kockelscheuer, and turn left after exiting on N31 to cross the freeway and head east. Again take the first exit to the right, it is about 1.6 kilometers to this turn, at a road labeled Bettembourg-Kockelscheuer. You'll soon see the signed entrance road to the campground and sports complex on your right.

TOURNAI (DOORNIK OR TOURNAI), BELGIUM

Population 68,000

Tournai is Belgium's second oldest city, only the small town of Tongeren is about two hundred years older. Tournai was founded by the Romans in the third century AD. Today it still has an impressive medieval center. The **Museum of Fine Arts** displays some of the masterpieces produced by artists who have called the town home. Also worth a look is the **Cathedral of Notre Dame**, which is Romanesque. Near Tournai you might enjoy seeing Belgium's version of Versailles, the **Château de Beoeil**.

Tournai Campground

✦ CAMPING DE L'ORIENT

Address: Vieux Chemin de Mons,
B-7500 Tournai
Telephone: 069 222635
Price: Inexpensive

Open all year

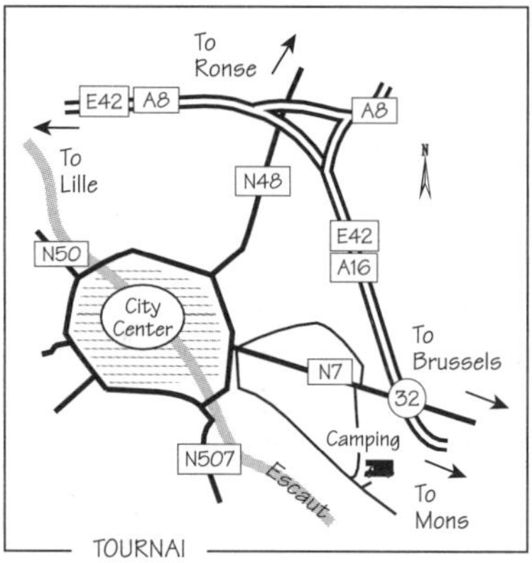

This campground is medium-sized with sites arranged off paved driveways. All are numbered and assigned. They are grass covered with brick parking pads and surrounding hedges. Electricity (French plugs, 10 amps) is convenient to most sites. The two shower/toilet buildings are new and well maintained, the one at the reception office is heated in winter. They have adjustable hot water for showers (payment required), bathroom basins, dishwashing areas, and a laundry with coin-operated machines. A small nearby lake offers restaurant and bar, fishing, picnic areas, a walking path, and a playground. There is also a swimming pool complex with a cafeteria. A shopping center is located less than a kilometer in the direction of the town.

Central Tournai is about three kilometers from the campground, a pleasant walk. There is also a bus (Number 1) to the center that makes hourly stops near the campground entrance.

The campground is located on the east side of Tournai. From the E42 freeway take Exit 32 onto Highway N7 and proceed west toward town. At the first stoplight turn left, the campground is about a half kilometer down this road on the left, there is an easy-to-miss sign at the turn on N7.

ZANDVOORT AND HAARLEM, THE NETHERLANDS

Population Zandvoort 16,000, Haarlem 153,000

Zandvoort is a popular Dutch resort on the coast just west of Haarlem. You may be familiar with the name because it is home to a well-known automobile racing circuit. There are miles of sandy beach backed with dunes and bike trails. This is a good place to just kick back and relax if you've been playing tourist a little too hard. The campground is actually located in the **Kennermer Dunes Natural Reserve (Kennemerduinen)** which has miles of bike and horse trails. This is also an area with several golf courses.

Haarlem is a center of the tulip bulb growing industry in Holland and has many flower-oriented events. The **Grote Markt** (market square) is surrounded by 17th and 18th-century architecture. There are two good museums: the **Frans Hals Museum** and the **Tylers Museum**. Haarlem also has the **Grote Kerk** which has one of Europe's best-known organs, it was played by both Handel and Mozart.

Zandvoort and Haarlem Campground

✦ CAMPING DE LAKENS

Address: Zeeweg 60, NL-2051
Bloemendaal aan Zee
Telephone: 023 251902
Price: Moderate

Open April 1 to September 30

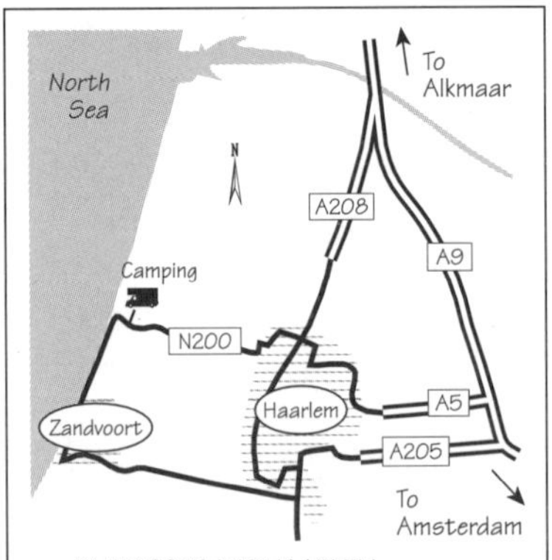

ZANDVOORT AND HAARLEM

This is a large campground set in the dunes about 200 meters from the ocean. There are quite a few long-term campers here but also lots of room for tourists. Camp sites are on sand and are of different types, some are nicely secluded while other spots are crowded. Electricity is available to some sites (CEE17 plugs, 4 amps). The shower/toilet facilities are Spartan but adequate, hot showers are free. The campground has a camping shop and restaurant. There is a path through the dunes to the ocean, many bike paths in the park, a small fresh-water pond, and even a nearby restaurant.

Busses from a stop near the campground entrance service both Haarlem and Zandvoort. Both towns are also within bike range, Haarlem at 6 kilometers and Zandvoort at 4 kilometers.

To find the campsite follow signs to Zandvoort and then follow the beach north. In about 3 kilometers the road will turn away from the beach and almost immediately you'll see the campground entrance on your left. If you're on foot you can take the number 81 bus from the NS-Haarlem railway station.

Side Trips from Zandvoort and Haarlem

The **tulip bulb growing area** of The Netherlands stretches from Haarlem south to Leiden, a distance of some 20 kilometers. The **Keukenhof Gardens** are a great place to see a riot of blooms. They are located near Lisse, about 10 kilometers south of Haarlem and are the largest gardens in the world. Keukenhof is open only when the tulips are in bloom, late March to late May. When Keukenhof is open there are signs pointing the way posted throughout the area, there's lots of parking. You can also stop at one of the area flower growers and buy bulbs.

Even closer to Haarlem is the **Linnaeushof Amusement Park** just off Highway N208 south of town.

TULIPS NEAR HAARLEM

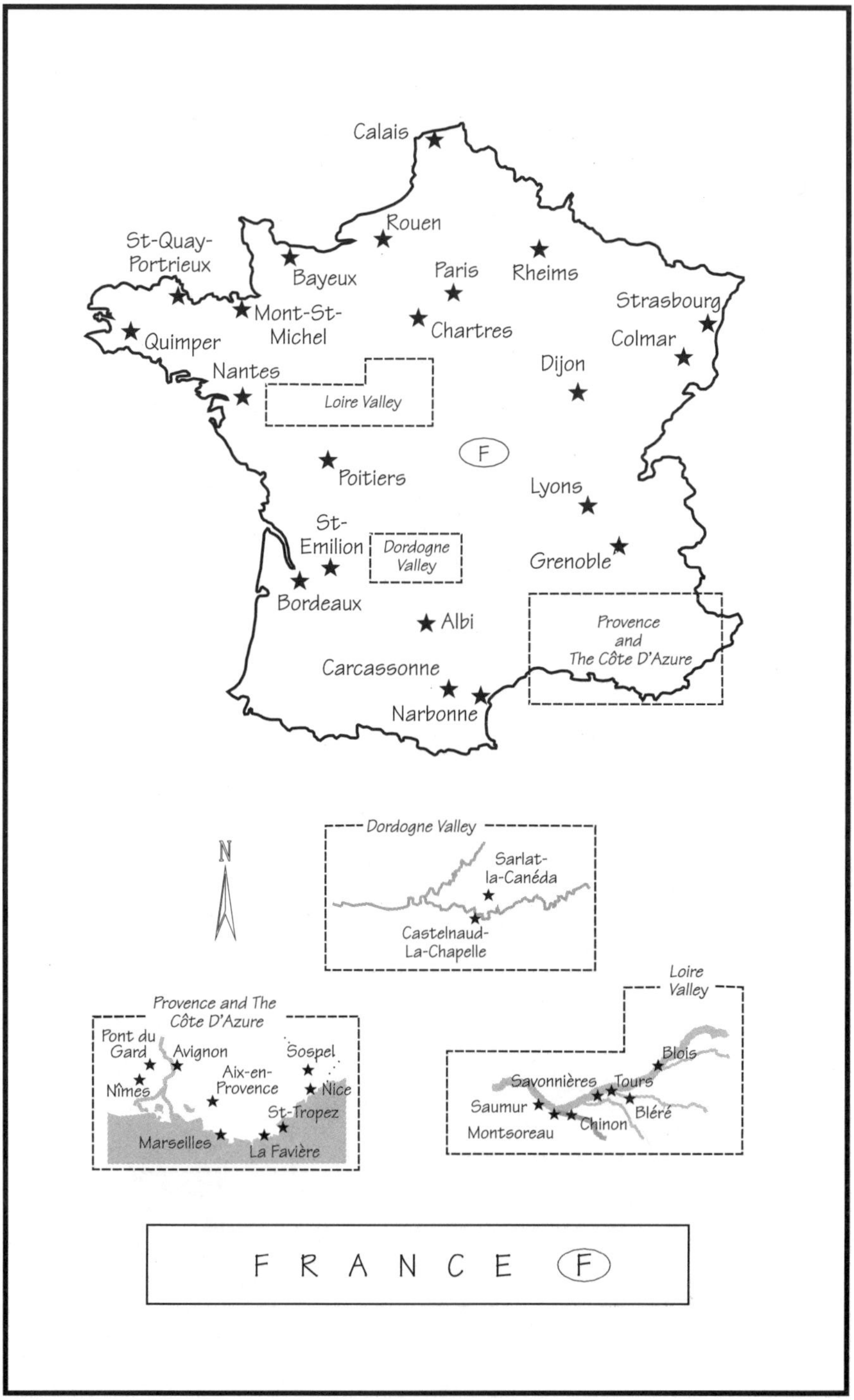
Calais
Rouen
St-Quay-
Portrieux
Bayeux
Paris
Rheims
Mont-St-
Michel
Chartres
Strasbourg
Quimper
Colmar
Nantes
Dijon
Loire Valley
F
Poitiers
Lyons
St-
Emilion
Dordogne
Valley
Grenoble
Bordeaux
Albi
Provence
and
The Côte D'Azure
Carcassonne
Narbonne
N
Dordogne Valley
Sarlat-
la-Canéda
Castelnaud-
La-Chapelle
Loire
Valley
Provence and The
Côte D'Azure
Pont du
Gard
Avignon
Sospel
Nîmes
Aix-en-
Provence
Nice
St-Tropez
Marseilles
La Favière
Blois
Savonnières
Tours
Saumur
Bléré
Montsoreau
Chinon
FRANCE
F

CHAPTER 7

FRANCE

INTRODUCTION

France is in such a central location and has so many attractions that you will probably spend more time here than in any other country in Europe. With the magical city of Paris, a lush countryside, world-famous wine regions, a variety of coastlines and tons of art, architecture, history, and food you'll find much more to see and do than you'll ever have time for. Best of all France is an excellent place to camp, there are good convenient campgrounds virtually anywhere you would want to go.

Roads and Driving

The roads in France rate second only to Germany. There is an extensive system of autoroutes or freeways. Unfortunately these are toll roads and the tolls mount up quickly. Fortunately, there is a great road system of "N" and "D" roads also, and they are free. In most places you can make good time on secondary roads. On maps autoroutes are designated as "A" roads, Routes National (red) as "N" roads, Routes Departmental (yellow) as "D" roads, and small local roads (also usually yellow) as class C roads. It pays to use the autoroutes through major towns, you can pass through quickly and usually there are no tolls on the urban sections.

The autoroute toll rates are not all the same, but they are uniformly expensive. Cars travel at the lowest rate, cars with caravans are more expensive and camping vans and motorhomes are more expensive still. Plan on between 5 and 8 U.S. cents per kilometer for an automobile and between 10 and 13 U.S. cents per kilometer for vans and motorhomes. Tolls are generally collected when you leave the autoroute although there are some collection stops en route. Credit cards are accepted at the toll booths.

French drivers can generally be characterized as good but aggressive. They are accustomed to sluggish motor homes, we've never had any unpleasant experiences with

French drivers. Although not as much a problem as in the past you should be aware than many French intersections have no traffic-control signs, the person on the right has the right-of-way. This is called *priorité à droite*. You must be alert to this. Major roads and arterials usually have *passage protegé* or right-of-way. This is indicated by either a small yellow white-bordered diamond-shaped sign or a pyramid-shaped, red-bordered, white sign with an upward pointing arrow posted frequently along the road. Don't assume you have the right of way over entering vehicles unless you see these signs. Caution is never a bad idea.

While touring France you may notice route signs carrying the word Bis. This stands for *Bison Futé*, these are routes to be used during peak traffic periods like the end of August when everyone in the country seems to be driving back to Paris after the holidays. Actually you can expect the roads to be full of holiday drivers at the beginning and end of July and August and also on the 14th, 15th and 16th of those months.

Bicycles are very popular in France and drivers are accustomed to dealing with them. Dedicated bicycle paths are infrequent but the extensive secondary road system offers some of the best bicycle touring possibilities in Europe.

Breakdown help on the autoroutes is organized by the police, motoring organizations are not allowed to respond first. The emergency number for the police is 17. Automobile Club National (ACN) (01 44 51 53 99) has a reciprocal agreement with the AAA but expect to be charged for breakdown service (0800 08 92 22).

Camping

France is reported to have more than 10,000 campgrounds. This may be true, almost every village seems to have a municipal campground of some kind. These municipal campgrounds are one of the treasures of France, they are often inexpensive and comfortable without unnecessary facilities to drive up prices, and they are invariably in convenient locations with good public transportation available when necessary.

Another side of the campground scene in France is the commercial campground chains. **Airotel de France**, **Castels and Camping Caravanning**, and **Campéole**, among others, all have many campgrounds scattered around the country with most located in vacation areas. When you first visit a location belonging to one of these chains be sure to pick up a guide to the rest of their locations. Commercial French campgrounds often have lots of extra amenities and are aimed at vacationing families. It is often easy to reserve ahead with campground chains.

French tourist and information offices, even in smaller towns, almost always have lots of free information about campgrounds in the surrounding region, often in the form of attractive high-quality booklets.

Free camping is widely prohibited but sometimes tolerated in France. Many campers like to use the autoroute rest areas as campgrounds. When in doubt about whether free camping is allowed you should always ask permission.

Camping International Cards are not required in France but are helpful. They will usually be accepted in lieu of a passport as security for payment.

Shopping, Currency, Credit Cards and Fuel

Even by European standards France is an expensive country. Taxes are high and France usually tends towards being a "hard" money member of the European Community. Gasoline prices are higher than anywhere else in Europe. There are, however, offsetting money-saving strategies that you can use.

France is famous for her hypermarkets, huge supermarkets selling almost everything. If you shop in the hypermarkets you'll find that you have the best selection at the best prices. You can also often buy gasoline at hypermarkets, many have their own stations in the parking lots with much lower prices than those along the autoroutes.

The small food shops in France are one of the country's luxuries. You will want to do some shopping in them even if the things you buy cost you a little more. A boulangerie is a bread store, fresh batches of bread are baked twice a day, morning and early afternoon. French bread is delicious but doesn't keep long so you'll often see people along the road with a fresh baguette (called a French stick by the English) under their arm. Patisseries are often colocated with boulangeries, they sell delicious pastries. For picnic and camping treats try a charcuterie selling prepared meats like hams, sausages, terrines and pâtés, as well as delicious salads. There are also often cooked dishes like cassoulets. A butcher shop is a boucherie.

Credit cards are widely used in France and become more popular each year. Many hypermarkets and gas stations accept cards, Visa seems to be the most popular. Cash machines are everywhere, many hypermarkets have a machine.

Suggested Itineraries

It seems almost ludicrous to suggest an itinerary in France, the entire country is a park with lots of intriguing destinations and activities. Paris is the most popular destination, of course, but the nearby Loire Valley also attracts may people. In addition to almost all major cities we've included detailed descriptions of the camping scene and attractions of three popular regions in this book: the Loire River Valley, the Cote d'Azure and Provence, and finally, the Dordogne River Valley. Any of these regions would easily keep you busy for at least a couple weeks.

France is cold in the winter, even the southern coast has almost no camping during December through March. In the south camping starts in April, farther north April is cold and you won't really be comfortable until May. May and June are the best months for camping in France, school holidays mean that campgrounds are crowded in July and especially August, particularly along the coasts. If you stick to the towns and cities and avoid the seashores you will find plenty of room in the campgrounds even during the vacation months. Fall camping in September and October is also good, especially if you luck out on weather.

You can request information about touring France from the **French Government Tourist Office, 444 Madison Avenue, 16th Floor, New York, NY 10022-6903 (212 838-7800)**. In Canada the address is **1 Dundas St. West, Toronto, ON M5G 1Z3 (416 593-4723).** Check our internet site at www.rollinghomes.com for links to information sites.

FRANCE
DISTANCE TABLE

In Kilometers

Kms X .62 = Miles

	Aix-en Provence	Albi	Avignon	Bayeux	Bordeaux	Calais	Carcassonne	Chartres	Colmar	Dijon	Grenoble	La Favière	Lyons	Marseilles	Mont-St-Michel	Nantes	Narbonne	Nice	Nîmes	Paris	Poitiers	Pont Du Gard	Quimper	Rheims	Rouen	Sarlat-La-Canéda	Sospel	St-Emilion	St-Quay-Portrieux	St-Tropez	Strasbourg
Albi	355																														
Avignon	75	299																													
Bayeux	1040	858	1015																												
Bordeaux	642	323	580	577																											
Calais	1067	1068	975	359	874																										
Carcassonne	303	107	242	912	339	1082																									
Chartres	803	655	736	212	532	349	738																								
Colmar	734	793	659	774	859	673	860	632																							
Dijon	500	553	425	612	618	561	637	381	231																						
Grenoble	244	461	230	831	663	861	439	589	485	303																					
La Favière	114	488	199	1138	755	1167	418	944	834	610	366																				
Lyons	318	412	243	722	536	753	445	485	418	195	106	418																			
Marseilles	29	373	93	1035	647	1065	310	776	730	510	272	104	315																		
Mont-St-Michel	1114	829	1086	155	510	468	845	331	887	692	944	1251	835	1030																	
Nantes	970	630	904	313	328	594	663	289	858	619	710	1079	606	971	177																
Narbonne	243	167	187	959	397	1096	60	753	805	581	384	362	389	254	904	721															
Nice	165	534	240	1192	809	1222	471	933	738	664	332	110	472	189	1187	1133	416														
Nîmes	101	254	45	970	535	1001	197	691	666	442	245	227	250	119	1041	859	142	280													
Paris	777	707	702	263	581	290	790	83	443	310	570	877	461	774	337	385	804	931	709												
Poitiers	703	433	647	353	248	627	583	241	676	446	527	854	424	687	356	183	642	844	602	336											
Pont Du Gard	102	274	27	990	555	986	217	676	651	427	230	226	235	120	1026	879	162	267	20	694	622										
Quimper	1188	865	1122	416	546	736	881	470	991	844	1083	1311	831	1176	273	219	940	1326	1077	553	400	1097									
Rheims	922	842	734	421	717	274	926	228	328	289	602	909	493	806	482	521	880	963	854	145	472	839	689								
Rouen	914	796	880	145	617	217	879	133	576	451	703	1012	594	907	254	378	893	1064	842	137	372	827	504	237							
Sarlat-La-Canéda	501	186	485	619	166	834	289	490	732	491	527	707	399	599	625	457	349	760	440	542	268	460	712	678	631						
Sospel	213	582	288	1240	858	1270	519	981	786	712	380	158	520	238	1235	1181	464	48	328	979	892	315	1374	1011	1112	808					
St-Emilion	650	318	566	618	41	915	344	560	818	597	642	784	515	663	551	369	408	795	550	622	289	570	587	734	687	145	843				
St-Quay-Portrieux	1198	841	1132	249	556	627	891	377	933	738	990	1297	881	1076	129	223	950	1233	1087	460	402	1107	194	611	394	671	1281	597			
St-Tropez	120	475	195	1160	756	1170	423	923	831	620	364	37	438	141	1234	1090	363	93	221	897	823	222	1308	1042	1034	621	141	770	1318		
Strasbourg	806	871	736	766	936	619	938	573	72	310	548	911	495	808	827	866	882	801	743	490	817	728	1034	348	582	809	849	915	941	894	
Tours	745	541	670	251	347	529	682	139	677	414	549	847	445	737	284	198	741	894	652	237	102	672	417	373	273	368	942	388	330	865	718

SELECTED DESTINATIONS AND CAMPGROUNDS

ALBI, FRANCE

Population 50,000

A friendly medium-sized town, Albi, located on the Tarn River in southeast France, makes an pleasant destination for a one or two day visit. Your overwhelming impression of the town's two main sights, the Romanesque **Cathédrale de Ste-Cécile** and the **Palais de la Berbie** with its Toulouse-Lautrec museum, is one of masses of red brick. The cathedral was built just after the Albegension Crusade in 1209 directed against heretics in the region, and appears to be as much fortress as church, necessarily so since the local population was often quite hostile. The Palais de la Berbie (bishop's palace), located next door, definitely was a fortress, and was the home of the unpopular Catholic bishop, Bernard de Castenet. It now houses the **Musée Henri de Toulouse-Lautrec**.

Albi's old town is a good place to spend the rest of the day. Check at the information office next to the museum for information about walking tours around town. The narrow streets are for pedestrians only, and the cafes make a good place to relax in the afternoon heat.

Albi Campground

✦ PARC EUROPÉEN DE CAMPING DE CAUSSELS

Address: Rue du Go, 81000 Albi
Telephone: 05 63 60 37 06
Price: Moderate

Open April 1 to October 10

Camping de Caussels, located just outside the city, is the only campground in the immediate area. It is medium-sized with sites scattered under large shade trees. Some sites are separated by concrete curbs, others are not. Electricity (4 and 10 amps) is available to most sites. The shower/toilet facilities are older but clean, hot showers are free. There is an indoor swimming pool located next door and a large supermarket within easy walking distance.

Access to central Albi is not great, there is no bus service. The distance is about 3 kilometers so you can walk it in a half hour or 45 minutes or use a bike.

To find the campground follow signs east from downtown toward St. Juery. You'll soon see campground and piscine (swimming pool) signs. The two are located next door to each other and are not both listed on every sign so follow signs for either one. The final few hundred meters are a little complicated so watch closely. There is a large supermarket across from the campground entrance road.

Side Trips from Albi

From Albi you can drive 25 kilometers northwest to **Cordes**. The town is a beautiful hilltop bastide village, similar to Domme in the Dordogne valley.

If you are in the mood for a little longer expedition you might want to drive east on D999 about 150 kilometers to the spectacular **Gorges du Tarn** and **Canyon de la Dourbie**. The area has many campgrounds, you might try the Castels & Camping Caravaning campground LE VAL DE CANTOBRE near Nant in the Dourbie Valley, open from May 15 to September 15.

BAYEUX, FRANCE

Population 15,000

Bayeux's small size belies its interest to visitors. First, the town is the location of the **Bayeux Tapestry** which depicts the story of the Norman invasion of England in 1066. You shouldn't miss the opportunity to examine it, assisted by a running commentary through a set of headphones. Second, Bayeux is a great base for touring the **Allied invasion beaches of World War II**. They are all just a few miles away, and Bayeux has a museum and information to orient you properly. You'll need to use your vehicle or take an organized tour, public transportation is just too inconvenient. There are many additional campgrounds along the ocean nearby.

Bayeux Campground

✦ BAYEUX-CAMPING MUNICIPAL

Address: Bd. Périphérique d'Eindhoven,
14400 Bayeux
Telephone: 02 31 92 08 43
Price: Inexpensive

Open March 15 to November 15

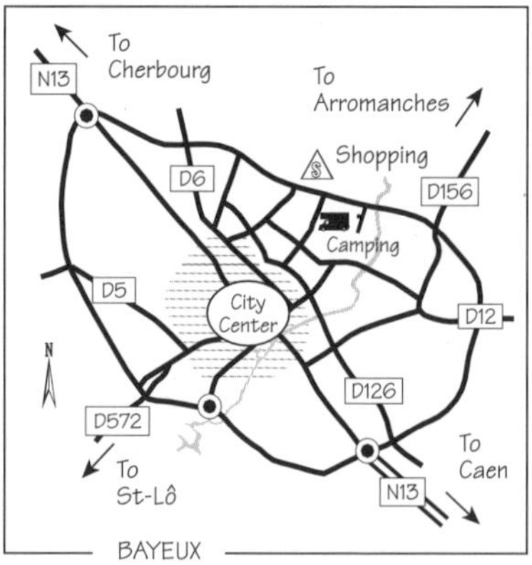

Bayeux's attractive campground has all the features you want in a city campground: great location, nearby shopping, good facilities, and extreme cleanliness. This makes it a popular place. English campers throng to the coastal region.

Bayeux-Camping Municipal has curbed gravel driveways and neatly-clipped grass sites. The few trees are mostly ornamental. It is a fairly large place. Electrical boxes (CEE17, 5 amps) are near most of the sites. The modern shower/toilet buildings are very clean. They have hot water showers. There is a municipal swimming pool next door and a supermarket across the street. A small kiosk sells limited supplies and food in the campground. Central Bayeux is a fifteen-minute walk or bike ride.

The campground is located north of town on Bd. Périphérique d'Eindhoven, also called N13, it is a portion of the small ring road that runs all the way around the village. There are several signs, the campground is just across the street from the Champion supermarket.

BORDEAUX, FRANCE

Population 215,000

Bordeaux is well known, not because of the city itself but because it is the center of a region that is the source of the world's best wine. While Bordeaux is a fine city, it has little that is unusual to offer the visitor. It has impressive 18th-century neoclassic facades in its center but overall seems kind of grimy and doesn't offer a lot to see or do. No wine lover, however, would pass up a chance to tour the famous wine region surrounding Bordeaux.

The **CIVB** wine information office has lots of information about Bordeaux wines and châteaux. They'll give you addresses of the local wine information offices in the various wine-growing regions, those offices will have information about which châteaux are open to visitors on any given day. This can all be kind of complicated, especially in view of the fact that some châteaux charge a visiting fee, most expect purchases, and some of the largest and most famous are not open to visitors at all. You can simplify by taking a wine area bus tour, check at the tourist office across from the CIVB for details.

If you are willing to deal with the châteaux yourself or if you will be satisfied with just touring through the region and visiting the major villages you can take driving trips in almost any direction. Probably the most attractive wine town in the region is **St-Emilion**, which happens to have a good campground and is described separately in this chapter.

North on D2 (the "wine road") is the **Haut-Médoc** region, home of the best Bordeaux wines, four of the five "premier cru" wines come from here. The villages of **Margaux** and attractive **Pauillac** are the important wine villages on the route. Farther north is the less prestigious **Bas-Médoc** region.

Circling the city of Bordeaux on the west and southwest is the **Graves** region. Graves is home of the fifth "premier cru", **Haut-Brion**. The château that produces this wine is virtually inside the city of Bordeaux itself.

South from Bordeaux around the small village of **Sauternes** the sweet white wines named after that village are produced. From there you can follow D8 east to the D10 and follow it north along the scenic river through **Loupiac** and **Cadillac**, this region also produces sweet whites and they are much more affordable than the sauternes.

Bordeaux Campground

✦ LES GRAVIÈRES

Address: Villenave-D'Ornon, 33140
Pont-de-la-Maye
Telephone: 05 56 87 00 36
Price: Moderate

Open all year

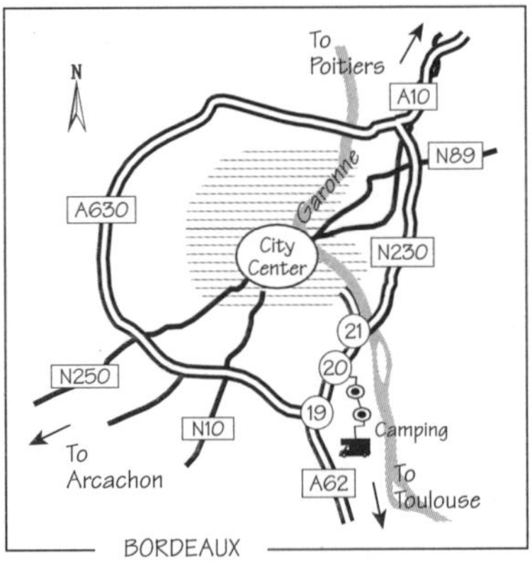

Les Gravières is a good base for a visit to Bordeaux itself. It is located just outside the ring road on the south side of the city and there is convenient bus and rail transportation nearby.

The campground is older but well managed and located between a series of small lakes, gravel pits we suspect, thus the campground name. It is a medium-sized campground with some permanently-situated caravans. Electrical boxes are scattered (3 amps or 5 amps) but available to most sites. The shower/toilet facilities are older but adequate, hot showers are free. The campground has a grocery shop and snack bar. There is no swimming in the lakes but fishing is possible. You'll find a supermarket and rail station for the train into Bordeaux nearby.

To reach the campground take the Begles Exit from the Bordeaux ring road on the southeast side of town. Head south away from Bordeaux and follow the signs to the campground.

Side Trips from Bordeaux

West of Bordeaux is a wild stretch of Atlantic coast that is very popular with French campers. Starting in the north at Pointe de Grave and the town of **Soulac-sur-Mer** and stretching south for 150 kilometers is a region of sand dunes, backed by pine forest or "landes" and several lakes. You'll find many good campgrounds and bike trails in this region. Try AEROTEL DE L'OCEAN north of Lacanau-Océan, open from May 1 to September 30.

CALAIS, FRANCE

Population 78,000

The channel crossing from Calais to Dover is the shortest and therefore the least expensive between the British Isles and the Continent. There are so many ferries on this route that you probably won't even need a place to camp while waiting to cross, but Calais does have a convenient campground. In addition to the campground described below there is a special "Port Sleeping Area" near the ferry terminal where you can park and sleep in your rig. If you get into town late in the evening you might overnight here so you can cross in the daylight hours or, heading the other way, start your continental tour refreshed after a relaxing evening. Calais is also near the French entrance of the EuroTunnel or "Chunnel" which is now a good alternative to the ferries, even for RV's.

Calais Campground

✦ **CAMPING MUNICIPAL**

Address: 62100 Calais
Telephone: 03 21 97 89 79
Price: Inexpensive

Open all year

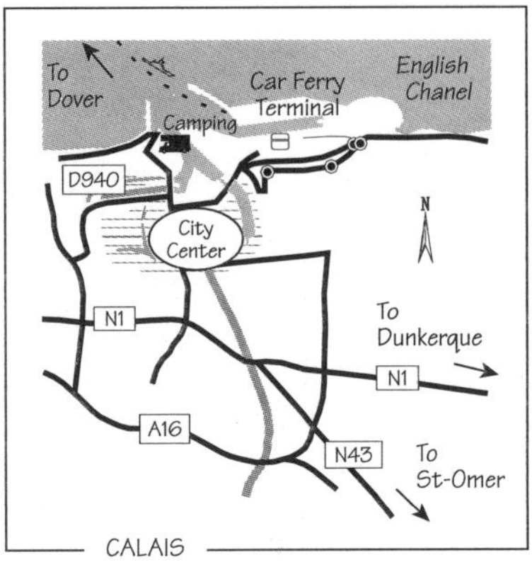

The campground sits at a point just opposite the car ferry docks. You can watch the ferries arriving from your lounge chair and occasionally get to your feet to watch a giant hovercraft roar by offshore. The wide sandy Calais beach is within easy walking distance.

Camping Municipal has a great location and decent facilities. There aren't a lot of extras here, but who needs them when you have the beach nearby and the shipping activity for entertainment. It is a large campground with grassy sites separated by hedges, there is no shade but the breezy waterside location usually makes shade unnecessary anyway. Sites that offer electricity don't require long cords, many also have their own water faucets. The large shower/toilet building is heated and was nice at one time, now it needs maintenance. It does have hot showers and hot water in bathroom basins, dish, and hand clothes washing areas.

The campground is located on the point at the western side of the entrance to the Calais ferry harbor. You can reach it by following signs north from the central area of town. Although the campground is very close to the ferry you must drive a long distance around the downtown and boat basins to reach the loading docks. You can avoid the central area traffic by following the outer boulevards.

CARCASSONNE, FRANCE

Population 45,000

From the campground you can follow a good walking trail up to the old walled city of Carcassonne. It starts at the campground gate, follows the fence around to a small canal, and then along the bank to the foot of the hill. By approaching the Cité this way you'll be able to best appreciate the famous walled town without interruption from crowds of tourists. Signs lead you through narrow streets and up a path to the Port d'Aude, the back door to the most complete and best preserved walled city in Europe.

Carcassonne is a restored town, some people think too perfectly restored, but the out-of-the-way backwater location has meant that significant modern development and destruction of the old city never occurred. What you see, for the most part, is the true ancient city, built over a period of 1800 years, and restored in the 19th century.

Today Carcassonne is a popular tourist destination. The city is filled with tourist shops, restaurants, and people, but at times you will feel as you've gone back 500 years in time, making a visit a worthwhile experience.

Carcassonne Campground

✦ CAMPÉOLE LA CITÉ

Address: Route de St. Hilaire, 11000 Carcassonne
Telephone: 04 68 25 11 77
Price: Moderate

Open March 1 to October 10

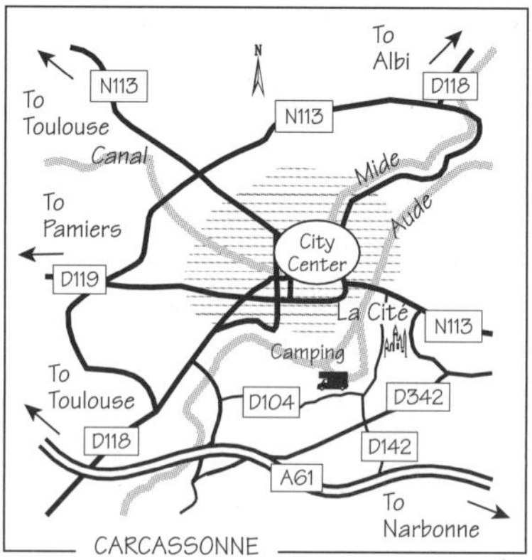

There are several campground choices in Carcassonne, but this is the closest to the walled city. It is run by the Campéole chain. La Cité is a large area with grassy individual sites separated by small hedges. There is little shade but that is good, the trees won't block your view of the floodlit city in the evening. Electricity (CEE17, 10 amps) is convenient to most sites. Sanitary facilities are more than adequate, nice and clean with free hot showers. There is shop, a bar and a small restaurant near the gate. The campground also has a pool and tennis courts.

You're main destination from the campground is probably going to be the walled city. You can walk the distance in 20 minutes or catch a bus near the campground.

The route to the campground from town is well signed. If you head south on D104 from its intersection with N113 just east of the bridge over the Aude River you'll soon pick up the signs. Alternately you can head southwest out of Carcassonne on D118 and then follow signs to the left across the river and back toward the walled city.

CHARTRES, FRANCE

Population 40,000

The town of Chartres is synonymous with its early Gothic cathedral, the **Cathédrale de Notre Dame**. As you approach Chartres the spires of the cathedral are visible from miles away, and once there they dominate the town itself. This cathedral was a true 13th-century building project, it was finished in only a quarter century. Other cathedrals you'll see in Europe have been under construction for centuries and aren't finished yet. When you tour the cathedral note the mostly original "Chartres blue" stained glass windows, they're awesome!

Chartres Campground

✦ CAMPING MUNICIPAL DES BORDS DE L'EURE

Address: Rue de Launay, 28000 Chartres
Telephone: 02 37 28 79 43 Fax: 02 37 23 41 99
Price: Inexpensive

Open April 21 to September 3 (dates vary)

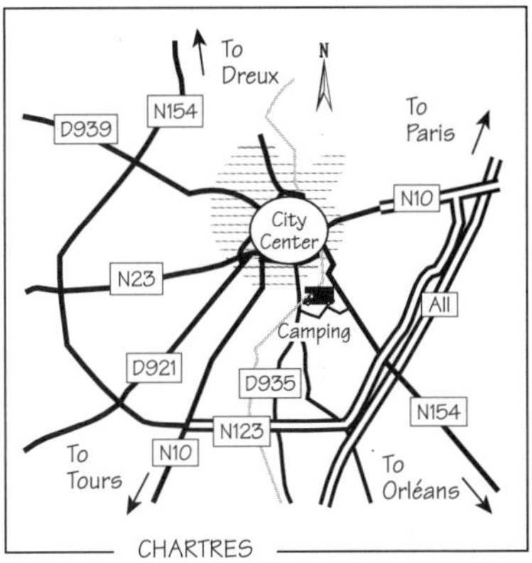

CHARTRES

Bords de l'Eure is pleasant medium-sized campground with a great location. Chartres is near enough to Paris that it is possible to take day trips to the big city by train if you wish. You can walk to the cathedral or train station easily, fifteen minutes or so to the cathedral and a few more to the gare or train station. There is also bus service around Chartres.

The campground is in a valley next to the river. Camping sites are grassy with a few hedges for separation. Electricity (varies, to 10 amps) is available to most sites. Sanitary facilities include free hot showers. There is a small grocery shop and a playground.

You'll find that the routes to the campground are well signed from N154, the highway running southeast towards Orléans.

CHARTRES CATHEDRAL

COLMAR, FRANCE

Population 65,000

An Alsace town, to the visitor Colmar is like a smaller, friendlier version of Strasbourg. It has the same half-timbered buildings, the same great restaurants, and the same half French, half German culture.

Colmar, however, has its own set of sights. The **Unterlinden Museum** with medieval art work from the area, pewter and earthenware, medieval arms, and even an Alsatian wine cellar is very well known. You can visit the old Dominican church to see Schongauer's famous painting The ***Virgin and the Rosebush***. Frédéric Bartholdi of Statue of Liberty fame was from Colmar and has his own museum, the **Musée Bartholdi**. Finally, and best of all, there are the traffic-free streets of the central area, the old **Tanner's quarter**, and **Petite Venice**, all in a small, convenient package.

Colmar Campground

✦ CAMPING INTERCOMMUNAL DE L'ILL

Address: Rte. de Neuf Brisach, 680000 Horbourg-Wihr
Telephone: 03 89 41 15 94
Price: Inexpensive

Open February 1 to November 30

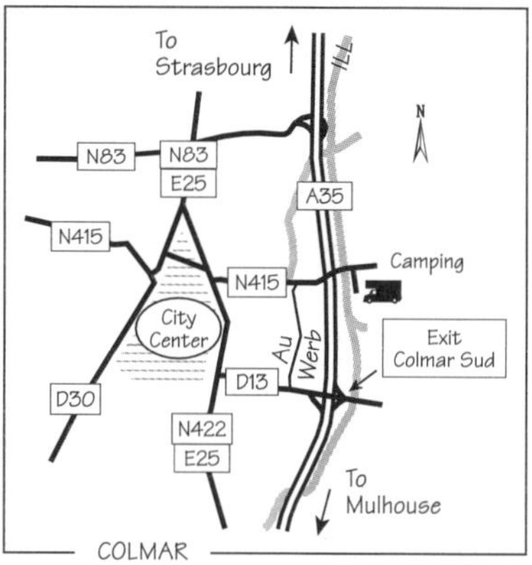

Camping Municipal is a short distance from the center of town. It sits on the banks of the Ill River, which is very small at this point. There's a freeway on the far side of the river but a large berm keeps the noise down.

The campground is a long grassy plot situated along a raised dike next to the river. Many large trees provide quite a bit of shade. Camping sites for wheeled vehicles are numbered and arranged on the dike and in front of it. A large tent area stretches down to the river. Electrical outlets are either 3 amps and some 5 amps. The three shower/ toilet buildings provide free hot showers (push valves, not adjustable), and hot water for shaving sinks and dishwashing sinks. There is a nice little restaurant and a small grocery shop. About 1 kilometer toward Colmar there is a giant supermarket.

Access to central Colmar is good. You can walk on good sidewalks or ride your bike, the distance is 2 kilometers. There is also a convenient city bus, the stop is just outside the campground entrance, bus Number 1.

The campground is located on Highway 415 just east of where it crosses over Highway A35 and the Ill River. It is on the west border of the small suburb of Horbourg. If you are traveling on Highway A35 take the Colmar Sud Exit and drive west toward Colmar. Take a right on Au Werb to parallel the freeway heading north. You will meet Highway N415 after 1.4 kilometers. Turn right and cross over the freeway, the campground will be on your right.

DIJON, FRANCE

Population 150,000

You probably think of mustard when you hear the name of this town, but there's lots more to Dijon than mustard. It is located at the north end of the famous Côte-d'Or, home of some of the most famous wines in France, the burgundies. The city also has a great deal of historical interest since it was the capital of the powerful Dukes of Burgundy during the fourteenth and fifteenth centuries.

Dijon's epicurian side is represented by more than mustard. The city is also well known for cassis liquor, gingerbread, and snails; not to mention wine from the surrounding vineyards.

The architectural and monumental side of the city reflects the glory days of the Dukes of Burgundy. The **Hôtel de Ville** or city hall incorporates portions of the old **Palais des Ducs de Bourgogne**. It was substantially rebuilt in the 17th century but houses a museum with many of the treasures acquired by the Dukes. There are also many mansions, often with the trademark patterned-tile roof of the region, from later periods. The **Notre-Dame Cathedral** has two memorable features: the **gargoyles** on the facade and the **owl (chouette)** on the north side which brings luck when touched.

Dijon Campground

✦ TERRAIN DE CAMPING DU LAC

Address: 3 Bd. Chamoine Kir, 21000 Dijon
Telephone: 03 80 43 54 72
Price: Inexpensive

Open April 1 to October 15

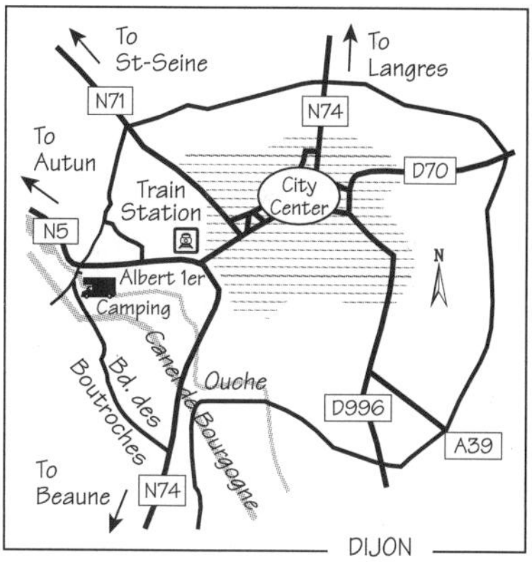

Terrain de Camping du Lac is located within walking distance of this fascinating town next to the Ouche River and near a nice lake. With all this near at hand you might enjoy an extended stay. There's also bus service into Dijon if you don't feel like walking the 2 kilometers.

The campground is a large grass field segmented by paved driveways. There is a gravel area just inside the entrance where more permanent units are parked. Tourists in good weather are usually assigned the better marked sites on grass in the inner area. Electricity is handy and readily available to those that want it. The shower/toilet buildings are older but clean and have hot showers. During busy months a kiosk sells some groceries and snacks, including fresh bread of course. Paved paths run along the river and around the lake. They're great for walking or riding a bike.

From central Dijon follow Ave. Albert 1er (Ave. Albert 1st), the road running west from the south side of the railroad station. In about 2 kilometers you'll see the campground sign.

Side Trips from Dijon

Burgundy is wine country. 130 kilometers to the northwest of Dijon is the small **Chablis** region, famous for the scarce and often unsuccessfully-copied dry white Chablis wine. South from Dijon is the even more famous Burgundy wine region. Follow N74 toward Lyons through the **Côte d'Or,** and **Beaujolais** region. Consider spending the night 40 kilometers south of Dijon in **Beaune** at the pleasant and convenient municipal campsite, CAMPING MUNICIPAL DES CENT VIGNES, open from March 15 to the end of October and located just northeast of town. Don't miss Beaune's **Hôtel-Dieu** and wine museum.

About 100 kilometers west of Dijon is **Vézelay** with its basilica of Mary Magdalene, restored by Viollet-le-Duc. Vézelay is where Bernard of Clairvaux, head of the Cistercian order of monks, preached the Second Crusade in 1146 to pilgrims including Louis VII of France, and inspired him to lead it. The Third Crusade, in 1190, also departed from here.

GRENOBLE, FRANCE

Population 160,000

Home of the 1968 Olympics, Grenoble seems more like a modern industrial town than a mountain ski resort. This is a city, not a town, and the countryside around Grenoble is in many ways more attractive than the town. Grenoble does make a good base for exploring the surrounding mountains and as a university town and commercial center this is an engaging city.

The central part of town around the **Place Grenette** is the center of the action. There's a cable car that climbs to the **Fort de la Bastille** for the view. You can walk down to the **Musée Dauphinois** regional museum. Back in town take in the **Musée de Grenoble** with its surprisingly complete painting collection.

Grenoble and especially the Vercors region to the west were centers of the resistance during World War II. Tour the **Musée de la Résistance** if this interests you. Book people may enjoy the **Musée Stendhal**, the great novelist was from Grenoble.

Grenoble Campground

✦ CARAVANNING LES 3 PUCELLES

Address: 58 Rue des Alobroges, 38170 Seyssinet-Parisset
Telephone: 04 76 96 45 73
Price: Inexpensive

Open all year

The campground is a medium-sized site about 7 kilometers from downtown Grenoble. It is nothing fancy but is the closest site and has handy bus/tram service into Grenoble.

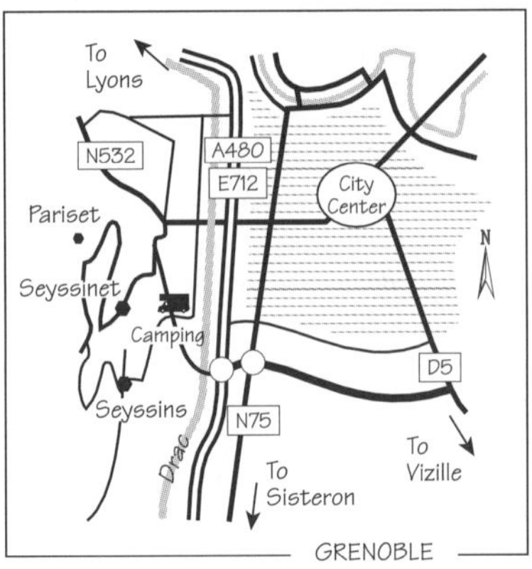

Camp sites are on grass with quite a few trees for shade. While this is primarily a tourist campground there are many trailers that are here for long stays. Electricity (French plugs, 5 amps and 16 amps) is available, the warden will unlock the box to let you plug in. The hot showers and toilets are in a large heated building near the entrance, check out the toilet with the automatic seat-washing system. The campground has a good swimming pool and there's a supermarket nearby.

Caravanning Les 3 Pucelles is located in the suburb of Seyssinet some 7 kilometers southwest of Grenoble on the far side of the Drac River. From Grenoble head south on N75 toward Sisteron. Turn right and cross the river on N82 following signs for Seyssinet-Parisset. At the first roundabout after the river near an Intermarché supermarket you'll find the first of a series of camping signs which will direct you to the campground.

Side Trips from Grenoble

North from Grenoble on the D512 only 20 kilometers or so is the mountainous **Chartreuse region**. Chartreuse liquor originated at the **Grand Chartreuse Monastery**. It is now produced in the town of Voiron where you can visit the **Chartreuse Distillery**.

West of Grenoble is the **Vercors regional park**. Follow D531 up into the park where you'll find mountain villages, waterfalls and deep dark gorges. Don't take a trailer or large rig, some of the roads are narrow with low rocky overhangs.

Lyons (Lyon), France

Population 425,000

France's second largest city, Lyons, is something of a crossroads. If you are traveling south to the Riviera or Italy or east to the Alps you are likely to pass through the town. Stop and take a look around. There's a campground north of the city with frequent easy bus service downtown. Once there you'll find that most of the places you want to go will be within easy walking distance. If not, Lyons has a subway system.

You might take a stroll toward the **Basilique Notre-Dame de Fourvière**, visible on the hill to the west. At the foot of the hill you'll find the **Vieux Lyon**, the old section of town, filled with old mansions, restaurants, and shops. Since the city is famous for its food you may get sidetracked and never make it up to the Basilique with its fine view of town. If you do climb the hill you can also take in the **Théâtres Romains**, two excavated amphitheaters built by the Romans and still in use. They're located a few blocks behind the basilica.

Lyons also has France's second-largest museum after the Louvre. It's called the **Musée des Beaux Arts** and is located in a 17th-century convent on the place des Terraux.

Lyons Campground

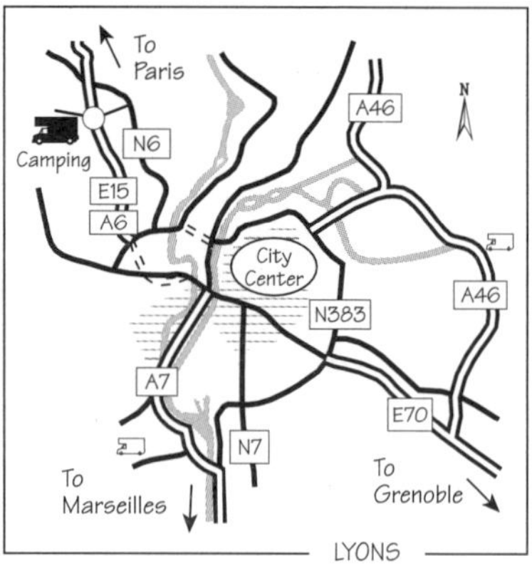

✦ LA PORTE DE LYON

Address: Porte de Lyon, 69570 Dardilly
Telephone: 04 78 35 64 55
Price: Moderate

Open all year

Camping Lyon is part of a large tourist lodging complex about 9 kilometers north of Lyons. The campground is surrounded by hotels and a large supermarket. The people staying here seem to be doing business in Lyons or making a quick stop on their way to somewhere else.

The campground is large, sites are arranged along paved avenues. Sites without electricity are very good, grassy and separated by trees with lots of shade. Sites with electricity (French plugs) are on gravel and closer together with no separation. There are several shower/toilet buildings, the main one in the reception building is heated for winter use and has adjustable hot showers. Other facilities include a swimming pool, television room, bar, restaurant, small store, and playgrounds. A large Mammoth supermarket is on the far side of the freeway about a kilometer from the campground.

Bus number 19 will take you to the Hôtel de Ville area in the middle of town. Going the other way the campground is the next-to-the-last stop, called Camping International.

The easiest way to find the campground is from A6 even if you normally don't use the toll roads. Take the Limonest Exit north of Lyons. Follow signs for Porte de Lyon to the west , then the Complexe Touristique, and then the campground. The campground is close to the freeway.

Side Trips from Lyons

The great monastery of **Cluny** is located about 80 kilometers north of Lyons near the city of Mâcon. Not much is left today of this most important of French monasteries but for 500 years, until the building of St. Peters in Rome, the abbey church here was the largest and most impressive building in Europe and the monastic order based here the most powerful.

MONT-ST-MICHEL, FRANCE

If you decide to visit **Mont-St-Michel**, and you should, don't do it on a weekend or holiday. This world-famous abbey and cathedral, situated on an offshore rock, attracts so many people that the line of cars sometimes runs down the rock from the abbey, across the causeway to the mainland, and then five kilometers inland. You can beat the crowds and enjoy the site by picking the time for your visit and by doing something that the majority of the tourists can't do. You can spend the night just outside the walls of the island village.

Almost-Free Camping In The Mont-St-Michel Parking Lot

There is a public parking area along the causeway just outside the city entrance. A large area is set aside for campers. There is a parking fee that covers a twenty-four hour period, but you can actually park for free from 7 PM to 6 AM (or maybe a little later). We call it "almost-free camping". There are no facilities except a public toilet just inside the city gate (small fee). Things slow down considerably when the tour busses leave in the evening. This isn't a great place to stay when the weather is bad, also, watch where you park. The incoming tides here are known for their height and speed.

NANTES, FRANCE

Population 245,000

Astride the Loire River but west of the area generally known as the Loire Valley is the city of Nantes. While it is large, Nantes has a relaxed pace, a very good municipal campground and a medieval district next to the river. Historically Nantes was part of Brittany but today the city is the capital of Pays de la Loire and is a major inland seaport.

The massive **Château des Ducs de Bretagne** seems more castle than château. You can walk the walls and visit the **Musée des Salorges**, a naval museum that deals primarily with the slave trade, Nantes shippers were heavily involved in it. The nearby **Cathédrale St-Pierre** is late Gothic and contains the tomb of Françoise II, the Duke who was largely responsible for building the Château des Ducs in its present form.

The Erdre and Sèvre Rivers enter the Loire at Nantes and boats cruise the rivers which have many châteaux along the shores. This is also Muscadet wine country.

Nantes Campground

✦ CAMPING DU PETIT PORT

Address: 21 Boulevard de Petit-Port,
44300 Nantes
Telephone: 02 40 74 47 94 Fax: 02 51 84 94 50
Price: Moderate

Open all year

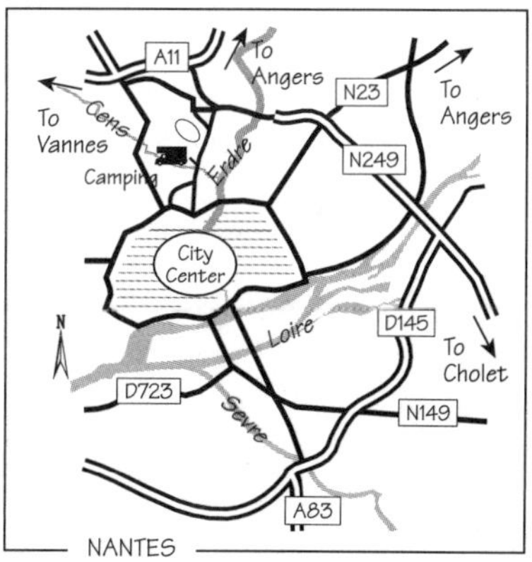

Val de Cens is a large above-average municipal campground, and in France that is saying a lot. It is only 3 kilometers from the city's center, by far the most convenient campground in Nantes.

The campground sites are arranged along two long parallel driveways. The sites for wheeled vehicles are separated from each other by hedges and shrubs. There are no permanent resident rigs. Tent sites are in a separate area. Electricity (6 or 10 amps) is available to most wheeled-vehicle sites, as is water and a drain. The shower/toilet buildings are well maintained and have hot water for showers and basins. The campground has a small shop during the summer. There is a nice walking path along a small stream (the Cens) that passes the campground and a swimming pool, restaurant, and shops are nearby. Tram service to the center of town is just outside the campground gate.

Find the campground by following signs north from the center of town. It is in the same area as the university. The hippodrome (horse track), which is often better signed, sits just northwest of the campground.

NARBONNE, FRANCE

Population 43,000

Narbonne was once the most important Roman port in southern France. Even after it was eclipsed by other Roman towns farther east and through the Middle Ages it continued to be a prosperous place, but like several other old ports you'll see in Europe, its river silted up and it went into decline. Here you can actually see evidence of the flight of prosperity. The grandiose **Cathédrale St-Just et St-Pasteur** has only a chancel, the transept was abandoned when the money started to dry up. Also take a look at the **Horreum**, underground Roman grain storage bins under the city's restored medieval quarter.

Narbonne Campground

✦ CAMPING LES ROCHES GRISES

Address: 11100 Narbonne
Telephone: 04 68 41 75 41
Price: Moderate

Open all year

Camping Les Roches Grises is open all year and close enough to the freeway to make a good overnight stop as you are traveling across southern France. It's also a good place to stay while taking a look at Narbonne.

This is a medium-sized campground with sites on gentle terraces above the main services building. Pine trees provide shade. The sites are numbered but not separated, the surface is hard dirt and gravel with some grass. Electricity (CEE17plugs, various amps) is available but boxes are quite a distance apart. There are two shower/toilet areas, one has hot water for showers (push-button, premixed), bathroom basins, and for dishwashing and clothes washing. The main building also houses a snack bar/shop and laundry equipment. There is a swimming pool and playground.

Narbonne is about 5 kilometers from the campground. There is bus service but this isn't really a difficult parking town. There seem to be enough supermarkets on

Narbonne's outskirts to serve three towns this size so shopping is easy.

From Narbonne or the Narbonne Sud Exit of the freeway follow N9 toward Perpignan, you'll see the campground sign pointing up the slope to the right about 4 kilometers out of town.

PARIS AND THE ILE DE FRANCE

Population 9,000,000

Many people think that Paris is the most fascinating city in the world. You could easily spend a year visiting Paris and still not see and do everything. Long before you were finished you'd be ready to start over.

The sights of Paris are well documented elsewhere, the listing here is very incomplete. We will try to give you a mental picture of the region's arrangement and an idea of where you might camp and how you can get around. There are many guides to the city available, you'll definitely need one of them as well as a good map. McDonald's puts out a popular tourist map and sells it in their hamburger stores.

Paris is a giant city, the greater Paris area, called the Ile de France, has over 9 million people. There is a 35 kilometer ring road around the center of Paris, the Ville, which has over 2 million inhabitants. You'll probably have no reason to drive inside the ring road which is good since traffic is terrible. All of our campgrounds are located outside it. Paris has a wonderful subway or Metro system, it is said that no point inside the ring road is more than half a kilometer from a Metro station.

The Seine River winds its way through the Ile de France and the city. It provides a reference for keeping track of where you are. The geographic center of the city is an island, the **Ile de la Cité**. On this small island you will find several important tourist sites: **Notre Dame Cathedral**, **Sainte-Chapelle**, the **Conciergerie** and the **Crypte Archéologique**.

The **Left Bank** of the Seine (facing downstream of course) near the Ile de la Cité is the student quarter, the **Sorbonne** is located here. The **St-Germain-des-Prés** quarter, and the **Luxembourg Gardens** are nearby. As you move downstream along the river you'll pass the **Musée d'Orsay**, **Les Invalides**, and the **Eiffel Tower**.

On the right bank near the Ile de la Cité are the **Marais** and **Beauborg** quarters where you'll find the **Pompidou Center**, and the **Musée Picasso**. Downstream is the **Musée du Louvre,** probably the world's most complete and impressive art museum. From the Louvre you can pass through the **Jardin des Tuileries** and across the **Place de la Concorde** to the head of the Champs-Elysées. Strolling up the boulevard you'll eventually reach the **Arc de Triomphe** and be able to see **La Défense** in the distance at the far end outside the ring road.

Everything mentioned above except La Défense is in a fairly compact central area. Farther afield but still inside the ring road are the **Sacré-Coeur** and **Montmartre**, **Montparnasse** and the **Cimetière du Père Lachaise** and the **Cité des Sciences** museum.

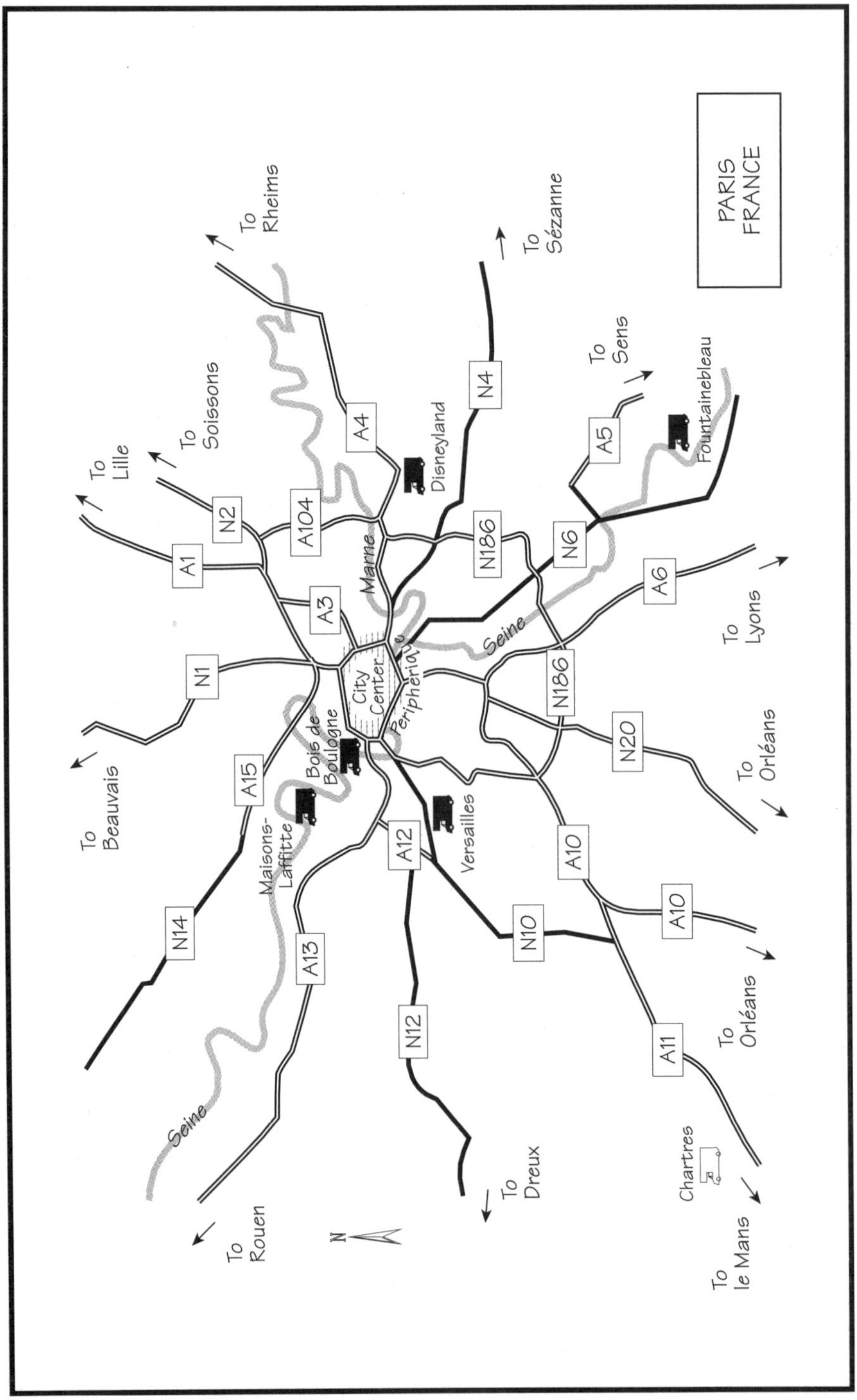
PARIS
FRANCE
To Rheims
To Sézanne
To Sens
Fountainebleau
To Soissons
To Lille
Disneyland
To Lyons
To Orléans
To Beauvais
Bois de Boulogne
Maisons-Laffitte
Versailles
City Center
Periphérique
Marne
Seine
To Dreux
To Rouen
Chartres
To le Mans
N
A1
N2
A104
A4
N4
A5
N6
N186
A6
A3
N1
N20
A15
A12
A10
N14
A13
N10
N12
A11

To go even farther afield, outside the ring road, you can still use public transportation. The RER (suburban rail lines) and the SNCF (national railroad) are well integrated with the Metro subway system. RER tickets can be purchased from easy-to-understand machines and will take you well outside the city. In fact, three of the four campgrounds we describe below are conveniently tied to the Metro stations of central Paris by the RER.

You may want to consider visiting some of the following destinations in the surrounding countryside: **Versailles** (description with campground below), **Fontainebleau** (description with campground below), the **Château de Vaux-le-Vicomte**, or even **Euro Disney** (description with campground below).

The Bois de Boulogne campground is the closest to Paris. The four others we've described are located near popular destinations and make convenient bases for visiting Paris and the Ile de France.

Paris Campground

✦ CAMPING DU BOIS DE BOULOGNE

Address: Allée du Bord de l'Eau, 75016 Paris
Telephone: 01 45 24 30 00 Fax: 01 42 24 42 95
Price: Moderate

Open all year

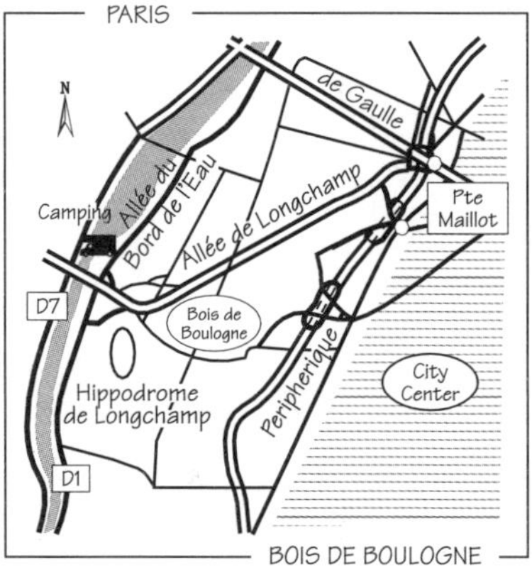

Camping du Bois de Boulogne is probably most people's first choice for a stay in Paris. You should give it at least one visit. It is located in the Bois de Boulogne just outside the Paris ring road and is really the only campground actually in Paris. It is set right on the bank of the Seine River, is large, and is usually crowded. Sites have been being upgraded lately, almost all now are separated by hedges and most have convenient electricity (French plugs, 10 amps), water, and even drains. Grass is scarce, most sites are gravel or dirt. You probably won't spend much time in your rig or tent however, Paris beckons. The shower/toilet building is old but serviceable, it has hot (premixed, push button valves) showers, dishwashing facilities and a laundry area. The campground offers a good grocery store and a bar/cafe.

Access to the city is convenient. During the summer there is a shuttle bus from the campground to the Port Maillot metro station, at other times city bus service is about half a kilometer away, with convenient metro connections. The walk to the subway line is not impossible, in forty minutes you can walk across the park to the Port Maillot station or, more easily, down the river to the Pont de Neuilly station which is quite a bit closer.

Finding the campground is not a difficult challenge if you have some notion of where it is. Take the Port Maillot Exit from the ring road and then follow the campground signs. Bear in mind that the campground is on the far side of the Bois de Boulogne from the freeway exit, at some points the signs are a little confusing but there are so many routes through and around the park that you'll eventually be successful. Probably the worst traffic is on a sunny weekend afternoon in the spring when every person in Paris seems to be in the Bois.

VERSAILLES

When you visit Paris it is not really necessary to camp in Paris itself. You will find that use of the RER (suburban rail line) makes Versailles just as convenient as the Bois de Boulogne. Here you have the added convenience of being close to the most impressive château and gardens in France.

The **Versailles Château** is huge, when it was built it was so admired by other European monarchs that you will find it the model for similar palaces throughout Europe. It is the most popular destination in France outside Paris and the crowds can be terrible. If you camp nearby you can get there early or late to avoid long lines. Don't miss the huge gardens.

Versailles Campground

✦ CAMPING MUNICIPAL DE PORCHEFONTAINE

Address: 31 Rue Marcelin-Berthelot, Porchefontaine, 78000 Versailles
Telephone: 01 39 51 23 61
Price: Moderate

Open April 1 to October 31, varies slightly

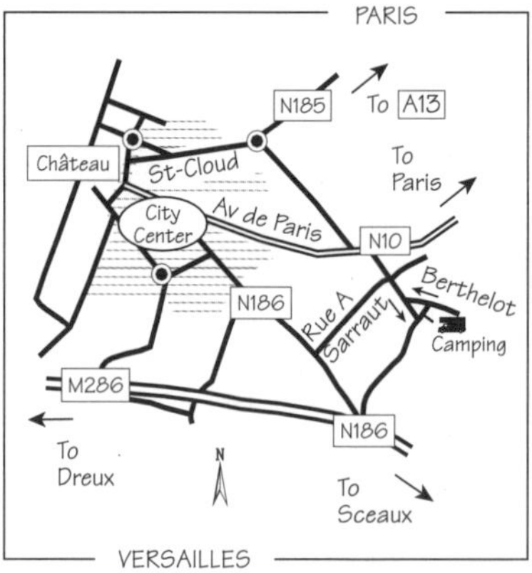

The campground sits in a grove of trees that slopes towards Porchefontaine, a Versailles suburb. Some of the sites with electricity (6 amps) sit in a grassy area outside the trees, otherwise you just park where you can find a flat spot in the mossy gravel under the trees. The campground is large, and since sites are not demarcated, there are lots of them, although you'll have trouble finding a flat one if the campground is crowded. Small toilet buildings with continental toilets are scattered around the campground, a large building with adjustable hot showers and areas for dish and clothes washing is at the foot of the slope near the entrance. A small trailer kiosk provides some supplies. There is a sports facility next door with swimming pool and running track and a forest above the campground with hiking paths. Restaurants are within easy walking distance.

Public transportation to Versailles and to Paris are conveniently located near the campground. The Porchefontaine station for bus B is nearby, it will take you to the Versailles Chateau. RER train service to the Paris-Invalides station is accessible at the Porchefontaine station only a half kilometer from the campground. The walk to the château is about 4 kilometers.

The campground has good signage making it easy to find. It is just off Avenue de Paris which is the large boulevard which starts at the château and heads east, eventually becoming N10 to Paris. If you start at the château and drive east on Avenue de Paris you'll want to turn right after about 2 kilometers. Signs for the campground will say Camping Parc des Sports de Porchefontaine.

FONTAINEBLEAU

Historically **Fontainebleau Château** preceded that at Versailles. Many kings made contributions to the château but today it reflects mostly those of Françoise I and Napoléon. Smaller than Versailles and not quite so over-the-top, the château and surrounding gardens are a pleasure to visit. It is also usually not nearly as crowded as Versailles.

Fontainbleau Campground

✦ SAMOREAU CAMPING CARAVANING COMMUNAL

Address: 77210 Samoreau
Telephone: 01 64 23 72 25
Price: Moderate

Open summer only

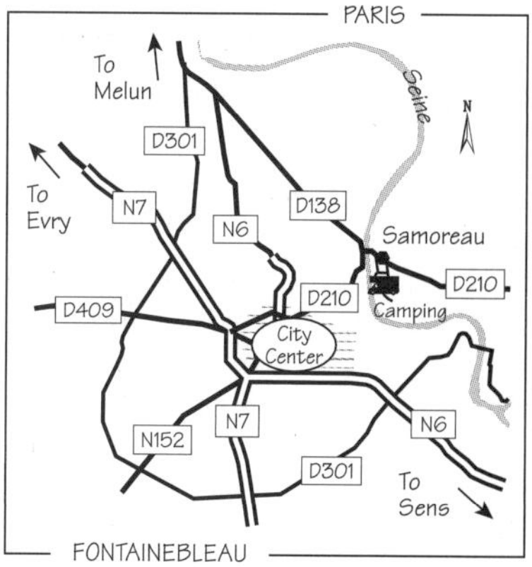

There are several smaller campgrounds on the banks of the Seine to the east of Fontainebleau. This is a small quiet one, yet there's bus transportation to Fontainebleau and train transportation to Paris nearby.

The Samoreau Campground is a grassy field that slopes to the banks of the Seine. There are generally a few long-termers here, not really permanents, but close. The river is pretty quiet but it's nice to watch the occasional barge pass. Sites are in two fields separated by a hedge, both sides have electricity. The shower/toilet area is older but adequate, hot showers are available. This small town has a few restaurants and shops, most of the action is in Fontainebleau, about 4 kilometers to the west.

The local bus is infrequent, you'll have to plan your trips carefully if you wish to use it. There's a train station within a kilometer but trains to Paris from it are also infrequent, more planning. A busier train station about 3 kilometers in the direction of Fontainebleau is probably more convenient if you wish to travel in to Paris.

To find the campground examine your Fontainebleau area map carefully and find the Seine. Samoreau is one of the small towns along the river, once you reach it you can't miss the campground.

MAISONS-LAFFITTE

The small prosperous town of Maisons-Laffitte is located next to the Seine to the northwest of Paris. It has shops and restaurants and makes a very pleasant base for your Paris visits. An added bonus is the town's **Maisons-Laffitte Château.** It was built by the architect Mansard (you've seen his roofs) and finished in 1651 during Louis XIV's reign. The town also has a horse-racing track.

Maisons-Laffitte Campground

✦ **CAMPING CARAVANING INTERNATIONAL MAISONS-LAFFITTE**

Address: Ile de la Commune, 1 Rue Johnson, 78600 Maisons-Laffitte
Telephone: 01 39 12 21 91 Fax: 01 34 93 02 60
Price: Moderate

Open all year

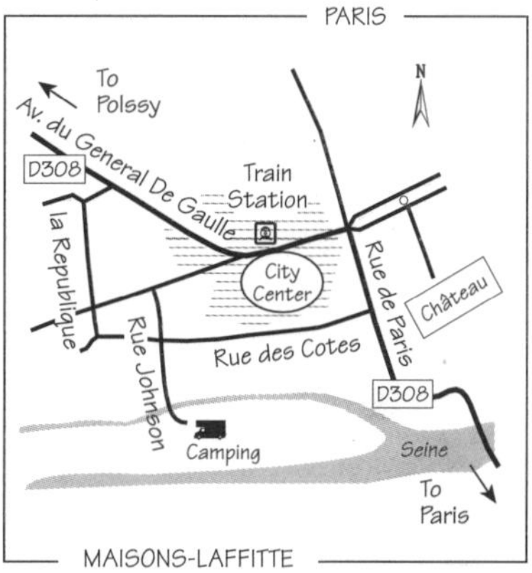

Camping International is another popular base for exploring Paris. Located on the bank of the Seine some 15 kilometers outside the ring road it has the advantage of being in a relaxed small town while having very convenient public transportation to Paris.

The large campground occupies flat ground that is actually an island. Sites are large and mostly separated by small hedges, surfaces are grass or packed dirt, many trees provide quite a bit of shade. There are many rental mobile homes here, they occupy about a third of the sites. Electricity (4 or 10 amps, French plugs) is available but outlets are widely spaced. The shower/toilet buildings are older but clean, premixed hot water is piped to push button valves in showers, bathroom basins, dishwashing sinks, and laundry tubs. The campground has a bar/pizzeria/restaurant and grocery shop on the bank of the river. Other amenities include a playground and laundry facilities. The campground is a ten minute walk from central Maisons-Laffitte with it's train station and shops. The trip to Paris on RER trains is inexpensive and connects you directly with the subways. There are supermarkets near the train station in Maisons-Laffitte and the château is about five minutes on the far side of the train station.

To find the campground you can drive one of many routes to Maisons-Laffitte which is located northwest of Paris and a short distance northeast of St-Germain. The campground is well signed from all of the major routes into town. It lies on the river bank just upstream from the central part of town.

DISNEYLAND PARIS

Would you go all the way to Europe and then visit Disneyland? You might enjoy it, if only to see how Disney translates into French. The theme park is located about 25 kilometers east of Paris just off the A4 autoroute. And disneyland Paris has its own campground!

Disneyland Campground

✦ Davy Crocket Ranch

Address: BP 117, F-77777
Marne-la-Vallée Cedex 4
Telephone: 01 60 45 69 00 Fax: 01 60 45 69 33
Price: Very, very expensive

Open March 30 to October 31

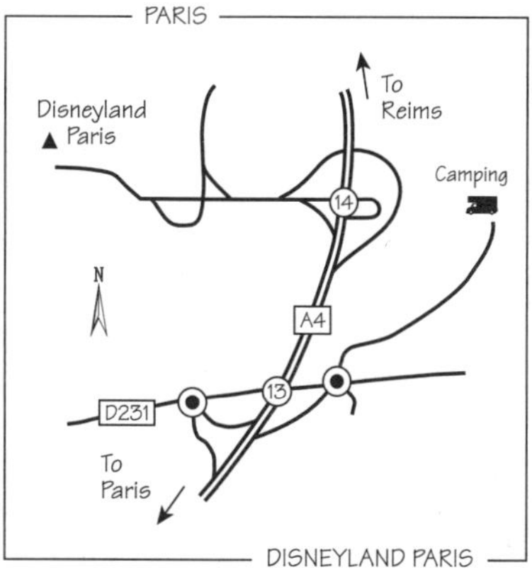

This must be the most expensive campground we've ever visited, over $60 U.S. (in French francs of course) during the fall. We had to spend the night here just so we could say we'd done it.

Davy Crocket Ranch is located several kilometers from Disneyland on the far side of the autoroute. There's really more than just a campground. Most of the visitors stay in prefab mobile units guissied up to look like log cabins. There's a central village with Crocket's Tavern, the Saloon, the Alamo Trading Post, and the Blue Springs Pool. Disney characters including Goofy and Mickey visit the village square and meet the kids. There's also horseback riding, pony rides, a small animal park, and tennis.

The actual camping area must be the most interesting part of the operation to the European visitors. It is much like a North American campground, nothing like you'd see anywhere else in Europe. Rigs back into individual sites separated by undisturbed natural buffer areas, much like you'd see in a government campground in the U.S. Each site has it's own paved parking; electrical (CEE17 plugs, high amp), water, and sewer hook-ups; and even a North American-style wooden picnic table. The sanitary facilities are more French-style. They're modern with unlimited hot water in showers (push-button valves) and sinks. Access to Disneyland is by shuttle bus. If you want to stay here it is a good idea to make reservations, the campground is very popular. There's also a nearby golf course.

To find the campground just head east from Paris on the A9. Take Exit 13 which immediately enters a roundabout. The entrance drive to the campground is the third exit from the roundabout.

Poitiers and St-Maixent-l'Ecole

Poitiers Population 85,000

Poitiers is known for it's charming historic area along the Clain River. Especially admired are its churches: **Notre-Dame-le-Grande**, the **Cathédrale St-Pierre**, the **Eglise Ste-Radegoned**, **The Baptistère St-Jean** and the **Eglise St-Hilaire-le-Grand**. Poitiers is 45 kilometers northeast of St-Maixent on the A10 autoroute.

St-Maixent in not only a good base for exploring the Poitiers area, the village is an attraction itself. It has a medieval old town and its Flamboyant Gothic **abbey church** is one of François Le Duc's most admired reconstructions.

St-Maixent-l'Ecole Campground

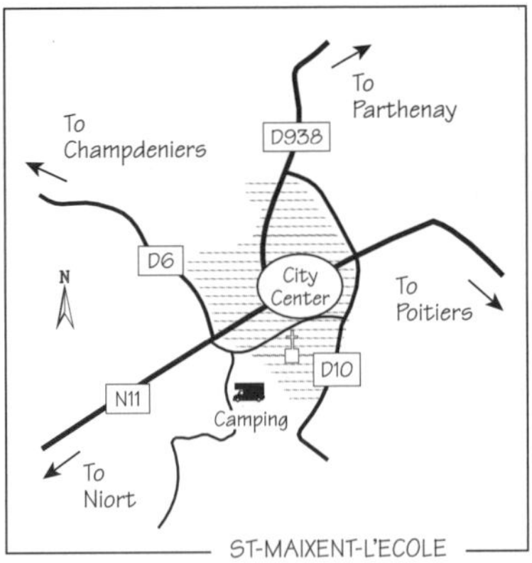

✦ CAMPING MUNICIPAL DU PANIER FLEURI

Address: 79400 St-Maixent-l'Ecole
Telephone: 05 49 05 53 21
Price: Inexpensive

Open all year

If you are traveling the A10 autoroute between Paris and Spain, especially in the winter when most campgrounds are closed, this little municipal campground is a great find.

The medium-sized campground is set in a municipal park along with a swimming pool and several large sports fields. The campground is mostly flat with manicured grass sites. Electricity (French plugs, 5 amps) is available to most sites from widely-spaced boxes. Shower/toilet buildings have hot showers, bathroom basins, and dishwashing sinks. In winter they are closed and a small prefabricated unit is substituted. It is kept toasty warm and has free hot showers (adjustable), bathroom basins, and dishwashing sinks. In winter the warden is only around in the morning and evening, you can set up and plug in, he'll come around and collect later. If the gate into the campground is locked you can walk in and find someone at the house near the reception window. The campground is about a kilometer up the hill from the old town so a bus isn't really necessary. You'll find several supermarkets near the old town with good parking.

The town and campground are about 15 kilometers off the A10 autoroute on the N11 secondary road about 12 kilometers north of Niort. Take either Exit 31 or 32 and follow signs to St-Maixent. The campground is located near the top of the hill at the southwest end of town. The turn is at a stoplight, Highway D6 goes in one direction and the road to the campground the other. The campground is not signed at this turn if you are heading north but is if you are heading south.

Side Trips from Poitiers and St-Maixent-l'Ecole

Forty kilometers from St-Maixent-l'Ecole on the far side of industrial Niort is the small town of **Coulon**. Coulon is the gateway to the **Marais Poitevin regional natural park**, an area of marshes known as the **Venise Verte** or Green Venice. Full of weedy canals, orchids, and water lilies, they can be toured in small boats either with or without a guide.

Futuroscope is a giant theme park built around several futuristic cinemas. It is just off the A10 north of Poitiers. Kids love it.

QUIMPER, FRANCE

Population 61,000

Quimper is a Breton cathedral town located on the south coast of Brittany. The Steir and Odet Rivers flow through Quimper which has a pleasant riverside promenade. The **Vieux Quimper** area nearby is pedestrianized and a good place to shop for Quimper's most famous product: faïence hand painted pottery. A short stroll down the river is the **Faïenceries HB-Henriot** factory which has tours and a museum. Worth a look is the **Cathédrale St-Corentin**, also in the Vieux Quimper area. Something to watch for–it is reported that during bad storms people in Quimper can feel the waves hitting the rocky coastline 19 miles away.

The quiet municipal campground is close to town and reasonably priced. Quimper is also home to L'ORANGERIE DE LANNIRON, a large campground belonging to the Castels and Camping Caravaning organization. It is farther from town and much more expensive.

Quimper Campground

✦ CAMPING MUNICIPAL BOIS DU SEMINAIRE

Address: 29000 Quimper
Telephone: 02 98 55 47 21
Price: Inexpensive

Open all year

The municipal campground site is in a wooded area with quite a bit of shade but also some sun. Sites are separated and most have electricity available. The shower/toilet building is older but in good repair and has hot showers on payment.

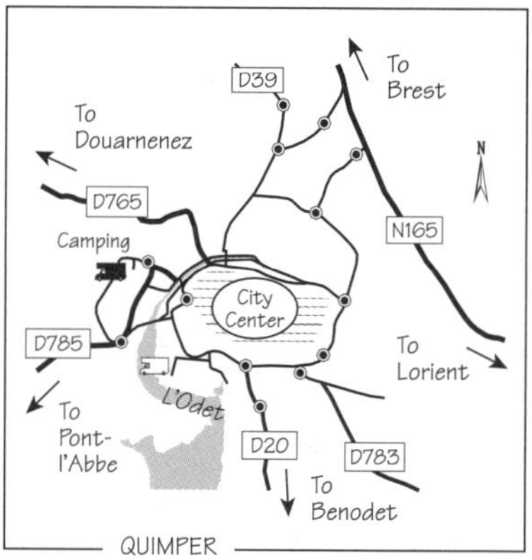

The city of Quimper has all the shopping and restaurants you could wish. Access by bus is convenient, the number 1 bus stops at the Chaptal stop near the campground entrance. If you are willing to walk or ride a bike to the city center the distance is about 1.5 kilometers.

You can most easily find the campground by starting on the right bank of the river below the central business area. Follow signs for Pont l'Abbé away from the river on Rue de Pont l'Abbé, go straight ahead where the main road turns at the second intersection, you'll see the campground on the left just after this turn.

RHEIMS (REIMS), FRANCE

Population 185,000

Located about 145 kilometers northeast of Paris, Rheims offers two good reasons for you to visit. It is home to one of France's most important Gothic cathedrals, the **Cathedral Notre-Dame**. This is the traditional site where the kings of France were crowned. It is also the center of France's champagne industry. The town is home to the major producers and cellar tours are available. Try **Mumm** and **Taittinger**. The rolling countryside around Rheims is covered with yellow flowers and grape vines. World War II buffs will want to see the **Salle de Reddition** where the German surrender was signed in Eisenhower's post-war headquarters.

Rheims Campground

✦ CAMP MUNICIPAL VAL-DE-VESLE

Address: 51360 Val-de-Vesle
Telephone: 03 26 03 91 79
Price: Inexpensive

Open April 15 to October 30

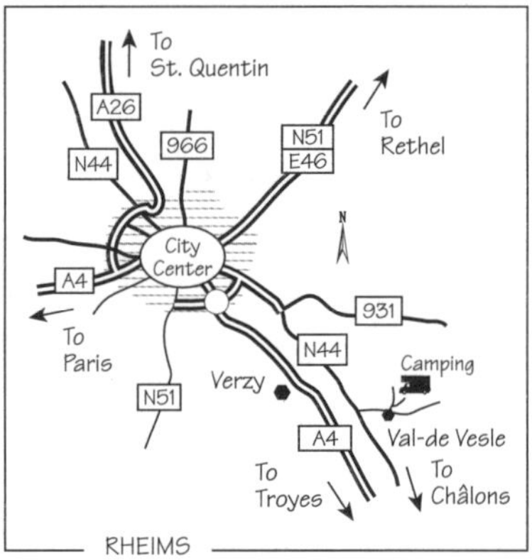

While there is no longer a convenient campground in Reims there is an excellent municipal campground in the very small village of Val-de-Vesle about 15 kilometers southeast.

This is a typical medium-sized French village municipal campground with room for about 100 rigs or tents. It is a large grassy field with shade trees located in the middle of farming country at the outskirts of the village. Parking is on grass, spaces are not delineated or assigned. Electrical boxes are widely spaced (French, 6 amps). The bathroom building is older but has hot water for showers and sinks. You can wander into town to find a small store and restaurant and say hello to the locals.

To reach the campground drive southeast from Reims on N44. After approximately 14 kilometers you will see a couple of tall grain silos across the fields to your left. These mark the village. The road left to the village is signed Val-de-Vesle. Follow it into town and then take the signed left in the center of the village to the campground.

ROUEN, FRANCE

Population 105,000

You may be surprised to hear that this inland city is France's fifth largest port. Rouen is conveniently located between Paris and the Normandy coast and was the city where Joan of Arc was executed by the British during the 100 Years War. You will find her well remembered here, most strikingly by the **Eglise Jeanne d'Arc** on the **Place du Vieux Marché** where she was burned at the stake. The city suffered quite a bit of damage during World War II so a lot of it is new, but there are also many older buildings that were either undamaged or that have been restored. One of these is the **Notre Dame Cathedral**, one of France's best known Gothic cathedrals, perhaps because of

Claude Monet's series of impressionist paintings of its' facade. The old town around the cathedral has old half-timbered houses, shops, restaurants, and walking streets.

Rouen Campground

✦ Camping Municipal

Address: 76250, Déville-lès-Rouen
Telephone: 02 35 74 07 59
Price: Inexpensive

Open March 1 to December 31

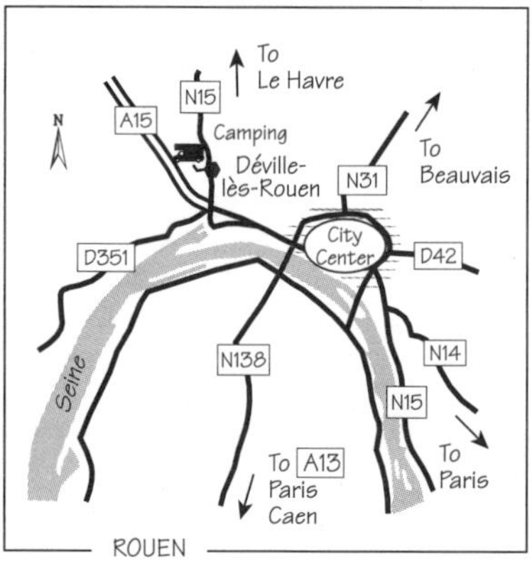

Camping Municipal has no outstanding features but it is convenient and clean. It is a small facility with parking for vans, coaches, and caravans arranged on gravel around the outside walls and a grassy tent area in the middle. There's no shade and the vehicle spaces are not separated by shrubbery. Electricity is provided around the circumference, long cords are necessary for some sites. The shower/toilet building is located at the entrance, adjustable hot showers are provided. There is a small supermarket nearby, also smaller shops.

The number 2 bus passes by the campground frequently. From downtown you want to get off at the Marie stop in the suburb of Déville-lès-Rouen.

Finding the campground is not difficult although there are no signs from downtown. Follow the street that runs along the north side of the river toward the west. It is variously named Quai du Havre, and Quai Gaston-Boulet. This road will become N15 as it leaves town, do not let yourself be shunted onto the A15 autoroute. In the suburb of Déville-lès-Rouen, about 4 kilometers from the city center where you started, you'll see a camping sign pointed down the hill to your left. The campground is about a block down this hill on the right.

St-Emilion, France

This beautiful little town is everything that you would expect in a Bordeaux wine village but that most are not. It has old stone houses and vineyards surrounding it on all sides. There are lots of wine shops and restaurants. The fact that the town is frequented by tourists is good, not bad. You can enjoy the atmosphere and avoid the high prices by staying at the great campground just north of town.

You can take a ride on the wine train through some of the nearby vineyards. One of the best, **Château Ausone,** is just outside town. Check at the tourist office for vineyards open for guests. The town also has an underground church called the **Eglise Monolithe** and a castle built by Henry III of England, the **Château du Roi.**

St-Emilion Campground

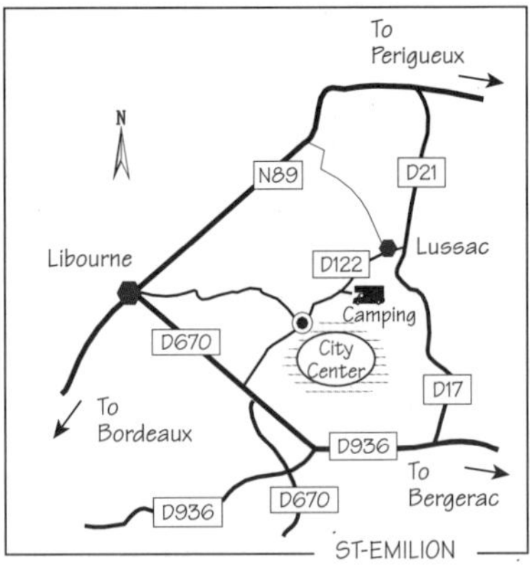

✦ CAMPING LA BARBANNE

Address: 33330 St-Emilion
Telephone: 05 57 24 75 80
Price: Moderate

Open April 5 to October 10

The campground is large, about 150 sites. They are placed in a grassy field with a paved access road and shade trees. Sites are not numbered, separated, or assigned. There are no permanently situated caravans. A small lake is adjacent to the campground and some of the nicer sites are facing it. Electricity (6 amps) is available to about half the sites. Hot water is provided for showers (adjustable) and bathroom basins. There is a small bar/restaurant and a grocery shop. Other facilities include a swimming pool, fishing in the small lake, tennis courts and bicycle hire. There's a nice walking path around the lake although the distance is only about half of a kilometer. The campground also has its own wine label, you'll probably want to buy a bottle.

St-Emilion is about 3 kilometers south of the campground along a country road. You can easily ride a bicycle or walk to town, there is no bus.

St-Emilion is located just east of Libourne. The campground is about 2.5 kilometers north of St-Emilion just off Highway D122 to Montagne and Lussac.

ST-QUAY-PORTRIEUX, FRANCE

St-Quay-Portrieux is a small town on Brittany's rocky eastern coast. It has a picturesque boat harbor that goes dry at low tide and an engaging easygoing atmosphere that makes it a fine place to relax and forget sightseeing. Just enjoy the view from your campsite and wander along the cliffs until you've recharged those batteries and are ready to hit the road again.

St-Quay-Portrieux Campground

✦ CAMPING BELLEVUE

Address: 68, Blvd. du Littoral, 22410 St-Quay-Portrieux
Telephone: 02 96 70 41 84 Fax: 02 96 70 55 46
Price: Moderate

Open May 1 to September 15

Camping Bellevue is an ocean-side campground perched on a rocky bluff above the Brittany coast. You can easily lose several days here while you hike the trail above the bluff and explore the tide pools in the rocky coves.

This is a medium-sized family-run campground. It sits at the top of a bluff and on terraced sites below. Many of the sites have great views, especially the lower ones without electricity. The shower/toilet facilities are older but clean and in good repair, hot water is provided for showers, bathroom basins, and dishwashing. There's a great trail that runs for miles above the ocean and the nearby cove is used by many for sun bathing. Shopping and restaurants in St-Quay are within one kilometer.

To reach the campground follow signs from near the St-Quay harbor. They'll take you north on small roads just back from the coast for about 1 kilometer to the campground.

STRASBOURG, FRANCE

Population 430,000

Strasbourg, located just a short distance from the Rhine, is in a much-disputed area, the Alsace. Both France and Germany have controlled the city at various times, and the influence of the two cultures on the town is what makes it unique. The Alsace is an important wine-growing region, and as you would expect Alsatian cuisine is outstanding.

The tourist center of the town is the **Cathédral Notre-Dame** with its one lacy tower and pink sandstone. Surrounding the cathedral and its square is the old town, which is in turn surrounded by water. The Ill River separates and runs on both sides of Strasbourg. The old town is full of museums and pedestrian shopping streets. Don't forget to stroll through the small **Petite France** section which has cobblestone streets and restaurants along the river.

Strasbourg Campground

✦ CAMPING MONTAGNE VERTE

Address: 2 Rue Robert Forrer,
67200 Strasbourg
Telephone: 03 88 30 25 46
Price: Moderate

Open all year

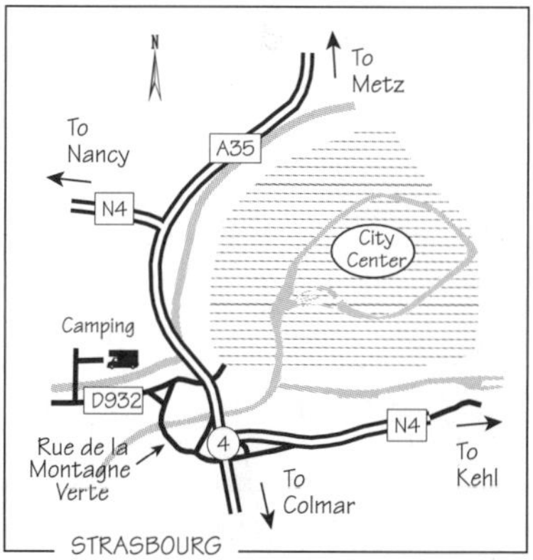

Camping Montagne Verte is located in the suburb of Montagne Verte just southwest of Strasbourg. The walk to the old city takes 40 minutes, there's also convenient and frequent bus service.

The large campground has sites arranged on grass off paved driveways that circle around a field with scattered trees, some quite large. Individual sites are numbered and assigned at the reception office. Electricity is available at widely scattered boxes (CEE17 plugs, mostly 4 amps). The two shower/toilet buildings are modern and clean with plenty of facilities for the size of the campground. Hot showers are free (push-button valves, not adjustable). Hot water is also available in bathroom basins and dishwashing sinks. The campground has coin-operated washers and dryer. It also has a small kiosk selling limited groceries and meals, tennis courts, a playground, and a volleyball court.

To reach the city from the campground you must walk about 500 meters to the main street running through Montagne Verte. Catch the 3 or the 23 bus. Alternately you can walk the 4 kilometers in to town, the route has good sidewalks the entire distance.

Finding the campground is not difficult if you remember that it is located in the suburb of Montagne Verte just southwest of town. Both the A35 highway and N4 highway have off ramps for Montagne Verte but have no campground signs until you leave the freeway. Montagne Verte is located near the junction of A35 and N4. Once you leave the freeway (Exit 4 from A35) you will see campground signs that will lead you directly to the site.

Side Trips from Strasbourg

The well-signed **Route du Vin** (wine road) begins at Marlenheim to the west of Strasbourg. It runs south past Colmar to Thann, just west of Mulhouse. You'll pass through vineyards and small medieval towns with timbered houses, winstubs, restaurants and churches. There's even a castle or two. Try hiking some of the **sentiers viticoles**, these are trails through the vineyards.

THE ROMAN PONT DU GARD NEAR NIMES

THREE OUTSTANDING REGIONS AND THEIR CAMPGROUNDS

PROVENCE AND THE CÔTE D'AZURE

Provence and the Côte d'Azure together make up the most visited region in France, it is full of fascinating towns, Roman ruins, mountains, gorges, cliffs and beaches. The area stretches from the Rhône River in the west to the Italian border in the east, a distance of over 250 kilometers. If you follow the twisting mountain or coast roads your driving route can easily be twice that distance, yet modern freeways make it possible to drive from one end to the other in three hours.

While the area is rich in natural features like seashores and mountains it also offers historical and cultural attractions. You'll probably not visit many cathedrals in this region but you will see Roman antiquities and also find that the area has many good art museums. Of course there is also the people watching along the Riviera.

NÎMES, FRANCE

Population 130,000

Just west of what is properly Provence is the thriving modern city of Nîmes. If you take a closer look, however, you'll find that Nîmes has a Roman past and today contains one of the finest collections of Roman monuments in France.

Les Arènes is the best preserved Roman amphitheater in France, it is still used for concerts and bull fights. French bull fights are different than Spanish and Mexican ones because the bulls are not killed. The **Maison Carrè** (Square House) is a Roman temple used as a model by Thomas Jefferson in his design for the Virginia capitol and the **Porte Augustus** and **Tour Magne** were both once part of the Roman walls. Also visit the pleasant 18th-century **Jardin de la Fontaine**, the site of the spring that was the reason Nîmes was located here and where you'll also find a view over the town.

Nimes Campground

✦ CAMP MUNICIPAL DE LA BASTIDE

Address: 30000 Nîmes
Telephone: 04 66 38 09 21 Fax: 04 66 38 09 21
Price: Moderate

Open all year

This campground is a convenient place to spend the night if you are entering the Provence region from the west. It is also a good place to use as a base while touring the attractions of Nîmes since traffic in town is heavy and park-

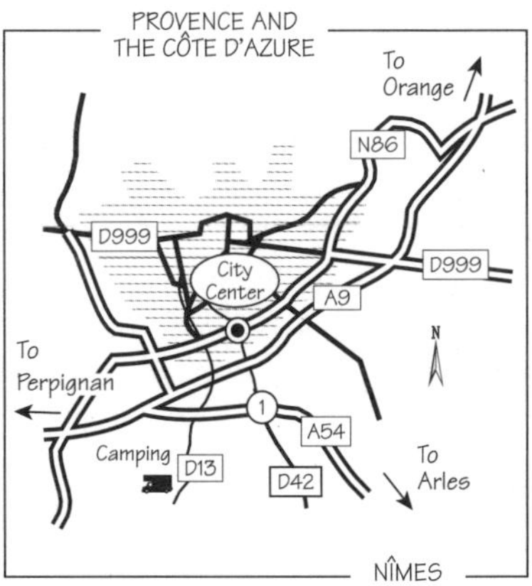

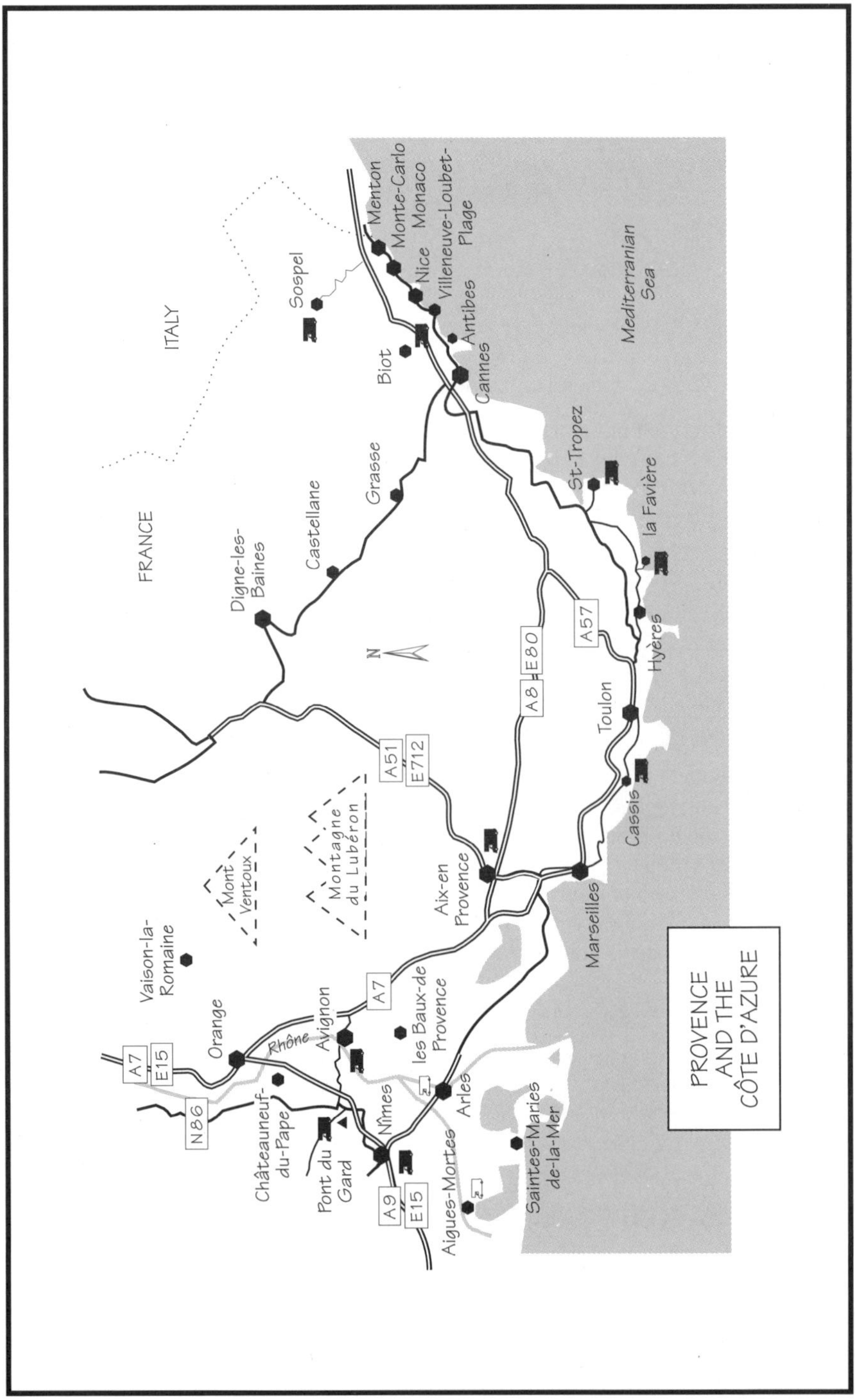
PROVENCE AND THE CÔTE D'AZURE
ITALY
FRANCE
Mediterranian Sea
N
Menton
Monte-Carlo Monaco
Nice
Villeneuve-Loubet-Plage
Antibes
Biot
Sospel
Cannes
Grasse
Castellane
Digne-les-Baines
St-Tropez
la Favière
Hyères
Toulon
Cassis
Marseilles
Aix-en Provence
Mont Ventoux
Montagne du Lubéron
Vaison-la-Romaine
Orange
Avignon
Rhône
les Baux-de Provence
Arles
Nîmes
Pont du Gard
Châteauneuf-du-Pape
Aigues-Mortes
Saintes-Maries de-la-Mer
A7
E15
N86
A9
E15
A7
A51
E712
A8
E80
A57

ing is near to impossible for large rigs.

Domaine de la Bastide campground sits outside of town surrounded by vegetable and sports fields. The facility is quite large with the spaces arranged in circles and separated by hedges. There are lots of electric and water hook-ups so you can get by with a short cord even if the campground is busy. Sanitary facilities are good with lots of hot water. There is also a small store, a bar, and a restaurant.

The campground is located about 7 kilometers south of central Nîmes. You'll see signs for it in town, including one near the Roman amphitheater, but they are a little hard to follow. Signs pointing south from N86 as it passes just south of the downtown area are better. There are also signs from the Nimes-Oest Exit of the A9 autoroute. You want to head south on D13 toward Générac, the campground will be on your right. Bus service to the campground is good, it is the final stop on the route and busses park for a few minutes before starting back to Nîmes.

Side Trips from Nîmes

Forty kilometers south of Nîmes is **Aigues-Mortes**, western entrance to the **Camarague** or Rhône Delta. The Camarague is an area of marshes, pasture land, dunes and salt flats. This large natural area is ideal for bird watching. The walled town of Aigues-Mortes (dead waters) has more than an interesting name. It is surrounded by walls built during the 13th century by St. Louis (King Louis IX). The best view of the flats surrounding the town is from the **Tour de Constance**. There's also a museum, the **Musée Jadis Aigues-Mortes**. You can drive out to the coastal town of **Saintes-Maries-de-la-Mer** where Gypsies from all over Europe gather in May. Aigues-Mortes has its own campground, CAMPING LA PETITE CAMARGUE, good if you decide that the Camargue deserves more of your time.

Twenty-five kilometers southeast of Nîmes is **Arles**. Arles, too, has its own campground, CAMPING DES ROSIERS, but the city is easily visited on a day trip. The **Roman Amphitheater** is Arles' most popular tourist site, it was built over a century before the Coliseum in Rome. Like the one in Nîmes it is used for bull fights. French bullfights are not like those in Spain, here the bull survives. Another Roman ruin is the **Théâtre Antique** (Roman Theater). There's not much of it left standing, but it is still used for performances.

From Arles you can easily drive northeast about 20 kilometers to **les Baux-de-Provence**. The town is immortalized as the place where bauxite was discovered, but has other attractions. It is a hilltop town with tiny streets and great views, but also has the **Ville Morte** (Dead Town), an area of deserted medieval ruins formerly occupied by a powerful castle. The citadel here was destroyed under the orders of Louis XIII in 1632 because it had become a troublesome Protestant stronghold.

Leaving les Baux drive north five kilometers to St-Rémy-de-Provence where Van Gogh painted *Wheat Field With Cyprus* and turn west towards Nîmes. Nîmes is forty kilometers directly west, you'll cross the Rhône where Tarascon and Beaucaire sit on opposite banks. Both of these towns have well known châteaux.

PONT DU GARD (REMOULINS), FRANCE

When you leave Nîmes to set up a new base 40 kilometers northeast in Avignon you'll want to stop along the way at the **Pont du Gard**. This well-preserved Roman aqueduct is in a peaceful country setting bridging the Gard River near Remoulins. The bridge/aqueduct is spectacular. It was built to help carry water for a canal that ran 50 kilometers from Uzés to Nîmes and was the highest bridge ever built by the Romans. You can even walk right across the top in the empty water channel.

Pont du Gard Campground

✦ CAMPING CARAVANING LA SOUSTA

Address: Avenue du Pont du Gard, 30210
Remoulins, France
Telephone: 04 66 37 12 80
Fax: 04 66 37 23 69
Price: Inexpensive

Open March 1 to October 31

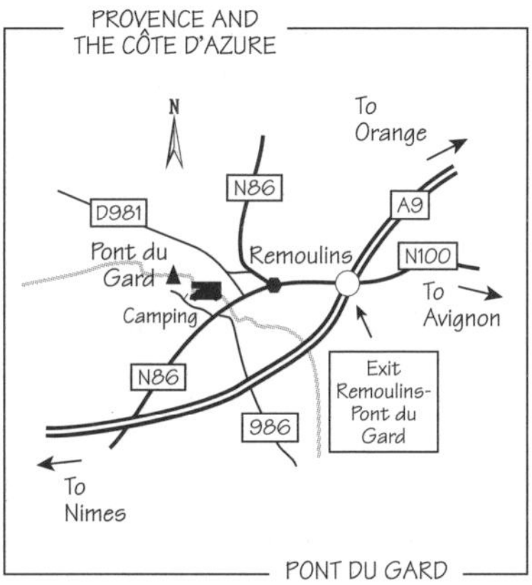

This campground makes an excellent place to stay on the evening of your visit to the Pont du Gard. You can easily hike the kilometer to the Pont du Gard or swim in the Gard River running next to the campground. You may decide to stay another week. This campground could also be a good base for exploring Avignon, the distance is about 22 kilometers.

This is a large campground with sites on grass or dirt off gravel drives. There is lots of shade. Most vehicle spaces are numbered and there is also a huge grassy tent-camping area. Electricity boxes are widely spaced and have both CEE17 and French outlets (6 amps). The shower/toilet facilities are modern, showers have push-button controlled hot showers and there is hot water at the shaving sinks, most dish and clothes sinks have cold water although there is one with hot. There is also a clothes-washing machine. Other amenities include a large swimming pool, tennis court, restaurant, basketball court, mini-golf, and a barbecue area. There are some rental trailers and cabins.

You'll have no trouble finding the campground. Follow signs to the Pont du Gard. If you are on the A9 autoroute take the Remoulins-Pont du Gard Exit. Just remember that the campground is on the right bank (rive droite) of the river, if you follow the left bank signs you can't access the campground. It is located very near the right bank parking area, just a little less than a kilometer from the Pont.

AVIGNON, FRANCE

Population 92,000

From 1309 to 1377 Avignon was an important religious town, this is where the pope lived. Today Avignon is a walled town which still shows some signs of the wealth brought by these high-living ecclesiastics. The **Palais des Papes** is their fortress-like palace and Avignon's most important sight. The **Petit Palais** was the home of a later Archbishop and is now a museum with medieval paintings. The famous **Pont St-Bénézet** is the bridge of the children's song *Sur le Pont d'Avignon*. Today it stretches only halfway across the river which is good because otherwise it would pass right through our campground which is located on an island in the river.

Avignon Campground

✦ CAMPING MUNICIPAL SAINT BÉNÉZET

Address: Ile de la Barthelasse, 84000 Avignon
Telephone: 04 90 82 63 50
Price: Moderate

Open March 10 to October 31

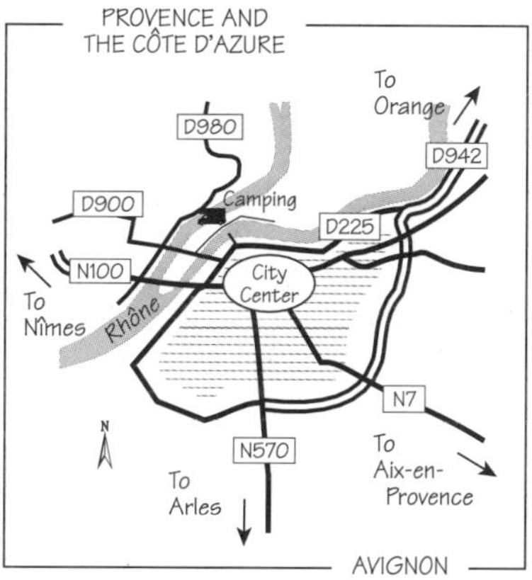

The most convenient place to stay when you visit the Pope's palace in Avignon is on the Ile de la Barthelasse, just across the river from the palace. There are actually two campgrounds there, this one and CAMPING BAGATELLE. Take your pick, they're both good.

Camping Municipal Saint Bénézet is large. It sits next to the river and has grassy, shaded sites with hedges for separation. A dedicated tent area is next to the river. Electricity (6 amps and higher) is available at most sites although you'll sometimes need a long cord. The sanitary facilities are good with free premixed hot water in the showers and bathroom basins. There is a store and bar/restaurant as well as a couple of nice tennis courts.

Getting in to town is easy. Bus service (Number 10) is available but most people make the 20-minute walk. The campground is actually located exactly where the famous Pont St. Bénézet used to cross the island — this is where the people in the song dance. You can get a great picture of the bridge and palace from the campground.

The easiest way to locate the campground is to follow the road running around the outside of the old town's walls until you are on the river or west side. Follow N100 west towards Nîmes onto the island and then follow signs for the campground.

Side Trips from Avignon

Twenty-five kilometers north of Avignon is the town of **Orange**. On the way north you may want to stop briefly in the wine town with the famous name, **Châteauneuf-du-Pape**, home of some of the finest of the **Côtes du Rhône wines**. Orange itself is known for wine, but it also has two important Roman sites: the **Roman Theater** and an impressive **Triumphal Arch**. If you're interested in seeing more if slightly less spectacular Roman ruins continue northwest another 35 kilometers to Vaison-la-Romaine where you'll find an excavation called the **Roman City**.

Near Vaison-la-Romaine is the tallest mountain in the region, **Mont Ventoux**. There's a road all the way to the top, in fact, this has been one of the tougher venues of the

Tour de France bike race. Petrarch's description of his climb up the mountain in 1336 is one of the earliest known mountain climbing chronicles. There are spectacular views from the top.

Fifty kilometers east of Avignon is the wild limestone mountain range known as the **Montagne du Lubéron**. This is a region that has been designated a regional nature park and a good place for hiking. It has recently become famous because the writer Peter Mayle has written about it in his popular series of books about Provence.

AIX-EN-PROVENCE

Population 127,000

As you travel south from the Avignon and Pont du Gard region toward Marseilles you may want to stop in **Aix-en-Provence**. While the city doesn't have a lot of important tourist sites it is pleasant and has the nickname "the city of a thousand fountains". Aix is a decent base for visits to Marseilles, the distance is about 29 kilometers. Another good base is Cassis, a resort town on the rocky coast just east of Marseilles.

Aix is a great base for exploring Marseilles and central Provence. The medium-sized city is more residential than industrial, it serves as a sort of bedroom suburb to huge Marseilles. It's also a university town with a huge number of students. Use the **Cours Mirabeau**, a tree-lined boulevard, as your reference. North is the old town, founded about 100 BC by the Romans. South is the new town dating from the 17th and 18th century. Sights include **Saint-Sauveur Cathedral** and the studio of Paul Cézanne, called the **Atelier de Cézanne**, he was born in Aix. The town is also known for its street markets in the central squares of the old town.

Aix-en-Provence Campground

✦ AEROTEL CHANTECLER CAMPING

Address: Famille Durand, Val St. André,
13100 Aix-En-Provence
Telephone: 04 42 26 12 98 Fax: 04 42 27 33 53
Price: Moderate

Open all year

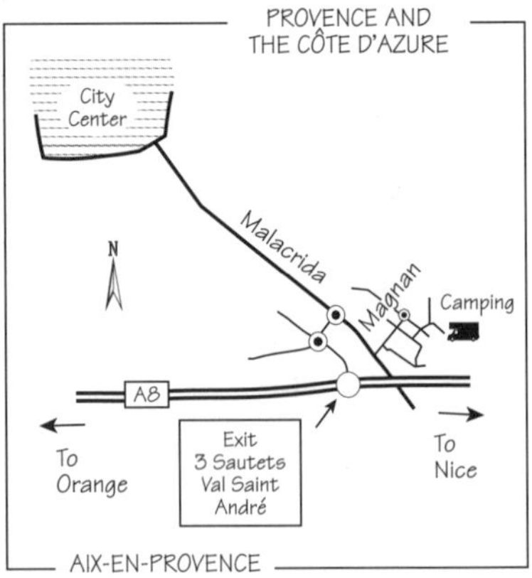

This large campground occupies the grounds of a hilltop country house some three kilometers south of central Aix. There are lots of trees and undeveloped grounds giving the campground a very rural atmosphere even though it is only a 30-minute walk from the center of town.

The sites are arranged off gravel roads. Camping is on grass, the sites are fairly level and many have conveniently-located electrical boxes (French plugs, 5 amps). Several good-quality heated shower/toilet buildings have adjustable hot showers and hot water in shaving, dishwashing, and laundry sinks. There is a laundry area with automatic washers and dryers. The campground also has a swimming pool, grocery shop, restaurant/bar, playground, and dump station. There is a small local grocery store within easy walking distance. You can walk in to town in about 30 minutes or take the bus (the Saint André Number 3).

Chantecler Camping is located south of Aix in the suburb of Val St. André. The N8 from the south runs right through Val St. André and the campground is signed from Ave. H. Malacrida, which is what N8 is called in the town. The easiest access to the campground is from the A8 autoroute south of Aix. Take the exit labeled Les 3 Sautets and Val Saint André. At the roundabout immediately after you exit take the first right. When you reach the next roundabout at Ave. H. Malacrida go right. The left turn to the campground off this avenue is well signed and only a short distance from the roundabout. Other signs will take you up through a residential area to the campground.

MARSEILLES (MARSEILLE) AND CASSIS, FRANCE

Marseilles Population 900,000

Marseilles has an unfortunate reputation as an unpleasant and sometimes dangerous place to visit. The many immigrants, mostly North African in recent years, give the city a crowded and exotic atmosphere which can sometimes be a little frightening. Give yourself some space by staying in the nearby fishing village and resort of Cassis and make easy day trips to Marseilles.

Marseilles is France's oldest large town. Now France's second largest city, it was founded in about 600 B.C. and called Massalia. Ships from the city are thought to have traded far into the Atlantic. The city also sits astride the most direct route to northern Gaul, up the Rhône Valley. When Rome became a power the city remained a center of Greek culture and influence.

Actually, the street life in Marseilles isn't a reason to stay away, it's the city's biggest attraction. Tourist sites are few and far between but the visitor will hardly notice. The **Notre-Dame de la Garde** church, reminiscent of the Sacré-Coeur in Paris or the Fourvière in Lyons, offers great views of the city. The **Vieux Port** (old port) area is the focus of the city, just to the south of it is an area of restaurants where you can find your obligatory and essential bouillabaisse fix. The history of the city can be found at the **Musée de l'Histoire de Marseille**. You might also consider a boat trip from the Vieux Port to the **Château d'If**, the prison island featured in Alexandre Dumas' novel *The Count of Monte Cristo*.

Marseilles Campground

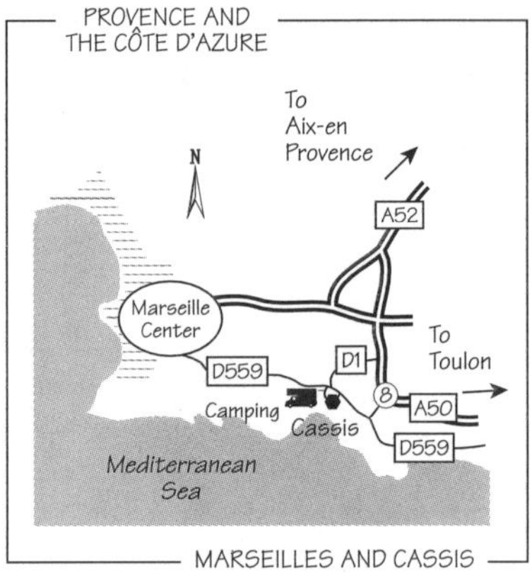

✦ LES CIGALES

Address: Rte. de Marseille, 13260 Cassis
Telephone: 04 42 01 07 34
Price: Moderate

Open March 15 to November 15

While there are no campgrounds in Marseilles itself you can easily visit the city by basing yourself in a nearby town. One of the best places to do this is the seaside resort of Cassis.

Cassis is a world away from Marseilles, about 20 kilometers to the southeast. It sits at the foot of Cap Canaille, Europe's highest cliff at 1,300 feet. There's a small boat harbor and several beaches. Small cafes and shops provide plenty of entertainment between visits to Marseilles.

Les Cigales is a large campground located near the entrance to Cassis. Sites are all separated by hedges and are numbered. There are quite a few permanently situated rigs here but they are not intrusive. Electricity (French plugs, 7 amps) is available throughout but the boxes are not very abundant, there are not enough outlets to service all of the sites. The one shower/toilet building is large and well maintained, hot water is provided for showers (premixed, push button), bathroom basins and dishwashing. There are coin-operated clothes washing machines. The campground has its own grocery store, bar/restaurant, and snack bars. A good supermarket is about 1 kilometer down the hill toward the center of town.

To get to Marseilles you can use either the bus or train. The Marseilles bus stops just outside the entrance of the campground, it takes about 40 minutes to reach the Castellane or St. Charles stations in the city. The train station is about 2 kilometers from the campground.

The campground is located on the outskirts of Cassis near the point where D559 from Marseilles enters town. Coming from Marseilles on D559 you will turn right toward town and see the campground immediately on your right. If you are on the A50 autoroute take Exit 8. After the exit drive toward Cassis on D559. Stay on D559 ignoring signs pointing to the left for Cassis until you reach an intersection in 4.7 kilometers. Turn left here, the campground will be on the right almost immediately.

LA FAVIÈRE, FRANCE

From Cassis we'll follow the coastal road east along the Riviera through Toulon and Hyères to our next base campground near le Lavandou. Toulon is an industrial city and has little of interest, Hyères is an older resort, you'll see lots more as you travel east. The coast between Hyères and St-Tropez is less built-up than the area farther along the coast, there are actually a few campgrounds along here that are on the beach.

Camping le Domaine is to the west in La Favière while Les Tournels is much closer to St-Tropez. Both are nice large holiday campgrounds, Camp du Domaine is on the beach while Les Tournels is a kilometer or so away on country roads through vineyard country.

The la Favière area is less developed and crowded than most of this coast. Recently several large developments and a marina have been built. The area has all the services you will need but little in the way of attractions other than the beach.

La Favière Campground

✦ CAMP DU DOMAINE

Address: B.P. 207, la Favière, 83234 Bormes-Les-Mimosas
Telephone: 04 94 71 03 12 Fax: 04 94 15 18 67
Price: Moderate

April 1 to October 30.

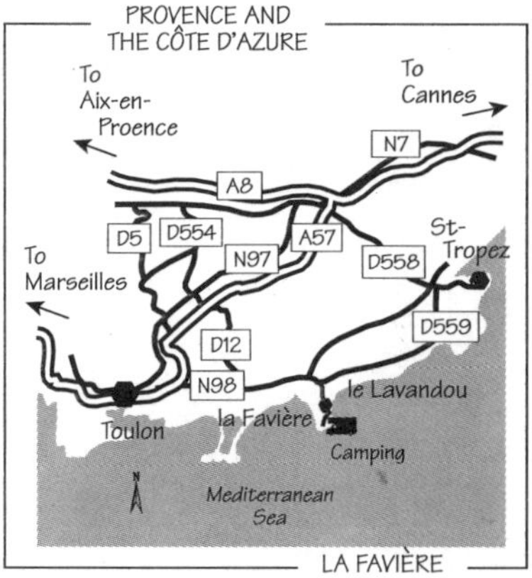

An enormous site, Camp du Domaine sits right on the beach near the small town of la Favière which is just south of le Lavandou. The campground sprawls over a pine-covered hill and down to the ocean. There are quite a few campgrounds in this area, this one has the advantage of having its own sandy beach.

The campground must have at least 500 camping sites. In the flat area near the beach the sites have electricity and the area becomes a busy little beach-side community. Farther back on the hillside the sites are more primitive with no electricity and some are difficult to access with a larger rig or caravan. Those with tents or vans may prefer this area because it has more privacy. There are sanitary facilities scattered throughout the campground, all are modern and have premixed hot water showers. There are two restaurants, a bar, stores, tennis courts, and of course a nice beach. Bus service is available nearby but the campground is not really near any large population centers. This is a family holiday campground.

Le Lavandou, the largest nearby town, is about 20 kilometers east of Toulon. Access to the campground is from the coastal highway, D559, at a roundabout just west of le Lavandou. There is a sign for the campground, the road is also signed la Favière, Bénat. Follow signs for about 2 kilometers down this road, the campground is on the left.

Side Trips from La Favière

If the quiet around la Favière is getting on your nerves you can drive 30 kilometers east to **St-Tropez**. Just inland from la Favière is the **Massif des Maures**, a wooded mountainous area threaded by small roads, perfect for exploration.

ST-TROPEZ

Population 6,500

Little St-Tropez is famous for its laid-back glamour. It may no longer have Brigitte Bardot but there are lots of other members of the rich and famous to see in an environment of cafés and yachts. You may find St-Tropez more charming than you expect, especially if you visit during the off season. The **Musée de l'Annonciade** (modern art museum) has works by Bonnard, Dufy, Derain, Matisse, Rouault, Seurat, and Signac.

St-Tropez Campground

✦ CAMPING CARAVANNING LES TOURNELS

Address: Route de Camarat, 83350 Ramatuelle
Telephone: 04 94 55 90 90
Fax: 04 94 55 90 99
Price: Moderate

Open all year

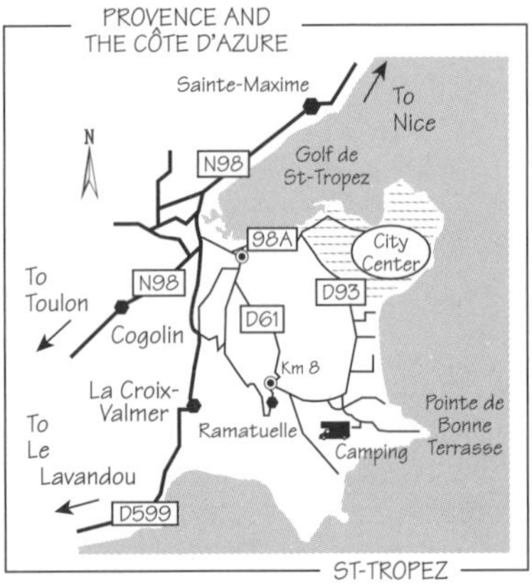

Les Tournels is one of several huge campgrounds located near St. Tropez. It is one of the nicest, and truly unique because it now remains open all year long. It would be easy to spend the entire winter in a place like this. The weather would be cool, but certainly comfortable in an RV.

The campground is scattered over a hillside and surrounded by vineyards. Campsites are assigned, they are generally well separated and shaded by olive trees and pines. Interior roads are paved, sites are dirt and electricity (French plugs) is convenient to most of them. There are lots of facilities. The shower/toilet buildings are very modern and have free hot water for showers (adjustable push buttons), shaving sinks, dishwashing and laundry sinks. There are washers and dryers, a huge swimming pool, tennis courts, playgrounds, rental storage boxes, a restaurant/bar, dump station, and even a good-sized supermarket just outside the gate of the campground that seems to be dedicated just to the campground. There's a pathway through the vineyards to the beach, about a kilometer away. St-Tropez is about 10 kilometers distant, easily reached by bicycle.

You will probably be approaching the campground from near St. Tropez. Follow signs for Ramatuelle, which is a small inland village about 10 kilometers south of St-Tropez. Once there you will see signs that will take you a few kilometers east to Les Tournels Camping Caravanning.

NICE, FRANCE

Population 350,000

Capital of the Côte d'Azur, largest resort on the Mediterranean coast, one of France's larger cities, Queen of the Riviera — these are all Nice. Nice is also congested traffic, a beach of rounded stones, and faded elegance.

You'll probably arrive in Nice by driving along the coast from either east or west. The **Promenade des Anglais** is a eight-lane boulevard along the beach with a strolling walkway on one side and old elegant hotels on the other. If you're driving your own vehicle perhaps you can snag a parking spot along the boulevard, but don't count on it. Arrive by public transportation if possible.

Nice's most atmospheric quarter is the **Old Town**. It's just west of the **Castle Hill (Colline du Château),** which in turn is just west of the yacht harbor. The quarter's narrow traffic-free streets and morning market in the **Cours Saleya** aren't to be missed.

Nice is exceptionally well endowed with museums. You'll find museums dedicated to both **Chagall** and **Matisse**, as well as a more general fine arts museum, the **Musée des Beaux-Arts Jules-Chéret** with works by Chéret, Monet, Rodin, Renoir and Degas. A modern art museum is the **Musée d'Art Contemporain**. There's a Roman antiquities museum, the **Musée Archéologique,** and a seashell museum, the **Musée International de Malacologie.** Finally, there's even a museum of Nice's history, the **Palais Masséna** (which also covers the Napoleonic era).

While you wander you'll come across many churches including the **Russian Orthodox Cathedral**, **Notre-Dame-de-l'Assomption monastery**, **Chapelle St-Giaume and St-François-de-Paule** with their famous Baroque interiors, and **St-Jacques** with a well-known painted ceiling. Finally, there's the **Cathédrale Ste-Réparate**, also Baroque, with a tiled dome and exuberant interior.

When you tire of Nice you'll find that even Villeneuve-Loubet has an attraction. There you'll find the **Fondation Escoffier**, the childhood home of the famous chef Auguste Escoffier. It is now a museum.

Nice Campground

✦ LA VIEILLE FERME

Address: 296 Bd. des Groules, 06270 Villeneuve-Loubet-Plage
Telephone: 04 93 33 41 44
Fax: 04 93 33 37 28
Price: Moderate

Open all year

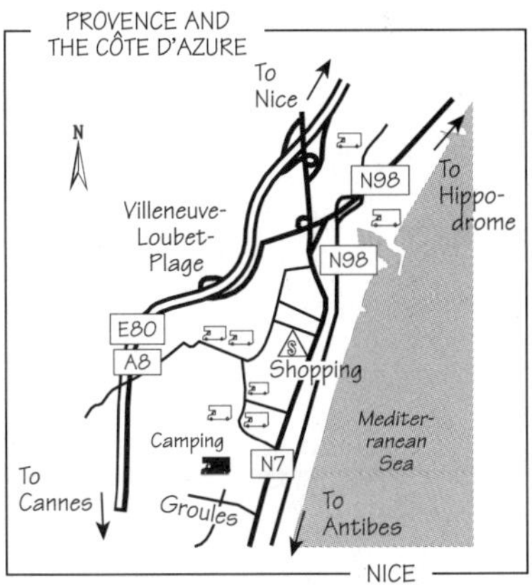

It is actually possible to find a campground near Nice. La Vieille Ferme and seven other campgrounds are located in the city of Villeneuve-Loubet-Plage, about 10 kilometers west of Nice along the coast. None of these campgrounds are on the beach, that would be too much to expect in an area with such high real estate values. They are within easy bus or local train range of Nice, however, and there are beaches nearby.

La Vieille Ferme is a medium-sized friendly campground that is popular because it has a covered swimming pool and is open all year. The sites are generally grassy areas separated by hedges although there is also a paved area for vans and motor homes. Electrical boxes (CEE17 plugs, various amps) are convenient for most sites, some will require longer cords. Water outlets are scattered throughout the campground. The shower/toilet buildings are not uniform having obviously been built at various times, but some are heated for winter use and there are premixed push-button valve hot showers. The large enclosed swimming pool is nice, there's also a small store, a TV room, boules, and Ping-Pong . A large, mostly undeveloped park with walking paths is located right next door and provides a good place to bike, run, or walk. Bus service and a train station are nearby giving you access to much of the coast without having to use your vehicle.

The campground is somewhat difficult to find because the highways are confusing in this neighborhood. The area is crossed by the A8 autoroute, N7 coastal highway, N98, D4 and several rail lines. Our map should make things a little easier on you. If you are on the Autoroute take the Antibes exit and drive south 4 kilometers to the N7 coastal highway. Turn left, toward the east, and drive another 4 kilometers. La Vieille Ferme is signed to the left, the campground is about 250 meters up the side road (Boulevard des Groules) on the right.

Side Trips from Nice

From this base there are good road and rail connections to all of the attractions along the coast east and west. **Cannes** is about 15 kilometers southwest, **Antibes** even closer, and **Nice** just to the east. Beyond Nice another 15 kilometers or so is **Monaco** and just beyond that **Menton** and the Italian border. The entire area is not particularly RV friendly. Many parking areas have height bars or restrictions on camping vehicles. You're much better off to leave the rig in the campground and use public transportation to get around. The Cote d'Azure is the world's playground, enjoy it.

There are several good excursions up into the mountains behind the coast. The entire region is rewarding, the small roads and rugged mountains make any drive a pleasant adventure. Here are some highlights.

An easy 5 kilometers from Villeneuve-Loubet-Plage is the small town of **Biot**. The hill town in known for the **Musée Léger** where Fernand Léger's ceramics are displayed.

About 25 kilometers behind Villeneuve-Loubet up Highway D2085 is the perfume town of **Grasse**. The perfume industry originated here because of the area's ideal growing conditions for aromatic herbs like Lavender, Jasmine, and Roses. There are several museums run by the perfume houses but **Musée Internationale de la Parfumerie** is a good place to start.

Also very near Villeneuve-Loubet-Plage, about 10 kilometers inland, are the towns of **Vence** and **St-Paul-de-Vence**. Vence is a town filled with holiday homes, St-Paul-de-Vence is an old walled hill village just above. Their proximity to Nice has made them a popular tourist destination with many art studios and galleries.

There are two gorges in the mountains behind the coast that are well known and well worth a driving tour. Closest to our base at Villeneuve-Loubet-Plage is the **Gorges du**

Loup. You'll find the Gorge just east of Grasse, head north from Châteauneuf-Grasse toward **Gourdon** where you should stop and see the **Château and gardens**.

Farther afield are the **Gorges du Verdon**. To reach them drive west from Grasse toward **Castellane**, a distance of about 65 kilometers along twisted but scenic N85, also called the Route Napoléon. From Castellane you can follow a circular route offering gorgeous views. Take D952 and then D955 south to Comps-s-Artuby, then D71 northwest to Moustiers-Ste-Marie. From there you can follow D952 back to Castellane with a brief detour south on D23 to the north rim of the gorge. You should pick up a good map of the region before attempting this trip. Highlights are the view from the **Pont de l'Artuby** and the star suspended on a chain above **Moustiers-Ste-Marie** during the crusades. There are hiking trails from **La Palud sur-Verdon** and **Point Sublime**.

SOSPEL, FRANCE

Another base option at this end of the Riviera, especially if you're ready for a quieter setting, are the campgrounds around Sospel, a small village nestled in a peaceful mountain valley some 20 kilometers behind Menton.

When you drive inland from Menton, after a dizzying climb you'll reach the small picturesque village. There are at least four campgrounds in the countryside around Sospel, it makes a pleasant contrast to the crowded seaside resorts below. This is a small town that is just sophisticated enough to be able to offer good cafes, bars and shops. Amazingly enough, the town's **Fort St-Roch** was part of the Maginot Line of forts built to protect France in the 1930's. Most of us tend to know of the portion of the line in northern France but it actually ran from Belgium to Corsica.

Sospel Campground

✦ CAMPING STE. MADELEINE

Address: Route de Moulinet, 06380 Sospel
Telephone: 04 93 04 10 48
Price: Moderate

Open April 1 to September 30

Camping Ste. Madeleine is a medium-sized campground arranged on a terraced hillside. It is a tourist site with no resident rigs other than rentals. Electricity is available to over half of the sites (French plugs, 6 amps). There is one shower/toilet block with older but clean facilities and hot water showers requiring payment but cold water to bathroom basins and dishwashing sinks. There is a big swimming pool. The nearest restaurants and stores are in Sospel about 4.5 kilometers away.

To reach the campground drive inland from Menton to Sospel and then follow the camping signs to the northwest on Highway D2566. The distance from Menton to Sospel is about 22 kilometers and from Sospel to the campground another 4 kilometers. The road from Menton climbs steeply with hairpin curves in places. It is very scenic but a little bit challenging.

LOIRE VALLEY

One hundred kilometers southwest of Paris by autoroute you will find one of France's best-loved regions. The Loire Valley has it all: beautiful countryside, history, wine and food, and of course the châteaux.

The Loire Valley is probably best known for the dozens of châteaux built here throughout French history. The oldest are really military castles. Later the valley's proximity to Paris made it a popular place for the rich and powerful to build their country homes. You'll find that there are quite a variety of different types of châteaux: some are isolated and almost deserted, others are crowded with busloads of visitors, some have museums and others are completely unfurnished. You'll probably find yourself trying to visit as many as possible, although not all in the same day. You'll probably also find yourself studying some French history, trying to see how all of these places fit into it. Many Loire châteaux have sound and light shows in the evening. The shows are popular and easy to enjoy if you're camped nearby.

Visiting the Loire is more than visiting the châteaux. There are pleasant and historical towns like Tours, Saumur, and Chinon. This is also wine country so you'll have lots of opportunities for tastings. Of course, like all wine areas the Loire has great food.

BLOIS

Population 50,000

Blois is an old industrial town that happens to be home to the historically important royal **Château de Blois**. This is a very heavily-visited château, probably because it is so easy to reach for railroad-restricted tourists. The château itself reflects the architecture of four centuries. The royal court often lived here until Henry IV moved it to Paris in 1598. The story of the murder of the Duc de Guise is a big part of a visit to Blois, check it out in a history book before your visit. The old town area between the château and the river and upstream to the cathedral is pleasant, there's a signposted walking tour called the **Route Royale**.

Blois Campground

✦ AIROTEL LAC DU LOIRE

Address: Base du Lac du Loire, 41350 Vineuil
Telephone: 02 54 78 82 05
Price: Inexpensive

Open April 1 to October 15

Located on the far side of the Loire from Blois and just to the east this large campground is pleasant but isolated. You'll have to drive if you want to visit any restaurant other than the small bar/cafe on the water near the camp.

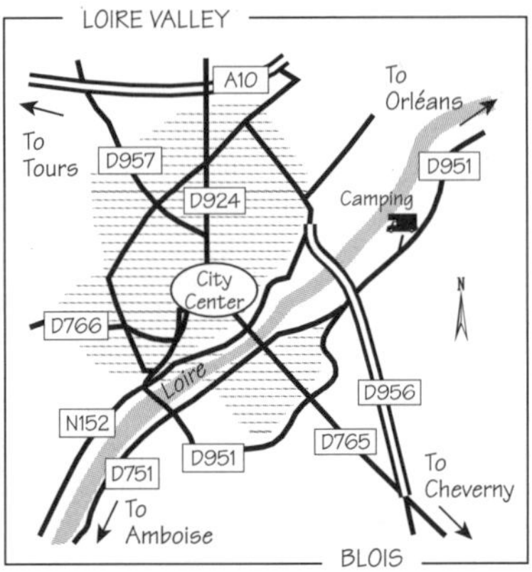

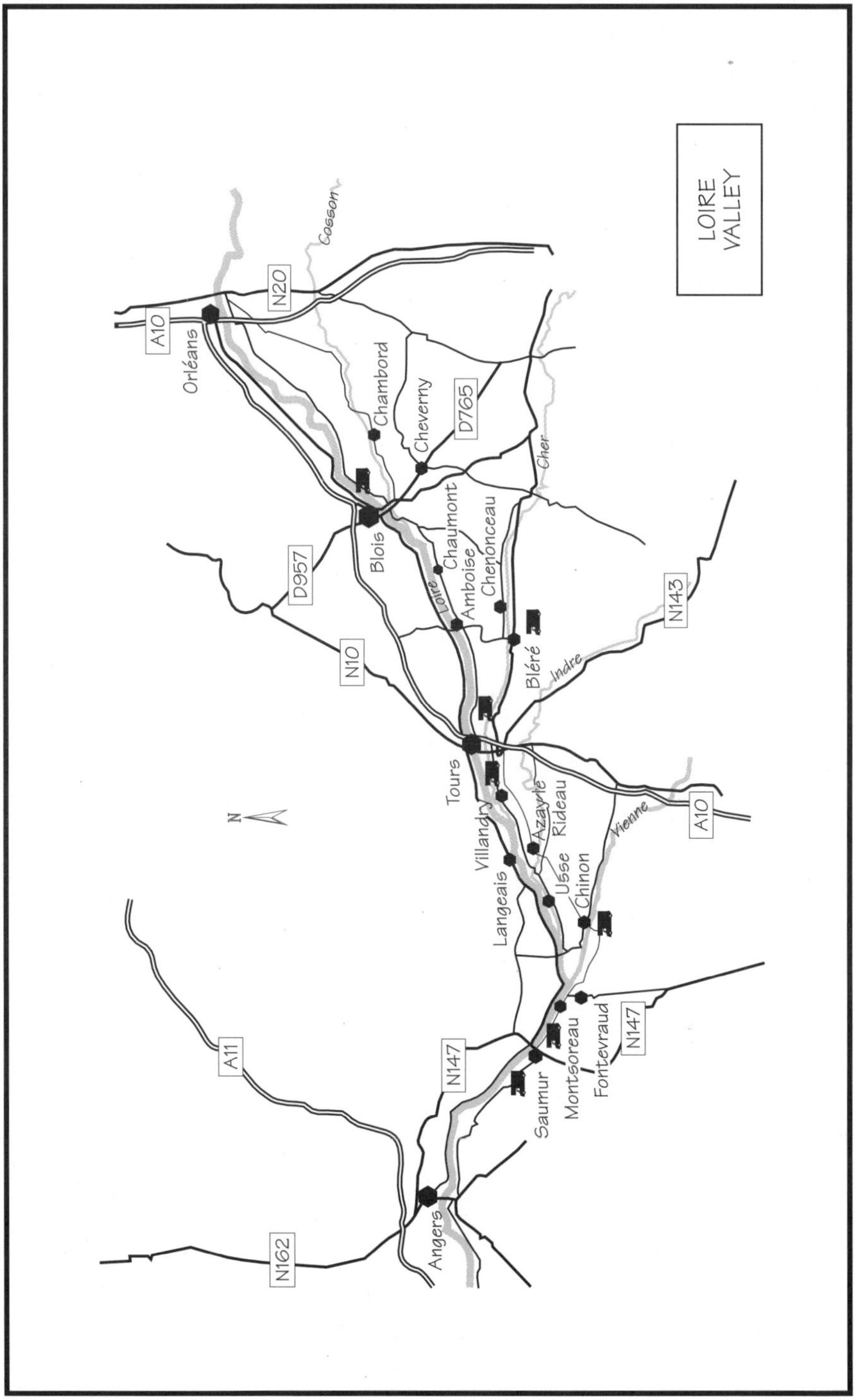
LOIRE VALLEY
Orléans
A10
N20
Cosson
Chambord
Cheverny
D765
Cher
Blois
Chaumont
Chenonceau
Amboise
Loire
D957
N10
Bléré
Indre
N143
Tours
Villandry
Azay-le-Rideau
Vienne
A10
Langeais
Usse
Chinon
Saumur
Montsoreau
Fontevraud
N147
N147
A11
Angers
N162
N

This is a large grassy campground in a grove of cottonwoods on sandy soil next to the river. Electrical outlets are available but widely spaced. Some sites are separated by shrubbery but others are in a large grass field. Sanitary facilities are clean and hot water is available for washing dishes and clothes, showers are preset but plenty warm. There is a bar/cafe/store that sits on the bank of the river nearby, it is not really dedicated to the campground, customers also come in from outside the campground and it is about a half kilometer from the sites.

To reach the campground drive south from Blois toward Vineuil on Highway D956 across the Loire River. On the south shore turn east (left) following campground signs another 2 kilometers.

Side Trips from Blois

The eastern Loire around Blois has many châteaux but the three best known are Chambord, Cheverny, and Chaumont. **Chambord**, sixteen kilometers to the east and about five kilometers south of the Loire is the largest and probably most impressive of the Loire's châteaux. It is a royal château, building was started by Françoise I in 1519, it was actually finished by Louis XIV. The Château has an isolated location and visitors come in cars and busses. On occasion we've had the whole place to ourselves with no other visitors. Leonardo da Vinci is said to have worked on the design, he was a visitor to the Loire at that time, and died in the valley.

Cheverny is located 12 kilometers south of Blois. It was finished in 1634 and is a luxurious country residence. The château is known for it's perfect classical-era design, the interior is beautifully furnished.

Chaumont-sur-Loire Château sits above the Loire about 20 kilometers southwest of Blois. This is the château that Catherine de'Medici acquired and forced Diane de Poitiers to accept in exchange for Chenonceau.

From Blois you may want to move down the valley to a location more convenient to several other popular châteaux. Bléré makes a comfortable base. The drive from Blois to Bléré along the Loire and then south to the Cher is 50 kilometers.

BLÉRÉ

Bléré has a large three-star municipal campground located next to the Cher River about six kilometers downstream from Chenonceau. This clean and well-run campground makes a great base for exploring with supplies only a short stroll away. Bléré is a small town right next to the campground with stores, restaurants, cafes, and several banks. Of the campgrounds in the general Chenonceau area we think this is the best.

Bléré Campground

✦ BLÉRÉ CAMPING MUNICIPAL

Address: 37150 Bléré
Telephone: 02 47 57 92 60
Price: Inexpensive

Open April 15 to October 15

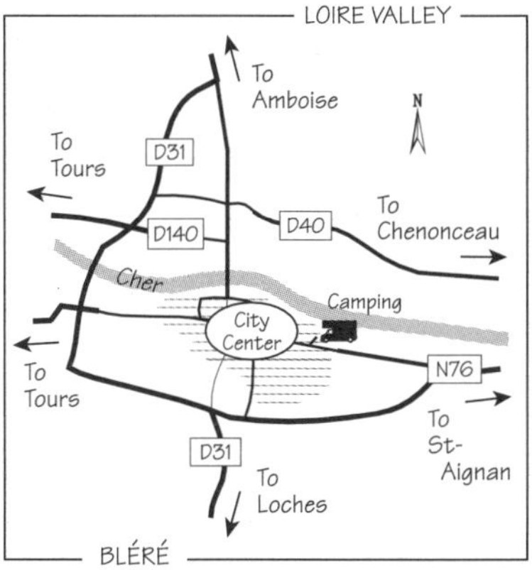

The campground is a large grassy field with scattered shade trees located next to the river with only a walking path intervening. The sites are not separated. Electrical boxes are set regularly around the campground, long cords would be necessary for most sites. The campground's pride and joy is a large control board behind the registration desk to remotely control each electrical outlet. It is covered with red and green lights and switches, be sure to compliment them on it. Sanitary buildings are clean and modern, showers have premixed hot water but clothes and dishwashing area have cold water only. There is a coin-operated washer and dryer. The campground has a small store and the location next to town makes many other facilities easily accessible. The campground is part of a municipal sports area that includes a swimming pool and tennis courts.

CHÂTEAU OF CHENONCEAU IN THE LOIRE VALLEY

Bléré is large enough to appear on most Loire area maps. The campground is on the east side of town next to the river, there are good direction signs on access roads into town.

Side Trips from Bléré

The château of **Chenonceau** is probably most people's Loire favorite. It is only a few kilometers from Bléré, the trip makes a nice bike ride. This is the château that is actually built out over the Cher and forms a bridge. It is a popular destination so you may find it more enjoyable to visit either early or late in the day, especially on weekends.

North 10 kilometers from Bléré on the south shore of the Loire is **Amboise**. The château here is another royal castle, its golden age was the fifteenth century under Charles VIII. Leonardo da Vinci spent time here as the guest of King Francis I, you'll find a museum here containing models of some of his inventions.

As we move down the Cher and Loire valleys we come to Tours. We've described two campgrounds here, one on the outskirts of town and the other in the small village of Savonnières to the west.

TOURS, FRANCE

Population 255,000

Tours has an enviable position in the heart of the Loire's château country. Unfortunately it is a large industrial city with busy crowded suburbs so camping visitors to the valley generally base themselves in more pleasant surroundings elsewhere. A visit to the city, however, is well worth the time and effort.

Tours occupies a peninsula some ten kilometers east of the point where the Loire and Cher rivers join. The old part of the city is on the south bank of the Loire. You can break this area into three smaller sections; these are the Cathedral District, the Rue Nationale or St-Julien District, and the Place Plumereau or Old Tours area.

The most eastern of these is the Cathedral area. There you'll find the **Cathédrale St-Gatien** and the château which houses **Historial de la Touraine**, a wax museum with figures of important historical figures of the Loire region.

The Rue National is a boulevard bisecting the older section of town. It is fronted by the city's major stores and shops. Near where it meets the Loire are two museums: the **Musée des Vins** (Wine Museum) and the **Musée du Compagnonnage** (Guild Museum). It is highly recommended.

Old Tours, farthest to the west has been heavily restored in recent years and is an area of walking streets, small cafes and shops. It is the district for an evening visit to Tours.

Tours Campground

✦ Camping Municipal des Rives du Cher

Address: St Avertin, 37170
Chambray-les-Tours
Telephone: 02 47 27 27 60
Price: Inexpensive

Open April 1 to October 15

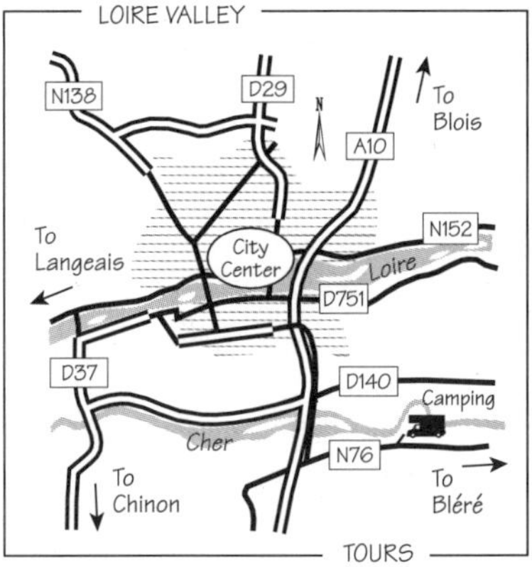

Rives du Cher is a municipal campground offering little more than well-managed basics in a pleasant riverside location in one of the nicer suburbs outside Tours. Everything you need is close by, and it is handy for visiting Tours.

The campground is situated on the south bank of the Cher River. Sites are on grass off paved access driveways. Electricity (4 and 10 amps) is available if needed. The shower/toilet facilities include free hot showers. You will find restaurants and groceries within a half kilometer.

Central Tours is about 5 kilometers from the campground. You can use your bike or the bus, there is a stop nearby.

To find the campground take N76 south from Tours. Watch for a campground sign as you cross the Cher bridge. The campground sits on the south bank of the river east of the N76 bridge.

Savonnières, France

Savonnières is a small village on the south bank of the Cher about 10 kilometers west of Tours. The Loire and the Cher haven't joined at this point, but they're getting close. The Château of Villandry is 2.5 kilometers west.

Savonnières Campground

✦ Camping Municipal de Savonnières

Address: 37510 Joué-les-Tours
Telephone: 02 47 50 15 71
Price: Inexpensive

Open June 15 to September 30

The municipal campground is a pleasant, conveniently-located two-star campground with no unnecessary expensive extra amenities. It is unlikely to be full and makes a good alternate for the Tours area.

The campground is a large grassy field, some parts are shaded. Camp sites are not separated or delineated. A very few boxes with electrical outlets are mounted on poles around the field, you'll need that long cord to use them. Scattered faucets provide water. The shower/toilet building is in one corner of the field and has free hot showers and hot water for washing dishes and clothes, there's even a coin-operated washing machine. There's a playground area for the kids and parents can enjoy watching canoes floating by on the river. The nearby town of Savonnières provides a bread shop and small grocery store, also a couple of small restaurants.

The campground is located just off Highway D7 on the eastern edge of Savonnières, next to the river.

Side Trips from Savonnières

Downstream from Tours along the Cher is **Villandry**. This château is known for its extensive gardens, including an unusual kitchen garden.

You can visit the next two important châteaux from Tours, or you can move 40 kilometers south to Chinon.

CHINON, FRANCE

Population 9,000

Chinon is an enchanting town on the banks of the Vienne river, some 30 kilometers southeast of Saumur. The medieval streets of the village along the river are overlooked by the **château**, really more of a fortress. Chinon's golden age was earlier than many châteaux in the Loire, Richard the Lion-Heart died in the town of Chinon in 1189 and Joan of Arc was presented to the Dauphin here for the first time in 1429. Most of the château has been dismantled over the years but the Royal Apartments of Charles VII and Joan of Arc's time remain.

Besides the château Chinon has a very good **wine museum**, the **States General House** where Richard the Lion-Heart died also has a museum of local history.

Chinon Campground

✦ CAMP MUNICIPAL DE L'ILE AUGER

Address: Quay Danton, 37500 Chinon
Telephone: 02 47 93 08 35
Price: Inexpensive

Open March 15 to October 15

When you visit the Chinon area there's no better place to stay than the town's municipal campground. It is on the banks of the Vienne River, just across from the château. The view is great!

The medium-sized campground is a grassy area on the river bank but with no direct access to the river, there is a fence. It is divided into several clusters of sites by low shrubs. Electricity (CEE17 plugs, 4 amps) is available. The clean shower/toilet facilities have hot showers. There is a playground in the campground and a boules-playing area. Stores, restaurants, and the château are a five to ten minute walk across the bridge. There's a swimming pool next to the campground.

To find the campground just look across the river from old Chinon below the château. Signs direct you across the bridge and then right to the gate.

Side Trips from Chinon

Azay-le Rideau is midway between Tours and Chinon. The small fairy-tale château is surrounded by water, it may remind you of Chenonceau. Nearby is **Ussé Château**, another very popular destination.

On the north bank of the Loire is **Langeais**. The first castle was built on this location in the 10th century but Louis XI finished the one that stands there today in 1469. It is unusually well preserved and a good château for a tour.

To get to our next campground you drive down the Vienne River from Chinon to the point where it flows into the Loire.

MONTSOREAU, FRANCE

Located on the south shore of the Loire River about 11 kilometers east of Saumur, this tiny village with its municipal campground makes a good place to spend the night while touring the Fontevraud Abbey which is just a few kilometers south of the river at this point.

Montsoreau has its own not very well known castle which dominates the point where the Vienne river meets the Loire. It has an unlikely museum about the Moroccan Goum cavalry regiments which was moved here in 1956 when Morocco became independent.

Montsoreau Campground

✦ CAMPING MUNICIPAL L'ÍSLE VERTE

Address: Avenue de la Loire,
49730 Montsoreau
Telephone: 02 41 51 76 60
Price: Inexpensive

Open May 1 to September 30

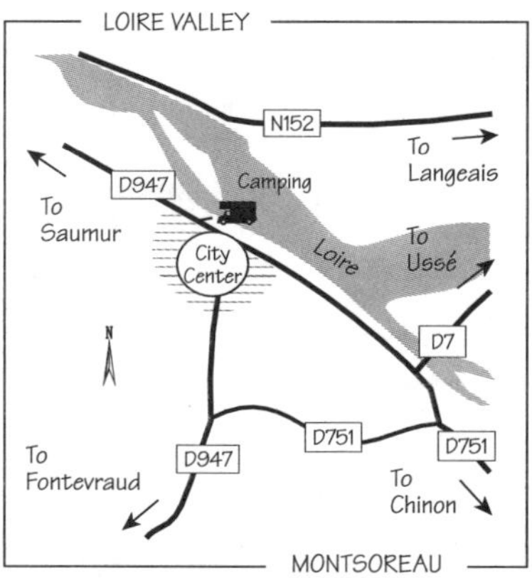

This campground, also known as Camping Municipal de Montsoreau, is a two-star campground which means it lacks some amenities, but it also means that you don't have to pay for them either. It is a medium-sized grassy meadow next to the river with scattered trees providing lots of shade. The bank of the river is fenced off, but there is access to it just east of the camping area for launching canoes, etc. The sites are not separated from each other although they are numbered.

Gravel access roads run through the area. Electricity and water outlets are widely scattered around the campground. The sanitary facilities are impressive for a municipal campground, hot water is free and available for dishes, clothes washing and showers. Other than the river, a children's play area, and a boules area there are no other facilities at the campground but the village, just across the street, has restaurants, a boulangerie, charcuterie, and a small supermarket. It also has several wine "caves". There is an information office in front of the campground and municipal tennis courts next door.

Montsoreau is easy to find. From Chinon follow the Vienne River down to the Loire or from Saumur take Highway D947 east along the south bank of the Loire for about 11 kilometers. You'll see the campground on your left next to the river just as you enter town. Watch for the information office.

Side Trips from Montsoreau

Montsoreau serves as a base for visiting the abbey at **Fontevraud**. Here you'll find the tombs of Henry II, Eleanor of Aquitaine, and Richard the Lion-Heart.

Eleven kilometers downstream is another great camping town, Saumur.

SAUMUR, FRANCE

Population 35,000

Saumur is a popular tourist destination and very camper-friendly. The municipal campground has great views of the château and a pleasant island location.

The **Château de Saumur** is very impressive from below, one of the best along the Loire for pictures. The old town below the Château has shops and restaurants. Saumur is home to the French cavalry academy and also the **École Nationale d'Équitation** with its **Cadre Noir** which puts on equestrian shows for visitors. Saumur is also a center for sparkling wine and for mushrooms, you can taste the wine and visit fascinating caves where mushrooms are grown.

Saumur Campground

✦ CAMPING MUNICIPAL L'ILE D'OFFARD

Address: Rue de Verden, 49400 Saumur
Telephone: 02 41 40 30 00
Fax: 02 41 67 37 81
Price: Moderate

Open January 15 to December 15

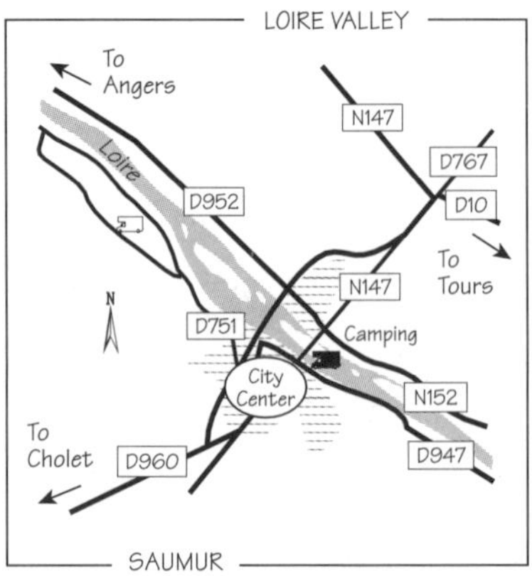

Camping Municipal is a four-star campground and the place to stay to be within walking distance of Saumur's restaurants and tourist sites. It is located on an island in the Loire and has a great view of the very photogenic Saumur Chateau.

The campground occupies a point of land on the east (upstream) end of the island. It is fenced so there is no direct access to the river although the location is very scenic. Grassy sites have quite a bit of shrubbery and shade but are not separated from each other. Electricity (CEE17 plugs, 6 amps and 10 amps) and water are available throughout but outlets are scattered. Sanitary facilities are good with hot water showers available. There is a restaurant/bar and small store at the campground, a municipal swimming pool is located next door as are municipal tennis courts. There are a lot of rental tents and rental caravans at the campground, the location makes this a popular place. This campground also has a dump station.

You can easily walk in to town, it should take ten to fifteen minutes to do so since you must walk to the center of the island and then cross the bridge.

To reach the campground follow signs from downtown Saumur across the river to the island and then right.

Side Trips from Saumur

A good side trip from Saumur is the town of **Angers**. It lies 45 kilometers downstream along the Loire and is a bustling town with a population of over 150,000. Angers has its own famous château, a 13th-century fortress which contains the medieval **Apocalypse Tapestry**.

DORDOGNE VALLEY

East of the Bordeaux region and St-Emilion is the Dordogne River Valley, the region is often simply called the Dordogne. It is an extremely popular vacation region, especially among the English, some say because it reminds them of their beloved Cotswolds. The Dordogne has a never-ending list of attractions. The lazy Dordogne River wanders through a countryside of lush fields and limestone outcrops. There are castles, hill towns, and caves filled with prehistoric paintings. Gastronomic specialties include foie gras, walnuts, and goose and pork delicacies. The river is popular for canoeing and kayaking. Best of all, campgrounds abound.

We use the town of Sarlat as a base as we explore the valley. It is approximately in the center. The western boundary of our Dordogne will be 75 road kilometers west in Bergerac, the eastern boundary will be 60 or so road kilometers east of Sarlat near the caves of Gouffre Padirac and Rocamadour. The brief listing of attractions that follows are just the highlights, there's something of interest around every corner.

SARLAT-LA-CANÉDA, FRANCE

Population 11,000

Sarlat-la-Canéda is located at the geographic center of the Dordogne region and is a most convenient town to use as a base for your explorations. Sarlat itself has many attractions, it also is the best place to buy supplies in the valley.

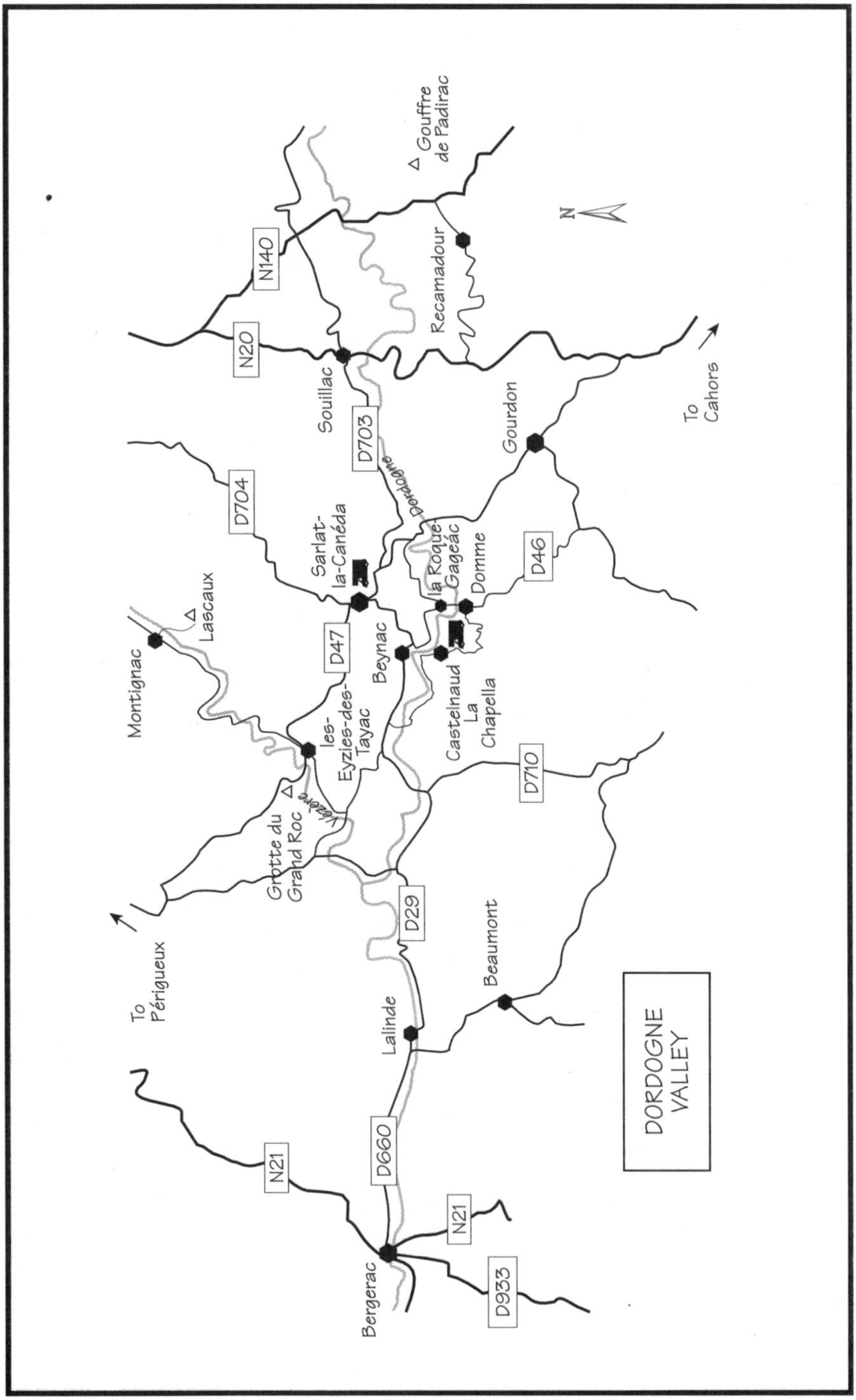
DORDOGNE VALLEY
N
Gouffre de Padirac
N140
N20
Recamadour
Souillac
D703
Dordogne
Gourdon
To Cahors
D704
Sarlat-la-Canéda
La Roque-Gageác
Domme
D46
Lascaux
Montignac
D47
Beynac
Castelnaud La Chapella
les-Eyzies-des-Tayac
Vézère
D710
Grotte du Grand Roc
D29
To Périgueux
Beaumont
Lalinde
N21
D660
N21
D933
Bergerac

Sarlat is said to have the highest concentration of Medieval, Renaissance and 17th-century facades of any town in France, today they are protected by law. The center of activities in Sarlat is the **place de la Liberté**, a square in the center of a district of walking streets. Each Saturday a street market famous throughout France is held in the place, on offer are those Périgord culinary specialties.

Adjoining the place de la Liberté is the **Cathédrale St-Sacerdos**, known for its organ. Another much-visited monument in Sarlat is the **Lanterne des Morts**, a conical-capped tower in the cemetery.

You'll find two small museums in town. **L'Homo Sapiens** has information about prehistoric man and the **Aquarium** spotlights the surprisingly large number of varieties of fish in the Dordogne River.

Sarlat-La-Canéda Campground

✦ CAMPING LES PÉRIÈRES

Address: Rte. Ste Nathalène, 24203 Sarlat
Telephone: 05 53 59 05 84
Fax: 05 53 28 57 51
Price: Expensive

Open Easter to September 30

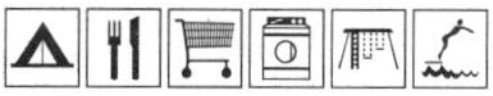

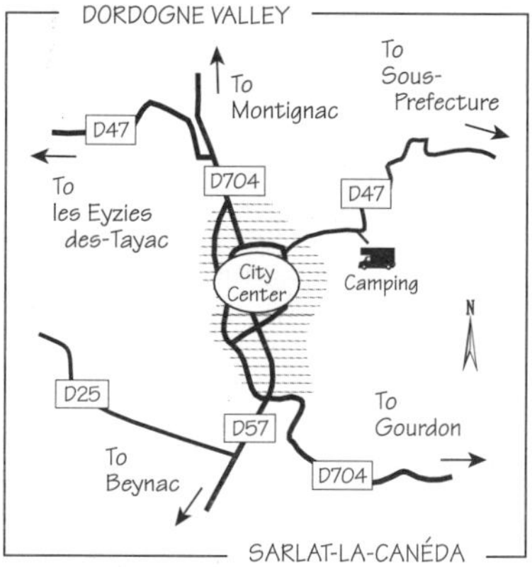

There are at least 35 campgrounds within a 20 kilometer radius of Sarlat, les Périères is the closest to town and the only one allowing you to stroll in on foot. The distance is about one kilometer.

Campsites are arranged on terraces in a semicircle overlooking the swimming pool and main buildings. All sites are covered with well-tended grass and most have convenient electrical and water connections. The five shower/toilet buildings are clean and well kept, hot water is provided for showers (adjustable), bathroom basins, and dishwashing. There is a beautiful swimming pool. Other amenities include tennis courts, a bar and snack bar, small shop, and library. Restaurants and shops are within walking distance.

To find the campground follow D47 toward Sous-Prefecture and Croix d'Alon. This small highway leaves Sarlat towards the northeast. You'll see the campground just a short distance up the hill.

CASTELNAUD-LA-CHAPELLE, FRANCE

Castelnaud, only 14 kilometers southwest of Sarlat, offers a quiet and scenic pastoral alternative. The village itself is little more than a few houses, a hotel, a couple of restaurants, and an imposing castle. The ramparts of **Castelnaud Castle** offer great views, there are also exhibits of medieval siege weapons.

Castelnaud-La-Chapelle Campground

✦ CAMPING CARAVANING MAISONNEUVE

Address: 24250 Castelnaud-La-Chapelle
Telephone: 05 53 29 51 29
Fax: 05 53 30 27 06
Price: Moderate

Open April 1 to Sept. 30

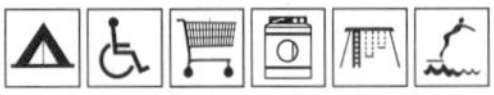

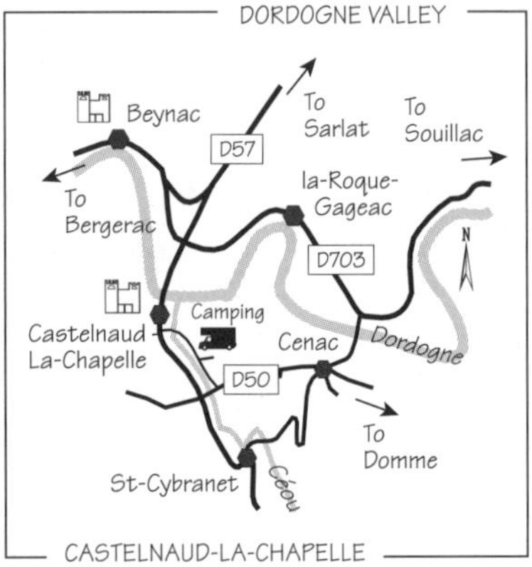

Maisonneuve is a beautiful, modern campground in a pleasant country setting. From most of the sites you have a great view of Castelnaud Castle on the hillside just a kilometer or two up the valley. This three-star campground is relatively new and offers a park-like atmosphere with large grassy sites separated by hedges and trees. Electrical outlets (CEE17 plugs, medium amps) are conveniently located near the sites. The shower/toilet facilities are in the main building and are quite nice with free hot showers. Maisonneuve also has a swimming pool, miniature golf, table tennis, a grocery shop and a bar. The stream running next to the campground has a very tempting swimming hole.

You'll need your own local transportation if you camp here, there is no bus service and the nearby village of Castelnaud-La-Chapelle offers little more than a few small restaurants. The town of Sarlat is about 14 kilometers away.

To reach the campground head south from Castelnaud toward Domme on D57. You'll see signs almost immediately. The campground is approximately 1 kilometer from the village.

Side Trips from Sarlat

Sarlat's immediate vicinity holds many attractions. Just 10 kilometers south-west of Sarlat two 13th century castles face each other from outcroppings on opposite sides of the river, just as they did during the 100 Years War. The French were in **Beynac**, which is restored and must be toured with a guide, and the English in **Castelnaud**, with its own self-guided tour. Castelnaud is described above and is near one of the area's two featured campgrounds.

You can follow the north bank of the Dordogne less than 5 kilometers east from Beynac to **la Roque-Gageac**, a small village on the riverside beneath an overhanging cliff. Here you can catch a boat for a ride on the river. If you drive a short distance on across the river the road climbs a small mountain to the hilltop bastide village of **Domme**. Domme is justifiably famous in literature for its views (Henry Miller) and is also known for the caves beneath the town, they can be reached by elevator from the central square.

Twenty kilometers northwest of Sarlat is **les Eyzies-des-Tayac,** a good place to start your exploration of the Vézère River valley, sometimes called the "cradle of mankind". In dozens of caves along this valley archeologists have discovered prehistoric cave paintings and living sites. The **Musée National de la Préhistoire** will introduce you to the subject, the **Abri Pataud** nearby is an actual cave dwelling. Three kilometers away is the **Grotte du Grand Roc** area where you'll find cave dwellings, limestone caverns, and even the **Musée de Spéléologie** which covers cave exploration. Twenty-five kilometers up the Vézère near Montignac is **Lascaux** where some of the world's most impressive cave paintings were discovered in 1940. The original caves have been closed to visitors because bacteria and algae introduced by the traffic were destroying the paintings but a replica cave has been constructed and is well worth a visit. The replica is called **Lascaux II**.

East of Sarlat at the eastern border of the region are two entirely different attractions. **Rocamadour** is a medieval pilgrimage town impressively situated on a cliff side. See if you can find Durandal, Roland's sword, plunged into the rock wall. **Gouffre de Padirac** (Padirac Chasm) is a giant series of limestone caves where visitors actually ride in a boat to view some of the more remote caverns. The underground regions are floodlit and elevators make access easy, these caves are some of Europe's finest. You can spend the night on this eastern edge of the Dordogne at CAMPING LES CIGALES or LE RELAIS DU CAMPEUR in l'Hospitalet just a kilometer east of Rocamadour.

If you find yourself with the itch to explore a little farther afield there are several towns that make excellent day trips from your Sarlat base. **Bergerac**, 75 kilometers west of Sarlat is known for its wine and, amazingly, tobacco. You may also be familiar with the town's namesake, Cyrano de Bergerac. The **Musée du Tabac** covers the tobacco industry very well, a drive 8 kilometers south to **Chateau Monbazillac**, home of the region's most famous wine, will round out your visit.

Sixty-five kilometers north of Sarlat is **Périgueux.** The town is know for its part Romanesque, part Byzantine **Cathédrale Saint-Front**. The **Musée du Périgord** will introduce you to the town's Roman ruins.

Finally, 60 kilometers south of Sarlat is **Cahors**, known for its "black" or deep purple wine. The scenic town is almost encircled by a bend of the Lot river. It was an important town in the Middle Ages and structures remaining from that time include the **Valentré Bridge** and **St-Stephen's Cathedral**. The Lot River Valley can provide you with several more days exploration, and has many campgrounds. In Cahors you might try CAMPING MUNICIPAL SAINT-GEORGES which is open April 1 to November 15 and within easy walking distance of the central town.

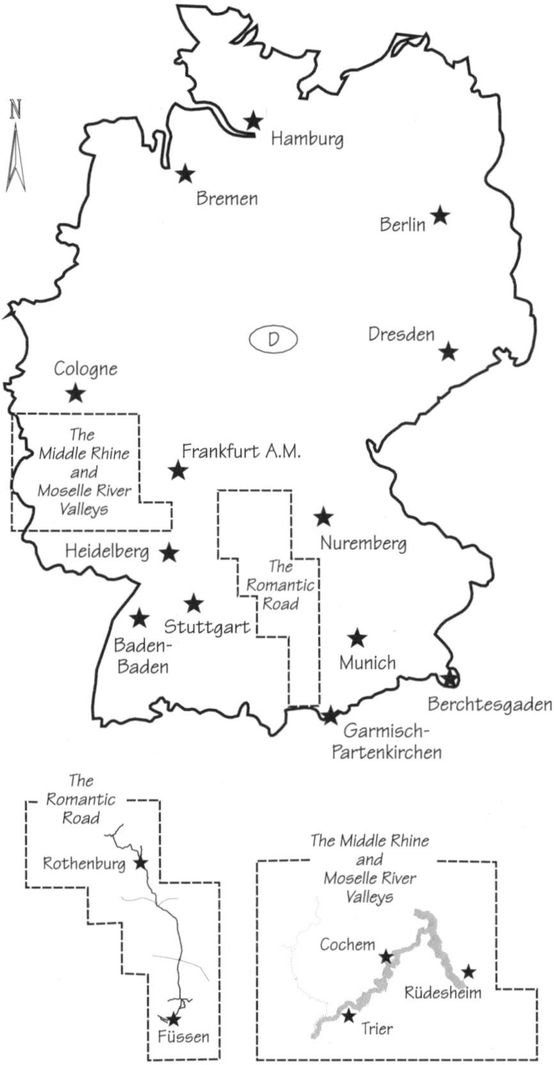
N
Hamburg
Bremen
Berlin
D
Dresden
Cologne
The Middle Rhine and Moselle River Valleys
Frankfurt A.M.
Nuremberg
Heidelberg
The Romantic Road
Stuttgart
Baden-Baden
Munich
Berchtesgaden
Garmisch-Partenkirchen
The Romantic Road
Rothenburg
Füssen
The Middle Rhine and Moselle River Valleys
Cochem
Rüdesheim
Trier

G E R M A N Y (D)

CHAPTER

8

GERMANY

INTRODUCTION

Germany may feel more like home to people from the United States or Canada than most places in Europe. The country is prosperous and organized. There are many people, yet much of Germany is not overly crowded. Roads are good, signage and traffic lights are similar to ours, and drivers are generally skillful and not overly aggressive, except on the autobahn. You'll find that Germans are outdoors enthusiasts so there are many campgrounds and natural areas with miles of bike and hiking trails. Many of the large German cities were destroyed during World War II and have been rebuilt so they often have a modern appearance. Efficient public transportation and traffic-free central areas are common. In West Germany, at least, English is widely spoken.

In a sense, of course, there are two Germanys. The former East Germany remains much different than the western part of the country. If anything, this makes Germany even more interesting, and the eastern part of the country offers many good camping opportunities. You will find that the roads are not quite as good as in the west and that gas stations are harder to find. These things are being rapidly improved, however.

Roads and Driving

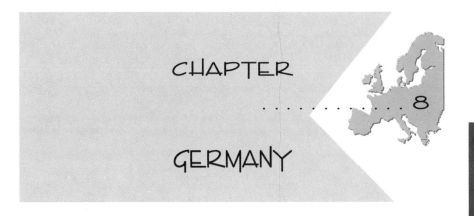

Germany is well known for its autobahns and the fact that many have no speed limits. You'll be smart to stay well to the right and keep an eye on your rear view mirror, the speed differential between an RV and a powerful Mercedes, BMW, or Porsche coming up behind can easily be more than 50 miles an hour. Don't let this intimidate you however, you'll have lots of company in the right lanes in the form of thousands of trucks traveling across the country, just like in the U.S. Many sections of the autobahns do have speed limits, a 120 kph (75 mph) limit is quite common. One of the best thing about the German autobahns is that they have no tolls. For this reason a drive across Germany is a great way to get from one place to another in Europe. For example, it is much less expensive to travel from the British Isles or the Benelux countries to Italy via Germany than via France. On maps the autobahns have an "A" prefix. Many are also labeled with an international "E" prefix, as are some "B" roads.

Secondary roads have a "B" prefix and in Germany they are usually good. Most are wide and have shoulders but when you get off the beaten track it is still possible to find narrow roads and cobblestones. Since autobahns are so common and are used for most long-distance travel you'll find that secondary roads tend to run through towns instead of bypassing them. Germans have lots of cars so you'll usually have plenty of company on the highway. Large RVs should have no trouble negotiating the roads, in fact, most of the larger RVs in Europe are manufactured in Germany and owned by Germans.

The general emergency phone number in Germany for both police and ambulance is 110. The AAA affiliated automobile club in Germany is ADAC (Allgemeiner Deutscher Automobil-Club E.V.). You can reach them at 089 76 76 0. There is also a nationwide breakdown service at 01802 22 22 22.

Camping

Germany has plenty of campgrounds, about 3,500 of them. Facilities are generally of good quality and clean with hot water and electricity available. You will find that many campgrounds meter electricity and charge by the kilowatt hour, some use coin-operated meters and others have an attendant read the meter before you hook up and when you leave. The CEE17 plug is the most common plug but the older German style is also used. In Germany more than anywhere else in Europe you will find many campgrounds full or nearly full of semipermanent resident caravans. Many are used only on weekends or during the July and August summer holiday. The campgrounds listed in this guide tend to cater to tourist campers, but many of them also have a large resident population with tourist sites intermixed with the permanent ones. Often no English is spoken by the reception person at German campgrounds, especially if he or she is older, but this is no problem, sign language always proves adequate. Campground reception offices are often closed for a couple of hours during lunch. Most campgrounds have a coin-operated washing machine and some also have clothes dryers.

An International Camping Card is usually not required in Germany, but you can often get a discount if you have one.

Free camping is something of an institution in Germany. Many Germans think that they are perfectly within both their rights and the law to free camp in any public parking space or lot. This is not strictly true and discretion is advised. Regulations vary from one area to another. It is usually permissible to camp for a few hours in autobahn rest areas but you are not allowed to set up equipment outside your rig (no tents).

Shopping, Currency, Credit Cards and Fuel

As a rich modern country you will find that Germany has plenty of shops and lots of variety. Supermarkets tend to be smaller than those in France and Great Britain but generally offer a good selection. A real problem in Germany is that opening hours in all stores are severely restricted by law. Finding time to shop has become a real problem for some working German families. Efforts are underway to change this but meanwhile you will find that most stores are only open during the week from 9 AM to 6:30 PM and on Saturdays from 9 AM to 2 PM. They are closed on Sundays.

Debit and credit cards are widely used, particularly Master Card, Visa, American Express and Diners Club. Our experience has been that Master Card is more useful than Visa in this country. Cash machines are widespread, even in small towns. Most gas stations now accept credit cards.

Itinerary Ideas

Good months for touring Germany are April through June and September and October. The school holidays that fall in July and August result in overflowing campgrounds so it is best to be somewhere else during those months. Winter weather on the North German Plain can be very cold and wet, however, there are many campgrounds in or near the Alps that remain open through the winter for snow enthusiasts.

Germany's major tourist cities are Munich and Berlin (each worth at least a week), other larger cities with tourist potential that are covered in this book are Bremen, Cologne, Dresden, Frankfurt, Nuremberg and Stuttgart. Some others that are not covered but still definitely worth a visit are Hanover, Constance, Leipzig, Lübeck, Rostock, and Weimar. Don't limit yourself to large towns, Germany abounds in interesting smaller villages, many with medieval centers.

The German tourist industry has developed a number of interesting driving routes for tourists. The best known of these is the Romantic Road which passes through many small towns with good campgrounds and is covered in this chapter. Others include the Castle Road from Mannheim to Nuremberg and the Fairy-Tale Road from the Frankfort A.M. vicinity to Bremen.

Some areas of Germany exude charm and make great places to enjoy the countryside and smaller villages while camping in rural settings. The Moselle and Rhine Valley are thoroughly covered in this chapter as an area, others include the Black Forest, Bavarian Alps, Harz Mountains, and the Baltic Coast. In this book Baden-Baden makes a good gateway to the Black Forest while Garmisch-Partenkirchen, Füssen, and Berchtesgaden are all in or near the Bavarian Alps.

Request touring and camping information from the **German National Tourist Office, Chanin Building, 52nd Floor, 122 East 42nd Street, New York, NY 10168-0072 (212-661-7200)** In Canada, **175 Bloor Street East, North Tower, Suite 604, 175 Bloor Street East, Toronto, Ontario M4W 3R8 (416 968-1570)**. Ask for their camping map, it has information about several hundred German campgrounds. Check our web site at www.rollinghomes.com for links to information about Germany.

GERMANY DISTANCE TABLE

In Kilometers

Kms X .62 = Miles

	Arnhem Netherlands	Baden-Baden	Basel Switzerland	Berchtesgaden	Berlin	Bremen	Cochem	Colmar France	Cologne	Dresden	Frankfurt A.M.	Füssen	Garmisch-Partenkirchen	Hamburg	Heidelberg	Innsbruck Austria	Luxembourg City Luxembourg	Munich	Nuremberg	Prague Czech Republic	Rottenburg Ober Der Tauber	Rüdesheim	Salzburg Austria	Strasbourg France	Stuttgart	Trier
Baden-Baden	517																									
Basel Switzerland	669	164																								
Berchtesgaden	897	472	566																							
Berlin	609	727	871	765																						
Bremen	263	628	780	911	390																					
Cochem	304	312	467	733	663	479																				
Colmar France	633	126	67	633	853	754	438																			
Cologne	172	345	490	738	583	325	132	471																		
Dresden	642	632	778	485	214	485	570	747	578																	
Frankfurt A.M.	351	172	330	551	564	467	173	298	190	471																
Füssen	760	312	310	264	697	812	577	317	588	604	425															
Garmisch-Partenkirchen	816	374	364	200	679	837	631	376	644	585	481	59														
Hamburg	382	663	815	949	285	120	574	789	430	485	490	856	866													
Heidelberg	422	85	243	487	639	543	218	206	260	571	100	333	383	581												
Innsbruck Austria	864	417	379	159	754	912	650	422	692	661	524	105	60	942	424											
Luxembourg City Luxembourg	344	269	316	682	756	572	119	247	200	663	219	599	623	667	227	627										
Munich	751	309	423	155	590	745	559	409	580	494	405	120	90	775	330	162	597									
Nuremberg	604	293	445	322	431	573	391	419	432	346	223	231	254	607	219	329	492	162								
Prague Czech Republic	794	567	772	394	366	640	665	693	689	152	497	505	453	638	493	537	766	378	274							
Rottenburg Ober Der Tauber	544	222	386	359	534	548	299	374	377	438	168	241	256	578	170	318	400	204	92	366						
Rüdesheim	318	181	343	615	619	493	112	310	146	526	79	462	508	588	105	538	181	447	279	553	237					
Salzburg Austria	896	457	552	38	733	891	713	585	725	457	537	250	239	930	473	145	665	141	308	368	345	601				
Strasbourg France	571	54	135	534	775	682	366	72	417	680	220	384	443	717	139	488	215	373	347	621	293	226	505			
Stuttgart	524	103	227	376	631	634	324	220	352	551	191	202	266	659	107	383	302	221	205	474	144	212	378	148		
Trier	329	230	385	629	709	525	72	359	158	616	172	551	615	620	188	580	47	550	445	719	403	174	615	284	295	
Zurich Switzer-land	752	255	83	475	873	857	538	150	580	780	412	217	293	887	326	296	399	340	447	718	405	426	461	221	210	468

SELECTED CITIES AND CAMPGROUNDS

BADEN-BADEN, GERMANY

Population 50,000

A popular health spa, Baden-Baden can also be considered the gateway to the Black Forest. The town is located near the Rhine and the French city of Strasbourg, and the forest rises to its south and east. Baden-Baden is the premier German resort with more millionaires per square acre than Palm Springs. Shopping and restaurants are excellent, of course, but could strain the budget.

While you're in Baden-Baden you might visit one of the baths. The two best choices are on Römerplatz near the old Roman bath ruins, naturally called the **Römische Badruinen**. Rather than touring the old baths, take a bath yourself. The **Friedrichsbad** will run you through a two hour series of showers and baths while the **Caracalla-Therme** just gives you the run of their pools and saunas. While the Caracalla is considerably cheaper you might base your decision on another factor. The Friedrichsbad allows no clothes on some days while the Caracalla always requires a bathing suit.

Besides the baths you may want to take advantage of the many hiking trails that run through the hills surrounding the town. There's also the casino.

Baden-Baden Campground

✦ CAMPING FREIZEITCENTER OBERRHEIN
Address: D-77836 Rheinmünster
Telephone: 072 27 25 00 Fax: 072 27 24 00
Price: Moderate

Open all year

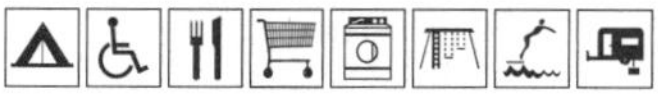

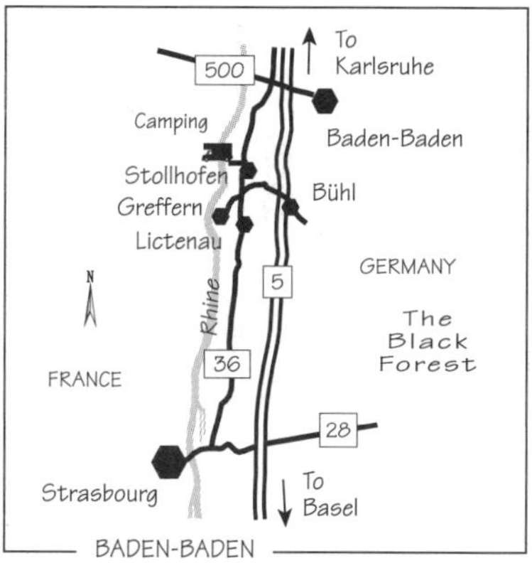

BADEN-BADEN

If you ask about campgrounds at the information office in Baden-Baden they'll hand you a list of six different places. Unfortunately, none of them is in Baden-Baden. Freizeit Center Oberrhein is one of the closest and not hard to reach if you have your own vehicle.

This is a giant campground. It surrounds two lakes about half a mile from the Rhine. There are many permanently-situated caravans here, but there is also lots of space for tourist rigs. Two areas are set aside for tourists, one is near the entrance and the second on the far side of the lakes. We prefer the one past the lakes because it is more scenic and has less one-night traffic. Sites are not marked, you can choose your own spot, an indication that there is usually plenty of room outside the busy July and August period. There are at least six shower/toilet buildings, two brand new ones are real Taj Mahals. They have self-opening electric eye doors, showers with glass doors that actually keep your clothes dry, and even special showers for the kids. Needless to say there is plenty of free hot water for showers, shaving and washing dishes and clothes. Coin-operated washers are available. The campground has two restaurants and a grocery shop.

Freizeit Center Oberrhein is 14 kilometers from Baden-Baden. To drive to town head north on Highway 36 for 8.5 kilometers then turn right at the sign for Baden-Baden. You'll reach town in another 5.5 kilometers on Highway 500.

You can easily find the camp from the autobahn, Highway A5. If you take the Baden-Baden exit proceed west until you meet Highway 36 and then turn south. If you take the Bühl exit head west to Highway 36 and turn north. The campground is located just north of the town of Stollhofen and is signed from Highway 36.

Side Trips from Baden-Baden

The **Black Forest** extends some 75 kilometers south from Baden-Baden and perhaps 30 kilometers east. This seemingly small area of pine forests is full of quaint villages and hiking trails. You can easily spend an extended time here visiting the most interesting sites and walking or skiing the trails. Incidentally, the Black Forest is equally accessible from Basel in Switzerland or Strasbourg and Colmar in France. All of these cities are within 100 kilometers of the city of Freiburg where we start our tour.

While there are many good driving routes through the Black Forest we'll suggest one that will allow you to see many of the sights. Once you've done this tour you can go back and spend a little more time at the places you admire most. This drive covers about 310 kilometers with the first 100 on good fast autobahn.

Head south on the A5 autobahn for about 100 kilometers to **Freiburg**. Freiburg is a good place to stop and do a little sightseeing. The **Münster** or Cathedral is a combination of Romanesque and Gothic that took three centuries to build and is sometimes called the finest in Europe. The medieval area around the Münster is also a good place to try some of the local Black Forest food specialties.

From Freiburg head east on B31 through the very scenic **Hell Valley (Höllental)** to **Hinterzarten**, an 800-year-old town that is the most popular resort in the southern Black Forest, and then a little farther to the **Titisee**, a beautiful mountain lake and resort with several campgrounds. Backtrack a little now and turn north on B500 to **Furtwangen** with its **clock museum** (cuckoo clocks originated in the Black Forest and are still a major shopping item), and **Triberg** where **Germany's highest waterfall** is located. So is the **Black Forest Museum** with more clocks and other exhibits about the Black Forest. A few miles north, just south of **Wolfach**, is the **Freilichtmuseum Vogtsbauernhof**, an open-air living museum showing the traditional way of living in the Black Forest. There are quite a few of this type of attraction throughout Germany and Scandinavia but this is one of the best.

Now take B294 toward Wolfach, and continue north through Schiltach, Alpirsbach, and Freudenstadt back to Baden-Baden on the Schwarzwald-Hochstrasse (B500).

If you fall in love with the Black Forest don't despair. There are several good campgrounds centered around Freiburg, Titisee, Wolfach and Freudenstadt. Some are open year round to take advantage of the winter ski season. You'll find CAMPINGPLATZ BELCHENBLICK just south of Staufen which is about 12 kilometers southwest of

Freiburg. The campground is open year round. One of the many campgrounds near the Titisee is TERRASSENCAMPING SANDBANK, open April 1 to October 20. Finally, near Schapbach about 20 kilometers southwest of Freudenstadt is SCHWARZWALDCAMPING ALISEHOF, open year round.

BERCHTESGADEN, GERMANY

Population 8,000

Berchtesgaden is a popular German resort that is located in a valley almost surrounded by Austria. If you've heard of Berchtesgaden it may be because this is the site of the **Eagle's Nest**, Hitler's alpine redoubt. Much of it has been destroyed but there's still a lot to see, with the bonus of a great view and good hiking. Take the bus from Berchtesgaden, this is a steep road and you'll have to park and take a bus for the last portion of the trip anyway. Another interesting destination is the **Salzbergwerk**, an operating salt mine which offers underground tours including a ride on an small underground railway and on a boat across an underground lake. Munich's Wittelsbachs had a palace here too, the **Schloss Berchtesgaden** is now a museum.

The **Berchtesgaden National Park** to the south of town is one of only a few German national parks. You can cross the **Königsee** on an electrically-driven excursion boat and then hike another kilometer or so to another lake, the **Obersee**, with its **Rothbachfall waterfall**. There are many other hikes in the park.

Berchtesgaden Campground

✦ CAMPING ALLWEGLEHEN

Address: D-83471 Berchtesgaden
Phone: 086 52 23 96   Fax: 086 52 63 50 3
Price: Moderate

Open all year

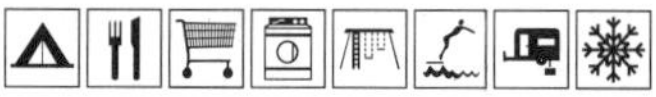

This is a large campground in a beautiful setting. It sits on a hillside with mountains on all sides. Perched high on the mountain behind the campground is Hitler's Eagle's Nest.

Allweglehen has several groups of sites, mostly with gravel surfaces, arranged on terraces. There are many semipermanent rigs here, but usually room for all the tourists that show up. Sites are numbered and assigned, electricity (CEE17 plug, 16 amps) is convenient to most sites and is metered. The shower/toilet facilities are arranged near the front gate, most in the main building and some in an adjacent building. Hot water is provided for showers (adjustable), bathroom sinks, and dishwashing. The laundry room has coin-operated machines. There is a swimming pool, a good restaurant, and very limited groceries. This campground also has a dump station.

Berchtesgaden is 4 kilometers from the campground. Frequent bus service is available at the main road about a kilometer from the campground.

The campground is located just off Highway 305, the Salzburg-Berchtesgaden road. This is the main access road to Berchtesgaden from the north. As you head toward Berchtesgaden you'll come to the road to Obersalzberg which heads up hill on your left. Just after this road you'll see the campground sign with the access road also heading uphill to the left. The campground is about a kilometer from the highway. The paved access road is steep with one steep hairpin. If your rig has problems with hills you might want to stop below and walk the hill first. A tractor is available to give assistance if requested. Most campers should have no problem.

BERLIN, GERMANY

Population 3,500,000

Berlin is an enormous city covering many times the area of Paris, in fact, it is the largest city, by area, in Europe. Population-wise, however, the city is quite small when compared with some other European capitals. This is not a high-rise city, it sometimes seems more of a park. Much of the area is covered by forests and lakes. Don't let the large area worry you, the city has an extensive and easy-to-use public transportation system.

Much of the recent history of Berlin is overshadowed by the **Berlin Wall**. Since the city was reunited in 1989 the wall has been mostly town down, there are still a few sections standing. The most central and easiest to visit is near the former Checkpoint Charlie on Friedrichstrasse. There is a wall museum there called **Haus am Checkpoint Charlie**. There's another museum housed in an East German watchtower in the Treptow district of former East Berlin.

The Unter den Linden was the central boulevard of prewar Berlin. When it was cut by the wall the West Berlin portion was renamed Strasse des 17 Juni. Now that traffic once more passes through the Brandenburg Gate Unter den Linden and Strasse des 17 Juni make a good way to orient yourself. Starting at the eastern end on Museum Island they run west through the **Brandenburg Gate**, past the **Tiergarten**, around the Grosser Stern with its **Victory Column**, and then on west to **Ernst-Reuter Platz**, a total distance of about 6 kilometers. Off the east end of the boulevard you can follow Karl-Liebknecht-Strasse a short distance to the **Alexanderplatz**, showcase of the former East Berlin. From Ernst-Reuter Platz you can follow Otto-Suhr-Allee 2 kilometers northwest to **Schloss Charlottenburger**, the impressive imperial palace and museums.

Another famous boulevard in Berlin is the **Kurfürstendamm**, relatively unimportant in the prewar city, but the center of the action in West Berlin after the division. It is not nearly as sparkling and upscale as you may expect, in fact before the war it was a kind of cabaret district. Bear in mind too that most of the buildings have been built since the war. This is the top shopping, gallery and restaurant street in Berlin although the former eastern sector has the **Friedrichstrasse**, which is now a major construction zone and coming rapidly along.

Berlin has an enormous number of good museums that are worth seeing. The **Museum Island** at the east end of Unter den Linden has the **Pergamon Museum** with its

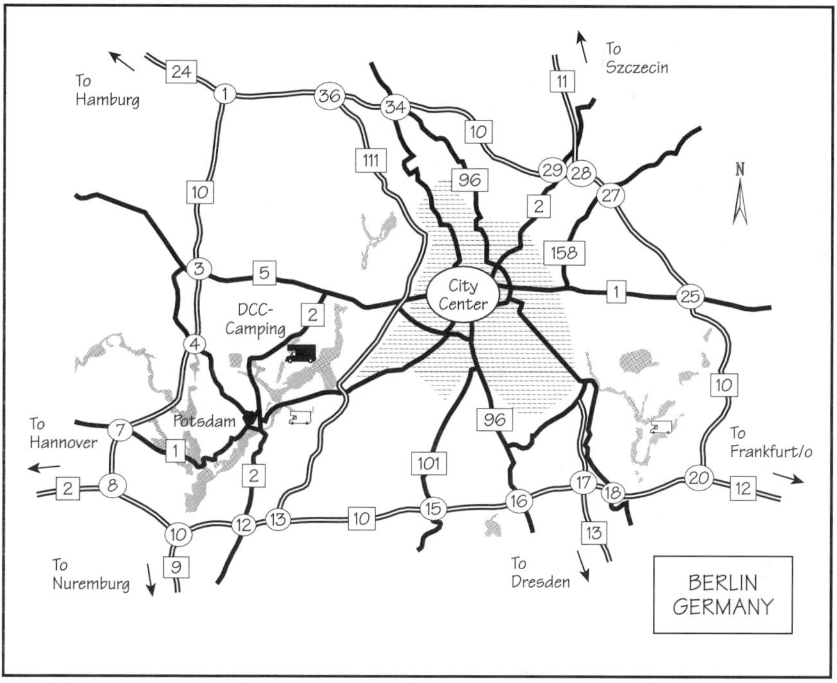

Pergamon Altar and Babylonian Processional Way, moved in their entirety from the middle east and reassembled inside the building. Museum Island also has the **Nationalgalerie** museum of painting and the **Bodemuseum** with its collections of antiquities and Italian Renaissance paintings. There's another group of museums in the south part of town, the **Dahlem Museums**. Accessible by subway, these include the **Gemaldegalerie** with a massive collection of paintings of the European masters through the eighteenth century; the **Museum für Völkerkunde** with exhibits of Mayan, Aztec, Inca, Polynesian, African and Asian artifacts; and the **Skulpturensammlung** with (you guessed it) a fine collection of sculpture. These two clusters of museums are just the beginning, there are lots more scattered around the city.

Since a large part of Berlin is water it only makes sense to spend some time on a boat. The Weisse Flotte (White Fleet) offers cruises on the Spree River and the lakes in southeast Berlin from near the Treptower Park S-Bahn station in Treptow (S-6 train line). Spree River trips are available from a dock in the Tiergarten. Boat trips on the large lakes in southwest and western Berlin go as far as Potsdam and depart from Wannsee and Tegel, accessible by S-Bahn (S-1) and U-Bahn (U-6) respectively.

When you've finished with all of the things mentioned above there's still the **Berlin Zoo** in the Tiergarten, and Sanssouci in Potsdam, which is covered as a side trip below.

There are actually quite a few campgrounds surrounding Berlin. These are primarily country caravan villages for Berlin residents but they do have tourist sites available. In addition to Kladow, described below, Berlin campgrounds include a group of sites in an area of lakes about 20 kilometers southeast of Berlin center including DCC CAMPINGPLATZ AM KROSSINSEE just west of Wernsdorf on the Krossinsee and open from early May to late September. In another direction CAMPINGPLATZ KOHLHASENBRÜCK and CAMPINGPLATZ DREILINDEN are located near Wannsee about 15 kilometers southeast of central Berlin.

Berlin Campground

✦ DCC-CAMPING ELSE-ECKERT-PLATZ

Address: Krampnitzer Weg 111,
D-14089 Berlin
Telephone: 030 36 52 79 7 Fax: 030 21 34 41 6
Price: Moderate

Open all year

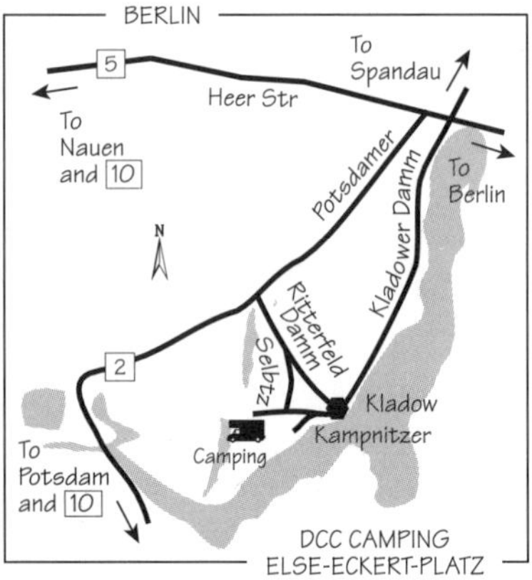

Berlin's campgrounds are really resident camps, they are full of caravans that don't move most of the year and are used by Berlin residents on weekends and during the summer. They are places that date from the period before the Berlin Wall was torn down. In those days you couldn't get far out of town, even to go camping. Kladow follows that pattern, however it has a large area for tourist rigs and tents and has quite nice facilities. Access to downtown Berlin is good.

Campingplatz Kladow is a very large campground located near a large lake called the Havel on the outskirts of the small town of Kladow between Potsdam and Berlin. The tourist camping area sits near the large services building quite a distance from the campground entrance. It comprises several hedge-surrounded site groupings with mostly gravel but some grass ground cover. Electrical outlets are all located at the entrances to the site groupings and are metered (CEE17 plugs). A warden will read the meter before you plug in and when you leave to determine your electricity usage. The showers, toilets, and other services are all in a two-story heated building. Showers are on the upper level and are adjustable, a 50-pfennig coin is required. Shaving sinks have hot water and there is hot water in the sinks in a special dishwashing room. The campground also has coin-operated washers and dryers. Near the campground entrance there is a nice little restaurant and also a grocery shop.

The bus journey in to central Berlin starts at a bus stop about 500 meters from the campground. The number 234 bus will take you some 2 kilometers in to Kladow. From the same stop in Kladow you then take the 134 north about 8 kilometers to Heerstrasse. Again from the same stop the 149 will carry you 11 kilometers through the western part of the city to the centrally located Zoo Station. This all sounds quite involved but usually takes only about an hour and is pretty painless.

The easiest way to find the campground is to take Exit 12 from the ring road south of Berlin near Potsdam. Follow Highway 2 from this exit north. It will take you right through the center of Potsdam (relatively light traffic) on one of several different routes following signs for Spandau and on north toward Berlin. After leaving Potsdam watch for campground direction signs, the first is at about 10 kilometers. You'll be directed to the right towards Kladow on Ritterfeld Damm and then right again to the campground.

Side Trips from Berlin

Potsdam and its **Sanssouci Park** are an essential side trip when you visit Berlin. If you followed our directions to the campground you drove right through the center of Potsdam (not a very large city) so you know how to get there by car. It is also possible to get there by boat from Wannsee or by S-Bahn from central Berlin. Sanssouci contains the rococo **Sanssouci Palace** itself, built by Frederick the Great, and several other palaces. The buildings, the park, and the water make this one of the most attractive palaces you'll see in Europe.

BREMEN, GERMANY

Population 540,000

For travelers in northern Germany Bremen can be a pleasant alternative to its rival giant Hamburg. Today Germany's oldest seaport has lost some of its seagoing traffic to smaller Bremerhaven which is closer to the ocean and can handle today's large seagoing ships, but there is still plenty going on here. The considerable damage that the central old town or **Schnoorviertel** received during World War II has been repaired and the area is full of restaurants and galleries. There's also the **Cathedral of St. Peter** (11th century), the Gothic **town hall**, rows of restored gabled houses, and the **Übersee Museum** with exhibits covering the places that Bremen traders visited around the world. Incidentally, Bremen is also the home of Beck's beer.

Bremen Campground

✦ CAMPINGPLATZ FREIE HANSESTADT BREMEN

Address: Am Stadtwaldsee 1, D-28359 Bremen
Telephone: 0421 21 20 02 Fax: 0421 21 98 57
Price: Moderate

Open March 23 to October 31, varies slightly

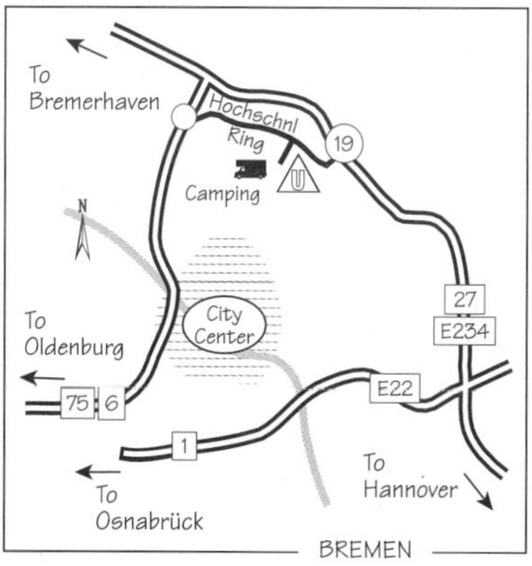

This campground is deceptive, due to the way that it is laid out it seems quite small, yet it will easily hold more than 150 campers, all with electricity. Campsites are grassy with many tree-separated glades holding 12 to 25 sites. There are also a few sites with hard surfaces for wet-weather camping. The shower/toilet building is near the front of the campground and also houses the other campground facilities including a store and restaurant. Showers are hot (adjustable push-button valve) as is the water in bathroom sinks and for dishwashing. Cook tops are provided in the dishwashing room for those with no stoves in their rigs. There is also a laundromat with coin-operated machines. The campground restaurant is quite large and provides relatively sophisticated offerings, the campground store is adequately stocked. There is a lot of municipal park land around the campground with a lake and lots of walking and biking trails.

Bremen's central area is about 5 kilometers away. If you don't feel like the hour walk or a bike ride you can use a convenient bus/tram combination. Details are available in the reception office.

The campground is most easily reached from Highway A27 which runs north of the city from the northwest to the southeast. Take Exit 19 towards Universitat. After a half kilometer turn right at the first stop light (there is a campground sign here). Proceed 1.5 kilometers and you will see the campground on your left.

COLOGNE'S DOM

Side Trips from Bremen

Bremen's port, **Bremerhaven**, is about 50 kilometers down the Weser River near the coast. It is home to the **Deutsches Schiffahrtsmuseum**, Germany's best maritime museum.

COLOGNE (KÖLN), GERMANY

Population 1,000,000

Cologne is an ancient city located on the banks of the Rhine river and, since it has always been a crossroads, you will probably pass near it. It is the fourth largest city in Germany, but the part of the city that will interest most visitors is a small easily-explored area near the cathedral.

The best reason to stop in Cologne is the cathedral, or **Kölner Dom**. Started in 1248 it wasn't finished until 1881 partly because work stopped for a 280 year interval during the construction. This is probably the most awe-inspiring Gothic cathedral in the world and the sight of its spires rising above the modern town will create a truly lasting impression.

Cologne has been an important city for many years, in fact it was an important Roman city, along with nearby Trier (Trèves). The **Römisch-Germanisches Museum** displays a large quantity of Roman artifacts from this period. It is conveniently located right next to the cathedral.

Also near the cathedral are two other important museums: the **Wallraf-Richartz-Museum** has paintings from 1300 to 1900 and the **Museum Ludwig** has paintings from 1900 to the present. Their collections of Dutch and Flemish masters and Picassos are especially outstanding.

The streets around the cathedral are designated as pedestrian only, and many stores and restaurants are located here. Crowds stroll along window shopping and watching street performers. There is a special restaurant area along the Rhine near the cathedral.

Cologne Campground

✦ CAMPING PLATZ BERGER

Address: Uferstrasse 71, D-50996 Köln-Rodenkirchen
Telephone: 0221 93 55 24 0
Fax: 0221 93 55 24 6
Price: Moderate

Open all year

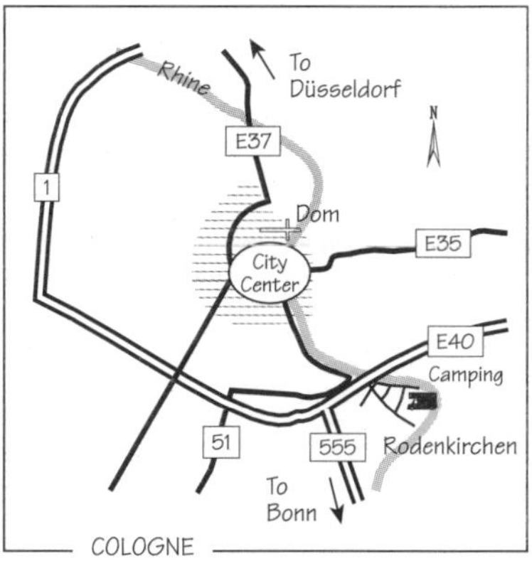

Cologne has three campgrounds that are convenient for visiting the central cathedral area. All are upstream along the Rhine, two are on the opposite or right bank. The last, Camping

Platz Berger is on the left bank in the town of Rodenkirchen about 7 kilometers from the cathedral. This is a good spot to enjoy the passing Rhine River barge traffic.

The large campground occupies a grassy area next to the river. There are large numbers of resident rigs here, especially during the middle of the summer. Camp sites are not numbered and are unassigned unless the campground is busy. Electrical outlets (CEE17 plugs, 10 amps) are in boxes hung on poles and are widely spaced, a warden will unlock the cover so that you can hook up. The large shower/toilet building is next to the entrance. Showers are hot and adjustable, there is hot water for the bathroom sinks, dishwashing sinks, and laundry area. Coin-operated washing machines are available. There is also a covered area with hot plates for cooking. The campground has a grocery shop and a good restaurant. There is a Jumbo supermarket in Rodenkirchen about 1.5 kilometers from the campground. A park along the river next door is convenient for children and for walks or bike rides.

There is a bus stop near the campground for getting in to Cologne but service is infrequent. A better option is the park-and-ride tram stop about 2 kilometers downstream from the campground, if you don't want to leave your rig unprotected you can easily walk the distance along a good bike path. Campers with bicycles at their disposal can ride the entire distance to the center of town, 7 kilometers, using the same bike path along the river.

The campground is located in the village of Rodenkirchen on the left bank of the Rhine about 5 kilometers upstream from Cologne. You can reach Rodenkirchen without driving through Cologne, Highway E40 crosses the river just north or downstream of the village. Once in Rodenkirchen thread your way through town to the river, you'll find the campground just upstream.

Side Trips from Cologne

Seventy kilometers west of Cologne on the E40 autobahn is another famous cathedral town, **Aachen**, also known as Aix-la-Chapelle. Charlemagne is king here, or was during the 9th century. After Charlemagne 32 of the following Holy Roman Emperors were crowned in Aachen and many of them gave a gift to the cathedral. As a result it has the most impressive and interesting **cathedral treasury** in Europe.

Bonn, former capital of West Germany, is only 26 kilometers south of Cologne along the Rhine. If you're staying at Camping Platz Berger it is even closer. While Bonn is not really much of a tourist destination you might want to take a quick drive down to take a look. The central part of the city is traffic free; there's a **Romanesque cathedral**, a university, a **Beethoven museum** (he was born here), and lots of **government buildings** along the Rhine south of the city.

DRESDEN, GERMANY

Population 525,000

Sitting way over in southeast Germany the city of Dresden seems to be in an inconvenient location, but it is really not. Dresden makes a great place to break a driving trip from Berlin to Prague. Mortally wounded by a heavy bombing raid late in World War

II many of the city's historical buildings have been rebuilt, particularly in the area along the Elbe. There's also a lot to interest the visitor in the surrounding vicinity, including Elbe River excursions and the region upstream known as Saxon Switzerland.

Museum lovers love Dresden. There's the **Zwinger palace** with no less than five different museums in one complex, most importantly the **Alte Meister Gallery** with old master paintings. The **Porcelain Museum**, featuring Dresden and Meissen china is also in the Zwinger. The new master paintings (19th and 20th century) are in the appropriately named **Neue Meister Gallery** in the **Albertinum** a short distance to the east. The Albertinum also houses the **Green Vault**, a museum with works of art fashioned of gold, jewels, and other precious materials. You might also find the **Karl-May-Museum** interesting. Karl May was a writer of westerns during the late 1800's and early 1900's, the museum helps explain curious German ideas about America's wild west. This museum is located in the town of Radebeul which is within tram-riding distance of central Dresden.

Dresden Campground

✦ CAMPINGPLAZ AM FREIBAD MOCKRITZ

Address: Boderitzer Str., D-01217
Dresden-Mockritz
Telephone: 0351 47 18 22 6
Price: Moderate

Open January 15 to December 15

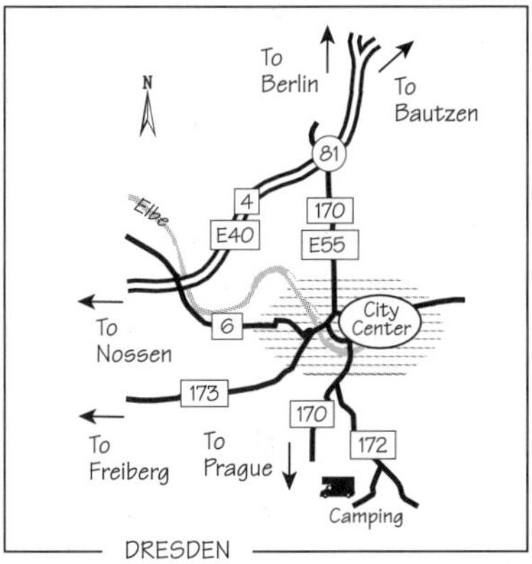

Dresden is rich in campgrounds, there are at least six within 15 kilometers of the city. Mockritz is one of the closest, you can reach the center of town using only one bus.

This is a medium-sized campground with few frills. Camping sites are on grass and are arranged between several parallel access roads on a slight slope. The campground has many rental bungalows, some sit around the border of the camping area. There is also a grassy tent-camping area surrounded by more bungalows. Many of the caravans here appear to be long-term tenants although they have not established their own fenced territories as in some other campgrounds. They have installed patios, however. Electrical outlets are located quite far apart, there are both German and CEE17 style plugs (10 amps). The shower/toilet building is old but clean and well maintained. There are free hot showers (adjustable) and hot water is available in the shaving sinks and at a small dishwashing station.

There is a bus stop next to the campground entrance. The number 76 will take you right to the Hauptbahnhoff (train station).

To reach the campground take Exit 81 from the E40 freeway running east and west to the north of Dresden. Travel south towards Dresden on Highway 170 (also called E55). This road will take you right through Dresden, in town it becomes Highway 172 and is signed as being the road to Pirna. About 3 kilometers out of the central area you'll see a campground direction sign pointing to the right down Gostritzer Strasse, you'll find the campground on the right in another 2 kilometers.

Side Trips from Dresden

Meissen, famous for its porcelain, is only 26 kilometers downstream from Dresden. The porcelain works here are open to visitors and there is a very good museum. Meissen wasn't damaged by bombing during the war so the central area is well preserved. It has a palace and a cathedral.

Saxon Switzerland (Sächsische Schweiz) is upstream from Dresden and just short of the Czech border. You get there on paddle-wheel excursion boats to Schmilka. This a very scenic area that is great for hiking. You can also get there by taking Highway 172 east from Dresden through Pirna.

FRANKFURT A.M., GERMANY

Population 650,000

Your overwhelming impression of Frankfurt will probably be how modern and well off it is. This is the business capital of Germany. The skyscrapers and the newness of the central area are the result of two bombing raids during World War II, the old town was practically leveled. Frankfurt has obviously recovered, this is arguably the busiest and most productive of German cities (Munich and Hamburg residents might not agree) and much of the resulting resources have gone into making the city a showplace.

Frankfurt has many museums, maybe more than any other German city, and that's saying a lot. A few of the best are the **Goethe-Haus** (the house where Goethe was born and also a museum), the **Städel Museum**, and the **Museum of Modern Art**. When your museum visits are finished the place to seek refreshment is the **Sachsenhausen** area a few blocks south of the Main River.

Frankfurt A.M. Campground

✦ CITY-CAMP E. SCHMITZT

Address: 35b Am der Sandelmühle, Alt Heddernheim, D-60439 Frankfurt am Main
Telephone: 069 57 03 32 Fax: 069 57 03 32
Price: Moderate

Open all year

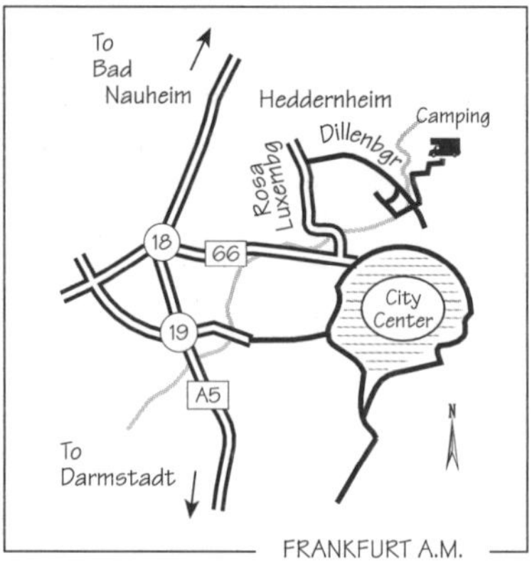

There are several campgrounds around Frankfort but this is the closest to the city. The location is not very scenic, but the convenient access to the U-Bahn makes up for a lot.

The campground is medium-sized with many permanent residents and also room for many tourist rigs. While facilities are adequate the campground seems a little run down. The management is friendly and helpful. Many of the folks staying here appear to be Germans with business interests in town. The campground can be crowded so the manager will probably assign you a place to park. Most camping sites are not clearly marked. There is an older shower/toilet building in the center of the site, hot showers require a token and shaving sinks have cold water as do the dishwashing sinks. There is another portable-type toilet building near the entrance to the campground, it has no showers but is convenient to the front area of the campground where most tourist rigs park.

Access to central Frankfurt is where this campground shines. The Heddernheim stop on the U-1,2 and 3 lines is about 500 meters from the campground. The trip to central Frankfurt takes about 15 minutes.

To reach the campground start on the A5 autobahn which runs north and south to the west of Frankfurt center. Take the A66 towards the east and then take the Nordweststadt exit. Following the signs toward Nordweststadt will put you on another elevated freeway heading north, this is Rosa Luxemburg Str. Take the Heddernheim-Industriegebiet exit and turn to the right onto Dillenberger Strasse. You'll see the first campground signs here and can follow them to the park. Just before the Dillenberger Strasse crosses the Nidda River you'll exit to the right and pass under the bridge to the left and to the campground.

Side Trips from Frankfurt

A colorful tourist route starts in Hanau, a suburb of Frankfurt, and runs north to Bremen. Called the **Fairy-Tale Road or Märchenstrasse**, it is a much more interesting way to drive north than the autobahn. Zigzagging north on back roads it passes through Steinau (**Brothers Grim childhood home**), Lauterbach, Kassel (**Wilhelmshöhe Palace and fountain**), Münden, Sababurg (**Sleeping Beauty's castle**), **Hameln** (of Pied Piper fame), and Bremen. The route appears on many maps and is marked with road signs. Long stretches can be bypassed using autobahns, otherwise this could be a week-long trip.

GARMISCH-PARTENKIRCHEN, GERMANY

Population 30,000

This town has name familiarity to many North Americans because it hosted the 1936 Winter Olympics and because it is a popular recreation destination for Americans serving their military tours in Germany. While the sister villages are attractive with many tourist facilities the real attraction is the countryside and mountains around them, particularly the nearby **Zugspitze**, Germany's highest peak. You can reach the top via either a cog railway or a cable car, there's skiing on the glacier at the top even during the summer. Other winter skiing areas in the surrounding mountains make great summer hiking destinations with convenient access provided by the lifts. There are even some good hiking opportunities in the flatlands below the Zugspitze, try the trail around the Eibsee near the lower Zugspitze cable car terminal.

Garmisch-Partenkirchen Campground

✦ CAMPINGPLATZ ZUGSPITZE

Address: D-82491 Garmisch-Grainau
Telephone: 088 21 31 80 Fax: 089 55 25 56 66
Price: Moderate

Open all year

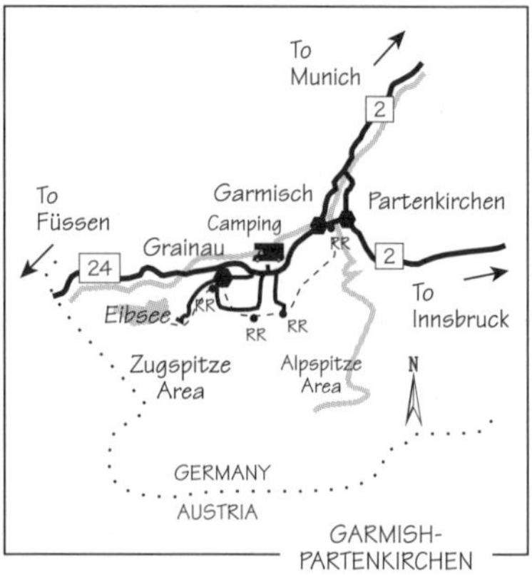

GARMISH-PARTENKIRCHEN

Camping Zugspitze is located about 4 kilometers west of the village of Garmisch in the direction of the Zugspitze lifts. This location is very convenient for all of the attractions associated with the mountain.

The campground is medium-sized with many permanent residents. The tourist sites are on grass in several rows near the highway and are not marked or separated from each other. Electrical outlet boxes are widely spaced (CEE17 plugs, 16 amps). The outlets are metered, you pay for the electricity that you use. The shower/toilet facilities are in an older building but are heated and in good repair. There is no free hot water, showers and dishwashing sinks require a coin and the bathroom sinks have no provision for hot water. There is a kiosk-style grocery store which has some restaurant take-out items. There is also a restaurant located across the street.

There is a bus stop next to the campground entrance for the bus that runs from Garmisch-Partenkirchen to the last lift station below the Zugspitze called the Eibsee. The bus stops at several villages between the two, there are access points to smaller lifts onto the mountain and to hiking routes that do not require lifts. Busses run approximately every hour, sometimes more often. A bicycle trail runs into Garmisch.

The campground is easy to find. Drive east from Garmisch-Partenkirchen on Highway 24 toward Ehrwald. About 4 kilometers out of town you'll see the campground on your right, you'll probably see the rigs before you see the small sign.

Side Trips from Garmisch-Partenkirchen

Two of the top destinations in Germany are within 20 kilometers of Garmisch-Partenkirchen. These are Schloss Linderhof, one of Ludwig II's three castles, and the town of Oberammergau. They're both in the same direction, Oberammergau is about 20 kilometers north on Highway 23, while Schloss Linderhof is reached by turning west at Ettal and driving about 10 kilometers on a narrow country road. While passing through Ettal you'll have the chance to tour **Kloster Ettal**, a monastery with a great rococo church.

Schloss Linderhof is the smallest of Ludwig II's castles, it is also the only one where he spent much time. That doesn't mean that it was a normal kind of place, check out the grotto in the garden, Ludwig's bedroom, and the hall of mirrors.

Oberammergau is a beautiful little Bavarian village known for two things: wood

GARMISCH-PARTENKIRCHEN STREET SCENE

carving and its Passion Play. The play is presented every day from May to September every ten years, 2000 will be the next performance year. Tickets are not easy to get. Woodcarving, on the other hand, is performed every year, you can see woodcarvers at work and buy as many carvings as you like.

Hamburg, Germany

Population 1,600,000

Hamburg is the largest city in northern Germany and one of the world's major ports, even though it is miles from the ocean. It is also the number three foreign tourist city in Germany, after Berlin and Munich. Arranged between and around the Elbe River and Alster Lakes with lots of green areas the central city is surprisingly pleasant for such a large town. Hamburg suffered during World War II but has been rebuilt, much of the central area is modern but there are many restored buildings too. A tour should include the area around the **Binnenalster Lake**, the **Jungfernstieg** shopping area, the **Rathausmarkt** square, and the many churches whose spires define the skyline. Hamburg is also famous for the **St. Pauli District** and its **Reeperbahn**, a very large and active red light district.

Hamburg Campground

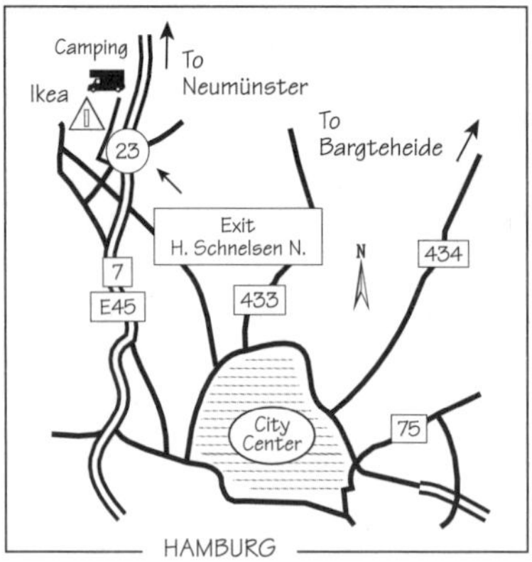

✦ CAMPINGPLATZ SCHNELSEN-NORD

Address: Wunderbrunnen 2, D-22457 Hamburg
Telephone: 040 55 94 22 5
Fax: 040 55 07 33 4
Price: Moderate

Open April 1 to October 31

This medium-sized campground is conveniently located just off the A7 autobahn and has bus and subway service in to the center of Hamburg. The camping sites are large and grass covered. Hedges separate groups of two or three sites, all are numbered and assigned at the reception desk. Electrical outlets are conveniently located (CEE17 plugs, 6 amps). The one shower/toilet building next to the entrance is modern and nice. Tokens are required for both showers and warm dishwashing water, sinks in the bathroom have free hot water. There are a few grocery items available in the reception office, including excellent beer. The campground has a playground, a laundry, and there is a golf course nearby, not to mention shopping at the Ikea store out front.

The trip in to town is easy to accomplish once you figure it out. The receptionist will explain, it involves a walk of about a half kilometer, a 10-minute bus trip to the subway station, and then a 15-minute subway ride.

To find the campground take the Schnelsen Nord exit from the A7 autobahn some 15 kilometers north of Hamburg. Head west following signs to an Ikea store and the campground. The campground is just behind the Ikea store which has a very high sign that you can easily see from the freeway.

Side Trips from Hamburg

Only 60 kilometers northeast of Hamburg via autobahn is the historic Baltic port of **Lübeck**. This was one of the Hanseatic ports and has so many preserved buildings that UNESCO lists it as one of the world's greatest cultural and national treasures.

HEIDELBERG, GERMANY

Population 135,000

Heidelberg is the oldest university town in Germany, the university dates from 1386. The town also has a **castle**, a very interesting **old town** area, and is full of students and tourists. The scenic location on the Neckar River is an added attraction. When you walk around town and see the foreign tour groups you will know that you are truly on the tourist road.

A favorite pastime in Heidelberg is just wandering around the old town. Heidelberg did not sustain damage in World War II so what you see is not reconstructed. It is a great place to take pictures, you'll see many people doing just that. The walk up the hill to the castle is worthwhile, if the idea of a lot of stairs bothers you there is a funicular railway that will take you to the top.

Heidelberg Campground

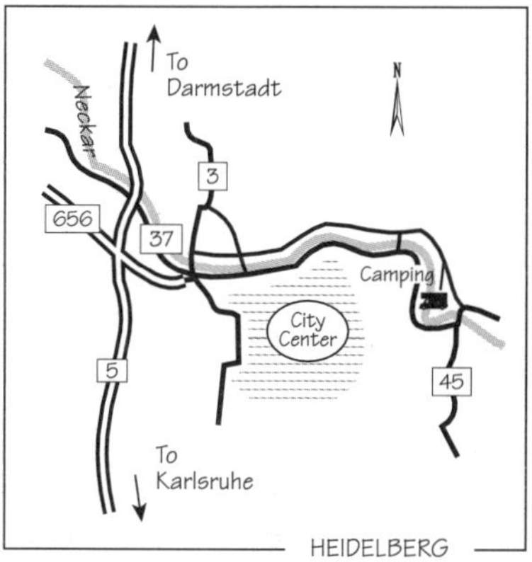

✦ CAMPING HAIDE

Address: D-69151 Neckargemünd
Telephone: 062 23 21 11
Price: Moderate

Open April 1 to October 31

Haide is a rural campground located along the right bank of the Neckar River about 6 kilometers upstream from Heidelberg. You'll notice noise from a railway and highway on the far side of the river at first but trains and traffic are not frequent enough to cause a big problem. The riverside location is very pleasant and scenic, especially in the evening, and there is interesting barge traffic on the river. You'll wonder how they manage to thread their way up this narrow river in the middle of the night with no lights.

The campground is a large narrow field that stretches along the river, sections farther from the reception kiosk are closed if it is not high season. Camping sites are located on grass on both sides of a central access driveway. Electrical boxes are widely spaced (CEE17, 16 amps). The shower/toilet buildings are older but clean, hot showers require a token and dishwashing is in cold-water stations located around the campground.

The town of Heidelberg itself sits just where the river emerges from the mountains. The Campground Haide is about 7 kilometers from town, a little far to walk, and it makes sense to take the bus in to town because it is difficult to find a place to park in Heidelberg. Ask at the campground reception desk about the best place to catch the bus.

To reach the campground from Heidelberg follow Highway B37 up the south side of the river past the old town. Cross the river to the north side on the bridge just outside of town and continue upstream. You'll see the campground sign on your right.

Side Trips from Heidelberg

Schwetzingen, 10 miles southwest of Heidelberg, has an impressive 18th-century palace and gardens. This is also Germany's asparagus center, something to bear in mind in the late spring and early summer.

The **Castle Road (Burgenstrasse)**, formally begins in Mannheim, but Heidelberg is where it really gets serious. If you follow the Neckar Valley upstream you'll find castles in or near the towns of Neckargemünd, Neckarsteinach, Zwingenberg, and Mosbach; and that's only the first 45 kilometers, the Castle Road now runs all the way to Prague.

MUNICH (MÜNCHEN), GERMANY

Population 1,300,000

Munich is pretty well known around the world as a fun town. Most people have heard of the Oktoberfest celebration which attracts beer lovers from everywhere for a two-week party. There is also the Fasching or Carnival before Lent. Some people think there's a little bit of the Italian in every Bavarian, something must be responsible for the personality difference between this part of Germany and all of the rest.

For orientation purposes you can consider the center of town to be the **Fussgängerzone**, a long stretch of pedestrian shopping streets and squares starting in the west near the Hauptbahnhof and running for two kilometers to the southeast. This is the center of shopping, eating, and tourism in Munich. Toward the east end you'll find the **Marienplatz** overlooked by the **Neues Rathaus** with its famous **Glockenspiel**. A few blocks off this end of the Fussgängerzone you'll also find the **Hofbräuhaus beer hall**.

Munich is, of course, famous for its beer. There are many breweries in town and the famous Hofbräuhaus is just one of a large number of beer halls, beer cellars, and beer gardens. The biggest party, the **Oktoberfest**, is really mostly in September, it runs for two weeks and always ends on the first Sunday in October. While there are people having a good time all over town the center of the action is the **Theresienwiese**. You

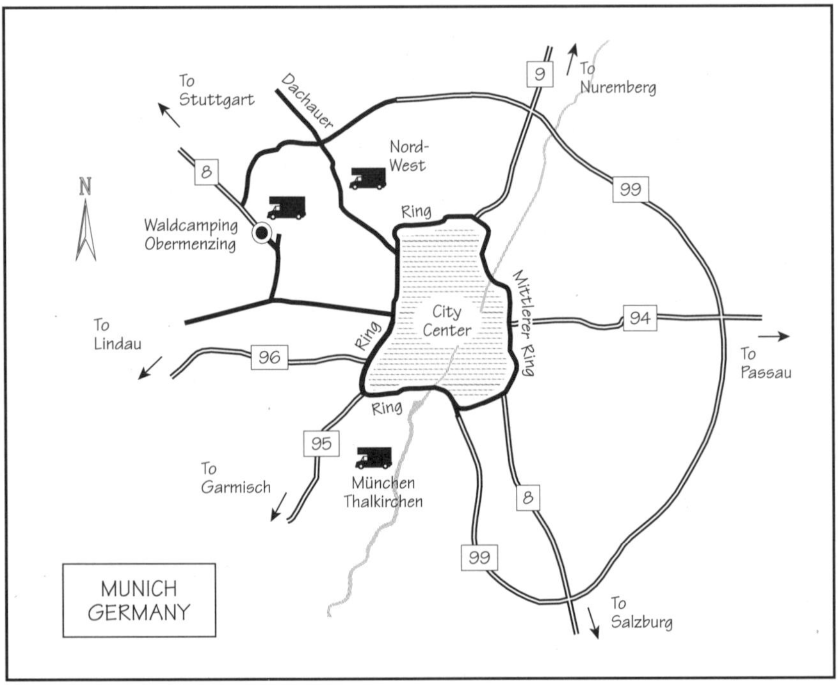

can reach it easily on the subway, there's a Theresienwiese stop on the U4/U5 subway line. Large beer hall pavilions are set up as well as circus rides and everything else it takes for literally millions of people each year to have a good time.

For 750 years until 1918 Munich and Bavaria were ruled by monarchs, the Wittelsbachs. The most famous member of this family is probably **Ludwig II**, not because he was a good king but because he wasted a lot of money building the ridiculously expensive castles that are some of Bavaria's top tourist attractions. Ludwig wasn't the only Wittelsbach builder, Munich is full of their palaces and government buildings. These include their town palace complex, the **Residenz** and their summer palace complex, the rococo Versailles-like **Schloss Nymphenburg**. During their long reign the Wittelsbachs had time to collect a great deal of art so Munich has some great museums. The **Alte Pinakothek** is considered one of Europe's best picture galleries, full of Italian, Dutch, and German masters. Across the street is the **Neue Pinakothek** with a more modern selection.

While there are other well-known art museums that are well worth a visit probably the most popular museum in Munich is the **Deutsches Museum**, located on Museum Island, as short walk from the Fussgängerzone. This is a huge science and technology museum full of such things as a walk-through submarine, airplanes and rockets, cars and trains, science experiments that allow you to participate, a planetarium and an IMAX theater. In all there are 30 different departments. No kid under the age of 90 will want to miss it. You may also be interested in the **BMW Museum** (Munich is BMW's home); the **German Hunting and Fishing Museum (Deutsches Jagd-und Fischereimuseum)** just across from the Michaelskirche on the Fussgängerzone; or the **Marstallmuseum** at Schloss Nymphenburg with its royal carriages and Nymphenburg porcelain.

Other interesting offerings in Munich are the **Englischer Garten**, the continent's largest city park; the **Olympiapark**, site of the 1972 Olympic games; and Dachau concentration camp, covered below as a side trip.

Munich has an excellent subway. It also has a good bike path system, you can pick up a bike path guide at the tourist office.

Munich Campgrounds

✦ WALDCAMPING OBERMENZING (WEST)

Address: Lochausener Str. 59,
D-81247 München
Telephone: 089 81 12 23 5
Fax: 089 81 44 80 7
Price: Moderate

March 15 to October 31

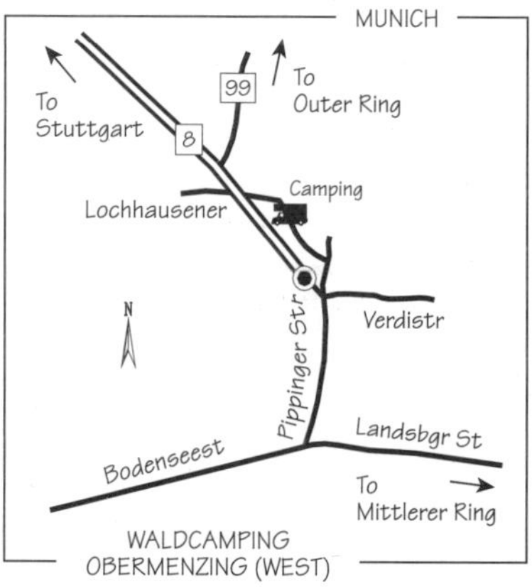

If you happen to be approaching Munich from the west, especially on the A8 from Stuttgart, you might want to give Obermenzing a try.

Thalkirchen, on the south side of town is much more difficult to find if you don't know exactly how to get there. You also have to negotiate a lot more Munich traffic.

Obermenzing is a large campground set on a heavily treed plot in the western outskirts of Munich. There are no resident campers. The A8 Stuttgart Autobahn runs just next door so there is some traffic noise. There is a large area with numbered sites for trailers and motor coaches with the sites separated by high hedges. Tent sites are located in a central circular area and there is room for more wheeled campers to park around the outside of that area. The reception person does not usually assign sites letting you park where you wish unless the campground is crowded. Individual electrical outlets are conveniently located next to many of the sites, they are metered (15 amps, CEE17 plugs), requiring you to deposit 50-pfennig coins. The shower/toilet building is older and a little grim but clean, hot showers require a token, free hot water is available in shaving sinks and for washing dishes and clothes. The campground has a coin-operated washer and dryer, a small grocery shop, and a tavern that offers snacks.

There is a bus stop about 800 meters from the campground for the number 76 bus that will take you to the Pasing S-Bahn station. From there it is clear sailing on in to central Munich.

The driving route to the campground begins at the roundabout before the beginning of the Stuttgart autobahn. Don't start down the autobahn, the first U-turn exit is 10 kilometers away. Turn north at the first turn east of the roundabout onto Pippinger Str. The campground signs are poor here at the roundabout but are fine once you get make this critical turn, you'll reach the campground in about 1.6 kilometers as the signs gradually lead you back towards the north side of the freeway on Lochhausener Str. From the other approaches to Munich follow signs toward the Stuttgart Autobahn, they'll lead you to that last roundabout where you can reverse and proceed to the campsite.

GERMANY

✦ CAMPINGPLATZ MÜNCHEN-THALKIRCHEN

Address: Zentralländstr 49, D-81379 München
Telephone: 089 72 31 70 7 Fax: 089 72 43 17 7
Price: Moderate

Open from March 15 to October 31

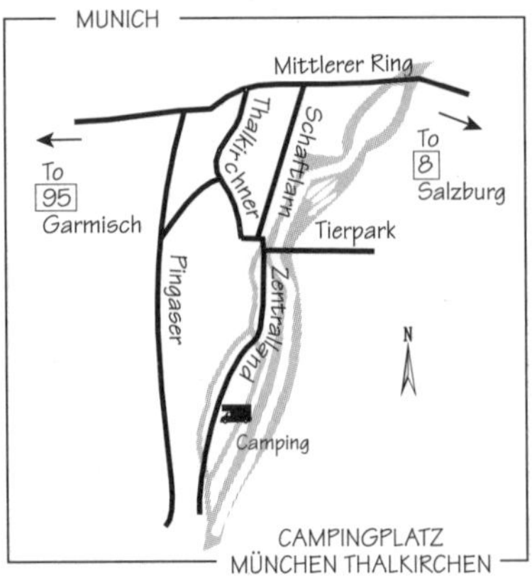

Thalkirchen is one of the best-known campgrounds in Europe, almost everyone passes through at one time or another, many during Oktoberfest. Its large size, decent facilities, and very convenient location make it Munich's best place to stay. During Oktoberfest you can count on it being overcrowded and noisy, that's part of the experience.

The campground is a large, partly-shaded field located in the Isar Valley Conservation Area about 4 kilometers from the center of Munich. Individual sites are of many kinds, most of those for wheeled vehicles are numbered and usually separated by pipe fences. Tents are pitched in large grassy areas, generally away from the owner's cars. Bus tour companies love this campground and there are often large areas covered with their identical small backpacking tents. The reception staff does not generally assign individuals camping sites, they just assign you a general area. Electrical outlets are widely spaced. Several shower/toilet buildings of various ages and quality service the campground, hot water always requires a token. There is a grocery shop, a snack bar, and a laundry room.

The Thalkirchen U-Bahn subway stop on the U3 line is about 2 kilometers from the campground. The number 57 bus does nothing but make a circuit from a stop near the campground to the subway station with the entire circuit taking about 20 minutes including a 5-minute stop at each end. The driver always seems polite but bored.

Finding Thalkirchen is a challenge despite numerous campground signs posted all over town. If you lose the thread while following the signs head for the Mittlerer Ring on the southwest side of town. The campground is well signed from this motorway. The zoo is nearby and you may see signs for it if you don't spot a camping sign.

✦ CAMPINGPLATZ NORD-WEST

Address: Schrederwiessen 3,
D-80995 München
Telephone: 089 15 06 93 6 Fax: 081 31 21 97 8
Price: Moderate

Open all year

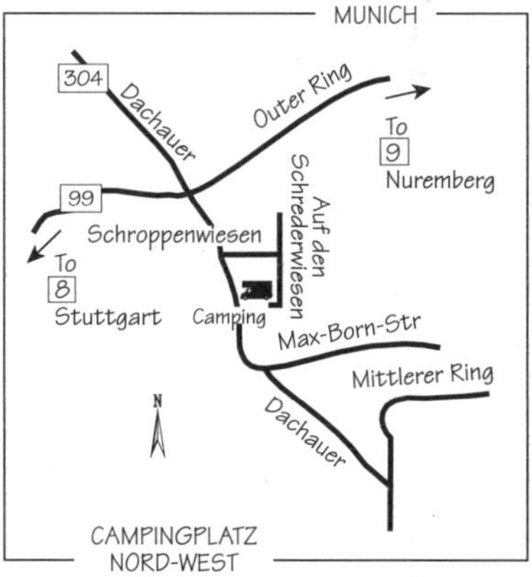

This is a medium-sized campground with grass-covered sites. It has many resident rigs, tourists with motorhomes are usually parked in small sites along the outside fence. Electrical boxes are widely spaced and metered, the warden will read the meter before you hook up and when you check out to determine your usage. The shower/toilet building is small but clean and heated in the winter. Showers are nice and hot.

Access to central Munich from the campground is by bus. There is a stop on Dachauer Str. not far from the campground.

To find Campingplatz Nord-West proceed northwest on Dachauer Str. This is a major arterial that runs northwest from the Hauptbahnhoff or railway station in the central part of town. After about 7 kilometers the street comes to a T and bears left to circle around a railway yard, just after this you'll see a campground direction sign pointing to the right.

Side Trips from Munich

Just 20 kilometers northwest of Munich is **Dachau**, the first Nazi concentration camp. It is one of the few that have been preserved. You'll find the walls, a museum, one of the dormitory buildings (and the foundations of the others), and the crematorium. To drive there from Munich take the autobahn toward Stuttgart and then the Dachau exit. Drive toward Dachau and watch for signs. There is a large parking lot. You can also easily reach Dachau from Munich on the S-2 suburban rail line.

Schloss Herrenchiemsee, one of Ludwig II's castles (really more of a palace), makes a good day trip from Munich. It was modeled after Versailles and never finished. Take the E52 autobahn towards Salzburg, the distance is about 90 kilometers. The castle is on an island in the Chiemsee, ferries depart frequently from the village of Stock, near Prien on the west shore of the lake.

NUREMBERG (NÜRNBERG), GERMANY

Population 575,000

Nuremberg is a large industrial town with a walled medieval center. This is another city that was almost completely destroyed during World War II, the old medieval city has been rebuilt here more extensively than anywhere else in Germany. You have to look closely to see that much of it is really quite new. You can easily walk to any of the sights inside the walls, they include the **Medieval Mall (Handwerkserhof), Imperial Castle (Die Kaiserburg)** and the house of the artist Albrecht Dürer, the **Dürerhaus**. Since this is said to be Germany's toy capital you might also want to visit the **Toy Museum (Spielzeugmuseum).** Nuremberg is also justifiably famous for its bratwurst.

Nuremberg Campground

✦ CAMPINGPLATZ IM VOLKSPARK DUTZENDTEICH

Address: Hans Kalb Str. 56, D-90471 Nürnberg
Telephone: 091 18 11 12 2
Price: Moderate

Open May 1 to September 30

Nuremberg's only campground is located in a large park area about 4 kilometers to the southeast of the center of town. A pleasant 1.2 kilometer walk on paths through the park takes you to the subway station for a ride into town.

This is a medium-sized campsite in a well-kept grassy meadow with large trees. There are very few permanent resident rigs. Campsites are not marked or assigned, campers tend to loosely cluster around the few electrical boxes. Electricity (CEE17 plugs, 10 amps) is metered, the boxes take 1 mark coins. The two shower/toilet rooms are clean and airy, showers require a token and shaving sinks have warm water. Cold water dishwashing facilities are scattered around the campground. There is a coin-operated washer and dryer. The campground also has a kiosk selling groceries and take-out food.

Access to the center of town is by subway. The Messezentrum station on the U1 and U 2 lines is a 1.2 kilometer walk through the park, the path is signposted. En route you will walk across a wide unused boulevard that looks like a good place to hold a military parade. Subway stations are conveniently located in the town center.

The campground could be difficult to find if it weren't signposted once you leave the autobahn. From the E50/A6 that runs east and west to the south of town take Exit 59 which is marked Nürnberg-Langwasser and proceed north following the camping signs which soon appear. They will take you north on Gleiwitzer Str., right on Beuthener Str. in a curve around the park where the campground is located, then three quick rights take you around and under Beuthener Str. and into the park where the signs will guide you to the campground. Just before turning into the park you'll see a rather spooky-looking old stadium that may remind you of video clips you've seen of Nazi rallies. This is the Zeppelinfeld and it was in fact used for those rallies.

From E45/A9 running east of town in a north and south direction take Exit 52 marked Nürnberg-Fischbach and proceed toward Nürnberg. After about 5 kilometers you'll see a campground direction sign pointing to the left. This left turn on Kalb Str. will take you into the park where signs will direct you to the campground.

STUTTGART, GERMANY
Population 560,000

Most of us know Stuttgart as the city where Mercedes Benz and Porsche build cars. You'll find the impression reinforced by the fact that the campground here is in the suburb of Bad Cannstatt is near the Mercedes plant.

Both Mercedes and Porsche have interesting museums. It is also possible to visit the production line at the Porsche plant. At the center of this mostly very modern town is the **Schlossplatz**. Nearby is the **Staatsgalerie** which has a collection of paintings by masters from the area as well as from the Low Countries, some French Impressionist canvases, and Germany's best Picasso collection.

Stuttgart Campground

✦ CAMPINGPLATZ CANNSTATTER WASSEN

Address: Mercedesstrasse 40,
D-70372 Stuttgart
Telephone: 0711 55 66 96 Fax: 0711 55 74 54
Price: Moderate

Open all year

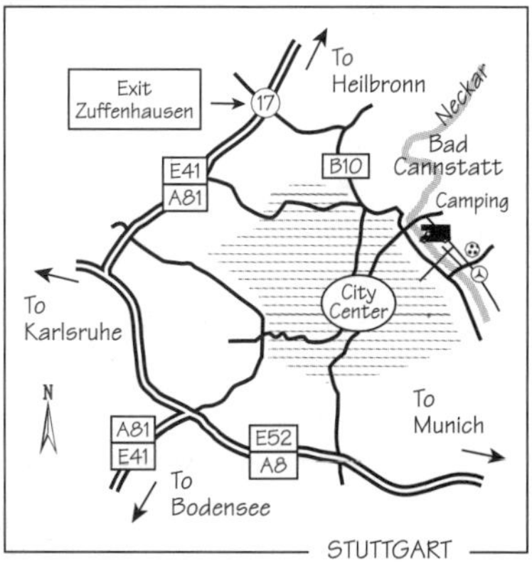

This city campground has a pleasant location next to the Neckar River in the Stuttgart suburb of Bad Cannstatt. It adjoins the Cannstatter Wassen (Canstatter Meadows) where the Oktoberfest-like Cannstatter Volksfest is held each autumn for two weeks encompassing the end of September and the beginning of October. The campground will probably be full at the time of the festival but additional temporary camping areas are provided.

The campground is medium-sized with vehicle parking off a circular paved drive on lattice bricks. Electricity is convenient to the sites. There is a grass-covered tent area at one corner of the campground. the moderns shower/toilet building has hot showers with unlimited free hot water and hot water in bathroom sinks and laundry sinks. There is a small store at the campground as well as a small bar/restaurant. A bike path runs next to the campground on the bank of the Neckar River.

The campground sits quite a distance from the two freeways that run south (E52) and west (E41) of Stuttgart. Best access is from E41. Take Exit 17 and follow Highway 10 southeast into Stuttgart. You will see Bad Cannstatter and Stadion direction signs, the campground is near the stadium in Bad Cannstatter so follow these. Eventually you will begin seeing camping signs and these will lead you the campground on the east bank of the Neckar near the stadium. By tram number 2 or U1 from downtown in the direction of Bad Cannstatt get off at the Mercedesstrasse stop. If you are using the surface lines (S1, S2, or S3) get off at Bahnhof Bad Cannstatt. The campground is about a kilometer south along the river.

KING LUDWIG II'S NEUSCHWANSTEIN CASTLE

TWO OUTSTANDING REGIONS AND THEIR CAMPGROUNDS

THE ROMANTIC ROAD

The Romantic Road is the best of several driving routes through the country, others include The Fairy-Tale Road (see Side Trips under Frankfurt) and The Castle Road (see Side Trips under Heidelberg). The Romantic Road starts in Würzburg, about 100 kilometers east of Frankfurt, and runs southward for about 360 kilometers to the town of Füssen near the Swiss border. The major points of interest and distances between them are as follows:

Würzburg	0 KILOMETERS
Rothenburg	95
Dinkelsbühl	48
Nördlingen	30
Donauwörth	31
Augsburg	43
Landsberg	38
Shongau	30
Schwangau-Füssen	45

These are only the larger and more important towns. You'll drive through many smaller villages and scenic areas between them. There are campgrounds in Würzburg, Bad Mergentheim, Creglingen, Rothenburg, Schillingsfürst, Dinkelsbühl, Donauwörth, Augsburg, Landsberg, Rottenbuch, and in the Schwangau-Füssen neighborhood. There are complete descriptions of campgrounds in both Rothenburg and Schwangau-Füssen in this chapter. Some people "do" the Romantic Road in one day, others spend two weeks.

Würzburg marks the beginning of the route and has several attractions. The most important sight is the **Residenz**, a world-renowned baroque palace that was built during the early eighteenth century. While the exterior is restrained, the enchanting interior is considered one of the finest examples of rococo decoration in the world. If you have the energy after touring the Residenz you'll also want to walk across the **Old Main Bridge** and climb to the **Marienberg Fortress**. It houses a museum which contains sculptures by the great German woodcarving sculptor Tilman Riemenschneider. You'll see many additional examples of his carvings in churches as you travel south. The nearest campground to Würzburg is CAMPINGPLATZ KALTE QUELLE, open from the middle of March to the end of November and located about 5 kilometers south of town toward the village of Winterhausen.

Heading south from Würzburg on the Romantic Road you'll pass through the Tauber Valley and the town of Bad Mergentheim and eventually reach **Rothenburg**. Sometimes the roads are confusing but follow signs for the Romantische Strasse. There are

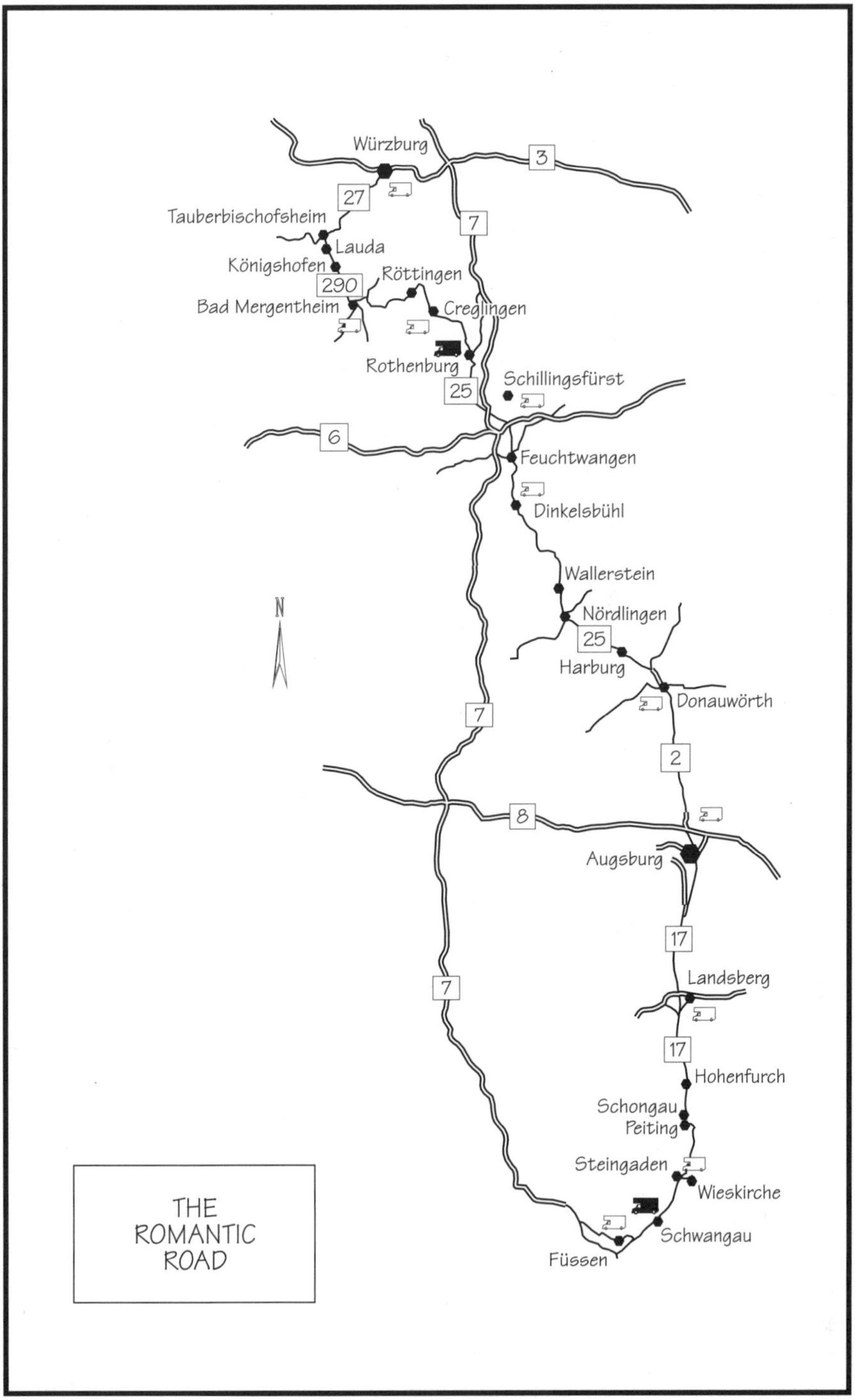
Würzburg
3
27
Tauberbischofsheim
7
Lauda
Königshofen
290
Röttingen
Bad Mergentheim
Creglingen
Rothenburg
Schillingsfürst
25
6
Feuchtwangen
Dinkelsbühl
Wallerstein
Nördlingen
N
25
Harburg
Donauwörth
7
2
8
Augsburg
17
Landsberg
7
17
Hohenfurch
Schongau
Peiting
Steingaden
Wieskirche
Schwangau
Füssen
THE ROMANTIC ROAD

a couple of good campgrounds in Rothenburg, it is one of the highlights of the route.

ROTHENBURG OBER DER TAUBER, GERMANY
Population 12,000

The walled city of Rothenburg is probably the most realistic and tasteful walled-city preservation in all of Europe. Nothing important seems to have ever happened in Rothenburg, and as a result the town hasn't changed. For campers Rothenburg is particularly pleasant because there are two great campgrounds in the very scenic village of Detwang in the valley just below the city walls.

You'll want to spend most of a day just wandering around the extremely picturesque streets. In addition visit the **Kriminalmuseum**, climb the **city hall tower** for the view, and tour the **Toppler Castle** outside the city. You can walk around much of the town on the **city walls** and take a tour in the evening with the night watchman. Even Detwang, your home base, deserves a look. The village is even older than Rothenburg and is the home of the **Church of St. Peter and St. Paul** with a carved Crucifixion Alter by Riemenschneider and a yard full of interesting headstones.

Rothenburg Campground

✦ CAMPINGPLATZ TAUBERROMANTIK

Address: Detwang 39, D-91541
Rothenburg o.d.T.
Telephone: 098 61 61 91 Fax: 098 61 86 89 9
Price: Moderate

Open March 1 to October 31 and December 1 to January 2

Camping Tauberromantik is large, well run, and has facilities designed to match the ambience of Rothenburg perfectly.

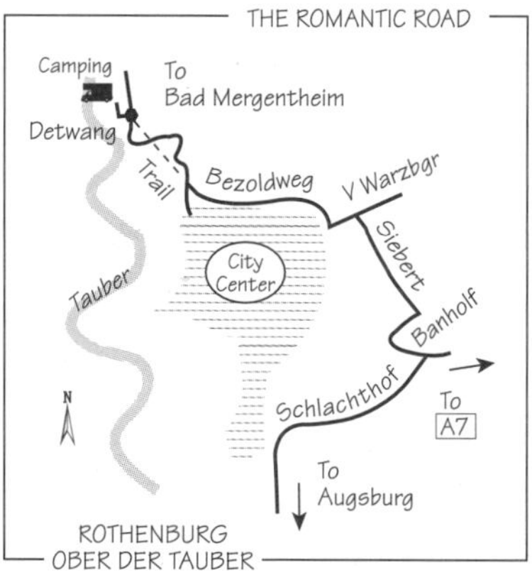

This is a tourist campground with no resident campers. The sites are unmarked and unassigned on grass with gravel driveways. Some are terraced below the entrance and others are in a large, well-shaded field below. Electrical distribution posts are quite a distance apart, you'll need that long cord. The shower/toilet building is very modern and has hot showers, hot water in basins, and hot water for washing dishes and clothes. In fact, this campground wins the prize for the best campground shower that we've seen in Germany. There's a laundry room with coin-operated washer and dryer, a camp shop, and a very good restaurant overlooking the campground.

The walk up to Rothenburg is not long, about 1 kilometer, but the first half kilometer is up hill so it is strenuous. There's a bench for resting about half way up, the path borders an apple orchard. Bus service up to town is available from a stop just outside the campground entrance but busses are extremely infrequent. You can drive up to town, there is lots of parking just outside the city walls.

Instructions for finding the campground are almost unnecessary. If you're following the Romantic Road from the north you'll pass through Detwang just before heading up the hill towards Rothenburg. The campground is well signed and just off the main road.

After leaving Rothenburg you can take a look at the **old square** in **Feuchtwangen** and then drive on to **Dinkelsbühl**. Dinkelsbühl also has a good campground nearby and is, in some ways, just as interesting as Rothenburg with fewer tourists. The campground is DCC CAMPINGPLATZ ROMANTISCHE STRASSE, open all year and located about two kilometers north of town on a small lake.

While **Nördlingen**, the next stop on the route, has old city walls and half-timbered houses like the towns farther north, a most unusual stop here is the **Rieskrater Museum**. The town sits in a fifteen-mile-wide crater, the Ries Depression, which resulted from the impact of a huge meteorite. You won't be able to see the crater, it has eroded too much, but the museum is interesting nonetheless.

Augsburg, south of Nördlingen, is a major city, Bavaria's third largest. To a large extent the history of this town is dominated by one family, the Fuggers. They were a family of merchants and bankers, and they were active throughout Germany and Europe in the fifteenth and sixteenth centuries with offices as far afield as Lisbon and Seville. Probably the most interesting sight is the **Fuggerei**, a Fugger housing project providing housing for the poor. Annual rent even today continues to be less than five dollars, unfortunately there is a waiting list. Residents are also required to pray for the soul of Jakob Fugger.

Both of the campgrounds near Augsburg are about 4 kilometers north of the city near the Augsburg-Ost exit of the Munich to Stuttgart autobahn. CAMPING AUGUSTA is open year round while CAMPING LUDWIGSHOF is open from the beginning of April to the end of October.

Heading south again you begin to near the mountains. You'll pass through **Landsberg** where Adolph Hitler wrote *Mein Kampf* while in jail; **Schongau**, another walled town; and **Rottenbuch** with its **monastery**. The extraordinary rococo **Wieskirche** is well worth a 14 kilometer round trip detour near Steingaden. Finally, off the left of the road you'll see the white **St. Coloman** pilgrimage church in a field and might even spy the **Neuschwanstein Castle** on the mountainside beyond. You're now in the Schwangau-Füssen neighborhood, a playground with good campgrounds and lots to see and do.

FÜSSEN, GERMANY

Population 15,000

The real attraction in Füssen isn't really in town at all. About 5 kilometers to the east are two of the most famous castles in the world, Ludwig II's **Neuschwanstein** and his boyhood home **Hohenschwangau**. These castles aren't the only attractions in the area however. There is another castle in Füssen itself, the **Hohes Schloss**. There are many kilometers of trails in the mountains and along the lakes around the town, the Forggensee is good for sailing and windsurfing, and this is also an important winter sports area with downhill skiing possibilities.

Füssen Campground

✦ FERIENPLATZ BRUNNEN AM FORGGENSEE

Address: Seestr. 81, D-87645
Schwangau-Brunnen
Telephone: 083 62 82 73 Fax: 083 62 86 30
Cost: Moderate

Open December 15 to November 15

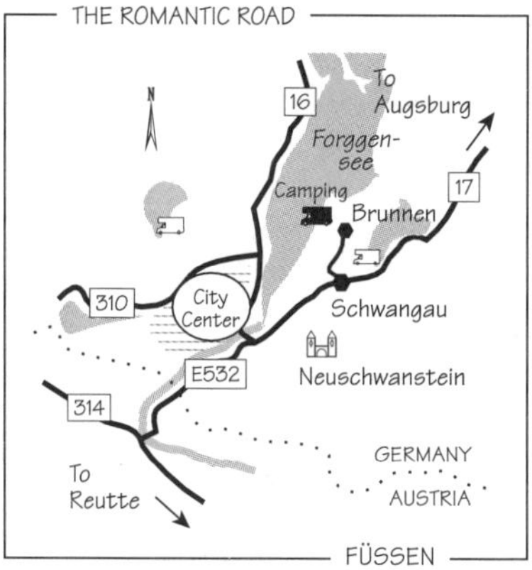

Ferienplatz Brunnen is located in Brunnen on the shore of the Forggensee, a large lake. The campground is about 5 kilometers north of the castles and 6 kilometers from Füssen.

It is a large campground with few permanent rigs. All sites are on gravel and are separated from each other by rows of small trees or bushes. Electrical boxes are widely separated, you may need a long cord (CEE17 plug, 16 amps). The shower/toilet building is a strong point here. The building is modern, heated, and spacious, there are lots of showers and they are free, hot water is also provided to the bathroom sinks, dishwashing sinks and laundry sinks. There are several coin-operated washers and dryers and there are hot plates in the dishwashing room. The campground has its own small grocery shop and a playground. There is also a dump station. Swimming in the lake is popular in the summer and many people use small boats. There is a good restaurant near the campground and a Spar supermarket about 2 kilometers away in the town of Schwangau. This campground is very popular and can be busy, get there as early as you can.

There is only one bus stop in Brunnen so you can't go wrong. It is about 300 meters from the campground. The bus services both the castles and Füssen. You can also easily use your bike or walk to either destination. There are good bike trails all over the area. An especially nice trail follows the lake shore to Füssen.

To find the campground take Highway 17 northeast from Füssen to Schwangau. In the middle of Schwangau you will see the signs pointing left for Brunnen or Forgensee and for camping. Follow the signs to the campground.

THE MIDDLE RHINE AND MOSELLE RIVER VALLEYS

The Rhine River runs northward through western Germany from the border with Switzerland to the border with Holland. Near Frankfort, where the towns of Rüdesheim and Bingen sit on opposite banks of the river, it enters the Taunus Mountains. For about 100 kilometers, until it reaches the town of Koblenz where the Moselle River flows in from the west, the Rhine Valley is a land of ancient robber baron castles, spectacular scenery, and tourists. Barges and cruising pleasure palaces chug upstream

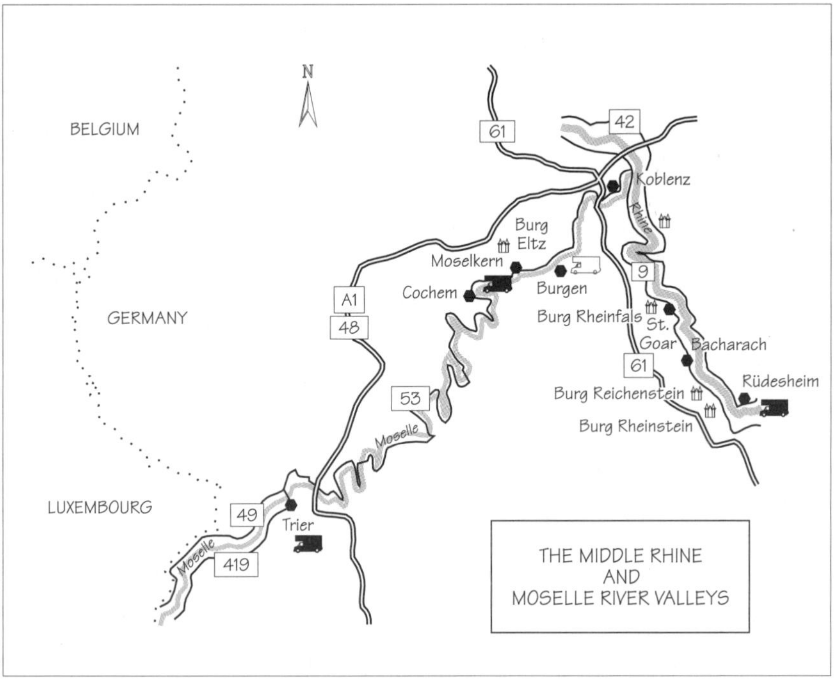

or shoot downstream as the Rhine is squeezed between its banks and rail and automobile traffic stream along both sides of the river.

The Moselle is a different story altogether. It is a smaller, dreamy, meandering river. As it flows from the Luxembourg border toward the Rhine it passes between hillsides covered with vineyards, passing through small scenic towns, some of them dating back to the Romans.

Together these two river valleys make up a destination region known around the world with many campgrounds and lots to see and do. Mark Twain introduced the area to Americans in his book *A Tramp Abroad* and the first modern written travel guide, by Baedeker, was written to cover the area in 1834. Even today it is considered one of the top destinations in Europe.

Cruise boats ply both rivers and are one of the most popular ways to see the Rhine and lower Moselle. One of the campgrounds covered in this book, the one in Rüdesheim, is an excellent place to embark on such a trip. Boats that cruise the Moselle can be boarded near another campground you'll find here, the one in Cochem.

The Moselle is famous for its wine, vineyards cover the hillsides, especially on the south facing slopes. The Rhine too, of course, is a famous wine area with the wine towns of **St. Goar**, **Bacharach** and **Rüdesheim** along this stretch of river.

The Rhine castles are world famous. Most were built during the 11th to 13th centuries. Many were homes to barons who would stop traffic, sometimes using chains stretched across the river, and levy tolls. The most famous today are **Burg Eltz**, perched far above Moselkern on the Moselle, and the Rhine's **Burg Rheinstein**, **Burg Reichenstein**, **Burg Rheinfels** in St. Goar, **Burg Katz, Burg Maus** and **Marksburg**. There are few bridges across this section of river but that is not a real problem, small ferries run frequently at several locations.

We cover three campgrounds in this region in detail, all in interesting towns. There are many others along these rivers.

TRIER (TREVES), GERMANY

Population 96,000

Trier is thought to be the oldest town in Germany, founded in about 2000 BC. Much later it was an important Roman town and remains the German city with the deepest Roman imprint. Sights include the famous **Black Gate (Porta Nigra)**, the **Imperial Baths (Kaiserthermen)**, **Rhineland Archeological Museum (Rheinisches Landesmuseum)**, a **Roman amphitheater**, and churches dating from the time of the Emperor Constantine. Trier was also the birthplace of Karl Marx and has a **Karl Marx Museum** in the house where he was born. The central area of town has pleasant pedestrian malls in the area of the Porta Nigra and the Hauptmarkt.

Trier Campground

✦ CAMPINGPLATZ TRIER-CITY

Address: Luxemburger Strasse 81,
D-54294 Trier
Telephone: 065 18 69 21
Price: Moderate

Open April 1 to October 31

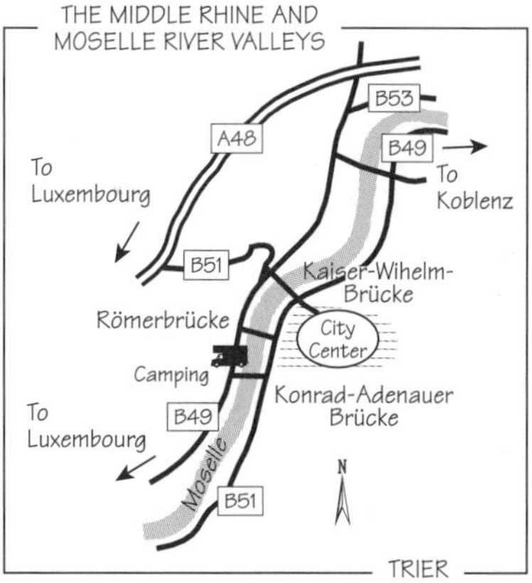

Campingplatz Trier-City is located next to the river just opposite central Trier. A fifteen minute walk will take you across the Römerbrücke and in to town.

The medium-sized campground is a narrow grassy area with lots of shade sitting just above a bike path next to the Moselle River. Individual sites are not numbered or marked, you park where you like. Electrical service is limited, the few plug boxes (10 amps, CEE17 plugs) are widely scattered, you'll need a very long cord if you can't find a place near one of them. An older shower/toilet building provides hot showers (push button valves), with hot water for the shaving and dishwashing sinks. There's a restaurant next to the campground and a supermarket about 1 kilometer north along Luxemburger Strasse. Walkers and bike riders will enjoy the paved trail that runs for miles along the river.

Finding the campground is easy. It sits on the left bank of the river between the Römerbrücke and the Kaiser-Wilhelm-Brücke (bridges). The sign is small, just an international camping site sign, so watch carefully.

COCHEM, GERMANY

Cochem is a popular tourist destination, probably because of its scenic location and extensive riverside promenade, restaurants, and docks. There is a castle sitting on a peak above the river and town, the **Reichsburg of Cochem**.

Cochem Campground

✦ CAMPINGPLATZ AM FREIZEITZENTRUM

Address: Stadionstrasse, D-56812 Cochem
Phone: 026 71 44 09
Price: Moderate

Open April 4 to October 31

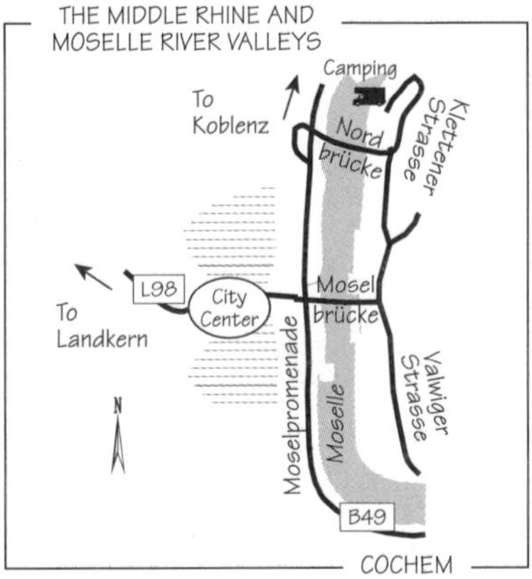

This is a well-organized municipal campground that is located on the banks of the Moselle River within easy strolling distance of downtown Cochem.

The campground is a large one that sits next to the river. It is long and narrow with paved driveways and grass covered sites. Electrical outlets are in pole-mounted boxes, you'll probably need a very long cord (CEE17 plugs, 16 amps). The two toilet/shower buildings have coin-operated hot showers (adjustable), cold water in the bathroom basins and coin-operated hot water available in the dishwashing sinks. The campground has its own restaurant.

You can easily walk downtown from the campground, the distance is about 1.5 kilometers. The path along the river is flat and scenic, best access to town is over the upper bridge, the Moselbrücke.

The campground sits next to the river on the right bank downstream from the town. Easiest access with a rig from town is across the new downstream bridge. Follow signs to the Freizeit Zentrum (sports center) and then down the hill to the campground.

RÜDESHEIM, GERMANY

Population 11,000

There is a cluster of towns situated near the point where the Rhine enters the Taunus Mountains: Wiesbaden, Eltville, Geisenheim, Bingen, and Rüdesheim. Rüdesheim is a wine town and a tourist town and makes a great base for exploring. This area, the **Rheingau**, is famous primarily for its wine, Riesling.

In Rüdesheim itself you'll probably spend at least one evening in the **Drosselgasse**, a narrow weingasse or wine alley full of restaurants. You can combine your interests in wine and castles by visiting the **Schloss Brömserburg**, home of the **Weinmuseum in der Brömserburg**, a wine museum located in a castle. High above Rüdesheim is the **Niederwald-Denkmal**, a statue and memorial to united Germany dating from 1883 which offers great views of the river below. There's a chair lift from the center of town up to the memorial or you can walk or drive.

Rüdesheim Campground

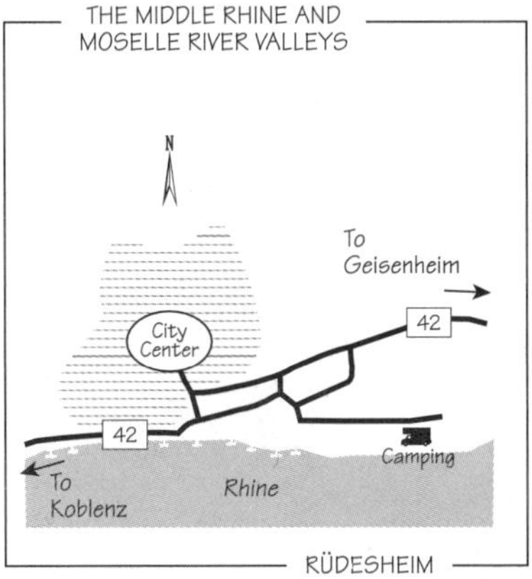

✦ CAMPINGPLATZ AM RHEIN

Address: D-65385 Rüdesheim am Rhein
Telephone: 067 22 25 28
Price: Moderate

Open May 1 to October 3, varies slightly

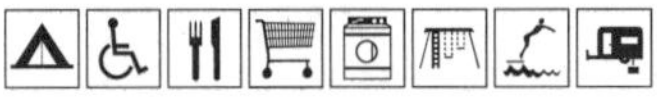

Campingplatz am Rhein is one of the nicest campgrounds in the region and it is well worth your time to spend at least one night here if you are nearby. An added benefit is that many Rhine tour boats leave from Rüdesheim and you can leave your rig in the campground while you cruise the river. Unfortunately there are several islands offshore here and most of the river traffic passes on the other side, too far away to really enjoy it.

This large campground is a grassy field on the banks of the Rhine. There is a tree-covered promenade between the river and the campsite. Most sites are on grass although there is also an attractive brick paved area. Many sites are not marked but a warden will guide you to a parking spot. This is a tourist campground with no resident campers. Electrical service boxes (CEE17 plugs, 16 amps) are on scattered poles, this is another campground where you will want to have a long electrical connection cord. The shower/toilet building near the entrance is an attraction in itself, both men's and women's sides are large with vines growing along the ceiling, displays showing the region's attractions, and even an old wine keg. The token-operated showers have hot water (not adjustable), shaving sinks and dishwashing sinks also have hot water but don't require a token. There is a small grocery store. A good-sized supermarket is about 1 kilometer away, ask at the reception kiosk for directions. Toward town along the river are tennis courts and a large swimming pool.

Access to central Rüdesheim is by foot, the 1 kilometer walk along the Rhine is scenic and interesting. The tree-shaded pathway runs past the docks for several of the Rhine cruise boats.

To find the campground head east from central Rüdesheim along the river. The road will run inland and almost immediately a campground sign will point toward the water. You may take this route if your rig is less than 2.8 meters high (there is a low railroad underpass), otherwise you may want to take the next right by the McDonald's and work your way towards the river, then left to the campground.

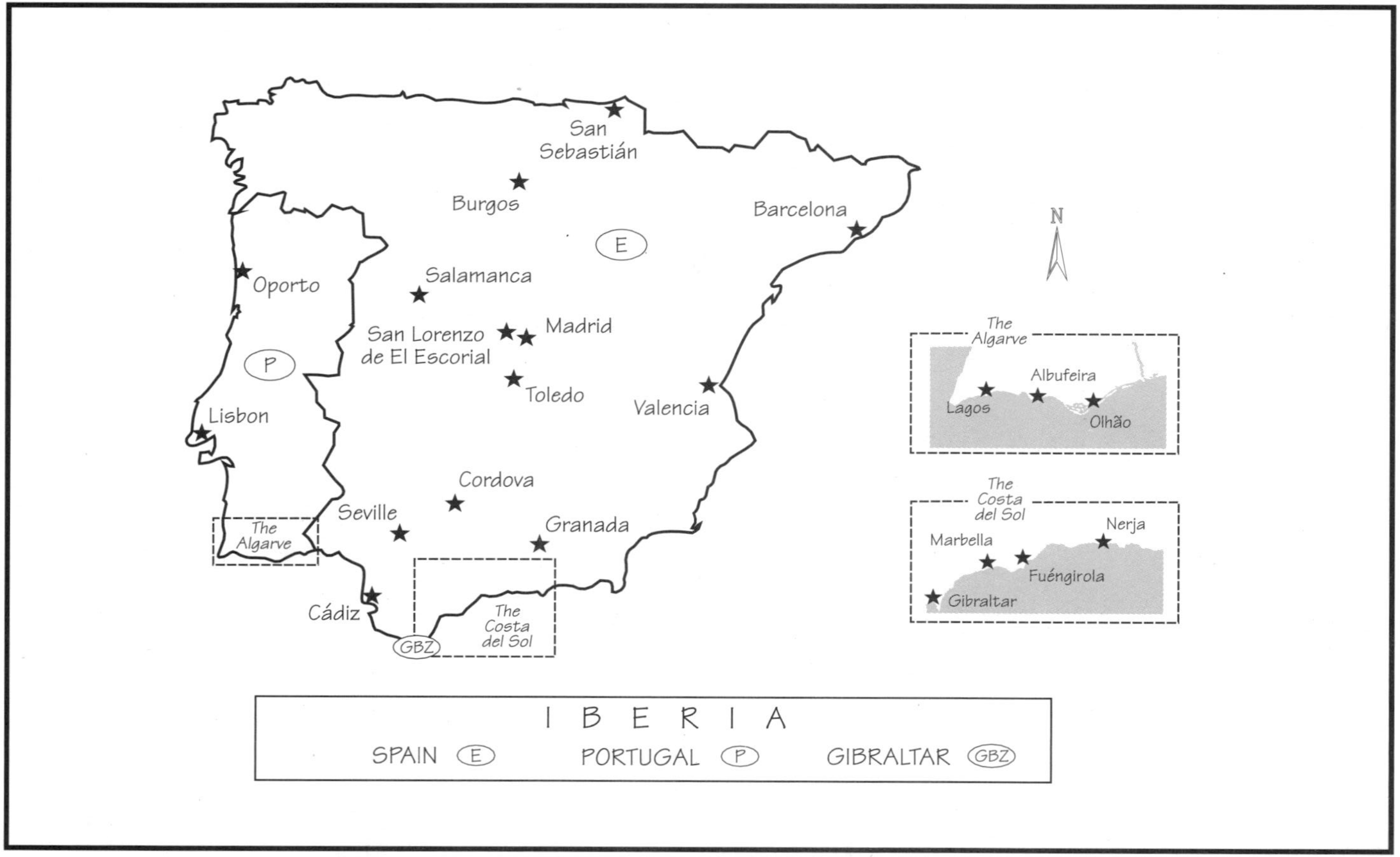
San Sebastián
Burgos
Barcelona
N
E
Oporto
Salamanca
San Lorenzo de El Escorial
Madrid
P
Toledo
Valencia
Lisbon
Cordova
Seville
Granada
The Algarve
Cádiz
The Costa del Sol
GBZ
The Algarve
Albufeira
Lagos
Olhão
The Costa del Sol
Nerja
Marbella
Fuéngirola
Gibraltar
I B E R I A
SPAIN E
PORTUGAL P
GIBRALTAR GBZ

CHAPTER

9

IBERIA

INTRODUCTION

Spain and Portugal share the Iberian Peninsula, isolated from the rest of Europe by the Pyrenees Mountains. While there are similarities in the cultures of the two countries there are also differences. Portugal has been a separate country since 1143. The Spanish and Portuguese languages have the same roots but are quite different. Both countries are now members of the European Union but Spain is noticeably more modern, has a higher per capita income and also slightly higher prices.

Spain is reported to be the second most popular tourist destination in the world with only France having more visitors. A good part of the travelers to Spain and Portugal are from Northern Europe, and they usually head for the beaches of the Mediterranean and Atlantic Coast: the Costa Brava, Costa Daurada, Costa Blanca, Costa del Sol, Costa de la Luz, and the Algarve. As you might expect, many of these visitors come as campers, and as a result Spain and Portugal are well equipped with campgrounds.

You might also think of Spain and Portugal as the Florida and Arizona of Europe, the European equivalent of North America's snowbirds like to spend their winters on the southern coast of these countries.

Roads and Driving

Roads are generally pretty good in both Spain and Portugal. Both countries are building freeways (autopistas in Spain, auto-estradas in Portugal) and many miles of them are open. Spain has a freeway along the Mediterranean coast from the French border to Murcia and there is also one from the border crossing from France on the Atlantic coast as far as Burgos. Another connects the two coasts across northern Spain. Some of these are high-priced toll roads, especially E15 along the

Mediterranean. The cost of a drive from Barcelona to Valencia, a distance of 350 kilometers, is about $29 for a car or van. Portugal has a freeway from Lisbon to Oporto, this is also a toll road. The cost of a trip on the Lisbon to Oporto toll road, a distance of 313 kilometers, is about $15 for a car or car with trailer and $27 for a van or two-axle motorhome.

The major secondary roads that are the alternative to the toll roads are for the most part decent. Many, especially in central Spain outside the immediate vicinity of Madrid don't have much traffic and you can move right along. Others, particularly along the Mediterranean can be terribly crowded, you'll count yourself lucky to have the E15 toll autopista handy.

In both countries the freeways are designated with "A" prefixes and the major secondary roads have "B" prefixes. Smaller roads in Spain have a "C" prefix. The international "E" prefix is also used.

The quality of Spanish driving is just fine (it has improved in recent years). The only difference you'll notice from North America is a slightly more aggressive technique, just as in the rest of Europe. Portugal is another story, however. Many drivers are not quite as experienced as on the rest of the continent and vigilance is advised.

The AAA-affiliated auto club in Spain is Real Automóvil Club de España (RACE) at 91 4473200 and government breakdown assistance is available throughout the country at 91 5933333 or 900 112222. In Portugal you can call Automóvel Club de Portugal (ACP) at 01 3563931. The national number for emergencies in Portugal is 115. Breakdown service in the north is 02 8340001, in the south 01 9429103.

Camping

Both Spain and Portugal have quite a few campgrounds. They've been developed with sun-seeking tourists from the rest of Europe in mind so most are located along the southern coasts. They tend to be large and dedicated to family campers with lots of facilities on-site.

In Portugal you should be aware of the Orbitur chain of campgrounds. There are at least eighteen of them spread throughout the country and they are generally well equipped and well run. You can pick up a guide for the chain at the first one you visit. In this guide we describe an Orbitur campground near Lagos in the Algarve region. You can make reservations at an Orbitur campground for other sites in the chain, there is also an Orbitur Camping Club you can join to get discounts on your fees. There are large discounts available for long stays during the winter. For information or reservations contact Orbitur-Central de Reservas, Rua Diogo do Cuoto, 1-8°, P-1100 Lisboa (telephone 01 8117000).

In the last decade or so many Iberian residents have begun to buy campers to take advantage of the camping facilities. Some leave their rigs in the campgrounds so there are increased numbers of semipermanent resident campers in some campgrounds, especially near larger cities.

Free camping is very common, especially in Portugal where it is supposedly illegal. Many people think that this is the cheapest way to spend the winter but it is important to remember that gas costs tend to be higher for a free camper who is often forced to search out a new spot or travel to get to shopping areas. Like in North America discounts are often available at campgrounds for extended stays.

Winter camping is really practical in Iberia, especially along the southern coasts. Many campgrounds, even those in the interior, are open all winter long. Often their amenities, like restaurants and stores, are closed for the winter but this is less of a problem in Iberia than in many other parts of Europe. We've made a special effort to describe only campgrounds that are open all year long for this section of the book.

You'll find a grab bag of electrical connectors in use here. Most newer campgrounds use the CEE17 plug, but many have French or German style plugs. Older places sometimes have a variation on the Swiss type plug, a Swiss adapter works fine for these.

A Camping Card International is usually not required in Spain but is often helpful if you wish to avoid handing over your passport to the reception desk. Quite a few Portuguese sites do require the card.

Shopping, Currency, Credit Cards and Fuel

Now that Spain is part of the European Community the prices are really not much different from those in the rest of Europe. The currency is slightly softer than Germany and France, prices are more like England and Italy. Hypermarkets are common in larger cities and even smaller towns have medium-sized supermarkets.

Portuguese prices tend to be slightly lower than those in Spain and supermarkets much harder to find. You may often find yourself shopping in small shops and markets in Portugal.

Credit cards are easy to use in both countries. Spaniards, in fact, seem to use credit cards more than the citizens of any other country in Europe. You can almost always buy gas and groceries with credit cards in Spain. Cash machines are ubiquitous in Spain and common in tourist areas of Portugal.

Any visitor to Spain should be aware of the Paradors. They are located in tourist towns throughout Spain, always in prime locations, many are actually in converted castles. The attraction for campers is not the hotel, it is their restaurants. They specialize in local cuisine. While Parador restaurants are not inexpensive they are very good for the occasional splurge. We like to drop in for lunch whenever it is convenient, and frequently it is since there are over 70 of them scattered around the country.

Spanish telephones follow the normal European conventions except that area codes are preceded by a 9 instead of a 0. Include the 9 if dialing from Spain, leave it off if calling from outside the country. Portugal uses the normal 0 prefix.

Itinerary Suggestions

Spain is a large country and the climate varies spectacularly. The central plateau is very hot in the summer and sometimes very cold in the winter. Along the coasts the weather is milder, the north has a temperate climate while the

Mediterranean Coast is semitropical.

Portugal has a mild maritime climate with short summers in the north and long ones in the south.

Many campgrounds in Spain and Portugal are open all year and the weather really is pleasant in southern areas during the winter. July and August can be unbearably hot.

Since distances are relatively short it is feasible to base yourself on the Costa del Sol or Algarve during the winter and make short three or four day trips to places like Madrid when the weather looks like it will be reasonable for camping.

Here's a month-long tour of the Iberian Peninsula. Barcelona is a fascinating city and shouldn't be missed. Fortunately it is located near a convenient entry point from France. After driving along the coast south to Valencia an easy half-day drive will take you inland to Madrid. The Madrid area is full of worthwhile destinations, besides the city itself there is the El Escorial district, Toledo, and Segovia. By driving south from Madrid you reach Moorish Spain. Cordoba and Granada claim two of the most important attractions in the country, the Mezquita and the Alhambra. From there the Costa del Sol is close. You can spend some time in the sun and then head for Portugal, stopping in Cádiz and Seville along the way. The Algarve is another good place to recharge your batteries before visiting Lisbon and then Oporto. Finally, you can cross northern Spain through Salamanca, Valladolid, Burgos, and San Sebastian to reenter France. You'll see just enough of Iberia to tempt you back for more.

You can obtain tourist and camping information at the **Spanish National Tourist Office, 666 Fifth Avenue, New York, NY 10103 (212 265-8822)**. In Canada the address is **2 Bloor Street West, 34th Floor, Toronto, Ontario M4W 3E2.**

For information about Portugal contact the **Portuguese National Tourist Office, 590 Fifth Ave., Fourth Floor, New York, NY 10036-4704 (212 354-4403 or 800 767-8842)**. In Canada the address is **Portuguese Trade and Tourism Commission, 60 Bloor Street West, Suite 1005, Toronto ON M4W 3B8 (416 921-7376)**. Check our internet site at www.rollinghomes.com for links to information about Spain and Portugal.

IBERIA
DISTANCE TABLE

In Kilometers

Kms X .62 = Miles

	Albufeira Portugal	Barcelona Spain	Bordeaux France	Burgos Spain	Cádiz Spain	Cordova Spain	Fuéngirola Spain	Gibraltar	Granada Spain	Lagos Portugal	Lisbon Portugal	Madrid Spain	Marbella Spain	Narbonne France	Nerja Spain	Olhão Portugal	Oporto Portugal	Salamanca Spain	San Lorenzo de El Escorial Spain	San Sebastián Spain	Seville Spain	Toledo Spain
Barcelona Spain	1254																					
Bordeaux France	1483	637																				
Burgos Spain	959	590	466																			
Cádiz Spain	360	1165	1369	865																		
Cordova Spain	376	880	1106	640	263																	
Fuéngirola Spain	468	1093	1353	888	238	373																
Gibraltar	481	1210	1750	986	121	384	117															
Granada Spain	488	880	1140	675	335	160	213	330														
Lagos Portugal	45	1301	1471	1004	405	421	513	526	533													
Lisbon Portugal	279	1250	1247	780	555	510	639	656	675	267												
Madrid Spain	777	625	706	240	663	400	647	764	434	822	625											
Marbella Spain	497	1122	1382	917	209	402	29	88	242	542	668	676										
Narbonne France	1509	255	397	711	1420	1135	1348	1465	1135	1556	1486	880	1377									
Nerja Spain	509	992	1252	787	339	352	101	218	112	554	680	546	130	1247								
Olhão Portugal	36	1220	1390	923	324	340	431	445	452	81	315	741	461	1475	473							
Oporto Portugal	599	1190	1097	625	805	710	889	906	870	587	320	591	918	1336	930	635						
Salamanca Spain	713	800	760	240	599	540	703	720	631	758	535	212	732	945	743	677	390					
San Lorenzo de El Escorial Spain	831	679	706	294	717	454	701	818	488	876	679	54	730	934	600	795	645	174				
San Sebastián Spain	1189	530	237	235	1132	875	1179	1196	903	1234	1010	469	1145	476	1015	1153	860	469	523			
Seville Spain	239	1015	1244	720	125	139	229	246	256	284	410	538	258	1270	270	203	660	474	592	950		
Toledo Spain	689	690	777	305	583	345	610	727	397	734	615	71	639	951	509	653	625	234	125	540	450	
Valencia Spain	904	350	832	520	808	530	706	823	519	949	980	352	735	605	605	868	960	564	406	595	665	420

SELECTED CITIES AND CAMPGROUNDS

BARCELONA, SPAIN

Population 1,800,000

Barcelona is very different from other cities in Spain. It could almost be located in another country. This might be explained by the fact that Barcelona was occupied by the Moors for less than 100 years. Sitting in the far northeast corner of the country, very near the border with France, Barcelona feels much more cosmopolitan, busy, and modern than Madrid. Much of the polish of Barcelona is due to the recent summer

WORK CONTINUES ON THE SAGRADA FAMILIA CHURCH IN BARCELONA

Olympics, held here in 1992, but Barcelona has always been a remarkably inviting city for the visitor.

It is hard to think of Barcelona without thinking about Moderniste (Modernismo) architecture, a turn of the century offshoot of Art Nouveau. The best known of the Moderniste architects was Gaudí. Examples you won't want to miss are the uncompleted **Sagrada Familia Church**, which looks a little like it is melting, Parc Güell, and several office and apartment buildings along **Passeig de Gràcia** boulevard near the American Express office.

Another well know attraction in Barcelona is the **Rambla**, a long boulevard linking the harbor with the central **Plaça de Catalunya**. This walking street is a colorful bazaar for casual strollers with flower stands, pet kiosks, news and book stands and street performers. If you leave the Rambla about half way down its length you can explore the narrow streets, shops and restaurants of the Gothic Quarter. The **harbor area** at the end of the Rambla is the site of a lot of recent development and improvements with harbor side walks and a large shopping center.

The hill of **Montjuïc**, to the west of the central area of the city, is serviced by both a funicular and a cable car. It was the site of much of the 1992 Olympics and is also home to a park, an amusement park, a castle, and several museums. Another museum that you won't want to miss is the Picasso Museum in the Gothic Quarter, one of the world's best devoted to this prolific Spanish artist.

Barcelona Campground

✦ CAMPING MASNOU

Address: Camilo Fabra 33, E-08320
El Masnou, Barcelona
Telephone: 935 551503 Fax: 935 551503
Price: Moderate

Open all year

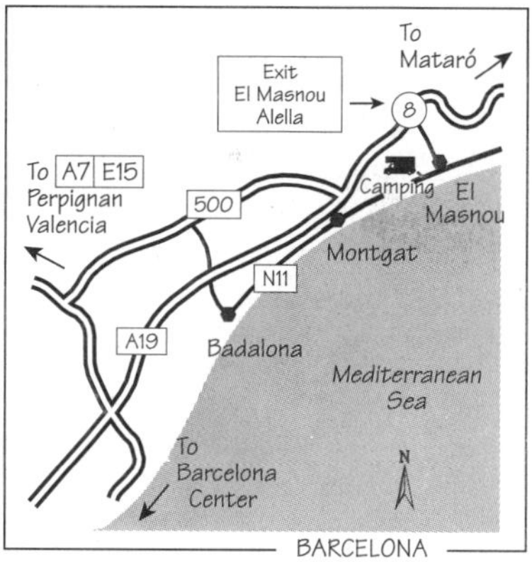

This is a suburban campground set across the highway from a sandy beach with good rail access to Barcelona. It is in the small town of Masnou, about 6 kilometers east of the city. In camping guides it is sometimes listed as being located in Badalona which is really a couple of kilometers to the west.

Masnou is a medium to large campground with its sites in three areas: a large lower area near the entrance and two smaller upper terraces. Some of the sites on the upper terrace overlook the ocean. Sites are on grass under good shade, they are numbered but not physically separated. Electricity (4 amps, German) is available to most sites with long cords. The shower/bath facilities in the main building near the entrance have adjustable hot showers. Bathroom basins and dish and clothes washing sinks have cold water only. The campground also has a swimming pool, restaurant/bar, shop, and playground. A nice sand beach is across the road and railroad tracks, to reach it you must walk about 500 meters east to an underpass.

You can easily take the train in to Barcelona from the campground. The Masnou station is about a kilometer east of the campground and frequent trains will deliver you to Catalunya Square in the middle of Barcelona in about 20 minutes.

Camping Masnou is on the secondary coastal road N11 at kilometer post 633. There is a short coastal freeway that comes east from Barcelona, A19. From this freeway take the Masnou (no. 8) exit, drive down to the coastal road, turn right toward Barcelona, and you'll see the campground on your right in about 500 meters.

Side Trips from Barcelona

The hillside **Monastery at Montserrat** with its Black Virgin and impressive setting among the crags makes a good day trip from Barcelona. This Benedictine monastery is located near the Barcelona suburb of Terrassa and the drive takes less than an hour from the campground.

Amazingly, a day trip to Andorra is also possible from your Barcelona base. Andorra is primarily a ski resort in the winter and a tax free shopping opportunity in the summer, but it is an addition to your life-list of countries so why not drive on up. The distance is about 200 kilometers on secondary roads so get an early start or plan to spend the night. There are at least five campgrounds within a few kilometers of the main town, Andorra-La-Vella.

There are numerous holiday-style campgrounds on the coast both north and south of Barcelona. The coast to the north is called the Costa Brava, it has a rocky coastline but many beaches. The **Salvador Dali Museum** in Figueras shouldn't be missed. The drive from Tossa de Mar northeast along the coast to Sant Feliu is another highlight that should only be attempted in maneuverable vehicles. Top resort towns are Lloret, Tossa, the three coastal villages near Palafrugell (Tamariu, Llafranc, and Palamos), l'Estartit, and Cadaqués. There are a huge number of campgrounds all along the coast but most are open only during the summer, if you are looking for sand and sun you might try the giant CAMPING LAS DUNAS near L'Escala in Empúries, open from the middle of May to the end of September.

South from Barcelona are **Tarragona** and the **Costa Daurada**. Tarragona, 100 kilometers from Barcelona, was a Roman city, the Archaeological Museum will give you a suitable background for exploring the city's **Roman Forum** and **Necropolis**. There are many campgrounds along the Costa Daurada, CAMPING LA BALLENA ALEGRE is a well-known and very large campground only 15 kilometers south of Barcelona in Castelldefels. It is open from the beginning of April to the end of September. Nearer Tarragona PARK PLAYA BARÁ is on the coast near Roda de Bera and open from the middle of March to the end of September. Roda de Bera is about 25 kilometers up the coast from Tarragona.

BURGOS, SPAIN

Population 160,000

Burgos was the capital of old Castile until supplanted by Madrid in the 16th century. Most of the city's sights date from this period of importance. Burgos is on the pilgrimage route to Santiago de Compostela and is well supplied with churches, monasteries, and convents. These include the magnificent 13th-century **Cathedral** and nearby **Arco de Santa María**, the **Cartuja de Miraflores** Carthusian monastery and the **Convento de las Huelgas**. All have impressive architecture and art treasures. The Spanish hero El Cid was born near Burgos and you can find traces of this legendary citizen throughout the town including some of his bones in the cathedral (since 1921) and a statue on the Arco de Santa María.

Burgos Campground

✦ CAMPING CABIA

Address: Ctra. Burgos-Valladolid, Km. 15, E-09196 Burgos
Telephone: 947 412078
Price: Inexpensive

Open all year

This is a basic campground sitting next to the freeway about 16 kilometers west of Burgos. Although lacking personality it has comfortable facilities and is a good place to spend the night while traveling through the area. There's nothing in the immediate neighborhood but the freeway, a set of freeway service stations, the campground and empty fields. You may feel as if you've stopped at a campground somewhere on the Great Plains in the states.

Camping Cabia is a medium-sized campground on flat ground. Sites are unmarked, grass covered, and have no shade or separation. There are quite a few permanent resident campers but not an overwhelming number. Electricity (German plugs, 10 amps) is in widely-spaced boxes. The one shower/toilet building is modern, it has hot showers requiring a token and cold water in bathroom basins, dishwashing sinks and laundry tubs. There is a decent restaurant and bar at the front of the campground, also a swimming pool. To get in to Burgos you'll have to use your own vehicle. Fifteen kilometers from the campground, on the near side of Burgos next to the freeway, is a large new Pryca supermarket and shopping center.

The campground is just off the N620 freeway west of Burgos. Take Exit 17 heading west or Exit 18 heading east. Both have campground signs on the freeway but if you are heading east there is an easy one kilometer long dirt access road to negotiate.

CÁDIZ (CADIZ) AND JEREZ DE LA FRONTERA, SPAIN

Population 160,000 (Cádiz), 180,000 (Jerez)

Today's Cádiz is an attractive port city with whitewashed houses, narrow streets and small squares. During the eighteenth century things were much grander, Cádiz was the port for Spain's treasure ships from the Americas. You'll find reminders of those days in the **museum of the cathedral**.

Sherry is named after Jerez de la Frontera, and this is where the authentic stuff comes from. You may want to visit one of the **sherry bodegas** here and take a tour. The major houses are Domecq, Harvey, Gonzáz Bypass, and Sandeman. Another memorable destination is the **Real Escuela Andaluza del Arte Ecuestre** where you can watch well trained-horses perform a show much like that of the Spanish Riding School in Vienna.

Cádiz Campground

✦ CAMPING GUADALETE

Address: Ctra. N IV, Km. 655, E-11500 Puerto Sta. Maria (Cádiz)
Telephone: 956 861749
Price: Moderate

Open all year

This campground is located almost exactly half way between Cádiz and Jerez de la Frontera, about 20 kilometers from each. It, therefore, can be used as a base for exploring both.

Guadalete is a large campground set on flat ground under large trees that provide lots of shade for some clusters of sites. Some individual sites are marked and numbered but you can generally choose your own parking spot, not necessarily in a proper site. There are a lot of permanent resident caravans, they have the shady sites. Electricity (German plugs, medium amps) is available at widely-spaced boxes. The shower/toilet buildings are adequate but not particularly clean or well maintained, hot showers are free and there are bathroom basins, dishwashing sinks, and laundry tubs all with cold water only. During the summer season the campground has a swimming pool, restaurant, and grocery shop. There is a pretty good sandy beach about one kilometer from the campground down a quiet road.

The campground is located next to the Carretera Nacional IV near kilometer 655 which is not a freeway at this point. It has good signs on the road and sits on the west side of the road.

CORDOVA (CÓRDOBA), SPAIN

Population 300,000

Cordova's glory days were during the tenth century when the Moorish city was one of the world's greatest. Today the city is about a third the size that it was then and a much less important player on the world's stage. Cordova remains one of Spain's most-visited cities. People come to see the **Mezquita**, the large mosque that was later converted to a church. You'll also enjoy the narrow streets and squares of the old city near the Guadalquivir River.

Cordova Campground

✦ CAMPAMENTO MUNICIPAL EL BRILLANTE

Address: Avda. del Brillante No. 50,
E-14012 Córdoba
Telephone: 957 282165
Price: Moderate

Open all year

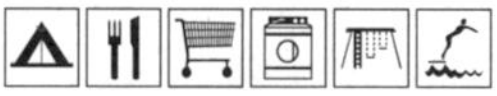

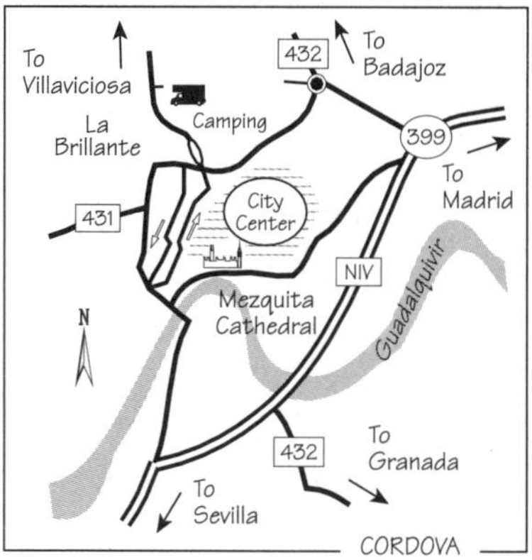

Long an institution in Cordova, Campamento Municipal is the most convenient campground for visiting the city's sights. We first stayed here in 1973, and the place hasn't change much over the years. Expect hot weather if you're here in the summer, the pool is very popular.

This is a medium-sized campground with sites on packed dirt under trees, some are olive trees. There are also some frames and netting for artificial shade. Electricity (German plugs, medium amps) is convenient to many of the sites. The shower/toilet buildings are older but clean and well maintained, they have free hot showers, hot water in bathroom basins, and cold water for dishwashing sinks and laundry tubs. They are crowded when the campground is full. There is a beautiful swimming pool at the campground which is also open to people not camping here, it has a separate entrance for them. There is also a restaurant and a small grocery shop. A brand new large shopping center with supermarket is about 1 kilometer from the campground.

Bus service to the old town and Mezquita cathedral is from a stop about a half kilometer from the campground. Bus number 12 runs every 20 minutes or so. You can also walk through town toward the river to the old town, the distance is about 3 kilometers and the walk takes about 40 minutes.

This campground is not well signed and the way that roads are directed around the old town make it somewhat difficult to find. It is on the north side of Cordova where the road to Villaviciosa begins, unfortunately this road is not well signed either. If you have a central city map you will see that it takes off to the north west from the Plaza de Colón. The best and most easily identified place to begin your drive to the campground is headed west on the riverside road in front of the cathedral and old town. Take the right turn onto the main north/south boulevard (Avenida Conde Vallellano) and head north on it. This is signposted Ciudad Central at the turn. The name changes and you will be shunted to the right onto Avenida. Ronda de los Tejares and then left onto Avenida. del Brillante which is the road that the campground is on. You can follow signs for the Parador, which is in the same direction, when you see them. They are almost hidden in the long stack of hotel signs that are mounted on almost every important corner.

GRANADA, SPAIN

Population 265,000

Granada, like Cordova, has a rich Moorish history, but Granada's golden age was later than Cordova's. To evoke the period of Moorish splendor during the 13th, 14th, and 15th centuries try reading *Tales of the Alhambra* by Washington Irving, which is also the best introduction to the **Alhambra**, Granada's most important attraction. Sitting high on the mountainside above Granada the Alhambra has palaces, towers and gardens with names you've heard all your live: Generalife, Alcazaba, and Court of the Lions. You'll also want to explore the city's old quarter or **Albaicín** and drive up the **Camino del Sacromonte** past gypsy cave houses to the monastery near the top of the mountain.

Granada Campground

✦ SUSPIRO DEL MORO

Address: N 323, Km. 145 (Cruce Carretera Almuñécar), E-18630 Granada
Telephone: 958 555105
Price: Inexpensive

Open all year

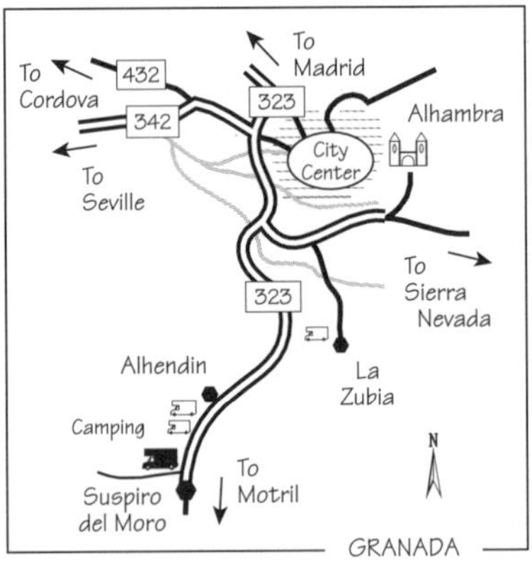

As you drive south on N 323, the main road to the coast from Granada, you'll see a series of campgrounds along the road. Suspiro del Moro offers the most convenient access and best accommodations, in the summer you'll appreciate the slightly cooler temperatures that the Sierra Nevada foothills offer. If you don't think the heat near the city will bother you there is a campground in La Zubia, CAMPING REINA ISABEL, which is quite nice.

The campground is located on a flat shelf with a large pool area and restaurant between it and the highway. Camp sites are on gravel and sparse grass with some shade trees. The sites are numbered and hedges provide some separation between small groups of sites. Electricity (German plugs, medium amps) is available at widely-spaced cement vaults that service groups of sites, about half of the sites can use electricity at one time. There are two clean and well maintained shower/toilet buildings, they have hot showers (premixed push-button valve), and cold water for bathroom basins, dishwashing sinks and laundry tubs. The large pool on a terrace between the roadside restaurant and the campground is the social center of the campground, there is also a small grocery shop.

Bus service to Granada is on pretty much an hourly schedule, you'll want to try to catch an express as they takes only about 20 minutes to make the run versus three times that for the others. The reception desk has the details as well as lots of visitor information about Granada.

COURT OF LIONS IN GRANADA'S ALHAMBRA

To reach the campground from Granada drive south on Highway N 323 towards Motril and the Costa del Sol, it is on the right near kilometer 145, about 12 kilometers south of Granada.

LISBON (LISBOA), PORTUGAL

Population 850,000

Lisbon is located on the north shore of the Tagus River estuary some 35 kilometers from the ocean. The central city occupies a sort of valley with **Saint George's Castle (Castelo de São Jorge)** overlooking it from the east and the **Bairro Alto** on the high ground to the west. Down the river about 6 kilometers is **Belém** (Bethlehem) where many of Lisbon's most visited monuments are located. The city has an extremely good transportation system of trams and busses, there's also an underground Metro but its usefulness for visitors is limited.

The central area of the city is called the **Baixa** (lower town). This is the fashionable shopping district and the central business area of the city. From here you should make judicious use of public transportation as you move around the city because almost all your destinations are either above you or quite a distance away. For a great view of the city take a tram or taxi up to the Castelo de São Jorge. From there you can walk back down to town through the very old **Alfama** district. The **Sé** (cathedral) dating from 1120 is located in this district.

Once you reach the Baixa again it is time to climb back up to the **Bairro Alto** on the far side. There are elevators and a funicular to help you accomplish this. The Bairro Alto is a jumble of coffee houses, restaurants, shops and churches.

The best way to reach Belém from the Baixa is tram or bus. Lisbon has some very sharp new trams running on this route, also some of the oldest you'll see in Europe, take your pick. In Belém you may want to see **Mosteiro dos Jerónimos** and the **Torre de Belém**, two of the best examples of Manueline architecture in existence. Manual I, king during the successful Portuguese voyages of discovery to India and Brazil is buried at the monastery. So are Vasco da Gama and the great Portuguese poet Camões.

Most visiting campers stay in the Parque Municipal de Campismo de Monsanto because it is convenient. Another possibility is ORBITUR CAMPING COSTA DE CAPARICA, about 20 kilometers south of Lisbon on the coast near Caparica. You can use bus transportation to get into Lisbon from there. You might also consider the ORBITUR CAMPING GUINCHO near Guincho on the coast near Sintra.

Lisbon Campground

✦ PARQUE DE CAMPISMO MUNCIPAL DE LISBOA/MONSANTO

Address: Estrada da Circunvalação, P-1400 Lisboa
Telephone: 01 702061 Fax: 01 702062
Price: Inexpensive

Open all year

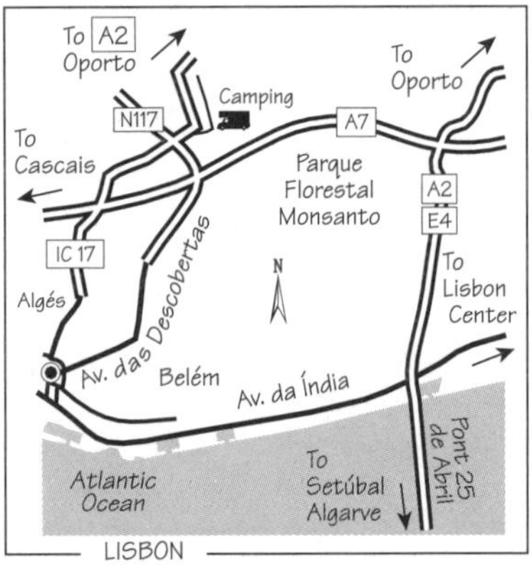

This is a very large municipal campground conveniently located for visiting the city. There are over 2,500 sites here and you can count on finding a place somewhere although there are many resident caravans and this is a popular place. The campground spreads over a west facing slope on the edge of the Parque Florestal da Monsanto. Sites are well shaded and generally of packed dirt or grass. They are not separated or numbered, even in very busy times the reception people only assign you a general area of the campground leaving you to find a suitable site. Electricity (German plugs, medium amps) is surprisingly convenient to most sites. The many shower/toilet buildings are older and could be better maintained. They have very hot adjustable showers and cold water for bathroom basins. Dishwashing sinks and clothes washing tubs are in separate buildings, also with cold water. The campground has many amenities including a large swimming pool, restaurant, grocery shop, TV lounge area, cash machine, tennis court, and laundry room with machines. There is a large shopping center about 1.5 kilometer west of the campground which can be spotted across the intervening valley from the campground entrance.

Bus service to both central Lisbon and the Belém area is good. The number 43 takes about 20 minutes to get you downtown while the 50 takes about 10 minutes to reach Belém.

While there are many signs for the campground when you approach Lisbon from all directions the best way to approach the campground is from the N7 freeway that runs west toward Estoril from Lisbon. The proper exit for the campground is signed from both directions on this highway. Using other approaches can be tricky because many apparently logical routes are obstructed by freeways.

Side Trips from Lisbon

The area to the east of Lisbon is full of interesting destinations. Drive west on N6 along the water from Belém to **Estoril** and **Cascais**, a distance of about 15 kilometers. These ritzy resort towns have a seaside promenade that is 5 kilometers long and we think the best way to see the towns. It starts in São João do Estoril which is east of Estoril proper. Estoril's big attraction is a casino overlooking the sea.

Back in the car, drive on through Estoril and Cascais to **Boca do Inferno (Mouth of Hell)**, a grotto on the shoreline where the ocean pounds into the rocks. From here you can drive about 10 kilometers north along the coast to the beach at **Guincho**. At Guincho the road cuts inland to Sintra although you can take a side road to **Cabo de Roca**, the most western point on the European continent.

Sintra was for many years a favorite haunt of Portuguese royalty and is known for it's castles. There is much to see here so you should stop at the tourist office for a local map. If you like walking you can see almost everything by hiking but you will cover quite a bit of ground. You'll want to see the **National Palace (Palácio Nacional de Sintra)**, the **Moorish Castle (Castelo dos Mouros)**, **Pena Palace (Palácio Nacional da Pena)**, the **Parque Liberdade** and the gardens of **Monserrate**.

As you head back for Lisbon there is one more important stop. In **Queluz** you will find the baroque **Queluz Palace (Palácio Nacional de Queluz)**, really worth at least a half-day visit.

If you decide that you would like to spend more time in this area you can stay at the CAMPING ORBITUR GUINCHO near Guincho Beach about 10 kilometers from Cascais and open year round. There is also a campground near the beach between Praia Grande and Praia das Maças to the north of Cabo da Roca and about 11 kilometers from Sintra. It is called PARQUE DE CAMPISMO PRAIA GRANDE and is open all year.

Madrid, Spain

Population 3,200,000

For a European capital Madrid has few well known attractions. Don't let the lack of monuments keep you away, however. Once you are in Madrid you will find that the street, cafe, and bar scene is the real attraction, and there are many good day trips into the surrounding countryside. The central city is relatively compact and accessible. If you don't feel like walking there is a good subway system.

Most visitors to Madrid would be surprised to learn that the city was little more than a country town when Philip II decided to make it his capital in 1561. Even after that he spent much of his energy building El Escorial nearby, and in 1588 the defeat of the

Spanish armada signaled the end of Spain's glory years and imposed limits on the city's growth and wealth. Only the Plaza Mayor was actually planned as a plaza, the others grew from crossroads.

Number one on most visitor's reasons for coming to Madrid is probably the **Prado Museum**. It is one of the top two or three museums in the world and houses an enormous collection of paintings collected over the centuries by Spanish royalty. Nearby you'll also find the **Centro de Arte Reina Sofía** which houses **Picasso's** famous painting entitled **Guernica**. In the other direction is the **Archaeological Museum (Museo Arqueológico)** which has an underground replica of the Altamira cave paintings.

You can have a good look at central Madrid with a walking tour that connects its plazas. Start at the **Plaza de Oriente** on the western edge of the central area and work your way east. The Plaza de Oriente is bordered by the **Royal Palace** and is the site where Franco gave many of his speeches. The Royal Palace is enormous and well worth touring. To the southeast the **Plaza Mayor** is one of the largest town squares in Europe, it is surrounded by arcades and dates from 1620. Around the Plaza Mayor is the older section of Madrid, especially just to the west. There are narrow streets and small plazas to explore. The **Puerta del Sol** to the northeast of the Plaza Mayor is the center of traffic in town. It is the zero kilometer point for Spain's highways and has the central metro station underneath. The **Plaza Cánovas del Castillo** has a statue of Neptune in the center of a traffic circle with the Paseo del Prado boulevard stretching north and south. The Prado Museum is on one side of this plaza and the **Museo Thyssen-Bornemisza** on the other. North of this is the **Plaza de la Cibeles** with the well-loved statue of Sybil in the center of another traffic circle. Even farther north is **Plaza de Colón** with a statue of Columbus in the center. Finally, just down the top shopping street in town, **Calle de Serrano**, is the **Plaza de la Independencia** and the entrance to the **Parque del Retiro**.

Madrid is known for its late dinner hour and late night partying. No one would think of going to a restaurant before nine o'clock, ten is better. Before dinner you can visit the tapas bars of **Cava de San Miguel**, just west of the Plaza Mayor. After dinner try the **Malasaña district** near the Plaza dos de Mayo which is near the Noviciado (line 2), Bilbao, and Tribunal (line 1) metro stops just north of central Madrid.

Madrid Campground

✦ CAMPING ALPHA

Address: Carretera Andalucia, Km. 12.4, E-28906 Getafe-Madrid
Telephone: 91 6958069 Fax: 91 6831659
Price: Moderate

Open all year

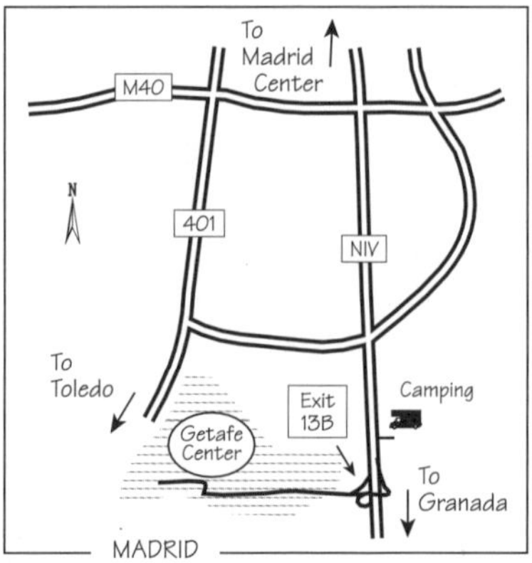

The city of Madrid is served by several campground, none are exceptionally nice, but Camping Alpha has decent facilities, can be easily accessed without driving in heavy traffic, and has public transport available to downtown Madrid. Many people prefer to stay in Toledo or San Lorenzo de El Escorial while visiting Madrid since both have nice campgrounds with transportation to Madrid available.

Camping Alpha is a large campground with many permanent resident trailers. Space for tourists is limited but generally available, especially in the off season. Sites are dirt, mud is a problem if it is raining. Electricity (CEE17 and German plugs, various medium amps) is available at all sites, water and gray-water drains are also available at many. The shower/toilet building is modern and clean, hot showers require a token and water in bathroom basins, dishwashing sinks, and laundry sinks is cold. There is a coin-operated washing machine. The campground has a swimming pool, playground, bar/restaurant, and grocery shop. The bar/restaurant and grocery shop remain open all winter. The Cerro de los Angeles shrine is on a hill nearby and has a pine forest and walking paths.

Transportation to Madrid is by a combination of bus and subway. The number 447 bus stops about a kilometer from the campground at a stop on a freeway ramp. You have to walk along the freeway from the campground to get to it. A fifteen-minute bus ride will bring you to the Legazpi subway station on line three, the central Sol station is five stops away.

Camping Alpha is situated near the N IV freeway south of the city. You can only enter the campground if you are traveling north on the freeway, use the Getafe off-ramp (number 13b) to turn around if you are heading south, the turn-around route is simple and has campground signs to lead you around. Watch carefully for the campground sign when heading north, it is right at the 12.4 point and about 1 kilometer north of the off-ramp for Getafe. You'll turn right into a dirt access road and find the campground in about 200 meters on the left.

Side Trips from Madrid

Castile, the area around Madrid, provides the opportunity for many side trips. **Toledo** and **San Lorenzo de El Escorial**, described elsewhere in this chapter because they are important destinations in their own right, also make good excursions from Madrid. Each has its own campground, however, so you may wish to spend the night. Toledo, especially, deserves to be visited in the evening when the tourist hubbub dies down. El Escorial and Toledo also make good bases for visiting Madrid.

Aranjuez, the Spanish Versailles, is described in the Toledo section of this chapter but also is a good side trip from Madrid.

About 90 kilometers northwest of Madrid is **Segovia**. This walled town dates from Roman times and has a rich history that is reflected in monuments that include one of the last **Gothic cathedrals** to be built in Spain, the 12th-century Romanesque **San Millán church**, and one of he finest surviving **Roman aqueducts** in the world. It's over a kilometer long. The **Alcázar** overlooks Segovia and was Isabella's favorite castle. Eleven kilometers southeast of Segovia is the **Royal Palace at La Granja (Palacio Real de La Granja)**. The gardens are the draw here, especially the fountains. Segovia's campground is CAMPING ACUEDUCTO located about 3 kilometers from town on N601 toward La Granja. It is open from early May to late September.

About 55 kilometers west of El Escorial is the walled town of **Ávila** which is also easily accessible from Salamanca. CAMPING SONSOLES is located about 2 kilometers south of town on N403 toward Toledo and is open from early June to late September.

OPORTO (PORTO), PORTUGAL

Population 340,000

Of course Oporto is known for Port wine, but there's lots more. If Port wine is of interest to you the **wine lodges** are located in the town of **Vila Nova de Gaia**, which is just across the River Duoro from Oporto itself. Tours and tastings are easily arranged.

Oporto itself rises steeply from the river bank to the plateau above. The twisting passages of the **Ribiera** are lots of fun to explore with steep stairways and the occasional open door giving a glimpse of the interiors of these jumbled houses. At the top of the slope is the bustling shopping district and the **Sé** (cathedral). As you wander around town notice the attractive white and blue ajulejos (tiles) on the face of many of the churches and other buildings.

Oporto Campground

✦ PARQUE DE CAMPISMO DA PRELADA

Address: Rua du Monte dos Burgos,
P-4200 Porto
Telephone: 02 812616 Fax: 02 723718
Price: Inexpensive

Open all year

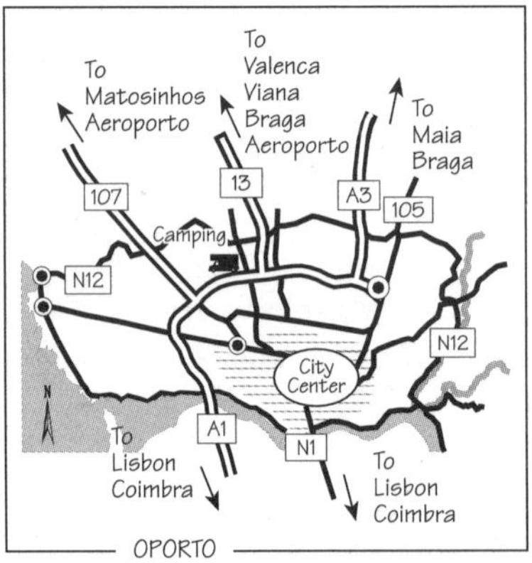

This large campground is only three kilometers from central Oporto and generally is not crowded. Tall trees provide lots of shade with many sites or groups of sites separated by high hedges. Ground cover is sparse grass or packed dirt. Electrical outlets (German plugs, 6 or 2 amps) are widely spaced. The two shower/toilet buildings are showing their age. Barely warm showers (when we visited) require a token, cold water is provided for bathroom basins, dishwashing sinks and laundry tubs. There is a nice garden in the rear of the campground with a circular pool with fish and a tower on the island in the middle. The campground also has a restaurant, bar, grocery shop, and tennis court. There are quite a few shops and restaurants in the general area, especially toward central Oporto. About a kilometer in this direction is a small but modern and well stocked Pingo Doce supermarket.

Bus service to central Oporto is frequent and convenient. The stop is just outside the campground entrance.

To find the campground most easily take the Matosinhos exit from the N13 freeway

MARKET IN PORTUGAL

which runs north and south on the north side of town. Matosinhos is the first junction north of the point where the N13 freeway meets the A1 freeway. After the exit you will find yourself heading west. The first traffic light (in about .7 kilometer) is Rua du Monte dos Burgos. Turn left here, the campground is on the right in half a kilometer. In Oporto there are many signs scattered around town directing you to Prelada, unfortunately we've not found any on the freeways where they would be most useful.

SALAMANCA, SPAIN

Population 168,000

Salamanca has been known for centuries for its **university** which was founded in the

13th century and had 10,000 students during the 16th century. It was at least equal in importance to other major universities of the day like Paris, Bologna and Oxford. Salamanca's university was important in acquainting the western world with Arabic philosophy and reintroducing classical Greek and Roman thought. Today the university is still active and respected, and the city is filled with life and history.

The best place to start your tour is the old **Roman bridge** spanning the River Tormes which is outside and below the old city. Parking is impossible in the old town. When you climb the hill toward the sandstone-colored city you will find yourself near three of the most important sights: the **Catedral Nueva** (Gothic) and **Catedral Vieja** (Romanesque) and the university. Make sure you note the Catedral Nueva's west facade and the university's **Patio de Las Escuelas**.

After leaving the university walk toward the northwest to the center of the old town, the **Plaza Mayor**. It is one of the largest and most gracious squares in Spain and its arcades offer many good places to stop and take a relaxing break, on nice days there are tables spread out into the square.

Salamanca Campground

✦ CAMPING REGIO

Address: Carretera Salamanca-Ávila Km. 4, E-37009 Santa Marta de Tormes, Salamanca
Telephone: 923 130888 Fax: 923 130044
Price: Moderate

Open all year

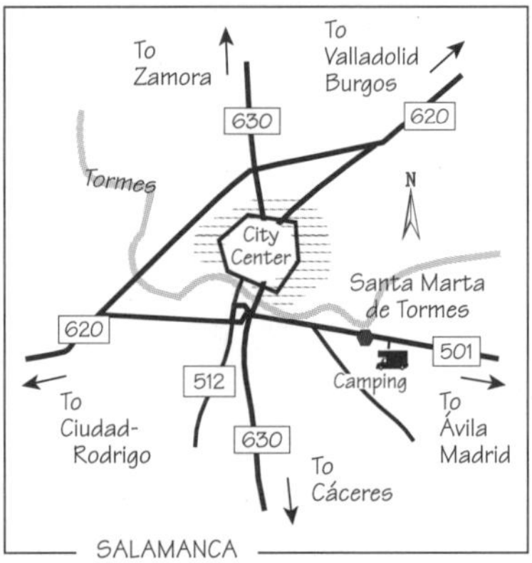

Placed as it is in north-central Spain on a frequently-used route to Portugal, Camping Regio is a popular stop for travelers heading south. Even in winter you'll probably have several fellow campers.

This is a large campground sitting behind a nice hotel. It is a flat campground with many trees that provide some shade. Sites are grass-covered and most allow caravanners to park without unhooking. Electricity (German plugs, 10 amps) is readily available but sockets are widely spaced. The large shower/toilet building has hot showers (adjustable push-button valves) and hot water for bathroom basins, dishwashing and laundry tubs. In winter there is no hot water in the building but hot showers are provided inside the hotel. The campground shares a large swimming pool with the hotel and there is a also a bar, a restaurant and a cafeteria in the hotel. Other amenities include a small shop, tennis and a playground.

Central Salamanca is about 5 kilometers from the campground. Bus service into the city is convenient.

The campground is located just off Highway N501 from Salamanca to Ávila and Madrid. It is about 4 kilometers from Salamanca on the far side of the suburb of Sta. Marta de Tormes. It is well signed, in fact you'll be reminded of Burma Shave signs.

Side Trips from Salamanca

The old walled town of **Ávila** is 100 kilometers southeast of Salamanca toward Madrid. The surrounding wall, built in the 11th century, has 86 towers and 9 gates. See the Ávila side trip from Madrid for information about a campground in the town.

SAN LORENZO DE EL ESCORIAL, SPAIN

Population 6,000

There are two important sights in the neighborhood of this small town. The first is **El Escorial** itself, a huge combination monastery and palace built in 1584 by Philip II. Some historians consider it the first massive government office building. Inside the enormous pile you'll find tombs, an important art collection, a library, and royal apartments. About 10 kilometers from El Escorial (on the opposite side of the campground) is the **Valley of the Fallen (Valle de los Caidos)** with its 485-foot-high cross and a crypt hollowed out of the mountainside. It is a monument to the people killed during the Spanish Civil War.

San Lorenzo de El Escorial Campground

✦ CAMPING CARAVANNING "EL ESCORIAL"

Address: Ado de Correos No. 8, Carretera de Guadarrama a El Escorial Km. 3.5, E-28280 El Escorial, Madrid
Telephone: 91 8902412 Fax: 91 8961062
Price: Moderate

Open all year

This is an enormous campground located about 6 kilometers from the town of San Lorenzo de El Escorial. It is generally considered the nicest campground in the Madrid area and makes a good base for exploring the region and the city of Madrid. Although not promoted as such, if you wander the small roads surrounding the campground you'll find that it is in the middle of a large bull breeding ranch.

The campground has over a thousand sites and is being expanded. There are a large number of permanently located rigs but they are in an area isolated from the tourist sites and are not really a factor, except that they justify the large variety of amenities in the campground. Tourist sites are on sparse grass and are numbered but not separated by vegetation. Most have shade in the form of a metal frame with mesh cover. There is also a large grassy field for overflow and tent sites. Electricity (German plug, about 5 amps) is available to most sites but there are enough sockets for about half the sites and the boxes are widely spaced. Shower/toilet buildings are modern and well maintained, heated when necessary, and have free hot water for showers (adjustable, push button valve), bathroom basins and dishwashing. There are a limited number, considering the campground size, of coin-operated washers. Other amenities include a large grocery shop, restaurant/bar, disco, tennis courts, three swimming pools, and lighted basketball and soccer areas. There is a supermarket near the entrance to the town of El Escorial about 6 kilometers from the campground.

Both Madrid and San Lorenzo de El Escorial are serviced by the number 664 bus which stops at the campground entrance. The bus runs from near the El Escorial monastery to the Moncloa metro station in Madrid and stops at the campground en route so you can reach either one with it. Madrid is about an hour away.

You will find the campground on Highway M600 about 6 kilometers from San Lorenzo de El Escorial, near the 15-kilometer marker. Coming from Madrid take the number 2 exit from Highway A6 and follow signs for El Escorial. The campground will be on your left from this direction.

SAN SEBASTIÁN (DONOSTIA), SPAIN

Population 180,000

San Sebastián is a sparkling resort city in the northeast corner of Spain. It is the country's premier ocean resort, with wide boulevards, elegant restaurants, and even a casino. The city makes a great base for exploring the Basque region, during the warm season you can stroll along La Concha promenade or even stretch out on the beach between side trips. You should be aware that during the hottest months the Spanish government moves to San Sebastián to escape the heat of Madrid so things get pretty crowded.

San Sebastián Campground

✦ CAMPING IGUELDO

Address: E-20190 Igueldo
Telephone: 943 214502 Fax: 943 280411
Price: Moderate

Open all year

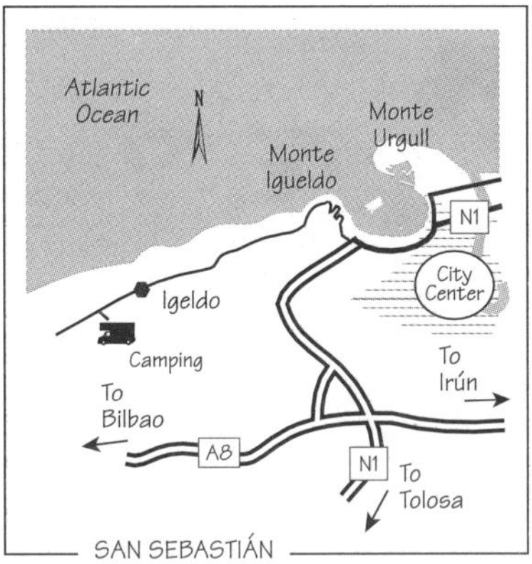

This is an attractive large campground covering a south facing slope about four kilometers west of San Sebastian. Sites are on large terraces, they are mostly covered with thick grass, numbered, and separated from each other by small hedges. Even in the slowest season sites are assigned at the reception kiosk. There are no permanent resident caravans at this campground. The electrical sites have convenient outlets next to each space, some also have water and drains. If you decide on electricity you'll be issued a small key at the reception desk to turn on a switch that activates the electricity(5 amps) at your site, an unusual arrangement but a good innovation because it allows the campground to control access to the electricity but lets the camper get to the breaker switch in case it is accidentally tripped. The shower/toilet buildings have free hot showers (push button valve, not adjustable) and cold water for bathroom basins, dishwashing sinks, and laundry tubs. Near the campground entrance there is a small shop and a restaurant/bar.

Transportation to San Sebastian is by hourly local bus. You can easily walk in to town but will probably want to catch the bus back because most of the distance is up hill. The road is narrow and has too much traffic to be a comfortable bike route.

To find the campground head for Mt. Igueldo, the mountain at the west end of town next to the ocean. Camping signs will direct you up the mountain and along its crest toward the west. The campground is on the left about four kilometers from where you start up the hill.

SEVILLE (SEVILLA), SPAIN

Population 675,000

Always a great city to visit, Seville is looking good after being spruced up for EXPO 92. Improvements include new highways, a new bus and train station, and a new riverfront promenade. However, the real attractions continue to be the historic buildings, vivacious people, and old neighborhoods or barrios surrounding the city center.

The most important buildings are clustered a short distance from the Guadalquivir River. Seville's **cathedral**, quickly built in just over 100 years, is the largest in Spain and the third largest church in the world (after Rome's St. Peter's and London's St. Paul's). Next door is the **Giralda Tower**, originally a Moorish mosque's minaret and now the cathedral's bell tower. The tower affords great views of the cathedral's gargoyles. Nearby is the **Alcázar**, a Moorish-style palace actually built by the Christian king Pedro I in the 14th century. It has a delightful garden.

Just north of the Alcázar is the **Barrio de Santa Cruz**, today rather upscale. Here you'll catch glimpses of flower-filled patios behind wrought-iron gates. The **Calle de las Sierpes** is a favorite shopping and strolling street.

Seville Campground

✦ CAMPING "SEVILLA", S.A.

Address: Apdo de Correos 938,
E-41080 Sevilla
Telephone: 954 514379
Price: Moderate

Open all year

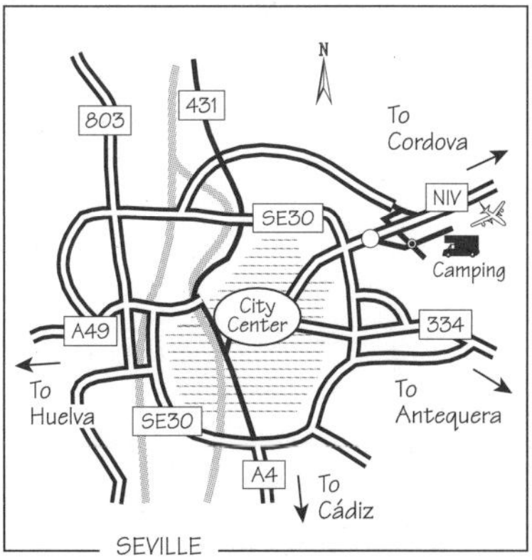

Camping Sevilla is a medium-sized campground located next to the N4 Cádiz-Madrid freeway east of Sevilla near the airport. It is a flat field with packed sand and grass sites. A few trees provide some shade. Most sites have convenient electricity (German plugs, 7 amps). The shower/toilet building is older but well maintained, it has free hot showers (adjustable) and cold water for bathroom basins and dishwashing sinks. The campground also has a swimming pool, a bar/restaurant, and a grocery shop. The airport next door has jet traffic and is noisy during takeoffs, fortunately Seville doesn't get many flights.

Bus transportation to Sevilla (about 10 kilometers to the west) is frequent but you must walk about a kilometer to the stop. Check at the reception desk for details.

Access to the campground is from a side road next to the freeway. While the campground is at kilometer 534 you must exit the freeway at the exit at kilometer 535 (west of the campground). There is a traffic circle just south of the freeway at this exit, the side access road leads east from this circle along the south side of the freeway. Follow it past the back of the gas station to the campground. There are campground signs showing the proper freeway exit and pointing (a little ambiguously) at the proper exit from the traffic circle.

Side Trips from Seville

From the campground you can drive some 25 kilometers east to **Carmona**, a very old walled hillside village. Take a look at the **Roman Necropolis** and the town's fortifications. There is a Parador here in the ruins of the **Alcázar de Arriba**.

Just north of Seville on N630 is **Italica**, an ancient Roman city that is being excavated. This is no Pompeii but there is a large **amphitheater**. The town may not look like much now but three important Roman emperors were born here: Trajan, Hadrian, and Theodosius.

The **Parque Nacional de Doñana** is Spain's largest national park and very popular with bird watchers and nature lovers. Drive west on E01 toward Huelva and then south at Exit 10 toward Almonte. Near the coast you'll find the Reception and Interpretation Center, starting point for very popular jeep tours of the park. Total distance from Seville is about 100 kilometers.

You can drive west along the coast from the park to see the point where Columbus departed on his first voyage to America near Huelva. The actual point of departure is **Palos de la Frontera** but the monastery of **La Rábida** is known to Spaniards as the "birthplace of America" because Columbus used it as a base and received much of his political support from the friars here. A good nearby campground is CAMPING ROCIO PLAYA on the beach near the village of Mazagón between Matalascañas and Huelva.

TOLEDO, SPAIN

Population 61,000

The first thing to do when you arrive in Toledo is to drive the **Carretera de Circunvaleción** which follows the Rio Tajo around the south side of the city. There are several places where you can park and take advantage of memorable views of the city across the river gorge. You'll be able to see most of the important monuments in the town and appreciate the military advantages of Toledo's site.

The city has justifiably been designated a national monument. It is a well-preserved medieval town and as such is probably best enjoyed by wandering the narrow streets in the morning before the tour busses arrive or in the evening after they leave. This is a good reason to spend several days at the campground here. The tourist sights include the **Cathedral**, the **House and Museum of El Greco**, **El Alcázar**, and **Santo Tome**, which houses El Greco's *The Burial of Count Orgaz* in a chapel with its own entrance.

Toledo Campground

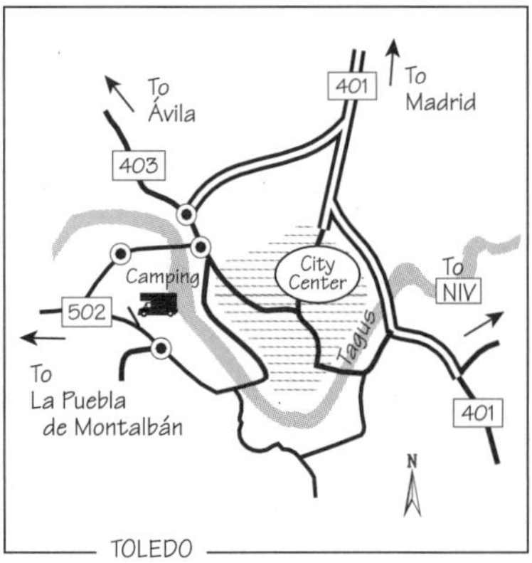

✦ CAMPING "EL GRECO"

Address: Carretera. Comarcal 502,
E-45004 Toledo
Telephone: 925 220090
Price: Moderate

Open all year

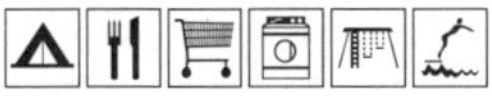

El Greco is a medium to large campground situated on the bank of the Tagus River about 2 kilometers west of Toledo's old town. Camp sites are on packed dirt under a grove of trees, shade is important here in the summer and you may wish the trees were bigger. Hedges separate about half the sites. Electricity (German plugs, high amps) is available but outlets are widely spaced and sockets are limited. The shower/toilet buildings are well maintained and have adjustable hot showers with cold water for bathroom basins, dishwashing and laundry tubs. There is a coin-operated washer and dryer. The campground has a nice swimming pool, a restaurant and bar, and a grocery shop.

You can walk to the foot of the old town in 20 minutes from the campground or take a bus. The Number 7 stops just outside the gate and runs hourly.

The campground entrance is on Highway C502 to the west of Toledo and it is well signed once you get to the west side of town. This highway is signposted as going to La Puebla de Montalbán. As you approach Toledo from any direction follow signs to Highway 502 and then signs to Camping El Greco.

Side Trips from Toledo

The equivalent of Versailles for the 18th-century Spanish Bourbons was Aranjuez, about 50 kilometers northeast of Toledo. The **Palacio Real** is Versailles-style and there are extensive gardens. The **Casa del Labrador**, located nearby, is a smaller palace well worth a tour to see the interior.

VALENCIA, SPAIN

Population 800,000

Spain's third largest city sits at the mouth of the Turia River on the Mediterranean Coast about halfway between Barcelona and Madrid. Extensive irrigation makes this an important area for growing lots of oranges. Probably the best known tourist sight in town is the **Lonja de la Seda (Silk Exchange)**, an important example of non-ecclesiastical Gothic architecture. The **Cathedral** itself is also Gothic, it is said to house the Holy Grail and its tower offers good views of the city.

Valencia Campground

✦ FUNDACION MUNICIPAL CAMPING "EL SALER"

Address: El Saler, E-46012 Valencia
Telephone: 961 830023
Price: Moderate

Open all year

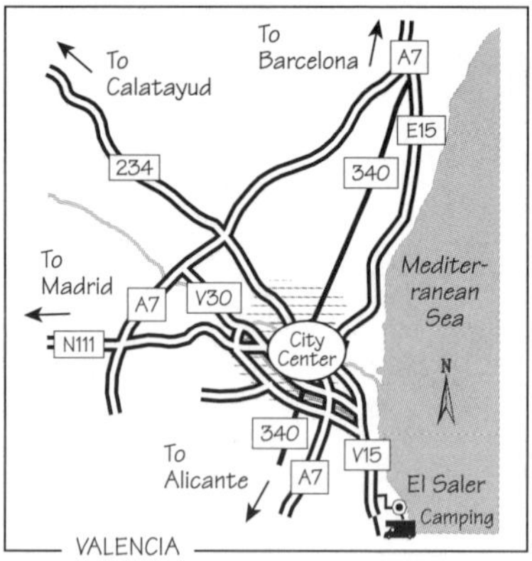

Several campgrounds are located along the beach south of Valencia in the small seaside resort of El Saler. This is one of the largest and best equipped, it also has convenient bus service in to Valencia.

El Saler Municipal is a large campground with sites on sand (mostly packed but some soft) in a grove of scattered pine trees. There are many permanently-based trailers but also a large area for tourists. Electricity (Swiss and CEE17 plugs, various amps) is in widely-spaced switch blocks. The shower/toilet buildings have free hot adjustable showers and hot water in bathroom basins, dishwashing and laundry sinks have cold water only. The campground also has two bar/restaurants, a large grocery shop, a swimming pool, and a playground. The beach is across the street and has several open air restaurants during the summer. Buses to Valencia stop at the campground entrance.

From central Valencia there are signs to the beaches at El Saler that point the way out of town to the southeast to the short V15 freeway. You probably won't want to take your rig into Valencia, however, and don't need to. Use the freeway bypass, a combination of A7 and V30, which extends around the town and connects with V15 a few kilometers north of the El Saler exit. When you do reach the El Saler exit from V15 follow signs to El Saler. In the middle of the small town a sign for the campground and beaches will direct you to the east, you'll soon reach a traffic circle at the beach, turn right and in a short distance you'll see the campground on the right across from the beach.

TWO OUTSTANDING REGIONS AND THEIR CAMPGROUNDS

THE COSTA DEL SOL, SPAIN

The Costa del Sol is just about as far south as European snowbirds can go without climbing onto a ferry to Africa. Many camping enthusiasts winter here as do thousands of northern Europeans and Americans who haven't yet discovered camping and therefore stay in expensive hotels and condos. The beaches, restaurants and shops help to pass the time comfortably and the weather is nice but not too hot. Campers can keep expenses in check by limiting driving miles and checking into campgrounds on a monthly basis.

For our purposes the eastern end of the Costa del Sol is Almuñécar. This is where the road from Granada reaches the coast. Almuñécar is a small beach resort. Driving west along the coast the next stop is Nerja.

NERJA, SPAIN

Population 13,000

Nerja is a small and relatively unspoiled seaside town. It is located at the eastern end of the Costa del Sol and the location may explain why it remains unspoiled, intense development just hasn't reached it yet. The town sits above the ocean on a rocky shoreline with several small beaches below. There are good restaurants and small shops. Nerja is known for the **Balcón de Europa**, a viewpoint above the ocean near the town square.

Just east of Nerja you'll find the **Cuevas de Nerja**, a large limestone cave system that is equipped with paths and lighting for tours.

Nerja Campground

✦ NERJA CAMPING

Address: Carretera N 340, Km. 297, E-29787 Maro-Nerja, Málaga
Telephone: 952 529714
Price: Moderate

Open all year

Nerja Camping is a small pleasant campground perched on a high ridge overlooking the coast. Sites are hard dirt and scattered grass under olive trees. There are frames for shade netting in the summer. Sites are numbered and separated by trees and rows of bricks set in the ground. About half of the sites have electricity (German plugs, 15 amps) available. The shower/toilet building is modern and clean, it has free hot showers (adjustable, push-button valve) and cold water in bathroom basins, dishwashing sinks, and laundry tubs. The campground has a swimming pool, a small bar/restau-

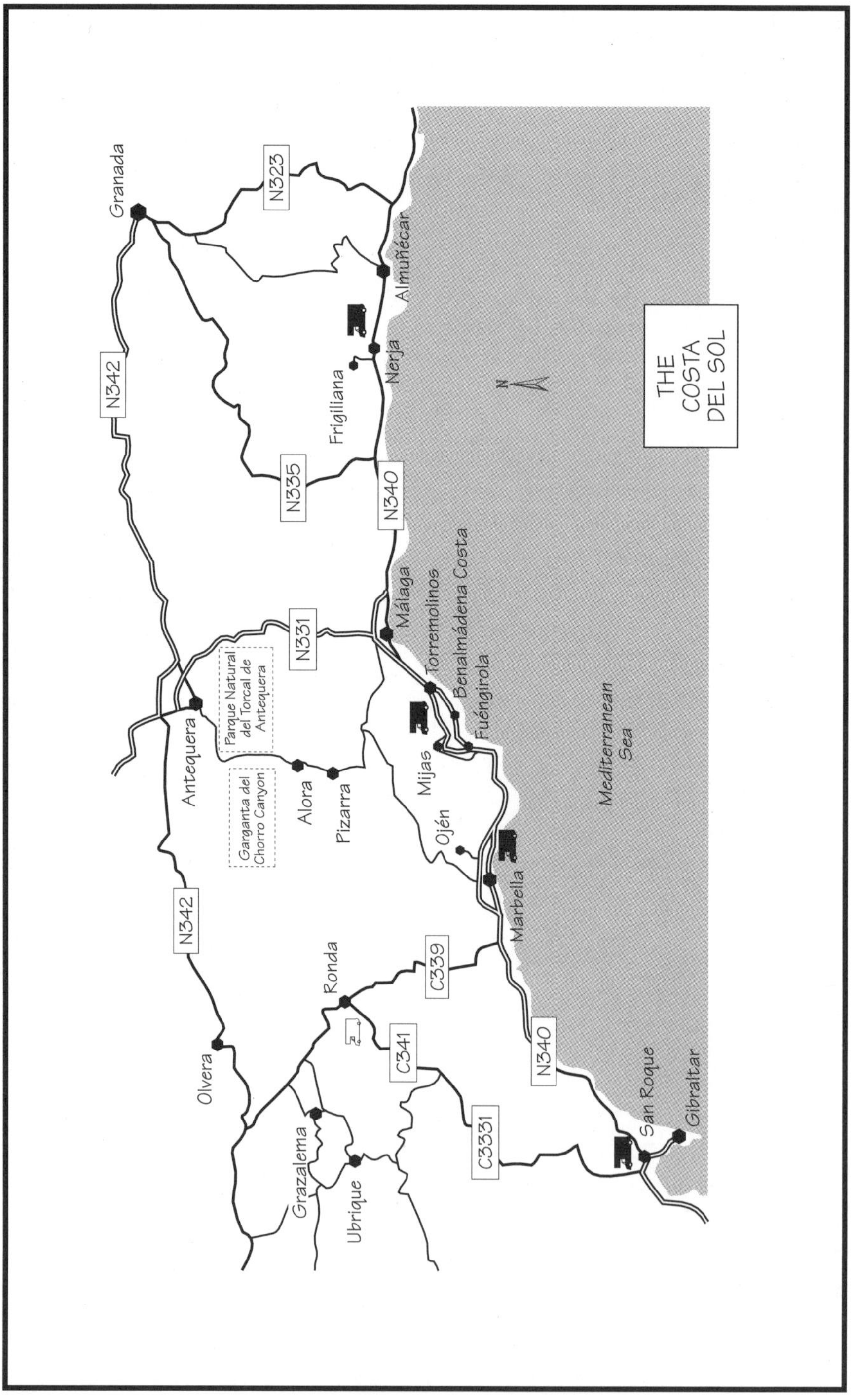
THE COSTA DEL SOL
N
Mediterranean Sea
Granada
N323
Almuñécar
Nerja
Frigiliana
N342
N335
N340
Málaga
Torremolinos
Benalmádena Costa
Fuéngirola
N331
Parque Natural del Torcal de Antequera
Antequera
Garganta del Chorro Canyon
Alora
Pizarra
Mijas
Ojén
Marbella
N342
C339
Ronda
C341
N340
Olvera
C3331
San Roque
Gibraltar
Grazalema
Ubrique

rant, and bread is delivered each morning. It is owned and run by a Spanish/Irish family.

This is an easy campground to find, in fact you can't miss it. Traveling along the coast on Highway N340 you'll find it near kilometer 297, sitting just above the highway about 4 kilometers east of Nerja.

Traveling westward, the city of **Málaga** has about 600,000 inhabitants and is by far the largest city on the coast. You'll probably be tempted to ignore it but central and eastern parts of town near the water are quite nice. You'll find gardens, churches, restaurants, and beaches. Málaga is also famous both for its sweet wines and as the birthplace of Pablo Picasso.

Fifteen kilometers west of Málaga is **Torremolinos**. This town is usually cited as an example of the worst that the Costa del Sol can offer. There are dozens of ugly high-rise hotels catering to Northern Europeans on package holidays. Vacation life for these visitors means lying on the beach during the day and discoing away the night. There's lots of action here and it can be a fun place if you know what to expect. **Benalmádena Costa** and **Fuéngirola** to the west are smaller and quieter versions of Torremolinos.

FUÉNGIROLA, SPAIN
Population 70,000

In this quieter and smaller version of "Terrible Torre" the high rises tend to be condominiums, not hotels. There's a long stretch of pretty good beach backed by a sidewalk promenade. You'll find plenty of inexpensive foreign food restaurants and tourist shops.

Fuéngirola Campground

✦ CAMPING LA ROSALEDA

Address: Apdo 288, Los Boliches, E-29649
Fuéngirola, Málaga
Telephone: 952 460191 Fax: 952 581966
Price: Moderate

Open all year

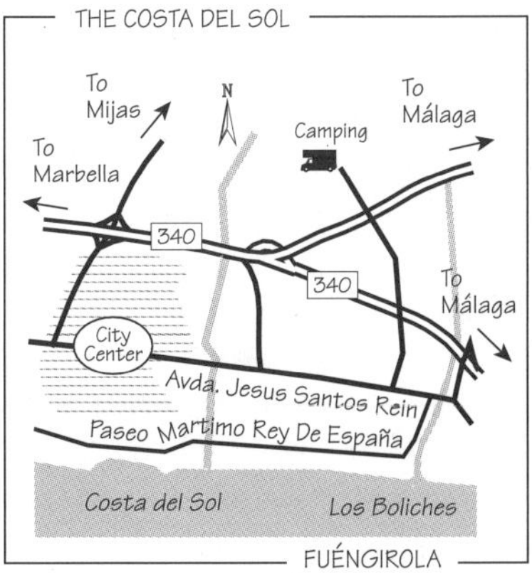

Sitting on a flat terrace on the hillside above Los Boliches, just east of Fuéngirola, La Rosaleda is filled with English, German, and Scandinavian snowbirds taking advantage of big discounts for long stays. La Rosaleda is popular because the facilities are decent, Fuéngirola and the beach are within walking distance, and there is a railway station nearby with trains to Torremolinos and Marbella.

The campground is medium to large with enough shade trees that no one has thought it necessary to put up frames for shade nets. Sites are on packed dirt and gravel, they are numbered but not generally assigned. Electricity (German plugs, 5 amps) is available to most sites using longer cords. The two shower/toilet buildings have free hot showers and cold water for bathroom basins, dishwashing sinks, and laundry tubs. There is a large swimming pool, a restaurant, and a grocery shop.

Many more restaurants and supermarkets are located in Los Boliches and Fuéngirola. When you walk directly down the hill on Avda. Salinas you'll find the railroad station at about 500 meters and the beach at about 800 meters. Turning right and walking along the beach promenade will bring you to Fuéngirola with the shops and restaurants starting almost immediately.

To reach the campground take one of the off-ramps as the N340 freeway passes through Fuéngirola near kilometer 211. Drive down the hill until you reach the street with the railroad tracks, Avda. Jesus Santos Rein. From most off-ramps you'll turn left and drive until you reach Avda. Salinas, then turn uphill and pass over two freeways to the campground. There are many campground signs, you'll find them marking every turn you need to make, beginning at the freeway off-ramps.

Side Trips from Fuéngirola

A good tour route starts at Málaga and follows C337 inland to **Pazarra**, **Alora**, the spectacular **Garganta del Chorro** canyon, and the **Parque Natural del Torcal de Antequera** where you can hike through the sandstone landscape. After the park complete the loop by passing through **Antequera**.

The next stop along the coast is Marbella.

MARBELLA, SPAIN

The jet set on the Costa del Sol hangs out in Marbella. This large town hasn't caught the high rise disease. Most of the hotels and condominiums here are garden style. The town stretches for almost 30 kilometers east and west along the beach, however, there really is a central Marbella. The most attractive part of town is not the waterfront, it lies several blocks inland and centers on the **Plaza de los Naranjos**.

About 7 kilometers west of central Marbella you'll see the turnoff for **Puerto Banús**, the port where the rich and famous keep their yachts. The road down to the marina is called the **Golden Mile**, you'll see why.

Marbella Campground

✦ CAMPING CARAVANNING MARBELLA PLAYA

Address: Carretera N 340, Km. 192.8, E-29600 Marbella, Málaga
Telephone: 952 833999 Fax: 952 833999
Price: Moderate

Open all year

This is the place to settle down for a few days (or weeks) to recharge your batteries. There's not much to do here except sit in the sun at the beach or pool. The campground has a couple of restaurants and a good supermarket just outside the entrance. If you get really ambitious you can catch the bus into Marbella for the day.

This is a large campground with about 400 sites. It is about 12 kilometers east of Marbella. The sites are numbered and assigned but campers are allowed to pick their own. Electricity (mostly German plugs, some CEE17, 10 amps) is available to most sites but sometimes requires a long cord. Shower/toilet buildings are clean and well maintained, they have free hot adjustable showers and hot water in bathroom basins. Dishwashing sinks and laundry tubs have cold water. There is a restaurant overlooking the large swimming pool and just outside the entrance are another small restaurant and a well-stocked small supermarket. We found that it carried a good selection of items selected with the many foreign visitors to the campground in mind. A decent beach is about 300 meters from the campground down a quiet country road.

Marbella is actually quite a distance away and there are no good bicycle routes. The bus runs on the freeway about 300 meters from the campground, this is the best way to visit town.

Marbella Playa is located on the ocean side of the N 340 coastal freeway at kilometer 192.8. Traveling eastward the exit is obvious and well marked. Traveling westward there is no exit and no sign. You must proceed a small distance past the 192.8 kilometer point, turn around at the next overpass, and enter the campground traveling eastward.

Side Trips from Marbella

Ronda is the most important and most often visited of the **Pueblos Blancos** or white villages. A few miles west of Marbella C339 winds up into the Serranía de Ronda mountains for 50 kilometers to the village. It is perched on a mountain top and is divided by a deep ravine called **El Tajo**. The spectacular mountain location and rich history of this town make it one of Spain's top tourist attractions. The **Puente Nuevo** over the ravine is spectacular, **La Ciudad** has Moorish features, the **Plaza de Toros** is one of the oldest bullfighting arenas in Spain and has its own museum, and the **Almeda del Tajo** gardens make a good spot to rest and enjoy the mountain air. You can camp near Ronda at CAMPING EL SU, 3 kilometers southwest of town on C341 toward Algeciras and open all year.

Surrounding Ronda in most directions are other pueblos blancos. These include **Grazalema**, **Ubrique**, **Olvera** and many others. Each has its own specialties and personality. You could easily spend several days exploring this small region.

From Marbella to Gibraltar is the up-and-coming part of the Costa del Sol. Now that Gibraltar can be entered from Spain tourists and winter residents can reach this coast easily from the airport there and also use Gibraltar as a supply base.

GIBRALTAR

Population 30,000

In some ways Gibraltar is a piece of England transported to the Costa del Sol, but the Rock has its own important place in history and geopolitics.

After a quick look around town (remarkably British) the prime attraction is the huge **Rock** itself. Taxi drivers will try to talk you into a tour but there's a **cable car** to take you to the top and from there it is a pleasant walk on paved roads back down to town. You'll no doubt see at least one of the two troops of **Barbary apes** and also have a chance to visit **St. Michael's Cave** which is filled with limestone stalactites and stalagmites.

You'll probably want to visit Gibraltar in your vehicle at least once even if your tourist excursions are by bus. It is worth the occasionally lengthy delay at the border in each direction because gas prices in Gibraltar are about a third less than in Spain (no VAT tax) and there is a brand new Safeway where you can restock from a fantastic selection of British items. Make sure you time your visit to avoid the morning and evening cross-border commute traffic.

Gibraltar Campground

✦ CAMPING MOTEL SAN ROQUE

Address: Carretera Algeciras-Málaga Km. 121, Apdo 87, E-11360 San Roque, Cádiz
Telephone: 956 780100
Price: Moderate

Open all year

Located in an area of gentle hills some 4 kilometers east of San Roque and 7 kilometers from Gibraltar this campground is the closest to Gibraltar. It serves well as a base for visiting because there is bus service to Gibraltar.

This is a large campground covering the rounded crest of a hill, there are many permanent caravans used by weekenders from Gibraltar. Sites are on dirt and sparse grass with some large trees providing a little shade. There are a few tourist sites in the back corner with views across the country side to the northwest. The shower/toilet buildings are small and simple, hot water showers (adjustable) are provided, as well as cold water in outdoors bathroom basins and dishwashing sinks. This is also a motel and has a restaurant/bar, a small store, and a swimming pool.

The bus to La Linea (The Line) stops at the campground gate every couple of hours. The trip takes 20 minutes and is inexpensive. From La Linea you walk about 200 meters across the border into Gibraltar where you can catch a Gibraltar local double decker that will take you the two kilometers into town.

There is a freeway under construction in front of the campground so access may become more difficult soon. Currently you will find the campground located on the south side of Highway N 340 near the 121 kilometer marker about two kilometers west of the first turn off for La Linea and about 4 kilometers east of San Roque.

THE ALGARVE, PORTUGAL

If you arrive in the Algarve from Spain's Costa del Sol it may seem to you that the two coastal tourist areas are very much the same. They really are very similar: they both occupy a southern coast that runs east and west, the architecture in both regions reflects a history of Moorish occupation, they have both developed a tourist economy in an area that previously had only fishing and agriculture.

The differences, however, are telling. The Algarve has not been developed to as great an extent, there are still some relatively unspoiled coastal villages. The water is not as warm on the Algarve, the Atlantic is much cooler than the Mediterranean. The Algarve's beaches are better, in many places there are miles of golden sand, not gray pebbles as on many Costa del Sol beaches, and finally, the Algarve continues to be less expensive, although not as much as it once was.

Think of the Algarve as having three different sections: the low area to the east with offshore islands, the stretch from Faro to Lagos with most of the tourist development, and the rocky coast from Lagos to the Cabo de São Vincent. Highway N 125 extends the entire length of the coast, usually a few kilometers inland. A new four-lane highway is being built and some of it already open.

The first town at the eastern end of the Algarve is right next to the Spanish border. **Vila Real de Santo António**. The border is actually the River Guadiana, and there's

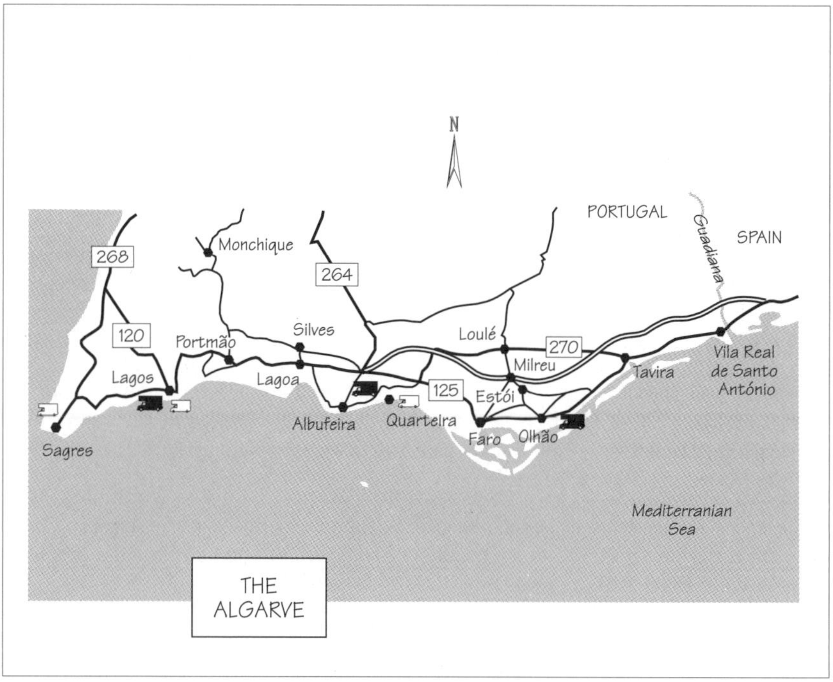

a bridge here as well as a ferry. Quickly heading east on N 125 (the coastal road) you'll soon reach **Tavira**. This small fishing village straddling the Gilão River is considered by many to be the most attractive town on the Algarve coast. A little farther west is **Olhão**.

OLHÃO, PORTUGAL

Population 35,000

Olhão is often thought to resemble a North African town more than a European one. This is because some of the residential areas have high whitewashed walls lining the street, the houses face inwards. The inhabitants are definitely Portuguese, however, and many are fishermen. You'll probably find yourself frequenting the **fish market** near the water and the simple seafood restaurants nearby. Tourist sights are limited here, but it is a great place to relax.

Olhão Campground

✦ CAMPING OLHÃO

Address: Apdo 300, P-8703 Olhão Codex, Algarve, Portugal
Telephone: 089 7001300 Fax: 089 7001390
Price: Inexpensive

Open all year

This is a popular, modern campground located about a kilometer east of the fishing port of Olhão. Olhão pretty much marks the eastern end of the Algarve camping district. Beaches here are on offshore islands that must be reached by small ferries.

Olhão, also known as Parque de Campismo e Caravanismo do Sindicato dos Bancários do Sul e Ilhas, is a very large campground with plenty of amenities. There are lots of tourists and few permanent rigs. Camp sites are marked off with small thin hedges. Most sites are pretty small and larger motor homes and trailers park on paved areas alongside the access roads. During slower seasons the campers tend to spread across two or three sites. Some shade is provided by trees. Electricity (German plugs, 5 amps) is available to all sites but outlet boxes are widely separated. There are lots of shower/toilet buildings, all have at least one free hot shower each for men and women with cold water in the bathroom basins. Some of these buildings also offer dishwashing sinks and laundry tubs, both with cold water only. Other amenities include a large swimming pool, wading pool, tennis courts, grocery shop, game and TV room, restaurants and bar. There is a railroad track along the bottom edge of the campground that gets a lot of use, you'll probably want to choose a site away from it.

Olhão can be reached by bus, there is a stop near the campground entrance. Alternately it is a 2-kilometer walk or bike ride to the center of town for shopping or the port area for boats to the offshore beaches. From Olhão you can take the bus to the larger town of Faro farther west.

You'll find the campground just off the coastal Highway, EN 125, about a kilometer east of the edge of Olhão. There's a sign on the road pointing south toward the water, the campground is about 300 kilometers down the road on the left.

Side Trips from Olhão

Some ten kilometers west of Olhão is **Faro**, the largest town on the Algarve coast and the best place to pick up supplies. Interesting sights in Faro are the Gothic **Sé (Cathedral)** with an interior covered with tiles and the **Capela dos Ossos (Chapel of Bones)** which is decorated with real bones.

A short distance inland from Faro are a number of destinations. **Estói** has the **Palácio do Visconde de Estói** with its gardens. Nearby are the **Roman ruins** at Milreu. Finally there is the small mountain town of **Loulé** with its **Saracen castle**.

The next section of coast is heavily developed and also has some fairly exclusive resorts This is the most heavily touristed section of the Algarve. Near the town of **Quarteira** near a long beach is the very large CAMPING ORBITUR QUARTEIRA, open all year. If you continue west you'll soon reach the turnoff for Albufeira.

Albufeira, Portugal

Albufeira is the flat-out resort and party capital of the Algarve coast. Once a small fishing village filling a coastal ravine it now has spread to cover the adjoining hills. Somewhat limited by having a small beach the town has compensated by building restaurants, bars, and shops. You'll never have any trouble finding a place to eat, drink, or dance, but to find a good beach go about 15 kilometers to the west to the fishing village of **Armação de Pêra**.

Albufeira Campground

✦ Parque de Campismo de Albufeira

Address: Estrada de Ferreiras-Alpouvar, P-8200 Albufeira, Algarve-Portugal
Telephone: 089 587629 Fax: 089 587633
Price: Moderate

Open all year

This campground is just up the hill from the tourist village of Albufeira. It has lots of amenities and also allows you to enjoy the nearby delights of the town.

This is a giant campground with the sites ringing a small hill. On the hill are most of the amenities: swimming pools, restaurants and bars, and a disco. The sites are on sandy grass with some shade, they are unmarked and not separated from each other. Larger rigs won't need to worry about small sites. Electricity is available (German plugs, medium amps) but you may need a long cord. The shower/toilet buildings have adjustable hot water showers, cold water in bathroom basins, and one hot-water tap in each of the separate buildings for dish and clothes washing. A laundry room with coin-operated machines is in one of the shower/toilet buildings. The grocery store is as large as anything you're likely to find in town. There are also a water slide, tennis courts, a playground, and dump stations.

Albufeira is 2 kilometers from the campground. You can easily walk down the hill on the wide shoulders of a fairly busy road or take the bus from a stop near the campground entrance.

You can find the campground by taking the Albufeira exit from the EN 125 coastal road and driving south toward the coast. The campground will be on your left in about 2 kilometers. It is also signed from the roads nearer Albufeira. Don't take your rig into town, the streets are very narrow and parking impossible.

Heading west from Albufeira on N 125 the next significant town is Lagoa, an inland market town with little to offer other than supplies. After Lagoa you'll reach Portmão, an important fishing port and one of the first towns to be developed for tourism along the coast. Another large fishing port, Lagos, is the next stop.

LAGOS, PORTUGAL

Population 15,000

This town is historically important as the departure point of the exploration voyages sponsored by Henry the Navigator along the African coast. Today it is a tastefully growing tourist town. Points of interest include the **old quarter**, a **statue of Henry**, and the **old slave market**. Just south of town is the impressive **Ponta da Piedade**. A good beach runs for miles to the east of town. Just west of Ponta da Piedade is IMULAGOS CAMPING which is close to town and an alternative to Camping Valverde Orbitur, described below. Imulagos is also open year round.

Lagos Campground

✦ CAMPING VALVERDE ORBITUR

Address: Praia da Luz, P-8600 Lagos, Algarve-Portugal
Telephone: 082 789211 Fax: 082 789213
Price: Inexpensive

Open all year

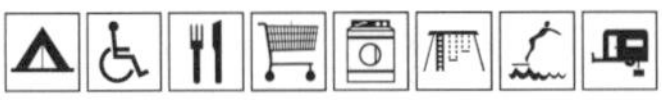

This is a very large campground that is part of the extensive Orbitur chain. Located about 4 kilometers west of Lagos and about 1 kilometer from the ocean it is well situated for exploring the western Algarve.

Valverde has about 1,000 sites, but this isn't obvious because they are spread over a large area and the shrubbery here has had time to grow to the point that it provides a lot of separation. Individual sites are mostly enclosed by hedges and have sandy dirt surfaces. Electricity (German plugs, medium amps) is available for most sites but plug boxes are widely spaced. There are several shower/toilet buildings, they have hot showers and cold water for bathroom basins, dishwashing sinks, and laundry tubs. There are coin-operated clothes washing machines available. Since this is a large campground it has lots of extras: restaurant and bar, disco, supermarket, pool, water slide, tennis court, bike rental, and playground.

Lagos is too far for walking, the bus stop is just outside the campground entrance. The small ocean-side village of Praia da Luz, which has a good beach, is just a little more than a kilometer down the road in the opposite direction.

To drive to the campground head west from Lagos toward Sagres on N 125. About three kilometers out of Lagos turn left to follow the sign to Praia da Luz, you'll see the campground on the right in about two kilometers.

Side Trips from Lagos

After Lagos the coast becomes even more rugged. You will soon reach **Sagres** where Prince Henry the Navigator's school was located and where high cliffs fall to the Atlantic far below. There's a campground on the road out to Cabo de S. Vicente called PARQUE DE CAMPISMO DE SAGRES which is open all year except December.

When you tire of the sun and sand on the coast there are several good day trips to sights located not far inland. From Portmão you can drive about 25 kilometers inland to the mountain town of **Monchique** and the nearby spa town of **Caldas de Monchique**. Take a look at the Manueline portal of the **Igreja Matriz** in Monchique or take the waters at the spa. There's a good eight-kilometer hike from Monchique to the peak at Fóia.

North from Lagoa only 8 kilometers is the ancient Moorish capital of the Algarve, **Silves**. You can tour the restored fortress and the **Cathedral of St Mary (Santa Maria da Sé)**.

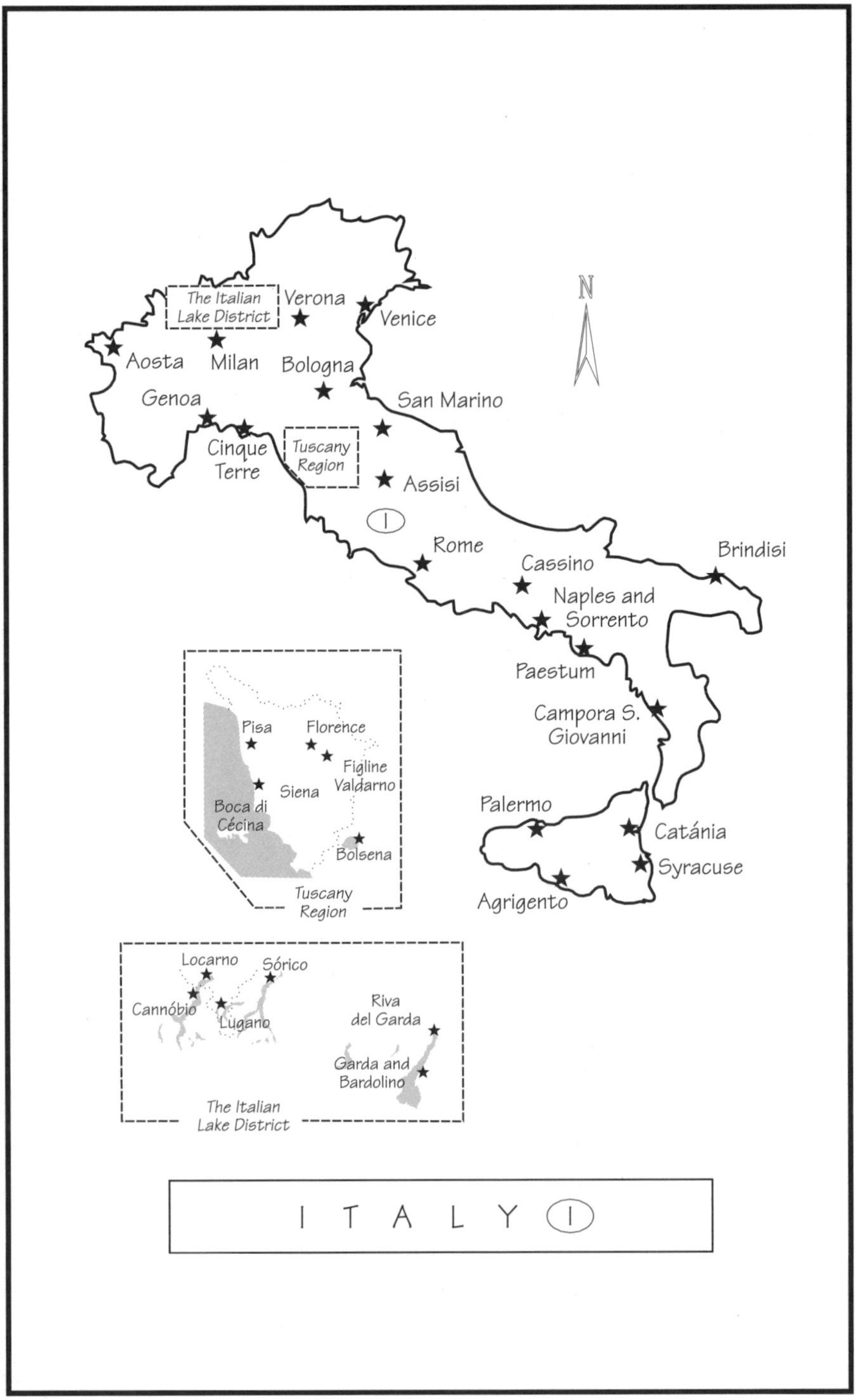
N
The Italian Lake District
Verona
Venice
Aosta
Milan
Bologna
San Marino
Genoa
Cinque Terre
Tuscany Region
Assisi
I
Rome
Cassino
Naples and Sorrento
Brindisi
Paestum
Campora S. Giovanni
Palermo
Catánia
Syracuse
Agrigento
Pisa
Florence
Figline Valdarno
Siena
Boca di Cécina
Bolsena
Tuscany Region
Locarno
Sórico
Cannóbio
Lugano
Riva del Garda
Garda and Bardolino
The Italian Lake District
ITALY I

CHAPTER

10

ITALY

INTRODUCTION

Italy is a wonderful country for a visit. Camping is very popular here, Italians own and manufacture lots of motorhomes, their small Italian-built class C's are some of the nicest in Europe. There are over two thousand campgrounds in the country, almost any town or city of any size will have one.

This is not a homogenous country. In general, the farther north you are the more affluent the people. Northern Italy may remind you of Germany while southern Italy is more like Portugal or even rural Mexico. The whole country, however, offers great food and wine and many things to see. Remember that Italy was home to the Roman Empire and the Renaissance, not to mention the Catholic Church.

Roads and Driving

Italian driving has a certain reputation, just as German driving does. When we picture the German driver we see a large powerful car speeding down the autobahn. When we picture Italian driving we see crowded roads with aggressive drivers in small cars honking their horns and shaking their fists. The stories about crazy Italian drivers are largely an exaggeration, but many of them are aggressive. Most Italian drivers are very good, the driving environment is just less structured than the one we are accustomed to. You're likely to see Italian drivers making some maneuvers that will astound you by their audacity. On the other hand, we've found Italian drivers to be amazingly considerate when it comes to putting up with comparatively large and slow RV's. Just make sure to "check your six" for passing traffic before making any left or right turns.

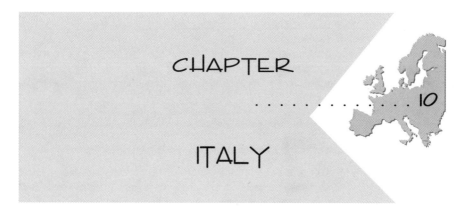

Italy is also motor scooter country. They're more common here than in any other west European country and they often disregard the traffic rules. It is entirely normal for scooters and mopeds to thread through traffic ignoring lights and signs. You must never change lanes, even a little, without double checking to see that a scooter isn't coming up behind you in a blind spot.

Italy has a fine system of freeways, called autostradas. Since this is a mountainous country you will see very impressive highway engineering in the form of huge bridges, viaducts, and tunnels. Autostradas are toll roads, you can expect to pay about five cents per kilometer for an automobile, a little more for vans and motorhomes, and cars with trailers pay a little more still. Secondary roads are also pretty good, but they are often crowded and they tend to run through many small towns. If you want to travel any longer distance in Italy you will probably soon find yourself on an autostrada, and you will be glad to be there.

On maps and signs the autostradas are designated with an "A" prefix, other state roads have a "SS" prefix with one, two, or three digits in the numeric designation. A smaller number of digits indicates a larger and better road.

It is not advisable to take your vehicle into the cities, particularly the larger ones. Traffic is heavy and roads are sometimes narrow. Parking is very difficult and even if you should find a space your vehicle will probably not be safe while you are away. Break-ins are very common. The best strategy is to leave your RV in a campground and use public transportation.

There's a good chance you'll do some traveling by ferry in Italy. The crossing from Réggio di Calábria to Messina in Sicily takes only about 45 minutes and the price is quite reasonable. You can take a ferry from Poimbino to the island of Elba where you will find several campgrounds. The normal route to Greece for campers is by ferry from Italy. You can travel from Trieste, Venice, Ancona, Bari, or Brindisi. Finally, you may decide to pay Sardinia a visit, there are ferries from Genoa, Livorno, and Civitavécchia. You may want to make reservations in advance at a travel agency for these longer trips so that you don't have to wait long for an open slot when you arrive in the port town.

The AAA-affiliated automobile clùb in Italy is the Automobile Club D'Italia (ACI) at 116 for breakdown service. The emergency number for the police in Italy is 113.

Camping

The overall level of quality of Italian camping facilities is somewhat uneven. There are modern campgrounds with excellent sanitation standards and there are older places where standards are barely passable. Most localities do have campgrounds, cities tend to be well serviced since many Italians use their motorhomes for business travel. A general rule with many exceptions is that the north has better and more modern campgrounds than the south.

Since temperatures are mild in southern and central Italy the shower/toilet buildings often are not fully enclosed or heated. Continental toilets are common. Showers are sometimes preset at coolish temperatures but are usually free. Cleaning can be hit-or-miss.

Electricity is usually inexpensive. This is possible because Italian campgrounds often have very low ampere breaker settings. Three amperes is not uncommon. That's just enough to run lights and a refrigerator. You'll find CEE17 plugs in common use with German style plugs in the older campgrounds.

Free camping is common in Italy as long as local regulations do not prohibit it. You'll often see large numbers of people camping in public parking lots. Sometimes they've been moved out by the next day but frequently the parking lot is really a designated camping area.

A Camping Card International is not usually required in Italy but if you don't have one you will probably have to give up your passport for the length of your stay in the campground.

Shopping, Currency, Credit Cards and Fuel

You should be able to easily find large supermarkets in Italy. They are usually located in the suburbs near major arterials. In the central areas of cities the stores tend to be much smaller, try looking in department stores; they often have a grocery section. In smaller towns and villages, particularly in the south, the traditional small meat, vegetable, bread, hard good, and even milk shops, will be your source of groceries.

You should often be able to use your credit or debit card. Look for a sign saying Carta Si indicating acceptance of Visa and Master Charge. Many gas station will accept cards, even American Express and Diners Club (very popular). Cash machines are common in cities and in tourist towns and we have not had any problems using them.

Itinerary Suggestions

Italians take their vacations during the school holidays just as most other Europeans do, campgrounds will be very crowded during July and August. The best months to visit are April through June and September through November. It is also very possible to spend the winter in Italy although you'll have little company in the campgrounds. Winter weather south of Rome is usually mild but not warm, north of Rome the winters are cold. Most of the campgrounds in this chapter are open year round.

The big three tourist destinations in Italy are Rome, Florence, and Venice. All of these cities are well supplied with campgrounds, and all have good public transportation connections between the campgrounds and the sights. Each of these places is worth at least a week.

The Italian countryside is justifiably famous. Two regions stand out: Tuscany and the Lake District. We've written special descriptions of these areas including detailed descriptions of several campgrounds in each. We're also very fond of the region surrounding the Sorrento Peninsula, including Naples, the Amalfi Coast, and Capri. We've written about many side trips in this region in our section on Naples and Sorrento.

For information about Italy contact the **Italian Government Tourist Board, 630 Fifth Avenue, Suite 1565, New York, NY 10111 (212 245-4822)**. In Canada the address is **1 Place Ville-Marie, Suite 1914, Montreal, QC H3B 2C3 (514 866-7667).** Check our web site at www.rollinghomes.com for links to information about Italy.

ITALY
DISTANCE TABLE

In Kilometers

Kms X .62 = Miles

	Agrigento	Aosta	Assisi	Bologna	Bolsena	Brindisi	Campora S. Giovanni	Cannóbio	Cassino	Catánia	Cécina	Figline Valdarno	Florence	Garda and Bardolino	Genoa	Innsbruck Austria	Lévanto (Cinque Terre)	Locarno Switzerland	Lugano Switzerland	Milan	Naples	Nice France	Paestum	Palermo	Pisa	Riva del Garda	Rome	San Marino San Marino	Siena	Sórico	Syracuse	Venice
Aosta	1700																															
Assisi	1131	633																														
Bologna	1335	400	268																													
Bolsena	1084	649	110	284																												
Brindisi	715	1180	731	780	684																											
Campora S. Giovanni	412	1340	771	975	724	320																										
Cannóbio	1667	231	600	352	616	1267	1302																									
Cassino	853	869	289	498	242	484	500	830																								
Catánia	165	1535	966	1170	919	550	247	1502	709																							
Cécina	1240	455	225	235	211	845	880	467	688	1075																						
Figline Valdarno	1199	506	149	141	167	816	839	473	367	1034	141																					
Florence	1230	470	163	105	179	830	870	437	398	1065	117	36																				
Garda and Bardolino	1495	334	428	175	444	1100	1135	291	658	1330	365	301	265																			
Genoa	1455	245	388	295	404	1060	1095	251	623	1290	215	261	225	284																		
Innsbruck Austria	1724	533	657	404	673	1324	1359	383	887	1559	594	530	494	270	549																	
Lévanto (Cinque Terre)	1420	334	353	255	369	1020	1060	340	577	1255	175	226	190	264	89	549																
Locarno Switzerland	1649	250	582	334	598	1249	1284	18	812	1484	450	455	419	273	259	368	333															
Lugano Switzerland	1611	237	544	296	560	1211	1246	56	774	1446	411	417	381	235	221	327	295	38														
Milan	1530	180	463	215	479	995	1165	137	693	1365	330	336	300	154	140	367	200	119	81													
Naples	760	955	391	590	344	370	400	922	100	595	500	459	490	750	715	979	669	904	866	785												
Nice France	1651	327	584	491	600	1251	1291	447	819	1486	411	457	421	480	196	703	285	448	417	336	911											
Paestum	710	1043	474	678	427	334	250	1010	187	545	583	542	573	838	798	1058	758	992	954	873	98	994										
Palermo	125	1675	1106	1310	1059	690	387	1642	828	205	1215	1174	1205	1470	1430	1699	1395	1624	1586	1505	735	1626	685									
Pisa	1325	400	234	190	220	930	965	412	493	1160	55	131	95	315	160	539	120	394	356	275	585	356	638	1300								
Riva del Garda	1549	345	482	229	498	1149	1189	277	712	1384	400	355	319	46	305	230	335	259	221	170	804	501	889	1524	345							
Rome	960	745	171	380	124	560	600	712	118	795	285	249	280	540	505	769	459	694	656	575	220	701	303	935	375	594						
San Marino San Marino	1268	538	227	143	310	936	914	490	494	1103	295	214	178	318	438	547	368	472	434	353	523	634	603	1243	273	372	376					
Siena	1185	535	124	170	110	785	825	502	348	1020	101	61	70	330	295	559	260	484	446	365	440	491	528	1160	110	384	230	180				
Sórico	1623	265	558	305	574	1225	1265	112	788	1468	442	431	395	189	245	268	334	94	56	103	880	441	963	1608	375	205	670	448	460			
Syracuse	215	1595	1026	1230	979	610	307	1562	748	60	1135	1094	1125	1390	1350	1619	1315	1544	1506	1425	655	1546	605	260	1220	1444	855	1163	1080	1528		
Venice	1485	450	334	160	444	870	1125	407	643	1320	385	301	265	150	400	374	364	389	351	270	740	596	828	1460	330	204	525	220	320	305	1390	
Verona	1460	340	393	140	409	925	1100	297	623	1295	330	266	230	35	290	279	270	279	241	160	715	486	803	1435	280	89	505	283	295	195	1355	115

SELECTED CITIES AND CAMPGROUNDS

AGRIGENTO, SICILY, ITALY

Population 52,000

Agrigento is the site of the ruins of five Greek Doric temples. They are located at the **Valley of the Temples**, a ridge near the town. The best preserved is the Temple of Concord dating from about 430 B.C. A visit to the temples isn't complete without a visit to the nearby **National Archeological Museum** to get an idea of what these temples looked like in ancient times. Agrigento's older central area, north from the museum across an area of excavations of Roman ruins, is worth a brief tour.

The beach town of **San Leone** situated below Agrigento is home to several campgrounds and makes a good place to spend some time on the beach.

Agrigento Campground

✦ CAMPING NETTUNO INTERNATIONALE

Address: San Leone, Via Alessandro Giuliana Alaimo, I-92100 San Leone, Agrigento
Telephone: 0922 416121
Price: Moderate

Open February 1 to October 30

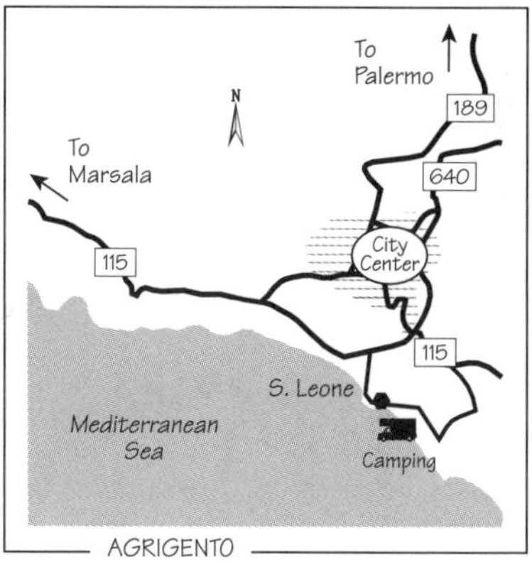

AGRIGENTO

There are actually two campgrounds here, INTERNAZIONALE SAN LEONE is almost next door and is open only during summer months. The campgrounds sit above a beautiful sandy beach.

This is a large campground built on terraces sloping down to the beach. Site surfaces are dirt, they are not separated. Electricity is available to most sites (CEE17 plugs, 4 amps). The shower/toilet area is in the center of the campground. Some of the showers have hot water (really just warm) but not the bathroom basins, which are outdoors. The campground has a snack bar, bar, and grocery shop. There is direct access to the beach with a gate which is closed at night.

The most convenient way to visit the temples is to drive, there is lots of parking. Bus service, however, to the temples and the town of Agrigento is good. There's a stop just outside the campground entrance, take bus number 9.

Find the campground by following signs from Agrigento or the coastal road toward San Leone. Once you reach the ocean follow it the east about three kilometers until the road turns to go inland. The campground sign and entrance road are on the right at the turn.

AOSTA, ITALY

Population 38,000

Aosta is a small town in the valley of the same name. Since the completion of the **Mont Blanc Tunnel** in 1965 the valley is a throughway to Italy from France, but once off the freeway the area has considerable charm. Aosta has Roman roots, it is a walled town and was an important military base since it controlled access to two important trade routes. It still does today, the steep road to the **St. Bernard Tunnel** and Pass meets the Mont Blanc route here. In Aosta you'll want to see the **Roman Arco di Augusto** and **amphitheater** ruins and the **Collegiate de Sant' Orso church** with its cloister. There is a market in the **Piazza Chanoux** at the center of town where the region's crafts are offered. During the winter the chain of small villages in the valley beginning with **Courmayeur** at the top are an important Italian ski resort. In summer it is a region offering hiking and castles including the castle of **Fénis** 14 kilometers down the valley from Aosta.

Aosta Campground

✦ CAMPING VILLA D'AOSTA

Address: Viale Grand San Bernard 37, I-11100 Aosta
Telephone: 0165 32878
Cost: Inexpensive

Open June 1 to September 30

This is a small campground within walking distance of Aosta. A big attraction is that the campground takes no permanent units, most campgrounds in this area are full of them. The town of Aosta and the valley above toward Courmayeur have many campgrounds. There are also some on Highway SS27 toward the St. Bernard Pass.

There are room for about 50 units, parking is on grass. Electricity (CEE17 plugs, low amps) is available to most camping sites. The shower/toilet building is near the entrance and has free hot showers. The campground has a small grocery shop and a bar.

To get to the campground follow signs from Aosta for the St Bernard Tunnel, Highway SS27. The campground is a short distance up the hill on the left.

Side Trips From Aosta

The ski village of **Courmayeur** is about 40 kilometers up the valley from Aosta. From La Palud, just beyond Courmayeur, you can ride a cable car up past Monte Bianco (Mount Blanc) and across the Alps to Chamonix in France. You switch cable cars at Helbronner (about 11,000 feet), and then climb to Aiguille du Midi (about 12,200 feet) and descend into France. In good weather this is the most impressive trip of its type in Europe but it is expensive, only go if the weather is superb.

If you drive down the Valle d'Aosta past the castle of Fénis for 26 kilometers, turn left at Châtillon, and climb for 30 kilometers up a side valley you will reach the village of **Breuil-Cervinia** at the base of the Matterhorn. This is another world-renown ski resort and in the summer you can ride cable cars into the mountains for views of the Matterhorn.

The **Parco Nazionale del Gran Paradiso** almost overlooks Aosta. Head up valley for six kilometers, turn left, and climb into the park. This is one of the most untouched natural parks in Europe, the park has both ibex (a wild goat) and chamois (an antelope).

ASSISI, ITALY

Population 25,000

Like many important tourist towns in Europe, Assisi is much more enjoyable and attractive when the streets aren't thronged with busloads of tourists. An excellent strategy is to base yourself nearby so that you can explore in the morning or evening. This is true of Assisi, and also of Mont-St-Michel, Rothenburg, Toledo, Delft, Bruges, Tournai and other destinations in this guide.

Assisi is a walled town situated on the slope of Mt. Subasio. The streets are narrow and necessarily somewhat car free, making this a pleasant town for pedestrians. It is full of churches and convents, but also of tourist-oriented novelty shops full of kitsch.

Without a doubt the most important site in Assisi is the **Basilica of St. Francis**. This huge conglomeration is really two churches, one over the other, both with celebrated artistic works covering the walls. It is without a doubt the spiritual, historic, and tourist center of the town. Also worth a visit are the **Church of St. Claire** and the **Rocca Medioevale** castle above the town which is an excellent viewpoint. There are Roman traces in Assisi also in the form of the **Tempio di Minerva** on the main piazza, the Piazza del Comune and also the **Roman Theater** between the Rocca Maggiore and the Rocca Minore. There are two very important pilgrimage days for Assisi, October 4 is the feast day of St. Francis, and August 12 is the feast of St. Claire.

Assisi Campground

✦ CAMPING FONTEMAGGIO

Address: Via Eremo delle Carceri 8,
I-06081 Assisi
Telephone: 75 813636 Fax: 75 813749
Price: Inexpensive

Open all year

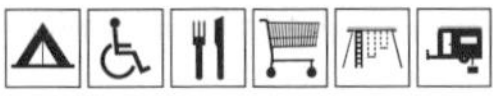

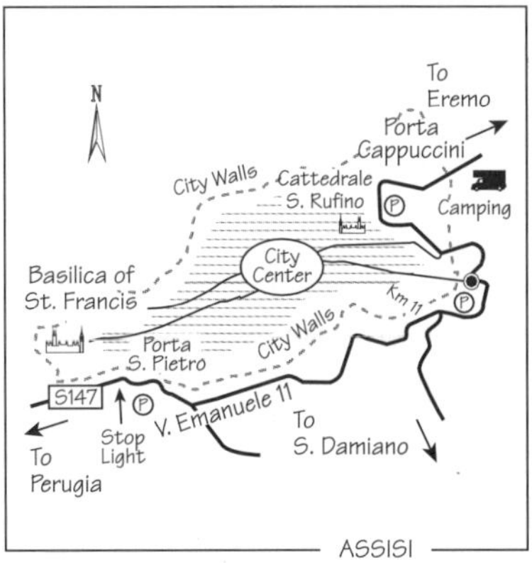

The long and winding access road up to Assisi, around the town, in and out through a couple of gates, and on up the mountain to this campground may be a little intimidating but most rigs should have no problem. Just forge ahead. The location is very convenient once you are there.

Camping Fontemaggio is both a hostel and campground. When you arrive check in at the desk in the main building. The campground is located behind and down the hill. Access roads are mostly gravel, sites are mostly flat with good shade on terraces. Electricity (German plugs, 10 amps) boxes are widely scattered. Restroom facilities are old and OK but not great, there may not be enough showers when the campground is full, they are free and the water is adjustable. The campground has a shop for groceries and also a restaurant. There is a nice country road/trail that runs the 1 kilometer to Assisi so the walk in to town is very pleasant.

To find the campground follow Highway SS147 from the direction of Perugia. You'll see an alternative Assisi campground, CAMPING INTERNATIONALE, between the 6 and 7 kilometer markers. Continue up the hill toward Assisi. You'll start passing below the walls and come to a stop sign near the Porta S. Pietro. From here there are small campground signs so watch carefully. The road curves to the right around below the walls of the city. following Viale G. Marconi and then Viale Vittoro Emanuele 11. You'll probably see the 11 kilometer sign and then pass by a bus parking lot. The road then comes to an intersection where you turn sharply left, then almost immediately to the right just before a gate into town. The road then curves around and does enter the town through another gate, passes by a parking plaza, then again turns right to pass out the Porta Cappuccini. The campground entrance is on the right in about a kilometer.

Side Trips from Assisi

Twenty-five kilometers west of Assisi is Perúgia. Perúgia is another old Etruscan hill town. There are Etruscan ruins in the city and tombs just outside of it. A prime attraction is the **National Gallery of Umbria** in the **Palazzo Communale** with an excellent collection of Perugian painters. The nearest campground is CAMPING PARADIS D'ETE, about 6 kilometers northwest of town and open all year.

BOLOGNA, ITALY

Population 460,000

Bologna has a convenient central location on the main autostrada between the north and Rome. It also has a good, convenient campground and sights enough to make a stop an inviting idea. Bologna is a rich town famous for its food. Window shop along its 21 miles of covered arcades and make a visit to a good restaurant. You can do some sightseeing in the neighborhood of the central **Piazza Maggiore**, make sure to see Bologna's leaning towers, the **Torre degli Asinelli** and the **Torre Garisenda**. They are similar to the ones in San Gimignano, there were once almost 200 of them in Bologna. The **Pinacoteca Nazionale** art gallery has many Italian masters. Bologna was a leading university town in the Middle Ages, at one time over 10,000 pupils were registered.

Bologna Campground

✦ CAMPEGGIO CITTÀ DI BOLOGNA

Address: Via Romita 12/4a, I-40127 Bologna
Telephone: 051 325016 Fax: 051 325318
Price: Moderate

Open all year, closed for Christmas period

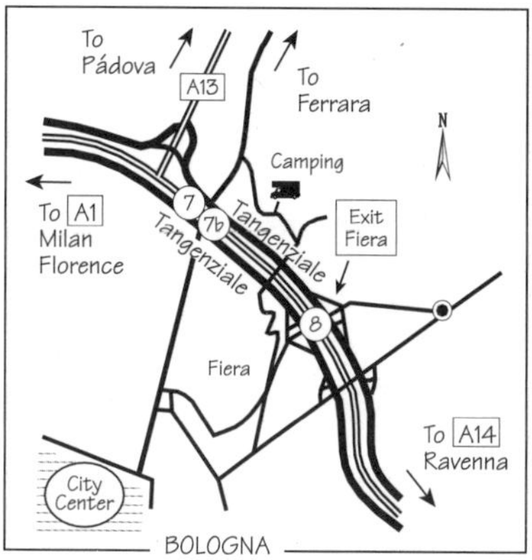

This is a relatively new site that is located near a trade fair and exhibition center to the north of the city. The campground is a large flat grassy field in the middle of other grassy fields with quite a few very modern and substantial rental bungalows in the center. Individual sites are numbered and assigned when the campground is busy, electricity (CEE17 plugs, 6 amps) is available to most of the sites. The central shower/toilet building is beautiful to behold, showers (not adjustable) require a token but bathroom basins and dishwashing sinks have free hot water. There are laundry machines and a dump station.

Bologna can be reached by bus, the stop is about a kilometer away. Ask for directions at the reception desk.

The campground can most easily be reached by traveling to the north of the city on the ring road (Tangenziale), then take the Fiera exit (Exit 8) toward downtown Bologna, the campground is well signed from this point and not far from the freeway.

BRINDISI, ITALY

Population 94,000

Brindisi has been an important port since Greek and Roman times. Its location on the heel of the Italian boot directly across from Greece and its large harbor insure that it will continue to be one. For travelers Brindisi is the main port for ferries to Greece, the distance across the Adriatic is shortest from Brindisi and therefore this is the most inexpensive and popular route.

There is little in the way of tourist sites in Brindisi. It is the end point of the Appian Way from Rome and there is a 65-foot **Roman column** near the harbor to celebrate this. There's also a **castle** built by the Holy Roman emperor Frederick II in the 13th century and an 11th-century **cathedral**.

If you arrive in town without ferry tickets you'll find most of the ferry offices on the Corso Garibaldi near the harbor. Many ferry lines service Greece. We found little difference in price but it doesn't hurt to do a little shopping, it won't take long with all the offices so close together. The closest and cheapest destination in Greece is Igoumenitsa. Also popular is Patras which is much closer to Athens. The island of Corfu is a stop on the Igoumenitsa - Brindisi run but not all boats stop there, many only do so on the return run from Greece so check this out if you want to visit Corfu which has many campgrounds. We've had no trouble getting reservations to travel on the same day we purchased tickets during September and October, this is probably not the case during busier months. The ferries run at night to accomodate truckers.

Brindisi Campground

✦ PINETA AL MARE VILLAGGIO

Address: Pineta al Mare,
I-72012 Specchiolla di Carovigno
Telephone: 831 9680571 Fax: 0831 987829
Price: Moderate

Open all year

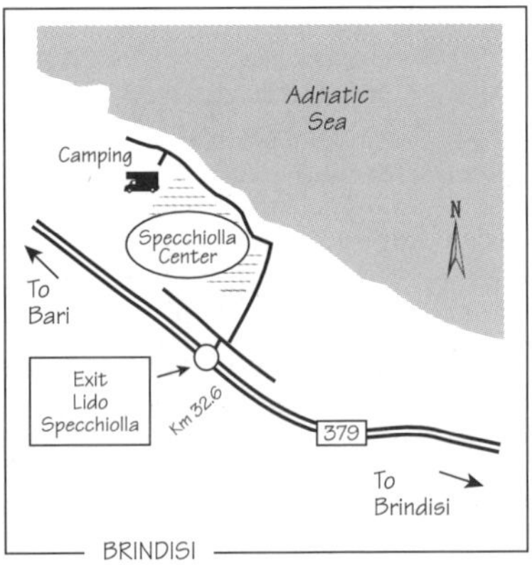

There are at least six huge campgrounds along the coast north of Brindisi. Most, however, are open only for a few months in the middle of the summer. Pineta Al Mare Villaggio is the exception, you may be the only visitor while you are there. The campground is also unusual in that it is located in a small village. Most the houses here are holiday rentals, but there are some restaurants and small shops.

The campground sits across from a small beach. It is a large holiday campground with many caravans that stay all year although they are used only for a few weeks in the summer. Restrooms are large and modern and have adjustable hot showers. Laundry sinks and dishwashing sinks have only cold water. Electricity is widely spaced (CEE17 plugs, 5 amps).There is a huge swimming pool, a beach across the street, a restaurant, a store, clothes washing machines, and a dump station.

Disregard most of the above in the off season. The store, restaurant, and swimming pool are all shut down. One restroom, normally used as the handicapped restroom, remains open. It is heated and has hot water for the shower and sink, quite satisfactory. There is also an available dish/clothes-washing sink and a washing machine. A short stroll will take you to a small store in town with basic grocery items.

The campground is in Lido Specchiolla which is on the coast near SS379 between Bari and Brindisi, about 30 kilometers north of Brindisi. The exit is near Km. 32.6 and there is a campground sign near the exit. Follow signs the kilometer or so to town, drive straight on to the beach, turn left to head south and you'll soon see the campground on the left. In the winter the campground direction signs are changed to take you to the back gate where you ring the bell for access. Someone will let you in and register you.

CAMPORA S. GIOVANNI, ITALY

We bet you've never heard of this place. Located on the west coast, just where the foot of the Italian boot starts, this campground is a place to spend the night if you're heading for Sicily. There's a beach here and the campground is open all year. Other nearby campgrounds close in the winter.

Campora S. Giovanni Campground

✦ MOTEL CAMPING LA PRINCIPESSA

Address: Variante SS 18, I-87030 Campora San Giovanni
Telephone: 0982 46903
Price: Inexpensive

Open all year

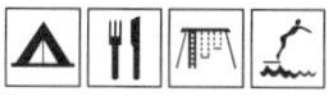

The medium-sized campground is located on the grounds of the Motel la Principessa, a quite polished establishment. The campground is grass and well shaded but not nearly as polished. Sites are not separated or assigned and electrical boxes are scattered around the grounds. Shower/toilet facilities are basic but adequate. Showers are free and hot (push-button valve, premixed), toilets are continental type. The motel has a restaurant and there is an access tunnel to the beach on the far side of the two-lane highway.

The campground is located on coastal Highway SS18 about three kilometers south of the town of Campora S. Giovanni. Look for the motel sign, the facility is on the left as you drive south. From the autostrada exit at Falerna, about 5 kilometers north, and head for the coast.

CASSINO, ITALY

Population 35,000

The main reason to stop in Cassino is the great **Benedictine monastery** overlooking the town from the top of Monte Cassino, just to the north. The name is familiar to most Americans because Monte Cassino was an important strong point of the German Gustav Line which blocked the advance of Allied forces up the Italian Peninsula toward Rome during the winter of 1944. Bombers destroyed the monastery then but it has been rebuilt and is a popular destination. A good paved road leads from the town up 1,700 feet to the monastery.

The town of Cassino was also heavily bombed during the war but it has certainly recovered. Today Fiats are assembled here, but several military cemeteries dot the surrounding countryside.

Cassino Campground

✦ **CAMPING TERME VARRONIANE**

Address: Via Terme 5, I-03043 Cassino
Telephone: 0776 22144
Price: Moderate

Open all year

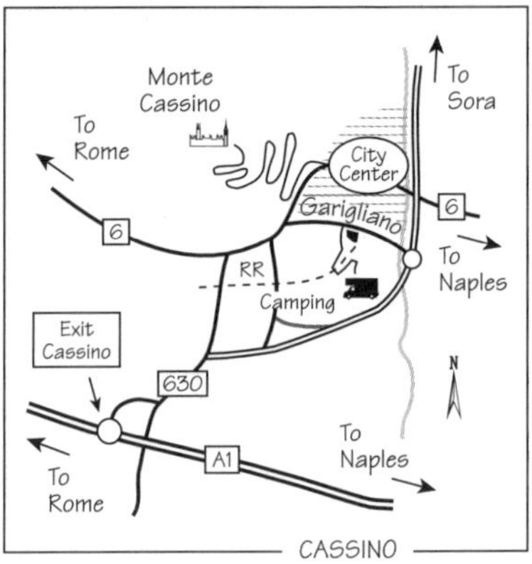

Cassino's campground occupies the site of a Roman villa and bathing area. Underground springs come to the surface here and form a small river that flows along the border of the camping area. It is pleasant to stroll along the crystal-clear steam and spot the places where the many springs flow out of the ground.

In late fall we found the campground to be a little run down with the grass in need of a good mow. Trees provide plenty of shade. Campsites are on grass off a gravel loop, they are not marked or delineated. Electricity (CEE17 plugs, 4 amps) is available to many of the sites. The shower/toilet building is clean and fairly modern, it seems to have no provisions for heating water although the water coming out the ground is slightly warm. There are dish-washing and clothes-washing sinks and a washing machine.

Most visitors to Cassino probably arrive on the A1 autostrada between Rome and Naples. Take the Cassino exit and follow SS630 toward Cassino. This highway forms a bypass route running south of Cassino. If you zero your odometer at the exit to the autostrada you will find yourself at the Cassino Center exit after 4.1 kilometers. You may spot a new entrance to the campground off to your left just before the exit but access to it is difficult. Instead, take the center exit and follow signs toward the center of town. You'll find yourself on Via Garigliano and after .7 kilometers pass the Piazza Garibaldi and spot the railroad station off to your left. The left turn for the campground is .2 kilometers beyond and is marked with a sign. A small road curves under the tracks and around the railroad yard to the campground.

CATÁNIA, SICILY, ITALY

Population 385,000

Catánia is a large city on the east coast of Sicily. It is not visited much by tourists. The walk along the seaside promenade from the campground towards the central part of the city, including a chance to watch the fishermen at the small harbor near the campground, is a good way to pass the time. The town is also know for its baroque buildings built in the 18th century after the city was mostly destroyed by eruptions and earthquakes from nearby Mt. Etna. The best reason for a visit is that Catánia is a good place to use as a base for visiting the volcano.

Catánia Campground

✦ CAMPING IONIO

Address: Via Acque Casse No 38, I-95126
Catánia Ognina
Telephone: 095 491139
Price: Moderate

Open all year

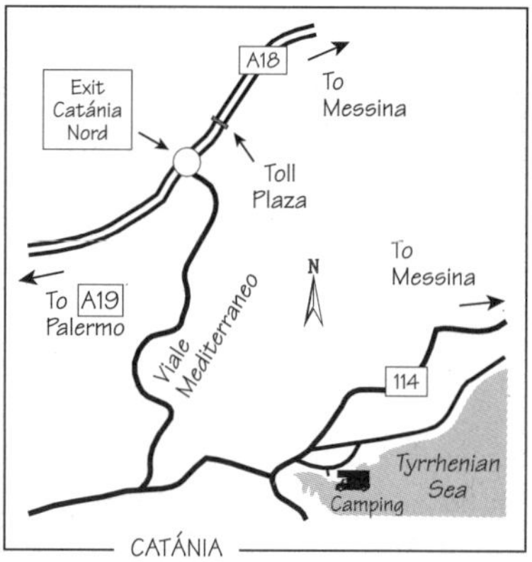

Camping Ionio is a waterfront campground, but the volcanic rock shoreline has no beach. The campground sits on a flat shelf some 15 feet above the waves. This is a medium-sized campground with quite a few permanent caravans, there is a separate area for tourists. Many of the sites have their own individual bath houses with toilet, basin, and cold shower, although these tend to go to longer-term guests. Electricity is available to the remainder of the sites but may require a long cord. The shower/toilet building is older and not in great repair, but usable. Hot showers are available and require a token. The campground has its own grocery shop and small playground. There are restaurants and a supermarket nearby.

You can reach central Catánia either by bus or bicycle. The bicycle ride or walk downtown along the seawall is pleasant, the distance about 5 kilometers.

You can most easily find the campground by driving to the waterfront in Catánia and then heading north. You'll see the campground signs just at the end of the promenade where the road leaves the coast. The small entrance road running behind the houses on the coast is very narrow if you attempt to enter from this southern end, if you have a trailer or larger rig you'll do better to take the north entrance which you will see on the right a little farther along just after passing the supermarket.

Side Trip From Catánia

A good way to visit **Mt. Etna** is to leave your car at the campground in Catánia and take a bus. At 7:30 AM a bus leaves from the main train station in Catánia and goes to the base station of a cable car at the Rifugio Sapienza. From there the cable car will take you part way up the mountain, to about 2,500 meters, where you can catch a small bus to a point near the top. You can also walk from the bottom of the cable car, the hike will take from three to four hours.

CINQUE TERRE, ITALY

The Cinque Terre, a series of five tiny towns perched above the Gulf of Genoa, has become a top destination for travelers searching for an unique experience. The five villages: **Riomaggiore, Manarola, Corniglia, Vernazza, and Monterosso;** seem isolated but are in fact linked by walking trails, rail, and even narrow winding roads.

The roads are virtually unnoticed because they approach from high above and do not actually enter most of these towns. The rail is almost entirely inside the cliffs so it is equally unobtrusive. The tracks only make a fleeting appearance in each village and then disappear again into the tunnels. Visitors hike the breathtaking trails between the towns, pause for rest and refreshment when they wish, and use the frequent trains for cheap and convenient backup transportation. The usual strategy is to use the train to get to either Monterosso or Riomaggiore, walk until you are tired, and then hitch a train ride home.

The trail between the towns varies in difficulty. Riomaggiore to Manarola is a flat wide path that takes about 30 minutes. Manarola to Corniglia is a little more strenuous but still pretty easy, plan on about 45 minutes. Corniglia to Vernazza and Vernazza to Monterosso are both relatively difficult with lots of up and down sections, they will take from an hour and a half to two hours each. These are, of course, just average times. It is also possible to follow an even more difficult trail north to Lévanto from Monterosso, but the route is not well marked. It takes at least two hours.

Lévanto Campground

✦ CAMPING ACQUA DOLCE

Address: Via Guido Semenza 5,
I-19015 Lévanto
Telephone: 0187 808465 Fax: 0187 807365
Price: Moderate

Open March 1 to November 15 and December 5 to January 7

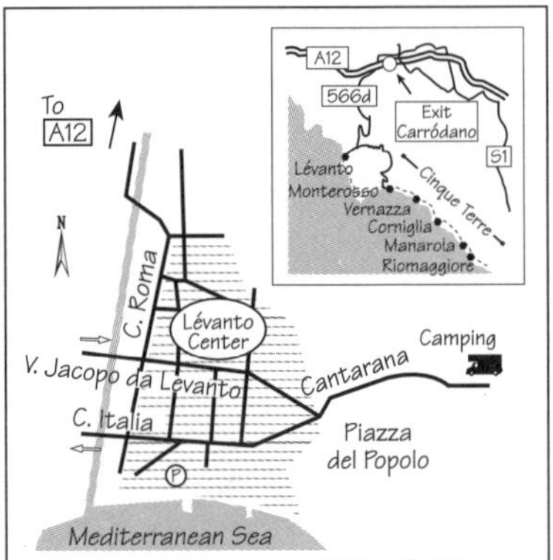

CINQUE TERRE

Lévanto is not really part of the Cinque Terre, but it could easily be. It is the next town to the north and sits in a narrow valley fronted by a nice sandy beach. The train blasts out of the mountain here for only a hundred meters or so just as it does in the Cinque Terre towns to the south. There are several campgrounds so Lévanto is a great base for exploring. The Cinque Terre walking paths actually come as far as Lévanto or the local train can give you access to any Cinque Terre town in just minutes.

Acqua Dolce is a medium-sized campground set on terraces on the south side of Lévanto. Olive trees on the terraces provide shade. The area can be crowded in the summer months but the extended opening dates of this campground give you a good opportunity to visit during the shoulder season when there is more room. Camping sites are numbered but not physically separated, electricity (3 amps, CEE17 plugs) is near all of the wheeled-vehicle sites, there are also sites for tents. The shower/toilet building is simple but modern with hot showers requiring payment. Sinks for shaving, dish washing, and laundry all have free hot water. The campground has a bar/pizzeria and dump station. Restaurants, shopping (groceries and other), and the beach are all within easy walking distance.

Lévanto itself is most easily reached by taking the Carródano exit some 25 kilometers north of La Spézia on the A12 autostrada. Once you reach the town the fun has just begun. Although small, it is a maze of one-way streets and the campground signage is poor. Your best bet is to follow the main road (Corso Roma) all the way to the beach, turn around and head back looking for the first one-way road to the right. This is V. Jacopo da Levanto. Turn right here and drive to the end, two blocks, then bear right toward the beach and then left at a park to head inland along the tiny Piazza del Popolo and into Via Cantarana. The campground is just ahead on the left. You'll probably see some campground signs along the route, it is actually easier to drive than to explain.

GENOA (GÉNOVA), ITALY

Population 760,000

Genoa is crowded, chaotic, and fascinating with a reputation of being somewhat difficult to visit. This is not the case for campers, thanks to a good campground with excellent bus transportation to town. The city has the largest **medieval section** in Europe near the harbor and that is where you'll probably spend your time. Christopher Columbus was born here and there is a reconstruction of his home. Around the perimeter of the old city, especially on **Via Garibaldi**, are the palaces of the rich from the fifteenth and sixteenth centuries. The hills above town with cog railway and elevator access offer great views of the city and its busy harbor.

Genoa Campground

✦ CAMPEGGIO VILLA DORIA

Address: Via al Campeggio Villa Doria 15n, I-16156 Génova-Pegli
Telephone: 010 6969600
Price: Moderate

Open all year

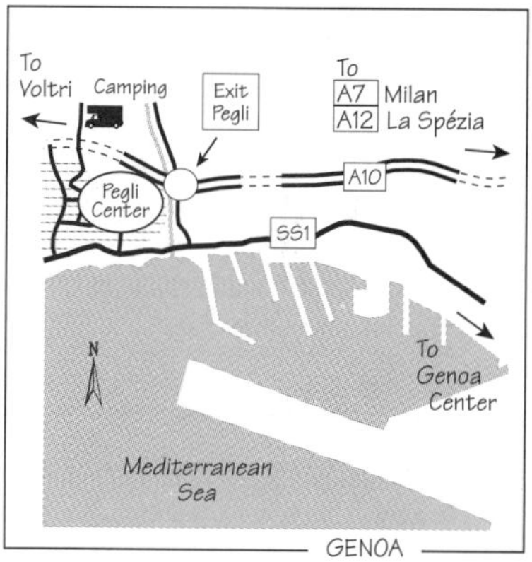

Villa Doria is actually located in the suburb of Pegli about 10 kilometers west of Genoa. Since there is good bus service into Genoa this is an advantage, Pegli is a friendly-sized waterfront town with supermarket, shops, restaurants, and an ocean-side promenade.

The campground sits in a small valley up the hillside from Pegli. Sites are in two areas, below the reception/bar building is a flat grassy terrace, above it is a long string of sites along the access road running back up the valley. Electricity (CEE17 plugs, medium amps) is next to all of the sites, many also have drains and water. The two shower/toilet areas are modern and very clean, there is free adjustable hot water to showers, bathroom basins, and dishwashing sinks. The nice bar area is also used as a TV room, serves limited food, and has some supplies. The campground also has a dump station. A supermarket is about 500 meters down the hill.

The Genoa busses run frequently along the waterfront about 700 meters down the hill from the campground. Numbers 1, 2, and 3 will all take you into the city. There's also a less frequent local bus that comes up the hill.

From the A10 autostrada take the Pegli exit west of Genoa. Drive down to the waterfront and turn right toward the west on SS1, the waterfront highway. Very soon you'll see the campground sign pointing right up the hill. Follow the signed route, it twists uphill through sometimes narrow streets to the campground. Take it easy with big rigs and trailers.

MILAN (MILANO), ITALY

Population 1,650,000

Milan is the center of Italian business, the largest city in Italy after Rome. Many of the well known sights are in a central area that is quite compact for such a large town. If you decide to wander a little farther afield there is a good subway system.

The place to start your tour is the **Piazza del Duomo** which has its own subway station. The **Duomo** is Gothic and quite unique, it is a forest of spires, belfries, and statues. A prototype of today's shopping malls is the **Galleria Vittorio Emanuele** which branches off the square in front of the cathedral. North of this are high fashion shops filled with Italian designs. Milan is also home to Leonardo da Vinci's painting ***The Last Supper*** which is in a somewhat isolated location about a kilometer and a half west of the Piazza del Duomo and south of Milan's impressive **Castello Sforzesco**. The Castello Sforzesco itself houses a museum with paintings, sculpture, and more. **La Scala opera house,** located just north of the Galleria, is best seen by attending an opera, the season is from December to May. If you're in Milan out of season or if you just can't get opera tickets you can also generally take a look by visiting the museum in the building. Finally, Milan's most famous art museum is the **Pinacoteca di Brera** with a fine Italian Renaissance collection. The Brera quarter is also the place to find less expensive restaurants.

Milan Campground

✦ CAMPEGGIO "CITTÀ DI MILANO"

Address: Via Gaetano Airaghi 61,
I-20153 Milan
Telephone: 02 48202993
Price: Moderate

Open all year

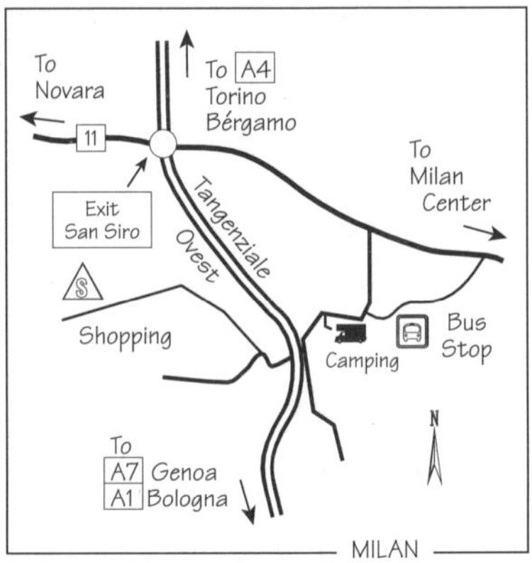

Choices for campgrounds in Milan are very limited, surprising for such an important city. Campeggio Città di Milano is located a considerable distance from the city center but does have public transportation in the form of bus, then metro service, to Milan center. Don't be surprised if you see a platoon of men in business suits leaving the campground each morning, many Italians use RV's in lieu of business hotels and Milan is Italy's business city.

This is a large campground located on the grounds of a commercial aquatic park (Aquatica). The facility was built to good standards but has deteriorated. The camping area itself sits behind the park, camping is on grass or gravel between a series of parallel access driveways of gravel or asphalt. There are a considerable number of semipermanent residents. Sites are not numbered, separated, or assigned. Electrical boxes (CEE17 plugs, 10 amps) are convenient to many sites and are in good repair but there are not enough outlets so there is some competition involved in getting one. There is no additional charge for electricity here, amazing in view of the high amperage and northern location of the campground, and this explains why everyone tries to use as much as possible, particularly in winter months. There are two shower/toilet buildings, originally very nice but now in need of restoration. Showers, bathroom basins, and dishwashing sinks all have provision for free adjustable hot water but the supply is erratic. The aquatic park has a restaurant. There is a small Coop supermarket about a kilometer from the campground and a much larger brand new one about two kilometers in the opposite direction on the far side of the nearby ring road.

To travel to Milan center you must walk about a half kilometer and catch the number 72 bus to the Place de Angeli Metro station. Once there traveling around the city on the underground Metro is convenient. The bus portion of the trip should take about 20 minutes, the metro trip to the Duomo station in the center of town takes another 10. Tickets can be purchased at the newsstand across from the Coop supermarket near the campground, the bus stop is behind the supermarket. Tickets are good for 75 minutes so one ticket will take you all the way downtown on both bus and metro.

The campground is located on the west side of Milan very near the Tanganziale Ovest (ring road), in fact you will see the Aquatica sign from the freeway if you approach from the south. Take the San Siro exit and then proceed east toward the city. The route to the campground is signed with Aquatica signs, if not aware of this you might miss them because they are not the more normal camping pictograph type. After 1.9 kilometers turn right, then right again in another half kilometer. You will soon see Aquatica on the left, the campground is entered through the water park's main entrance.

Side Trips from Milan

Having seen Northern Italy's biggest city you may want to see number two. Turin (Torino) is 140 kilometers east on the A4. Now an industrial town Turin is known as an early example of excellent town planning, particularly in the area of the **Piazza San Carlo** and its churches and palaces. The **Cathedral of San Giovanni Battista** houses the somewhat suspect **Holy Shroud**. There are Roman ruins in Turin including the **Palatine Gate** and the **Old Theater**. The **Royal Armory** is one of Europe's top arms collections and has **Napoleon's sword**. A good campground that is convenient to Turin is MILL PARK. It is in Caselette, about 15 kilometers west of the city center and is open year-round.

NAPLES (NÁPOLI) AND SORRENTO, ITALY

Population 1,300,000 (Naples), 18,000 (Sorrento)

A visit to Naples is best accomplished by camping in Sorrento or perhaps one of three campgrounds near Pompeii. Transportation around the bay on trains, busses and boats is easy and convenient. You can base yourself in Sorrento and make easy day trips to Naples, the island of Capri, the Amalfi Coast, Mt. Vesuvius or the Roman ruins at Pompeii and Herculaneum. This is a spectacular region with lots to see.

Sorrento itself is a well known resort town that perches on cliffs above the Bay of Naples with views of Mt. Vesuvius and Naples. Walks around the town of Sorrento and its two marinas are enjoyable, and there are restaurants, shops, banks with cash machines, and even travel offices if you would like to book a professional tour from Sorrento to one of the nearby attractions. The Marina Grande is a fishing port with small boats pulled up on the beach while the Marina Piccola to the east is the departure point for boats to Naples and Capri. The craftsmen in the town specialize in inlaid wood furniture.

Naples is a large, crowded, and somewhat intimidating town with a bad reputation. Guidebooks commonly warn about pickpockets and car break-ins. Still, you don't want to miss this city. One solution is to camp in Sorrento and visit on a day trip using

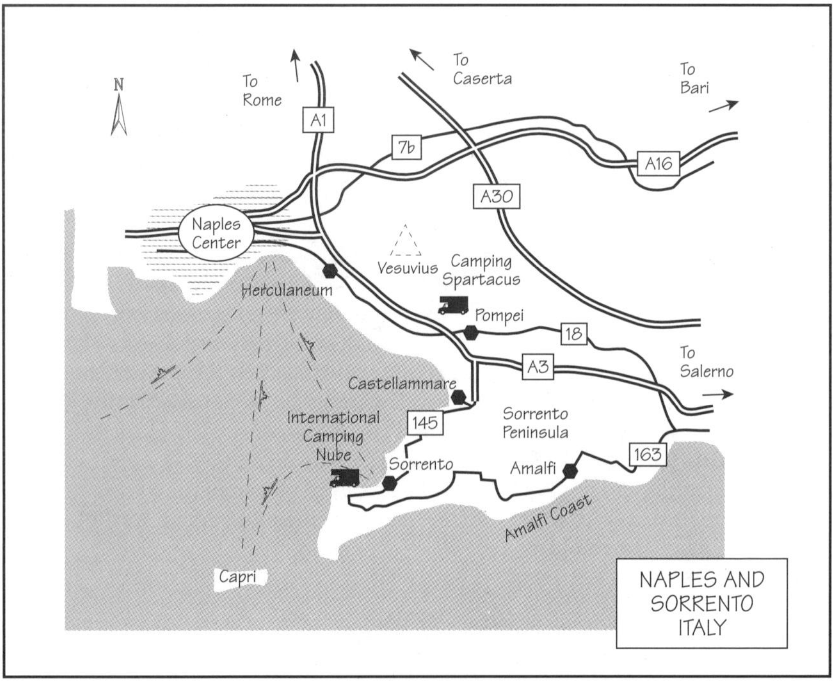

either the convenient hydrofoils from the Marina Piccola or the Circumvesuviana train line from the train station right in Sorrento. Both take an hour or so, the train is especially economical and runs frequently. About half way between Sorrento and Naples on the Circumvesuviana is Pompeii. There are three campgrounds here, Naples is even more convenient to Pompeii than it is to Sorrento and the ruins are extremely convenient to these campgrounds.

When you arrive in Naples your first priority is to obtain a map. With it in hand make your way to the eastern end of the **Spaccanapoli**. This small street cuts right through some of the most fascinating neighborhoods in town and is variously called (from east to west) Via Vicaria Vecchia, Via San Biagio dei Librai, and Via Benedetto Croce. A walk from one end to the other is the best introduction you could possibly have to Naples. Near the point where the Spaccanapoli crosses Via Toledo is the **Museo Archeologico Nazionale** which is filled with exhibits from the excavations at Pompeii and Herculaneum and which makes a good introduction to those sites. Also near the end of the Spaccanapoli is the funicular station for a trip up the hill to the **Castel Sant'Elmo** and the **Certosa de Martino monastery**, worth the trip even if you only go for the view. From the hill you can pick out other points of interest, perhaps the grouping of buildings near the harbor including the **Castel Nuovo** and **Palazzo Reale**. When you're ready to call it a day you can catch the metro from many locations including the lower funicular station back to the railroad station for the trip home.

Sorrento Campground

✦ INTERNATIONAL CAMPING NUBE D'ARGENTO

Address: Via Capo 21, I-80067 Sorrento
Telephone: 081 8781344 Fax: 081 8073450
Price: Moderate

Open all year

The Sorrento area has at least six campgrounds, this one has an enviable location and stays open all year long. Late fall isn't a bad time to visit the Naples area.

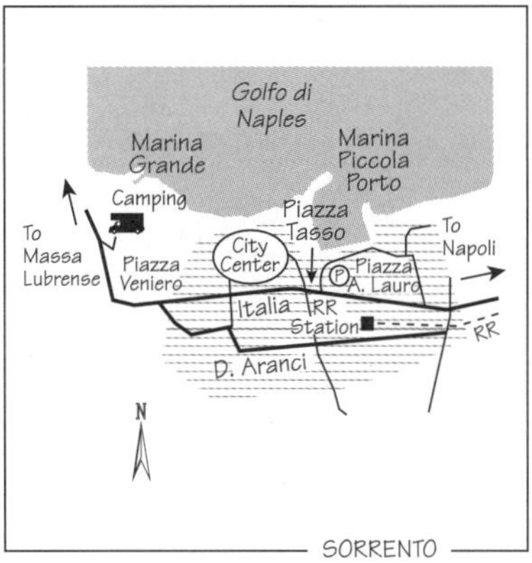

Camping Nube d'Argento spills down a terraced cliff above the small Marina Grande just west of Sorrento. Many of the camp's sites have a great view across the bay to Naples. Most sites are on packed dirt under olive trees, they are numbered but not separated except that groups of sites occupy different terraces. Electricity (CEE17 plugs, 4 amps) is available to many sites but long cords may be needed. The showers/toilets have doors opening to the outside and all sinks are in a covered outside area. Hot showers are free. The campground has a restaurant and grocery shop as well as a playground and swimming pool. Sorrento is only a kilometer or so to the east and has a small supermarkets, restaurants, and shops. There is bus service into town if you want it.

The drive from the A3 highway along the north shore of the Sorrento Peninsula on the SS145 takes a good 45 minutes, the distance from the Castellammare exit on the A3 to the campground entrance is 27 kilometers and the route runs through the crowded streets of several town. Larger rigs shouldn't have a problem, it just takes a while. The campground is right off the main road out of the west end of Sorrento. The entrance is on the right or ocean side but requires a very sharp turn, you'll probably have to go past it and turn around before entering. The entrance road is steep and has a sharp switchback, if you have a larger rig you might consider walking it before venturing down.

Naples Campground

✦ CAMPING SPARTACUS

Address: Via Plinio 117, I-80045
Pompei Scavi, Napoli
Telephone: 081 5369519
Price: Moderate

Open all year

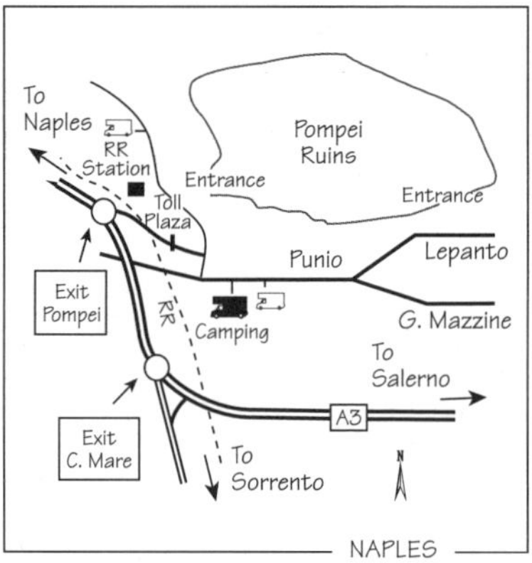

There are three good campgrounds clustered near the ruins at Pompeii. These are Camping Zeus, Camping Pompeii, and Camping Spartacus. Our favorites are Zeus and Spartacus with Spartacus having a slight edge because it is a family-run operation and is used less as a parking site than the others. Zeus is larger and therefore less crowded. All are within easy walking distance of the ruins and the Villa Misteri train station.

The campground is medium-sized with some 50 sites arranged off paved drives with parking on dirt. The sites are separated by hedges. There is lots of shade (orange trees) and electrical outlets are convenient to most sites (CEE17 plugs, 10 amps). This campground also has several rental cabins. The shower/toilet building is well maintained and has adjustable hot water showers with water from a boiler; shaving, dish-washing and clothes-washing sinks have cold water only. There are several coin-operated washing machines for clothes. The campground also has a pizzeria, a bar/restaurant, small grocery store, and a dump station. The reception kiosk is at the entrance so security is pretty good and there is a large supermarket about a kilometer away with a McDonalds about a kilometer in the other direction.

To reach the campground take the Pompeii exit from the A3 autostrada just south of Naples. You do not want the Scafati-Pompeii exit which is 2 exits south of the Pompeii exit, access is difficult from that exit. Watch closely for the Pompeii exit, it is a small one and easily missed, particularly when heading north. Once off the autostrada you pass a small toll booth. Turn right after the booth and then immediately left. Camping Spartacus will be on your right just after the turn.

Side Trips From Sorrento and Pompeii

The ruins at **Pompeii** and **Herculaneum** are easily accessible from Sorrento by taking the Circumvesuviana train line. The Pompeii stop (Pompeii - Villa Misteri) comes first, Herculaneum is a few stops farther along at the Ercolano station. Pompeii is the larger and more famous of the two buried cities, excavation is mostly complete and it is easy to spend the entire day here and feel like you'd like to come back tomorrow. Herculaneum is also a Roman town that was buried during the Vesuvius eruption of 79 AD at the same time as Pompeii, but it was buried deeper by mud and lava. It was discovered after Pompeii and is not as well known or as completely excavated, but the structures that have been excavated are better preserved.

Mt. Vesuvius is almost as convenient to visit as Herculaneum, in fact you can take the Circumvesuviana to the same stop. From there take a bus to the Seggovia station. Unfortunately these busses only run in the morning; approximately every 2 hours from 8 to 12 or so. From the Seggovia station it is a half-hour walk to the crater. Only make this trip when the weather is clear, otherwise you'll be in the clouds and see nothing. It is easy to keep an eye on whether the mountaintop is clear from Sorrento or Pompeii.

The **Island of Capri,** said to be the most beautiful island in the world, is only a boat ride away. From the Piccolo Marina in Sorrento the trip takes about 45 minutes. Many kilometers of paths along the cliffs, the **Blue Grotto**, and even a ancient **Roman villa** combine to make this a memorable day trip. There are also many excellent restaurants.

The **Amalfi Coast**, on the opposite side of the Sorrento Peninsula, is best visited by bus. You can catch one at the railroad station in Sorrento. It is advisable to take a bus because parking in the hillside towns of **Positano** and **Amalfi** is practically nonexistent. Besides, you'll enjoy watching a master at work as the driver negotiates the traffic and curves along the rocky cliffs. Once in Amalfi pick up a copy of *Walks From Amalfi* by Julian Tippett and explore the villages and olive groves above the town. That will get you away from the crowded town and up where you can appreciate what is probably the most spectacular coast you've ever seen. While Amalfi is now a small tourist town, it was an important trading city during the 10th and 11th centuries. Wealth provided by trade funded construction of the Lombard-Norman-style **Cathedral of Saint Andrew** in the 11th century.

PAESTUM, ITALY

Paestum is likely to surprise you. You'll be cruising through flat farm country south of Salerno when suddenly, out the side window of you car, you'll catch a glimpse of the Athenian Acropolis. Actually, it is not the acropolis, just three almost perfect **Greek temples**, sitting in the middle of nowhere in southern Italy. No, they're not copies, these are for real. Add to this the fact that there are a number of large campgrounds just a few kilometers away on a beautiful sandy beach and Paestum becomes a great destination. There's a museum across the street from the temples as well as an information office so you'll be able to look into how they happen to be here.

Paestum Campground

✦ CAMPING VILLAGGIO DEI PINI

Address: I-84063 Paestum
Telephone: 0828 811030Fax: 0828 811025
Price: Moderate

Open all year

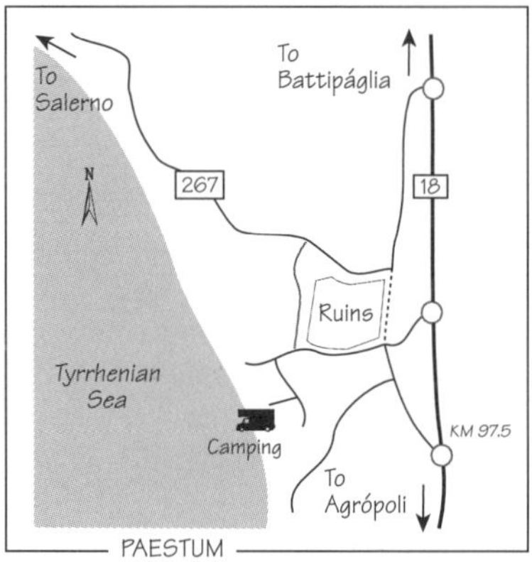

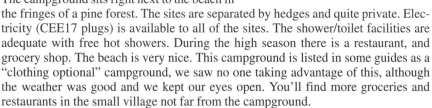

Camping dei Pini is one of a number of very similar large holiday campgrounds along this stretch of coast. It is unusual because it is open all year.

The campground sits right next to the beach in the fringes of a pine forest. The sites are separated by hedges and quite private. Electricity (CEE17 plugs) is available to all of the sites. The shower/toilet facilities are adequate with free hot showers. During the high season there is a restaurant, and grocery shop. The beach is very nice. This campground is listed in some guides as a "clothing optional" campground, we saw no one taking advantage of this, although the weather was good and we kept our eyes open. You'll find more groceries and restaurants in the small village not far from the campground.

The archeological site is about two kilometers inland from the campground. You can easily walk or bike the distance, parking is also available at the ruins.

GREEK TEMPLES IN PAESTUM

To reach the campground as you are headed south on SS18 take the Paestum exit just past the 97.5 kilometer point. Drive west and north to the stop light at 2 kilometers from the exit. The ruins are directly ahead, you want to turn left toward the coast. After another 1.2 kilometers you should turn left toward Torre de Paestum and the campground (there is a campground sign here). After another .4 kilometers a road leads right to the campground and beach.

PALERMO, SICILY, ITALY

Population 700,000

Located on the north coast of Sicily, Palermo makes a fascinating city to visit. While the city is obviously not very well off today, its streets and buildings reflect an unexpected history. The city has been Arab, Norman, and Spanish; at one time it was one of the richest and most elegant cities in Europe. Today you can inspect the churches and buildings from that period while enjoying the vibrant streets and markets.

The main streets of central Palermo are lined with impressive baroque palaces, legacy of her past. Behind them you will find a much less impressive warren of small streets and alleys. The dual Arab/Norman past is probably best reflected in the city's churches; you must see the extremely ornate interior of the **Cappella Palatina** which is located in the Palazzo dei Normanni and also **La Martorana** and **San Cataldo**, situated next to each other near the **Quattro Canti** or "four corners". Don't miss the **Vucciria**, an extensive street market that will probably remain your most vivid memory of Palermo.

Palermo Campground

✦ CAMPING DEGLI ULIVI

Address: Via Pegaso 25, I-90148 Sferracavallo
Telephone: 061 533021
Price: Inexpensive

Open all year

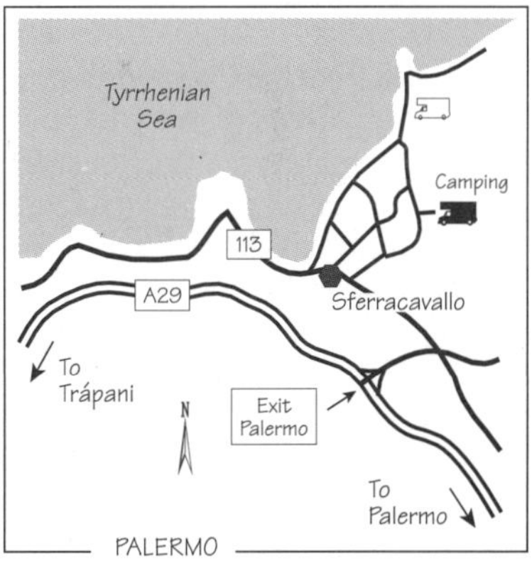

This is a very small, friendly campground, a haven after hectic Palermo. Since it is so small it may be full, if so try the much larger CAMPING INTERNATIONALE TRINACRIA just a few hundred meters away and across the road from the ocean. Both campgrounds are in the waterfront village of Sferracavallo, convenient to Palermo yet still a small town away from the sometimes intimidating streets of the city. You'll find both restaurants and grocery stores within strolling distance of the campgrounds.

Degli Ulivi is located off a back street, it has a single access driveway with campsites separated with small trees and shrubs on either side. Electricity is available but you'll probably need to borrow an adapter plug from the very helpful owner. The shower/toilet facilities are clean and well maintained, hot showers are free.

You can easily take a bus into Palermo from Sferracavallo. The bus stop is on the main road through town, Highway 113. Service is frequent.

Sferracavallo is located about 12 kilometers northwest of Palermo on the coast. From Highway 113 running right through the village you'll see camping signs pointing east, both campgrounds in this town are nearby and well signed. You can't get off the A29 freeway in Sferracavallo, the best exit is a few kilometers to the west.

ROME (ROMA), ITALY

Population 2,900,000

All roads really don't lead to Rome, but many Italian autostradas do lead to the GRA autostrada, Rome's ring road. Once established on the GRA you have a number of campgrounds to choose from, many actually have signs right on the autostrada. You can easily drive directly to any of the three Rome campgrounds that we describe below without really getting involved with heavy Rome city traffic.

After you've signed into the campground and set up your camp it is time to see Rome. One good first day strategy is to head for the Piazza del Popolo which is situated at the north end of central Rome. From Camping Tiber or Camping Flaminio you can catch the north suburban rail Metro line directly to the Piazza, from Camping Roma it is two busses and 45 minutes away.

Once at the **Piazza del Popolo** you have a choice. You can transfer to the metro line and go west toward (but not all the way to) the Vatican or you can head the opposite direction and get off at the Colosseum stop. Save those possibilities for later and just stroll south from the Piazza on Via del Corso. Many of the famous sights of Rome are located short distances to the left and right of this narrow city street. About 800 meters after leaving the Piazza you'll reach a cross street named Via Condotti. If you turn left here you'll be walking down a famous shopping street and soon reach the **Piazza di Spagna** and the **Spanish Steps**. Returning to Via del Corso and continuing south you'll see signs directing you left to the **Trevi Fountain**, right to the **Pantheon** (and on its far side the **Piazza Navona**), and finally reach the **Piazza Venezia**. Facing you across it is the **Vittorio Emanuele Monument** with the **Capitoline Hill** just behind it. To the left is the **Forum** and if you walk down Mussolini's Via dei Fori Imperiali for about a kilometer you'll arrive at the **Colosseum**. Join the crowds to take a look and then catch the subway back to the Piazza Popolo. You've just taken a four kilometer walk that passed right through the heart of Rome. You'll probably find yourself following variations of this path many times during your visit.

Rome is truly full of things to see. Besides the Roman excavations and landmarks you'll find dozens of churches (many with great masterpieces inside), hundreds of Renaissance and baroque architectural triumphs, and many piazzas full of fountains and tables where you can relax and enjoy the passing show.

The **Vatican City** is a venue which can easily occupy you for a day or days. You can walk there from the Piazza dei Popolo, or use the metro or bus system. Try attending a mass in **St. Peter's**, be blessed by the Pope in the **Piazza San Pietro**, lose yourself in the **Vatican Museums** and the **Sistine Chapel**.

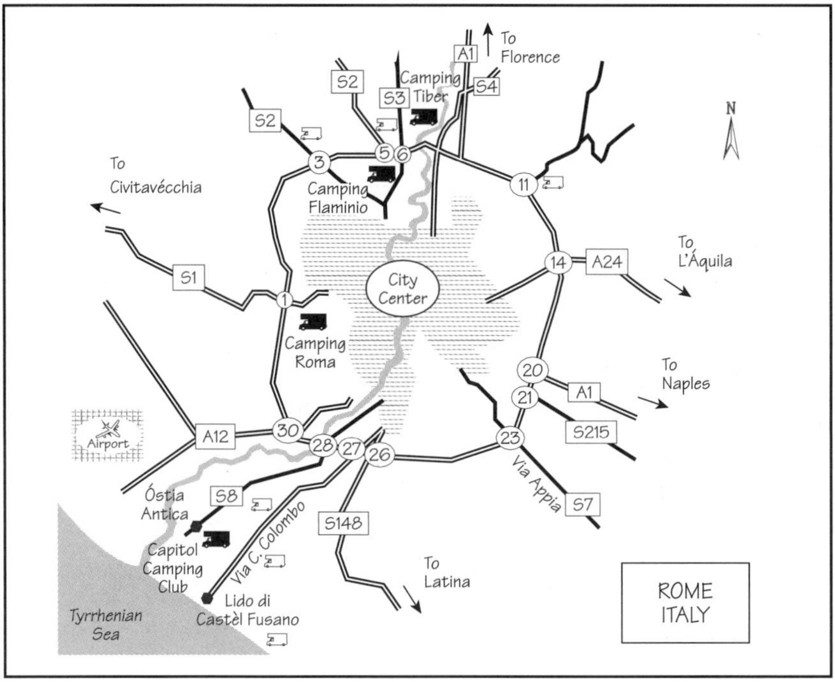

When you are temporarily overcome by monuments and museums sample the cafes and trattorias in the piazzas. Try the piazza in front of the Pantheon or the nearby Piazza Navona. After dark visit the Piazza di Spagna with its Spanish Steps or the Trevi Fountain. The **Trastevere district** on the far side of the Tiber is a good place to find reasonably priced restaurants and an active street scene.

If you tire of crowded Rome there are two good day trips in the region; Tivoli and Óstia Antica. See the side trip section which follows our description below of four Rome campgrounds for information about them.

Rome Campgrounds

✦ CAMPING TIBER

Address: Via Tiburnia Km. 1.4, I-00188 Roma
Telephone: 06 33612314 Fax: 06 33612314
Price: Moderate

Open March 1 to November 3

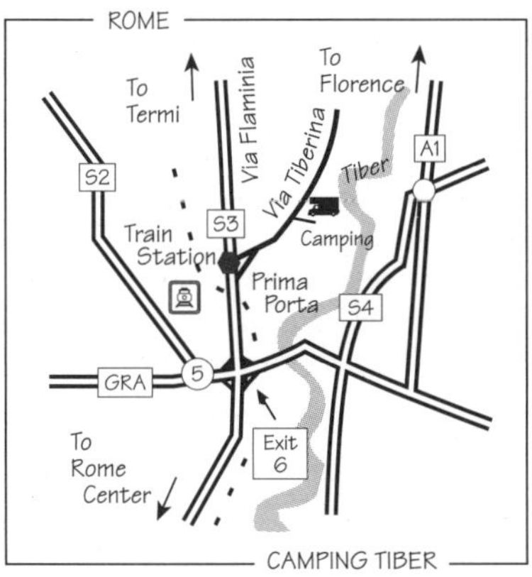

Camping Tiber is a good choice as your first campground when visiting Rome. Its location on the outside of the GRA near where you'll probably arrive on the A1 autostrada means you can quickly exchange your rig for public transportation while still well outside the city traffic.

The campground is a large grassy field next to the Tiber River. There are very few permanent rigs, this is a tourist campground. Camping sites are not marked or assigned. Electrical boxes (CEE17 plug, medium amps) are scattered but there are quite a few. The shower/toilet facilities are rustic, they are enclosed and covered but not inside a building. Hot water for showers (not adjustable) is free. The campground has a restaurant, bar, grocery shop, and swimming pool. There is a laundry room with coin-operated washer and room for hanging clothes to dry.

Access to Rome from this camping area is easy. The campground has its own minibus, which will deposit you at the Prima Porta subway station for a very small fee. Walking to the station is an easy twenty minutes, but why not ride, you'll walk plenty once you get in to town. The Metro in to the center of the city runs every ten minutes or so, tickets are available at the station. The train runs above ground until just before reaching central Rome so you can get some idea of what the countryside looks like. This line runs only as far as the Roma-Viterbo station. The station is located just north of the Piazza di Popolo, you can walk down the Via Del Corso from here or catch the A line of the subway. There are stalls at the station selling maps and guidebooks.

To find the campground take the first Exit 6 (heading west), the one going north, not far west of where the A1 highway from the north intersects the GRA. You will be on a four lane highway (Via Flaminia) for about a kilometer and then exit to the right. The campground is about 1 kilometer from the exit, follow the campground signs which actually start on the GRA itself.

✦ CAMPING FLAMINIO

Address: Via Flaminia 821, I-00191 Roma
Telephone: 06 3331429 Fax: 06 3330653
Price: Moderate

Open all year

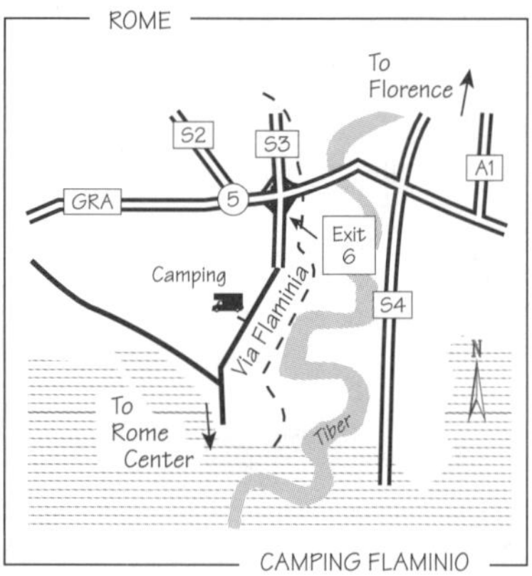

Camping Flaminio is an extremely large campground occupying a large south sloping wooded hillside and the flat area below it. Camping sites are unnumbered and unassigned. Many trees provide quite a bit of shade. There are very few permanent residents at this campground. Electrical outlets are provided for many of the sites. The shower/toilet building is older and not luxurious, hot showers (push-button, premixed) are free. Most of the toilets are continental. The campground has a restaurant, bar, and store together on a site on the hill, there is also a pool and playground. Laundry facilities with coin-operated machines are at the shower/toilet building.

If you are a runner, bike rider, or just want to stretch your legs, there is a great bike path just on the far side of the nearby Due Ponte station. It runs along the top of what must be a dike, and it appears to run quite a distance. A map posted on the trail showed that it runs along the right bank of the Tiber from GRA towards Rome, ending just short of the downtown area, with a planned extension across the river and into the Villa Borghese Gardens. If you have a bike this might make a nice way to get into town. Distances were not posted on the trail but I would assume that the total length must be in the neighborhood of 15 kilometers with Campground Flaminia near the midpoint. There were always quite a number of bikers and joggers on the trail, and the scenery included a golf driving range, sheep dogs working herds of sheep, small aircraft making approaches to a nearby airport, and soccer matches.

Access to downtown Rome from Campground Flaminio is similar to that from Campground Tiber. The same metro line runs just across the street from the campground, get instructions at the reception desk on how to walk to it because it is really quite difficult to find. Exercise caution crossing the highway. This station, Due Ponti, is very small and unattended. It is a request stop, heading out from Rome make sure to push the button to let the driver know that you want to stop at the Due Ponti station. Heading in to town the train will stop when the driver sees you waiting. Campground Flaminio has decent bus service, you can use it to get in to downtown Rome, it just will take longer than using the train. Bus tickets are available at the reception desk, you can't buy metro tickets at the campground but should be able to get day passes good on all public transportation.

To reach Campground Flaminio you take Exit 6 from the GRA on the north side of Rome, just as for Camping Tiber, but this time take the Exit 6 that leads south and head towards downtown Rome on the Via Flaminia Nuova. Immediately get in the left lane. Follow the campground signs, in three kilometers the road splits with the right fork appearing to go into a tunnel (actually an underpass), you take the left fork, still following Via Flaminia Nuova. It is easy to get stuck in the right lane, that's why you got into the left as soon as you were established on Via Flaminia Nuova. Immediately after this fork you will see the sign for the campground, it is located on the right side of the road.

✦ Roma Camping

Address: Via Aurélia 831, I-00165 Roma
Telephone: 06 6623018
Price: Moderate

Open all year

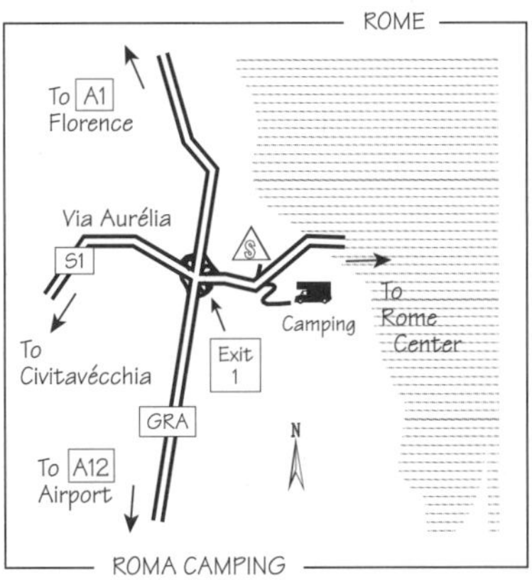

The advantage that Camping Roma has over Camping Tiber and Camping Flaminio is that it is really easier to find. You don't have to negotiate the maze of off-ramps and camping signs on the GRA (ring road) in the vicinity of Exit number 6. Camping Roma is also nice because it has a large supermarket just across the highway with a convenient pedestrian overpass.

This is a medium-size campground situated on a small hill above the Via Aurelia, which is really a four-lane freeway at this point. Traffic noise is a fact of life here, you get used to it. Sites are on grass off gravel and dirt circular access roads, they are unmarked and unassigned. Many trees provide shade. Electricity (6 amps, CEE17 plugs) is available but you'll need a long cord for some sites. The shower/toilet buildings are very basic, hot water showers are available for a price but there is no hot water in bathroom basins or for dishwashing. There are just a few stool-type toilets, most are continental. The campground has a small grocery shop and a snack bar. There's also a dump station.

Access to Rome from the campground is by bus. The Number 246 stops at the gate every 15 minutes and quickly drops you at the Largo Boccea where you switch to the 46, 49, or 490. These three busses will drop you just about anywhere in Rome that you could wish to visit. The time from the campground to Piazza del Popolo is about 45 minutes.

To reach the campground take Exit 1 from the GRA ring road to the west of Rome. Head towards the city on Via Aurelia for about 2 kilometers. When you see the big supermarket on the left take the off-ramp to the right, the campground entrance is on the right just after you exit the Via Aurélia. The entire route is well signed.

✦ CAPITOL CAMPING CLUB

Address: Casal Palocco, Via di Castelfusano 195, I-00124 Óstia Antica
Telephone: 06 5662720
Price: Moderate

Open all year

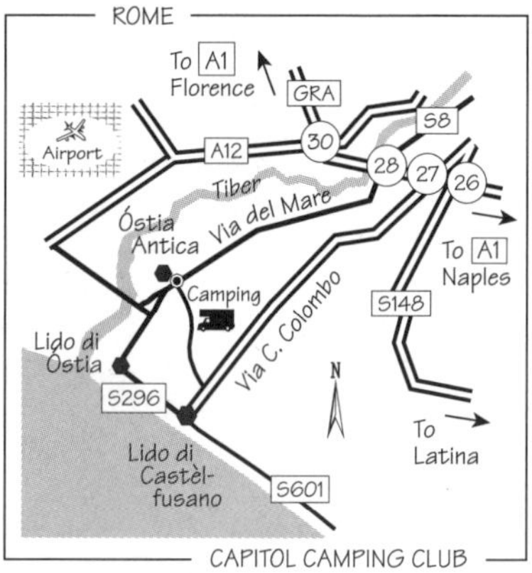

There is a group of campgrounds near Lido di Óstia and Lido di Castélfusano some 20 kilometers from Rome near the coast. For visitors to Rome their advantage is that they are near the Roman ruins of Óstia Antica. While they do have decent transportation in to Rome the campgrounds nearer the city are nicer and more convenient.

ITALY

Capital Camping Club is a good example of a type of Italian campground you often encounter near the ocean. It has room for about 1200 caravans, most of them remain permanently on site although they are not used much except during the short summer holiday season. While the campground has many amenities, most are not open except during those holidays. There is a grassy field near the entrance for tourist campers. Electricity is available (various plug types, medium amps) but not plentiful. The shower/toilet buildings are very basic, hot water is available for showers only. Amenities include a grocery shop, restaurant, large swimming pool, tennis courts, and playground.

This is a good base for exploring Óstia Antica. The ruins are 3.5 kilometers from the campground, it is a decent hike or bike ride although the road has no sidewalks. The number 5 bus stops near the campground and will take you most of the way to Óstia Antica or to the Óstia Lido area where you can catch frequent inexpensive trains in to Rome.

From Rome's GRA take the number 28 exit and head for the coast on Via del Mare. As you approach Óstia Antica watch the kilometer markers. Just after kilometer 23 you'll see a campground sign apparently pointing right, you really want to turn left here but traffic is directed around a very small convoluted interchange that is part traffic circle, part stop light. Once you've negotiated this turn and are established on Via di Castélfusano you'll find the campground on your left in about 2.5 kilometers.

Side Trips From Rome

Óstia Antica is an excavated Roman city which rivals Pompeii. It was the ancient seaport to Rome, gradually abandoned and covered by silt from the Tiber. It has now been excavated and covers a large area. Many people find it much like Pompeii and a lot easier to visit. See the description for Capitol Camping above for directions on how to get there.

Tivoli, about 30 kilometers from the GRA on the northeast side of Rome, has two well-known attractions. The first is the excavations of the emperor **Hadrian's Villa**. These can be rewarding and uncrowded, particularly if you are visiting on a week day outside the high season. Pick a good weather day. You will also find the **Villa d'Este** in Tivoli. It is famous for its gardens and hundreds of fountains. The Villa d'Este dates from a much later time than Hadrian's Villa, they were built by a Catholic cardinal in the sixteenth century. To reach Tivoli take the number 13 exit from the GRA and follow Via Tiburtina (SS5) northeast. Approaching Tivoli you will see signs for Villa Adriana (Hadrian's Villa).

San Marino, San Marino

Population 5,000

If you collect stamps it is hard to pass up a chance to visit San Marino. Every stamp collector is familiar with the beautiful stamps issued here. Another good reason to visit is that San Marino is not just another town, it is a country (of sorts). They'll even stamp your passport if you want.

The Republic of San Marino is just south of Ravenna near the Italian Adriatic coast. If you've been visiting Venice it is a 150 kilometer easy day's drive south along the coast to get here. Once you leave the vicinity of Venice you won't see much ocean, this is flat farming country until you reach San Marino.

San Marino is very small, 61 square kilometers, which we calculate to be a square about six miles on each side. The country really is almost square, and is centered around **Mt. Titano**. If you've seen pictures of this country they probably show the three castles that sit on a ridge at the top of the mountain. The old town of San Marino extends down the mountainside from these castles.

The entire economy of the country appears to be dominated by tourism, and most of it centers around visits to this town, which we must warn you, seems pretty modern for a medieval town. San Marino, however, does have a rich and varied history. It is the oldest state in Europe having been a sovereign territory for over 1,400 years. San Marino gave refuge to Giuseppe Garibaldi in 1849 and the U.S. president Lincoln accepted honorary citizenship here in 1861. The tiny country was invaded by both the Germans and Allies during World War II.

San Marino Campground

✦ CENTRO TOURISTICO

Address: Strada S Michele 50, I-47031 Cailungo, RSM
Telephone: 0549 903964 Fax: 0549 907120
Price: Moderate

Open all year

Centro Touristico is a large campground located some 4 kilometers down the mountain from San Marino. It sits on the side of the mountain with great views from most camping sites toward the east. While there are many campgrounds in the Ravenna/San Marino area few are open in the winter, this is the exception.

The individual sites are on terraces and are separated by hedges and plantings. Electricity is convenient to the sites (CEE17 plugs, 5 amps) The shower/toilet building used in the winter is modern and clean, hot water showers are free. There is a restaurant, a grocery shop, and a large swimming pool. The campground is open all year with limited facilities in the winter.

You don't want to try to walk or ride a bike up the hill to the town, traffic and lack of sidewalks or paths would make the effort foolhardy. Fortunately there is a bus stop just outside the campground entrance.

You can most easily find the campground from the Rímini area to the east. Just follow the San Marino signs and you'll soon start seeing the campground signs also.

Side Trips from San Marino

Ravenna is 75 kilometers north of San Marino along the Adriatic coast. Ravenna has wonderful mosaics in the **church of San Vitale**, the **tomb of Galla Placidia** and the **basilica of Saint' Apollinare Nuovo**. They date from the days when the Eastern Roman Empire, based in Istanbul, ruled the area.

SYRACUSE (SIRACUSA), SICILY, ITALY

Population 124,000

Anyone who has read much Greek history has already heard of Syracuse. This was the location for an important battle of the Pelopennesian War when the Athenian fleet was destroyed in the large bay just south of the city. There are still Greek ruins to see here, particularly the beautiful **Greek amphitheater** carved out of a limestone hillside and the nearby **quarry** that served as a concentration camp for the Athenian captives.

Other than the antiquities in the archeological zone most attractions are in the old town on the island of **Ortygia**. You should probably snag a parking spot near the short bridges onto the island and then wander around on foot, there's not a lot of room for parking or driving on the island. Sights include the **cathedral** which incorporates a Doric temple to Athena which originally stood on the site, the **Piazza del Duomo**, and **Arethusa Fountain**.

Syracuse Campground

✦ AGRITURIST RINAURA
Address: I-96100 Rinaura
Telephone: 0931 721224
Price: Moderate

Open all year

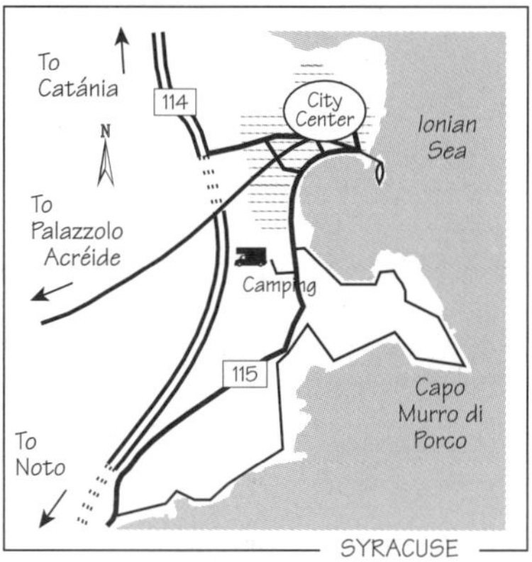

Agriturist Rinaura is a very small campground some four kilometers to the west of Syracuse. Camping is in a grass-covered field that badly needed mowing when we were there and facilities are limited to a few electrical outlets and a very small shower/toilet building. The one shower produced only a trickle of warm water. There is bus service to Syracuse available on the main road about a half kilometer from the campground, but you will probably have no problem finding parking in Syracuse.

To find the campground leave Syracuse on Highway 115, the road to Noto. After about 3 kilometers you'll see the camping sign pointing right. Follow the signs on the narrow country lanes for about a half kilometer, you may have to thread your way through a herd of sheep as we did, the campground is on the left.

VENICE (VENÉZIA), ITALY

Population 345,00

Venice really needs no introduction. Everyone knows the delights of the city of canals. What everyone doesn't know is that Venice is one of the best cities in Europe to visit as a camper. The city is surrounded by campgrounds, many with convenient boat transportation into town. We'll give you information about two of these, one on the mainland west of Venice and the other at Punta Sabbioni on the peninsula between Venice's lagoon and the ocean.

The real joy of Venice is the atmosphere. This is a town that has never known automobiles and for that reason it really is a city out of the past. While there are many things to see, the most enjoyable pastime is just wandering the streets. Keep a good map in hand but don't worry, getting lost is half the fun.

The most enduring image of Venice is probably the gondolas. You may not feel that a visit is complete until you have taken a ride in one. Be warned, they are very expensive! You do not have to worry about being stuck on shore, however. The busses of Venice are the vaporetti, covered boats that ply the canals. They're easy to use and convenient.

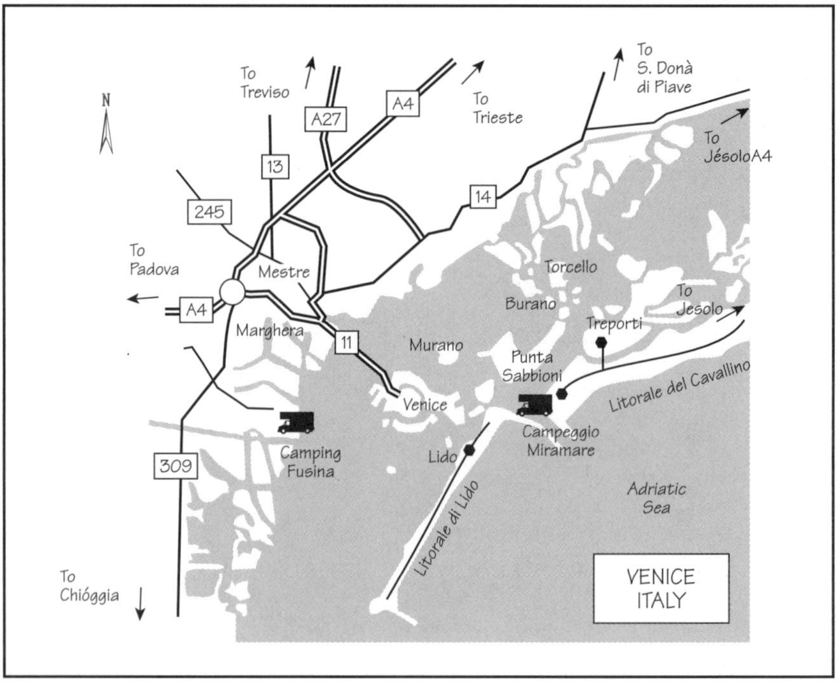

Venice Campgrounds

✦ CAMPING FUSINA

Address: Via Moranzani 79,
I-30030 Fusina, Venezia
Telephone: 041 5470055 Fax: 041 5470050
Price: Moderate

Open all year

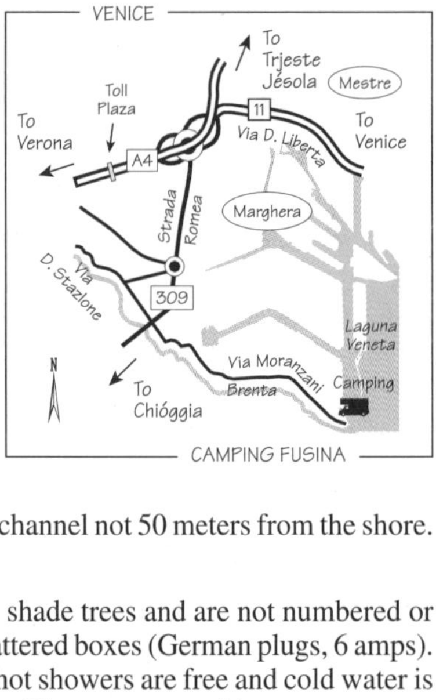

Fusina is a large campground located on the edge of the Venice lagoon near the industrial town of Marghera. There is a great view of Venice across the water and the only intrusion from the surroundings is the large ships passing directly in front of the campground in a ship channel not 50 meters from the shore. Free entertainment!

Camp sites are on a grass field with quite a few shade trees and are not numbered or assigned. Electricity is available from widely scattered boxes (German plugs, 6 amps). Toilet/shower facilities are rustic but adequate, hot showers are free and cold water is provided for bathroom basins and dishwashing. The campground has a restaurant, grocery shop, and also a dump station.

The campground runs a ferry service over to Venice in small boats. Runs are made every hour or so and the trip takes about a half hour. It is convenient.

The campground is well signed and easy to find from both the A4 autostrada and from Highway SS11. From the autostrada take the first off-ramp after the toll booth and take the first right on the traffic circle under the freeway. This should put you on SS309. At the next traffic circle take the third exit (actually by doing this you continue straight). You should see the first campground sign about here and will find them at every turn until you reach the campground. After the circle continue for .7 kilometer, turn left. In .6 kilometer turn right at a T. In 1 kilometer turn left and in another 4.5 kilometer you'll be at the campground.

✦ CAMPEGGIO MIRAMARE

Address: Lungomare D. Alighieri 29,
I-30010, Punta Sabbioni
Telephone: 041 966150   Fax: 041 5301150
Price: Moderate

Open March 21 to November 3 and for Carnevale (10 days before Ash Wednesday)

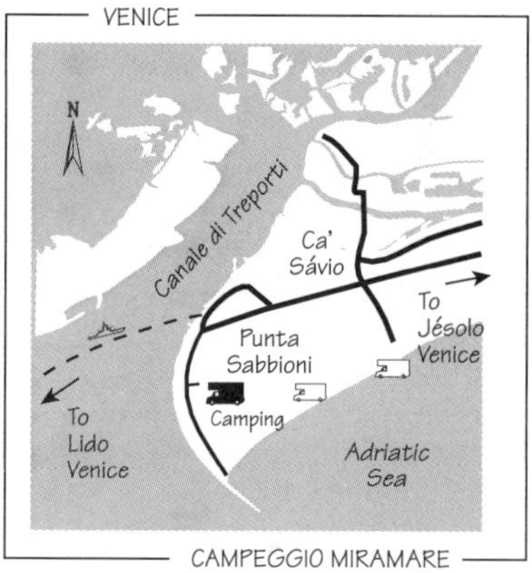

The Litorale del Cavallino, a long peninsula stretching from Jésolo to Punta Sabbioni, encloses a large part of Venice's lagoon. There are campgrounds standing shoulder to shoulder all along this beach for miles and miles. One of the smaller but most convenient of these is Camping Miramare with about 150 sites. Just to give you some idea, the Marina de Venezia just down the road has 3,000 sites.

Camping Miramare is a walled compound sitting across the street from the promenade at the end of the peninsula. Camping is on grass, sites are separated by shrubs and trees. There are no permanent units here. Electricity (various plug types including CEE17, 5 amps) is available to most sites. The shower/toilet buildings are the cleanest we've seen in Italy. Free hot water is provided for showers, bathroom basins, and dishwashing. There's a shop, laundry machines, a playground, and a dump station. A restaurant is located next door and a supermarket is next to the ferry dock a half kilometer stroll down the promenade.

Transport to Venice is extremely convenient. The ferry dock is a half kilometer from the campground, boats run every half hour during daylight hours and every hour or so at night. The trip takes about forty minutes including a stop at the Lido. The dock in Venice is just east of St Mark's square near the Bridge of Sighs. Take the Punta Sabbioni boat when leaving Venice for the campground.

Drive to the campground by heading around the east side of the lagoon and then follow signs to Punta Sabbioni. Go all the way to the end of the peninsula where you'll find the ferry and bus terminal. Turn left along the water, you'll see the Miramare entrance in under a kilometer.

Side Trips from Venice

The countryside inland from Venice was used by her wealthier families for country villas. During the 16th century many were designed by Andrea Palladio in a style called Palladian. In the U.S. both Monticello and Mount Vernon have elements of this style. **Vicenza** is the best place to see his work.

Padua (Padova), 25 kilometers west of Venice on the A4, makes an excellent day trip. One of Italy's oldest university towns, Padua's patron saint is St. Anthony. Since he's also the saint of lost things many pilgrims who have lost something of importance visit the city's **Basilica del Santo** for help. In addition to being a charming place to wander the streets Padua has the **Scrovegni Chapel** with frescoes by Giotto, it is one of Italy's top artistic attractions.

VERONA, ITALY

Population 260,000

When you come down out of the Brenner Pass from Germany and Austria you are faced with a tough decision at Verona. Should you go east to Venice, west to Milan and the Lake District, or hurry south to investigate Florence? Verona is a good place to stop and think about your decision. Meanwhile take a look around.

Verona, of course, is famous as the setting of Shakespeare's Romeo and Juliet. Some of the sights to see are from that period. **Juliet's home** is a tourist magnet, there is a statue of Juliet and you can take a picture of her balcony. We also found the 14th-century **Scaligeri Castle** and the **fortified bridge** over the Adige River to be interesting. The castle was the home of the Scaligeri family, the rulers of the town during the period in which Shakespeare set the play.

Verona was also an important Roman town. There is a huge **Roman amphitheater** now used for opera performances, and Roman ruins have been excavated in the old town near the **Piazza delle Erbe**. Tourist action centers around this piazza, near Juliet's home, which has cafes with outside seating and vendors stalls set up in the middle of the square. The streets around the square form a pedestrian area with shops and restaurants.

Verona Campground

✦ CAMPING ROMEO E GIULIETTA

Address: Via Bresciana 54, I-37139 Verona
Phone: 045 8510243
Price: Moderate

Open March 1 to November 30

This is a large campground totally devoted to tourist campers. Campsites are on grass and are divided by hedges. Electricity (CEE17 plugs, 6 amps) is convenient to the sites. The shower/

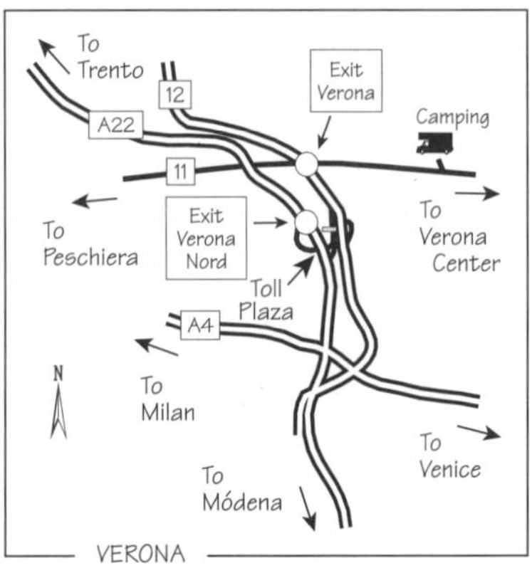

toilet building is modern and clean, hot water is provided for showers (push-button valves), bathroom basins, dish and clothes washing sinks. The campground also has a swimming pool, a very small grocery shop, and a dump station. On the road toward town you'll find two large supermarkets with lots of parking.

There is a bus stop just outside the campground with service to town. Busses run approximately every hour, you want the number 51. The distance to town is 5 kms.

The campground is most easily reached from the Verona Nord exit of the autostrada coming south from the Brenner Pass. Upon exiting the toll plaza continue straight ahead so that you are driving north along the side road (SS12) next to the freeway. Take the first right onto SS11 (signed Borgo and Milano) toward Verona. The campground will be on your left in 1.7 kilometers near kilometer 295. From Verona take SS11 toward Peschiera. The campground is near kilometer 295 on the right.

VENICE'S ST. MARKS SQUARE

TWO OUTSTANDING REGIONS AND THEIR CAMPGROUNDS

THE ITALIAN LAKE DISTRICT

The Lake District straddles the Italian/Swiss border, some of the towns we'll talk about in this section are actually Swiss. The dual nationality of the area is one of its charms, you'll find the differences between the two sides of the border to be quite educational. This is such a popular area that you must be careful about when you visit. Avoid July and August at all costs, the crowds are just too large. September and early October are great, you'll have no problems getting into campgrounds and the weather will probably be good.

The major lakes in the district are, from west to east, Lago Maggiore, Lago di Lugano (really mostly Swiss), Lago di Cómo, and Lago de Garda. They cover a large area, the east/west distance is 275 kilometers or so, but this is as the crow flies. The small crooked lakeside roads, mountains, and long tunnels make distances much longer. Each of these lakes has its own personality and attractions. Each has its head in the foothills of the Alps and its foot on the plains. The climate here is unusually mild, you will find semitropical vegetation right at the foot of the Alps. There are lots of campgrounds in the Lake District, the ones described below are just a small sampling.

ITALY

The westernmost lake, Lake Maggiore, is about 75 kilometers long. It is part Swiss and part Italian. The western shore, starting at the town of **Stresa**, has most of the tourist attractions. Stresa, about half way down the west side of the lake, is an old resort town and has the **Villa Pallavicino**, a huge garden and zoo with some freely-roaming animals and great views. Stresa is also the place to catch a boat to the **Borromean Islands**, owned by the same family since the 12th century. Each of the three islands offers something: a palace, a garden, or a scenic fishing village. If you wish to camp near Stresa try one of the lakeside campgrounds north of town near Baveno, both the LIDO and the PARISI are open from the first of April to the end of September. Traveling up the west shore of the lake you'll pass through small resort towns until you reach Cannóbio, the site of one of our favorite campgrounds.

CANNÓBIO, ITALY (LAKE MAGGIORE)

Cannóbio is located on the northwest shore of Lake Maggiore just south of the Swiss border. It is a small town with a typically Italian lakeside promenade and small town ambiance, especially if you arrive outside the high season. There are a number of campgrounds just north of town, the campground described here is one of the best.

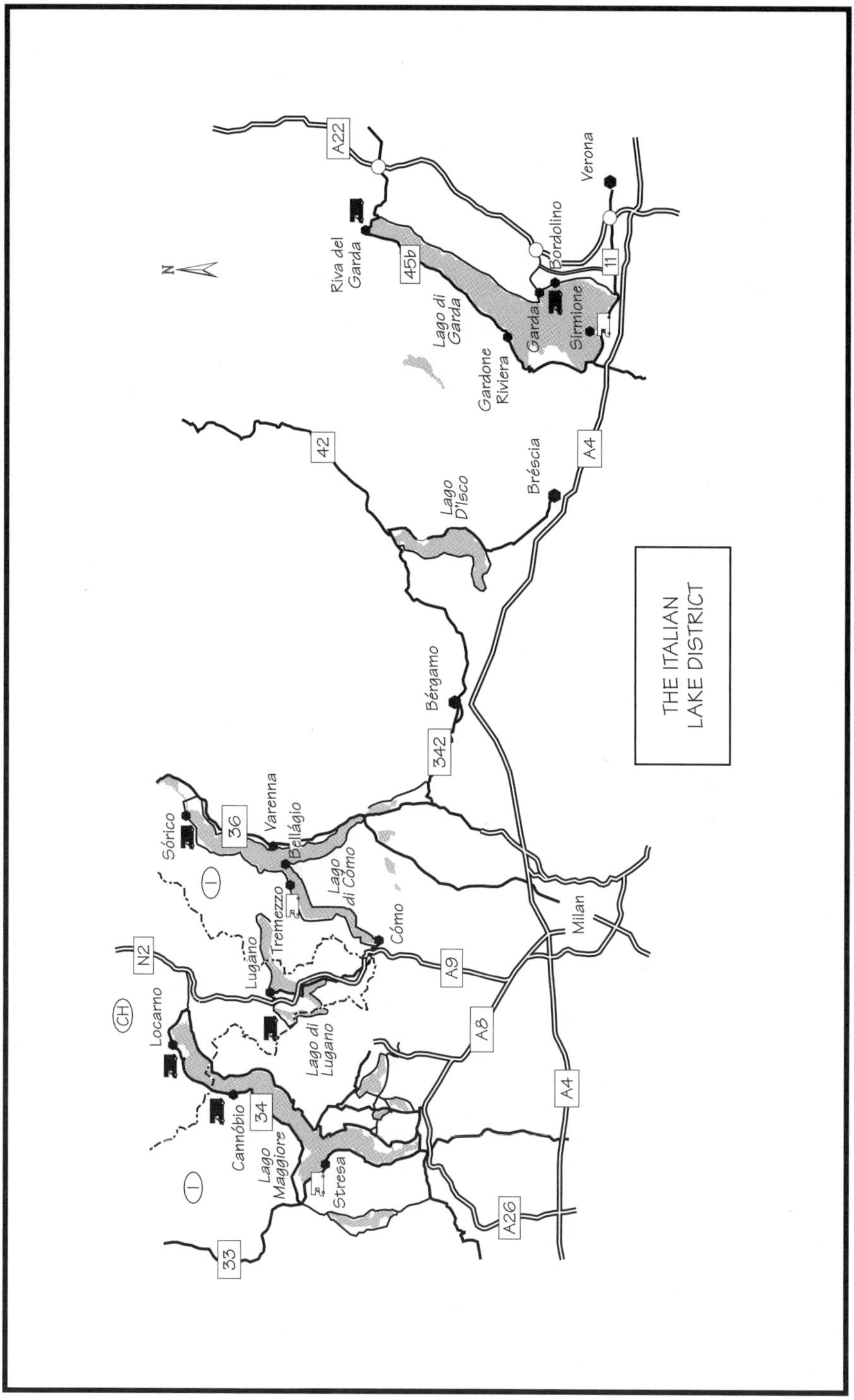
THE ITALIAN LAKE DISTRICT
N
A22
Riva del Garda
45b
Lago di Garda
Gardone Riviera
Garda
Bordolino
Sirmione
Verona
11
A4
Bréscia
Lago D'Isco
42
Bérgamo
342
Sórico
Varenna
36
Bellágio
Lago di Cómo
Tremezzo
Cómo
Milan
A9
A8
A4
A26
N2
CH
Locarno
Lugano
Lago di Lugano
Cannóbio
34
Lago Maggiore
Stresa
I
I
33

Cannóbio Campground

✦ CAMPING RIVIERA

Address: Via Casali Darbedo, I-28052 Cannóbio
Telephone: 0323 71360
Price: Moderate

Open April 1 to October 15 (varies slightly)

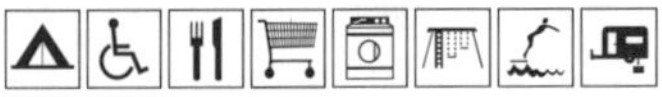

Camping Riviera is a large lakeside campground with sites set in a bewildering array of different kinds of trees and shrubs. All of the camping sites are separated from each other by plants. The surface is mostly dirt although the owner is industriously trying to grow grass, we think he needs fewer customers if he is going to be successful. Electricity (CEE17 plugs and German, 4 amps) is available in widely-spaced boxes. The shower/toilet buildings are not fully enclosed because the region has quite mild weather but are modern and clean. Free hot water is provided for showers (adjustable), bathroom basins, and for dishwashing. A grocery shop, restaurant/bar, pizzeria, large beach area, playground, and dump station round out the facilities. Cannóbio itself, about 1 kilometer from the campground, has supermarkets, restaurants, and shops.

The entrance road to the campground is on the right (lake) side as you drive north out of Cannóbio. It is immediately north of the bridge over the river so watch closely so you don't have to find a place to turn around.

A little farther north is the Swiss border and soon after that the town of Locarno, home to another of our campgrounds.

LOCARNO, SWITZERLAND (LAKE MAGGIORE)

Population 14,500

Locarno is a Swiss town at the north end of Lake Maggiore. After walking along the lake from the campground you'll find that the center of town is the **Piazza Grande**. You can walk or take a funicular up the mountain behind town to the sanctuary for a great view of the lake. From there you can ride a cable car and then a chair lift up to **Cimetta** which is a ski and hiking area.

Locarno Campground

✦ **CAMPING DELTA, LOCARNO (LAKE MAGGIORE)**

Address: vi G. Respini 7, CH-6600 Locarno
Telephone: 091 7516081 Fax: 091 7512243
Price: Expensive

Open April 1 to October 20 (varies slightly)

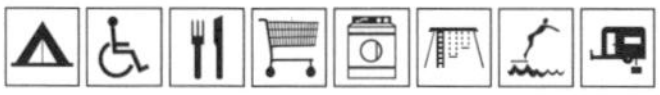

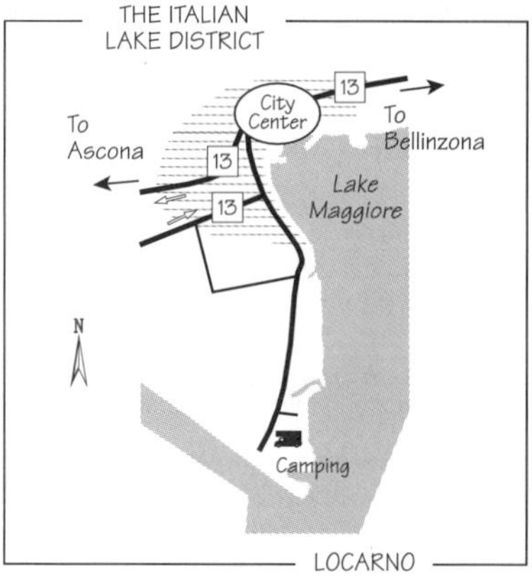

When you visit Locarno you'll want a convenient campground, and you can't get much more convenient than Camping Delta, located on the waterfront about 1 kilometer from the center of town. The only drawback is the price.

Camping Delta is a large facility with no static caravans. Individual sites are on grass, they are numbered but not separated in any manner. Buildings, fences, and an inlet from the lake with a boat-mooring dock make the layout attractive. The beach is fenced from the campground and there is an access gate. Electrical boxes are available throughout the campground. The shower/toilet building is large and clean with hot water for showers (adjustable) requiring payment but hot water for bathroom basins and washing dishes is free. There is a restaurant/bar, a grocery shop, cooking and laundry facilities, and a dump station.

You can easily find Camping Delta by driving to the waterfront and then following it south. The campground is just past the Lido. There are plenty of signs.

Side Trips From Locarno

Just west of Locarno and almost a suburb is the small village of **Ascona**. This is a world-renowned artist colony with an active waterfront.

An short day trip from Locarno is the valley city of **Bellinzona**, only 20 kilometers to the east. This fortified city historically guarded the St. Gotthard Pass route into Italy and has three impressive castles

---

From Locarno it is not far to the second of the lakes, Lago di Lugano, which is much more Swiss than Italian. Lago di Lugano is a smaller lake with few attractions beyond the town of Lugano itself.

LUGANO, SWITZERLAND (LAKE LUGANO)

Population 30,000

Much larger than that other lakeside Swiss town on the south side of the Alps, Locarno, Lugano is also a tourist town, but with much more to do. On the east end of the lakeshore promenade is the **Parco Civico** (Town Park) with a casino, gardens and a small zoo. West along the lake front are the **Piazza Rezzonico** and **Piazza della**

Riforma, behind them is the old town and the shopping streets. On along the bay is another park, the **Giardino Belvedere**.

Lugano is home to the **Thyssen Art Collection at La Villa Favorita**. The collection has been split and much has gone to Spain but Lugano still has an impressive collection of 19th- and 20th-century paintings by both American and European artists.

Lugano has several good hiking areas. **Monte San Salvatore** on one end of town and **Monte Brè** on the other can both be reached by lifts and offer good routes.

Lugano Campground

✦ TCS CAMPING LA PIODELLA

Address: CH-6933 Muzzanno
Telephone: 091 9947788 Fax: 091 9946708
Price: Expensive

Open all year except first half of March and all of November

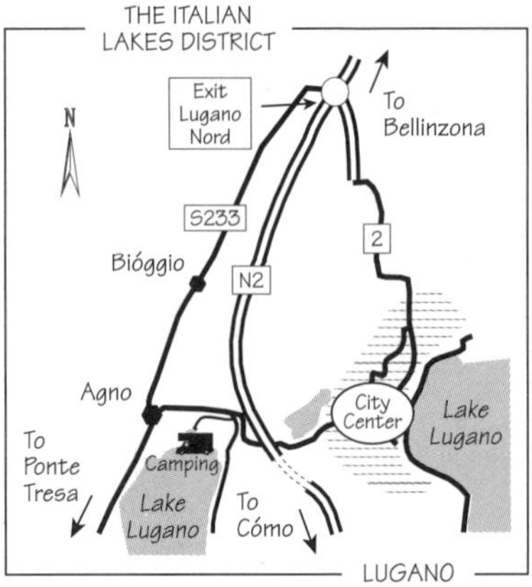

This large well-equipped campground is a good one for using as a base to visit Lugano. It is located about 6 kilometers from the city in an area where there are several other campgrounds, this is the nicest of them.

The campground is a large flat parcel of land on the lake shore. There are large trees on the older section next to the lake, farther back the trees need some time to grow before they will produce much shade. The campsites are numbered and assigned but there is no shrubbery to separate them from each other. The surfaces are grass and dirt, electrical boxes (Swiss, varying amps from 4 to 10) are widely spaced. There are two shower/toilet buildings, both nice. Showers (adjustable), bathroom basins, and dishwashing facilities have free hot water. The campground has lots of amenities: grocery shop, restaurant/bar, beach, swimming pool, tennis courts, playground, laundry facilities, TV room, cooking facilities, and a dump station. There is a large supermarket about .5 kilometer from the campground.

It is easy to travel into Lugano. There is a railway station about 1 kilometer from the campground for a small local train into town.

Camping Piodella and most other campgrounds near the city of Lugano are located on the lake shore west of town. There is a low hill between Lugano and the Agno area where the campgrounds and city airport are located. From Lugano take the Ponte Tresa road west to Agno and then turn left at the TCS Camping sign to the campground. It sits just south of the airport, across a river from several other campgrounds. When you pass the south end of the airport you've gone too far. Alternately, from the N2 freeway take the Lugano Nord exit, then drive west for .4 kilometer. Turn left towards Ponte Tresa and head south following the Ponte Tresa signs for 4 kilometers to the intersection in Agno where you turn left toward Lugano, you'll soon see the airport runway on your left and just beyond it the TCS campground sign on the right.

Lake Cómo has the distinction of being Europe's deepest lake, over 1,300 feet deep. The most beautiful portion of the lake is the middle where the towns of **Tremezzo**, **Bellágio**, and **Varenna** all have villas with beautiful gardens. DEGLI ULIVI is a campground just 1 kilometer south of Tremezzo near the west shore of the lake, it is open from the first of April to the end of October. Ferries plying this lake let you see some beautiful estates not visible from the shore roads, particularly in the southwest arm of the lake near Cómo. The northern end of the lake is by far the quietest area. There, in the town of Sórico, is another campground.

SÓRICO, ITALY (LAKE CÓMO)

Sórico is the first town you come to when you approach the north end of Lake Cómo from the east. The countryside is relatively flat here when compared with the north end of most of the other lakes. There is a string of campgrounds and small towns along the north shore making it a popular camping destination.

Sórico Campground

✦ CAMPING VILLAGGIO "AU LAC DE CÓMO" (LAKE CÓMO)

Address: Via Cesare Battisti 18, I-22010 Sórico
Telephone: 0344 84035 Fax: 0344 84802
Price: Moderate

Open all year

On the grounds of the Camping Hotel au Lac de Cómo you'll find a hotel, many small rental cottages, and quite a few permanent caravans. A large grass field next to the lake shore, however, is reserved for tourist campers.

If you consider only the tourist sites this is a medium-size campground. Sites are on the flat grass field, they are not separated. Electrical outlets are in a few scattered boxes (CEE17 plugs, 3 amps). The shower/toilet facilities are varied. Near the shore at one end of the tourist-camping field are some older quite rustic toilets and showers. The hotel building also has a few toilets. Finally, in the rental cottage area there is a heated shower/toilet building with showers (premixed) and basins both requiring tokens to get hot water. Dishwashing sinks also require tokens. There is a restaurant in the hotel and a grocery shop on the main road in front of the campground with access through the campground's back gate. Other amenities include a playground, a beach, and a dump station. The campground rents bicycles, canoes, and kayaks and there is a sports field and tennis courts next door.

The campground is located on the north shore of Lake Cómo just off SS38. You'll find that approaching from the east it is one of the first campgrounds on the lake that you come to, you'll find many others as you drive west.

The lake farthest to the east is Lago de Garda. It is the largest of the lakes and seems to have been popular the longest, you'll find some traces of the Romans as you tour the lake. Good bases for your visit are the town of Riva del Garda at the north end of the lake and the southeast shore near Garda and Bardolino. If you drive around the lake take a look at the **Vittoriale** in Gardone Riviera. This was the home of Gabriele d'Annunzio. Even if you've never heard of this modern Italian poet who was a friend of Mussolini you'll find this a worthwhile stop. At the south end of the lake be sure to stop and tour **Sirmione**, a small rocky peninsula which as been a tourist center and bathing spot since the time of the Romans. There's a large campground about 3 kilometers south on the lake which is called CAMPING SAN FRANCISCO, it is open from the first of April to the end of September.

RIVA DEL GARDA, ITALY (LAKE GARDA)

Riva del Garda is a charming town at the north end of Lake Garda. It is a relatively old town, the **Torre Apponale** dates from the twelfth century. The center of the action in town is the **Piazza 3 Novembre** which is on the lakefront. There are also yacht harbors and a nice lakeside park with a walking promenade. Riva del Garda is a windsurfing center due to its consistently good winds.

Riva del Garda Campground

✦ CAMPING BAVARIA (LAKE GARDA)

Address: 101 Viale Rovereto, I-38066 Riva del Garda
Telephone: 0464 552524 Fax: 0464 553636
Price: Moderate

Open April 1 to October 30

You'll find many campgrounds in the area around this town. Several, including this one, are on the waterfront.

Camping Bavaria is a medium-sized campground on the eastern outskirts of the town of Riva del Garda. The city's lake-side park is just in front of the campground with a nice gravel beach and walking paths. This is a tourist campground with no permanent trailers but during the summer some people make long stays. Campsites are dirt and grass between three parallel paved driveways running from the restaurant in front to the park-side fence near the lake. The sites are not separated or numbered. Electrical boxes provide enough outlets (CEE17 plug, 3 amp) for about half the sites, they are conveniently located. The shower/toilet building is in the middle of the campground, free hot water is provided for showers, bathroom basins and dishwashing. There is a restaurant at the front of the campground and a popular wind-surfing school at the back. Access to the beach is through a gate next to the school. Groceries, shops and restaurants are plentiful in town which is within 1 kilometer.

You can find the campground by driving east along the waterfront from town. Watch carefully, you don't want to pass it and have to turn around, the campground is on the right. If you reach the tunnel you've gone too far.

Garda and Bardolino, Italy (Lake Garda)

The southwest Lake Garda shoreline from Garda in the north to Lazise in the south is prime holiday camping country. In the early fall (September) the crowds have thinned and it is a good spot to relax and enjoy the Italian atmosphere. Garda, the largest town is also the oldest. Bardolino has a well-known wine named after it. Lazise is surrounded by mediaeval walls. A lakeside walk, some 15 kilometers in length, connects the towns. The area offers swimming in the lake, steamers and hydrofoils for lake tours, good restaurants and shops in the towns, and at least 8 very large campgrounds.

Bardolino Campground

✦ **La Rocca Camp**

Address: Loc. San Pietro, I-37011 Bardolino
Telephone: 045 7211111 Fax: 045 7211300
Price: Moderate

Open May 1 to September 30

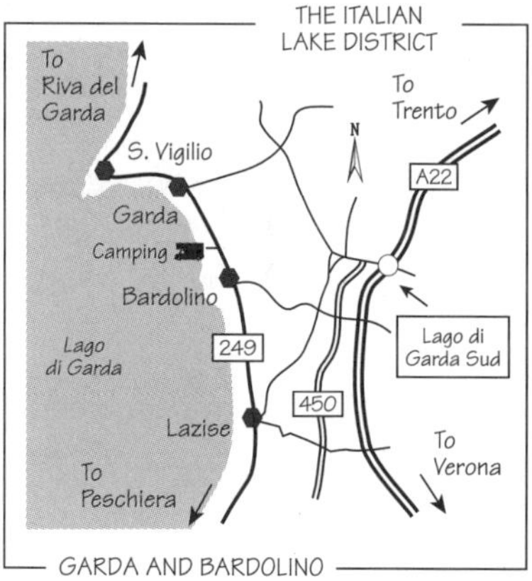

La Rocca is a huge campground located on the shore about 2 kilometers south of Garda and a kilometer north of Bardolino. It is the northern-most of the campgrounds in this immediate section of shoreline but there are many more north from Garda to Riva del Garda at the north end of the lake.

Campsites are located both above and below the highway on gentle terraces. Sites are set under olive trees and have conveniently located electrical outlets (CEE17 plugs). Bathrooms are fairly new with many continental-style toilets but a few stools. The showers are hot and adjustable, knobs not buttons. Shaving sinks are outside but under cover, they have hot water as do dish-washing and laundry sinks. Washing machines are available and there is a restaurant, pizzeria, a grocery store, fishing, and swimming in a large pool and in the lake.

You'll easily find the campground along the main road between Garda and Bardolino. The entrance and reception office are on the lake side. Try to get a camp site away from the road for a more peaceful night.

TUSCANY REGION, ITALY

To many people Tuscany is Italy at its best. The region really does have a great deal to offer: the art and architecture of Florence and the Renaissance; the rolling hills of Chianti with their vineyards and famous wine; hilltop towns and villages, each with its central plaza and churches filled with art treasures; and the purest form of the Italian language accompanied by some of Italy's best food, wine, and atmosphere.

Tuscany is located midway between Milan and Rome. It is home to several of the

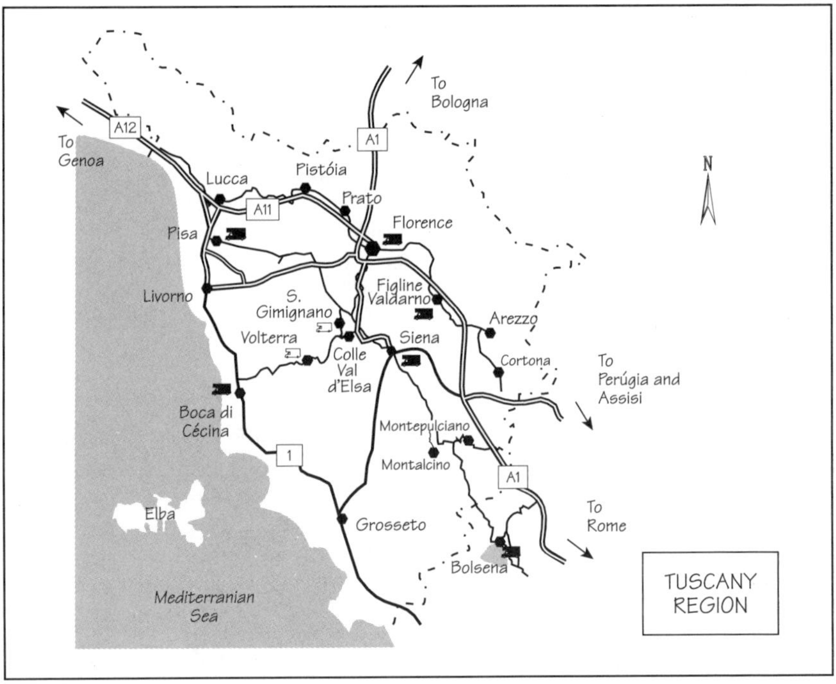

best-known towns in Italy. Florence and Pisa share the Arno River Valley in the northern part of the region while Siena is about 70 kilometers south via S2, or even better the winding S222. Between Florence and Siena you'll pass through the Chianti hills. In all directions from Siena are other hill towns to explore. Finally, there is the coastal region and the Island of Elba. We've described a campground on the coast in this area too.

FLORENCE (FIRENZE), ITALY

Population 455,000

If you go to Italy, you must go to Florence. The city is synonymous with the Renaissance, definitely one of the top destinations in Italy, some would say the most important stop in the country. The whole old town is a virtual museum.

Florence is a pleasure to visit. Besides the well know sights the town has a good English-language book store and also an English-language movie house. Restaurants around the central walking streets are expensive, but even a few blocks away there are nice places with reasonable prices.

During the Renaissance the Medici family was such an active patron of the arts that the city became the ultimate center of artistic endeavors. On the must-see list is the **Uffizi Gallery** which contains one of the world's great collections of Italian Renaissance Paintings. Nearby in the **Academy Gallery** the city's signature sculpture,

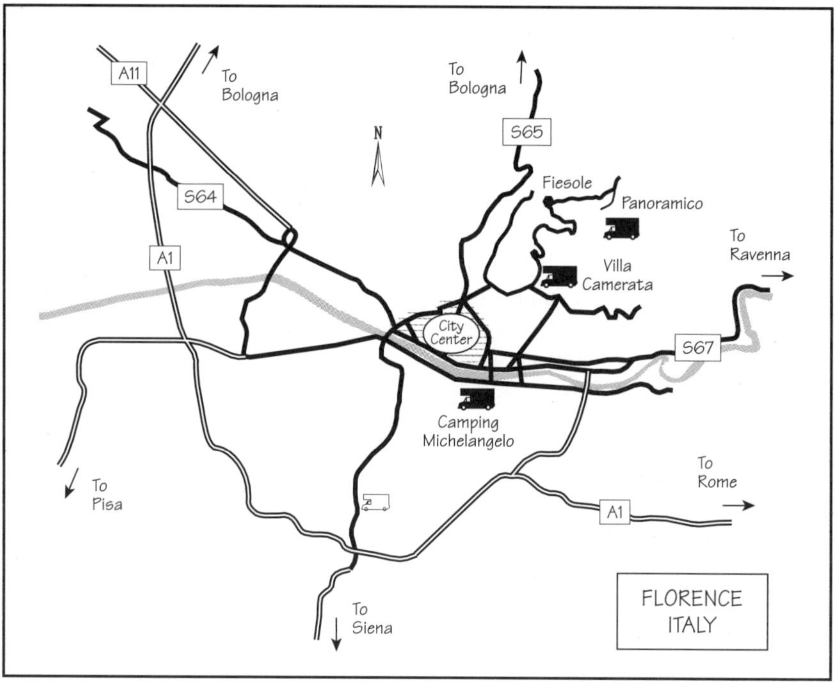

Michelangelo's towering **David,** attracts legions of admirers. Florence also has a great Romanesque Cathedral, known as the **Duomo**. It is the fourth largest in the world, and is known for its large dome, prototype for most of the others you'll see throughout Europe. The dome has unfortunately started cracking, and is being repaired. Don't let this stop you from climbing to the top and trying to spot your rig up in the campground. In front of the Duomo is the **baptistery** with its renown bronze doors. You can cross the mediaeval **Ponte Vecchio** to reach the **Pitti Palace** with its museum and the **Boboli Gardens**.

Florence Campgrounds

✦ CAMPEGGIO MICHELANGELO

Address: Viale Michelangelo 80,
I-50125 Firenze
Telephone: 055 681197 Fax: 055 689348
Cost: Moderate

Open December 15 to November 5

Camping Michelangelo is one of the best known and loved campgrounds in Europe. Don't even think of coming to Florence and staying anywhere else unless it is either full or

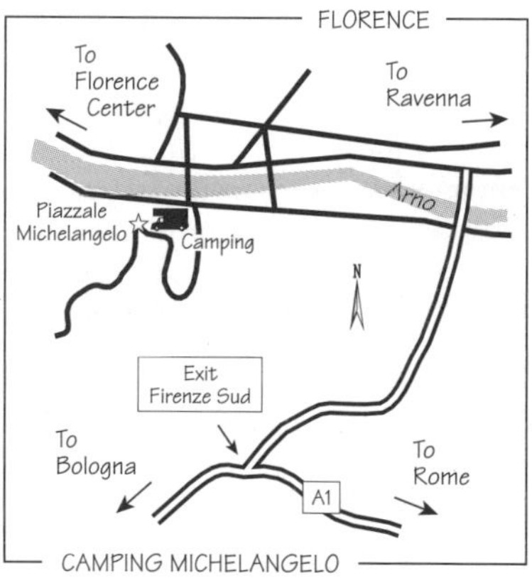

closed. The campground sits just below the Piazzale Michelangelo, a parking plaza south of the Arno river overlooking the old section of Florence. The Piazzale is reputed to have one of the best views in Europe, and the campground has almost the same view. It is within two kilometers of the centrally-located Ponte Vecchio so most of the things you will want to see are within easy walking distance.

Camping sites are unmarked and unassigned. They are on grass and under olive trees on terraces scattered down the hill from the entrance. Sometimes it is difficult to find a good flat parking spot, especially when the site is crowded. The largest flat sites are near the bottom. Electrical outlets (CEE17 plugs, 4 amps) are widely scattered. The shower/toilet building is older but clean. Hot showers are free. Most of the toilets are continental type but there are a few stools. The campground has a grocery shop and a snack bar. Arrive early in the day.

It is easy to walk into town from the campground but not necessary. There is frequent bus service from a stop just outside the entrance.

The easiest way to find Camping Michelangelo is to follow signs for Piazzale Michelangelo and then just look another 200 meters down the road for the campground. It is actually well signed. Just bear in mind that it is on the hill just south of the river.

✦ CAMPEGGIO VILLA CAMERATA

Address: Viale Augusto Righi 2/4,
I-50137 Firenze
Telephone: 055 600315 Fax: 055 601451
Price: Moderate

Open all year

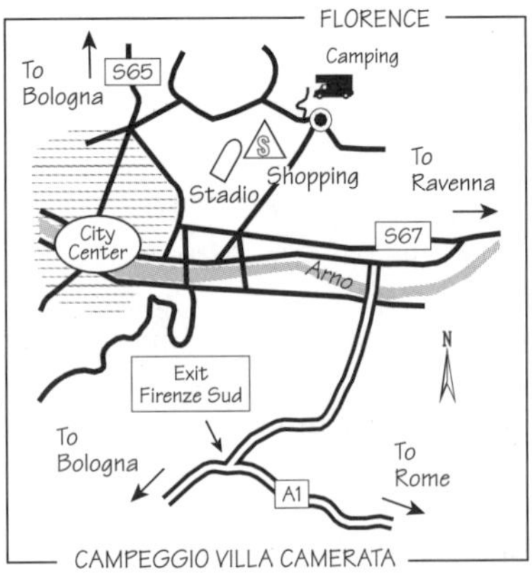

A good alternative to Camping Michelangelo is Camping Villa Camerata. The view is not as good but it is almost as convenient with good bus service (number 17B to/from the railway station) or a 45-minute walk in to town.

This medium-sized campground is located on the grounds of a large hostel. It is a tourist campground with no permanent residents. There are three different camping areas: a tent-only area, a tent/RV area with sites on grass that is often closed when the campground is not full, and a gravel and grass parking area for RVs. Sites are marked but not assigned, electrical outlets (CEE17 plugs, 6 amps) are widely spaced. The shower/toilet buildings are old and it is sometimes possible to use the nicer ones inside the hostel building. The showers (premixed, push-button valves) are hot, water to basins is cold, and the toilets are not continental. There is a good supermarket about a kilometer from the campground in the direction of downtown Florence.

Camping Villa Camerata is located northeast of central Florence. From the A1 Freeway take the Firenze Sud exit. After leaving the toll booth continue on the four lane highway north for 3.5 kilometers towards Florence until it terminates just after the

ITALY

Arno bridge. Turn left here and follow the Arno north bank for 1.9 kilometers, then turn right following signs for Fiesole. Proceed north on this road for 2.5 kilometers, you will see occasional campground signs. At 2.5 kilometers turn left at a small semi-roundabout and then almost immediately right into the campground/hostel driveway.

✦ CAMPING PANORAMICO FIESOLE

Address: Via Peramonda 1, I-50014 Fiesole
Telephone: 055 599069 Fax: 055 59186
Price: Moderate

Open all year

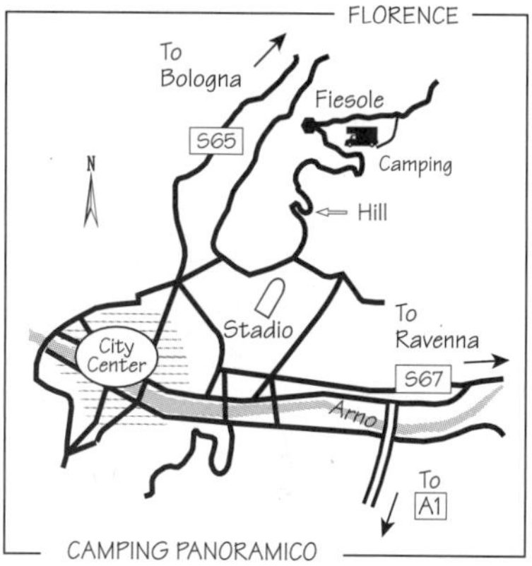

Camping Panoramico is located in Fiesole, a mountaintop suburb about 7 kilometers from downtown Florence. There is frequent city bus service up to Fiesole. The town is thought to be even older than Florence, inhabitants of this Etruscan village may have founded the city spread out below.

The campsite is located at the very crest of a hill some 1.5 kilometers beyond the village of Fiesole. The sites are arranged on terraces facing in all directions. The terraces are often narrow and might provide a maneuvering problem for caravans (trailers) or larger rigs. Many different species of trees provide shade and almost every site has a good view. Electricity (CEE17 plugs) is available to most sites. The shower/toilet buildings are older but well maintained and clean. Free hot water is available for showers (adjustable), bathroom basins, and dishwashing sinks. The campground has a grocery shop, snack bar/bar, and dump station.

Bus transportation to Florence is from the square in Fiesole. Reaching it requires a hike of about 1.5 kilometers. Using a bike to get into Florence is not advisable unless you are in good shape, the hill on the way back wouldn't be much fun.

To reach the campground follow the instructions given for Villa Camerata above. After passing Villa Camerata continue to the stop sign, then turn right and proceed up the hill. After 4 kilometers or so you'll pass through the village of Fiesole and in another kilometer you'll see the a campground sign pointing right up a small steep road. Follow this road for another half kilometer as it winds up to the campground entrance. The combination of the steep access road and limited maneuvering room in the campground make this a poor choice for trailers and big rigs.

Side Trips from Florence

Once you've had your fill of Florence it is time to see a little more of northern Tuscany. A good route to take toward Pisa is through the towns of Prato, Pistóia, and Lucca. Each is full of attractions requiring a stop. **Prato** has the 13th-century **duomo**, the **Museo Civico**, and the **Castello dell' Imperatore**. **Pistóia** also has its **Duomo** while **Lucca** is home to several important churches and museums as well as a 2.5-mile promenade along it's ancient walls.

PISA, ITALY

Population 105,000

About 90 kilometers west from Florence is the town of Pisa. Known around the world for its **leaning tower**, Pisa is easy for campers to visit. Of course you must see the tower, and the town's other major sights, the **duomo (cathedral)** and **baptistery**, are right next door. All are located on the very large grassy **Field of Miracles (Campo dei Miracoli)**, not a 15-minute walk from the Torre Pendente (Leaning Tower) campground.

Pisa Campground

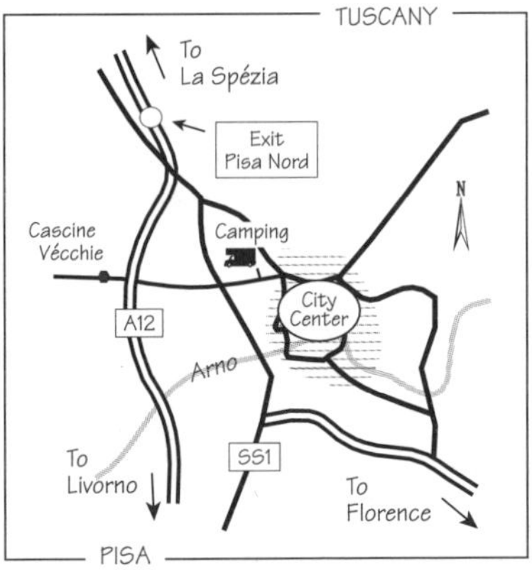

✦ TORRE PENDENTE

Address: Viale delle Cascine 86, I-56122 Pisa
Telephone: 050 561704 Fax: 050 561734
Price: Moderate

Open April 1 to October 15

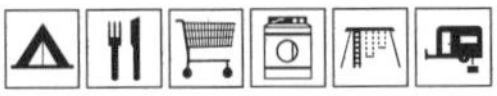

You can see the leaning tower peeking around the corner of the Duomo from this campground's entrance so its name appears to be justified. This is a large campground set in a grassy field on the western edge of Pisa. Electricity (CEE17 plugs, 5 amps) is available to most sites. There are free hot showers and the campground has a bar/restaurant, and playground.

The leaning tower is about 1 kilometer from the campground, a 15-minute walk. There is also a convenient bus to central Pisa.

Find the campground most easily from SS1, a secondary road which runs north and south on the western side of Pisa. Don't try to drive through the town, it is not worth it. Exactly 1.3 kilometers north of the Arno bridge, at about kilometer 336.5 you'll see a campground sign pointing east down Viale delle Cascine. The campground is .2 kilometer down this road on the left.

After your visits to Florence and Pisa you'll probably be ready for some quiet time in the country. The Chianti Hills are perfect for that. Using the Camping Villaggio Norcenni Girasole Club campground near Figline Valdarno as a comfortable base you can explore this famous wine area at your own pace.

Figline Valdarno Campground

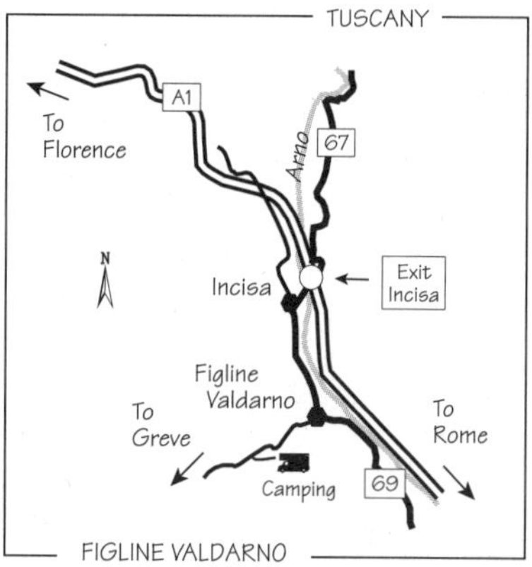

✦ Camping Villaggio Norcenni Girasole Club

Address: Via di Norcenni 7,
I-50063 Figline Valdarno
Telephone: 055 959666 Fax: 055 959337
Price: Expensive

Open March 1 to October 31

As one of the few four-star campgrounds in Tuscany this one makes a good long-term base for exploring the region, especially if you have younger members in your party who demand entertainment facilities. A shuttle bus or bus/train combo will take you into Florence, the remainder of the area sights are probably most easily visited with your own vehicle. The campground offers tours of Florence and the surrounding wine country. One real advantage of this campground as a base over the Florence campgrounds is that you do not have to thread through the city traffic each time you leave the campground.

The Camping Villaggio is a very large tourist campground built on expansive terraces on a south facing hillside in the Chianti Hills. There are many rental mobile homes and bungalows here, it is also popular with tour operators. The camp sites are on grass and gravel, separated by small hedges. They are not numbered. Electricity is available (CEE17 plug, 4 amps), the outlet boxes are widely spaced. The shower/toilet buildings are modern and clean, they have hot showers (premixed, push-button), and hot water in bathroom basins, dishwashing sinks, and the laundry area. There is a very upscale amenity area with a large swimming pool, tennis courts, fitness center, restaurant and bar, disco, grocery shop, and clothing store. Horses are available for rent and there is even a fishing pond.

The campground is most easily reached from the Incisa exit (the next exit south from the Florence Sud exit, about 19 kilometers) off Highway A1 south of Florence. Turn left after leaving the toll plaza towards Incisa and Figline Valdarno. After 4.7 kilometers, just after passing a Coop supermarket on the left, in the town of Figline Valdarno, turn right toward Greve and Siena. There is a campground sign at this corner. In another .3 kilometers turn right again, there's a sign here too. Follow this road another 2.2 kilometers up the hill and you'll see the campground sign and road on the left. The campground is another .2 kilometers down this entrance road.

Side Trips from Figline Valdarno

From Figline Valdarno you're within easy driving distance of several famous hill towns. San Gimignano, Volterra, and Col di Val d'Elsa are easy day trips.

San Gimignano is a 65 kilometer drive east of Figline Valdarno on small country roads. You'll pass through Greve, Castellina, and Poggibonsi en route. The hilltop village is known for its medieval streets and fourteen towers. There's a campground

SOME OF SAN GIMIGNANO'S TOWERS

about 2 kilometers southwest of town called IL BOSCHETTO DI PIEMMA which is open from the first of April to the middle of October.

Volterra, a pre-Roman Etruscan town, is located another 30 kilometers west of San Gimignano. Volterra also has a convenient campground, CAMPING COMMUNALE LE BALZE, just 1 kilometer northwest of town and open from early March to late October.

To explore southern Tuscany you might want to move your base of operations to Siena. The town has a good campground and makes an excellent base for day trips to the more southern hill towns of Arezzo, Cortona, Montepulciano, and Montalcino.

SIENA, ITALY

Population 65,000

How can you pass up the chance to visit a town that has a color named after it? A one-time rival to nearby Florence, Siena today is not as well known, which makes it a great place to visit. Today's Siena has only about a third the inhabitants that it did at the height of its power in the fourteenth century.

The life of the town revolves around the **Piazza del Campo**, a very large sloping plaza surrounded by cafes on the upper side and the Gothic **Palazzo Comunale** on the lower. Up the hill from the Campo is the **Duomo**, known as one of Italy's prettiest cathedrals with its black and white marble. The atmosphere in Siena is very quiet, particularly in the off season, you'll want to spend your time wandering the streets or sitting in a cafe on the Campo.

Siena Campground

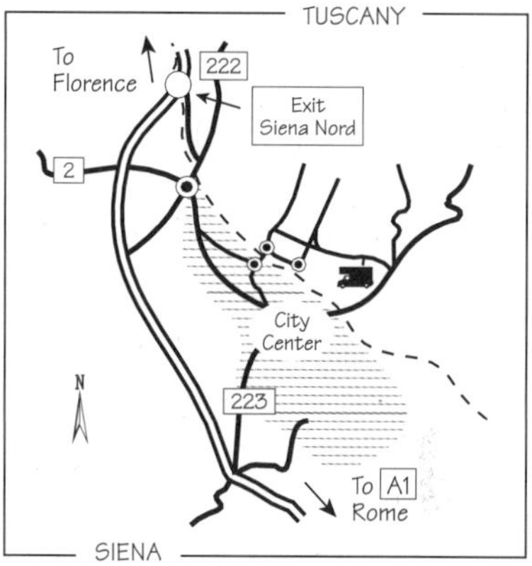

✦ SIENA COLLEVERDE CAMPING

Address: Strada Di Scacciapensieri 47,
I-53100 Siena
Telephone: 0577 280044 Fax: 0577 333298
Price: Moderate

Open March 21 to November 10

This is by far the most convenient campground for visiting Siena. It sits on a hillside about two kilometers northeast of town and offers fine views of the city across the intervening valley.

Camping Colleverde is a medium-sized campground on a sloping site, fortunately there are three large flat pads set aside for motor homes and trailers. The wheeled vehicle sites are numbered, others are not. There are many nice tent sites here. Electricity is convenient to the wheeled vehicle sites (CEE17 plugs, 3 amps). The shower/toilet buildings are clean and well maintained, hot showers (adjustable, push-button valve) are free in one of the buildings as is hot water in the bathroom wash basins. The campground has a small shop and bar with some take-out food. There is a large swimming pool and also a dump station and laundry machines. Just down the hill from the campground is a good supermarket.

Bus transportation to central Siena is convenient. Bus 8 stops near the campground and will take you to the Piazza Gramsci. You can also easily walk or ride a bicycle to the center of town, the distance is about 3 kilometers.

International camping signs are on all of the approaches to Siena, they direct you to this campground. It is located on the hillside on the far side of the train station from Siena. The easiest route is from the Siena Nord exit from the Florence to Siena highway. At the end of the exit ramp turn right and almost immediately (.2 kilometers) you will come to a traffic circle where you should turn left. In another 1.1 kilometer turn left again. After .8 kilometer at the roundabout turn left and cross the railroad tracks. In just .2 kilometer, turn right at the next roundabout. In another .5 kilometer turn left at another roundabout and proceed up the hill for 1 kilometer and turn right. The road will curve around toward Siena and at the T in .2 kilometer turn left. The campground is on the right in .6 kilometer. While this sounds complicated the route is well signed at the various turns and should present no problems. Traffic is not overly heavy as you never really get near the central part of town.

BOLSENA, ITALY

Population: 4,100

While not strictly a Tuscan town (it's actually just across the border into Lazio) this ancient lake-side village makes a very good base for exploring southern Tuscany. The town is known for a miracle in 1263 A.D. A doubting Bohemian priest was convinced of the doctrine of transubstantiation when blood appeared on the Host he was consecrating during a mass in the Church of Santa Cristina. The Feast of Corpus Christi is at least partially the result of this miracle. Bolsena has its own castle and an Etruscan and Roman museum. The Lago di Bolsena is a large lake, popular for water sports in the summer. Bolsena is a resort town with many campgrounds along the lake. One of these campgrounds often stays open all year, although it may not always be the same one. If no campgrounds are open folks seem to get away with free camping along the lake-shore drive for short periods.

Bolsena Campground

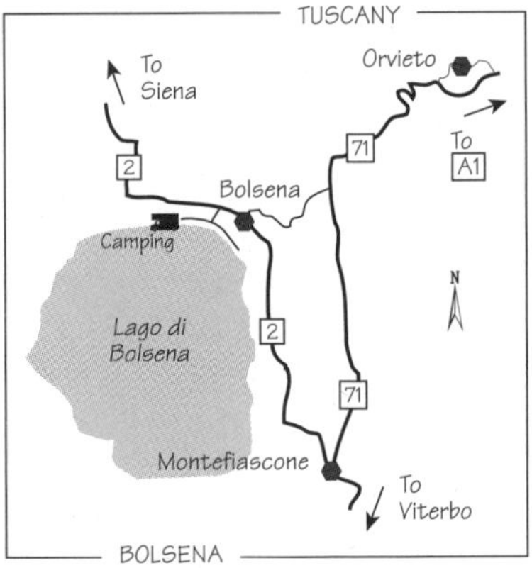

✦ CAMPING PINETA

Address: Bolsena I-01023

Price: Moderate

Open May 1 to October 30

This medium-sized campground has grassy spaces off gravel drives. They are not separated, electrical boxes (CEE17 plugs) are widely spaced. There are quite a few permanently-parked rigs but they are well kept. The shower/toilet building is modern and clean. It has hot water showers requiring a token, there is cold water in dish and clothes washing sinks. There is a restaurant and a coffee bar at the front of the campground and the lake is just across the drive in front. This lake-side drive and promenade runs for several kilometers along the lake and the walk along it toward town is very pleasant.

All Bolsena campgrounds are well-signed from town. It is best to follow the signs because sections of the lake-side drive are one way. For Camping Pineta start at the intersection where the road from Orvieto meets Highway 2 in town. Drive northwest on Highway 2 toward Siena for .5 kilometers and turn left. Follow the road another .5 kilometers to the lake, turn right and you'll see the campground on the right almost immediately.

Side Trips from Bolsena

Orvieto is about 23 kilometers east of Bolsena. The drive though verdant hill country is extremely scenic. Orvieto is an old Etruscan city built on a tufa hilltop, it is right next to the A1 south to Rome and anyone traveling the autostrada is tempted to stop and take a look. Orvieto is known for its cathedral, and also for the white wine named after it. The **cathedral** was built to celebrate a miracle that occurred in our base town of Bolsena. There are well-known wall and ceiling paintings by Fra Angelico, Benozzo Gozzoli, and Luca Signorelli. Another interesting site in Orvieto is the **Well of St. Patrick (Pozzo di San Patrizio)**. It is 200 feet deep and sixteen feet wide. Two spiral stairways descend into the well, one for down traffic and one for up. Windows in the walls of the well provide light.

Another much smaller hill-top town is **Cívita** located about 17 kilometers south of Orvieto near Bagnorégio. Many Americans have purchased homes here.

Finally, if you have time, you can visit coastal Tuscany. Perhaps the best way to do this is to take the coastal route on a visit to Rome. The Island of Elba is easily visited with an RV and has several campgrounds. On the mainland you'll find a good campground in Boca di Cécina.

Boca di Cécina Campground

✦ BOCCA DI CÉCINA

Address: Marina de Cécina, I-57023 Cécina
Telephone: 586 620509
Price: Moderate

Open all year

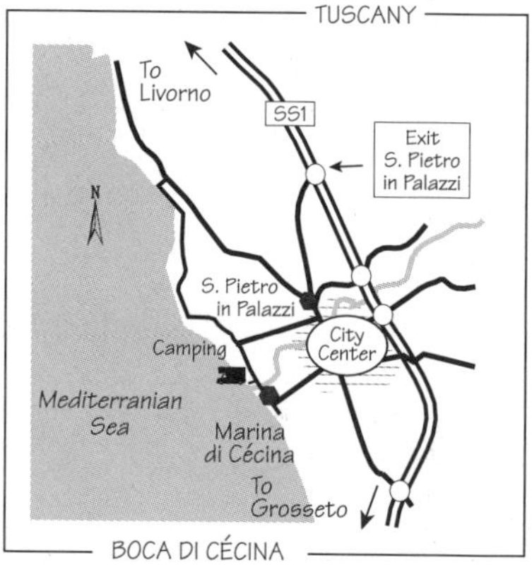

Bocca de Cécina campground makes a good base for exploring the western portion of Tuscany. It is also a convenient overnight stopping point if your are traveling the coastal route south to Rome. Cécina is about 30 kilometers south of Livorno.

This is a very large coastal holiday-type campground. It is unusual for this type of campground because the facilities are really quite nice, and if you visit in the off season it can be a pleasant stop. The individual sites are separated by hedges and there are enough trees to provide good shade. Electricity (CEE17 plugs, 2 amps) is convenient to most sites. The shower/toilet buildings are clean and modern, one is even heated in cooler weather. Hot showers are free and there is hot water to bathroom basins. There are lots of amenities although most are only open during the summer season. They include a grocery shop, restaurants and bar, playground, beach, laundry, and dump station.

After taking the middle Cécina off-ramp from the coastal freeway follow signs to the Marina di Cécina or Cécina Mare. Once you reach the coastal road you'll see signs for several campgrounds including Bocca di Cécina.

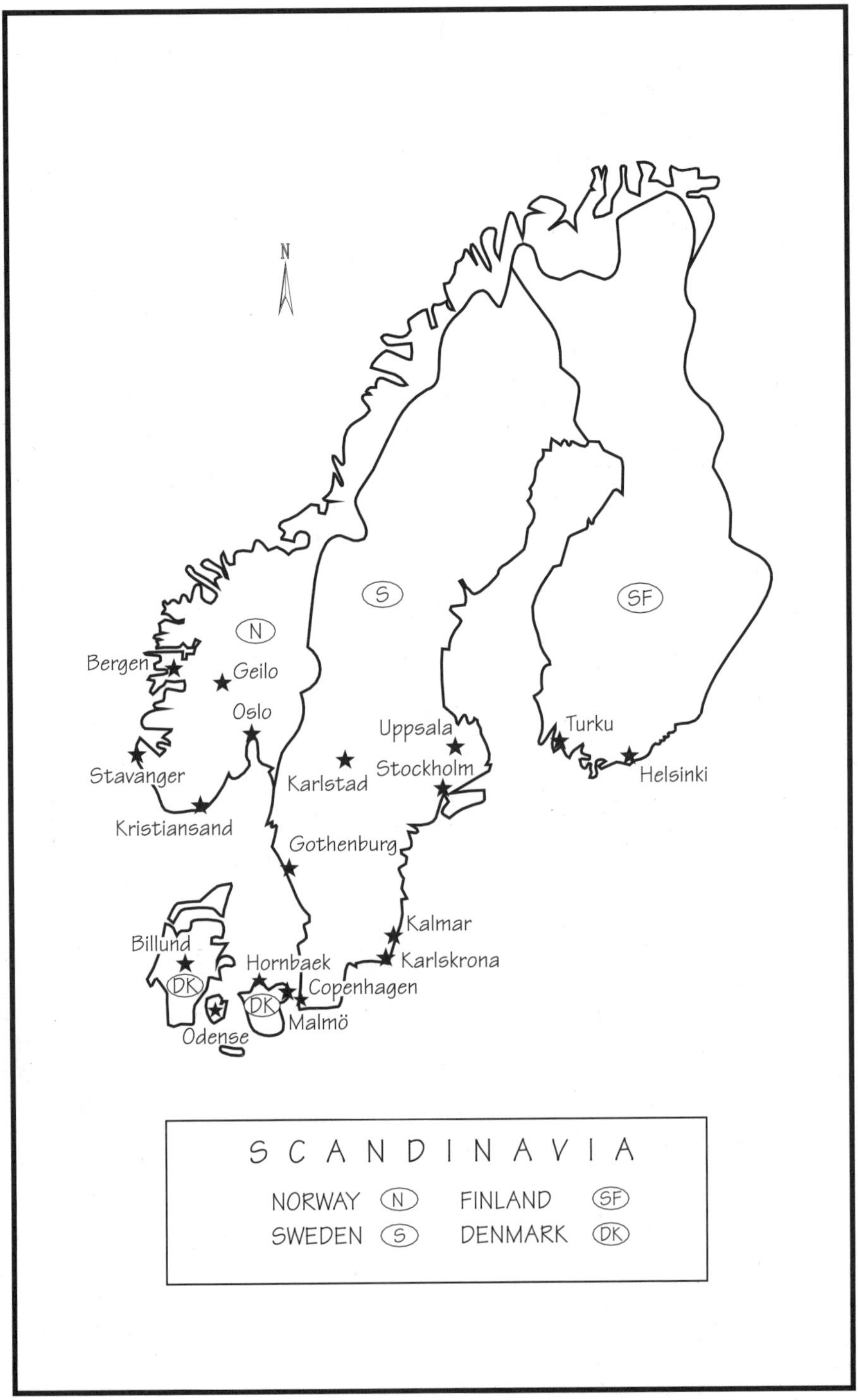
N
Bergen
Geilo
Oslo
Stavanger
Kristiansand
Karlstad
Uppsala
Stockholm
Gothenburg
Kalmar
Karlskrona
Billund
Hornbaek
Copenhagen
Malmö
Odense
Turku
Helsinki
S C A N D I N A V I A
NORWAY N
SWEDEN S
FINLAND SF
DENMARK DK

CHAPTER 11

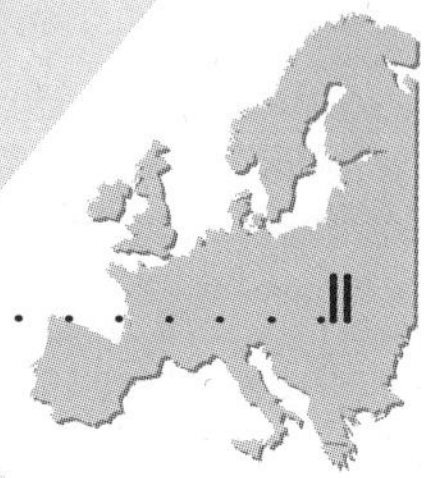

SCANDINAVIA

INTRODUCTION

We tend to think of the Scandinavian countries: Denmark, Sweden, Norway, and Finland; as being much alike. They are really quite diverse. In terms of terrain Denmark, Finland, and most of Sweden are mostly flat while Norway is just the opposite. Water plays an important part in the geography of all of them. Only three cities visited in this chapter (Odense, Billund, and Uppsala) are not located alongside the sea or a lake.

Politically, of course, they all share a relaxed form of socialism, or more properly, social welfare. The resulting societies are intriguing to an observer, if only because they may partially reflect our future. There are differences between them. All of these countries except Norway are members of the European Community (EC). Norway's citizens voted to stay out. Finland and Sweden are not members of NATO but Sweden maintains a strong military. Scandinavia's location close to Russia affects the politics of all of these countries, especially Finland.

One nice thing about Scandinavia for North Americans is that English is widely spoken.

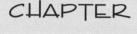

Roads And Driving

All of these countries have good roads. Where there are freeways they are not toll roads, however some tunnels, especially in Norway, have very high tolls. A very long, deep, and expensive tunnel under a fiord just north of Stavanger stands out. A Norwegian twist is that some cities, Oslo among them, have city tolls with booths at the entrances to the city. These city tolls, however, are not very high.

Ferries form an important part of the transportation network in this part of the world. A ferry is required to get to Norway or Sweden from the rest of Europe, and unless you are ready for a very long drive, another is required to travel on to Finland. The west coast of Norway between Bergen and Stavanger is traveled on a combination of ferries, tunnels, and short sections of road. For the most parts you won't need reservations, an exception is the 12-hour-long trip between Stockholm and Finland. The costs of the ferries and tunnels are not an insignificant budget item, you'll want to use them sparingly by carefully planning your itinerary. Keep the high cost of gasoline in mind, however, sometimes using a ferry can save considerable driving distance.

Since you will have to use a ferry to get to much of Scandinavia anyway you might consider saving some gas by using one to travel direct from the British Isles or the continent. Ferry connections include Newcastle, England to Bergen, Stavanger, Kristiansand, and Oslo, Norway; Amsterdam, The Netherlands to Stavanger; Newcastle and Harwich, England to Gothenburg, Sweden; Amsterdam to Gothenburg; and Newcastle and Harwich to Esbjerg, Denmark.

Scandinavian drivers tend to be courteous and quite good. Many countries require the use of headlights during the day, if you see others using their headlights be sure to join them. Automated radar systems are in use in some places. They capture a picture of your license plate on film and result in an automatic ticket. This means that most people obey the speed limits, you should do the same. Finally, drinking and driving is absolutely not tolerated in Scandinavia.

Sweden's air force plans to use the highways as a secondary landing strip in the case of a war. If you find long lengths of wide highway with large parking areas alongside you'll know what they are.

Bike riders will love Denmark. The country is flat and there are many back roads which are perfect for a bike tour. Campgrounds are plentiful.

For help on the road in **Denmark** you can reach the police by dialing 112, breakdown service for a fee is at 70 102030 or 70 108090. In **Sweden** the major AAA affiliated auto club is Motormännens Riksförbund (M) at 08 6903800 and road service is at 020 912912, a fee is charged. Police are at 112. In **Norway** the major AAA affiliated auto club is Norges Automobil-Forbund (NAF) at 022 341400. Road service is at 81000505, payment is required, and police at 112. Finally, in **Finland** the AAA affiliated auto club is Autoliitto, Automobile and Touring Club of Finland (AL), telephone number 09 77476400. Emergency road service is limited, the emergency number for police is 10022.

Camping

Scandinavia has many campgrounds, you'll usually have no problem finding one when you need one. Most have fewer amenities than campgrounds farther south but many provide cooking areas with hot plates, a welcome feature for tent campers. There are few swimming pools but many campgrounds are on lakes or salt water and the Baltic is warm enough for swimming in the summer. Electricity is usually either expensive or low amperage in Scandinavia, probably not a problem since it will most likely be warm and not very dark at night during a summer visit.

A large percentage of the campers in Scandinavia are tent campers and most campgrounds have large areas available for campers not needing electricity, even those with wheeled vehicles. If you are in an RV you should take a look at the available camping areas before deciding on an electric site, you might find that you prefer the ambiance of the area without services.

The Scandinavian camping season is short, spring comes late and winter early. In the northern countries the season is limited to the months of June, July and August, although you will find much less crowding if you can put up with cooler temperatures and fewer campgrounds in spring and fall months.

Free camping rules in Scandinavia vary from country to country. Most have laws against it but these are often ignored. Sweden and Norway have a tradition, called everyman's right, allowing free camping on unfenced land away from buildings, but this does not apply to RVs and there are strict laws against taking your wheeled vehicle off road.

A Camping Card International is required for most Scandinavian campgrounds. If for some reason you don't have one you can sometimes purchase a national card as a substitute.

Shopping, Currency, Credit Cards and Fuel

The Scandinavian countries are modern places. Credit cards, cash machines, and supermarkets are easy to find. Prices tend to be the highest in Europe, probably because the taxes are high. We find Scandinavian supermarkets to be the poorest in western Europe, the selections are surprisingly limited even if you can find a large supermarket. Finland is an exception and has good selection in large stores.

All of the Scandinavian countries except Denmark have strong alcohol control laws. You'll usually find only low alcohol beer in the grocery stores, for stronger stuff you must visit government liquor stores.

Gasoline prices in Scandinavia are high. Most gas stations are modern and self-service and accept credit cards.

Itinerary Ideas

In Denmark you will want to spend some time in Copenhagen. The city is on the island of Zealand which has many sights easily visited on day trips from the capital's campgrounds. The remainder of the country is pastoral and pleasant if not exciting. If you have time there are some great beaches and countryside campgrounds.

Sweden is quite spread out, you must do quite a bit of driving to reach Stockholm since it is located on the far side of the country from your likely entry point. Stockholm has much to see and you will want to spend several days. The southern coast has many nice seaside campgrounds and is good for a relaxing visit and as a base for visiting the crystal-producing country around Växjö. Värmland in the interior north of lake Vänern is popular with Swedish campers. The west coast north of Gothenburg is also a good camping destination.

Norway's capital, Oslo, is another great destination. Once you've seen the sights there you may want to do a circular tour running northwest to Bergen and then south around the coast back to Oslo.

The drive to the North Cape (Nordkapp) is a popular excursion for European campers. This is no day trip, the distance from Oslo to the North Cape is about 2,200 kilometers. The Cape is Europe's most northern point. It is a spectacular drive. The normal route would be to drive to Trondheim and then follow the coast north. You'll see lots of mountains, fjords, and empty country. Besides Trondheim the road passes through Mo i Rana, crosses the Arctic Circle, then Narvik, Alta, and Honningsvåg. Short side trips will add Bodø, the Lofoten Islands, Harstad, Tromsø, Hammerfest, and Karasjok. During July and early August you'll find that you are not alone in making this popular trip.

On your way to Helsinki you will probably have a chance to tour the country's second largest city, Turku. Helsinki is the equal to the other Scandinavian capitols in many ways although it is smaller and newer. The northern part of the county is extensive and not as easily visited.

The Scandinavian countries are good about providing tourist information and they all work out of the same New York address. The **Scandinavian Tourist Board**, representing all four countries plus Iceland, can be contacted at **P.O. Box 4649, Grand Central Station, New York, NY 10163 (212 885-9700).** For more information about Scandinavia check the links on our internet site at www.rollinghomes.com.

SCANDINAVIA DISTANCE TABLE

In Kilometers

Kms X .62 = Miles

	Bergen Norway	Billund Denmark	Copenhagen Denmark	Geilo Norway	Gothenburg Sweden	Hamburg Germany	Helsinki Finland	Hornbaek Denmark	Kalmar Sweden	Karlskrona Sweden	Karlstad Sweden	Kristiansand Norway	Malmö Sweden	Odense Denmark	Oslo Norway	Stavanger Norway	Stockholm Sweden	Turku Finland
Billund Denmark	--																	
Copenhagen Denmark	--	244																
Geilo Norway	244	--	--															
Gothenburg Sweden	823	--	--	579														
Hamburg Germany	--	292	444	--	--													
Helsinki Finland	--	--	--	--	--	--												
Hornbaek Denmark	--	309	65	--	--	509	--											
Kalmar Sweden	1169	--	--	925	346	--	--	--										
Karlskrona Sweden	1164	--	--	973	341	--	--	--	84									
Karlstad Sweden	734	--	--	490	245	--	--	--	431	460								
Kristiansand Norway	402	--	--	451	644	--	--	--	990	985	555							
Malmö Sweden	1104	--	--	860	281	--	--	--	284	211	504	925						
Odense Denmark	--	104	140	--	--	304	--	205	--	--	--	--	--					
Oslo Norway	505	--	--	261	261	--	--	--	664	659	229	326	599	--				
Stavanger Norway	147	--	--	331	331	--	--	--	1245	1240	810	255	1180	--	581			
Stockholm Sweden	1042	--	--	798	798	--	--	--	411	494	313	863	604	--	537	1177		
Turku Finland	--	--	--	--	--	--	165	--	--	--	--	--	--	--	--	--	--	
Uppsala Sweden	1023	--	--	779	779	--	--	--	447	530	289	839	641	--	518	1099	72	--

SCANDINAVIA

SELECTED CITIES AND CAMPGROUNDS

BERGEN, NORWAY

Population 215,000

Bergen is the second largest city in Norway and is located in the middle of fjord country on the west coast. It has a very compact city center that is easily explored on foot, especially if you camp at the Bobil-Senter. The town is well known for its rain, but ignore that and take a look around. Since this is a major ferry port for traffic from Newcastle in England you'll find the restaurants and shops are well prepared for English-speaking customers. From Bergen you are within easy striking distance of beautiful fjord country but the town itself deserves a good examination first as there is a lot of history and some good museums. Until the nineteenth century Bergen was Norway's big city.

Bergen's history as an important Hanseatic League port is evident in the **Bryggen** district, located between the campground and the central **Fisketorvet** (fish square). The row of **wooden gabled warehouses** along the north shore of the harbor has UNESCO World Heritage List status. You'll also find the **Hanseatic Museum**, the **Bryggen Museum**, and the **Schjøtstuene guild halls** just back from the harbor in this area. For a break from the museums try a ride on the **Fløibanen funicular** to the

THE BOBIL-SENTER IN BERGEN

Fløyen viewpoint above Bergen. There are hiking trails in the vicinity of the viewpoint.

Bergen is Norway's cultural capital and is known for its **Bergen International Festival** in late May and early June with music, dance and plays. Art museums include the **Stenersen Collection** and the **Rasmus Meyers Samlinger** collection.

You may also want to visit the **Fishery Museum** near the Bergenhus or the very good **Aquarium** on the point extending along the south shore of the harbor.

We've written below about the Bobil-Senter campground, a good alternative if you can get in and if you are in a van or motor home. Otherwise consider LONE CAMPING, 20 kilometers from the center of town on Highway 580. This campground borders Lake Haukeland and has bus transportation in to Bergen. It is easily accessible when you approach town from the east, watch for Highway 580 cutting off to the south from E16.

Bergen Campground

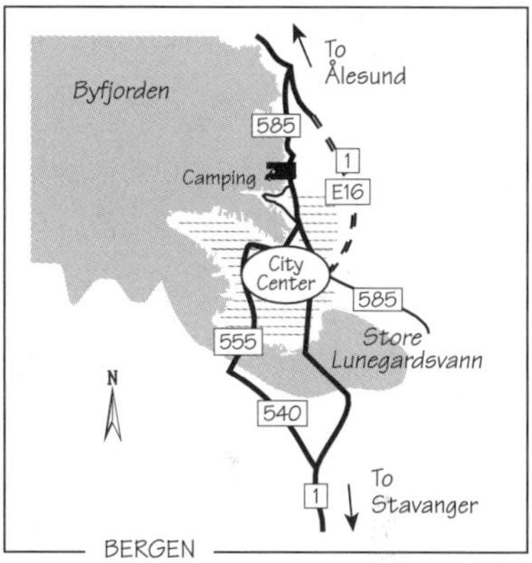

✦ BERGEN BOBIL-SENTER

Address: Skuteviksторget, Bergen
Price: Inexpensive

Open mid May to mid September

The best reason for staying at this campground is the location, in fact there are no other reasons. The Bobil-Senter is a city-run campground located within one kilometer of the city center. It is really just a paved parking lot on the water's edge with very few amenities, and for this reason it accepts only self-contained motor homes and vans, no tents and no trailers (caravans). The motor homes are parked about 3 meters apart so you aren't really overcrowded, but no space is wasted. Shower/toilet facilities are inadequate, there is one shower for the men and two for the ladies, but many of the rigs have their own, of course. Hot water is provided for the showers and bathroom basins. There is an oceanfront picnic area and a dump station. There are no provisions for reservations and spaces are in heavy demand so arrive as early in the day as possible.

You'll find the campground on the waterfront just a quarter of a kilometer north of the passenger ferry docks. The easiest way to get here is to follow the ferry signs as you come into town because there are no signs directing you to the campground. From the center of town at the head of the harbor you should follow the street running along the north shore around the Bergenhus point.

Side Trips from Bergen

Bergen has its own open-air museum, the **Old Bergen Museum**. It is located in the suburb of Sandviken and has a collection of Norwegian buildings from the 18th and 19th centuries designed to show traditional lifestyles.

A popular day trip from Bergen is the island castle of violinist Ole Bull, **Lysøen.** Follow E68 south to Fana, then follow Highway 546 to Buena Kai. You must take a ferry to the island.

Bergen was the home of composer Edvard Grieg. To visit his home, **Troldhaugen** (Troll Hill) drive south on E68 for about 5 kilometers taking the Fantoft Studentby exit and then follow signs.

Bergen is the fjord tour center of Norway. Check at the tourist office for information about what is available.

BILLUND, DENMARK

Population 5,000

If you have children in your rig you won't want to drive past Billund. This is the home of the Lego Company and their theme park — **Legoland,** one of Denmark's most popular tourist attractions. It is filled with models of almost anything you can think of, all constructed of tiny plastic bricks. The campground is less than a kilometer from the park. You'll also find a good **transportation museum** right next to the campground, as well as an airport.

Billund Campground

✦ BILLUND CAMPING

Address: Ellehammers Allé 2,
DK-7190 Billund
Telephone: 075 331521 Fax: 075 353736
Price: Moderate

Open all year

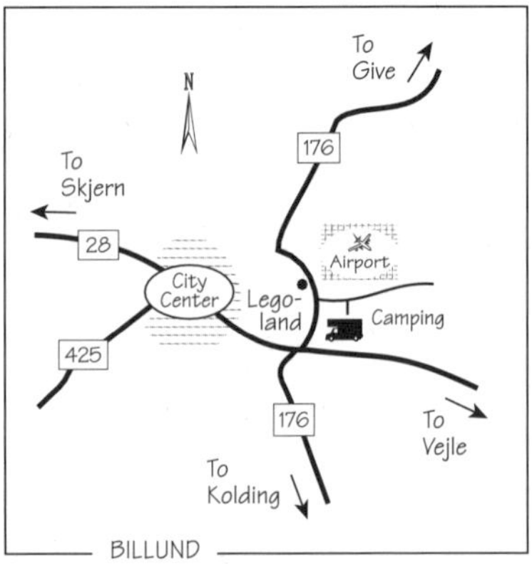

This is a large modern campground with first class facilities. The campsites are in small hedge-enclosed clearings, each holding about six rigs. The hedges are laid out in a kind of maze, the design works well to make you feel like you have some privacy. The sites are surfaced with a brick lattice (no, not Legos) that give you a firm parking surface with grass growing through them. The shower/toilet buildings are nice, showers and dishwashing require tokens, bathroom basins have free hot water. There is a good grocery store restaurant, a playground, nearby miniature golf, and a small petting zoo with goats and pigs.

You can easily walk the half kilometer to Legoland. Billund itself has stores and other necessary facilities, it is about two kilometers west.

To find the campground take Route 28 towards Billund from the east. Just before reaching Billund you'll come to Route 176, a north/south street. Turn north, there's a sign for Legoland and almost immediately you'll see the campground on the east side of the road. It is adjacent to both the airport and Legoland so following signs to either one will bring you to the right neighborhood.

COPENHAGEN (KØBENHAVN), DENMARK

Population 1,400,000

Think of Copenhagen and you'll probably think of its two marquee attractions: the little mermaid statue next to the harbor and the Tivoli Gardens amusement park. These are probably the top tourist draws, but Copenhagen also has a friendly-sized central city area, a relaxed and fun-loving pace, and many other attractions to visit.

Copenhagen is a low-rise city with most of the things of interest arranged in a small area at the center of town. There's good public transportation if you need to leave the central area. Consider using a bicycle to get around, the terrain is flat and bicycles are a common form of transportation.

The Indre By central district, usually just called the **Strøget,** is a large central pedestrianized shopping area where you'll probably spend quite a bit of time. The area is filled with shops and restaurants and makes a great place to just stroll.

Just east of the Strøget on what is really the island of Slotsholmen, is **Christiansborg Castle (Christiansborg Slot)** which houses parliament, the royal reception rooms, and the supreme court. Nearby is the **Børsen**, the world's oldest stock exchange still

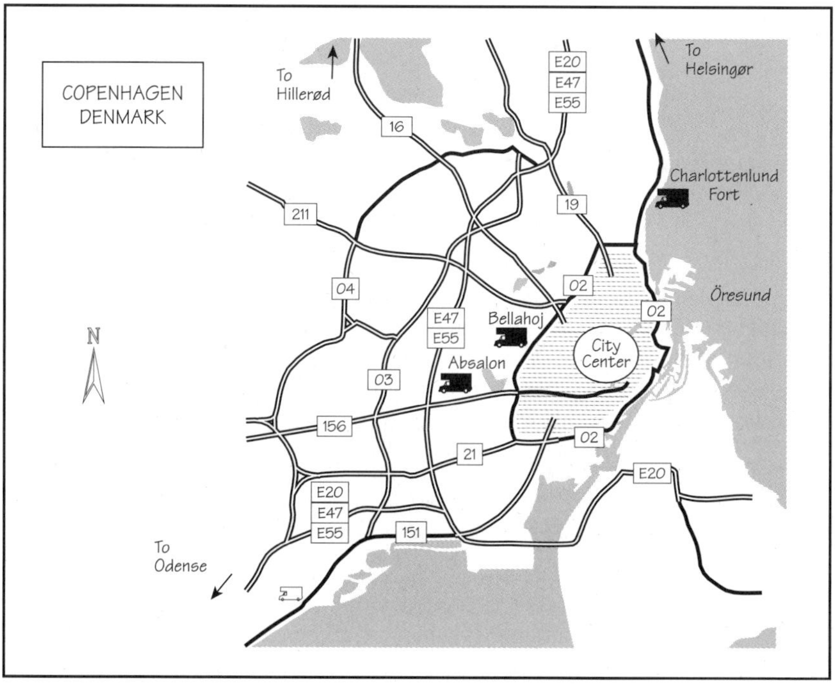

in use, known for the four dragon's tails forming its spire. Beyond the castle across a drawbridge is **Christianshavn,** a residential quarter that may remind you of Amsterdam. The **Vor Frelsers Kirke** (a church) has a tall spire with an outside staircase, braver visitors can climb to the top for the view. Beyond Christianshavn is **Christiania**, once an area of military barracks, now controlled by young and formerly homeless people and declared a "free city". It is an interesting community and has inexpensive shops and restaurants.

North of the Strøget you'll find the royal residence of **Amalienborg**. Beyond Amalienborg is **Churchill park**, formerly a military fortress, and on the far side of the park along the waterside promenade or Langelinie is the **Little Mermaid Statue** (**Den Lille Havfrue**) which has been there since 1913.

Finally, just south of the Strøget are the famous **Tivoli Gardens**, now somewhat faded and smaller than you might expect if you are accustomed to modern theme parks. The gardens have been world famous since being built in 1843 and the concept has been copied in many other countries. East of the gardens is **New Carlsberg Museum (Ny Carlsberg Glyptotek)**, a museum built and maintained by a foundation started by the founder of the Carlsberg Breweries. It has a good collection of Impressionist and Post-Impressionist paintings, as well as a large collection of Etruscan art.

Copenhagen Campgrounds

✦ DCU ABSALON CAMPING

Address: Korsdalsvej 132, DK-2610 Rødovre
Telephone: 036 410600 Fax: 036 440293
Price: Moderate

Open all year

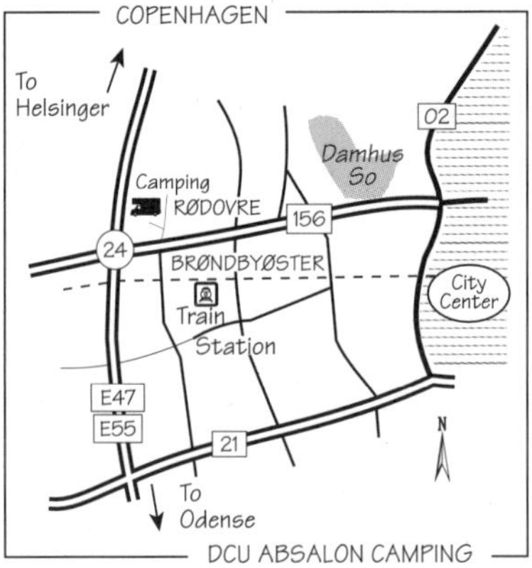

The second-closest campground to Copenhagen center with good transportation connections, Absalon is also large enough that you can almost always find a spot, even during July and August.

This large campground has various types of sites, all on grass, some in small groups separated by hedges and others in large fields. Electrical outlets may not be available if things are crowded, even if available they can be widely spaced. Shower/toilet facilities are in a large building, not modern but clean with hot water for showers, bathroom basins, and washing dishes. The dishwashing area also has hot plates. There is a large enclosed area with picnic tables for those camping in tents or looking for conversation. The campground also has a laundry room with coin-operated machines, miniature golf, playground equipment, and a grocery shop. There is a small booth selling food with tables on a patio. A couple of larger grocery stores are nearby near the rail station.

Surprisingly, considering that the campground is only about 8 kilometers from central Copenhagen, the best transportation is suburban rail. The Brøndbyøster station is only a half kilometer from the campground.

To find the campground take Exit 24 from the E55 freeway. Turn toward central Copenhagen. You'll see the sign pointing to the campground on the left within one kilometer.

✦ CHARLOTTENLUND FORT

Address: Strandvejen 144B,
DK-2290 Charlottenlund
Telephone: 031 623688
Price: Moderate

Open May 15 to September 30

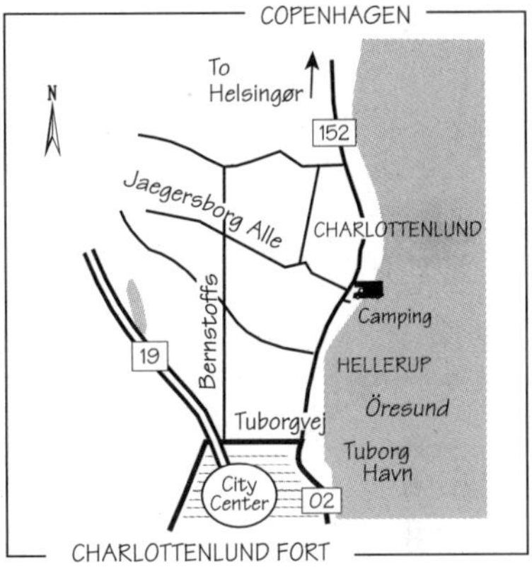

This campground sits inside the raised earthworks of an old coastal-defense battery. Some of the guns remain in place and the modern sanitary facilities are in one of the old storerooms inside the earthworks. The campground is fronted by a quiet beach park. Since this is a smaller but popular campground you'll probably want to make an advance reservation if you plan to stay here while visiting Copenhagen.

Charlottenlund Fort is a medium-sized campground with grass sites arranged on either side of one road that runs through the crescent shaped fort. Electrical outlets in some spots will require a long cord. The shower/toilet room is modern and clean, it has hot water. Areas are provided for dishwashing, cooking, and doing laundry with coin-operated machines. Tents have a preferred location here, they are pitched on grass above the RV area and have a nice sea view. There is a restaurant next to the tent area and a small grocery shop.

Access to downtown Copenhagen is by bus from near the campground.

The campground is located just off the coastal boulevard north of Copenhagen. Continue for about two kilometers after you pass the big Tuborg brewery, you'll see the campground sign pointing to the right.

✦ DCU BELLAHØJ CAMPING

Address: Hvidkildevej 66, Bellahøj,
DK-2400 København NV
Telephone: 031 101150
Price: Moderate

Open June 1 to August 31

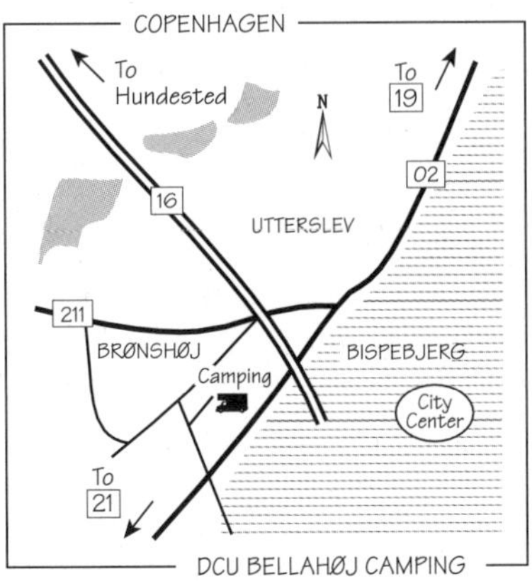

Bellahøj is the closest campground to Copenhagen center, it is full of the tents and vans of foreign visitors to the city. This is a little hard to understand since it is the least pleasant of Copenhagen's campgrounds, and only marginally cheaper or more convenient than the others. There is always room for one more camper here so it makes a good place to stay if everything else is full.

The campground is a very large sloping grass field with no shade, no numbered or assigned sites, and very few electrical outlets. Campers can set up wherever they desire so it is difficult to say what the maximum capacity is here, probably thousands. The shower/toilet facilities are clearly inadequate for thousands, there is one well-used older building. While showers are theoretically hot you should test the waters before committing, hot water is somewhat intermittent. Bathroom basins and dishwashing sinks have cold water and there are hot plates for cooking. The campground has a small grocery shop and an open-air kiosk/cafe. Access to downtown Copenhagen is by bus number 2 Bellahøj and takes about 15 minutes. Be careful coming from downtown because there are two different number 2 busses, you want the Bellahøj bus.

The campground is located just off the 02 ring road to the west of downtown. Follow signs for the Bellahøj Exhibition Halls and then campground signs. The place is so large that it is hard to miss.

Side Trips from Copenhagen

Copenhagen is on the east coast of the largest Danish island — **Zealand** (Sjælland). Zealand is 125 kilometer long and 100 kilometers wide, it provides opportunities for several good day trips.

North of Copenhagen along the "Danish Riviera" but south of Helsingør (see the Hornbæk write-up) there are two good museums. The **Karen Blixen Museum** is in Rungsted Kyst, near the coast about 25 kilometers north of Copenhagen's center. The second is **Louisiana**, a world-famous modern art museum. It is in Humlebæk, about 35 kilometers north of Copenhagen and also on the coast.

Inland, about 40 kilometers northwest of Copenhagen in the town of Hillerod is **Frederiksborg Slot**. The extensive castle houses a museum of Danish history and is often considered the Danish Versailles, but its Dutch Renaissance design and the fact that it is constructed on three islands make this palace unique.

Roskilde, 30 kilometers west of Copenhagen, is home to the magnificent **Roskilde Cathedral (Roskilde Domkirke)** where Denmark's monarchs are buried. It is also the location of the **Viking Ship Museum (Vikingeskibshallen)** where 5 reconstructed Viking ships are on display. They were actually found at the bottom of the nearby fjord and include men of war, freighters and even a ferry.

Connected to the south end of Zealand by bridges are three islands: **Falster, Lolland, and Møn**. The islands are mostly rural and have good beaches and several campgrounds. Møn is the most visited, it is covered with **Neolithic burial mounds** and has **chalk cliffs** on the east side, the only ones in Denmark and a good place to search for fossils.

GEILO, NORWAY

Population 3,000

The small village of Geilo is most well known as Norway's largest winter ski resort. The hills overlooking town are covered with downhill ski runs and lifts and the area also has lots of cross-country ski routes. In the summer Geilo provides a good base for exploring the **Hardangervidda**, a mountain plateau that is Norway's largest national park. Horse and hiking trails lace the area. Geilo also makes a good place to stop while driving from Oslo to Bergen as it is at the exact halfway point. At least four small campgrounds provide comfortable and scenic sites. You may want to ride the ski lift up to **Geilotoppen** for the view.

Geilo Campground

✦ SOLLI SPORTELL

Address: Skurdalsvegen 25, N-3580 Geilo
Telephone: 032 091111
Price: Moderate

Open June to September

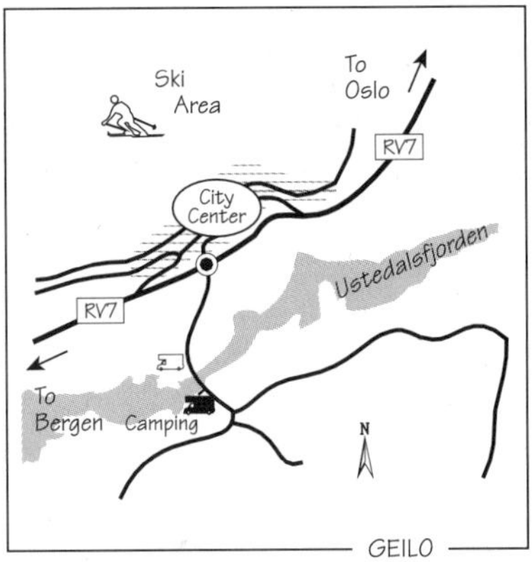

A small site on the shores of the Ustedals Lake outlet river, Solli Sportell has both assigned electrical sites and a large tent-camping field. The campground is run in conjunction with a hotel so amenities are pretty good. The shower/toilet facilities have coin-operated hot showers, hot water in bathroom basins, dish and clothes washing sinks with hot water, and a coin-operated washer and dryer. There is a grocery shop and a restaurant.

This is such a small town that instructions for finding the campsite are almost unnecessary. Just head down the hill toward the bridge over the river, the campground is on the far side. The distance to town is about one-half kilometer.

Side Trips from Geilo

You can drive 35 kilometers east to the town of **Torpo** which has a twelfth-century **stave church**.

On the far side of the Hardangervidda, 75 kilometers west of Geilo, Highway 7 drops dramatically to the valley of Måbødalen. Take the short side road to the **Vøring Falls (Vøringfossen)** which drop over 450 feet and perhaps walk down the old trail route to the bottom, there are many, many steps.

GOTHENBURG (GÖTEBORG), SWEDEN

Population 435,000

Gothenburg is Sweden's second-largest city and Scandinavia's largest port. The city rose to importance because it is located north of the Öresund, the channel between Denmark and Sweden, and Swedish goods shipped through Gothenburg could escape the seventeenth, eighteenth, and early nineteenth-century Danish tolls. Today Gothenburg is a modern industrial town and home to Volvo's manufacturing plant.

The city is well served by trams. After you take one downtown from the campground area you can board an open top tram for a city tour. Most things of interest are within walking distance of each other near the city center. You'll probably want to visit the **Nordstan**, a huge indoor shopping mall, and **Liseberg Nöjespark**, a giant, well-run amusement park.

Gothenburg Campground

✦ KÄRRALUND CAMPING AND DELSJÖ CAMPING

Address: Kärralund, Olbersgaton 1,
S-41655 Göteborg
Telephone: 031 840200 Fax: 031 840500
Price: Kärralund - expensive, Delsjö - moderate

Kärralund open all year, Delsjö open July 1 to August 13

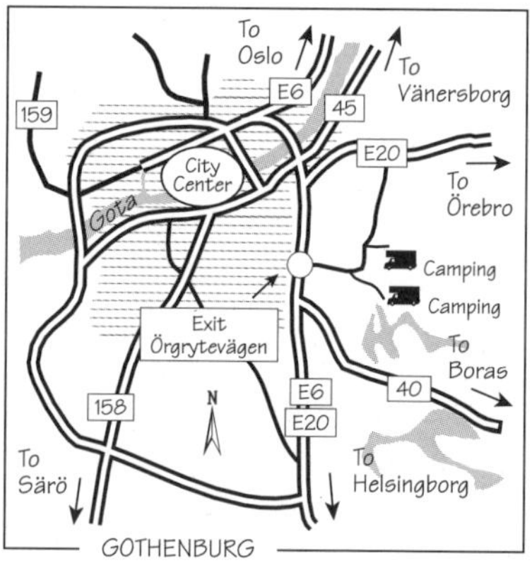

Both of these campgrounds are operated by Lisebergs Camping, in fact, almost every campground around Göteborg is run by this company. They also have ASKIM STRAND CAMPING and LILLEBY HAVSBAD CAMPING. Delsjö and Kärralund are the closest to the city and are both located in the Delsjö Recreation Area, a large park with jogging and bike trails, lakes, a golf course and, in fact, almost any outdoor recreation activity you can think of. Kärralund is the gold-plated first-class campground with price to match, Delsjö is nice but more in line with what you've come to expect in a campground. It is a little less convenient and open only in the summer, while Kärralund is open year-round.

Kärralund Camping is a high class affair with grass covered sites, first class shower/toilet buildings with free hot water, many sites with cable TV, and a grocery shop, laundry, and miniature golf.

Delsjö is a large campground set well into the recreation area. You can choose to camp on grass or on a gravel area that once was a large horse ring. There's shade available around the edge of the campground and electrical outlets are numerous. The shower/toilet buildings are not luxurious but they are adequate and have free hot showers, bathroom basins, and dishwashing areas. There is a small grocery store on site and a swimming area nearby.

Access to the central area from both sites is by the same city tram (5). The difference is that from Delsjö you must walk two kilometers across the park to get to the tram stop while from Kärralund the walk is only about one-half kilometer.

To find the campgrounds start on Highway E6 which runs through Göteborg from north to south just east of the city center. Take the Örgrytevägen exit which is marked with a sign for Kärralund Camping and is near the Liseberg amusement park. Follow the Kärralund Camping signs east for about two kilometers. You'll see a sign pointing right towards Delsjö camping first, then a sign for Kärralund about one-half kilometer farther along. The choice is yours.

Side Trips from Gothenburg

The coast from Gothenburg north to the Swedish border is heavily indented by fjords and is called **Bohoslän**. You can follow the small roads west from the E6 highway to explore the small villages and beaches. There are many campgrounds in the region.

The **Göta Canal** runs from Gothenburg to Stockholm across over 600 kilometers of rivers, lakes, canal cuts and sea. You can make the whole trip by boat in four days or take a short excursion over part of the distance. There is also a bike path along the canal if you care to make an extended bike trip.

HELSINKI, FINLAND

Population 990,000

The capital of Finland, Helsinki is located on the southern coast. It is not a giant city but is quite cosmopolitan. This and the coastal location with bays, inland waterways, and islands make it a fun city to visit. A metro system provides easy access to the center and most of the things you'll want to see and do can easily be reached on foot or by using the excellent public transportation system.

Central Helsinki spreads from the **Kauppatori** outdoor market and indoor **Kauppahalli** market at the head of the South Harbor. It is not an old city, frequent fires caused rebuilding, most buildings do not date earlier than the nineteenth century. In the central area a highlight is the **Senate Square** with its impressive surrounding buildings including the **Lutheran Cathedral (Tuomiokirkko)**. Other points of interest are the Russian Orthodox **Uspenski Cathedral**, the **Esplanadi** boulevard, and **Stockman's Department Store** and **Academic Book Store** (many English-language books).

Catch a tram and ride up Mannerheimintie to the northwest to see some of Helsinki's better-known architecture: the **National Museum**, **Finlandia Hall**, the **Helsinki City Museum**, and the **Olympic Stadium**.

There are two good island destinations some 3 kilometers from the city center. **Seurasaari** is an island **open-air Museum** with rural buildings from all over Finland. It can easily be reached by using the number 24 bus from the central area. **Suomenlinna** is a former island fortress (known as the Gibraltar of the North) now filled with museums and parks. You can reach it by ferry from the harbor near the Kauppatori.

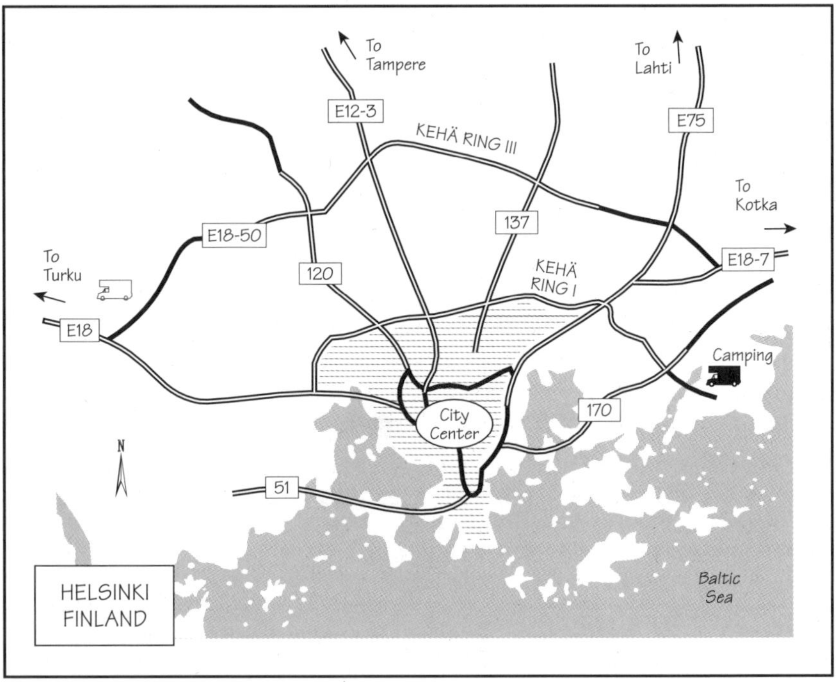

Helsinki Campground

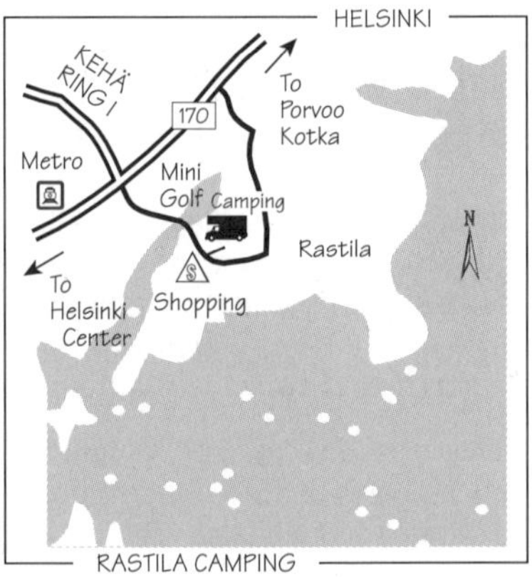

✦ RASTILA CAMPING

Address: Vuosaari, Nordsjö,
FIN-00980 Helsinki
Telephone: 09 316551 Fax: 09 3441578
Price: Inexpensive

Open May 15 to September 30

Rastila Camping is really your only choice for a campground with easy access to Helsinki. It is a very large campground spread over several large grassy fields with a few shade trees. Electrical outlets require very long cords for some sites. Campers are free to choose their own sites and the reception desk does not keep records so you'll have to make provisions to mark you site if you leave with the intention of returning. There's lots of room, however, even during the busy July vacation month. Shower/toilet buildings are clean and modern with plenty of hot water. Cooking/dishwashing cubicles are provided, there are also dishwashing and clothes-washing rooms. All of these have free hot water. There is a small grocery and restaurant at the campground and a supermarket with several small restaurants across the street. There is also a very large shopping center with large supermarkets 3 kilometers away near the subway terminal. A swimming beach is about a half kilometer from the campground and if you wander around the neighborhood you'll find others, as well as several basins full of yachts.

To get downtown catch the bus at the campground (number 90) which takes ten minutes to reach the subway station. Another ten minutes on the subway will see you in Helsinki.

Located toward the eastern edge of Helsinki's suburban sprawl Rastila Camping is most easily reached by following the inner ring road, Kehä Ring I, toward the east and Vuosaari. You'll eventually see campground signs and then the campground on the left after the road crosses an estuary with a swimming beach.

Side Trips from Helsinki

Porvoo, 50 kilometers east along the coast from Helsinki is an old trading village that recently has seen new life as an artist colony. The town has cobblestone streets and colorful wooden houses, Porvoo provides a peek at what Finnish life was like before Helsinki and the modern era.

Hämeenlinna, 95 kilometers northwest of Helsinki on excellent road is Finland's oldest inland town. The town is named after the **Hämeenlinna castle**, a thirteenth-century castle that is open for tours. The town is also the birthplace of the composer Sibelius and you can visit **Sibelius Childhood Home**. In the nearby town of Hattula you should visit **Hattula Kirkku**, one of the finest medieval churches in Finland. The interior is covered with hundreds of frescos of scenes from the bible. While driving out to Hattula you'll pass AULANKO CAMPING, an excellent choice if you don't feel like driving back to Helsinki.

HORNBAEK, DENMARK

The north coast of Zealand can be a pleasant change from the crowded Copenhagen area. This is also a good place to spend the night if you've just come across from Helsingborg in Sweden. Hornbaek is just 12 kilometers up the quiet coast from **Helsingør** and its **Kronborg Castle**.

Hornbaek Campground

✦ DCU HORNBAEK CAMPING

Address: Planetvej 4, DK-3100 Hornbaek
Telephone: 049 700223 Fax: 049 702391
Price: Moderate

Open April 1 to September 24

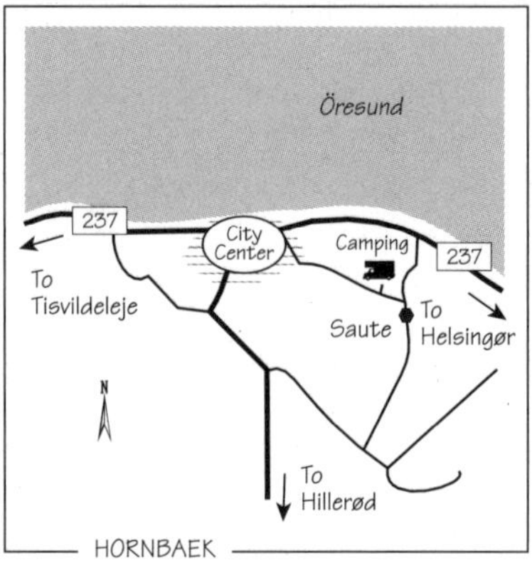

Hornbaek Camping is a large campground in a wooded setting about one kilometer outside the small town of Hornbaek. The campground covers several large grassy fields, campers choose their own unmarked sites. Shower/toilet facilities are in an older building but are well maintained. Hot showers require the use of two kroner pieces, hot water in bathroom basins and for dishwashing is free. There is a grocery shop in the reception building, coin-operated washing machines, a cooking area, and a playground. This large campground should always have room, especially if you're willing to camp without electricity. Bus transportation to Hornbaek stops nearby and a bus to Helsingør is available from Hornbaek.

The campground is well signposted so finding it isn't a problem. Follow the shoreside Highway 237 northwest from Helsingør. At ten kilometers you'll see a sign to the left for Saunte and the campground in one and a half kilometer. If you miss this turn continue to follow Highway 237 on in to Hornbaek and from there take the Saunte road to the left and follow it for about one kilometer to the campground. Both routes are well signed.

Side Trips from Hornbaek

Kronborg Castle in **Helsingør,** about 12 kilometers southeast of Hornbæk, was used by Shakespeare as the model for his Elsinore in Hamlet. Kronborg was really built in the sixteenth century and isn't nearly old enough to really have been Elsinore. It was built to help enforce the taking of tolls from ships passing through the sound between Sweden and Denmark. You'll want to tour it and see the dining hall and dungeons. Also consider visiting **Marienlyst Slot**, a French-style chateau also built in the sixteenth century and located about a kilometer north of Helsingør.

A few kilometers west along the coast from Hornbaek is **Gilleleje**, a fishing village famous as the place where Søren Kirkegaard pondered his philosophy while walking the paths through the dunes. You can do the same, the paths are still there.

KALMAR, SWEDEN

Population 57,000

Probably best known for its picturesque castle, **Kalmar Slott** and its museum, Kalmar is also the landfall for the long bridge from the island of **Öland** with its many holiday

SWEDEN'S KALMAR SLOT

campgrounds and the ruins of Borgholm Castle and Gråborg Fortress. Also in Kalmar is the **Kronan Exhibition** with artifacts recovered in the 1980's from the seventeenth-century warship called the Kronan. There is a large yacht harbor and a modern harbor-side mall with groceries and almost everything else. The town itself is just through the gates across the street from the mall and has pedestrian streets with restaurants and shops.

Kalmar Campground

✦ STENSÖ CAMPING

Address: Stensö Kalmar, S-39244 Kalmar
Telephone: 0480 88803 Fax: 0480 86086
Price: Moderate

Open April 1 to October 27

Stensö Camping is actually located on a small island on the outskirts of Kalmar. The sites are not arranged to take advantage of the seaside location, they are scattered over the interior of the island. Sites with electrical service are numbered and arranged on flat grass-covered areas. Other sites are scattered throughout the campground. Providing you can find a flat site you'll probably be quite happy on one of these because campers are not crowded together. The shower/toilet buildings are very rustic-looking from the outside but clean and modern inside. There's plenty of hot water provided for adjustable showers, bathroom basins and dishwashing sinks. Hot plates are located in the dishwashing room and there is a laundry area with coin-operated machines. The campground has a grocery store and restaurant, miniature golf and a nice beach area. It also has a monster croquet field.

Access to Kalmar from the campground is easy. You can drive in to town, parking facilities are convenient and adequate. Bus service from just outside the campground is frequent. You can bike or walk to town, the distance is about 3 kilometers on quiet streets.

The campground is located on the shoreline west of town. From Highway E22 watch for signs for the hospital (Sjukhus) which is near the campground. You'll start seeing camping signs by the time you reach the hospital area, if not before.

Side Trips from Kalmar

Småland, often nicknamed the **"Kingdom of Crystal"** is just west of Kalmar. Between Kalmar and Växjö, a distance of 110 kilometers, you'll find some 15 glassworks. They are small places with familiar names like Orrefors and Kosta Boda. Many are set up for visitors with catwalks above the working floor to let you watch the work in progress and stores selling almost perfect but inexpensive "seconds". Växjö's **Småland Museum** has a great collection of glassware.

KARLSKRONA, SWEDEN

Population 60,000

Karlskrona is a funny mixture, half navy town and half tourist Mecca. The town is spread over a series of rocky islands connected by bridges. Founded in the seventeenth century to be the home of Sweden's Baltic fleet, the town is considered a fine example of town planning. The Admiralty Church is the largest wooden church in Sweden. Karlskrona continues to have a navy presence. Yachtsmen and campers, however, also wander the streets and fill the bars and restaurants, especially during June, July, and August.

Karlskrona Campground

✦ DRAGSÖ BADOCH CAMPINGPLATS

Address: Box 205, S-37124 Karlskrona
Telephone: 0455 15354   Fax: 0455 15277
Price: Moderate

Open May 1 to August 31

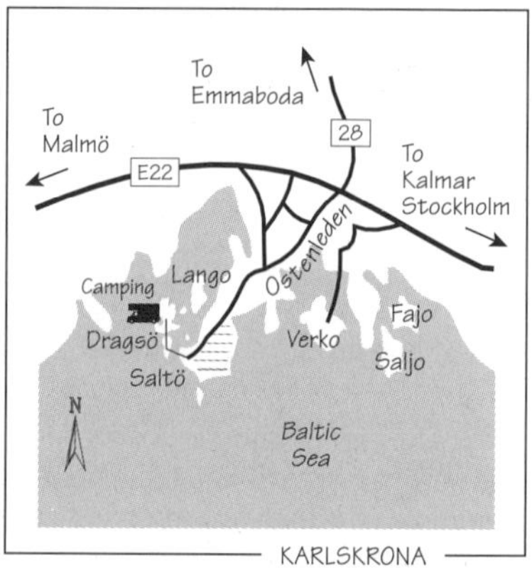

Located on its own island a short distance from the town of Karlskrona this campground is extremely popular during the Swedish summer holidays. You may find it easier to cope with the crowds if you visit during June or towards the end of August.

The camp sites are arranged along the shore of the island with the center reserved for a wooded area that contains trails and a few rental cabins. Sites are dirt or grass, numbered, and the tents and rigs are really packed together. Shower/toilet facilities are almost inadequate for the numerical pressure during high season. There's one larger building and several smaller ones scattered around the campground. Showers are coin-operated but hot water is not always forthcoming, check with someone coming out of the shower room before paying your money, unless you like cold showers. Bathroom basins and dishwashing sinks are cold water also. A laundry is available, coin-operated of course. There's a store and small restaurant. Two beach areas provide places to sun or swim.

The walk into central Karlskrona is about three kilometers, you cross another island en route and have views along the way of islands, water, and boats. Bikes work good as the roads aren't too busy.

To reach the campground you must actually drive through Karlskrona. From any direction follow signs to Karlskrona, then Saltö. Drive on across these two islands following campground signs for Dragsö. The streets are plenty wide enough for large rigs.

KARLSTAD, SWEDEN

Population 76,000

The rural town of Karlstad is located near the north shore of huge Lake Vänern on the delta of the Klarälvan River. This is the heart of Sweden's Värmland province. It is a great place to kick back and relax after visits to the more hectic urban attractions of Stockholm or Oslo. While the surrounding countryside lacks much in the way of "must see" sights or theme parks there are lots of more natural pursuits: hiking, fishing, rafting and canoeing, or just lying on the beach in the sun.

Karlstad is home to the **Emigrant Registry (Emigrant Registret)** which has information allowing North American emigrants from Sweden to trace their ancestry.

Karlstad Campground

✦ SKUTBERGS CAMPING

Address: S-65346 Karlstad
Telephone: 054 535139 Fax: 054 535170
Price: Moderate

Open all year

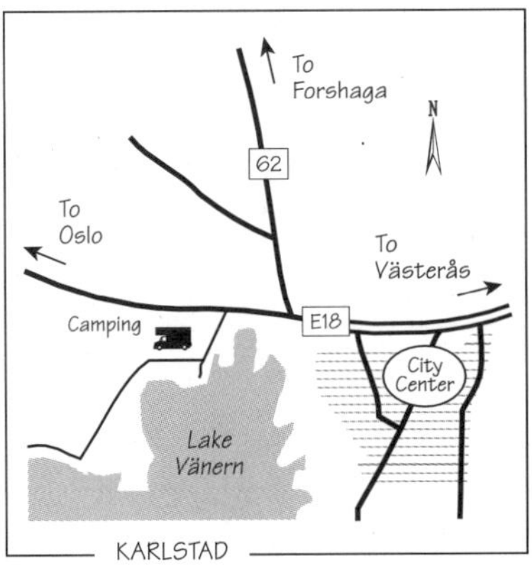

This very large holiday campground occupies a large flat field about a hundred meters from the shores of Lake Vänern. Karlstad, about eight kilometers distant by bus or bike trail is a good place to shop for supplies. The lake has good swimming beaches and cross-country ski trails cut through the nearby woods providing beautiful routes for walking. Skutbergets

Camping is one of two large campgrounds in the same area.

Most sites have electricity (10 amps), all are grass-covered and numbered. The reception office assigns each visitor a site. The shower/toilet buildings are clean, showers are in cubicles. Showers are metered but dishwashing areas have free hot water and cooking surfaces. A coin-operated laundry has several machines. There is a grocery shop at the reception building. Nearby you'll find the beach, a water slide area, hiking trails, and even a lake-side restaurant.

A good paved bike trail towards Karlstad will take you to a shopping center within four kilometers and the town in about eight kilometers. There is also bus service into town from the swimming beach area.

To find the campground follow Highway E18 west from Karlstad. After six kilometers or so you'll see camp signs pointing to the exit, follow them and then the sign for Skutbergs Camping.

KRISTIANSAND, NORWAY

Population 66,000

Kristiansand is another gateway to Norway. Ferries dock here from England and Denmark. This is a Norwegian beach resort area so campgrounds aren't hard to find, but they are very busy during July. Kristiansand is a town, like Bergen, that has a Bobilparkering motorhome camping area in a paved lot on the waterfront but we prefer Roligheden Camping, also conveniently near town.

As the largest town in far southern Norway Kristiansand is a popular destination for vacationing Norwegians seeking the sun. A facility designed to cater to these visitors is **Kristiansand Dyrepark**. Located eleven kilometers east of town it is really five parks in one: a water park, a forest park, an entertainment park, a zoo, and Cardamom Town modeled from a book by Swedish writer Thorbjørn Egner.

Other popular destinations are **Baneheia recreation area**, a park with lakes and walking paths just north of town and **Vest-Agder Fylkesmuseum**, an open-air folk museum.

Kristiansand Campground

✦ ROLIGHEDEN CAMPING

Address: Mauksveen 100, N-4601 Kristiansand
Telephone: 038 096722
Price: Moderate

Open June 1 to September 15

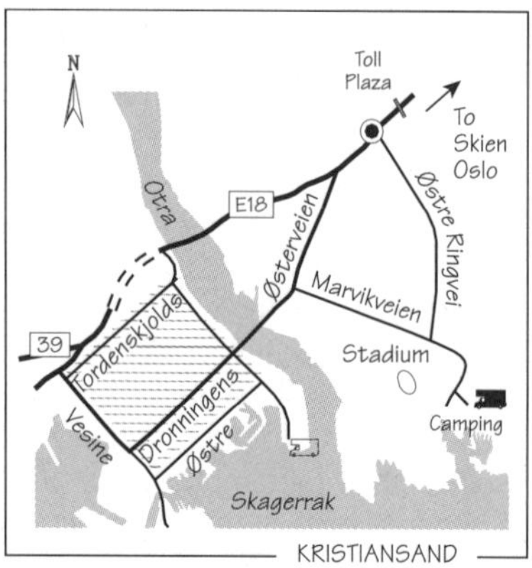

Roligheden Camping is set in a group of rounded rocks behind a yacht harbor and swimming area about two kilometers east of central Kristiansand. Grassy glades provide places to camp, all with electrical outlets widely spaced.

The undeveloped rocky areas give the campground a feeling of openness even when it is full. Shower/toilet facilities are modern. Showers require a token, dishwashing sinks have cold water only although bathroom basins have hot water. There is a grocery store, a restaurant overlooking the yacht harbor, and a good salt water swimming area with a small beach between the rocks.

The walk in to town is quite easy, no more than three kilometers. Alternately, a bus stop is located just outside the back gate of the campground with frequent service in to town.

The easiest way to find the campground is to follow Highway E18 east from town. After it crosses the Otra River you'll soon see campground signs pointing right toward the ocean. Alternately, if you follow Dronningens Gate east from town you'll also find signs to the campground.

MALMÖ, SWEDEN

Population 233,000

Malmö sits directly across the Öresund from Copenhagen, you can easily see Denmark. A long waterfront with ferry terminal and parks stretches between the central area of the town and the campground, some 12 kilometers south. The center of town is very attractive, historic and modern at the same time. It is surrounded by a canal and larger than you might expect, this is Sweden's third largest city.

Malmö Campground

✦ SIBBARPS CAMPING

Address: Strandgatan 101, S-21611 Malmö
Telephone: 040 155165 Fax: 040 159777
Price: Moderate

Open all year

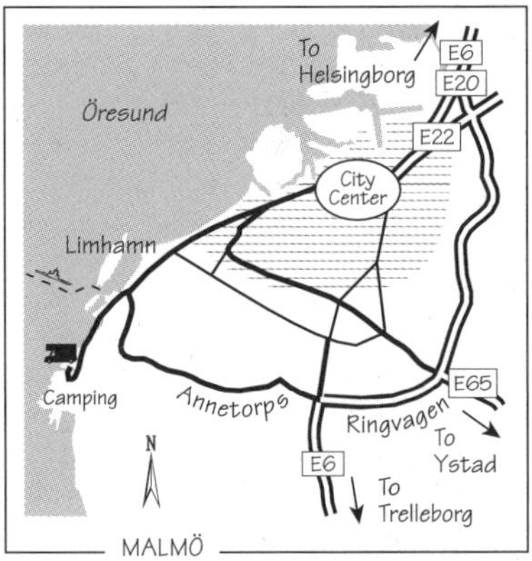

Sibbarps Camping is a large campground located next to the sea about 12 kilometers south of central Malmö. The grounds are grassy fields separated into glades by a few strips of trees with paved circular driveways . Like many Scandinavian campgrounds the electrical sites are numbered and assigned while those without services are not numbered and campers plunk down where they wish. Shower/toilet facilities are in large buildings near the reception area, there is hot water for showers and bathroom basins. Dishwashing sinks and hot plates are in a room together. The campground also has a grocery shop, restaurant, and miniature golf. There's a nice little beach on a protected inlet next to the campground entrance for sunbathing and swimming. Tougher and more aggressive swimmers can use the swimming piers on the open water north of the inlet.

Access to Malmö is by bus from just outside the campsite. The 8 kilometers to town makes a pleasant bike ride with trails and sidewalks most of the distance.

The best way to find the campground is to keep in mind that it is on the waterfront just about two kilometers south of the ferry terminal at Limhamn. The ring road around Malmö can be confusing but if you follow the ferry signs you'll eventually start seeing camping signs too. If all else fails just follow the shoreline south from Malmö center.

ODENSE, DENMARK

Population 175,000

Denmark's third largest city is Odense, main city of the island of Funen. Odense is best known today as the birthplace of Hans Christian Anderson. Anderson, author of many well-known fairy tales (including the one about the Little Mermaid), is the focus of most tourist interest in the city, you can visit the **Hans Christian Anderson Museum** and the **Hans Christian Anderson Childhood Home**. There is also a good outdoor museum, **Funen Village**, south of town. Odense has a gothic cathedral built in 1300 **(St. Canute's Cathedral)** and also a castle **(Odense Castle)**. This is a quiet city and a good place to stop on your way east to Copenhagen and the rest of Scandinavia.

Odense Campground

✦ DCU CAMPING ODENSE

Address: Odensevej 102, DK-5260 Odense
Telephone: 066 114702 Fax: 065 917343
Price: Moderate

Open April 1 to October 26

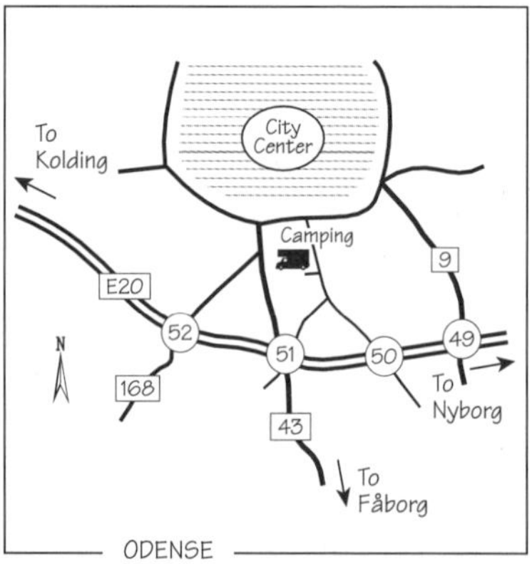

A large campground and very popular, in season you won't want to arrive too late or you might not find a spot. The campground has two types of site layouts. Sites with electricity tend to be the nicest with hedges separating and surrounding individual or groups of sites. There is also a large grassy field for those not needing electricity or for late arrivals. Small shower/toilet buildings are scattered around the campground, hot showers are not adjustable and require a token. Bathroom basins have hot water and a combination cooking and dishwashing area also has hot water along with hot plates. A central laundry area is equipped with coin-operated machines. There is a small grocery store.

Bus service to downtown Odense is good with a stop near the campground. The central part of town is within easy bicycle range.

To find the campground exit from Highway E20 at Exit 50. Drive north toward town and turn left into the campground entrance just after passing a Texaco service station.

OSLO, NORWAY

Population 460,000

Oslo sits at the north end of the Oslo Fjord surrounded by hills. It is a beautiful waterfront location, the fjord is an important part of the city's ambiance.

Karl Johns Gate, part pedestrian mall and part boulevard, defines the center of the city. It runs northwest from the Central Railway Station to the **Royal Palace (Slottet).** It is lined with restaurants and shops and is filled with strollers. Just a few blocks south of Karl Johans Gate is another place where people congregate, the waterfront with its docks and ferries and the brand new **Aker Brygge** development with offices, apartments, restaurants, and shops. From here you can catch ferries across the harbor to the Bygdøy peninsula and its unusual museums.

Near Karl Johans Gate to the east of the Royal Palace is the **National Gallery (Nasjonalgalleriet)** with a great collection of Scandinavian impressionists and an excellent collection of paintings by Edvard Munch. This is where his famous painting *The Scream* was stolen in 1984. If your interest is piqued by this display you'll want to catch the subway out to Tøyen Senter station and the **Munch Museum (Munchmuseet)** where there is a much larger collection.

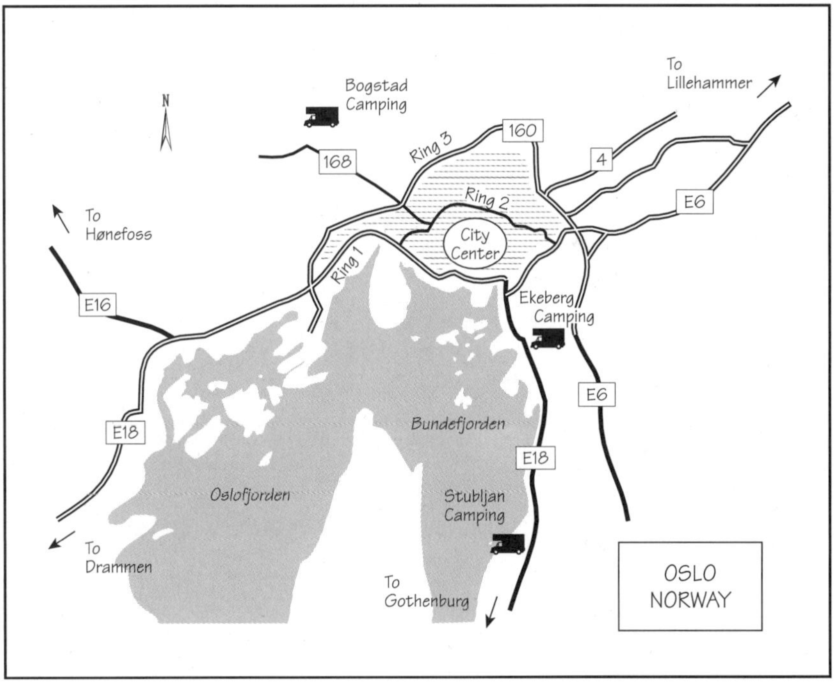

You'll also want to visit the **Frogner Park** with its fantastic **Vigeland Sculpture Park**. Gustav Vigeland spent his entire life filling the park with a controversial collection of huge sculptures. It is located northwest of the central area but is easy to reach by tram from the central city or by bus from the Munch Museum. Farther from town in the same direction and accessible by subway at the Holmenkollen station is the **Holmenkollen**, a huge ski jump offering a somewhat daunting view of the city and also an excellent ski museum.

The Bygdøy Peninsula has five museums clustered within walking distance of each other. These are the **Norwegian Folk Museum** with its own Stave Church, The **Viking Ship Museum**, the **Kon-Tiki Museum**, the **Fram Museum**, and the **Norwegian Maritime Museum**. You can get there by bus or by ferry.

Oslo Campgrounds

✦ **BOGSTAD CAMP AND TURISTSENTER**

Address: Ankervejen 117, N-0757 Oslo
Telephone: 022 507680 Fax: 022 500162
Price: Moderate

Open all year

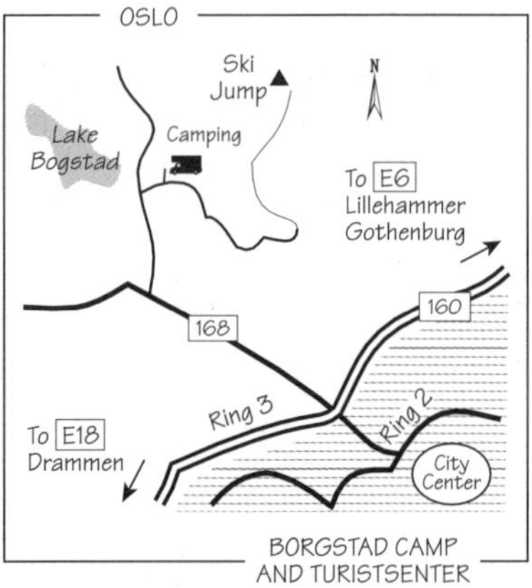

Bogstad is located about 9 kilometers north of downtown Oslo, much too far to walk but with excellent bus service. This is a large campground in an open field with few trees, there are both assigned electrical sites and unassigned sites without electricity. Shower/toilet buildings include a large building near the entrance with hot showers (adjustable), dishwashing and cooking facilities (hot water), and a coin-operated laundry. The grocery shop is actually at an Esso station in front of the campground and there's a restaurant in front also. There are great children's playground facilities and a swimming lake a short distance from the campground.

The bus downtown (32) stops at the campground entrance and will deliver you to the center of Oslo in about 20 minutes.

The campground is well signed from both Ring 3 and Ring 1 on the west side of town. Coming in to town from the south follow the signs taking you toward Drammen to the west. After passing the central area you'll see campground signs taking you north. From the west you'll see them before getting into the central part of town. From the north on E6 turn right on the ring road and pass north of town toward the west until the campground signs appear.

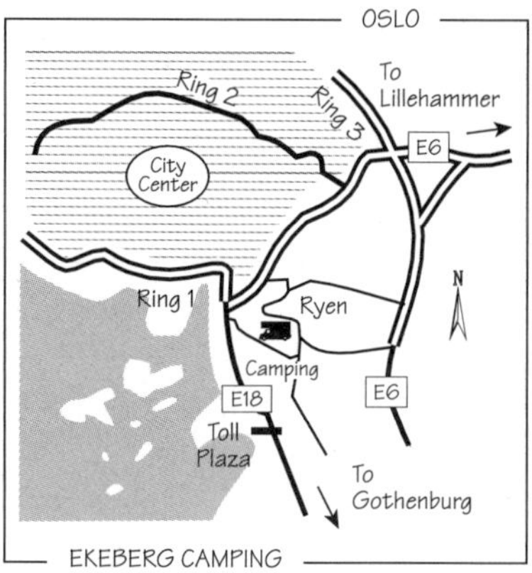

EKEBERG CAMPING

✦ EKEBERG CAMPING

Address: Ekebergveien 65, N-1181 Oslo
Telephone: 022 198568 Fax: 022 670436
Price: Moderate

Open June 1 to August 30

This is a large campground that sits on a high hill overlooking downtown Oslo. The campground is a large open grass field with little shade. There is no electricity available here. Camp sites are not numbered but when things are busy the staff will show you a spot to park. There is one very large modern shower/toilet building with showers (adjustable) and hot water in bathroom basins and dishwashing sinks. There is also a food-preparation area. The campground has a small grocery, a food kiosk, a video game area, and a post office.

Although this campground is within walking distance of downtown almost no one walks. The bus (number 24) is convenient and stops at the campground entrance. If you choose to walk downtown you can take a shortcut down the hill on trails, then follow a another trail along Ring I through the railroad yards. The distance is about 3.5 kilometers and the walk takes 45 minutes.

Finding the campground is easy if you follow the right route. From the south come in to town on E18 along the water. After passing the toll booths you'll see the campground signs pointing off to the right. From other directions proceed toward E6 on the east side of town, you'll see the campground signs just before E6 toward the south begins.

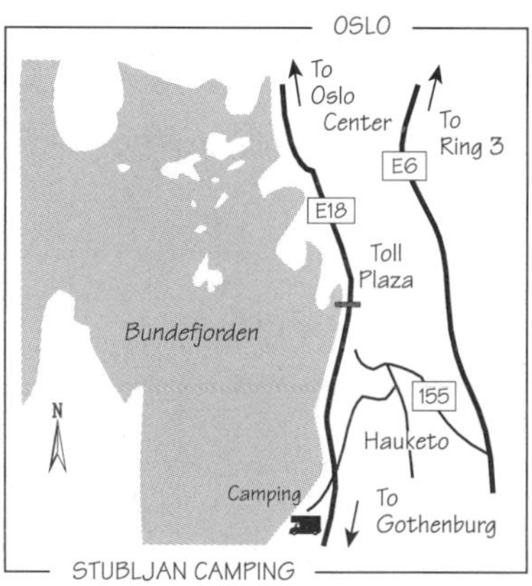

STUBLJAN CAMPING

✦ STUBLJAN CAMPING

Address: Ljabruvelen 1250, N-0112 Oslo
Telephone: 022 612706
Price: Moderate

Open May 15 to September 1

This is a medium-sized campground located near the Oslo Fjord some fifteen kilometers south of Oslo. Although not as convenient for visiting downtown Oslo as the other two campgrounds it is much quieter here and not nearly as crowded. The campground is located on a hillside with camping sites on sloping and flat grass. There are also some nice sites at the very top of the hill in a clearing. There is quite a bit of shade if you want it. Electrical plugs are well scattered. Electricity here is expensive so you'll probably want to find a way to do without. The shower/toilet building is older but in good repair and clean. Hot showers require a token but free hot water is provided for bathroom basins, dishwashing sinks, and clothes tubs. The reception desk has a few grocery items and there is a food kiosk nearby with things like hot dogs. Across the street is a park with swimming in the fjord and walking paths along the water.

There is hourly bus service to downtown Oslo, Bus 87 stops just across from the campground.

The campground is well signed from both E6 and E18 about 15 kilometers south of Oslo. It is just west of E18 and a cross road from E6 provides easy access from that freeway. It is outside the Oslo toll area so if you forgot to get currency at the border you can stay here to avoid a problem at the toll booth. The reception person can direct you to a shopping center with cash machines.

Side Trips from Oslo

Since the 1994 Winter Olympics **Lillehammer** has been a popular destination. The town is about 170 kilometers north of Oslo. In addition to the venues built for the games you will want to see the **Sandvig Collection at Maihuagen**, northern Europe's largest open-air museum which includes a stave church. The area also has lots of skiing in the winter and hiking trails in the summer. NAF STRANDA CAMPING is 11 kilometers south of Lillehammer on E6, it is open year-round.

STAVANGER, NORWAY

Population 100,000

As you drive north on the west coast of Norway the town of Stavanger is where you meet the fjords. From here you will constantly use tunnels and ferries with short stretches of road between them. While Stavanger has a long history as a fishing port today it is something of a boom town, making its living from the offshore oil patch and as a service center for island and fjord communities in the north. The central area near the harbor is attractive and bustling, it offers shopping and restaurants.

Stavanger Campground

✦ MOSVANGEN CAMPING

Address: Tjensvoll 1, N-4021 Stavanger
Telephone: 051 532971 Fax: 051 872055
Price: Moderate

Open May 24 to September 1

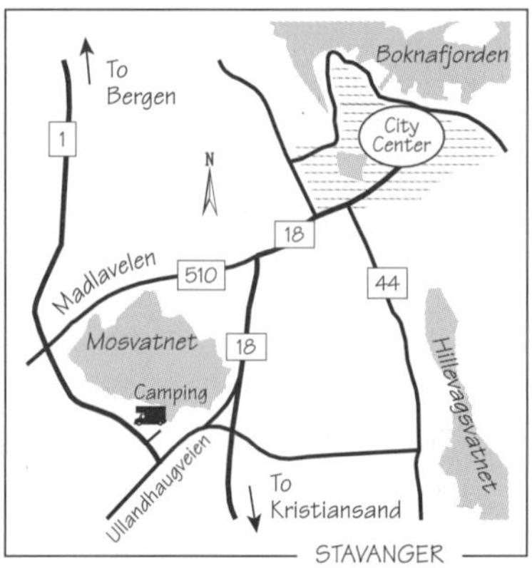

This is a medium-sized campground on a rolling meadow next to Mosvatnet Lake. Camping sites are not marked or numbered, electrical outlets are located in several areas. Quite a few trees give you a choice of sun or shade. The shower/toilet building has hot water with tokens required for the showers. There is only one dishwashing sink so you'll probably have to wait in line to use it. The campground has a children's play area and a dock on the lake but no swimming is allowed. A walking trail circles the lake. There is a small grocery store in the campground and a slightly larger one about 200 meters away.

Access to the central area of town from the campground is good. You can easily walk the 2.5 kilometers or you can take a bus, stops are located on two sides of the campground.

Both Highway 1 from the north and E18 from the south pass nearby, in fact they meet not far from the campground. You'll find campground signs on both.

Stockholm, Sweden

Population 1,535,000

Like the other Scandinavian capitals Stockholm is located next to the sea, in this case spread over mainland and islands at the outlet to Lake Mälaren. A huge archipelago of islands is scattered to the east towards Finland. There is a good public transportation system which includes subways, busses and boats. Much of your sightseeing can be done on foot but don't miss the chance to make some journeys by boat.

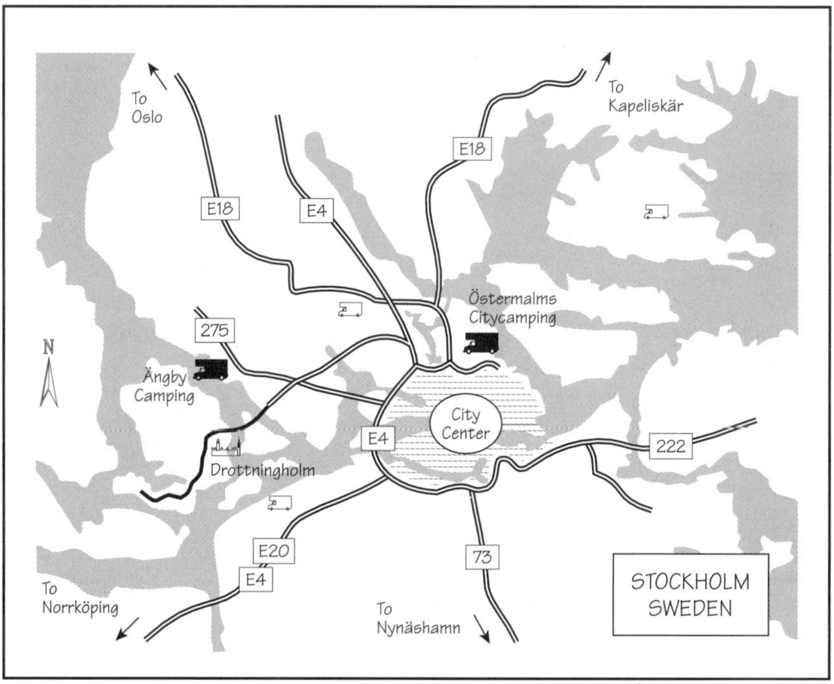

The center of the city is a modern square called **Sergels Torg**. Saving until later (if you have time) your exploration of modern Stockholm you'll want to walk directly south across the small **Holy Ghost Island (Helgeandsholmen)** with its **Parliament Building (Riksdagshuset)** to the **Old Town (Gamla Stan)**. Beyond the **Royal Palace (Kungliga Slottet)** are the **Great Square (Stortorget)** and small medieval streets full of boutiques, restaurants and people.

Directly east of Gamla Stan are both an island and a peninsula covered mostly by parks and filled with museums and recreational opportunities. Access is by bridges from the mainland, or by ferry. The first and smaller of the two is **Skeppsholmen** which has the **Museum of Far Eastern Antiquities** and is an excellent place for a relaxing stroll. Farther east and much larger is **Djurgården**. This is a good ferry destination, terminals are in Gamla Stan and in front of the Nybroplan on the main island. Djurgården has the **Vasa Museum**, the **Gröna Lund amusement park**, and the **Skansen open-air museum**. Skansen is said to be the world's first open-air museum, grandfather to those you've probably already toured in other countries.

For a fun water-borne excursion take the boat to Drottningholm Palace. This is a lake voyage, the boat departs from the mainland just west of Gamla Stan and crosses Mälaren lake in a 45-minute cruise to **Queen's Island Castle** (**Drottningholms Slott**). This palace has often been compared to Versailles, they were built during the same time but it is very much smaller. It is still the royal residence but much of the castle can be toured and the gardens and lakeside location are magnificent. The small court theater at Drottningholm is world famous, don't forget to take a look.

There are many other short boat trips available from Stockholm. For another lake trip take the steamer Mariefred to the town of **Mariefred**, an all day trip with the opportunity to tour **Gripsholm Castle**. For a trip through the **archipelago (Skägården)** take a ferry trip to Vaxholm, one hour each way. A longer trip is the ferry ride to **Sandhem**, an island community without automobiles but with lots of boats. Check with the ferry operators and local travel agents for other possibilities.

Stockholm Campgrounds

✦ ÖSTERMALMS CITYCAMPING

Address: Fiskartorpsv@gen 2,
S-11433 Stockholm
Telephone: 08 102903
Price: Moderate

Open approximately June 26 to August 20

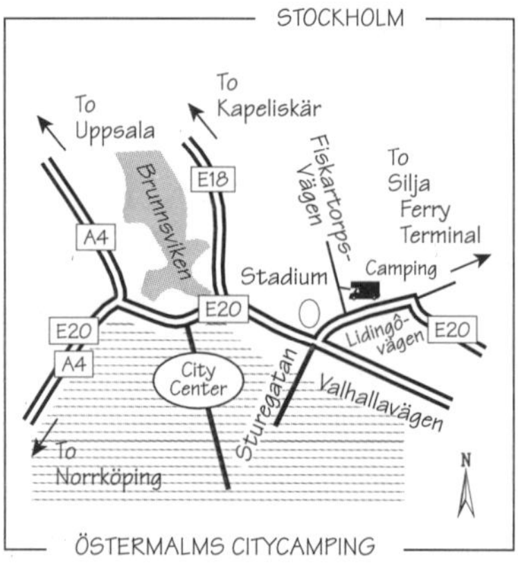

This campground has a great location and very poor ambiance. It is really just a large, unshaded gravel playing field in a sports stadium. On the other hand, it is only 1.5 kilometers from the city center and it is never full.

The campground is a large gravel field overlooked by bleachers. While it appears to be a parking lot it is actually used as a sports field and skating rink in the winter. Tenters have a grassy area with shade, their pitches are much more crowded than those for wheeled homes. There are just a few electrical hook-ups available. The sanitary facilities for the campground are located inside the bleachers, there are plenty of hot showers and bathroom basins with hot water. Dishwashing sinks and hot plates share a room. There is also a laundry room that must be reserved at the reception kiosk and a small snack bar with some grocery items.

To get downtown from the campground you can either use the subway which has a station about one-half kilometer from the campground or you can easily walk the 1.5 kilometers to the very center of the city.

To reach the campground follow signs for E20 as they wind their way through the streets north of the Stockholm central area. Your city map should clearly show the location of a stadium to the north of the downtown area. This stadium is near the one holding the campground. Watch carefully for camping signs, many are hard to see and are hand written since this is really just a temporary campground. Follow E20 as it takes a left onto Lidingovägen just after passing the stadium. Almost immediately (100 meters) turn left into Fiskartorpsvägen and follow it around the corner to the right where you'll find the campground entrance on your right. A bonus to this campground location is that it is very near to the terminal for the Silja Line ferries to Finland. You can easily spend the night here and be at the terminal at 7 AM the next morning for loading.

✦ ÄNGBY CAMPING

Address: Blackebergsvägen 24,
S-16850 Bromma
Telephone: 08 370420 Fax: 08 378226
Price: Moderate

Open all year

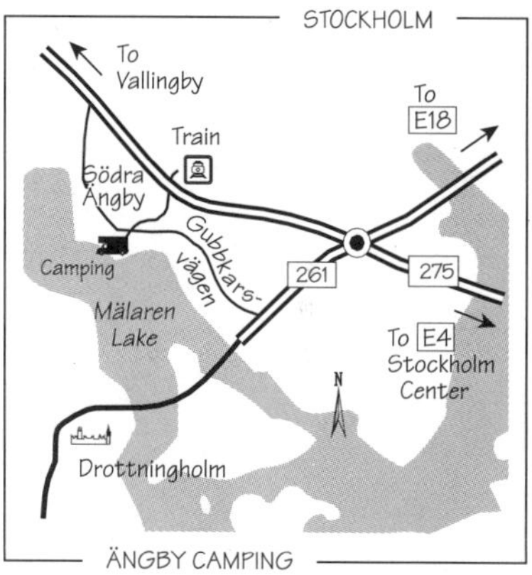

Ängby Camping is a more traditional campground than Östermalms Citycamping but it is more difficult to find a spot here, particularly if your rig is at all large. It is located in the suburb of Bromma near both Drottningholm Palace and the Ängbyplan subway station. You can walk or bike the three kilometers to the castle or be in downtown Stockholm in fifteen minutes on the train.

The campground is relatively large but often full during June, July and August with camping sites in two areas. You should aim for a weekday arrival and arrive early in the day. Those desiring a good flat spot with electricity are clustered close together near the reception building. Behind this area rises a rocky wooded hillside with several access roads. Tent campers pitch in the wooded area and there are some sites for wheeled vehicles along the roads. There are also cabins in this section. Two shower/toilet buildings are provided, they are clean and modern but hot water for any purpose requires a token. Cooking and laundry facilities are also available. The campground reception building has a TV room and some hot take-away food is sold. A small room full of electronic games will keep the children happy and there is a sauna. Next to the campground is a public swimming beach on Lake Mälaren which also has a large water slide. There is a small supermarket near the subway stop about one-half kilometer from the campground. This campground also has a dump station.

You can easily hike to Drottningholm Palace by following the lake shore from the swimming area to the left. After about one kilometer you'll see a bridge overhead. Climb to this bridge and cross it, you'll soon see the palace. Bikers should probably follow the street rather than taking the path as it is a little narrow.

To find the campground travel west on Highway 275 from Highway E4 where it runs north and south on the west side of Stockholm. You'll see a left for Drottningholm at a traffic circle after four kilometers and also a campground sign. After driving toward Drottningholm 1.5 kilometers turn right at a road just before a large bridge over an arm of lake Mälaren. There is a campground sign here also. You will see the campground on your left after 2.2 kilometers.

TURKU (ÅBO), FINLAND

Population 162,000

The town of Turku, or Åbo if you speak Swedish, is your likely point of arrival in Finland. The extremely scenic ferry route from Stockholm through the Stockholm Archipelago and the Åland Islands ends here. Central Turku lies on the banks of the Aura River giving it a pleasant open feeling and this is a university town so there is quite a bit of activity on the streets. Turku was Finland's capital until it was moved to Helsinki in 1812 so there are several worthwhile sites: **Turku Art Museum**, **Turku Castle**, and the **Cathedral** are good starters.

Turku Campground

✦ RUISSALO CAMPING

Address: FIN-20100 Turku
Telephone: 022 589249 Fax: 022 623255
Price: Moderate

Open June 1 to August 31

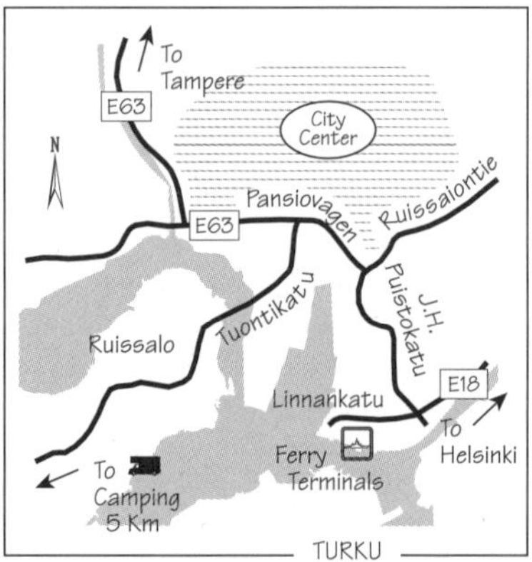

Ruissalo Camping is the place to stay while in Turku, you really have no other choice, but that's OK since this is a very nice campground. It is located about nine kilometers west of town on the Ruissalo Peninsula in a quiet park area with bike trails and beaches. Frequent bus service with a bus stop right in the campground makes it easy to visit Turku, although parking in town is easy if you would rather drive yourself.

The campground is large. The assigned electrical service sites are very nice with shade trees and well-spaced sites. Two large grassy fields for tenters have almost no shade but provide lots of room. Shower/toilet buildings are nothing special but do have hot water showers, bathroom basins, and dishwashing sinks. There are hot plates for cooking in some cubicles with their own sinks. The campground has a nice beach area and water slide and a small grocery. There is also a restaurant.

To find the campground from the ferry dock or town just follow the campground signs, they're everywhere. Incidentally, they're accustomed to late arrivals from the ferry so don't fret about finding an open campground when you arrive from Stockholm.

UPPSALA, SWEDEN

Population 160,000

Uppsala is Sweden's old university town, the University of Uppsala was founded in 1477. The town was the home of Carolus Linnæus, the father of modern biology and you can visit the **Linneträdgården** and see his home and gardens. **Old Uppsala (Gamla Uppsala)** is 5 kilometers north of town and was the Swedish Viking capital, the burial mounds there are known as the "Pyramids of Scandinavia"

Uppsala is located only 75 kilometers from Stockholm by good freeway. The town is full of life and is dominated by its huge **Cathedral (Domkyrka)**, old but restored many times and still very much in use. While the town is far from the sea there is actually boat service between Uppsala and Stockholm, the small **waterfront area** is a good place to spend some time.

Uppsala Campground

✦ FYRISHOV CAMPING

Address: Box 16045, S-75016 Uppsala
Telephone: 018 274960 Fax: 018 248314
Price: Moderate

Open all year

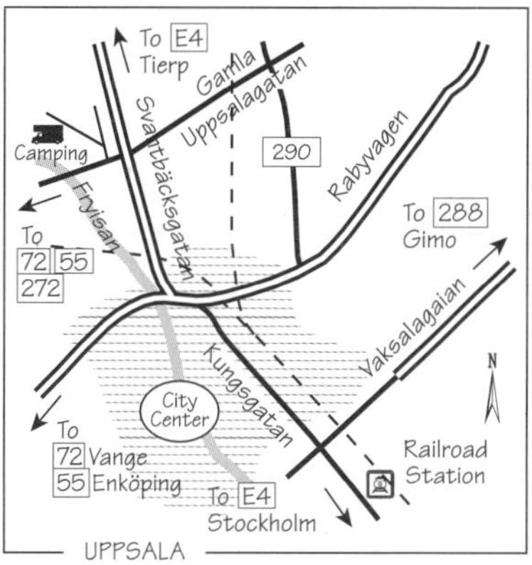

Fyrishov Camping is only one kilometer north of downtown Uppsala, and an easy walk. The campground is medium-sized and relatively new. Camping is on grass. Electrical sites are numbered and assigned, others are not. There are also lots of rental cabins. The shower/toilet building is modern with good showers that are metered. There is free hot water for bathroom basins and dishes however, and hot plates for cooking. There is also mini-golf and a good playground area. The reception office has a few grocery items. Next door to the campground is a large swimming complex and restaurant.

To reach the campground drive north from the railway station near the center of town on Kungsgatan. Follow camping signs through a jog to the left onto Svartbäcksgatan and then turn left on Gamla Uppsalagatan, the campground is a short distance down this road.

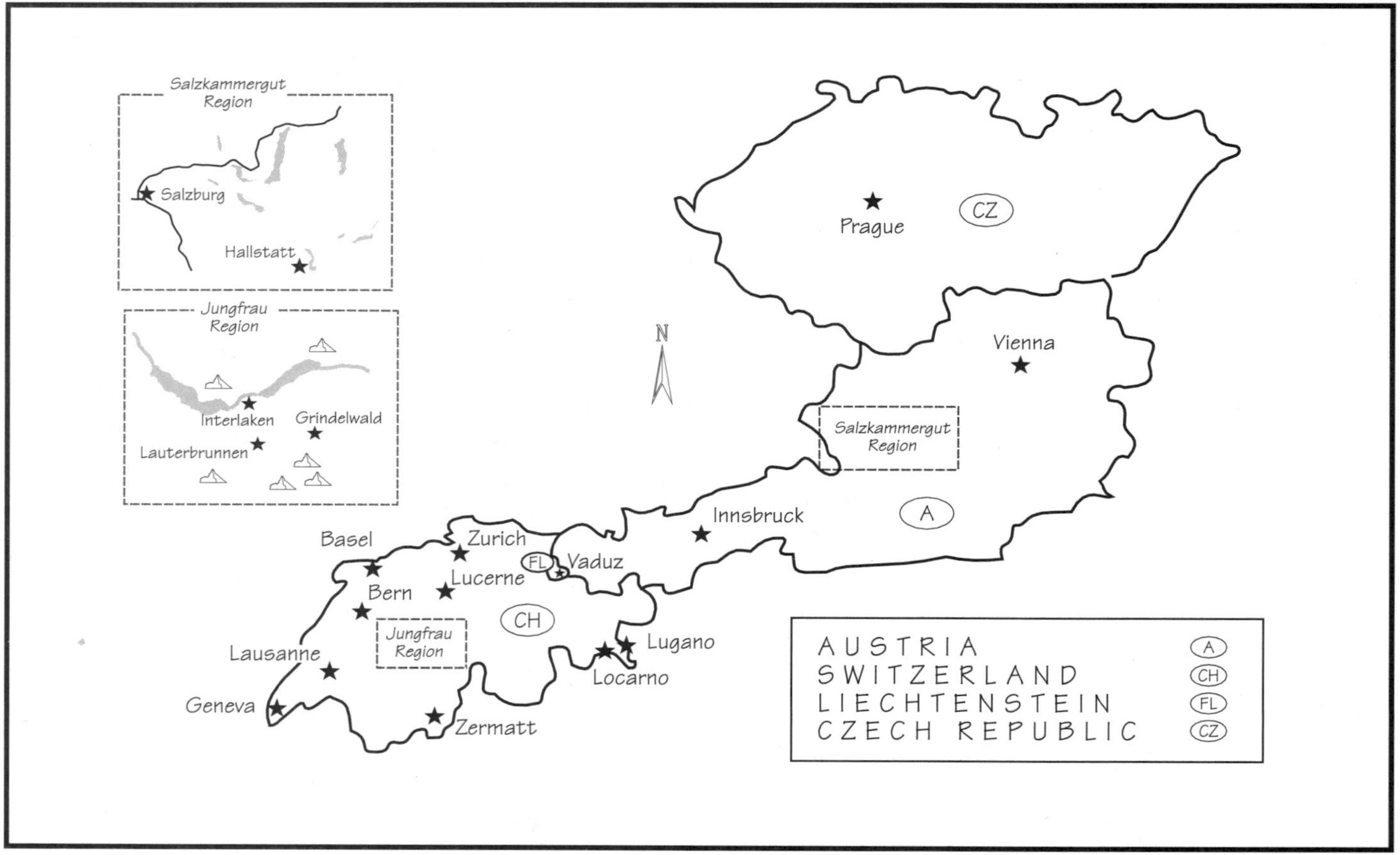
Salzkammergut Region
Salzburg
Hallstatt
Jungfrau Region
Interlaken
Grindelwald
Lauterbrunnen
N
Prague
CZ
Vienna
Salzkammergut Region
A
Innsbruck
Basel
Zurich
FL
Vaduz
Lucerne
Bern
CH
Jungfrau Region
Lausanne
Lugano
Locarno
Geneva
Zermatt
AUSTRIA A
SWITZERLAND CH
LIECHTENSTEIN FL
CZECH REPUBLIC CZ

CHAPTER

. . . . 12

SWITZERLAND, AUSTRIA AND THE CZECH REPUBLIC

INTRODUCTION

We've included Switzerland and Austria in the same chapter in the interests of convenience. In addition to being located next to each other the countries do have similarities: they are both mountainous, they are about the same size, they both have large German-speaking areas. They also have large differences: Switzerland's independence and neutrality, Austria's Austro-Hungarian Empire history.

Prague is included in this chapter only because it fits here better than anywhere else. Prague has become an important destination and is easy to visit, it would be a shame to leave the city out.

Roads and Driving

Switzerland has an excellent freeway system. This is a toll system but tolls are not collected at booths. Instead you pay an annual fee and receive a sticker that must be placed on you windshield. All users must have the sticker, even visitors. Theoretically you can buy the sticker at border crossings but this is not always possible since there are often no longer kiosks at Swiss borders. Try the gas stations near the border crossing. If you can't find a place to buy your sticker at the border just go to a post office, and stay off the freeways until you do. The cost of the sticker at publication is 40 Swiss Francs, the fine for not having one on a freeway is 100 Swiss Francs and you must also buy the sticker. A separate sticker is required for a trailer. There are additional tolls in some of the big tunnels.

Swiss secondary roads are good, but the mountains sometimes make driving a challenge. You can run into snow and ice at almost any time of the year. Many high mountain passes are closed to vehicles pulling trailers. There is always an alternative route, often a tunnel or rail shuttle service where your vehicle is actually placed on a flatcar for a short train ride. When driving in the mountains remember to pull off to let faster traffic pass. On narrow roads uphill traffic has the right-of-way over downhill traffic.

Austria has several excellent autobahns. The country has recently initiated a fee system like that in Switzerland using windshield stickers. Stickers can be purchased for 10 days or two months. There's a special two-month, two-trip ticket (called a Kombi) that can be used to transit the country on important trans-Europe routes like the Brenner Pass. Buy tickets at border crossings, gas stations near border crossings, and post offices, just as in Switzerland. Austrian roads, both autobahns and secondary, are well maintained but the mountainous character of the country means that many have steep grades with high passes and tunnels. The most famous of the high passes is the Grossglockner Alpine Toll Road (Grossglockner Hochalpenstrasse) running south to cross the high Alps from near Zell about 150 kilometers east of Innsbruck.

Roads in the Czech Republic are best characterized as adequate. Your drive to Prague from either Germany or Austria will be on a two-lane road and you will share it with many trucks, mostly slow moving. Just take it easy and enjoy yourself.

The AAA-affiliated automobile club in Switzerland is Automobile Club de Suisse (ACA) at 031 3283111. The telephone number for emergency road service is 140, there is a charge. The number for the police is 117. In Austria the AAA affiliated auto club is Österreichischer Automobil-, Motorrad- Und Touring Club (ÖAMTC) at 01 711990. The number for emergency service is 120 and the police emergency number is 133. In the Czech Republic the AAA-affiliated auto club is the Ustredni Automotoklub CR (UAMK;CR) at 02 6110433. The emergency road service phone number is 0123. The emergency police number is 158.

Camping

Campgrounds in Austria and Switzerland are excellent. Standards of cleanliness and quality of the improvements both tend to be very good. The campgrounds in Prague vary quite a bit in quality but on the whole are good

Swiss campgrounds use a electrical plug type that is entirely different than any other country. It has three prongs set on a diamond-shaped base. You should probably wait until you reach Switzerland to try to find one, most campgrounds and hardware stores can provide a compact adapter.

Free camping in Switzerland and Austria is generally allowed as long as you don't set up camping equipment outside the vehicle. In other words, be discrete. Some localities do, however, not allow free camping so you should check. Make sure to get permission if you camp on private property. Do not free camp in the Czech Republic, it is prohibited and fines are levied.

The Camping Card International is not required in these countries but often will get you a discount at the campgrounds.

Shopping, Currency, Credit Cards and Fuel

Prices in both Switzerland and Austria are extremely high, both of these countries, especially Switzerland, have strong currencies. In fact, we think that Switzerland is prohibitively expensive for travel if you aren't staying in campgrounds and cooking your own food. The Czech Republic, on the other hand, is one of Europe's bargain destinations. Prices are as low or lower than in the U.S.

In Switzerland many gas stations are closed on weekends. Many have automatic dispensers that can be used while they are closed. Some accept credit cards and many accept Swiss ten and twenty franc notes.

The credit card situation in Austria, Switzerland and the Czech Republic is much like Germany and France. They are widely accepted and cash machines are easy to find.

Itinerary Ideas

Like much of Europe, Switzerland fills up with vacationing Europeans in July and especially August. The shoulder seasons are best, May and June in the spring and September and October in the fall. October mountain camping can be wonderful if you are equipped to stay warm at night as the temperature dips into the high 30's and low 40's (Fahrenheit). Follow the general European rule and save July and August for your visits to the cities, plan to arrive early at campgrounds or make reservations.

All areas of these countries make excellent destinations. One of Austria's claims to fame is music, you'll want to visit both Vienna and Salzburg. Switzerland is synonymous with Alps, if the weather is good you want to be climbing one. The two regions discussed in detail in this chapter, Austria's Salzkammergut and Switzerland's Jungfrau, are outstanding in every way, don't miss them.

For information before you go about Switzerland contact **Switzerland Tourism, 608 Fifth Ave., New York, NY 10020 (212 757-5944).** Austria information is available from the **Austrian National Tourist Office, P.O. Box 1142, New York, NY 10108-1142 (212 944-6880)**. Finally, Czech Republic information is available at the **Czech Tourist Authority, 1109 Madison Ave., New York, NY 10028 (212 288-0830)** or in Canada at **Czech Tourist Authority, Suite 715, The Exchange Tower, 130 King Street West, P.O. Box 198, Toronto, ON M5X 1A6 (416 367-3432)**. Our web site at www.rollinghomes.com has links to information sites about Switzerland, Austria, and the Czech Republic.

SWITZERLAND, AUSTRIA CZECH REPUBLIC DISTANCE TABLE

In Kilometers

Kms X .62 = Miles

	Aosta Italy	Baden-Baden Germany	Basel Switzerland	Berchtesgaden Germany	Bern Switzerland	Colmar France	Garmisch-Partenkirchen Germany	Geneva Switzerland	Grindelwald Switzerland	Hallstatt Austria	Innsbruck Austria	Interlaken Switzerland	Lausanne Switzerland	Lauterbrunnen Switzerland	Locarno Switzerland	Lucerne Switzerland	Lugano Switzerland	Prague Czech Republic	Salzburg Austria	Vaduz Liechtenstein	Vienna Austria	Zermatt Switzerland
Baden-Baden Germany	471																					
Basel Switzerland	307	164																				
Berchtesgaden Germany	692	472	566																			
Bern Switzerland	204	261	97	673																		
Colmar France	374	126	67	633	164																	
Garmisch-Partenkirchen Germany	593	374	364	200	428	376																
Geneva Switzerland	142	404	240	736	175	307	574															
Grindelwald Switzerland	275	339	170	659	71	237	459	215														
Hallstatt Austria	75	534	629	86	764	662	82	828	668													
Innsbruck Austria	533	417	379	159	54	422	60	577	446	222												
Interlaken Switzerland	255	314	150	639	51	217	439	195	20	648	426											
Lausanne Switzerland	143	339	175	685	91	242	544	60	145	748	506	125										
Lauterbrunnen Switzerland	267	326	162	651	63	229	451	207	16	660	438	12	137									
Locarno Switzerland	250	449	285	527	240	352	428	300	210	590	368	190	265	202								
Lucerne Switzerland	296	258	94	527	92	164	345	245	94	590	348	74	185	86	190							
Lugano Switzerland	237	464	300	486	255	367	387	335	225	549	327	205	300	217	38	203						
Prague Czech Republic	1038	567	772	394	872	693	453	1047	868	445	537	848	928	860	928	770	943					
Salzburg Austria	678	457	552	38	687	585	239	751	591	77	145	571	671	583	513	513	472	368				
Vaduz Liechtenstein	470	354	182	416	244	252	215	374	243	399	257	223	309	235	182	149	192	760	402			
Vienna Austria	973	752	856	333	991	580	562	1046	886	288	469	866	966	878	808	808	767	270	295	697		
Zermatt Switzerland	173	469	309	673	212	376	559	207	175	743	521	155	176	167	159	184	194	943	666	256	961	
Zurich Switzerland	348	255	83	475	125	150	293	275	150	538	294	130	210	142	210	52	225	718	461	99	765	225

SELECTED CITIES AND CAMPGROUNDS

BASEL, SWITZERLAND

Population 175,000

Basel is a large industrial town and trade center in the far north of Switzerland that is also an old university town. It shares borders with both Germany and France and sits on the Rhine river, you couldn't ask for a location with better business prospects. For tourists the old town (**Grossbasel**) on the south bank of the river with its sandstone buildings is the most rewarding place to visit. Basel has several museums, the city's **Fine Arts Museum (Kunstmuseum)** is considered to be a world-class museum. The sandstone **Münster** (now Protestant) was consecrated in 1019 and has both Gothic and Romanesque elements, it has been largely rebuilt over the years.

Basel Campground

✦ CAMPING WALDHORT

Address: Heideweg 16,
CH-4153 Basel-Reinach
Telephone: 061 7116429Fax: 061 7114833
Price: Moderate

Open March 15 to October 10

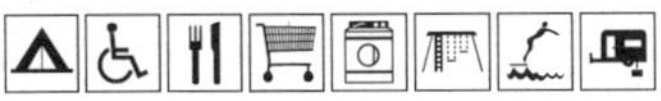

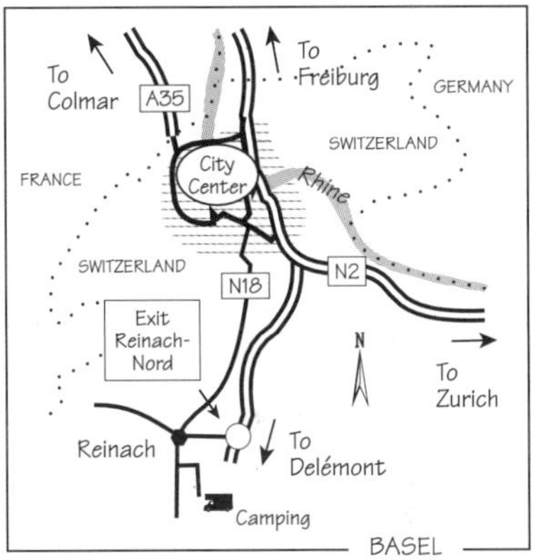

Camping Waldhort is a large campground located in a quiet area of Reinach, a suburb of Basel that is about 5 kilometers to the south of the central area of town. Trolley service into Basel makes this a convenient place to stay while visiting the city.

The campground is a large flat grassy field with small trees. There are many permanently-located caravans here but also quite a bit of room for tourist rigs. Electricity is convenient to the sites (CEE17 plugs, 6 amps). The showers have free hot water, other uses of hot water require payment. There is a grocery shop and a kiosk-style bar with terrace. The campground has a swimming pool and playground, as well as laundry facilities.

To located the campground follow the Delémont freeway and take the Reinach-Nord exit. Follow signs to Reinach/Aesch. They will take you about .6 kilometer west to N18 and then left or south on N18 for .7 kilometer. You'll see a camping sign here which will take you left onto small roads to the campground.

BERN (BERNE), SWITZERLAND

Population 141,000

Switzerland's capital city is unusual because it is one of the few Swiss cities that is not located next to a lake. It does have a river, however, the Aare. The river curves around the city, making the old town a peninsula. Bern is the Swiss capital and has the best-preserved historical city center in Switzerland. The central area's streets are lined with arcades and have many fountains. The city's mascot is the bear, and just across the Nydeggbrücke from the center of town are the **Bärengraben** (bear pits) where you can feed carrots to the bruin residents, they've been there since 1513. The town has several good museums including the **Swiss Postal Museum** covering the unusual Swiss postal system, the **Fine Arts Museum (Kuntsmuseum)** featuring the artist Paul Klee and others, and the **Swiss Alpine Museum**.

Bern Campground

✦ CAMPING TCS KAPPELENBRÜCKE

Address: Wohlenstrasse 62c,
CH-3032 Hinterkappelen, Bern
Telephone: 031 9011007Fax: 031 9012591
Price: Moderate

Open all year except early February

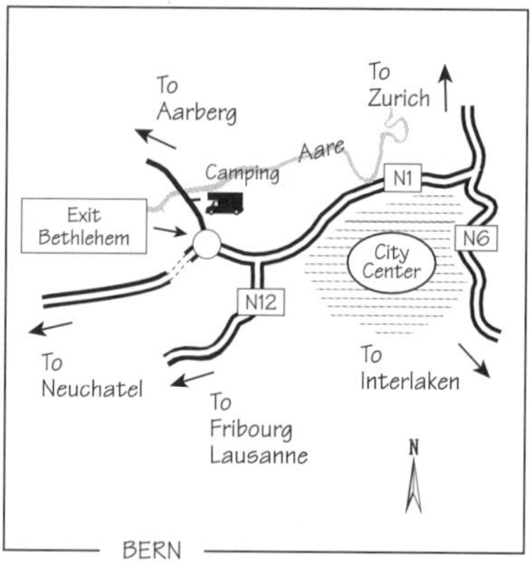

This is a large new campground located in a quiet area next to the Wohlensee inlet and near the Bremgartenwald (a forest park). While it is 6 kilometers from town there is good bus service.

Kappelenbrücke is a large campground with numbered but unseparated sites that are not usually assigned. Many sites are permanently occupied but there are large areas for tourist rigs. The sites are off gravel access drives and are grass surfaced. Electricity is from widely separated boxes (Swiss plugs, 3 amps). The shower/toilet buildings are new, heated, and quite nice. Showers (adjustable), bathroom basins, and dishwashing sinks all have hot water. There is a dump station. The campground has a grocery shop with outdoor bar, a TV room, a laundry room with coin-operated machines, a playground and a swimming pool. The outdoor terrace near the campground entrance and pool is popular, the campers here are a friendly group!

The bus to central Bern stops about 300 meters from the campground. The ride to town only takes about 10 minutes.

The campground is located on the west side of Bern. Take the Bethlehem exit from the N1 freeway and follow signs down the hill towards Aarberg. The campground is on the right just before the bridge.

GENEVA (GENÈVE), SWITZERLAND
Population 400,000

Geneva is a large bustling city that seems very French. The language, food, and culture reflect the fact that France surrounds this Swiss city which was in fact French until 1815. Roads in most directions, including east along the south shore of the lake lead to France. Geneva has an important role in religious history, it was sometimes called the Rome of the Protestants. John Calvin led Geneva to accept the reformation, you can see Calvin's Chair at **Saint Peter's Cathedral** or tour the **Church of Notre-Dame-la-Neuve** where he preached. While this large city has lots to offer in the way of museums and restaurants one of our favorite pastime is just walking the beautiful shores of Lake Geneva (Lac Léman) near its Rhône River outlet and the **Jet d'Eau** fountain.

Geneva Campground

✦ CAMPING POINTE A LA BISE

Address: Route d'Hermance, CH-1222 Vésenaz
Telephone: 022 7521296 Fax: 022 7523767
Price: Expensive

Open April 4 to October 25

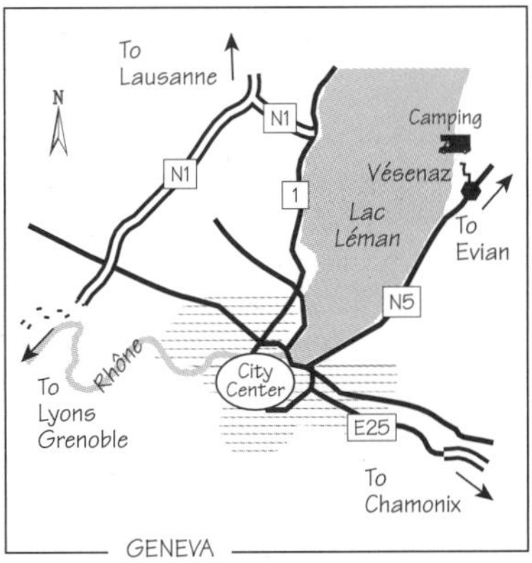

Camping PointeA la Bise has convenient bus service to central Geneva and also a quiet location on the east shore of Lake Geneva. It is a medium-sized campground with some permanent residents but also lots of room for tourists. The camp sites are on a large flat meadow next to the lake. Sites for tents are along the lake while wheeled campers occupy unmarked sites farther from the water. Electricity (low amps) is available to some sites. The shower/toilet building has free hot showers, cold water only in the bathroom basins, but hot water for washing dishes. There are also coin-operated machines for laundry. The campground has a small grocery shop and there is an off-site restaurant nearby. A shallow children's swimming pool is next to the lake shore and there is a playground. About 1 kilometer from the site in Vésenaz there is a supermarket.

The campground is about 7 kilometers from central Geneva. If you wish to ride your bicycle there is a good bike path along the water once you get back to the lake shore after leaving Vésenaz. Several busses service the campground, the stop is about a half kilometer up the hill toward Vésenaz.

Find the campground by driving along the east shore of Lake Geneva on N5 following signs for Evian. The road leaves the lake shore and climbs slightly into the village of Vésenaz, just after you pass a supermarket on the right and a traffic light you will see the campground sign pointing left. Follow the signs for another kilometer or so back down to the water and the campground on the shore.

Side Trips from Geneva

Geneva is only about 65 kilometers north of **Chamonix** and the Mont Blanc Tunnel. There's a **great cable car** there that will take you up over the glaciers near Mont Blanc and on into Italy. We've discussed this trip in more detail in our Aosta, Italy section.

INNSBRUCK, AUSTRIA

Population 117,000

Innsbruck straddles the most direct route from Germany to Italy, the Brenner Pass. From Innsbruck the freeway immediately begins its steep climb to the south, but Innsbruck is at a low altitude in the broad Inn Valley with peaks rising impressively all around. Don't be put off by the industrial appearance of the city from the autobahn, stop and look around. Innsbruck has a lot to offer and is a great central location for day trips into the surrounding Alps.

Most of the sights in Innsbruck itself are in the central **Old Town (Altstadt)** area. You'll want to see the **Olympic Museum's** famous **Golden Roof**, the **Imperial Palace (Hofburg)**, and the **Hofkirche** with Maximilian's mausoleum (he is actually buried near Vienna, against his wishes). You can also take the **Hungerburgbahn** funicular up the hillside to the north of town to see the **Alpine Zoo** or even higher to the lookouts at **Seegrube** or **Hafelekar**.

Innsbruck Campground

✦ CAMPING INNSBRUCK-KRANEBITTEN

Address: Kranebitten Allee 214,
A-6020 Innsbruck
Telephone: 0512 284180 Fax: 0512 284180
Cost: Moderate

Open April 1 to October 31

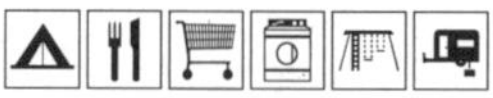

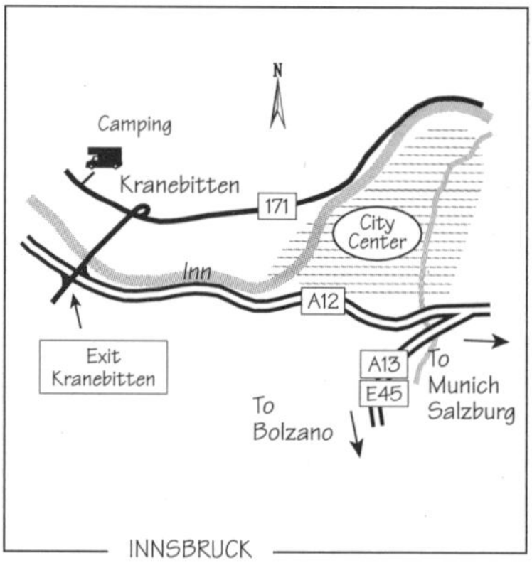

Kranebitten is a very small village just west of Innsbruck. The campground in the village is comfortable and provides good access to Innsbruck.

Camping Kranebitten is a medium-sized campground placed on a south facing hillside just above the Inn Valley. About half the campground is terraced to provide flat sites for four-wheeled vehicles and the other half slopes and has lots of shade, perfect for tents and trailers. All site surfaces are grass and are unnumbered and unassigned. Electrical outlets (CEE17 and German, 7 amps) are in large boxes on widely-spaced light poles. Shower/toilet facilities are in a building on one side of the campground, the building is older but in good repair and clean. Hot showers are free (mostly premixed with a foot-operated pressure valve), and there is also hot water in bathroom and dishwashing sinks. The laundry room with a coin-operated washer is located in the women's washroom. There is a nice restaurant and a kiosk-style grocery shop. There is also a large playground on the hillside just above the campground. You'll find a major shopping center 2 kilometers from the campground on the south side of the freeway, watch for the McDonald's arches.

Innsbruck is 4 kilometers to the east of the campground. There is a good bike route which runs along the road for 3 kilometers and then cuts over to the river. The stop for the most frequent bus route is a five minute walk from the campground, ask at the reception desk for directions.

From Highway A12 just west of Innsbruck near the airport take the Kranebitten exit and follow signs for Kranebitten and the campground. The distance from the freeway to the campground is only 1.5 kilometers.

Side Trips from Innsbruck

Schloss Ambras is just outside Innsbruck to the southeast and can actually be easily reached by bus from the city center. It is a popular castle dating from the 11th century and was rebuilt in the 16th century. You'll find an arms museum at the castle.

LAUSANNE, SWITZERLAND

Population 126,000

Lausanne is Switzerland's fifth largest city and has a hillside location above Lake Geneva. The museum to see here is the **Musée de l'Art Brut** with art by criminals and the insane (really). Lausanne also has two new museums worth a tour; the **Musée Olympique** and the **Musée Romain**. Both of these new museums are near the campground. The **Cathedral of Notre-Dame** dominates the town and is considered by many to be the finest Gothic structure in Switzerland.

Lausanne Campground

✦ CAMPING DE VIDY

Address: Chemin du Camping 3,
CH-1007 Lausanne
Telephone: 021 6242031 Fax: 021 6244160
Price: Moderate

Open all year

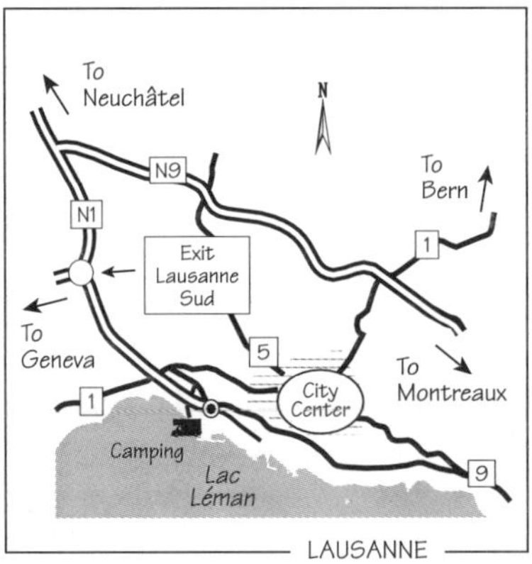

This is a large campground located next to the lake about 3 kilometers southwest of central Lausanne. It is quiet and well run, a pleasant place to stay while exploring Lausanne and the Swiss Riviera.

Camping de Vidy has about 450 campsites on a flat grassy field at the edge of Lake Geneva. The sites are numbered and assigned, electrical boxes are numerous and convenient (Swiss and CEE17 plugs, adapters available). There are some permanent rigs, perhaps 50, so most campers are tourists. The shower/toilet buildings are modern and clean, showers (premixed, push-button valve), bathroom basins, and dishwashing sinks all have free hot water. There is a laundry room with coin-operated machines. The campground has a grocery shop and a restaurant near the lake and also a dump station.

It is easy to walk into Lausanne. If you follow the lake shore and then walk up Avenue d'Ouchy from the port the hike takes about an hour and ten minutes, a more direct route up Av. de Montoie and Avenue de Tivoli takes 45 minutes. Alternately, Bus 2 stops about a half kilometer from the campground and runs along the lake shore and then up the hill to the train station.

To find the campground take the Lausanne-Sud exit from the N1 freeway. This stub freeway terminates in a very large traffic circle. There are campground signs from there. Take the third exit from the circle onto Rte de Chevannes and then turn left in about 100 meters. The campground is directly ahead.

Side Trips from Lausanne

Lausanne is a good base for touring the Swiss Riviera along the north shore of Lake Geneva with its vineyards and the **Château de Chillon** in Montreux, just 30 kilometers eastward along Lake Geneva's (Lac Léman's) north shore. The Château de Chillon was memorialized by Lord Byron in his poem *The Prisoner of Chillon*, it is now a national monument.

LOCARNO, SWITZERLAND

This town is included in our coverage of the Italian Lake District in Chapter 10.

LUCERNE (LUZERN), SWITZERLAND

Population 65,000

In direct contrast to nearby Zurich, Lucerne is undeniably a tourist town. There's lots to keep you occupied.

The old section of town with its pedestrian streets, shops, and restaurants is on the east side of the River Reuss, the outlet to Lake Lucerne (the Vierwaldstätter See) which is straddled by the town. The 14th-century **Chapel Bridge (Kapellbrücke)** across the river and adjoining **Water Tower (Wasserturm)** are popular attractions, the tower must be photographed since it is the city's premier landmark. Boats ply the lake and will take you almost anywhere, if you're interested in an effort-free view there's a cog railway up **Mt. Pilatus**. Near the campground is the **Swiss Transport Museum (Verkehrshaus)**, one of Switzerland's top tourist attractions.

Lucerne Campground

✦ **Camping Lido Lucerne**

Address: Lidostrasse 8, CH-6006 Luzern
Telephone: 041 3702146 Fax: 041 3702145
Price: Moderate

Open March 15 to October 31

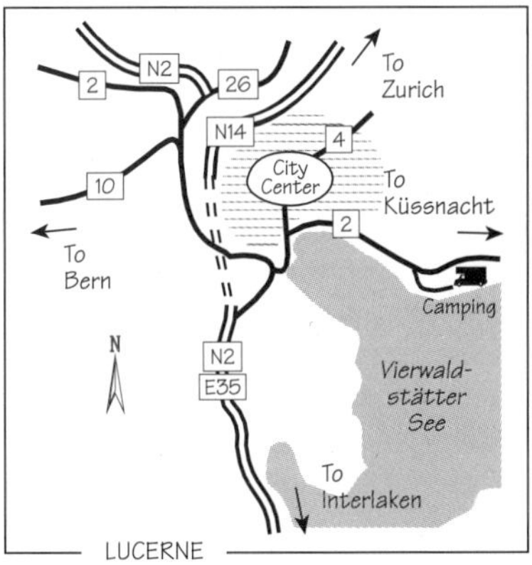

Camping Lido Lucerne is a large campground with a very good location for visitors to Lucerne. All sites are small without anything to separate them. Motorhomes and vans are parked in a separate area from trailers, and tents also have their own area. A warden will lead you to the proper area and usually let you choose your own site. Electricity (Swiss 3 pin, 10 amps) is metered, a 1 shilling piece buys you 2 kilowatt hours. The shower/toilet buildings can be heated during cooler weather, hot showers and hot water for dishwashing cost a half shilling while hot water in the bathroom basins is free. The campground has laundry facilities with coin-operated machines and a grocery kiosk with some take-away meals (broiled chickens). The Lido (beach) is across from the campground and the well-known Swiss Transport Museum is right next door.

Bus service to Lucerne is very good with busses at least every quarter of an hour from outside the campground. You can also easily walk the 1.5 kilometers along the lake in about 20 minutes. It is even possible to travel in to town by steamer from a dock nearby.

Find the campground by following the road that runs along the north shore of Lake Lucerne out of town to the east. The campground is well signed and is on the right after 1.5 kilometers. There's an access road that also serves the beach and transport museum.

Lugano, Switzerland

This town is included in our coverage of the Italian Lakes District in Chapter 10.

Prague (Praha), Czech Republic

Population 1,225,000

Prague represents the only real excursion into Eastern Europe in this book, if you don't count former East Germany. The city has become an extremely popular tourist destination. The attractions are many. There are excellent tourist facilities including hotels, restaurants and especially campgrounds. The city has not undergone the extremes of 20th-century development because it has been sheltered from the modern world behind the Iron Curtain. Prague is no high-rise city, the friendly scale and his-

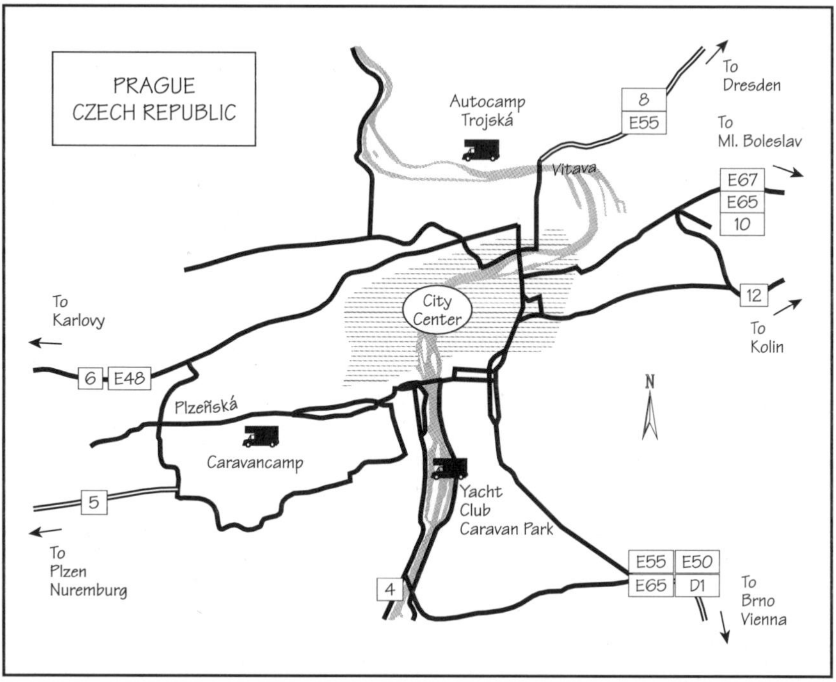

toric Gothic and Bohemian baroque facades along the city's streets make a visit a pleasure. Finally, the price is right. Even though prices are rising you'll find them much lower than in Western Europe. Add to all of this the fact that the Czech Republic is home to the world's best beer and it is no wonder that the city is popular.

Prague is bisected by the wandering Vltava River. On the west bank is Little Town (Mala Strana), the original settlement. Overlooking Little Town is the **Hradcany** (Prague) Castle where you'll find **St. Vitus Cathedral** and the **Royal Palace**. Below the castle is an outstanding example of Bohemian baroque architecture, the **Church of St. Nicholas**.

Across the **Charles Bridge** with its sidewalk vendors, street performers, and 30 18th-century statues is Old Town. This section of Prague centers around the Old Town Square which is surrounded by narrow medieval streets filled with shops and restaurants. In the square itself is the **Clock Tower** where you can watch the 16th-century mechanism toll the hour. This area of town is also home to the historic **Jewish Quarter (Joseph's Town)**, with its **Old Jewish Cemetery**.

Wenceslas Square (actually a boulevard) leads from the edge of the Old Town into the New Town, the bustling center of modern Prague. The square and streets off its lower end form a pedestrian shopping area and at the top of the square is the **National Museum** with a statue of St. Wenceslas overlooking the activities.

Prague has an excellent system of subways and trams so it is easy to get around. If you stick to the Old and Little towns you'll really only need the public transportation to travel from your campground. You'll also find that Prague has English-language movies with Czech subtitles.

Prague Campgrounds

✦ AUTOCAMP TROJSKÁ

Address: Trojská 157/375, CZ-17100 Praha 7
Telephone: 02 6886036 Fax: 02 5842945
Price: Moderate

Open November 1 to September 30

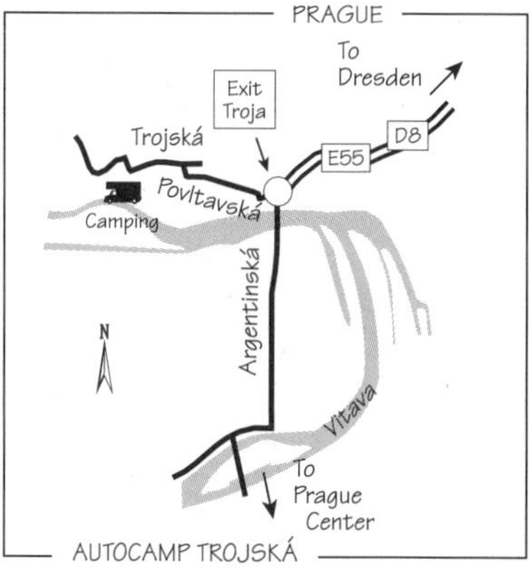

North of Prague, near the north bank of the Vltava where D8/E55 crosses, there is a cluster of small campgrounds. Many are situated behind residences under fruit trees. They make a good place to stay because they are pleasant and very convenient. Autocamp Trojská is one of the smallest, others include SOKOL TROJA, DANA TROJA and AUTOCAMP HAJEK.

CAMPING IN PRAGUE

Autocamp Trojská is a small campground with about fifteen spaces. The sites are on grass beneath apple and walnut trees, access to the campground is carefully monitored and sites are informally assigned. There are no resident rigs. Electricity (both CEE17 and German plugs, 10 amps) is available. The showers and toilets are clean, modern, more than adequate for the number of campers. Hot water is free and available to showers, shaving sinks, and dish and clothes washing areas. There are covered picnic areas and a limited snack bar and grocery shop. Bread and beer are both available.

Access to downtown Prague is extremely easy. You can either take the bus (number 112) which stops beside the campground driveway and runs to the north Metro station or you can walk about one-half kilometer and take the tram (number 5) directly in to town. The tram takes about 15 minutes and tickets are available at the campground reception desk. You'll find public transportation in Prague to be very reasonably priced, the tram tickets cost the equivalent of a U.S. quarter in each direction.

The campground is accessible from Highway D8/E55 north of town. If you've arrived from the direction of Dresden you'll probable be on this road already. If you're starting in Prague follow signs toward Teplice. From the highway take the exit for Troja and then proceed west, you'll soon see a number of campground signs. Take your pick.

✦ CARAVANCAMP MOTOL

Address: Pizeňská 279,
CZ-15000 Praha 5-Motol
Phone: 02 524714 Fax: 02 57215084
Price: Moderate

Open April 1 to October 31

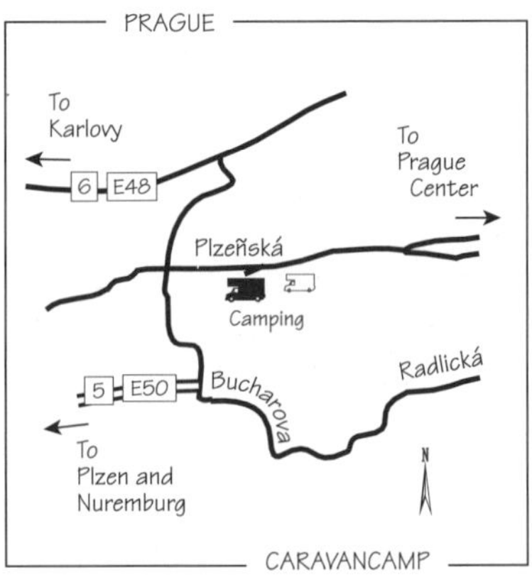

If you are approaching Prague from the west there are two conveniently located campgrounds. The two campgrounds are SPORTCAMP and Caravancamp. They are very similar and close together, we prefer the slightly larger and more conveniently located Caravancamp. The one major difference is that Sportcamp has rental bungalows while Caravancamp does not.

Caravancamp is a large campground in a grassy field located next to a major Prague arterial. Road noise is noticeable but not a big problem, especially later in the evening. Camping sites are on grass, they are not individually marked and campers choose their own sites. Electrical connections are widely spaced (German, 10 amps). The centrally-located services building contains everything: reception, washrooms, dishwashing, and restaurant. Showers have free hot water (adjustable), hot water is also available in the sinks. This campground also has a swimming pool and tennis and miniature golf are located nearby.

You can easily reach the Prague central area in about 15 minutes on tram 9 which stops just in front of the campground at a stop called Hotel Golf (the hotel overlooks the campground). Tickets are sold at the campground reception desk.

As you approach Prague from the west on 5/E50 you will find the sites well signed. Just as the freeway ends campground signs will take you on a 270 degree loop and send you north. After 1 kilometer take the off-ramp following signs for Centrum. This will put you on Plzeská heading east and in another 1.2 kilometer you'll see the campground on your right. The entrance is another 50 meters or so towards town.

✦ YACHT CLUB CARAVAN PARK

Address: Císarská Louka 599,
CZ-33333 Praha 5-Smíchov
Telephone: (02) 545925
Price: Inexpensive

Open all year

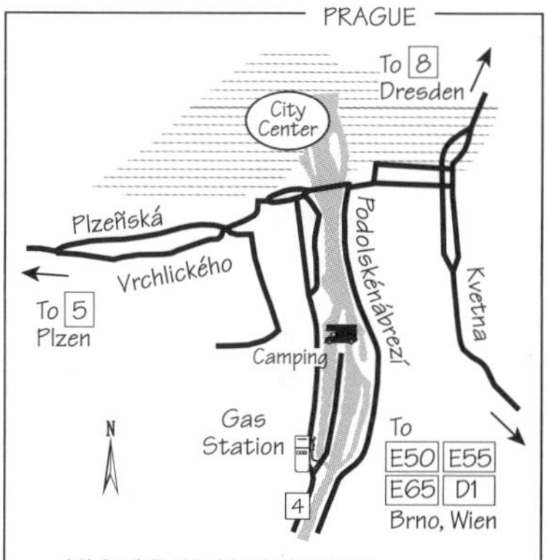

YACHT CLUB CARAVAN PARK

Císarská Louka is an island in the Vltava River that sits about three kilometers above the old town. There are two good campgrounds on the island, the Yacht Club Caravan Park is on the north end and has a great view of **Vysehrad**, the High Castle, on the right bank of the river. The quiet location is nice and a small private ferry giving easy access to the subway system makes it even better.

The campground is medium-sized and occupies a well-drained grass field next to the river. There are no permanently located rigs here. Camp sites are unmarked and electrical services (German, 10 amps) are far apart. The shower/toilet building is a prefab portable but is new and well maintained. It has hot water showers (10 crowns, adjustable), hot water in the bathroom sinks, hot water for dishwashing and a laundry room. There is a restaurant and nice clay-surfaced tennis courts. The campground also offers rental bungalows but they do not dominate the site. Sightseeing excursions on the river are offered.

The yacht club operates a small ferry that runs to the left bank every 30 minutes. The charge is 10 crowns, about 40 cents U.S. From the ferry landing it is a short five minute walk to the Smíchovské Nádrazi subway stop on the yellow metro line.

There is only one bridge onto the island. It is on the south end and can only be accessed from the northbound lanes of Highway 4 on the west or left bank of the river. You must watch carefully for the road to the bridge, it is marked but easy to miss if you are traveling too fast. About 1.2 kilometers after passing the large Barrandov Bridge interchange you'll see a gas station coming up on the right side. The island road is just before the station. Turn right, cross the small bridge, and follow a small paved road north past another campground on the right to the Yacht Club Campground at the end of the road.

Side Trips from Prague

Tours of the castles in the countryside surrounding Prague are very popular. You can do this in your own vehicle. Some of the most popular (in alphabetical order) are

Ceský Sternberk (45 kilometers southeast), **Hrad Karlstejn** (28 kilometers southwest), **Hrad Krivoklát** (45 kilometers west), **Konopiste** (45 kilometers southeast), **Nelahozeves** (30 kilometers north), and **Zbraslav** (15 kilometers south). Most have interesting exhibits.

The town of **Lidice** is 20 kilometers northwest of Prague. It is infamous because the Nazis razed the entire town in 1942 and either killed or shipped the inhabitants to concentration camps This was done as punishment for the assassination of Rheinard Heydrich, the Nazi official in charge of the so-called "final solution to the Jewish question". There is now a new village and a monument.

VADUZ, LIECHTENSTEIN

Population 5,000

Liechtenstein is a tiny country with an area of 61 square miles and a population of only about 30,000 people. The main administrative town is Vaduz, no corner of the country is really very far away. The countryside, customs and money are very Swiss. Believe it or not the river running through the valley here is our old friend the Rhine.

Unless you are planning to open a bank account (Liechtenstein is a financial center) you probably won't need a lot of time to look around. In Vaduz stamp collectors will enjoy the small **Postal Museum** and the art collection of the princes of Liechtenstein in the **Engländerhaus** including works by Dutch and Flemish painters.

Vaduz Campground

✦ CAMPING MITTAGSSPITZE

Address: Saga 29, FL-9495 Trieson
Telephone: 075 3922686 Fax: 075 3923680
Price: Moderate

Open all year

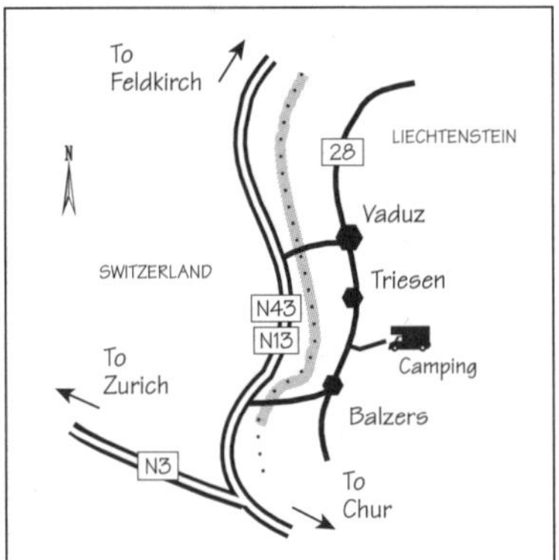

VADUZ

Camping Mittagsspitze is a medium-sized campground occupying a west-facing slope about 10 kilometers south of Vaduz. There are quite a few permanent rigs here, many with neat little cabins attached. Tourist sites are located on a series of grass covered terraces. Individual sites are not numbered or delineated in any way so the campground can get quite crowded during the high season. Electrical boxes are widely spaced and use the Swiss plug. The two shower/toilet buildings are very modern, heated, and provide free hot water for showers, sinks, and dishes. There are coin-operated clothes washers and dryers, a grocery shop, and a swimming pool.

There is bus service to Vaduz from a stop just below the campground.

To reach the campground travel south from Vaduz on Liechtenstein's main road, Highway 28. The campground is on the left after about 10 kilometers near the village of Trieson.

VIENNA (WIEN), AUSTRIA

Population 1,535,000

Vienna is one of the great cities of Europe. It is best known for its history: baroque architecture, coffee houses, music, and the monuments of the Habsburgs.

The layout of the city is simple, especially the central area where most of the sights are located. In the 19th century the city walls were demolished and a ring road, the **Ringstrasse** was built. This ring road is a boulevard, not a freeway, it circles the central district on all sides except the northeast where the border of the city is formed by the Danube Canal.

The central city inside the Ringstrasse is full of walking streets, churches and coffee houses. Many of the sights of Vienna are located here and walking tours are rewarding. The most centrally-located sight is the very unusual **St. Stephen's Cathedral (Stephansdom)** with its multicolored tile roof where you can climb or take an elevator up the **steeple (Steffel)** for an orientation view of the city. Coffee houses are a big

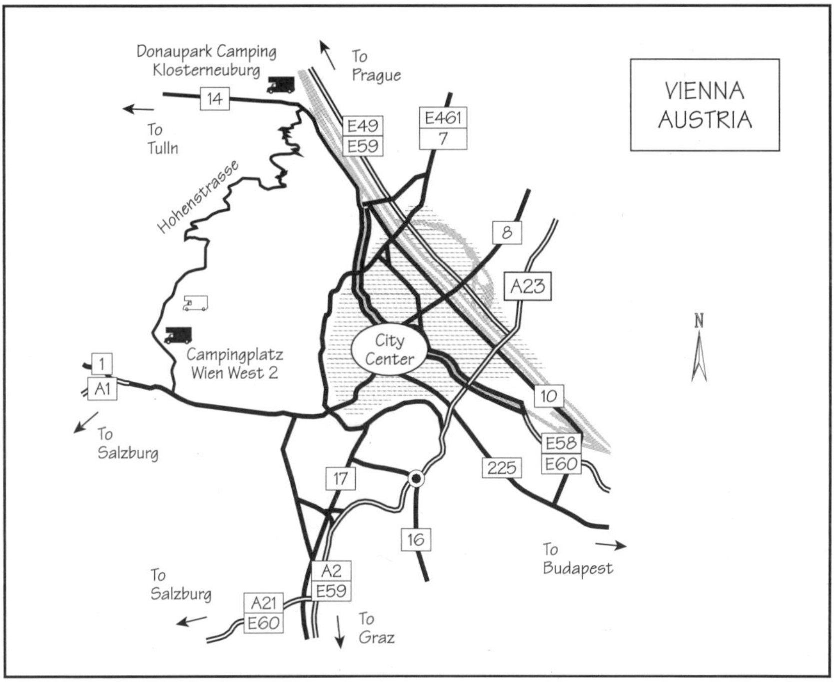

part of a visit to Vienna and the best are located in this district. Try the recently-restored **Café Central**, one of the city's most historic and one of Vienna's must-visit sites. The popularity of coffee in Vienna dates from 1683 when the city was introduced to the bean by a besieging Turk army.

The second major area of interest in Vienna is the Ringstrasse itself. Many majestic buildings were built along the street, the most impressive is probably the **Hofburg** or Royal Palace. It is really a group of buildings and houses many of the city's most popular attractions including the **Spanish Riding School** (**Spanische Reitschule**), the **Grand Hall of the National Library** (**Hofbibliothek Prunksaal**), and the **Imperial Apartments**. The **Kunsthistorisches Museum** is nearby and slightly farther out from the center is the **Belvedere Palace** which houses another museum with the works of nineteenth and twentieth-century Austrian artists like Gustav Klimt and Egon Schiele.

An important Viennese destination is farther outside the Ringstrasse. This is **Schönbrunn Palace** which is located in the western suburbs most easily reached by using the U4 subway line and getting off at either the Schönbrunn or Hietzing stop. This is the Habsburg's Versailles-style palace, built to outshine the original. The tour of the interior is a must but don't miss the gardens behind the palace. These gardens also house what is said the be the world's oldest zoo, the **Tiergarten**, founded in 1752.

Vienna Campgrounds

✦ DONAUPARK CAMPING KLOSTERNEUBURG

Address: A-3402 Klosterneuburg bei Wien
Telephone: 02243 25877 Fax: 02243 25878
Price: Moderate

Open all year

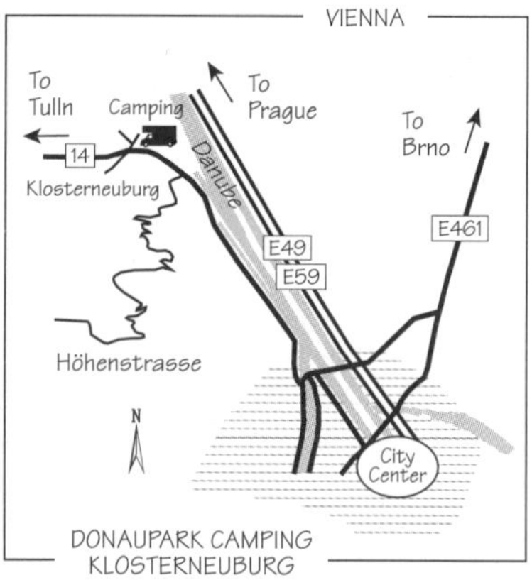

DONAUPARK CAMPING KLOSTERNEUBURG

Donaupark is a first class campground that is located west of Vienna on the south shore of the Danube in the small town of Klosterneuburg. You'll have decent access to Vienna with a base that offers small town amenities and bike trails along the Danube.

The campground is a large field that is mostly unshaded. The sites are marked and assigned when you check in. This is a tourist campground with no permanent residents. There is a special tent area set aside for cyclists biking along the Danube. The site surfaces are grass. Electrical outlets are convenient and numerous (CEE17 plugs, 6 amps). The shower/toilet buildings are modern, heated and clean. Hot water is provided for showers (push-button, adjustable), bathroom sinks, and dishwashing. Hot plates are provided in the same room as the dishwashing sinks. Coin-operated washers and dryer are available. The campground has a restaurant and a grocery shop and offers Vienna tours. There's even a large swimming park next door. In town, about 400 meters from the campground is a grocery store.

During the summer it is easy to visit Vienna, the campground runs a shuttle bus. During the rest of the year it is not much more difficult, a suburban train station is less than 250 meters from the campground, the trip to Vienna's Heiligenstadt subway station takes only 15 minutes, and from there the Green line will drop you at the Karlsplatz which is very convenient for starting your walking tour of Vienna. You can also ride your bike the 10 kilometers or so in to town. There is a bike trail along the river, part of the extensive Lower Danube Bike Route. For the first few kilometers the route is on back roads, then on a paved bike path.

The campground is easily reached from Highway 14 which follows the south bank of the Danube west of Vienna. Near the eastern edge of Klosterneuburg next to the railway station you'll see a campground sign pointing north toward the river. The road is easy to recognize because it immediately dives under a railway trestle. The campground is less than a half kilometer down this road on the right.

✦ CAMPINGPLATZ DER STADT WIEN, WIEN WEST 2

Address: Hüttelbergstrasse 80, A-1140 Wien
Telephone: 01 9142314 Fax: 01 9113594
Price: Moderate

Open March 1 to January 31

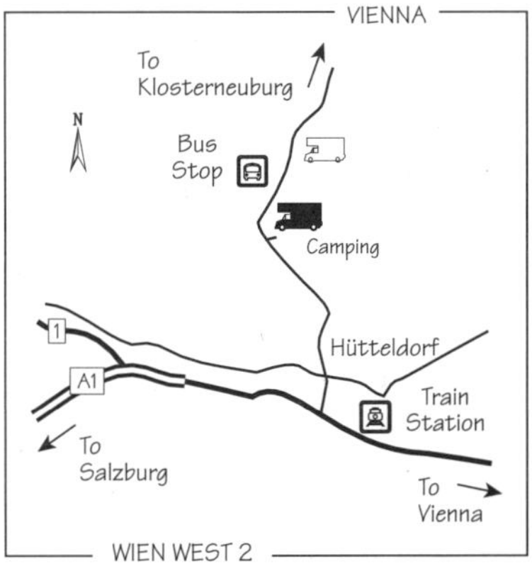

This is one of two city campgrounds sitting near each other in the western suburbs of Vienna. WIEN WEST 1 is only open during July and August, Wien West 2 is an all weather campground and stays open most of the year. Using a bus/subway combination you can conveniently reach the center of Vienna in about half an hour from these campgrounds.

Wien West 2 is a large campground with brick-surfaced camp sites for vehicles located around an oblong access road. Individual sites are not marked or assigned at the reception desk. There are two grassy tent areas. This is a tourist campground with no permanent rigs. Electrical connections are widely spaced (CEE17 plugs, 10 amps). The showers and toilets are in a modern two-story building at the center of the campground. Showers are hot (push valve, adjustable) and there is hot water in the bathroom sinks. Dishwashing with free hot water and cooking facilities including hot plates are available in the reception building. There is a grocery store and restaurant kiosk with a covered seating area located in the central building. A supermarket is conveniently situated just across the street.

The Hütteldorf subway station (U4 line) is a five-minute bus ride from the camp. Two busses, numbers 148 and 152 provide service every half hour or so. Once you know the route this also makes a nice walk. The U4 subway line will take you directly to the convenient Karlsplatz station near the center of things.

Easiest access to the campground is from the A1 autobahn. At the end of the freeway at the Aushof go straight, turn left at the first lights. Go straight through the next lights into Hüttelburg Strasse and follow this road up the hill to the campground which will be on your right. The route is well signed from the Autobahn.

Side Trips from Vienna

A boat trip on the Danube makes a good side trip. You can travel up the river to Krems, Melk, or Linz.

ZERMATT, SWITZERLAND

Population 4,000

Zermatt is a mountaineering and ski village that sits within sight of the Matterhorn. It is surrounded by mountains and is virtually traffic free, motorists must park in the village of Täsch some 5 kilometers away and take the train up to the town. Ski lifts rise in several directions, in summer they carry hikers onto the slopes to many excellent hiking trails. The views of the Matterhorn from the village and surrounding mountains are spectacular.

There's a cog railway from Zermatt to **Gornergrat** that is the highest in Europe. It provides even better Matterhorn views.

Zermatt Campground

✦ CAMPING ALPHUBEL

Address: CH-3929 Täsch
Telephone: 027 9673635 Fax: 027 9664647
Cost: Moderate

Open May 1 to September 30

This is one of two campgrounds that are convenient to the railway to Zermatt. Camping Alphubel is in the small village of Täsch, it is actually next door to the railway station. The other campground is 2 kilometers down the road toward the village of Randa, there are walking paths to the station.

Alphubel sits next to the mountainside on the west side of the valley. It is a medium-sized long flat campground with a paved access road to the grass sites. They are not separated, assigned, or numbered. There are no permanent residents here. Electricity (10 amps, Swiss plugs) is available at two boxes. The shower/toilet building also houses the reception office and is located at the campground entrance. Hot showers (adjustable) require payment, free hot water is available in the bathroom basins and for washing dishes. There is a grocery store and restaurants within 300 meters of the campground.

For all practical purposes the road stops at Täsch, to get to Zermatt you must either take the railway or walk, the hike takes about an hour and is pleasant, it follows the railway for the 5 kilometer distance. Alternately you can walk or bike up the paved road to Zermatt that is reserved for motor vehicles with special permission.

To drive into the campground watch for signs as you arrive in Täsch. Just past the big parking lot and railway station on the right you'll see the campground. You have to cross the tracks and a small bridge to enter the campground but even big rigs should have no problem if they take it slowly.

ZURICH (ZÜRICH), SWITZERLAND

Population 850,000

This largest city in Switzerland is known more for it is bustling business life than for its tourist attractions, but we don't travel just to see museums, do we?

Actually, Zurich does have its' share of museums and sights. The museums include the **Swiss National Museum** and the **Museum of Fine Arts**. The **Bahnhofstrasse** make a good place for a window-shopping tour. You'll enjoy walking around the older section of town along the Limmat River and also along the shore of Lake Zurich.

Zurich Campground

✦ CAMPING SEEBUCHT

Address: Seestrasse 559,
CH-8038 Zürich-Wollishofen
Telephone: 01 4821612 Fax: 01 4821660
Price: Moderate

Open May 1 to September 30

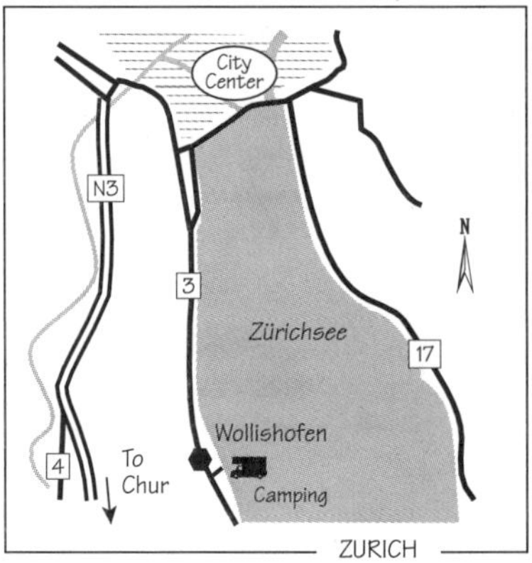

This is a very convenient campground for visiting Zurich. Downtown is only 4 kilometers from the campground and there is good bus service. Unfortunately the campground closes early in the fall and there are really no good alternatives close to the city.

Seebucht is a medium-sized campground in terms of the rigs that are accepted, small in terms of area. This means that things can be quite crowded, it is sometimes even necessary for trailer owners to park their cars away from their sites. The campground is located on the lake shore in a nice setting. Electricity (6 and 10 amps) is available, the outlet boxes are widely spaced. The shower/toilet rooms are in the same building as the reception and the grocery shop. Hot water for showers and bathroom sinks requires payment. There is a restaurant on the lake and it is also possible to swim.

Access to Zurich is great. Buses 161 and 165 stop just outside the campground entrance and provide service to central Zurich. There is a bike trail along the lake right in to town. The 4 kilometer distance also makes a pleasant hike.

To find the campground follow Highway 3 from Zurich along the west shore of the lake. At about four kilometers from Zurich you'll enter Wollishofen, the campground is on the left. Watch closely or you'll be past before you see it.

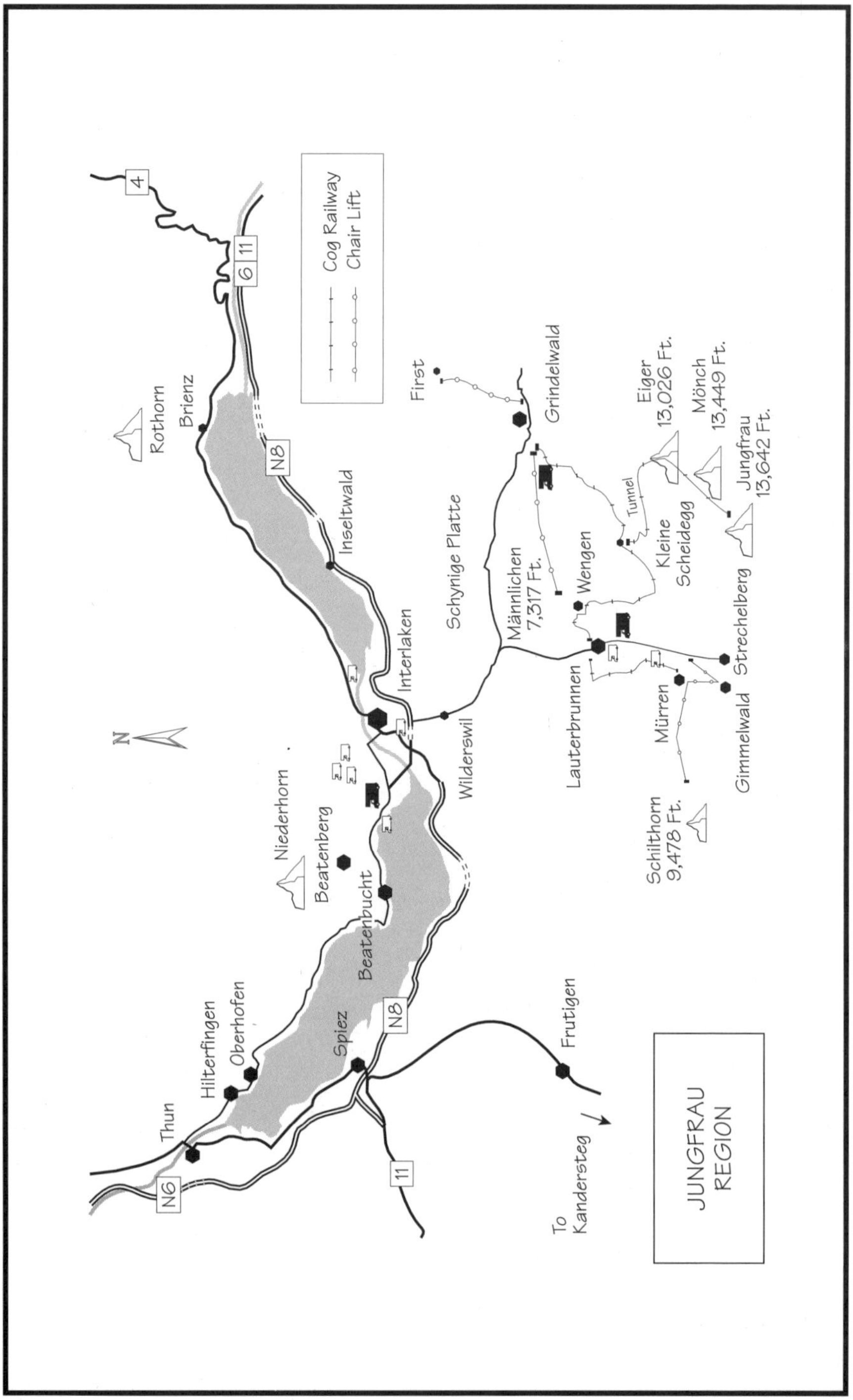
JUNGFRAU REGION
Cog Railway
Chair Lift
Thun
Hilterfingen
Oberhofen
Spiez
Beatenbucht
Beatenberg
Niederhorn
Interlaken
Wilderswil
Inseltwald
Brienz
Rothorn
Schynige Platte
First
Grindelwald
Männlichen 7,317 Ft.
Wengen
Lauterbrunnen
Kleine Scheidegg
Tunnel
Eiger 13,026 Ft.
Mönch 13,449 Ft.
Jungfrau 13,642 Ft.
Strechelberg
Gimmelwald
Mürren
Schilthorn 9,478 Ft.
Frutigen
To Kandersteg
N
N6
N8
6 11
4
11

TWO OUTSTANDING REGIONS AND THEIR CAMPGROUNDS

JUNGFRAU REGION

The draws in the Jungfrau Region near Interlaken are the mountains to the south: the Eiger (Ogre), Jungfrau (Virgin), and Mönch (Monk); the foothills and valleys below these peaks; and Lake Brienz (Brienzer See) and Lake Thun (Thuner See) on either side of Interlaken. The area is chock full of alpine railways, lifts of various sorts, hiking trails and boat routes on the lakes.

INTERLAKEN, SWITZERLAND

Population 5,200

Interlaken is the gateway to the Jungfrau Region. It is also an excellent base for your visit. Like all of the towns and villages in the Jungfrau Region Interlaken's business is tourism, you will be well taken care of. Supplies, banking, restaurants and diversions are all easy to find. Interlaken has been popular for years with the English, the town is often referred to as a Victorian resort town and was one of the first alpine resorts.

ARRIVING AT A SWISS CAMPGROUND

While the surrounding lakes and mountains are the prime attractions you will find some worthwhile sights in Interlaken itself. The oldest part of town is on the north side of the Aare River. You'll find the **Marktplatz** there, as well as the **Schloss Unterseen** and the **Stadthaus**. The **Touristik-Museum der Jungfrau Region** is a good introduction to the tourist industry in the region. Back on the south side of the river the **Höhematte Park** is the place for a nice stroll. You might also enjoy the demonstration of traditional Swiss cheese making at the **Chäs-Dörfli.** Finally, you'll find that Interlaken has its own **Casino**.

Interlaken has seven campgrounds. All of the them are numbered and there are sign-posts with the numbers all around town. The campgrounds with their numbers are as follows: CAMPING MANOR FARM (1), Camping Alpenblick (2), CAMPING HOBBY (3), CAMPING LAZY RANCHO (4), CAMPING JUNGFRAU (5), TCS-CAMPING SACKGUT (6), and CAMPING JUNGFRAUBLICK (7). In addition to these campgrounds there are also some in surrounding small villages.

Interlaken Campground

✦ CAMPING ALPENBLICK

Address: CH-3801 Unterseen/Interlaken
Telephone: 033 8227757
Price: Moderate

Open all year

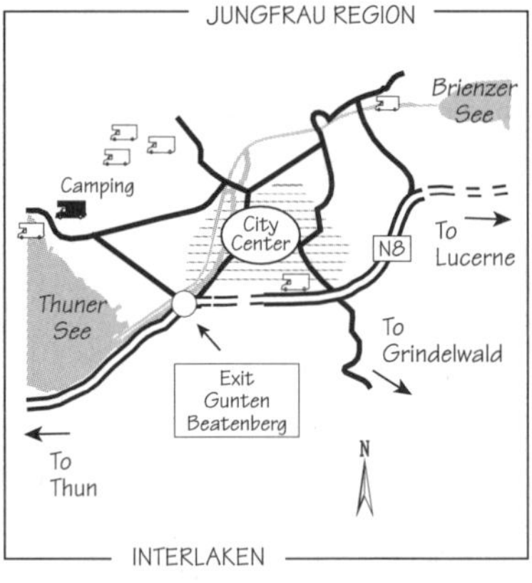

This is one of seven campgrounds in Interlaken. It is one of the farthest from the center of the town, but the distance is only two kilometers. One indication of this region's popularity is that all of the campgrounds have fairly high prices for the facilities that they offer, Alpenblick is one of the more reasonable.

The campground is a large grassy field with scattered trees. Gravel access roads cross the campground, sites are not numbered or assigned. Many permanent resident caravans are at the rear of the campground but there are large areas for tourist campers. Electricity is available at a few boxes (CEE17, German, and Swiss plugs, 10 amps). The shower/toilet building is rustic, hot showers are free and there is hot water in some of the bathroom basins, dishwashing sinks are cold water only. Laundry machines are available in the reception office. There are also a few grocery items. The Camping Manor Farm and the Motel Neuhaus are across the street, they offer restaurants, groceries, and a golf course.

Bus transportation to the center of Interlaken is convenient, the bus stops just outside the campground. The 2 kilometers to town is easily accomplished on foot or on a bicycle, there are trails the entire distance.

From the N8 freeway you can most easily reach the campground by taking the Gunten and Beatenberg exit at the west end of the tunnel. This is a spur road that runs right past the campground which will be on your right. From Interlaken itself follow the signs for Camp 2 from near the Interlaken West train station.

Side Trips from Interlaken

Interlaken covers the flat plain between the **Brienzer See** (Lake Brienz) and the **Thuner See** (Lake Thun). Both of these lakes are served by graceful lake steamers making circuits to places of interest on the shores. The Brienzer See stops include **Iseltwald** where you can take a beautiful hike to the **Gliessbach Falls** and **Brienz**. **Brienz** has a famous wood carving school where you can actually learn to carve small figures, and is the terminus for a cog railway up the **Rothorn**. Nearby is the **Ballenberg** open-air museum with 80 different traditional structures set in a 200 acre park. The Thuner See has even more, stops include **Spiez**, **Thun**, **Hilterfingen**, **Oberhofen** and **Beatenbucht**. Most of these towns have an interesting castle, Thun has a much-admired medieval square and unique shopping street that actually sits on the roofs of the shops of the street below. From Beatenbucht you can take a funicular up to **Beatenberg** where trails or a chair lift will take you even higher to the **Niederhorn** and great views as far as Mont Blanc. All of the lakeside towns mentioned above are also accessible by road.

If you plan to head south from the Jungfrau region to the Valais you can do it quickly and have some fun in the bargain by using a rail ferry. At the upper end of the Kander Valley, in Kandersteg, some 40 kilometers from Interlaken, is the northern terminal. Trains make a 15 minute run through the Lotschenpass Tunnel to Brig with your vehicle loaded on a flatcar. There is no road across the pass.

South of Interlaken the twin valleys of the Lütschine River afford access to the winter skiing and summer hiking of the high country below the Eiger, Mönch and Jungfrau. The left valley, that of the Schwartze Lütschine (Black Lütschine) climbs to the high resort town of Grindelwald. The right valley, that of the Weisse Lütschine (White Lütschine) doesn't climb as steeply so that when you reach the village of Lauterbrunnen you are surrounded by steep cliffs. Both of these villages and their surrounding attractions are described below.

GRINDELWALD

Population 4,000

This alpine village perched in the mountains south of Interlaken offers anything a mountain enthusiast could desire. It is much like the village of Zermatt except that automobiles are allowed. The sophisticated village has shops, restaurants, and even a sports center. Lifts of various descriptions will whisk you into beautiful high country containing hundreds of kilometers of hiking trails, or you can climb the hills under your own power. Towering over everything is the Eiger. The valley offers several campgrounds. Most are well signed from the entrance of the village. You can stop at the information map mounted on a board in a parking area on the road into town to orient yourself.

Grindelwald Campground

✦ CAMPING EIGERNORDWAND

Address: CH-3818 Grindelwald
Telephone: 033 8534227
Price: Moderate

Open all year

Eigernordwand is located on the valley floor below the village of Grindelwald. The Männlichen cable car passes almost over the site and views in all directions are spectacular.

This is a medium-sized site located in a slightly sloping field. All campsites are on grass and they are not separated or numbered. Electricity is available (Swiss plugs, 10 amps) from a few widely-scattered boxes. The shower/toilet building is modern and heated, hot water is free for showers (adjustable), bathroom basins, dishwashing and hand-laundry sinks. The laundry room has coin-operated machines and a heated drying room. There is a restaurant at the campground and a small grocery kiosk. There's also a dump station. Groceries are available in town and two small supermarkets about 1.5 kilometer from the campground but uphill.

As you drive in to Grindelwald you'll notice the Männlichen cable car on your right and below you. You'll probably also see the campground just beyond it. Turn right at the Y just after the Shell gas station toward the Grund railway station. You'll pass it at the bottom of the valley, then the signs will take you across a small bridge to the right and along narrow roads for about a half kilometer. The site is next to the Hotel Bodenwald.

Side Trips from Grindelwald

From Grindelwald it is possible to catch a cog railway up to **Kleine Scheidegg** at an altitude of 6,762 feet and then another on up to the **Jungfraujoch** at 11,333 feet. The second cog railway runs inside the Eiger, huge viewing galleries have been blasted in the side of the mountain and the train stops for an occasional peek on the way up. At the top is a viewing station with a restaurant and activities including dog sled rides and an ice sculpture museum. From Kleine Scheidegg you can continue on across to the village of Lauterbrunnen or return to Grindelwald.

LAUTERBRUNNEN, SWITZERLAND

Population 3,500

If you head south from Interlaken into the mountains and turn right at the fork you'll find yourself in the Lauterbrunnen Valley. Not far up the valley is the village of Lauterbrunnen. The village sits close below high cliffs on both sides of the valley, the **Staubbach Falls** make a very long drop from the top of the cliff just south of town. There are two campgrounds here: TCS Camping Schützenbach and CAMPING JUNGFRAU. Another few kilometers up the valley is another campground, BREITHORN, in the even smaller village of Stechelberg. Lauterbrunnen is a good place to catch a ride up into the high country, the cog railway heads uphill away from the road from here to Wengen and Kleine Scheidegg. On the other side of the valley you can catch the more reasonably-priced funicular and train combination to Mürren and Gimmelwald and many hiking trails above and below them.

Lauterbrunnen Campground

✦ TCS CAMPING SCHÜTZENBACH

Address: CH-3822 Lauterbrunnen
Telephone: 033 8551268 Fax: 033 8551275
Price: Moderate

Closed only a short period at end of November, beginning of December.

This is a medium-sized campground on flat ground just north of the village of Lauterbrunnen. Camping sites for caravans are on grass, those for motor campers on gravel. There are quite a few permanent resident caravans here but they are located in a separate area. Sites are not numbered and are not assigned. Electricity is available in widely-scattered boxes (Swiss plug, 10 amps). The shower/toilet building is heated, girls upstairs and boys down. Hot showers require payment but there is free hot water in the bathroom basins. Dishwashing sinks also require payment for hot water. There is a laundry room with coin-operated machines. A cooking area is outside but covered and has a couple of gas stoves. Prepared food is available at a snack bar and there is a small grocery shop. The campground also has a playground. More complete grocery shopping is available at the Coop supermarket in Lauterbrunnen about a kilometer from the campground.

You can find the campground by staying on the main road through Lauterbrunnen. It is on the left on the southern outskirts of the village.

SALZKAMMERGUT REGION

For most travelers Salzburg will probably be the gateway to the Salzkammergut. Many visitors to Salzburg have never heard of the region. Don't you be one of them.

SALZBURG

Population 145,000

Salzburg is a friendly-sized city with a beautiful location. The green glacial-colored Salzach River runs through the middle of the city and the **Hohensalzburg Castle** looks down from above the old town on the south bank. There are great views of the town from the castle. Mountains rise in almost every direction.

This is the town made famous in America by the movie *The Sound of Music*. Probably the most popular activity is the **Sound of Music Tour** which visits places seen in the movie, including some in the nearby Salzkammergut lake region to the east. You'll also want to see the baroque **Mirabell Palace** and visit **Hellbrunn Castle** just south

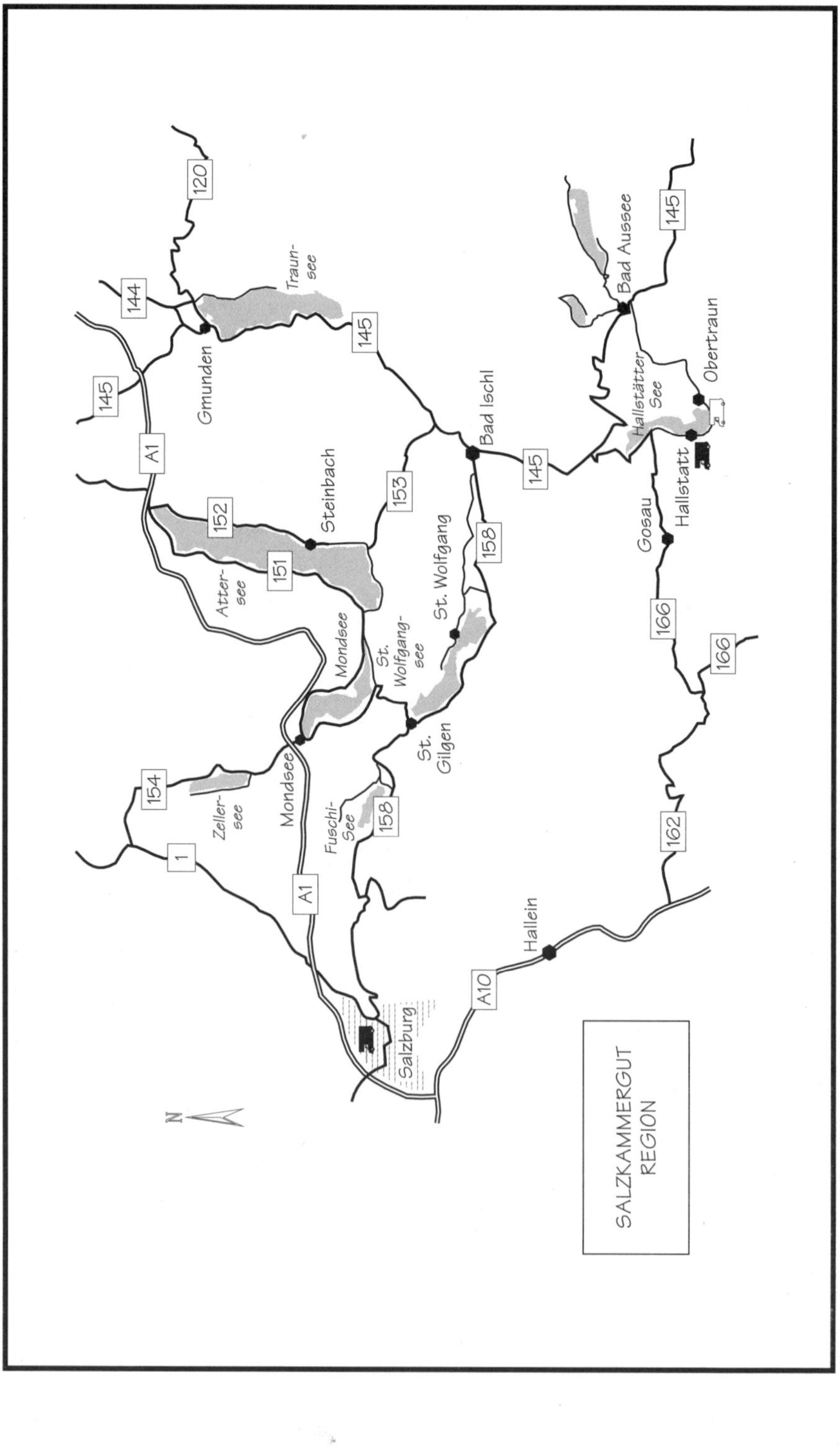
SALZKAMMERGUT
REGION
N
Salzburg
Hallein
A10
A1
1
154
Zeller-
see
Mondsee
Fuschl-
See
158
St.
Gilgen
Mondsee
St.
Wolfgang-
see
St. Wolfgang
Atter-
see
151
152
Steinbach
153
158
Bad Ischl
145
Gmunden
145
144
120
Traun-
see
145
Gosau
166
166
162
Hallstatt
Hallstätter
See
Obertraun
Bad Aussee
145

of town with its gardens and trick fountains. Take along some light rain gear or you'll get wet.

Salzburg is also a good place to take a salt mine tour. The **Durrnberg Salt Mines** in Hallein are about 12 kilometers south of Salzburg.

Salzburg Campground

✦ PANORAMA CAMPING STADTBLICK

Address: Rauchenbichlerstrasse 21, A-5020 Salzburg-Rauchenbichl
Telephone: 0662 450652 Fax: 0662 458018
Price: Moderate

Open March 20 to October 31

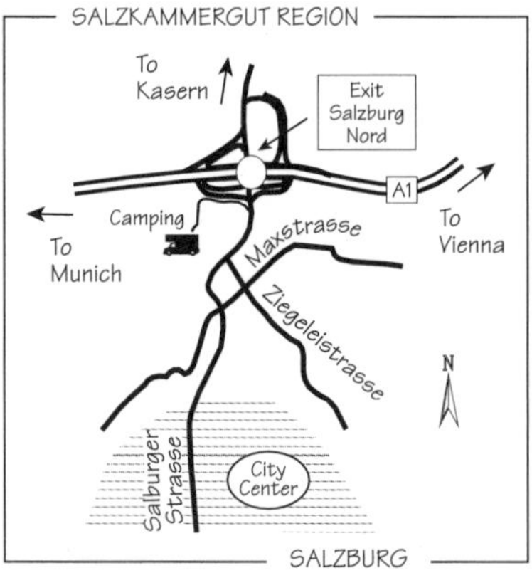

This is a very pleasant small campground overlooking Salzburg. It is easy to get to because it is just off the freeway and has a good bus connection to central Salzburg. There are three campgrounds in the general area of the Salzburg Nord autobahn exit so you'll have some other choices if this campground happens to be full.

The campground sits under tall trees at the top of a grassy slope. The camping sites are terraced so many have a great view of Salzburg and the Hohensalzburg Castle. There are no resident rigs here. The sites are either grass or gravel. Electrical outlets are widely spaced (CEE17 plugs, 6 amps). All of the facilities are in one building overlooking the campground. Free hot water is available for showers (adjustable), bathroom sinks and dishwashing. There are coin-operated washers and dryers, TV room, restaurant, and small grocery shop. About 1 kilometer from the campground toward town is a medium-size supermarket. Two hundred meters below the campground along a stream is a bike path and small city park with playground equipment for children.

The city bus stop is about one-half kilometer from the campground. The number 51 bus runs frequently, this stop is the end of the line for the bus so it waits for a few minutes every circuit. If you would like to ride your bike into Salzburg there is an excellent bike path that follows a small stream down to the Salzach River and then along it to the old part of town. The distance is about 4 kilometers.

From the east/west Munich-Vienna autobahn take the Salzburg Nord exit. You want to head south toward Salzburg. Almost immediately take a sharp right and follow a camping sign up a small lane to the top of the hill and the campground.

East of Salzburg only a few miles is a district of lakes and mountains known as the Salzkammergut. Today the region is known for its beauty, in earlier times salt was more important. The salt found here was so valuable that for many years the entire area was closed to visitors. In German the word Hall means salt and you'll see it in many of the names in the area.

The Salzkammergut is not a particularly large area. if you include Salzburg it makes a square that is 60 kilometers in each direction. In the north the lakes are shallower and warmer, the mountains are smaller. In the south the mountains get steeper and higher, the lakes deeper and colder.

The village of Hallstatt in the south makes a good base for exploring the Salzkammergut.

HALLSTATT

Population 1,200

This is a small but very old village with scenic location that won't quit. Originally Hallstatt was settled because of the nearby salt deposits, today the town is the perfect lake-side Alpine village. It can be crowded with tourist during the day but things quiet down in the evening. One reason the town is so popular is the rail access. The tracks run on the far side of the lake and a boat meets every train.

Hall has more history than most small towns. From 1,100 to 500 B.C. a group of Celts settled this region. They were so successful that that period of the iron age is now called the Hallstatt Period, largely because many archeological discoveries related to that period have been made around Hallstatt.

You'll want to visit the **salt works** perched on the mountain behind the village. You can hike up a very steep and scenic trail or take a funicular. Inside are an underground lake and railroad. South of Hallstatt in the town of Obertraun you'll find the **Dachstein Ice Caves**, accessible by cable car or trail, and in the surrounding mountains are many more miles of hiking trails.

Hallstatt Campground

✦ CAMPINGPLATZ KLAUSNER-HÖLL

Address: Lahnstrasse 6, A-4830 Hallstatt
Telephone: 061 348322
Price: Moderate

Open May 1 to October 15

This is a small campground with a great location just a half kilometer south of the center of Hallstatt. There is also a campground, CAMPING AM SEE, in the village of Obertraun at the south end of the lake. That is a good alternate campground if Klausner-Höll is full.

Klausner-Höll is two grassy fields separated by a row of trees and bushes. The front field has assigned spaces and electrical outlets (German and CEE17, 16 amps), the rear does not have electricity. The shower/toilet building is modern and clean. Hot showers are free and there is hot water in the bathroom sinks. Dishwashing sinks have cold water only. There is a small indoor lounge area and a restaurant. You'll find a supermarket about 200 meters towards town on the main road. There's a nice little park on the lake shore near the campground.

The campground is located some 500 meters south of Hallstatt. You need only wander down to the lake and head north to reach town. Finding the campground is equally easy. Traffic bypasses Hallstatt by way of a tunnel through the mountain behind town. From the south tunnel exit head south about a half kilometer, you'll see the sign for the campground on the right.

Side Trips from Hallstatt

From Hallstatt you can easily drive north to explore the northern Salzkammergut. Just 15 kilometers north is **Bad Ischl**, the central Salzkammergut town where Franz Josef held his summer court during his long reign in the second half of the 19th and early 20th centuries. You can visit his residence, the **Kaiservilla**. Bad Ischl is a spa town, the baths are called the **Kurhaus**.

East 12 kilometers from Bad Ischl is the **Wolfgangsee** and on its north shore is the town of **St. Wolfgang**. This resort village is one of the most popular in the area. From here you can catch a ride on a steamer for a tour of the lake or board a cog railway to climb the **Schafberg** for a view of the lake country. The town is also known for the carved altarpiece in the **Pfarrkirch** (Parochial Church) by Michael Pacher, a 15th-century woodcarver and painter. The **White Horse Inn (Im Weissen Rössl)** is much visited by tourists because it appears in a famous opera.

The next few towns on the tour are very popular with visitors from Salzburg, both tourists and residents, because they are so close to the city. They are more crowded and have less atmosphere but are well provided with restaurants and recreational facilities including beaches for swimming and water sports. **St. Gilgen** is on the north shore of the Wolfgangsee while **Fuschl** is just 6 kilometers north on the smaller **Fuschlsee**. About 20 kilometers north from Fuschl by roundabout small roads is the **Mondsee** (Moon Lake), warmest of the lakes for swimming. On the north shore is the town of Mondsee, the abbey church here was the setting for the wedding in ***The Sound of Music.***

The largest lake in the region, the **Attersee**, is just east of the Mondsee. From **Steinbach** on the east shore of the Attersee you can follow a small road 25 kilometers east to **Gmunden** on the north shore of another large lake, the **Traunsee**. Gmunden is the largest town in the area after Salzburg and has its own double castle, the **Schloss Orth** with one castle on the shore and another on a connected island. Lake cruises are possible and there's a cable car up the **Grünberg** for the view. From Gmunden you can head south for Bad Ischl and Hallstatt, a distance of 50 kilometers.

For some good hiking drive 14 kilometers west from Hallstatt to the town of Gosau. You can catch a bus or boat to Gosaumühl where trails start for hikes to the **Gosau Lakes** and surrounding mountains.

Bad Aussee, 15 kilometers east of Hallstatt, also makes a good day trip. Don't try this in a big rig, the road is very steep in places. Bad Aussee is a spa town and also a good base for hikes. Altaussee, on a lake about 4 kilometers higher, is both beautiful and historically interesting because mines nearby were used by the Nazis to hide and protect art treasures stolen throughout Europe.

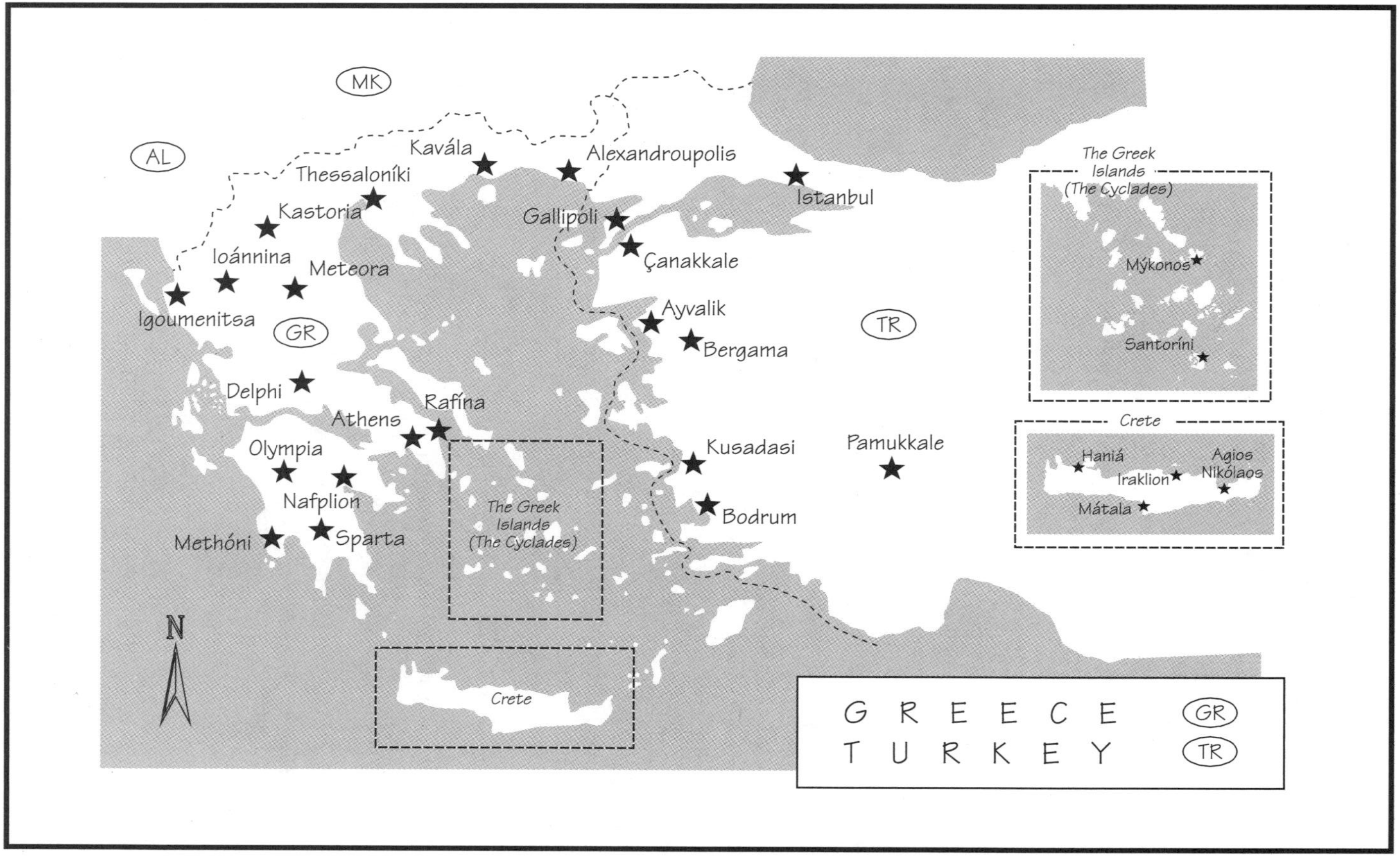
MK
AL
Kavála
Alexandroupolis
Thessaloníki
Istanbul
Kastoria
Gallipoli
Çanakkale
Ioánnina
Meteora
Igoumenitsa
GR
Ayvalik
TR
Bergama
Delphi
Rafína
Athens
Olympia
Pamukkale
Kusadasi
Nafplion
Bodrum
Methóni
Sparta
The Greek Islands (The Cyclades)
N
Crete
The Greek Islands (The Cyclades)
Mýkonos
Santoríni
Crete
Haniá
Iraklion
Agios Nikólaos
Mátala
GREECE GR
TURKEY TR

CHAPTER

13

GREECE AND TURKEY

INTRODUCTION

Both Greece and Turkey are great destinations for the camping traveler. Their excellent campgrounds, beautifully mild weather, many archeological sights, beaches, and low prices more than compensate for their relatively remote location. Once you're there you won't want to leave.

Don't suppose that our inclusion of Greece and Turkey in one chapter means that they are at all similar. The two countries do have a long history together and you will find as many ancient Greek archeological sites along the Turkish coast as you will find in Greece itself. On the other hand, through history Greece and Turkey have often been uncomfortable neighbors and today there is quite a bit of political animosity. The border is open, however, and travel between the two countries usually presents little problem if you show a little patience at the border stations.

Greece is a mountainous country with a very long coastline. The only large city that you are likely to visit is Athens. The Greek Islands are deservedly well known tourist destinations but you will find that the Peloponnese and northern Greece also have a lot to offer and are much easier to visit if you have your own vehicle. Tourist attractions include great beaches; ancient Greek, Venetian, and Byzantine ruins; and the Greek countryside, villages, and people.

Turkey is a much larger country than Greece, the campgrounds in this book are concentrated in what is the easiest to reach and most popular part of the country for tourists: Istanbul and the western coast. Istanbul is one of the world's most interesting cities, and along the rugged west coast of Turkey you'll find a variety of beaches, resorts, and world-class archeological sites. If you are traveling during the winter months this is one of the few areas included in this book where you will find truly comfortable weather.

You will find that Greece is more modern than Turkey and better off economically. Greece is a member of the European Community while Turkey is not. In religious matters there is a world of difference. Greece is largely Greek Orthodox while Turkey is Moslem.

Getting There

The shortest and least expensive ferry route from Italy runs from Brindisi, Italy to Igoumenitsa, Greece. Most boats make the run at night, it takes about 12 hours. You will not have access to your vehicle during the run and cabins are expensive. Once things quiet down after midnight most deck travelers find a place to stretch out somewhere inside or on deck, consider bringing along a sleeping bag.

It is possible to travel to Greece and Turkey from western Europe overland. This is a volatile area politically and it is important to take current conditions in each country into consideration when planning a route in the interests of safety. You may also want to check on visa fees, many countries assess them and you may find that the Brindisi ferry is the cheapest way to go. Also check your auto insurance, some Balkan countries may be excluded.

Roads and Driving

Greece has a decent road system composed largely of good two-lane paved roads. From Athens you will find good inexpensive toll roads leading north and west, but before long they narrow to two lanes. The mountainous terrain throughout the country means that you can't expect to move along the roads very rapidly, particularly since you will be sharing them with a lot of truck traffic. Many Greeks drive too fast, don't let them influence your own driving.

A word about Greek road signs. Place names on directional signs written in the Greek alphabet are almost impossible to decipher. Fortunately, the country gets a lot of visitors so there are often additional signs that the rest of us can read. When you approach an intersection you will see the Greek-language sign first, then just before the turn the second sign.

Turkey's road system is quite adequate, particularly away from the larger cities where traffic is not heavy. Most of the roads are two lane but there are also a number of larger toll roads, most notably between Istanbul and Ankara. The country is less mountainous that Greece in most areas which helps traffic move along, but there are also lots of trucks and tractors on Turkish roads, and they do obstruct traffic. Turkish drivers deserve special mention. Watch out for them, they are aggressive to a fault and entirely fearless. They can easily get you in trouble too if you aren't alert. It is important to watch your speed carefully in Turkey, police often set up speed traps using well-hidden radar guns and collect traffic fines on the spot.

Travel in Greece will probably involve the use of ferries. The majority of road visitors use a ferry from Italy to reach Greece, and ferries provide access to Crete and the rest of the Greek islands. See the Greek Islands section of this chapter for more information about ferry travel.

Travel to Turkey will probably involve crossing the Greece/Turkey border. Relations between Greece and Turkey are strained and this is often apparent while crossing the border. If things are going bad diplomatically you may find the border closed, or you may find an unofficial slowdown in effect. Patience is always an asset while crossing borders and yours may be severely tried while crossing this one. In 1998 we found a $45 U.S. per person visa fee in effect at the Turkish border for travelers from the U.S., the fee varies for other nationalities.

The Greek AAA-affiliated automobile club is the Automobile and Touring Club of Greece (ELPA), you can reach them at 0301 7488800. For breakdown assistance call 104, you can reach the police at 100 except in the suburbs of Athens where you must dial 109. In Turkey the AAA-affiliated automobile club is the Touring and Automobile Club of Turkey (TTOK) at 0212 2828140. Breakdown service is available only in northwestern Turkey, the Istanbul 24-hour service number is 0212 804449. The police emergency number in Turkey is 155.

Camping

Greek campgrounds are some of the nicest in Europe. As a general rule they are modern, clean, well run, and a good value. There are also a lot of them, particularly along the coast. International Camping Cards are not required but will often get you a discount. Most campgrounds keep your passport on file in the registration office during your stay, the camping card can usually act as a substitute. English is often spoken in Greek campgrounds.

We find that Turkish campgrounds don't compare well with those in Greece. Most are older and facilities are often in need of repair. Most use solar water heaters so showers are best taken in the evening. English is seldom spoken. The passport and camping card situation is similar to the one in Greek campgrounds.

Free camping is not recommended in either country. It is illegal in Greece and unusual enough to attract unwanted attention in Turkey.

Shopping, Currency, Credit Cards and Fuel

You will probably be pleased with the availability of groceries in Greece. There are few huge hypermarkets but there are many smaller supermarkets, and they have a pretty good selection of food, both fresh and processed. Credit cards can often be used to purchase groceries.

The food distribution system in Turkey is being modernized, but it does not compare with western Europe and Greece. There are a few hypermarkets but selection is poor. You will find row after row of soap powder filling the otherwise empty shelves, and much the same selection of goods that are found in much smaller stores. Processed foods are very expensive and selection is poor. You will always be able to find bread and vegetables, however.

Gasoline (leaded and unleaded) and diesel are readily available in both countries. There are an amazing number of large, modern stations in both countries, and most accept credit cards. Fuel is a relative bargain in Greece and Turkey compared with the rest of Europe, with Turkey offering the best deal.

The cash supply situation is similar in Greece to the rest of Europe. Cash machines are easy to find and seem to work well.

Cash in Turkey can be a challenge. Inflation is a huge problem, one U.S. dollar is worth several hundred thousand Turkish lira. It is a real job just keeping track of the number of zero digits on the bills. Cash machines are easy to find but we have had no success in using them, cards that work throughout Europe would not work for us in Turkey. Plan on using an alternate method for your visit, we found that exchanging travelers checks in banks gave a good exchange rate.

Itinerary Suggestions

September and October are the ideal months for a camping visit to Greece and Turkey. The weather is good and the campgrounds are not crowded. Rates for ferries have started to decline for the winter. Many folks decide to stay for the winter, the west coast of Turkey (the southern part) and Crete are good places to do this.

Both Athens and Istanbul are prime tourist destinations. Both are worth investing at least a week of your time and have decent campgrounds for a pleasant stay. For the rest of your visit just browse through the destinations and campgrounds in this chapter. There are places for beach lovers and places for culture lovers, also places suitable for both.

You will have to decide whether to visit the Greek islands. Doing this with a vehicle can be a bit pricey, consider leaving your rig in a campground on the mainland while you make a backpacking trip to the islands. Crete is the exception, you will find wheels very worthwhile there.

The Greek tourist office for the U.S. is at **Greek National Tourist Organization, 645 Fifth Ave., Olympic Tower, New York, NY (212 421-5777)**. In Canada the address is **Greek National Tourist Organization, 1300 Bay Street, Toronto, ON, M5R 3K8 (416 968-2220)**. For information about Turkey contact **Turkish Tourist Office, 821 United Nations Plaza, New York, NY 10017 (212 687-2194)**. In Canada try **Turkish Tourist Office, 360 Albert Street, Suite 801, Ottawa, ON K1R 7X7 (613 230-8654)**. Links to tourist information about Greece and Turkey can be found on our internet site at www.rollinghomes.com.

GREECE AND TURKEY DISTANCE TABLE

In Kilometers

Kms X .62 = Miles

	Ag. Nikólaos Greece	Alexandroupolis Greece	Athens Greece	Ayvalik Turkey	Bergama Turkey	Bodrum Turkey	Çanakkale Turkey	Delphi Greece	Gallipoli Turkey	Haniá Greece	Igoumenitsa Greece	Ioánnina Greece	Iraklion Greece	Istanbul Turkey	Kastoria Greece	Kavála Greece	Kusadasi Turkey	Mátala Greece	Meteora Greece	Methóni Greece	Nafplion Greece	Olympia Greece	Pamukkale Turkey	Rafina Greece	Sparta Greece
Alexandroupolis Greece	--																								
Athens Greece	--	872																							
Ayvalik Turkey	--	378	1250																						
Bergama Turkey	--	442	1314	64																					
Bodrum Turkey	--	782	1654	404	354																				
Çanakkale Turkey	--	192	1064	186	250	590																			
Delphi Greece	--	744	165	1122	1186	1526	936																		
Gallipoli Turkey	--	144	1016	234	298	638	48	888																	
Haniá Greece	192	--	--	--	--	--	--	--	--																
Igoumenitsa Greece	--	811	550	1189	1253	1593	1003	385	955	--															
Ioánnina Greece	--	710	504	1088	1152	1492	902	344	854	--	101														
Iraklion Greece	71	--	--	--	--	--	--	--	--	121	--	--													
Istanbul Turkey	--	303	1175	521	585	833	335	1047	287	--	1114	1013	--												
Kastoria Greece	--	575	496	953	1017	1357	767	370	719	--	304	209	--	878											
Kavála Greece	--	180	692	558	622	962	372	564	324	--	631	536	--	483	395										
Kusadasi Turkey	--	616	1488	238	188	156	424	1360	472	--	1427	1326	--	667	1119	796									
Mátala Greece	139	--	--	--	--	--	--	--	--	144	--	--	68	--	--	--	--								
Meteora Greece	--	615	353	993	1057	1397	807	227	759	--	226	125	--	918	143	435	1231	--							
Methóni Greece	--	1126	313	1504	1568	1908	1318	430	1270	--	815	783	--	1429	762	946	1742	--	619						
Nafplion Greece	--	956	147	1334	1398	1738	1148	267	1100	--	652	617	--	1259	595	776	1572	--	452	200					
Olympia Greece	--	1115	302	1493	1557	1897	1307	422	1259	--	807	772	--	1418	750	935	1731	--	607	131	189				
Pamukkale Turkey	--	784	1656	406	356	310	592	1528	640	--	1595	1494	--	835	1359	964	186	--	1399	1910	1740	1899			
Rafina Greece	--	886	25	1264	1328	1668	1078	198	1030	--	583	553	--	1189	542	706	1502	--	399	371	203	358	1670		
Sparta Greece	--	1042	229	1420	1484	1824	1234	349	1186	--	734	699	--	1345	677	862	1658	--	534	126	116	193	1826	285	
Thessaloníki Greece	--	379	541	757	821	1161	571	413	523	--	480	385	--	682	244	199	995	--	284	795	625	787	1163	555	711

SELECTED CITIES AND CAMPGROUNDS

ALEXANDROUPOLIS, GREECE

Population 36,000

Alexandroupolis makes a good place to spend the night before or after crossing the border with Turkey. The town is only 40 kilometers from the crossing near Ipsala. This relatively new town is a port and a resort, the promenade along the beach is its best feature. A huge lighthouse on the waterfront is hard to miss.

Alexandroupolis Campground

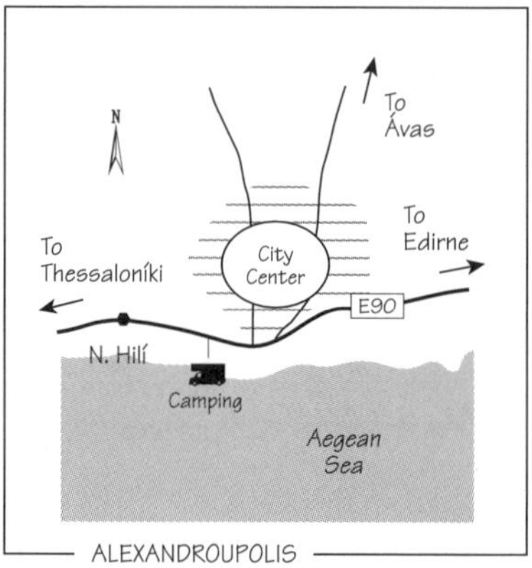

✦ CAMPING ALEXANDROUPOLIS

Address: GR-68100 Alexandroupolis
Telephone: 0551 26055
Price: Inexpensive

Open all year

This large beach-front campground is close to town and very nice. The sites are located off a grid of paved drives, they are separated by hedges and some have paved parking surfaces with large grass areas next to them, others are grass only. Sites are numbered and assigned. Electrical outlets are convenient to the sites, they have either 6 or 8 amp service and German plugs. There are big shade trees and lots of flowering bushes. Shower/toilet buildings have adjustable hot water for showers but cold water in the shaving sinks. Dish and clothes-washing sinks have hot water. The wide beach here is a combination of sand and gravel, the campground has a snack bar and store (closed in winter).

Camping Alexandroupolis is located just under a kilometer east of town on the main road west to Thessaloníki.

Side Trips from Alexandroupolis

Bird enthusiasts will want to drive north to the **Dadia Forest** about 75 kilometers north of Alexandroupolis. This pine forest is home and nesting site to 29 of the 36 European species of birds of prey.

ATHENS (ATHÍNA)

Population: 3,025,000

Few people visit Greece without a visit to Athens. The chaotic and smog-choked city may seem uninviting and intimidating compared to the attractive and easy-going Greek countryside but never fear. Athens has several campgrounds and they are on the outskirts of town. You will find that a camping visit to Athens is easy and fun.

The two big must-see attractions in Athens are the **Acropolis** and the **National Archeological Museum**. It is easy to see both in one day, but there is lots more to make a multi-day visit to Athens desirable. The city has several interesting neighborhoods as well as lots of museums and ancient Greek archeological sites.

Everyone loves the colorful old **Pláka** district with its relatively quiet streets, tavernas and restaurants, shops and studios. Located on the north slope of the Acropolis, the current buildings in this oldest section of Athens date from the Ottoman period. Next to Pláka to the west is the **Monastiráki** district which is probably best known for the flea market centered in the Plateía Avissynías.

After viewing the Acropolis you'll want to visit the nearby **Agora** which was the center of both commerce and government in ancient Athens. Don't miss the **Tower of the Winds,** located just to the east and actually in the Monastiráki district. Northwest of the Agora is the **Kerameikós**, ancient Athens' cemetery where you will see copies of tomb sculptures marking the grave sites. The originals are in the National Archeological Museum or the Oberlander Museum. A less well known ancient site is the **Temple of Olympian Zeus** dating from the Roman period and located east of the Acropolis and southeast of the Pláka district.

Athens is well supplied with museums. Top billing must go to the National Archeological Museum, but also definitely worth a look are the **Benáki Museum**, and the

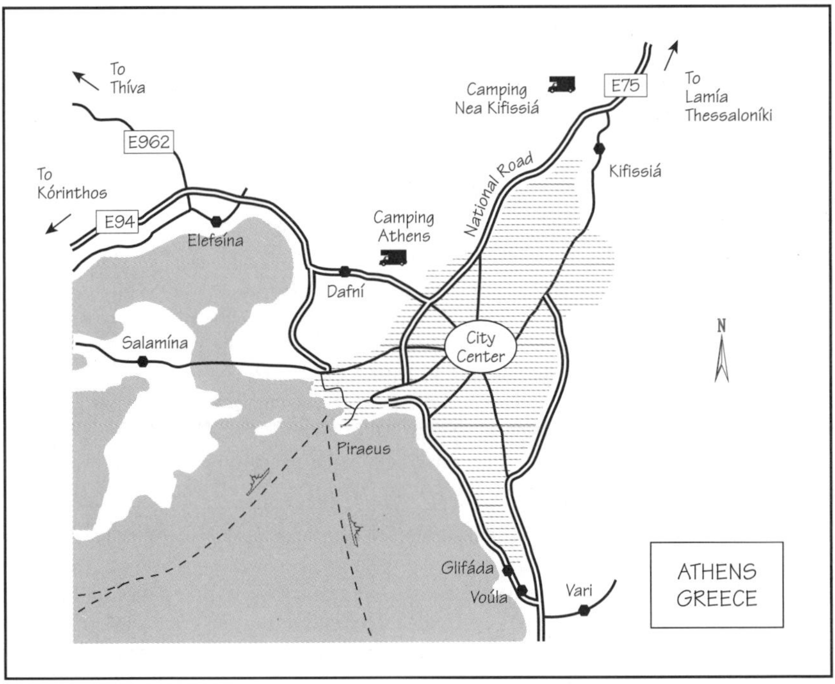

Museum of Cycladic Art. If you have time there is also the Acropolis Museum, National Gallery of Art, the Municipal Art Gallery, National Historical Museum, Byzantine Museum, Oberlander Museum, Theatrical Museum, Greek Folk Art Museum, War Museum, City of Athens Museum, and the Kanellópoulos Museum.

Most ferries to the Aegean Islands (Cylades, Dodecanese, Argo-Saronic, and Northeast Aegean) and Crete leave from **Piraeus**, the port of Athens since ancient times. Automobile access is easiest from the west of Athens, just follow the trucks. See the introduction to our section on Crete and the Islands toward the end of this chapter for more information.

Once your bus drops you in central Athens you will find that it is easy to get around. A metro system ties the main sections of the city together, including Piraeus. A multitude of bus routes complete the public transportation system.

Athens Campgrounds

✦ CAMPING ATHENS

Address: 198 Athinon Avenue,
GR-12136 Peristeri
Telephone: 01 5814114
Price: Moderate

Open all year

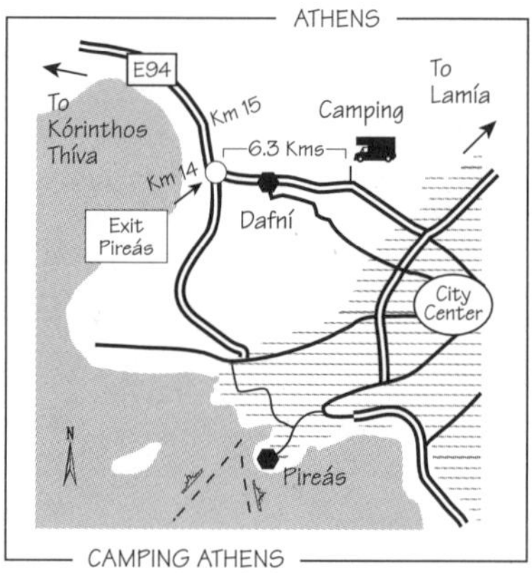

This is the best known and most crowded of the Athens campgrounds. If you are approaching Athens from the west this is probably the best choice for your Athens base. Unfortunately, the convenient location on the main access road to Athens from the west means that the campground tends to be very noisy, even during the night.

The campground slopes gently up from the busy Athens-Patras Highway. Sites types vary, some are back-in vehicle spaces and others tent sites, some with parking nearby. Most are on dirt. There is some shade although not for all sites. Electrical outlets are widely spaced (16 amps). Shower/toilet buildings are old but in good repair, hot showers are free, the dish washing and clothes washing sinks have cold water only. There is a small store and a restaurant at the campground. For a telephone you will have to go to a booth next to the road out front. There is a small supermarket near the campground. Access to Athens is by bus, the stop is just across the street from the campground and the trip to a stop near the Omonoias Square takes about 20 minutes to make the 7 kilometer run. Bus tickets can be purchased at the campground reception office. Try to arrive early since this campground tends to fill up.

To easily find the campground when arriving from the west on E 94 it is best to use your odometer. At about kilometer 15 you will be traveling along the waterfront west of the city. At kilometer 14 the road heads inland and you will see the off-ramp for Piraeus. Continue straight but zero your odometer at the overpass associated with this exit. At 6.3 kilometers from this point you will see the sign and entrance road for Camping Athens on the left.

✦ CAMPING NEA KIFISSIÁ

Address: Potamou 60, Adames,
GR-14562 Nea Kifissiá
Telephone: 01 8075579 Fax: 01 8075579
Price: Moderate

Open all year

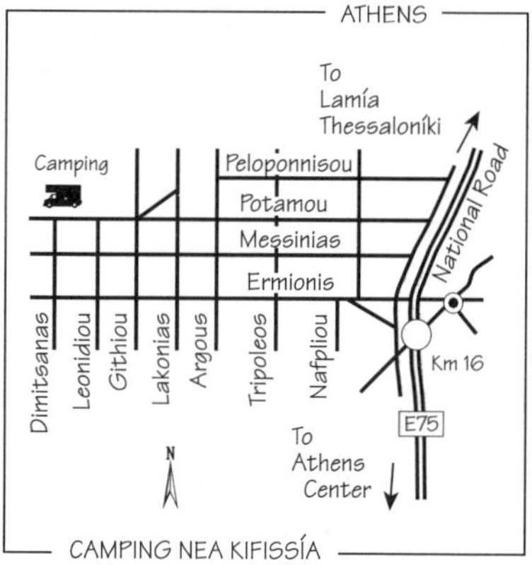

Less well known than Camping Athens, this campground can be an excellent base for visiting the city, particularly if you are arriving from the north on E 75.

This is a medium-sized campground with some permanents but room for tourist campers. It is quiet and well kept with gravel drives and sites with good shade, some from shade frames. The shower/toilet building is modern with adjustable hot showers. The campground has a swimming pool and restaurant and there is a grocery store nearby. Access to central Athens is by bus and metro or by bus, the bus takes about 45 minutes.

The campground is signed from near the 16-kilometer marker on E 75 north of Athens. The campground is situated to the west of the highway, about 6 blocks back into a residential neighborhood.

AYVALIK, TURKEY

Population 30,000

This small Turkish city occupies the coast opposite the Greek island of Lesbos. It is little visited by international tourists but is a popular Turkish resort. The island of Alibey Adasi is connected to the mainland north of town by a causeway. You can drive onto the island and will find yourself in a small town (also known as Alibey). There are many restaurants here, many people come by boat from Ayvalik to have a meal.

Ayvalik Campground

✦ ADA CAMPING

Address: Alibey Adasi, Ayvalik
Telephone: 0266 3121211
Price: Inexpensive

Open May 1 to October 15

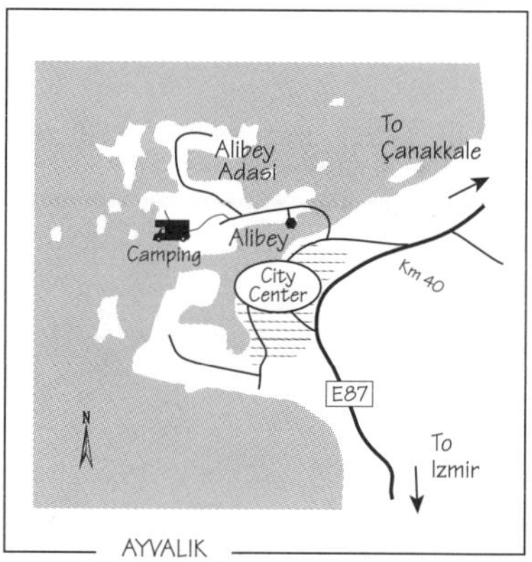

Ada Camping is the obvious choice for camping in Ayvalik, if only because there are signs for it everywhere. The campground is on the island of Alibey Adasi in a remote location past the village on the sea shore.

The campground is medium-sized with several grassy fields with scattered olive trees for camping. There are some sites with shade frames and a few right along the water next to the small rocky beach. Electricity is through German plugs and is very widely spaced. The shower/toilet facilities are older and could use some maintenance, there is one shower each for men and women, it does have hot water and requires a token. A kitchen room has a gas stove for the use of campers and dish-washing sinks. There is also a laundry area. The campground has a small restaurant, a playground and a basketball court. A few supplies can be purchased at the campground.

To reach the campground follow the Ayvalik road off the main highway near kilometer 40. You will probably see signs for the campground from there. The road will take you to the coast and Ayvalik, you will see the causeway to the offshore island off to your right. Make your way to it and cross, the road is paved and good. Once on the island zero your odometer. In 1.5 kilometer you will come to the cut-off to the left for the village, go straight. At the Y at 3.8 kilometers go left, then turn right at 4 kilometers up a narrow road. You will reach the campground at 7.8 kilometers.

BERGAMA, TURKEY

Population 50,000

Bergama was known in ancient times as Pergamum. Its period of greatest prosperity was during the years immediately following Alexander the Great. Today Bergama is known for the ruins of the Acropolis and Asciepion dating from that time. Otherwise this is an agricultural market town with most thing of interest to a visitor related to its past.

The **Acropolis** site is located at the end of a 4 kilometer road that leaves town near the Red Basilica at the eastern edge of the built-up area. There are great views over Bergama from the site which has many ruined and rebuilt structures. The **Asclepion** was an ancient medical center, and it too has many interesting structures dating from the first and second centuries AD. Access is by a road that leaves the highway just a short distance toward the city from the Mocamp Berksoy. The **Archeology Museum** at the center of town is very good.

Bergama Campground

✦ MOCAMP BERKSOY

Address: Izmir Yolu PK.19, Bergama
Telephone: 0232 6332595
Price: Inexpensive

Open all year

This medium-sized campground is associated with the Hotel Berksoy located nearby. Camping is in a grass-covered field with sites not marked or separated. Some trees provide shade. Electricity is available from a few boxes (Ger-

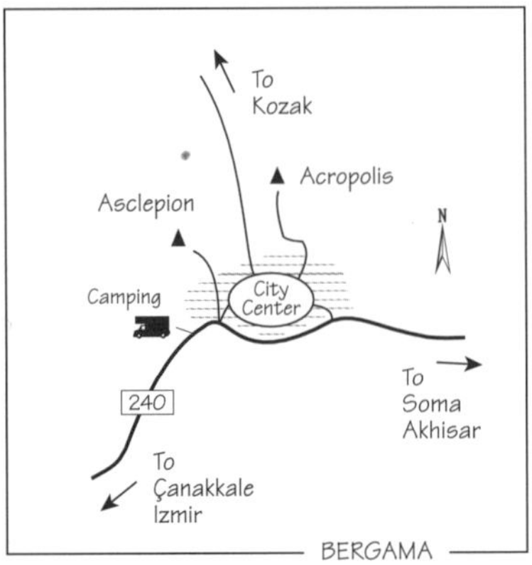

man plugs). The shower/toilet building offers adjustable hot showers and hot water in shaving, dish-washing, and clothes-washing sinks. A cooking area has propane burners for the use of the campers. The nice swimming pool, tennis court and restaurant at the hotel are available to campers.

As you approach Bergama from the southwest (toward Izmar) the Hotel Berksoy is easy to spot on the north side of the road about 2 kilometers outside town. The campground is just west of the hotel.

BODRUM, TURKEY

Population 25,000

Bodrum is a tourist town, and a relatively attractive one. It surrounds two bays with the impressive Castle of St Peter rising between them. Hundred of rental yachts dock in the western-most bay and pedestrian walking streets offer restaurants and shops aimed at visitors. Day trips on the yachts to remote swimming spots are very popular.

In ancient times Bodrum was called Halicarnassus and was known for the **Mausoleum**, the tomb of King Mausolus. It was built in the fourth century BC and was one of the Seven Wonders of the Ancient World. Unfortunately little of it remains today. There are exhibits, however, showing what it used to look like. The **Castle of St Peter** dates from the early 15th century and was built by the Knights Hospitaller. You can tour the castle, it houses the **Museum of Underwater Archeology**, the **Glass-ship Wreck Hall** and several other exhibits, actually a little bit of everything.

Bodrum Campground

✦ ZETAS CAMPING

Address: Gumbet, Bodrum
Telephone: 0252 3161407,
Reservations 0252 3162231
Price: Inexpensive

Open April 1 to October 31

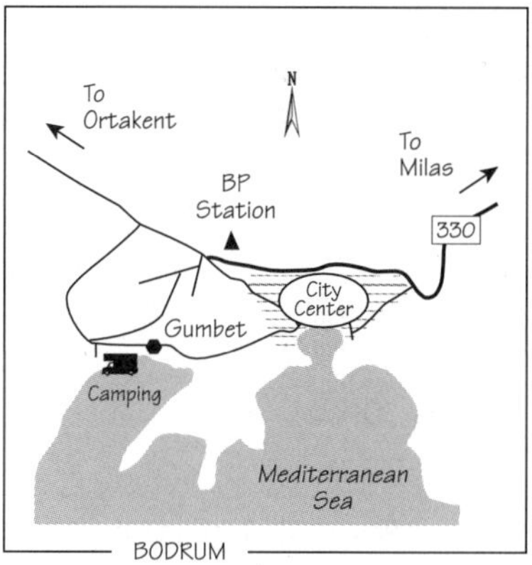

Zetas is a popular swimming and sun-bathing beach, it also has a restaurant, bar, and small store. It is located in the small resort town of Gumbet, really little more than a suburb of Bodrum with many hotels, restaurants, and discos.

The medium-sized camping area sits behind the beach and other structures, it is fenced and there is a manned gatehouse for security. Camping sites are scattered under big shade trees, they are not marked or physically separated. Electricity (German plugs, 16 amps) is from widely spaced boxes. The shower/toilet facilities are older but in relatively good repair, solar hot water is available in showers, shaving sinks, and for dish and clothes washing. A kitchen area offers gas burners for the use of campers.

VIEW OF HARBOR IN BODRUM

The beach out front is crowded but nice. It is a strenuous 45-minute walk in to Bodrum, busses are available.

The main highway descends into Bodrum and then curves around the inland side of town toward the west. Watch for a BP station on the right, just beyond is a road going left for Gumbet. Take this left turn and zero your odometer. At the first Y at .1 kilometer go right. At the next Y at .4 kilometers go left. Follow the road as it turns right at 1.3 kilometers. At the intersection at 2.1 kilometers go left and then immediately right down toward the beach, the campground entrance in on the left, it was unmarked when we visited.

ÇANAKKALE, TURKEY

Population 55,000

Çanakkale occupies an enviable position on the Asian shore near the head of the Dardanelles. This is the narrowest part of the strait and was the ancient crossing point for armies intent upon invading Europe or Asia as well as a good place for modern travelers to cross. A car ferry takes 25 minutes to cross from Eceabat on the Gallipoli Peninsula, it runs every hour and the cost is reasonable. Purchase tickets at the ferry dock.

Tour operators in Çanakkale take advantage of the short crossing to offer bus tours of the Gallipoli Peninsula, but most visitors with their own vehicles will be happier doing the tour on their own. The other popular destination from Çanakkale is the ruins of ancient Troy. They are situated 28 kilometers south of the city, see side trips below for information.

If you are interested in the Gallipoli campaign you may want to visit the museums in Çanakkale devoted to it. They are the **Naval Museum** and **Military Museum** located next to the Çimenlik fortress south of the ferry docks. There is also an **Archeological Museum** with artifacts from Troy located about two kilometers toward Troy from the ferry docks.

Çanakkale Campground

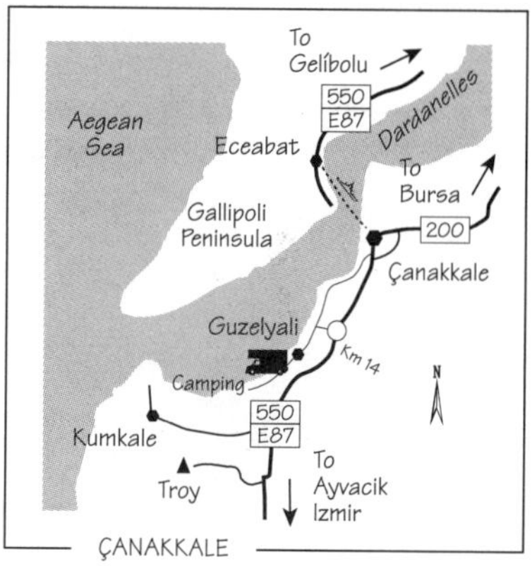

✦ MOCAMP TROVA

Address: Guzelyali, Çanakkale
Telephone: 0286 2328025
Price: Inexpensive

Open May 1 to October 31

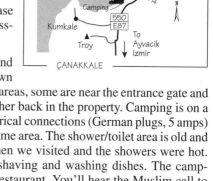

The Mocamp Trova is your best bet for a base to explore Troy or spend the night after crossing from Gallipoli.

Mocamp Trova is a medium sized campground sitting between the road through the small town of Guzelyali and the ocean. Sites are in two areas, some are near the entrance gate and reception office, others are under pines farther back in the property. Camping is on a hard packed dirt surface. Widely space electrical connections (German plugs, 5 amps) are provided. Rental motel units share the same area. The shower/toilet area is old and could use some repairs but it was clean when we visited and the showers were hot. Sinks with cold water were available for shaving and washing dishes. The campground has a sandy beach out front and a restaurant. You'll hear the Muslim call to prayer several times each day and evening and perhaps the thump from a nearby disco. There are small restaurants nearby and also a grocery store about 100 meters from the campground entrance.

The campground is on the coast about 14 kilometers south of Çanakkale. There are two roads, one along the coast that passes through several suburbs and villages, another slightly inland that is quicker and more direct. Watch for signs off this one for Guzelyali which is where the campground is located. You will see it on the sea side as you driver through town.

Side Trip from Çanakkale

Most visitors to the area want to take a look at ancient **Troy**. The site is really not too impressive, but it has interpretive signs and a replica of the famous Trojan Horse that makes a good subject for a photograph. The entrance road to the Troy site heads west from near the 28 kilometer marker which is 14 kilometers south of Mocamp Trova.

DELPHI (DELFÍ), GREECE

Population 3,000

The archeological site at Delphi occupies one of the most impressive locations in Greece. High on the side of Mt. Parnassus overlooking the Gulf of Corinth, both the archeological site and the campground have great views.

Modern Delphi is a small village dedicated to the legions of tourists that visit the archeological site. It has many restaurants and shops, there are three campgrounds nearby.

The Oracle of Delphi was in some ways the center of the ancient world. People from all directions came to consult the oracle. The site has a fourth-century BC Temple of Apollo, a theater, and a stadium as well as many other lesser structures and monuments. Everything is scattered up and down a steep slope, there's a museum at the lower end near the entrance.

Delphi Campground

✦ CAMPING APOLLON DELPHI

Address: Delphi GR-33054
Telephone: 0265 82762
Price: Moderate

Open all year

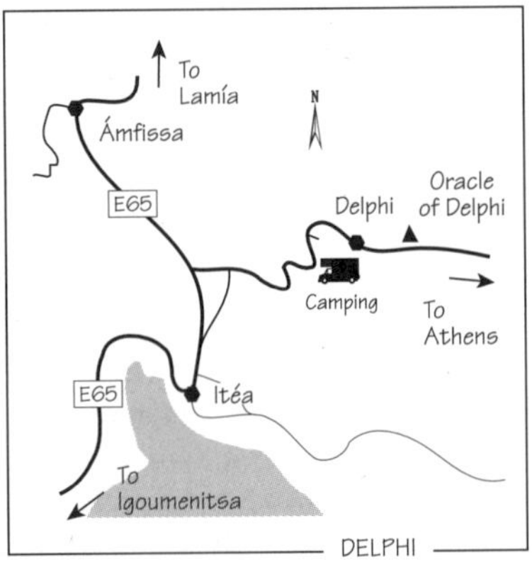

This is the closest campground to the village and occupies a very scenic location at the top of a ridge. Many sites, particularly those for tents, have wonderful views, the only drawback is that it is exposed to winds coming down the mountain.

The medium-sized campground has sites for wheeled rigs in the paved main yard near the entrance. These are back-in sites with electricity available (German plugs, 10 amps) and shade frames. Tent sites occupy terraces below the main restaurant building. Restrooms are small but clean and in good repair, showers are hot and there is hot water for shaving and dish and clothes washing. The campground has a restaurant/bar and a small store as well as a very nice swimming pool and a playground. The walk in to Delphi is about 1.5 kilometers, figure another kilometer or so to reach the archeological site on the other side of the village.

The campground is easy to find. It is on the right side of the road as you wind your way up the mountainside from the direction of Itéa. It is about 2 kilometers down the hill from the village, the archeological site is another kilometer or so on the far side.

GALLIPOLI, TURKEY

The Gallipoli Peninsula is one of the top tourist attractions in Turkey, particularly for visitors from Britain, Australia and New Zealand. The peninsula forms the north shore of the Dardanelles and was the location of one of the most fiercely fought battles of World War I. ANZAC troops (from Australia and New Zealand) were heavily involved. On the Turkish side Mustafa Kemal (Ataturk) began his rise to fame here by directing the bloody but successful defense against the Allied troops.

Today the peninsula is covered by pine forests and fields. There are dozens of cemeteries and war memorials. Some of the heaviest fighting and many of the monuments are at Anzac Cove on the west coast. There was another amphibious landing and battle at the south end of the peninsula and there are more monuments there.

The roads around this area of the peninsula are roughly paved and uncrowded so it is easy to drive to the various sites though you will do some walking once you arrive. The campground is between Anzac Cove and the south end of the peninsula.

On the east shore of the Gallipoli Peninsula the town of Eceabat is the best source of supplies and also the port for the car ferry that makes hourly crossings to Asia at Çanakkale. Tickets can be purchased at the dock.

Gallipoli Campgound

✦ HOTEL KUM CAMPING

Address: Kabatepe, Eceabat
Telephone: 0286 8141466
Price: Inexpensive

Open April 1 to October 31

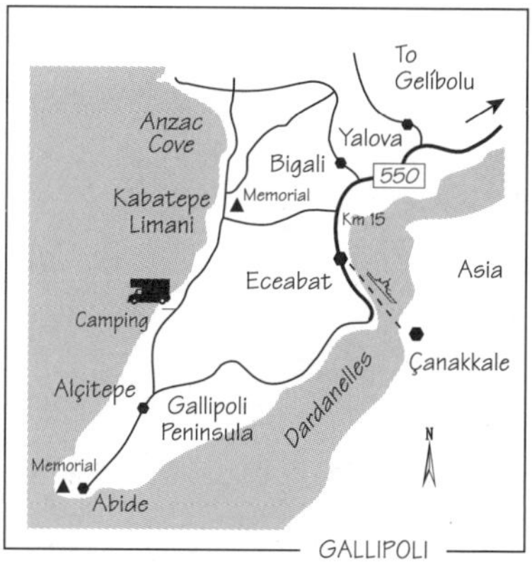

There is now a campground near the battle sites on the peninsula. The hotel and campground are frequently visited by busses of people touring the peninsula because this is the best place to swim in the area.

The campground occupies a fenced yard behind the hotel. Sites are in several long rows along curbs with electricity boxes (German plugs). The surface is grass. The shower/toilet building is in poor repair and was not clean when we visited, there was only cold water. Campers were allowed to use one of the hotel rooms for hot showers. The hotel has a large swimming pool, a restaurant, a café, a small store with limited selection, and a good sandy swimming beach.

To reach the campground follow the road west toward Kabatepe Limani where it branches off the main highway 1.4 kilometers north of Eceabat. Follow this road toward Kabatepe for 8.4 kilometers. You will come to an intersection, turn left and you will come to the campground in another 5.2 kilometers.

IGOUMENITSA, GREECE

Population 6,000

This small town serves as the nearest Greek mainland port for ferries from Italy. It offers the amenities required for ferry travelers. You'll find ferry ticket offices, bank machines, restaurants, a tourist office, and even a campground.

Igoumenitsa Campground

✦ CAMPING KALAMI BEACH

Address: Platariá, Igoumenitsa GR-46100
Telephone: 0665 71211
Price: Moderate

Open April 1 to October 15 (varies slightly)

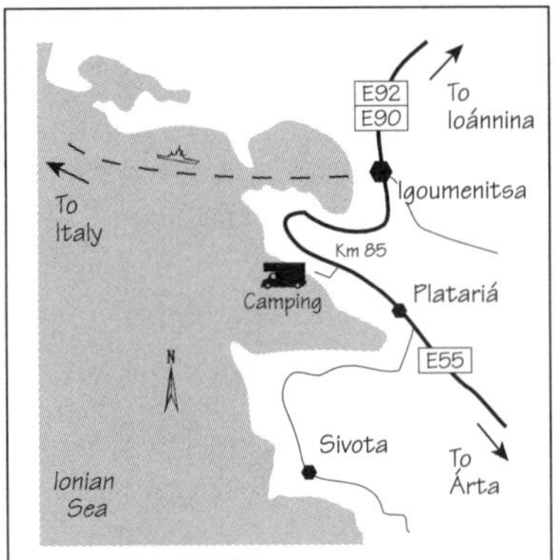

IGOUMENITSA

This campground is located about 5 kilometers south of town on E55. Sites are on terraces with good shade just above the sea shore. Electricity (German plugs, 10 amps) is available. Restrooms are clean and well kept and have free hot showers. There is a restaurant/bar, grocery shop, laundry with washing machine, and dump station.

To find the campground watch for the road down to the beach near the kilometer 85 marker.

IOÁNNINA, GREECE

Population 60,000

Ioánnina's period of glory was during Ottoman rule of Greece, particularly during the rule of Ali Pasha at the beginning of the 19th century. The town sits on the western shore of Lake Pamvotis and an old walled town occupies a peninsula projecting into the lake. During that period the city became a silver-working center and it is still a good place to buy silver filigree jewelry. There are several interesting museums in and around the walls of the old city: the **Popular Art Museum** in the **Aslan Pasha Mosque**, the **Byzantine Museum**, and the **Archeological Museum**.

Off shore is the island of **Nisí**. Boats run from the old city or fortress area. There is a village and several monasteries on the Island. The most-visited spot is probably the room in the **Panteleimon Monastery** where Ali Pasha finally met his maker after pushing the Turkish sultan just a little too far.

Ioánnina Campground

✦ LIMNOPOULA CAMPING

Address: Kanari 10, Limnopoula, GR-45500 Ioánnina
Telephone: 0651 25265
Price: Inexpensive

Open all year

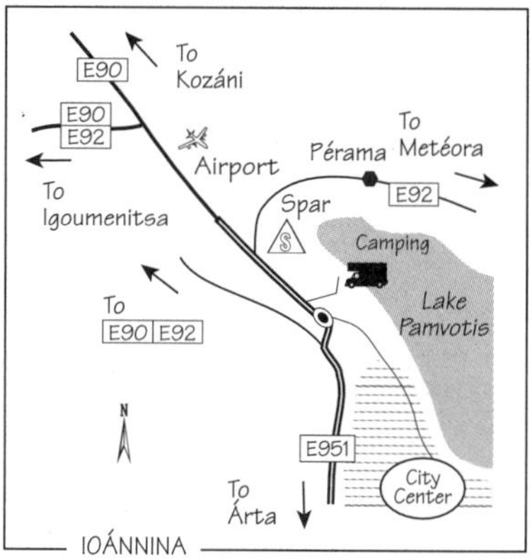

This medium-sized campground has a very pleasant location on the lake shore some 2 kilometers from the central part of town. The site is also a rowing club, it is fun to watch the action as local athletes launch and retrieve their shells. Campers park or set up their tents off paved drives on a well-trimmed lawn right next to the lake. Electrical boxes (German plugs, 10 amps) are conveniently located, there are two covered picnic pavilions. The shower/toilet building is modern and clean, showers are free and hot. There is an indoor laundry and dish-washing room with hot water. Next door is a restaurant and there is a Spar grocery store about a half kilometer away.

The roads from Métsovo (E92) and Kozáni. (E90) meet north of town near the lake shore. There is a Spar grocery on the corner. Travel south about .5 kilometer and take a left at the far end of a long oval roundabout. Immediately turn right and then left into the signed campground entrance road.

Side Trips from Ioánnina

The **Pérama Caves** lie near the village of Pérama about 4 kilometers north of Ioánnina. This is probably the largest network of limestone caves in Greece, there are tours through the caves.

Dodóni, 22 kilometers southeast of Ioánnina was the site of ancient Greece's second most popular oracle after the one at Delphi. It was even visited by Jason before he departed in search of the golden fleece. There is a huge Greek theater at Dodóni, as well as the ruins of a stadium, an acropolis, and a Byzantine basilica.

North of Ioánnina about 35 kilometers is the **Zagória** region. It is in the northern part of the Píndos Mountains and is home to the **Víkos Gorge**, a popular hiking route. There are some 40 small villages in the region, many can be toured by car on decent but small roads. There are many hiking routes, the most-traveled by far being the gorge. Most hikers start at the village of Monodéndri and hike the 14 kilometers to Megálo Pápigko.

GREECE & TURKEY

ISTANBUL, TURKEY

Population 12,000,000

Istanbul is not only Turkey's largest city, it is truly one of the world's great cities and should not be missed. It has history, architecture, and a wonderful street life. It is also very easy to visit as a camper, the two campgrounds we list below are easily reached in a camping vehicle and have excellent public transportation connections to the city.

Think of Istanbul as having two sections, the old and the new. The old section is also known as Eski Istanbul, it occupies the peninsula between the Golden Horn and the Sea of Marmara. New Istanbul, also called Beyoglu, is on the far side of the Golden Horn, connected by two bridges. If you are up to walking 4 or 5 miles during the course of a day you will have no problem getting around to the central sites on foot. The tourist areas are full of friendly touts who want to help you find their favorite shops, be advised.

Most of the sites that are on the must-see list for tourists are located near each other in the old city in what is called the Sultanahmet Area. These include **Hagia Sophia** (Aya Sofya), the **Blue Mosque** (Sultan Ahmet Camii), **Topkapi Palace**, the **Cistern Basilica** (Yerebatan Saray), and the **Covered Market**. Istanbul is well stocked with museums, besides those in the Topkapi Palace you may be interested in the **Textile**

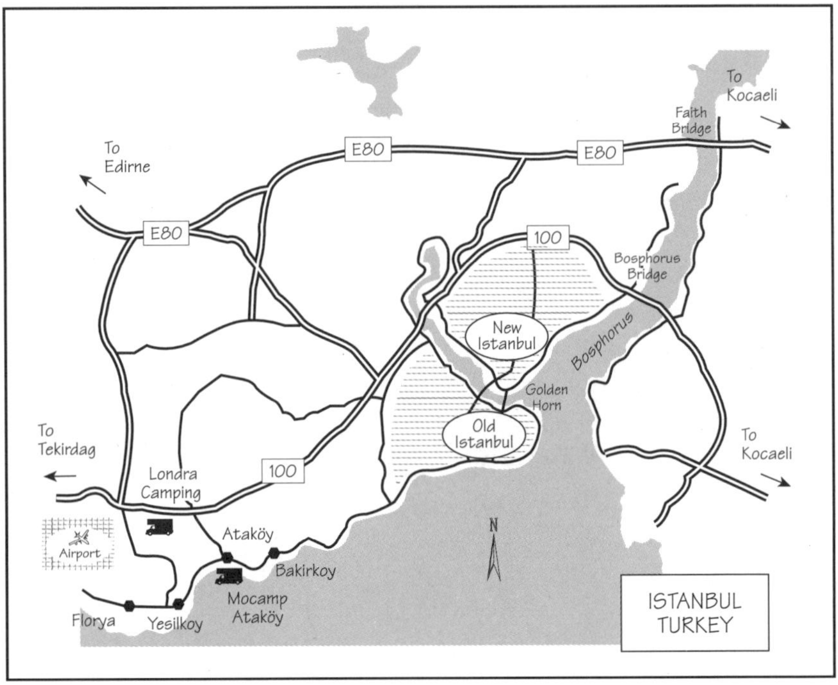

Museum, the **Mosaic Museum**, the **Turkish and Islamic Arts Museum**, the **Archeological Museum** and the **Museum of the Ancient Orient**. All are well worth a visit and all are near the most popular sites.

If you stroll across the Galata Bridge you will find yourself in the new city, Beyoglu. Traditionally, from very early times, this has been the foreign section of the city. It remains the section that is most European and has most of the hotels and embassies. Actually, your destination is at the top of that hill you see ahead. The easiest way to get there is via the Tünel, a short French-built subway that takes you to Tünel Square. This square marks the west end of **Istiklal Caddesi**, a walking street lined with hotels, embassies, stores, and restaurants, including virtually all of the American fast food chains. At its end is Taksim Square. About a kilometer north of the square is the very interesting **Military Museum**.

Transportation around Istanbul is not difficult, you just have to be flexible. There are subways, trams, busses, dolmusses, taxis, and even ferries. Getting from one place to another is a matter of picking the best means of transportation. If you don't mind walking most of the sights can be reached on foot with little difficulty, and your time en route is bound to be filled with interesting sights.

Istanbul Campgrounds

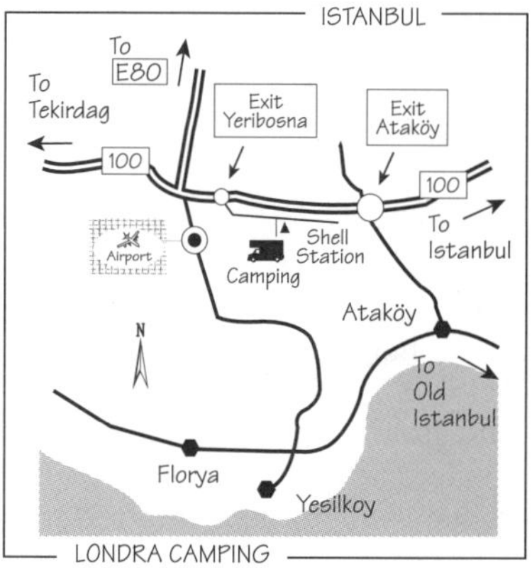

✦ **LONDRA CAMPING**

Address: Londra Asfalti,
Sutsanayi Karsisi, Istanbul
Telephone: 0212 5604200
Price: Moderate

Open all year

This very small campground is being squeezed out of existence. A new building occupies much of the former area of the campground, room for about 30 rigs remains. The location is handy but noisy since it sits next to one of the major highways into Istanbul.

The campground is located behind a Shell station and hotel. Camp sites are off paved driveways on grass under shade trees. A small fence surrounds the area in an attempt to keep a constant stream of visitors to the adjoining soccer fields from wandering through. Electricity (German plugs) is available from two plug boxes. The restrooms are in the lower floor of a large building, they are in poor repair and were not very clean when we visited. Showers were hot and free. There is a cooking room with gas burners and sinks with hot water for dishes, also a room with tables for eating. There is a swimming pool and a restaurant, both closed when we visited in October. The Shell station out front has a few grocery items. The reception office is in the hotel building, you can get instructions for the trip in to town there. The Yeribosna metro stop is only a half kilometer away and the subway will take you to Aksaray Square which is within walking distance of the Sultanahmet.

The campground is off Highway 100 which comes in to Istanbul from the west. Watch carefully for the Florya exit as you approach town near the kilometer 21 marker. Zero your odometer here at the Florya exit. You will soon see the airport exits and then at 4.1 kilometers from the Florya exit you will see a small exit marked Yeribosna. Take it. The campground is located along a lateral road on the right side of the highway that can only be entered from this exit. The campground is behind the Shell station that you will see after driving down the lateral .7 kilometers. If you miss the exit but see the Shell station it is possible but difficult to exit at the Ataköy exit just beyond, reverse direction, get back on the highway, exit at the airport exit, reverse again, and give it another try. A better idea would be to just head for the next campground, Mocamp Ataköy, since it is off the Ataköy exit.

✦ MOCAMP ATAKÖY

Address: Kennedy Caddesi, Ataköy, Sahilyolu, Istanbul
Telephone: 0212 5596014
Price: Moderate

Open all year

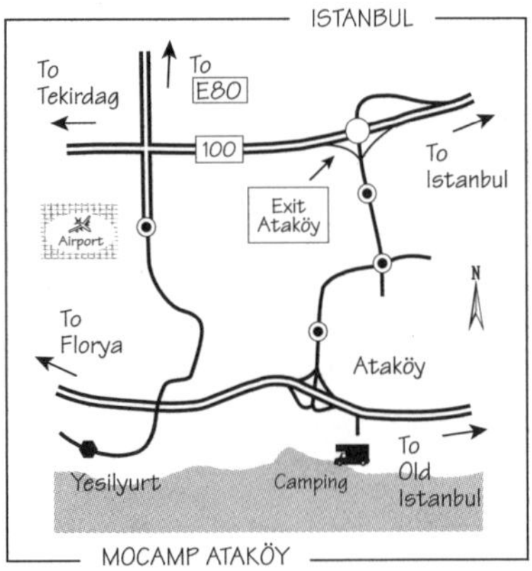

Mocamp Ataköy is our preferred campground for Istanbul. It is a large pleasant campground in a coastal location with decent access and good transportation in to town.

This is a large campground. It has a gated and guarded entrance. Camping is in several large grassy fields under shade trees. Electricity is from widely-spaced boxes (German plugs). Several restrooms are adequate with boilers providing free hot showers and hot water to shaving and dish-washing sinks. The campground is on the shore of the Sea of Marmara but swimming is inadvisable due to pollution. There is a small commercial area about a half kilometer from the campground with grocery stores and restaurants. There is a larger very modern shopping center about a kilometer away, it has a food court with most western fast food chains represented. Easiest access to central Istanbul is by modern double-decker bus from a stop near the campground to Eminönü which is conveniently located at the south side of the Galata Bridge.

This campground is actually not far from Londra Camping. Easiest access is off Highway 100 which comes in to Istanbul from the west. Watch carefully for the Florya exit as you approach town near the kilometer 21 marker. Zero your odometer here at the Florya exit. You will soon see the airport exits and then at 6.1 kilometers from the Florya exit you will see an exit marked Ataköy. Take this exit and once again zero your odometer. Immediately after the exit take the right. You will come to a traffic circle at .5 kilometers, go straight through. There is another traffic circle (actually more like a Y) at .9 kilometers, go right. At 1.3 kilometers the road curves left and goes over a bridge over railroad tracks. At another traffic circle at 2.7 kilometers go straight. The road immediately goes under an overpass, at the T on the far side take a left which is an on-ramp for the coastal road and you will immediately see the campground on your right.

KASTORIA, GREECE

Population 17,000

Little Kastoria is a little off the beaten path for most tourists but well worth a visit. Kastoria is known as one the most beautiful towns in Greece. It is located at the base of a peninsula that juts into Lake Kastoria (also called Lake Orestias). This is a fur town. Beavers lived in the lake at one time and when they eventually disappeared the locals continued to make fur garments for export out of fur brought in from other places. Wealthy furriers built mansions known as **arkhontika**. You can view the interior of one by visiting the **Kastorian Museum of Folklore** which is housed in an arkhontika built in about 1450 AD. Kastoria also has many small Byzantine churches that were originally private chapels for the arkhontikas. It is difficult to gain entrance to many of them but there is a **Byzantine Museum** in town with icons on display. An attractive feature of the town is 9-kilometer road that skirts the peninsula, it makes a great walking path.

Kastoria Campground

✦ BYZANTINE MONASTERY OF PANAYIA MAVRIOTISSA

Price: A contribution is expected (Inexpensive)
Open May 1 to October 31

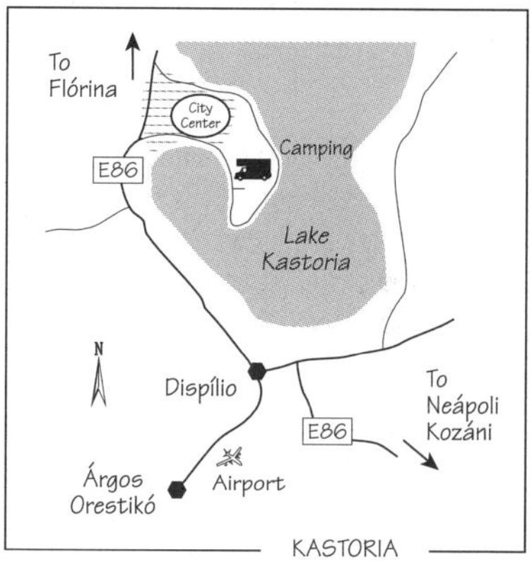

This is a small campground with few amenities, but it has a scenic location and is fun because it is unique. The campground is on the grounds of a monastery which sits on the shore of the lake mid way along the road that skirts the peninsula. Sites are on terraces that climb a grassy hill next to the buildings. Maneuvering room is limited, the sites on the hill are really only suitable for tents. There is room to park several wheeled camping vehicles in the parking area below. Facilities are limited to a small and rustic building at the top of the campground, it has a couple of toilets (continental) and cold showers. There is a restaurant nearby, a small tour boat stops there occasionally as do some of the many walkers who pass by as they hike around the peninsula.

When you arriver in Kastoria make your way to the lake shore and toward the obvious wooded peninsula. The campground is 2 kilometers from the last houses of town at the south entrance to the peninsula road. Ask at the monastery for permission before setting up. Their English is limited but they'll understand what you want.

KAVÁLA, GREECE

Population 55,000

Kavála is an attractive port town with a long history. In roman times it was called Neapolis and was the port for Philippi which is a short distance inland. The Apostle Paul landed here en route to Philippe where he founded the first European Christian congregation. The **Kavála Archeological Museum** located a few blocks west of the port has items from excavations around the region including Kavála, Avdira, Amphipolis, and Philippi.

Today the town is a fishing port and a ferry port for transportation to the northeast Aegean Islands. The area around the central port is full of life and the Panagia, the promontory west of the port, is an old town with a Byzantine Castle.

Kavála Campground

✦ CAMPING IRINI

Address: Perigiali, GR-65001 Kavála
Telephone: 051 229785 Fax: 051 22949
Price: Moderate

Open all year

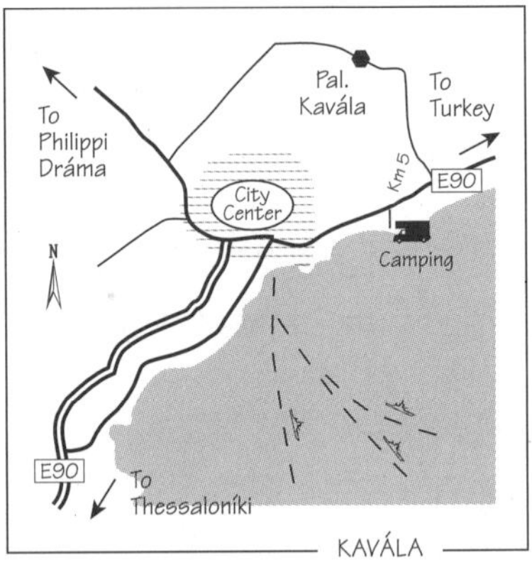

Camping Irini is a coastal campground just a few kilometers east of Kavála. This is a large campground with many of the sites (especially those along the beach) having paved parking pads and hedges to separate them. Electricity is convenient, plugs are English type. There is also lots of room for tents and parking on grass. Restrooms have adjustable hot showers but only continental-type toilets. There is a laundry room and a dish-washing and cooking room but no stoves are provided. The campground has an upscale restaurant, a small store, tennis courts, and a nice beach.

The campground is located 2 kilometers east of Kavála along the coastal road near the five kilometer marker.

Side Trips from Kavála

The ruins of ancient **Philippi** are about 16 kilometers northwest of Kavála. A theater and the ruins of the Agora remain. There is also a museum. Philippi is known as the site of the battle in 42 BC when the forces of Brutus and Cassius fought those of Octavian and Mac Anthony after the assassination of Julius Caesar.

KUSADASI, TURKEY

Population 50,000

Kusadasi is a southern Aegean tourist town. Cruise ships often stop here with all that that entails. The town is well prepared for them with lots of shops selling trinkets and nicer stuff, and many restaurants. There are also lots of hotels here, hosting hordes of vacationers from Europe. Despite all this the town has a lot to offer. It is an excellent base for excursions to local archeological sites, most importantly Ephesus.

Kusadasi Campground

✦ ÖNDER CAMPING

Address: Ataturk Bulvari 74,
TR-09400 Kusadasi
Telephone: 256 6142413
Price: Inexpensive

Open all year

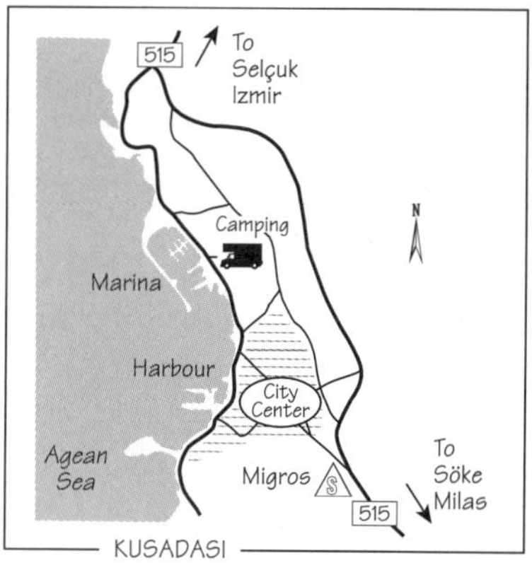

Two campgrounds sit side by side within easy walking distance of the center of Kusadasi. They are much alike, Yat Camping is on the north, Önder Camping on the south. They are across the street from a yacht harbor, just beyond the harbor is a beach, and a kilometer beyond that is the central walking district of town.

Önder Camping is a large campground. It is long and narrow, motel units line one side. Campsites are slightly terraced off a paved drive, there is lots of maneuvering room. Camping is on sparse grass under shade trees. Electrical outlets are widely scattered (German plugs). Restrooms are clean and modern by Turkish standards, they have adjustable hot showers and outside sinks for shaving and dish washing. The campground has a good restaurant/bar out front as well as a playground, swimming pool, and tennis court. There is a small shop at the campground and a better one just a block or so toward town.

The campground is located on the main road (Ataturk Bulvari) that comes into central Kusadasi along the harbor from the north. If you are coming from the direction of Selçuk and Ephesus (from the north) zero your odometer as you pass the Ephesus entrance road. You'll come to an intersection at 4.2 kilometers, turn left here. After 11.1 kilometers (15.3 on your odometer) the north entrance road to Kusadasi goes right. Turn here. You'll see the campground on the left at odometer 16.8 but will have to go beyond to a break in the median to turn back to the campground.

Side Trips from Kusadasi

Ephesus is considered the best-preserved and most extensive Greek ruin in Turkey, perhaps anywhere along the Mediterranean. It should definitely be on your tour card. The archeological site is about 2 kilometers outside Selçuk and about 17 kilometers from Kusadasi. There is lots of parking in the lower lot. Touts may try to get you to take a bus from there to the upper parking lot and then walk down through the ruins, this is unnecessary since the distances are not long and the elevation gain not large. There's an **Ephesus Museum** located near the center of Selçuk that adds much to a visit to Ephesus.

Pamacak Beach is directly seaward from Selçuk (don't turn toward Kusadasi at the intersection 4.2 kilometers west of Ephesus. It is a large and popular beach, you may find free campers parked there.

Priene, **Meletus**, and **Didyma** are all archeological sites located south of Kusadasi. While not up to the standard of Ephesus they are all well worth a look.

Samos is a large Greek island offshore from Kusadasi. Boats ply between the two, it is possible to go over for a day trip. Tickets are easy to get at local travel agencies, there are some formalities involving passports to go through as with any trip crossing the Turkish/Greek border but they are manageable.

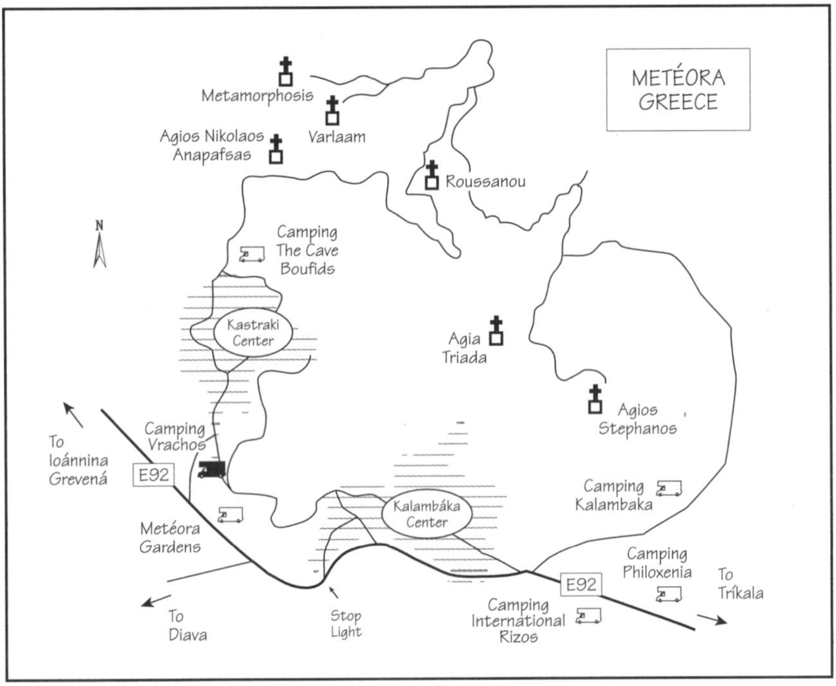

METÉORA, GREECE

Population Kalambáka 5,500, Kastraki 500

This is the name given to a region of northern Greece with a unique attraction. During the 13th to 15th centuries monasteries were built on top of huge sandstone pillars. The impressive and photogenic monasteries remain, today they are visited by thousands of travelers each year. The rock-top locations were defensive, there were no stairs, just winches used to lift visitors and provisions the hundreds of feet to the top.

Today there are 6 monasteries that will receive visitors. Stairways have been built, you won't need to arrive in a cargo net. A paved road some 15 kilometers long circles

MONASTERY NEAR METÉORA

through the area allowing access. There are also trails if you would rather hike. The two population centers are the town of Kalabáka and the small village of Kastraki. Several campgrounds serve the area, some in Kastraki, some located farther from the monasteries outside Kalabáka.

Visiting the monasteries is easy. There are parking lots at most that will accommodate vehicles up the size of a tour bus (many of these visit). Hours are usually from 9 A.M. to 6 P.M. although they do vary somewhat. Modest clothing is required for entry and this is monitored. At a minimum both men an women must have short sleeved shirts, long-sleeved ones are preferred, bare arms are not allowed. Long pants (or skirts below the knees) are required for both men and women, a skirt-like wrap is generally provided to you at the entrance if your clothing is not deemed to measure up.

Metéora Campground

✦ CAMPING VRACHOS KASTRAKI

Address: Kastraki, GR-42200 Kalambáka
Telephone: 0432 22293 Fax: 0432 23134
Price: Inexpensive

Open all year

Our favorite campground of the 5 or so in this area is Vrachos Kastraki. It is a modern campground with good facilities, lots of room, and a convenient location within walking distance of the shops and restaurants in Kastraki. Hikers will appreciate the location in Kastraki which is closer to the monasteries than most other campgrounds in the area.

This is a large campground. Camping is on grass or packed dirt off paved drives. Spaces are designated but not separated and many are shaded. Electricity (German plugs) is convenient to most sites. There are two facilities buildings housing both restrooms and dish- and clothes-washing sinks. Hot water is provided to showers and all of the sinks. There are covered cooking and eating areas with gas cook tops. There is also a huge swimming pool, a restaurant, and a small shop.

The campground is located on the outskirts of Kastraki on the road to Kalambáka. See the map for more information.

METHÓNI, GREECE

Population 1,300

Little Methóni has something unusual for a small Greek seaside village. On a point of land in front of the village is a huge Venetian fortress. Walls at least a kilometer long enclose an area that was once the port town, today it is mostly rubble and scrub. A small tower on an outlying island (reached from the fortress by a walkway) dates from the 16th century and is Byzantine. There is no entrance fee, explore to your heart's content.

Methóni Campground

✦ CAMPING METHÓNI

Address: Methóni, GR-24006 Messinias
Telephone: 0728 31228
Price: Inexpensive

Open May 15 to September 30

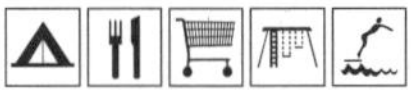

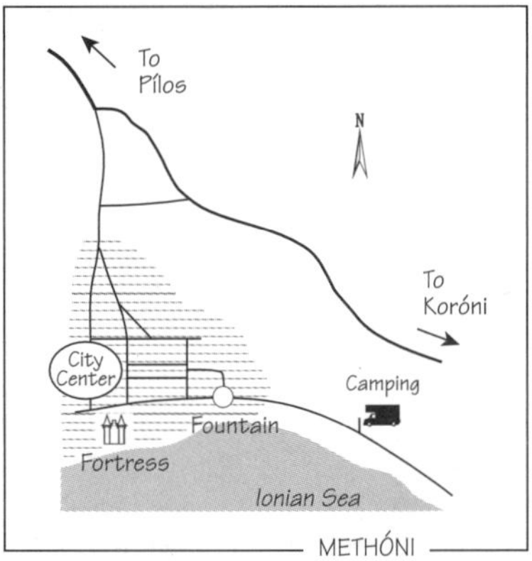

This is a municipal campground across the road from the beach. It is on the outskirts of Methoni within easy walking distance of restaurants, stores, and the fortress.

This is a large campground with campsites on sandy dirt. It can be a bit of a mess when it rains. There are metal frames with bamboo for shade, electricity (German plugs) is available to many of the sites. The restrooms are old and in poor repair but we found plenty of hot water for showers. All toilets are continental. Sinks are provided for shaving and for dish washing. The campground also has a restaurant, some grocery items for sale, and a playground. The beach across the street is used by swimmers and wind-surfers.

After taking the north exit for Methóni from the main highway you will come to a fork in the road. The easiest route through town leads to the left although either will work. Half kilometer from the fork you'll reach the beach, turn left and you'll soon see the campground.

NAFPLION, GREECE

Population 10,000

Nafplion was the Greek capital before it was moved to Athens. It is an attractive city with many interesting sights. More importantly, the campgrounds along the coast to the west make excellent bases for exploring the countryside around Nafplion, which is extremely rich in ancient Greek archeological sites and is known as Argolis.

The medieval section occupies a peninsula and dates mostly form the 15th and 16th centuries. The town was occupied by Turks and Venetians for long periods as they fought for control of this area. There are several mosques now converted to other uses. There is a prize-winning **Folk Art Museum** with exhibits showing the traditional textile production process, and also an **Archaeological Museum**. There are three different castle complexes in this town. The island of **Bourtzi** is fortified, it sits in the harbor. Just south of the old town is **Its Kale** which has four Venetian castles and the ancient acropolis. Finally there is the looming **Palamídi** which overlooks the town from 200 meters atop a high rock to the southeast. There are seven forts surrounded by a wall. The climb up to this fortress is said to have 1,000 steps, you can also drive up by taking a roundabout route.

Nafplion Campground

✦ NEW TRITON

Address: 21060 Plaka Drepano, Argolidos
Telephone: 0752 59369
Price: Inexpensive

Open all year

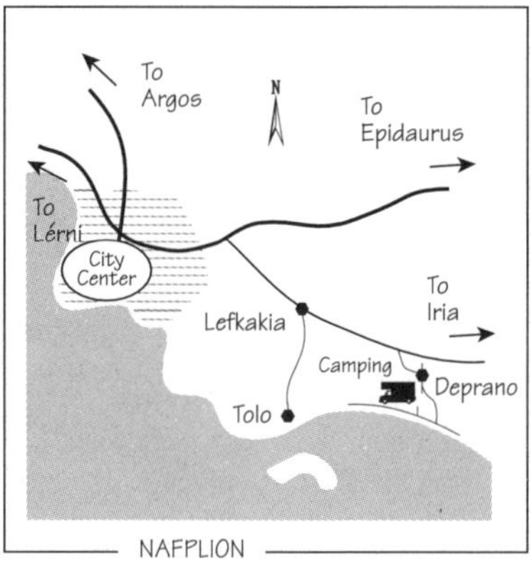

New Triton is a simple and well-run campground with everything you need close by. You can easily spend a lazy month here enjoying the beach with occasional visits to nearby archeological sites and towns. Several other campgrounds are nearby in case the New Triton is full, this beach area is called Plaka, it is one of several to the east of Nafplion.

The medium-sized campground has gravel sites separated by high hedges and covered by shade frames draped with vines. Electricity (German plugs) is convenient to all the sites, each also has an overhead light with an individual switch. The restrooms are immaculate and modern with adjustable hot showers. There is a dish-washing and food preparation room with hot water and gas cooking stoves, also a laundry room with hot water and a washing machine. A small store has supplies, restaurants are nearby and the beach is across the road.

You'll probably arrive in Nafplion from the north. The road from Argos meets the Nafplion - Epidaurus road a kilometer or so east of town. To reach the campground zero your odometer here and head east. At 2.7 kilometers you'll come to a Y. Go right toward Tolo and Drepano. Epidaurus is straight ahead. There is a Y at 5.4 kilometers, go left toward Iria. At 8.8 kilometers there is another Y, go right toward Drepano. Finally, at a T at 9 kilometers go right, then in another .3 kilometers turn left. Drive straight ahead to the beach, turn right, and you'll see the campground on the right.

Side Trips from Nafplion

Mycenae is well known to those familiar with Homer. This was the home of Agamemnon, leader of the Greeks during the invasion of Troy that is described in the Iliad. It was excavated by the controversial Heinrich Schliemann, who also excavated Troy. At Mycenae he found several tombs containing gold death masks that are exhibited in the Archeological Museum in Athens. Mycenae occupies an impressive location at the top of a hill, you'll have lots of company while here since a constant stream of tour busses also visit. Mycenae is located about 25 kilometers north of Nafplion, there is plenty of room for parking.

Tiryns, just 4 kilometers northeast of Nafplion, was a city much like Mycenae, but not built on a hill top. The site is not as often visited as Mycenae, but still interesting.

Epidaurus is best known for its huge Greek theater, but this large archeological site has many other ruins and also a small museum. The theater is the main attraction, it is known for its perfect acoustics and is still in use. Epidaurus is located about 30 kilometers east of Nafplion, a nice drive.

OLYMPIA, GREECE

Population 500

The small town of Olympia is home to the site of the original Olympic Games. They ran from 776 BC to 394 AD. Olympia today is a pleasant little tourist-oriented place with restaurants, shops, and several campgrounds. The **archeological site** is fairly large and has a very simple stadium as well as the ruins of temples and other buildings. There is an excellent **museum** right next door. The site and museum are located about a kilometer east of town, an easy walk from Camping Diana. There's another museum in town also, the **Historical Museum of the Olympic Games**, which has items commemorative items related to the games.

Olympia Campground

✦ CAMPING DIANA

Address: Ancient Olympia, GR-27065 Illia
Telephone: 0624 22314
Price: Moderate

Open all year

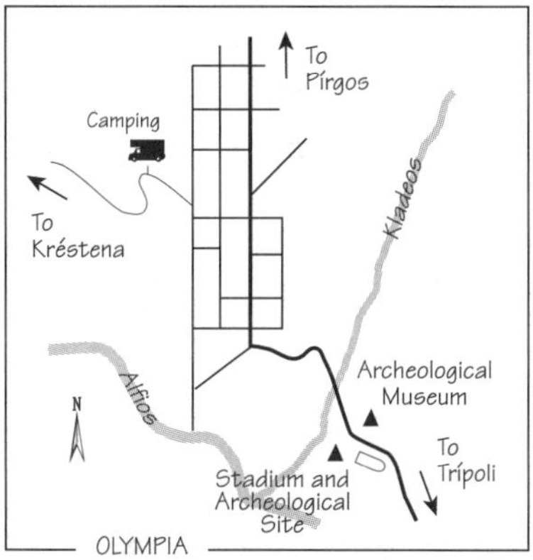

This is a small campground with good facilities, it is conveniently located on the verdant hillside overlooking the village. It takes less than 5 minutes to walk in to the center of town. You'll hear church bells in the morning and music at night.

The campground has about 30 sites, they are terraced and access for caravans is tight in some. The sites are shaded by fruit trees, there are scattered electrical outlets. The restrooms are in good repair and have hot showers and there is hot water for dish washing and laundry. This campground also has a small but nice swimming pool, a small restaurant, and a small store.

Watch for signs from the east (archeological site) side of the village. They'll take you right up the hill to the campground.

PAMUKKALE, TURKEY

One of the top tourist attractions of western Turkey is the huge travertine falls at Pamukkale. Calcium-rich water flowing down the mountainside has formed several square kilometers of white-stone cliffs that look like snowy waterfalls. This is now a national park called Pamukkale Örenyeri and during the last few years the area has changed considerably. Previously there were several hotels set near the travertines, some with campgrounds. All have been forced to move, the only camping now is in the nearby villages of Pamukkale Village and Karahayit. Formerly visitors were allowed to wander over the travertines, soaking in the occasional pools of warm water. Access is severely restricted now, only small sections are open to waders, these are quite crowded and somewhat unattractive. Development continues, so the situation will no doubt change. The ultimate objective is to protect the travertines and restore this as a park-like area.

This has been a popular bathing resort since Roman times, Romans called the city here Hierapolis. The ruins remain, and these are as much an attraction as the travertines. There is a museum and many ruins scattered over a large area. Hiking around the ruins can be entertaining, you can search out the necropolis, the Roman and Hellenistic Theaters, and various churches and temples.

Campgrounds at Pamukkale are mostly small back-yard affairs. There are several in Pamukkale Village, you'll see signs and touts will attempt to take you to others. Karahayit, five kilometers beyond, also has a campground. Karahayit is a spa town, the water here tends to be red because of the iron in it. Most of the new hotels that are being developed to replace those in the park are going into Karahayit.

Pamukkale Campground

✦ TERMOTES CAMPING MOTEL

Address: Pamukkale, Karahayit Köyü
Telephone: 0258 2714066
Price: Inexpensive

Open all year

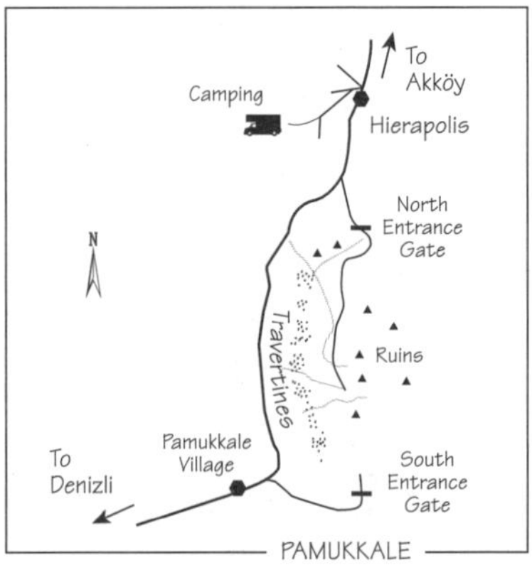

This is the largest campground we could find near Pamukkale. It is a small thermal bathing establishment with some simple motel units as well as the camping area. Two outdoor pools are used for bathing.

The camping is in two areas. A large campground is in a field below the motel and pool area. It has widely paced electrical outlets and small trees that do not yet provide much shade. The surface of drives and sites are dirt. Camping is also possible near the pool. Restrooms are small and simple but there is hot water (only) for showers and sinks for shaving and washing dishes. The motel has a restaurant and it is only a 1kilometer walk in to the town of Karahayit which has shops and restaurants.

As you near the center of Pamukkale Village you'll see the road to the south entrance of the park heading up to your right. Zero your odometer here. Don't take the south entrance road. Instead continue ahead and on out of the village. You will no doubt see several young men trying to flag you down, they will want to lead you to one of the local motels. At 4.3 kilometers you'll see the north entrance road going right, don't take it either. At 5.7 kilometers you'll pass under the arch marking the entrance to Karahayit and at 6.7 kilometers there is a Y. Go left here and then immediately sharply left again. In .4 kilometer you'll see the dirt Termotes entrance road going right and you will reach the motel in another .2 kilometer.

RAFÍNA, GREECE

Population 8,000

Rafína is Athens' second port. It has a large fishing fleet but also serves as a ferry port. Ferries from Rafína serve the Cyclades with connections to Crete and this may be a more desirable departure point than Piraeus since it is much quieter and less crowded. Tickets can be purchased from travel agencies in town and there are many restaurants and shops. Bus connections to Athens are excellent since they serve the ferries.

Rafína Campground

✦ KOKINO LIMANAKI CAMPING

Address: GR-19009 Rafína, Attiki
Telephone: 0294 31604 Fax: 0294 31603
Price: Moderate

Open April 1 to October 31

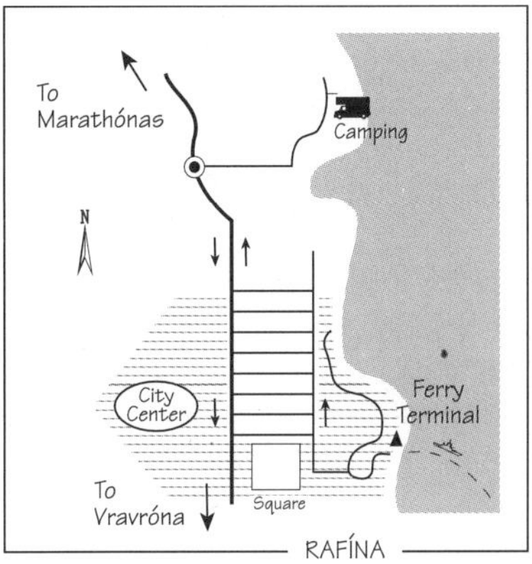

This family-run campground is our choice for a place to stay while visiting Athens. The hour-long bus ride is a small price to pay for the relaxed atmosphere of Rafína, and the advantage of being near the beach.

This large campground has several types of sites. Some are under shade frames in a courtyard-type area, others are above on a large tree-shaded terrace. Electricity is available to most sites (up to 16 amps). The large shower/toilet building is centrally located and is clean and modern. There is hot water for showers, shaving, and dish- and clothes-washing. There is also a washing machine. The campground has a small shop. There is a long set of stairs from the campground down to a good beach which is about 200 feet below.

The campground is above the beach some 1.5 kilometers north of town. Some streets are one-way so these directions seem more complicated than the route actually is. From the port you drive up a long ramp toward town. At the stop at the top zero your odometer. Drive straight ahead for a short block toward the central square. Turn right (north) and go 8 blocks. Turn left and go one block. Turn right and you will come to a traffic circle at 1.3 kilometers on your odometer. Take the first right off the circle and go .3 kilometers, turn left and you will see the campground on your right in another .2 kilometers.

SPARTA (SPÁRTI), GREECE

Population 12,000

This city in the central Peloponnese has one of the most familiar names in Greece. Warlike ancient Sparta was a successful rival to Athens, yet today the town is relatively unimportant. The **ruins of the ancient city's acropolis** lie to the north of town, but they really do not amount to much. There are the remains of a theater and a temple along with walls dating from Byzantine times.

On the other hand, a few kilometers east of Sparta are the extensive ruins of the Byzantine city of **Mystra (Mystrás)**. The ruins are so extensive that it takes most of a day to wander from bottom to top and back again. There's a castle at the top, then spilling down the mountain you'll fine the ruins of a good-sized city including palaces as well as churches, monasteries, a convent, and a museum.

The Mystra ruins are situated just above the village of Nea Mystrás. It is located some 5 kilometers east of Sparta and has a good campground, Camping Castle View, just outside of town as well as restaurants and a small grocery store. You can walk the 2 kilometers from the campground to the lower entrance of the ruins or you can drive up to the upper entrance. There is another campground, CAMPING MYSTRÁS, that is 2 more kilometers closer to Sparta.

Sparta Campground

✦ CAMPING CASTLE VIEW

Address: Mistrás, GR-23100 Lakonias
Telephone: 0731 93303 Fax: 0731 20028
Price: Moderate

Open May 1 to September 30

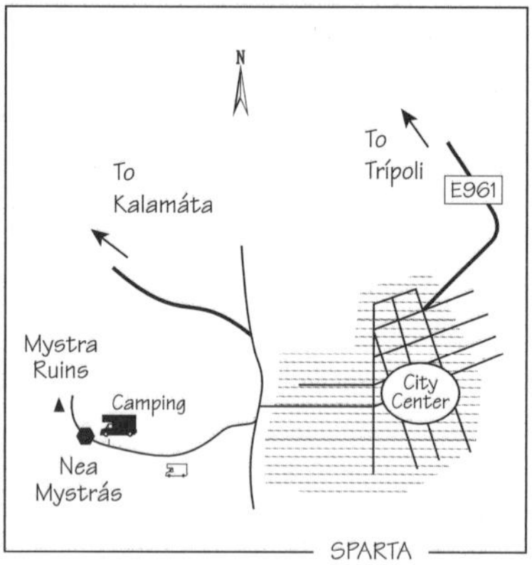

This is a pleasant country campground but with a great location. You can easily walk in to Nea Mistras to have dinner or visit the ruins.

The medium-sized campground occupies an olive tree grove. Widely space outlets (10 amps) provide electricity. The two shower/toilet buildings have adjustable hot showers but bathroom basins have cold water only. There is hot water for washing dishes and the campground has a washing machine. It also has a small swimming pool, a small grocery, and a restaurant. There is bus service in to Sparta from a stop across from the campground.

The road to Mystrás cuts off the road to Kalamáta very near the western outskirts of Sparta. The campground is 4.5 kilometers from the intersection.

THESSALONÍKI, GREECE

Population 800,000

This city is Greece's second largest and the country's largest port. Along the waterfront there is a promenade called the **paralía**, the White Tower that is located on the waterfront now houses the Byzantine Museum. The **Archeological Museum** exhibits the discoveries from the tomb of Phillip II, father of Alexander the Great. They include his gold burial casket and also his actual bones. Thessaloníki also has a number of **Byzantine churches**.

Thessaloníki Campground

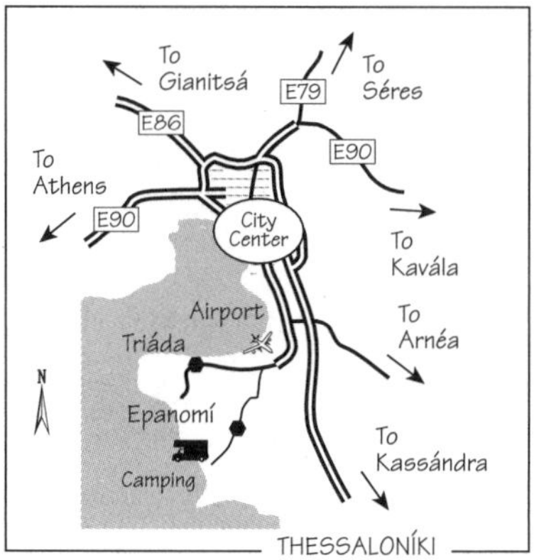

✦ E.O.T. CAMPING EPANOMÍ

Address: Epanomí, GR-57500 Thessaloníki
Telephone: 0392 41378
Price: Inexpensive

Open May 1 to October 31

Thessaloníki does not really have any conveniently located campgrounds for visiting the city itself. There are a couple of them located south of the city beyond the airport. This one is about 22 kilometers from the city near the village of Epanomí, easiest access to town is by bus.

Camping Epanomí is a very large campground located next to the ocean. There are paved driveways with curbs, sites are separated by hedges. Electricity (German plugs, 16 amps) is located near each site and there are large shade trees. The shower/toilet buildings are well maintained and fairly clean, they have hot water for the adjustable showers, and for the dish- and clothes-washing sinks which are located in their own rooms. The beach is sandy and looks across the bay at Mt. Olympus. The campground has a store and a restaurant.

To reach the campground head out of town toward the airport. You'll probably find it easiest to use the bypass road around the city rather than entering in your vehicle. If so you can drive south from the ring road on a major highway and when you reach the airport exit can jog west to pick up the Ag. Triáda road. Zero your odometer as you pass the airport on the road to Ag Triáda. At 4.9 kilometers you'll come to the road to the left to Epanomí. Follow the signs toward Epanomí and when you enter town at 14.1 kilometers start watching for blue signs marked Camping E.O.T. They'll lead you through town and southwest toward the beach which you will reach at about 18.7 kilometers. There is a T in the road, turn left, and you'll soon see the campground entrance on your right.

Side Trips from Thessaloníki

Pella was the birthplace of Alexander the Great. It lies about 40 kilometers northwest of Thessaloníki. It is know for its mosaics, there is a very good museum and also ruins with mosaic floors that you can explore.

TWO OUTSTANDING REGIONS AND THEIR CAMPGROUNDS

THE GREEK ISLANDS

No trip to Greece would be complete without a visit to the islands. There are over 2,000 of them and many are prime tourist destinations. On them you'll find great beaches, fascinating towns, wonderful weather, and lots more.

Here's a quick look at the Greek island archipelagos and larger single islands and what they have to offer the camping traveler.

The Cyclades are a chain of islands located between the Greek mainland and Crete. Some of the most-visited and famous islands in Greece are in this group. They include Santoríni, Mýkonos, Andros, Tínos, Sýros, Náxos, Páros, Ios, Amorgós and many smaller islands. Most of the larger islands have campgrounds and most campers are backpackers because vehicles are expensive to move between the islands and of limited use once you are there. We include information below about campgrounds on Santoríni and Mýkonos. The most important mainland ferry port for the Cyclades is Piraeus. There is also ferry service from Rafína and connections from Crete.

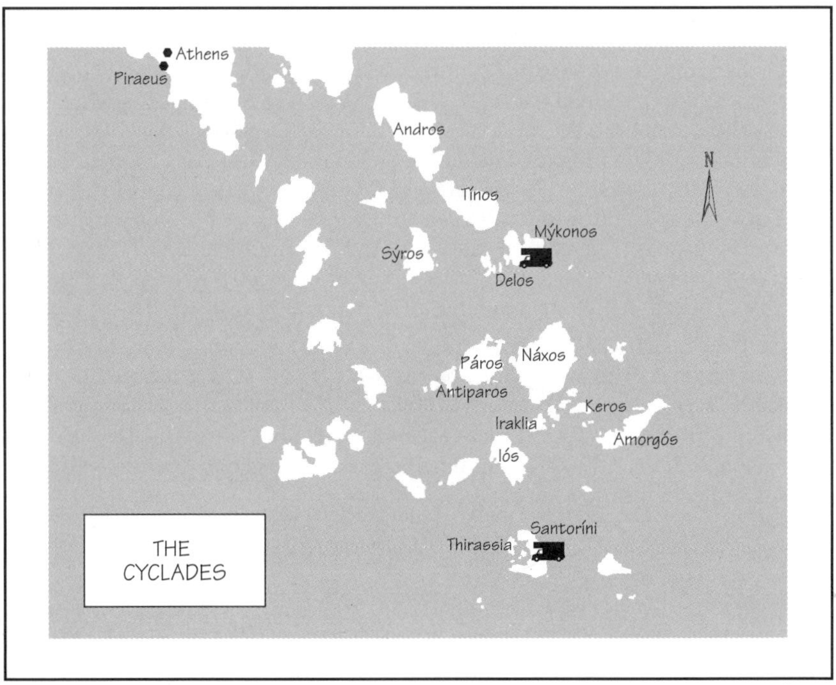

Crete - This large Greek Island is such an important camping destination that it has its own section below.

The Dodecanese are a chain of islands located between Crete and the Turkish coast. They are the most southerly Greek islands so they have the warmest weather. The major islands are Astypálaia, Chálki, Kálymnos, Kárpathos, Kastellórizo, Kos, Pátmos, Léros, Lipsí, Nísyros, Rhodes, Sými, and Tílos. Rhodes, Kos, Pátmos, Astypálaia, and Léros have campgrounds, ferry access to the islands is from Piraeus, the Cyclades, Crete, Samos (Northeast Aegean Islands), and even Turkey.

The Sporades and Euboea lie close to the east coast of the Greek mainland. They are easy to reach but not much visited by tourists. Islands in this group include Alónnisos, Euboea, Skiáthos, Skópelos, and Skýros. Ferry access is from mainland east coast ports. There are campgrounds on Euboea and Skiáthos.

The Northeast Aegean Islands are located along the Aegean Turkish coast and also near northeast Greece. They include Chíos, Ikaría, Lésvos, Límnos, Sámos, Samothráki and Thásos. Access to these islands is from Piraeus and several other mainland ports including Ayvalik in Turkey. There are campgrounds on Chíos, Lésvos and Thásos.

The Ionian Islands are located along the west coast of Greece. The best known of these islands is Corfu but they also include Ithaca, Keffalloniá, Lefkáda, Paxos and Zákynthos. Corfu is a stop for many ferries between Italy and Greece, while Patras is the other primary port for these islands. There are many campgrounds on Corfu and also some on Keffalloniá, Lefkáda and Zákynthos.

Most campers in the Greek Islands travel by ferry. It is easy to pick up tickets at travel agents on most islands, walk-on passage is very flexible. Between islands it is really not necessary to have a stateroom so deck passage is the norm. Travel with a vehicle is a little harder. Most ferries do carry vehicles but space is sometimes not available. The cost of passage for a vehicle can be surprisingly high, expect to pay the equivalent of about four deck passages for a small car, 6 deck passages for a camper van. Rates can vary considerably depending upon the season.

MÝKONOS, GREECE

Population 4,500

Mýkonos has the reputation of being the most tourist-oriented with the best nightlife of all the Greek islands. While the island is dry with few natural attractions it does have good beaches. The main village is Mýkonos Town. It is a picturesque white-washed cruise ship port with lots of restaurants and shops, it is also the ferry port. Bus transportation is available to villages and beaches away from Mýkonos Town.

While you are on Mýkonos do not miss taking a day trip by ferry to the island of Delos, one of the most important archeological sites in Greece.

There are two campgrounds on Mýkonos. They are both located on the southern shore of the island about 5 kilometers from Mýkonos Town. Mýkonos Camping has a quiet cliff-top location within easy walking distance of beaches, PARADISE BEACH is much more active (and noisy) and located just behind the facilities of one of the most popular beaches on the island.

Mýkonos Campground

✦ MÝKONOS CAMPING

Address: Drepano Paraga, GR-84600 Mýkonos
Telephone: 0289 24578 Fax: 0289 24578
Price: Inexpensive

Open April 1 to October 31

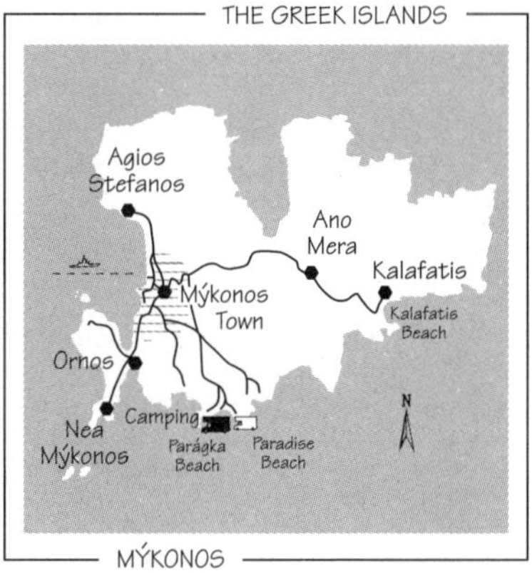

The campground sits on a headland between Parágka Beach and Paradise Beach. You can easily walk to Parágka, Paradise is a little more of a hike, about 1 kilometer. Mýkonos Camping has sites for both vehicles and tents on grass. Many sites have great views. The facilities are very nice and include restrooms with adjustable hot showers, a restaurant/bar, a small store, and a laundry/kitchen area with hot water.

To reach the campground follow the signs for Parágka. Unfortunately they are not at every intersection near town, as you near the beach you will see more of them. From the ferry turn right and follow the main road through town, you can follow airport signs at first. Zero your odometer as you leave the dock. At .2 kilometers there is a stop sign, go right. At .9 kilometers there is a Y, go right. At 1.3 kilometers go left and at the Y at 1.8 kilometers again go left. At 2.9 kilometers go right, the road to the left goes on to the airport. Follow the main road and signs to Parágka or Paradise from here until you reach the cut-off to the right for Parágka at 5.6 kilometers. The campground is 800 meters down this road on the left. If you miss that last turn you will end up at Paradise, the end of the road and the location of the island's other campground.

SANTORÍNI, GREECE

Population 1,500

Is your vision of a Greek Island one of a whitewashed village sitting far above the blue sea with visitors riding donkeys up the long winding path from the dock? You are picturing Santoríni, although these days ferries dock some distance from the town and are met by busses and a cable car serves the landing stage below the village.

In 1450 BC this island was blown apart by a huge volcanic explosion turning what was basically a round island into one shaped like a crescent. Today the crater is filled with water and represents one of the most fantastic views in all of the world. From the village of Thíra high on the cliff overlooking the bay there is a stunning vista of deep blue water dotted with cruise ships.

The campground below is in the village of Thíra which is about 7 kilometers from the ferry dock. Busses meet the ferries. This is the main town on the island. It is a cruise ship town with all that that means, but Thíra is the ultimate cruise ship town and not to be missed. As you would expect the narrow pedestrian-only streets (actually, donkeys are allowed too) are lined with shops and restaurants, some with stunning views.

Thíra has no beach, a good alternative for sun lovers is on the far side of the island, the town of Períssa. The campground here is PERÍSSA CAMPING.

Santorini Campground

✦ CAMPING SANTORÍNI (FORMERLY CALDERA VIEW)

Address: Thíra, GR-84005 Santoríni
Telephone: 0286 82010 Fax: 0286 81889
Price: Inexpensive

Open May 1 to October 31

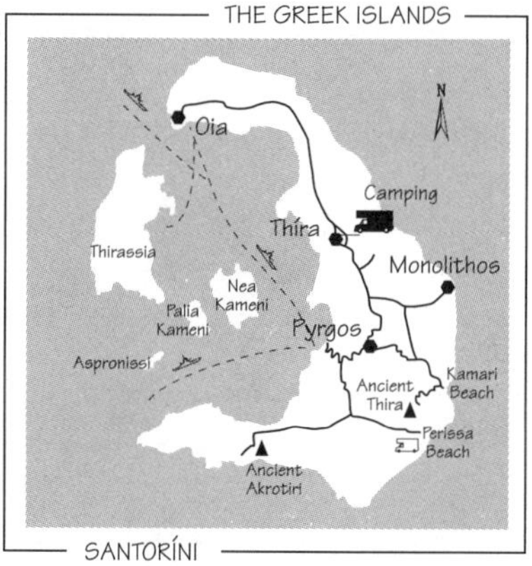

It is hard to beat the convenience of this campground. It is located in the town of Thíra, the central square is a short walk up the hill. If you wish to visit other villages or beaches around the island you can catch a bus from the square. The square is also the place to visit a travel agent to pick up ferry tickets. There's even a view of the eastern coast from the campground.

This is primarily a tent camping facility although there are a few spaces with electricity available for vans. The sites are on packed earth, trees and tall reeds provide shade. Some campers make do without tents under shade frames. There are adjustable hot showers and dish and laundry areas with cold water. The laundry area has a washing machine. The campground also offers a swimming pool, restaurant, and small store.

To find the campground just head up the hill from the ferry docks and follow signs to Thíra (sometimes spelled Fira). You'll also see many signs for the campground. When you reach the central square in Thíra campground signs will take you right and down to the campground entrance which is about 350 meters from the square.

CRETE

Crete is a large island, some 250 kilometers long. It has a well-developed system of paved roads with the main east-west route along the northern coast and spur roads leading south through the mountainous spine to the south coast. The largest town and main port is Iraklion, other large towns include Haniá, Réthymno, and Agios Nikólaos. Crete is known for Minoan archeological sites, particularly the palaces of Knossos and Phaestos, but the island has also been ruled by the Romans, Byzantines, Venetians and Turks and they have all left their marks in the form of palaces and forts. Crete is a very popular vacation spot offering many hiking opportunities and beaches.

Most camping visitors arrive in Iraklion by ferry from Piraeus. There are many boats each day, they carry automobiles and the non-stop run takes about 11 hours.

AGIOS NIKÓLAOS, GREECE

Population 10,000

This is a seaside tourist town, one of the most attractive on the island. Its most unusual

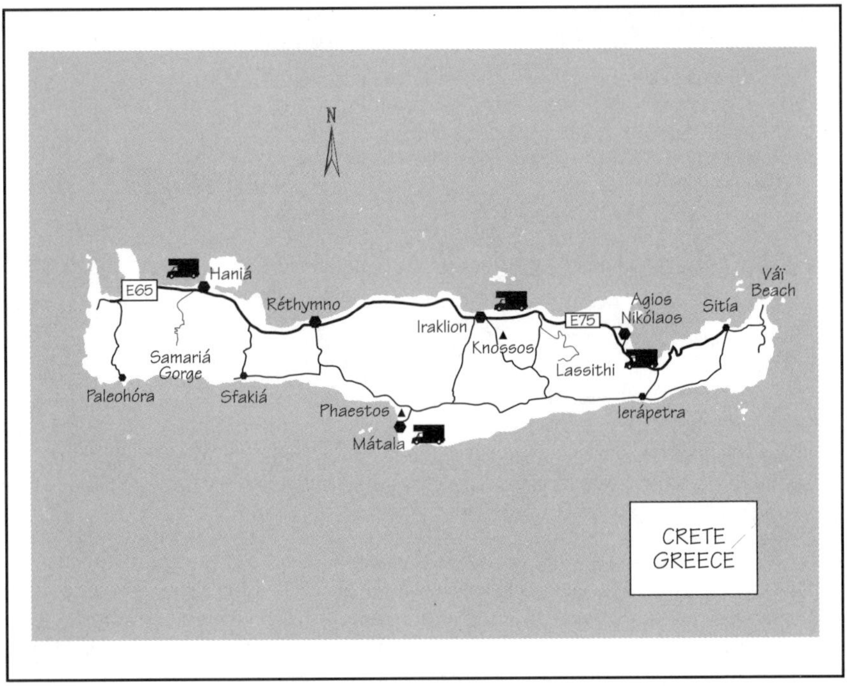

feature is Voulisméni Lake which is located near the center of town and fringed by a promenade and restaurants. The **archeological museum** here is very good with exhibits from the surrounding area. The lake is about 60 meters deep and joined to the harbor by a short canal. Excursion boats run from Agios Nikólaos to **Spinalógka Island** with its Venetian castle and **Aqioi Pántes**, which is a refuge for wild goats.

Agios Nikólaos Campground

✦ GOURNIA MOON

Address: Agios Nikólaos
Telephone: 0842 93243
Price: Moderate

Open all year

This medium-sized campground has an isolated but interesting location off the main road along the coast about 17 kilometers southeast of Agios Nikólaos. The Minoan site of Gournia is located just a kilometer or so past the campground along this same road.

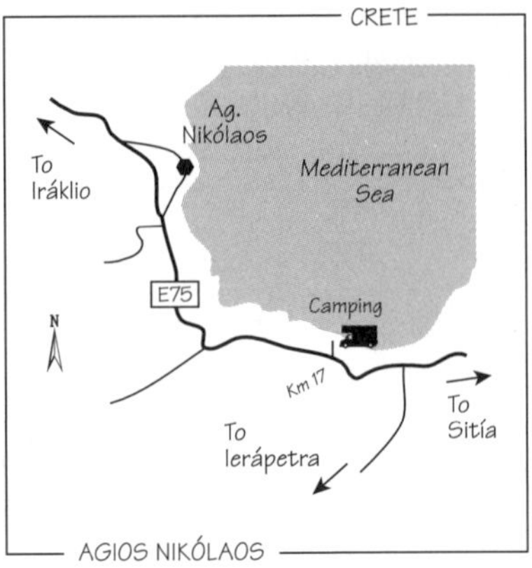

Campsites are arranged off two short parallel dirt roads at the rear of the site. Frames and a few trees provide shade. Electricity is available to these sites. There are also a few tent sites down the hill toward the water. The shower/toilet facilities are adequate, they have solar-heated showers and a dish washing area also with hot water. A clothes washing machine is available. There is a nice swimming pool, a small store, and a small restaurant. Below the campground is a small rocky cove where you can swim in the ocean, there is flat concrete area for lounging and a little gravel beach.

Gournia Moon is located right off the coastal highway at the 17 kilometer marker on the road toward Sitía.

HANIÁ (CHANIÁ), GREECE

Population 50,000

Haniá, in far western Crete, is probably best known in travel circles as the jump-off city for a hike through the Samariá Gorge. More about that later in the side trips section. The city does have more to offer, however. Originally a Minoan town, Haniá has also been Hellenistic, Roman, Byzantine, Genoan, Venetian, and Turk. The Minoan town is being excavated, the **excavations** are just west of the Old Harbor on the hill. The **streets around the old harbor** are full of restaurants and shops, the district is surrounded by **walls** and has a fort built by the Venetians. The fort houses the **Naval Museum**. There is an exceptional covered municipal **food market** in the city that you shouldn't miss. Haniá's **archeological museum** has Minoan and Roman artifacts from western Crete. The best beaches are west of the city near the campground.

Haniá Campground

✦ CAMPING HANIÁ

Address: Ag Apostoli,
GR-73100 Kato Daratso Khania
Telephone: 0821 31138 Fax: 0821 33371
Price: Moderate

Open April 1 to October 31

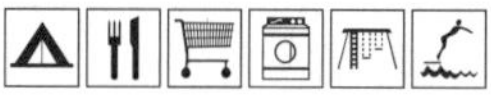

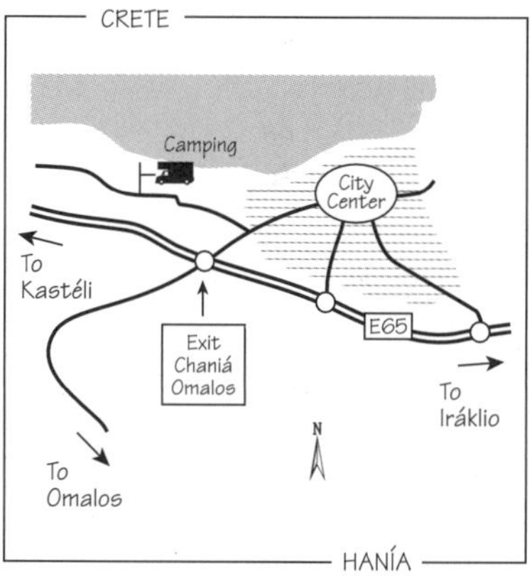

Camping Haniá is located west of the city in a suburb dedicated to small tourist pensions and hotels. The medium-sized campground is a walled olive grove with many rental tents, but it also has a good-sized area for transient campers. The sites are well shaded with convenient electrical connections. Maneuvering room can be a problem for units larger than a van, particularly caravans. The shower/toilet building is modern, there are adjustable hot showers and hot and cold water for the shaving sinks, but only continental-style toilets. A separate dish- and clothes-washing area has only cold water. There is also a washing machine. Other amenities include an excellent swimming pool, a bar/restaurant, a playground, and a shop for groceries. A nice beach is a block away, nice beaches are also located to the east and

GREECE & TURKEY

west between small rocky headlands. There is frequent bus service to central Haniá. Tours to the Samaría Gorge are available.

Easiest access is from the four-lane freeway that runs south of Haniá. Take the exit marked Chaniá 4, Omalos 36. This exit is west of Haniá and is the same one you would take to reach Omalos at the head of the Samariá Gorge. Turn toward the beach (north) and drive 1.4 kilometers to an intersection. This road is a two-lane highway that runs from central Haniá toward the west serving the small towns along the coast. Turn left here and drive 2.1 kilometers. Turn right (the campground is signed here) and drive toward the beach for .6 kilometers. Take the small lane to the right (signed for the campground) which makes a 140 degree angle and leads you back into an area of houses to the campground. While driving this route you will pass several supermarkets.

Side Trips from Haniá

Many of the people visiting Haniá do so just to hike the **Samariá Gorge**. This may be the most popular hiking route in Europe. The gorge is a national park. The route starts at over 1000 meters. Most of the altitude is lost in the first two kilometers as you descend down a rocky zig-zag trail (with safety fences). Then you follow the gorge another 16 kilometers to the coast at Agía Rouméli. Along the way the trail passes the abandoned village of Samariá and passes through the Iron Gates where the walls squeeze to less than 10 feet apart. A boat then takes hikers along the coast to access the road system and travel back to civilization.

If you plan to hike the entire gorge (most people do) you will want to use a bus to reach the upper end of the gorge since you will return another way and would have to retrieve your car. Busses run from central Haniá to the start of the hike at Xylóskalo. After the hike you catch a boat to Hora Sfakion where busses meet the boats to travel back to Haniá.

It is also possible to drive to Xylóskalo and walk into the gorge and out. The drive between Haniá and the start of the trail is very scenic, you climb well into the mountains. Don't plan to walk all the way to the Iron Gates (12 kilometers each way) unless you are in shape for a marathon, the climb out of the gorge is a killer. Make sure to bring good sturdy shoes because the footing is very rocky.

IRAKLION (IRÁKLEIO), CRETE

Population 100,000

Iraklion is the capital of Crete and the largest town by far. Your ferry will probably arrive in Iraklion but you'll probably not spend a lot of time in the city. While there is a lot of history here the town isn't exactly inviting. The campground is quite a distance outside of town so you'll visit to see the important attractions. These include the most important Minoan archeological site in Crete, Knossos, and the excellent Archeological Museum. Crete was the birthplace of El Greco, usually associated more with Spain than Greece. There is only one of his paintings displayed in Crete, it is in the **Historical Museum**.

Knossos is the most important and impressive Minoan site. Much of the palace has been reconstructed, there's more to see here than at most ancient sites. Knossos is located about 5 kilometers southeast of the city. The easiest way to visit is by using your own vehicle. Parking is available in several small lots near the site.

Iraklion Campground

✦ CRETA CAMPING

Address: Gouves, Hersonissou, GR-70014
Crete
Telephone: 0897 41400 Fax: 0897 41792
Price: Moderate

Open May 1 to October 30

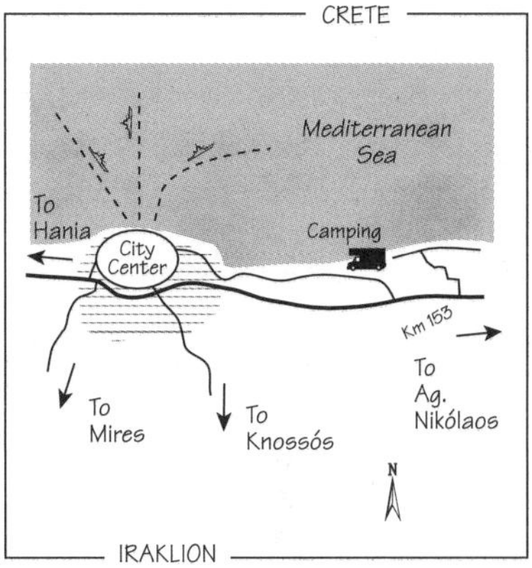

This is a medium-sized campground located near the beach in a small resort town about 15 kilometers east of Iraklion. It makes a good base for a visit to the city while providing a beach and a quiet atmosphere.

The campground sites are on grass in several areas divided by bamboo plantings. These provide some shelter when the wind blows from the north. Camping is on grass with gravel drives. Electric plugs and water faucets are scattered throughout the campground. A few spaces near the front have shade frames, otherwise there is little shade. The shower/toilet buildings are older but in decent repair, they have adjustable hot showers and hot water in the shaving sinks. There is a room for washing dishes and one for laundry, cold water only. The campground has a restaurant/bar and a shop. There is a beach across the access road out front and next door some government land that has a good sandy beach and is open during the day for the public to use.

To find the campground head east from Iraklion on the main highway toward Ag. Nikólaos and Sitía. Just after the 153 kilometer marker Creta camping is signed to the left. Turn and follow the road toward the beach through vineyards and small hotels and homes for about a kilometer. When you reach the beach turn left, the campground is at the end of the beachfront road, a distance of .8 kilometers.

MÁTALA, GREECE

Population 500

The southern coast of Crete is different than the north coast. There is no road running along most of it as there is in the north. Instead, individual roads stretch south to the often rocky coast, many through mountain passes. There are good beaches on the south coast and the water is warm enough for swimming even during the winter.

One popular southern village is Mátala. This small resort village sits next to a small but beautiful sweep of sand. On the opposite side of the cove sandstone cliffs pockmarked with caves overlook the town. These were once used as camp sites but the area is now fenced. The village is a busy and popular place with small hotels and many restaurants and tourist shops. It is closed to traffic, a large parking lot at the outskirts of the village provides parking for rental cars and tour busses.

Mátala Campground

✦ KOMOS CAMPING

Address: I. Kiprakis S.A., GR-70200 Komos, Iraklion, Crete
Telephone: 0892 45596
Price: Moderate

Open April 1 to October 31

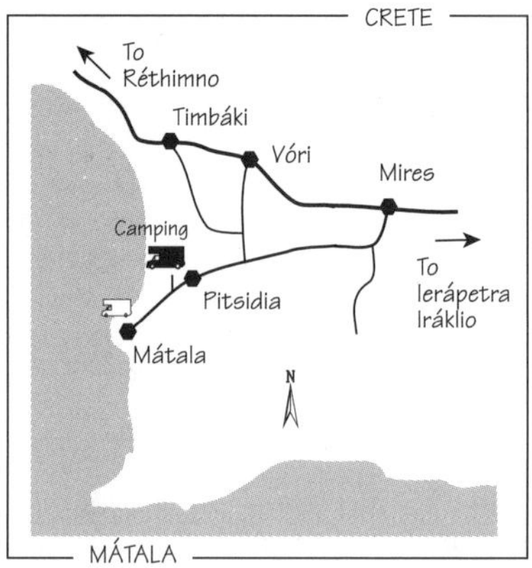

This very nice campground is located at the top of a hill overlooking the southern coast. It is just outside the village of Pitsidia, about 2.5 kilometers up the hill from Mátala. A 1 kilometer walk down the hill in the other direction is Komos Beach which is much larger and much less crowded than the beach at Mátala.

Camping is on packed sand with sites separated by small trees and bushes, most sites have shade. Modern electrical boxes are spaced about 25 meters apart. The shower/toilet buildings are very modern and clean, they offer adjustable hot showers and outdoor shaving sinks with hot water. There is a separate kitchen building with an outside seating area, it has gas cook tops and sinks with hot water. There is also a laundry area. Near the entrance is a beautiful swimming pool, a restaurant, and a mini market.

Mátala appears on most maps. As you approach the south coast you will pass through the town of Pitsidia. On the far side, about a half kilometer from the town you will see a sign for the campground pointing to the right. There is also a simple campground just behind the beach in Mátala, MÁTALA CAMPING, but Komos Camping is much nicer.

Side Trips From Mátala

Among the Minoan palace sites **Phaestos** is second only to Knossos. It is located about 10 kilometers from the campground. Phaestos occupies a very impressive hilltop site and is much less crowded than Knossos.

TEXT INDEX

ABOUT THE AUTHORS

Several years ago Terri and Mike Church decided to do some traveling. Their savings wouldn't cover hotels and restaurants for anything like the length of time they wanted to be on the road. On the other hand living out of a backpack wasn't a particularly attractive idea either. RVs turned out to be the perfect compromise.

In their time on the road the Churches have toured the continental U.S., Europe, Alaska, and Mexico in one type of RV or other. During the course of their travels they noticed that few guidebooks were available with the essential day-to-day information that camping travelers need when they are in unfamiliar surroundings. *Traveler's Guide to European Camping*, *Traveler's Guide to Mexican Camping*, and *Traveler's Guide to Alaskan Camping* are designed to be the guidebooks that the authors tried to find when they first traveled to these places.

Terri and Mike now have a base of operations in the Seattle, Washington area but they continue to spend at least nine months of each year traveling. The entire first edition of the Europe book and most of the Mexico and Alaska books were written and formatted using laptop computers while on the road.

MEXICO

Traveler's Guide To Mexican Camping

by Mike & Terri Church

6" x 9" Paperback

416 pages, over 200 maps

ISBN 0-9652968-1-4

How would you like to spend your winter camped near crystal clear blue water on a white sand beach? Mexico has many world–renown beach resorts, and they all have campgrounds. Try Cancun, Acapulco, Ixtapa, Mazatlan, or Puerto Vallarta. If you are looking for a beach, but not a resort town, Mexico has miles and miles of beautiful, empty beaches and many of them also offer camping opportunities.

If beaches aren't your thing, don't despair. The interior of Mexico is full of attractions. Many North Americans are drawn to superior climate and cultural attractions of Guadalajara, Lake Chapala, San Miguel de Allende, Alamos, Guanajuato, and Cuernavaca.

Visit Mexico City, the largest city in the world. Or see the Pre-Columbian Mesoamerican archeological sites scattered throughout the country. There are so many sites you may even discover one yourself!

Traveler's Guide To Mexican Camping will give you all the information to cross the border and travel Mexico like a veteran. The book features:

- ❑ Complete descriptions of over 200 campgrounds, accompanied by maps and detailed driving instructions for each campground listed. You'll know the exact location of virtually every campground in Mexico.
- ❑ Coverage of the entire Mexico mainland and the Baja Peninsula.
- ❑ Four possible itineraries including the Baja Peninsula, the Grand Coastal Tour, Colonial Mexico, and Down the West Coast.
- ❑ Border Crossing Information including maps of the major border crossing cities.
- ❑ Descriptions of sights to see and things to do in every city covered by the guide.

ALASKA

Traveler's Guide To Alaskan Camping
by Mike & Terri Church
6" x 9" Paperback
416 pages, over 100 maps

ISBN 0-9652968-2-2

Alaska, the dream trip of a lifetime! Be prepared for something spectacular. Alaska is one fifth the size of the entire United States, it has 17 of the 20 highest peaks in the U.S., 33,904 miles of shoreline, and has more active glaciers and ice fields than the rest of the inhabited world.

In addition to some of the most magnificent scenery the world has to offer, Alaska is chock full of an amazing variety of wildlife. You are likely to see bald eagles, dall sheep, moose, bison, brown bears, caribou, beavers, black bears, a wide variety of marine birds and waterfowl, whales, porpoises, sea lions, sea otters, and even more. Some of these animals may even pay a visit to your campsite.

Alaska is an outdoor enthusiast's paradise. Fishing, hiking, canoeing, rafting, hunting, and wildlife viewing are only a few of the many activities which will keep you outside during the long summer days.

Traveler's Guide To Alaskan Camping makes this dream trip to Alaska as easy as camping in the "lower 48". It provides details on:

- ❑ Over 400 campgrounds throughout Alaska and on the roads north in Canada with full campground descriptions and maps showing the exact location of each campground.
- ❑ Complete coverage of the routes north, including the Alaska Highway, the Cassiar Highway, and the Alaska Marine Highway.
- ❑ RV rental information for both Alaska and Canada.
- ❑ Things to do and see throughout your trip, including suggested fishing holes, hiking trails, canoe trips, wildlife viewing opportunities, and much more. There's even a full chapter on off-road camping trips for those who want to venture away from the beaten path!

ORDER FORM

To order complete the following and send to:

Rolling Homes Press
P.O. Box 2099
Kirkland, WA 98083-2099

Name____

Address______________________________________

City____________________State__________Zip__________

Description	Qty	Price	Subtotal
Traveler's Guide To Alaskan Camping	____	$19.95	______
Traveler's Guide To Mexican Camping	____	$19.95	______
Traveler's Guide To European Camping	____	$19.95	______
3 Book Set (Alaska, Mexico, Europe)	____	$49.95	______

Method of Payment

- ❑ Check
- ❑ Visa
- ❑ Mastercard

Order total: ______
Shipping: 4.00 *
Total: ______

Credit Card # ______________________ Exp. date ________

Signature ________________________________

To order by phone call toll free from the U.S. or Canada 1-888-265-6555
Outside the U.S. or Canada call (425) 822-7846
Have your VISA or MC ready

U.S. Dollars or MC/VISA only for non-U.S. orders

Rolling Homes Press is not responsible for taxes or duty on books shipped outside the U.S.

*$4 shipping regardless of quantity order for all orders sent to the same address

Visit our web site at www.rollinghomes.com